SOME GEORGIA COUNTY RECORDS
VOL. 3

BEING SOME OF THE LEGAL RECORDS
OF
BIBB, BUTTS, FAYETTE, HENRY, MONROE
AND NEWTON COUNTIES, GEORGIA

96 - 1218

COMPILED BY:
THE REV. SILAS EMMETT LUCAS, JR.
PUBLISHED BY:
SOUTHERN HISTORICAL PRESS

SOUTHERN HISTORICAL PRESS, INC.
c/o The Rev. Silas Emmett Lucas, Jr.
275 West Broad Street
Greenville, South Carolina 29601

ISBN 0-89308-058-6

INTRODUCTION

As previously stated in both Volumes 1 and 2 of "Some Georgia County Records", this book and the other two in this series are an attempt to meet some of the growing need for new Georgia source material.

As Publisher of this series of books, as well as Editor of The Georgia Genealogical Magazine, the oldest genealogical quarterly on Georgia source material, I have found that the Quarterly genealogical magazine subscribers are by-and-large an entirely different group of people from those who purchase genealogical books.

Therefore, to try and meet the needs of both groups of people, I have taken source material that has run in past issues of the Georgia Genealogical Magazine and put it together as one block of material for each particular county covered. However, some of the material appearing in this book, as well as Volumes 1 and 2 has never appeared in print in the magazine.

The original plan I started out with in this project envisioned at least three (3) volumes of Georgia county records. This being the third in the series, although I cannot state presently that this volume will conclude the series. There may be future volumes over the next several years.

Comments and contributions of original source material from readers will be appreciated for possible use in future books.

The Rev.Silas Emmett Lucas,Jr.
Publisher
August 1978

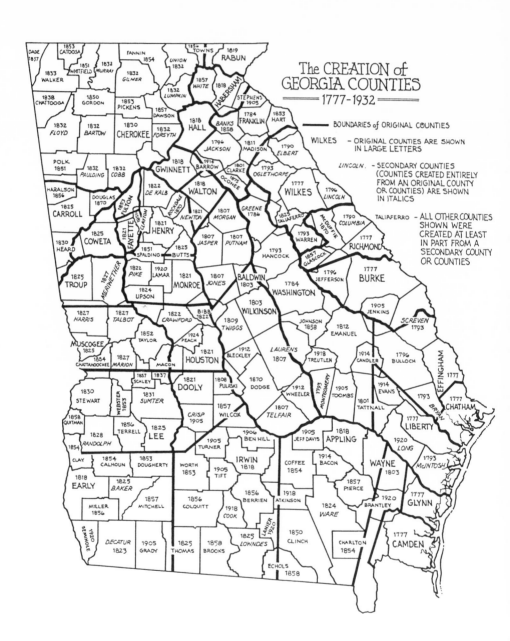

The CREATION of
GEORGIA COUNTIES
1777–1932

——— BOUNDARIES of ORIGINAL COUNTIES

WILKES – ORIGINAL COUNTIES ARE SHOWN
IN LARGE LETTERS

LINCOLN. – SECONDARY COUNTIES
(COUNTIES CREATED ENTIRELY
FROM AN ORIGINAL COUNTY
OR COUNTIES) ARE SHOWN
IN ITALICS

TALIAFERRO – ALL OTHER COUNTIES
SHOWN WERE
CREATED AT LEAST
IN PART FROM A
SECONDARY COUNTY
OR COUNTIES

TABLE OF CONTENTS

JEMISON, HENRY
    March 19, 1822 Baldwin County, Georgia. March 10, 1823 Monroe
County, Georgia. To wife Susanna, four negroes, Rachel and her three
children Ned, Joshua and Dolly; household furniture, plantation tools.
To children Sara Sophia, Robert William and Susanna Margaret, remainder of property both real and personal to be owned as a joint
undivided property until each one becomes of age. Children to live
with their Mother. Executors: Wife Susanna and her brother Tomlinson
Fort. Wit: Tomlinson Fort, J. Bozeman, Appleton Rosseter. (p. 1)

SMITH, HENRY
    January 19, 1823. June 5, 1823 Monroe County, Georgia...being
weak in body... to wife Dolly Smith two negroes viz. Lucy a negro
woman about thirty years old, Janah a girl about thirteen years old;
tract of land No. 330 in 13th District Monroe County, also $2000 in
notes and cash; stock, cattle, household and kitchen furniture, all
my working tools. To eldest son Daniel Smith, negro fellow Isaac
about forty years old, also one bed and furniture. To daughter
Loty Brady, two negroes, one a woman about forty years old, one girl
three years old which she has now in possession. To daughter
Susanah Howard, two negroes, one a woman Rose about thirty and her
child Emory about seven years old, also one bed and furniture. To
daughter Esther Smith, one negro girl Marthy about twelve years old,
also one bed and furniture. To daughter Mary Tompkins, one negro
girl Rose about fourteen years old, also one bed and furniture. To
son John Smith, two negro boys Jordan and Harry each about eight
years old, also one bed and furniture. To son Henry Smith, one negro
boy Moses about ten years old and one negro boy Ben six years old,
also one bed and furniture. To daughter Martha Smith, two negroes
Anthony and George each about two years old, also one bed and furniture. Executors: son Daniel Smith and wife Dolly. Wit: James
Golightly, H. H. Howard, Mary B. Tompkins. (p. 3)

WILLIAMS, JOHN D.
    October 2, 1821. May 6, 1822. Will made in Twiggs County,
Georgia. True copy recorded in Bibb County, Georgeia July 14,
1823...being sick in body... to wife Sally, all property real and
personal during her natural life, then to be divided between two
sons John and Joseph. To son Samuel S. Williams, fifty dollars. To
James Moore, one lot of land containing 70 acres being at or near
Camp Hope, also two negroes Lewis and Adaline. Executrix: wife,
Sally. Wit: Thomas Horn, John Harden. (p. 5)

SCOTT, JOHN
    November 13, 1824 Bibb County, Georgia. May 1, 1826 Jones
County, Georgia. I, John Scott, of Bibb County... of sound mind...
to Quincy Shankley, $500 to be paid from estate at wife's death.
To wife Christian Scott, remainder of estate. Executors: wife
Christian Scott, John Davis, and William Johnson. Wit: Peter
Rockmore, James Gates, Senr., Stephen Renfroe. (p. 6)

LIQUEUX, PETER
    October 15, 1827. November 5, 1827. ...of sound mind... to
wife Martha Liqueux, all estate real and personal. To mother Hannah
Germany, an annuity of fifty dollars per year. Executrix: wife
Martha Liqueux. Wit: Thos. Campbell, Geo. W. Ellis, R. W. Foster.
(p. 7)

JETER, ANDREW
    February 19, 1828. July 7, 1828. ...being sensible of my
approaching dissolution, being of sound mind and memory. Austin my
horse, bridle and saddle, my watch, furniture of every description,
cattle and land be sold for purpose of paying just debts and balance,
if any, be given to Massillian P. Stovall. To granddaughter Mary H.
Birdsong, negro Jim. To granddaughter Louisa Jane Stovall, negro

Hannah and child Amy. To daughter Betsy Stovall, use of the negroes given to the two girls until they arrive at age or marries but in no case to be taken to pay George Stovall debts and the Execution I hold against George Stovall. I give unto Massillia Pleasant Stovall and Joseph Aljanon Stovall equally. Executor: Robert Birdsong, Esq. Wit: Joseph Fluker, Eziekle Coffin, John R. Garland. (p. 8)

BURNETT, JOHN
    January 15, 1828. September 1, 1828. ...of sound mind and memory. To wife Soffhian Burnett all property real and personal during her widowhood or life. After her marriage or death, to be equally divided between children Martha Rache Susan Elizabeth John Surrader and Mary Drop Burnett. Executrix: wife Soffhrian Burnett. Wit: Edward C. Beard, Edward Wilder, John Audolf. (p. 9)

BURTON, ROBERT
    December 13, 1827. January 5, 1829. ...weak in body but of sound and disposing mind. To William Burton, two dollars. To William Hunt, two dollars. To John Burton, two dollars. To Alunson Burton (son of Archer Burton), land whereon I now live containing 105 acres being south half of lot No. 299 with three acres added; also negro woman Chaney and her three children Jackson, Josephine and Polly. To John Roff (son of Edward Roff), all debts due me in state of Virginia. To friend David S. Booth, my horse saddle & bridle. Executor: friend Benjamin B. Lamar. Wit: Martin H. Brown, Daniel Smith, R. H. Howard. (p. 10)

FLUKER, BALDWIN
    January 2, 1829. March 2, 1829. To wife Sarah Q. Fluker, and to children Robert O. T. Fluker, Baldwin M. M. Fluker, Rebecca M. Fluker and Ann E. Fluker, all my real and personal estate, each inheriting one fifth of my whole estate. Executors: wife Sarah Q. Fluker, Thomas Pace, son Robert O. T. Fluker, James Willis, and Isaac B. Roatland. Wit: Nicholas Childers, Walter L. Campbell, Edwin E. Campbell. (p. 12)

SAPP, HENRY
    October 26, 1829. November 3, 1829. ...of sound and perfect mind and memory. To wife Remellesant Sapp, all estate real and personal. After her death, to go to Henry Spears, Archibald Spears, Remellesant Hester, Martha McKinsy, Eliza Powel and Patience Barnes. To negro male slave Chance now about 35 years of age, his freedom after he shall hade arrived at the age of 50 years. Executors: grandson Henry Spears and Archibald Spears. Wit: P. Stubbs, Peter Stewart, John Baily, J.P. (p. 13)

SUMMERLIN, SARAH
    Will attested to verbally October 16, 1829. Sworn in open court November 3, 1829. Sarah Summerlin who died in said county on fifteen day of July last and was taken ill suddenly at her place of residence at which she had lived nearly five years previous to her death. To sons James and Allison, all property real and personal. (p. 14)

WELLS, NICHOLAS W.
    November 30, 1829. December 12, 1829. ...of sound and disposing mind. To sister Nancy, negro girl Easter now in possession of my brother Fletcher. To sister Winney, negro girl Lilly also in possession of my brother Fletcher. To sister Martha, negro girl Maria also in possession of my brother Fletcher. To sisters Winney and Martha, negro woman Sarah, and it is my wish that she be retained in the family until the marriage of all my aforesaid sisters. To brother Marion and James, the tract of land upon which my family now resides in Putnam County. To sisters Winney and Martha, all the beds and furniture in the house occupied in Putnam by my father's family to be equally divided among my said three sisters. To nephew Nicholas Smith when he shall attain the age of twenty one years, a negro boy of the value of $300 and a horse, saddle and bridle of the value of $200. Executrix: wife Susan. Wit: Nicholas Childers, Henry G. Ross, A. Durragh, Edw. D. Tracy. (p. 15)

KING, JOHN
    March 7, 1825. March 10, 1825. Baldwin County, Georgia. To
wife Winefer King, the whole of my property, land, negroes, household and kitchen furniture. To children Caroline King, Parnale
King, James H. King, and Jackson Esly King as they come of age, the
share coming to them by a proper appraisement made by three free-
holders. Wit: Samuel Smith, John Flewellen, James C. Humphries.
(p. 17)

SMITH, JAMES
    April 28, 1830. June 24, 1830. ...of sound mind and senses.
To wife Mary Jane Smith, negro boys Ben and Mingo, cattle and hogs,
lot of land No. 117 in 3rd District originally Houston now Bibb
County. After death or intermarriage of wife, the said land and
stock of cattle and hogs to become the property of my youngest child
Martha Jane Smith and her legal representatives. To wife, my stock
of horses, household and kitchen furniture, plantation tools. To
Martha Jane Smith, the negroes Harry, Sawny, Eady, and Mariah. To
Thomas Smith, James Jessop, Stephen Smith, Hiram McCullers and Jacob
Lewis, land in 32d District Lee County No. 14. Also two negroes
Willis and Milly to remain in possession of the widow until the 25th
Dec. next after which time the said lot No. 14 and the two negroes
Willis and Milly be sold by the Executor and the proceeds divided
between Thomas Smith, Stephen Smith, James Jesop, Hiram McCullers,
and Jackson Lewis. To Milborn Farmer, two dollars. Executors:
John A. Tharp and Joshua Jordan. Wit: Wm. Bowden, Wiley A. Thomas,
B. G. Riddle. (p. 18)

CROCKETT, DAVID
    April 1, 1830. May 3, 1830. ...being in low state of health...
putting trust and confidence in my friend John D. Singletary to
manage my business after my decease. All perishable property to be
sold and proceeds go for the use of my wife Elizabeth Crockett.
She also to get negroes Ned, Caty, Sarah, Bill, Edmond and Mariah.
To brother's son Archibald Crockett, land after my wife's decease.
Executor: friend John D. Singletary. Wit: Henry Clem, Durham
Singletary, M. M. Griffin. (p. 20)

DICKSON, THOMAS
    October 27, 1830. March 7, 1831. ...of sound mind but feeble
body. Property be kept together for support and education of my
family while wife Anna lives and remains single. If she should marry
before the youngest child comes of age or marries, then I desire the
property be sold to highest bidder and divided equally between wife
and children except lame daughter Elizabeth should have $200 (more)
than the rest. Children to get $200 as they come to twenty one
years of age or marry. Executors: Brother Benjamin Dickson and
wife Anna. Wit: Patrick McCallum, Josiah Dickson, Robert Dickson.
(p. 21)

ROGERS, WILLIAM B.
    January 5, 1833. May 6, 1833. ...of sound mind and memory
but of infirm health. Property real and personal be kept together
and managed by Executors for joint benefit of wife Jane M. Rogers and
infant daughter Catharine S. Rogers, as long as they both remain
unmarried, but in event of either marriage, property be divided
equally between them. At wife's death, her portion of estate to go
to daughter Catharine S. Rogers, or in event of her death then it
shall descend to her heirs, if any--if none, then that portion of
estate be inherited by children of Isaac Harvey begotten of his
present wife Eliza Harvey. If daughter Catharine S. Rogers dies
without issue, her portion of estate to go to wife Jane M. Rogers
during her celibacy or before she marries, but after her marriage or
death to be equally divided between my niece and nephew Martha
and Isaac Harvey, Jr. Executors (also Guardians of daughter Catharine
S. Rogers): Isaac Harvey, Senr., Everard Hamilton, John S. Childers.
Wit: Robt. Augst. Beall, A. T. Holmes, Josiah S. Law. (p. 22)

HUFF, EDWARD
     April 28, 1832. February 25, 1833. Chatham County, Georgia.
...of sound mind and memory. To John C. Nicole, Esq., Judge of
Court of Common Pleas of Savannah and Oyer and Terminer for city of
Savannah, my mulatto woman Dianna and her female child Eliza Jane.
My few debts be paid by John C. Nicole Esq., when can be raised
from the hire of said mulatto woman. Believe all I owe is $2.50 to
John Carter and seven or ten cents to James Lamar, my doctor's bill.
Executor: John C. Nicole. Wit: Margaret Pendergast, Ben Sheftall,
J.P. (p. 24)

OWENS, BENJAMIN FRANKLIN
     June 14, 1833. ...feebile in body but of sound mind. To wife
Elmyria A. Owens, the use of all my property real and personal, to
educate my sons Benjamin Franklin Owens and William Henry Owens and
her son Charles Williamson Hargrove until my son William Henry Owens
shall arrive at age of twenty one years and then I give to wife
Elmyria A. Owens one third part of said property real and personal
remaining and balance to be divided between son Benjamin Franklin
Owens, William Henry Owens, and Charles Williamson Hargrove. To wife,
family Bible. To son Benjamin Franklin Owens, my collar button,
containing a portion of the binding of General Washington's Revolu-
tionary Marquee. To son William Henry Owens, my sleeve buttons. To
stepson Charles Williamson Hargrove, my pencil case. To father-in-
law Rev. Charles Williamson, my picket Bible. Executors: wife,
Elmyria A. Owens, friend Charles Williamson, R. Blount. Wit:
Richd. McGolrick, Thos. T. Wyche, Judith C. Tucker. (p. 26)

RUTLAND, REDDEN
     September 9, 1833. ...in ill health but sound mind and memory.
To wife Mary, use of negro girl Harriet and her increase until my
son Rufus King Rutland becomes of age then said negro girl and her
increase to be equally divided amongst all my children then living.
Lands and stock to be sold and after paying just debts the remainder
be equally divided between wife and children. Executors: Blake B.
Rutland and Johnson Welborn. Wit: Z. Cowart, Wm. Griffin, Wm.
Farrmington. (p. 28)

VICTORY, THOMAS
     September 15, 1833. November 4, 1833. ...of sound and disposing
mind. To daughter Elizabeth A. Billups, negro slaves Ann, Jacob,
Tom, Jackson, Lucinda, Robert and Lydia with their children and
increase--at her death to be equally divided among her children. To
daughter Ellen H. Harris, negro slaves Nace, John, Charlotte,
Ephraim, Katy, Spencer, Jack. To son John Victory, negro slaves
Becca, Job, Turner and Andrew. Executors: Charles D. Stewart and
John Fountain. Wit: Edw. D. Tracy, Jacob Shotwell, David B.
Butler. (p. 29)

CHAMBLESS, HENRY
     August 12, 1834. November 3, 1834. Property real and personal
be kept together for purpose of raising and educating my children
subject to control of wife Rachel Chambless during her natural life
or widowhood or until youngest child becomes of age at which time,
should she be living and be a widow, she to have Anachy(?) and Brown
together with lot of land I now live on. Children: Lawson G.
Chambless, Andrew D. Chambless, William H. Chambless, Joseph B.
Chambless, John F. Chambless, Sarah Ann Chambless. Executors: wife
Rachel and Lawson G. Chambless. Wit: Benjamin Russell, John Parks,
Elizabeth Russell. (p. 31)

THARP, JOHN A.
     November 24, 1834. ...of sound mind memory and understanding.
To wife Elizabeth A. Tharp, land, negroes, household and kitchen
furniture, horses, cows and hogs. Mentions Mary Boon, James Madison
A. Tharp, William A. Tharp, Caroline Reynolds, Elizabeth Rogers,
Catherine A. Tharp, Cicero A. Tharp, Obedience A. Tharp, Henrietta A.
Tharp, Mathew A. Tharp, John Vinson A. Tharp, Robt. A. Tharp.

Executors: wife Elizabeth A. Tharp and children William A. Tharp and Robert A. Tharp. Wit: Richard Fish, William Stackey, Henry S. Ross, Johnson Reynolds. (p. 32)

GODFREY, FRANCIS H.
June 20, 1835. November 2, 1835. ...of perfect mind and memory. To wife Nancy Godfrey, household and kitchen furniture with exception of two beds bedsteads and furniture for the same, and a dressing table and stand, also my plantation tools, saving and excepting a set of Blacksmith's tools, also a horse called "true blue." To daughter Godfrey Virginia Godfrey, one bed and bedstead and furniture, also my african negro woman Hannah call short Hannah. To grandson Francis Harrison Godfrey Powledge, one shotgun. To relative living with him, James W. Harrison, one year horse colt Bellfast. To friend and brother Mason, Henry G. Lamar, my Masonic Royal Arch diploma, my mark or jewel and other Masonic articles. Daughter Martha Susan Powledge. After my death, my Executors to sell balance of property and proceeds together with debts due me, after paying my just debts, be appropriated as follows--to daughters Frances H. Godfrey and Godfrey Virginia Godfrey, $300 each over and above the portions allotted to my wife Nancy Godfrey and daughter M. Susan Powledge, then balance be equally divided between wife and three daughters. Executors: friends Henry G. Lamar and Doctor Ambrose Baber. Wit: J. L. Owen, Thos. R. Lamar, John L. Mustian. (p. 33)

BEALL, ROBERT AUGUSTUS.
July 14, 1836. July 21, 1836. Body be decently interred according to rites of Methodist Episcopal Church. Just debts be paid as soon as possible. A fair valuation or appriasement to be made by my neighbors, Col. E. Hamilton, Mr. J. Cowles, and Mr. Robt. M. Fort. Wife Carolie S. Beall. To daughter Florida Jane Beall, negro girl Amelia. My gold watch be sold and money to be used to mark graves of my parents. Executors: wife Caroline, friend Henry Lockhart of Warren County, and Edward B. Young of Twiggs County. Guardian for daughter Florida Jane Beall to be wife Caroline, my mother Elizabeth Beall, and friend Henry Lockhart. Wit: E. Hamilton, Thos. Hardeman, Edw. R. Ballard. (p. 35)

HOWARD, JOHN
March 29, 1836. October 10, 1836. ...in good health and sound mind. To wife Susan P. Howard, negroes Addy, Mary, Josiah, Daniel, Adam with the House and out Houses, one acre land, house and furniture, horse and surry. To daughter Susan A. Smith, negro girl Margarett. To daughter Caroline, my girl Hester with all her issue, with bed and furniture and Bureau to be given her at her marriage or age of twenty one years. To daughter Lydia Anciaux, my girl Kitty Ann with her issue, bed and furniture, with a Bureau to be given her at her marriage or age of twenty one years. To daughter Mary, at time she reaches age of sixteen, my boy Silas, with bed and furniture, and a handsome Bureau, or sooner, if she marry. To son Thomas at age twenty one, my boy William. To son John at age twenty one, my boy Josiah. To son Edwin at age twenty one, my boy Alexander. Laura (a cripple) to remain in possession of wife with her mother Aggy until my daughter Mary shall marry. To son Thomas Coke, my silver watch and all my papers. Executors: wife Susan and friend Thomas Hardeman. Wit: William Fort, Luke Bliss. (p. 37)

DARRAGH, ARCHIBALD
February 3, 1836. November 21, 1836. ...weak in body but of sound mind. Executors to collect all debts due me, after paying my debts in state of Pennsylvania, pay over any surplus, one half to Daniel Darragh, other half to Mrs. Beard. My friend Major Davis of Pittsburgh should make a gratuity of the lot of which I now live to my natural daughter Mary Darragh. My trunk and all my clothes and papers to be sent to Pittsburgh to my Executor. Persons indebted to me in this county should pay over to Charles J. McDonald the amount due, and he to apply it to my funeral expeses, and forward any surplus to my nephew Neil Darragh of Pennsylvania. Executor: nephew Neil Darragh. Wit: Charles J. McDonald, John Loving, H. H. Howard. (p. 39)

SMITH, GEORGE A.
December 23, 1835. To wife Angess, all my property. She
allowing my children in her body begotten a maintenance and so
forth. At her death, property to be equally divided among children.
Ip. 40)

ASBURY, JONATHAN.
April 16, 1837. May 1, 1837. ...of sound mind but feeble
body. My property should remain on the plantation for the raising
and schooling of my two children. To wife Jane, all household
furniture, stock of cattle & hogs. Two youngest children, James
Houston and Jane Caroline. To oldest daughter Nancy, two dollars.
Executor: wife. Wit: Charles McCardle, William Dickson, David
Moncreaf. (p. 41)

LANIER, JOHN I.
July 3, 1837. July 26, 1837. To my beloved mother, the house
and lot where we now live, also my negro man Tom. After her death,
the property to be sold and equally divided between N. B. Beard,
Josephine and Sarah Beard, Susan Lanier, John M. Simmons and Caty
Ann Dopson daughter of Thomas B. Porter. To N. B. Beard, my negro
man Peter, also my interest in stock of goods of firm J. Lanier &
Co. To Josephine Beard, my negro man Bob. To Sarah Beard, my negro
woman Fanny and two hundred and fifty dollars. To Sarah Simmons and
her heirs, my negro woman Milly and two hundred dollars. To John
M. Simmons, four hundred dollars. To Caty Ann Dopson, two hundred
dollars. Executors: Mathew Sicks, Aaron Lessel. Wit: Hampton H.
Howard, Samuel Pace, William M. Hill. (p. 42)

HARREL, HARDY
October 8, 1837. October 30, 1837. ...weak in body but of
sound and disposing mind. To son James Jardy Harrel, two lots on
Walnut Street in city of Macon adjoining each other and making
together a swaure of an acre and bordering on the reserve at the
end of the street; also my negro fellow Bob. To son Green Berry
Harrell, the lot on Bridge Street whereon I now live, being composed
of one half of two half acres lots and containing one half acre
more or less, adjoining lot of Mrs. Long. Executor to deed title
to said lot to said son according to the description contained in
the deed to the same to me from Nathan C. Monroe, Esq. To son Green
B. Harrell, my negro woman Betty and her four children Maria, Lucy
Ann, Ned and Phillis. To daughter Malinda Strickland, the lands I
own in Upson County, being fifty acres of land adjoining the Factory
lot, and nine acres where I formerly lived after the death of my
wife. To my children in equal proportion, the sum of ten thousand
dollars in money and notes. Children among whom said sum to be
divided are Sarah Keown, Rachael Lyons, Polly Mathews, Betsy
Mathews, Nancy Hearn, John Harrell, Susan Park, Rebecca Hammock,
James H. Harrell, Green B. Harrell and Malinda Strickland. To son
James H., a note of five hundred dollars which I hold on him.
Executor: friend Charles J. McDonald. Wit: James M. Green, Wm. E.
Harrell, George Vigal. (p. 43)

WEED, JOSEPH D.
September 16, 1838 Monroe County, Georgia. November 10, 1838
Bibb County, Georgia. ...of sound mind but greatly in body and
expecting soon to die. All of my estate of any and every kind to my
three sisters Amelia Frances Weed, Mary Elizabeth Weed, and Sarah
Ann Weed. Executors: my brothers Henry D. Weed and Edwin B. Weed.
Wit: Simri Rose, Henry J. Chalmers, Thomas Taylor. (p. 45)

NAPIER, THOMAS
February 17, 1832. October 29, 1838. ...in good health and
sound and disposing mind and memory. To wife Nancy, my right title
and interest in certain tract of land in Putnam County containing
202½ acres adjoining Hardy Waller; also negro Minty and her child
Aberdeen, Nelly, Becky and her two children Flora & child with all
their increase since the year 1826. I confirm a gift of six negroes
heretofore made by me to my youngest son William W. Napier and

delivered over to Singleton Holt his Trustee. Have already given
and advanced to my sons Thomas T. Napier, Leroy Napier & Skelton and
my daughters Martha and Tabitha, money and property to amount of
ten thousand dollars each. Also advanced to daughter Sarah Harvey
property estimated at three thousand dollars each making in all to
her and her children twelve thousand dollars. Executors: sons
Thomas Leroy and Skelton Napier and son-in-law Nathan C. Munroe.
Wit: Scott Cray, J. Washburn, Robt. W. Fort. (p. 46)

JOHNSTON, WILLIAM
     March 2, 1837. November 1838. ...beinf of health of body and
sound in mind and memory. To wife Million S. Johnston, two lots of
land in the Fourth District originally Houston now Bibb County and
known as lots No. 232 and 231. Also lots of land No. 3 in square 24
in City of Macon, also negroes Rose, Venus, Robert and Squire. Also
to wife, the use of lots of land No. 183 in 5th District originally
Houston now Bibb County until son Luther R. Johnston is 18 years of
age and No. 232 in 4th District originally Houston now Bibb until
son Morgan P. Johnston is 18 years of age. To son Gideon Johnston,
all property I have heretofore given him. To son Caleb Johnston,
property heretofore given including $550. To daughter Mary Ann Turk,
property heretofore given including negro woman Amelia. To daughter
Rebecca Turk, property heretofore given including negro Jim. The
wife and child of my deceased son Joel Mac Johnston, property heretofore given him. To son Asa Johnston, property heretofore given
including negro man May. To son Loyd Johnston, property heretofore
given including negro Frank. To son Albert Johnston, property
heretofore given including $550. To son William B. Johnston, negro
man Sam, girl Sal, land on which he now lives in Bibb County. To
daughter Susan Clark, three negroes Allen, Peggy and Nancy. To
daughter Eliza Harrington, three negroes Maria, Harriet and Caroline.
To daughter Vastile Johnston, four negroes Fanny, Mourning, Viney
and Orange. To son Luther R. Johnston, three negroes Spencer, Tom
and Matilda. To son Morgan P. Johnston, four negroes Jack, Maria and
her two children. To daughter Millison H. Johnston, four negroes
young Ben, Daniel, Mary and Jean. To daughter Ann Miriam Johnston,
four negroes Wiley, Powell, Julius and Sopha. Executrix: wife
Millison S. Johnston. Executors: Peter Stubbs and son Gideon
Johnston. Wit: Charles J. McDonald, Alexr E. Patton, Abner P.
Powers. (p. 53)

WILLIAMS, JOHN
     July 31, 1839. August 6, 1839. ...of sound mind and dispos-
ing memory. To wife Ann R. Williams, my plantation known as the
swamp plantation in Baldwin County. At her death, the plantation
to go to son Green and his heirs. To son Nathaniel G. Williams, the
mill plantation in Baldwin County. To son Reuben S. Williams,
plantation lands now in his possession in Lee County. To son John
J. Williams, plantation lands now in his possession in Lee County
and adjoining the lands of Reuben S. Williams. Negroes Milly and her
child Rachael, Anabella & Eliza and Major to my son Reuben S.
Williams. in trust for my daughter Eliza W. Ward. Negroes Jack,
Anaka, Julia, Grace to sons Reuben S. Williams, John J. Williams
and Nathaniel G. Williams in trust for my daughter Sarah C. Cowles.
Negroes Betsey and her child Maria, Louise & Jefferson to sons in
trust for daughter Mary Ann Cowles. To son Reuben S. Williams,
negroes Jordan, Mathew, Meshack and Mary now in his possession.
To son John J. Williams, negroes Man and his wife Sally Dick & Mary,
their two children Angelina & Simon Frances & Floyd. To son Nathaniel
G. Williams, negroes Amos and Redd. Sum from proceeds of estate to
be used for education of my grandson John W. Van Wagnon. Executors
to sell furniture in Central Hotel and proceeds to be applied to
discharge of such debts assumed for and on account of said Hotel and
Horace R. Ward. Executors: friend Richard H. Randolph and sons
Reuben S. Williams, John J. Williams, Nathaniel G. Williams. Wit:
Edw. D. Tracy, John J. Gresham, S. C. Lippitt. (p. 57)

FORT, ROBERT W.
     May 27, 1839. July 9, 1839. I Robert Fort of the City of

Charleston and State of South Carolina but at present in City of
Macon... desire body to be interred according to ceremonies of
Methodist Episcopal Church. To wife Adeline W. Fort and minor
daughter Julia L. Fort, forty thousand dollars share and share alike.
In event of death of Julia L. Fort during her minority, ¼ amount
bequeathed to her to be equally divided among my brothers Benjamin,
Marand, William, Ira E., Edward L. & James Fort and my brother-in-
law, Thomas J. Shinholser. Also out of said child's portion in the
event of her death, $1000 to Missionary Society of the Methodist
Episcopal Church to be used at the South. Also out of said portion,
$1000 to Archibald W. Martin and Mrs. Antionette Beall wife of Col.
Thomas N. Beall and William H. Scott son of Wm. F. Scott of Baldwin
County. To brothers Edward L. and James Fort, $4000 each. To
brother Ira E. Fort, $1500. Executors: friend Everard Hamilton of
Macon and John R. Hayes of Charleston, S. C. Wit: J. B. Wiley,
James Wimberly, Thos. J. Cater. (p. 62)

DANIEL, WILLIAM
     December 27, 1839. January 6, 1840. Just debts be paid and
any balance from estate to be equally divided between wife Ellen and
son William Lafayette. If son die unmarried or without children,
whole estate to go to wife. In event of death of wife and son being
unmarried and without children, estate to go half to wife's relatives and half to my relatives as would inherit under the laws of
this state. Charles Hutchins appointed Guardian of son William
Lafayette. Executor: Charles Hutchins. Wit: Ossian Gregory,
W. L. Wright, Levi Calhoun. (p. 65)

LAMAR, BENJAMIN B.
     November 28, 1835. February 1, 1836. ...of sound mind.
Executors: James Lamar, Henry Lamar, John Lamar, wife Eliza Lamar.
They to purchase land to put my negroes upon and that they be kept
together and given to the children as they become of age. To Rev.
John Robinson, my religious books. Wit: Dan'l S. M. Carter. Wm.
Simmons, W. C. Eubanks. (p. 66)

CHURCH, RODMAN E.
     December 14, 1839. May 21, 1840. ...feeling apprehensive
that my dissolution is near at hand. Desires monument for himself
and my dear Maria (who has just preceded me to the tomb). A neat
fence to be erected around the three graves after the same plan and
construction as the one around the grave of Charles A. Jones except
the brick work be not quite so high. Executors to make full inventory of stock in trade of Church & Strong. Appoint brother-in-law
Lewis L. Strong as Guardian for two only sons Lewis Sheldon &
Robert Rodman Church. As much as my brother L. H. Church has provided for my dear mother in her declining years, I do give him such
portion of the estate of Sarah Church, as may fall to my share at
her decease, said property as may fall to my share at her decease,
said property being in Town of Bethlen State of Connecticut.
Executor: brother-in-law Lewis P. Strong and neighbor John L.
Jones. Wit: E. B. Weed, Henry Williams, Jas. A. Wallis. (p. 68)

NIXON, WILLIAM
     July 26, 1838. May 7, 1840. Having heretofore justly provided
for my children by my first wife...to wife Pricilla Nixon formerly
Pricilla Pickett, the house and lot whereon I reside in Vineville,
furniture, family carriage, carriage horses and driver John. Estate
real and personal to be equally divided between wife and my children
born of her body to wit. Eliza Ann, Francis Lee, Mary Ellen,
Elizabeth Caroline, George Henry, Mertimore and Caroline Winn. Wife
to have management of my carpenters Syrus, Jim and Tom and my brick-
layer Davy. Executors: wife: Pricilla Nixon and friends John D.
Winn, William B. Parker. Wit: Christopher B. Strong, William A.
Pearce, Jr. T. Strong. (p. 71)

HOLT, TARPLEY
     November 29, 1839. Steptember 7, 1840. ...weak in body but
sound in mind and memory. To wife Betsy Lane Holt, my mansion house

with the square of land on which it is situated known by lot No. 318 in 13th District originally Monroe now Bibb County containing 202½ acres with two fractions No. 323 containing 28 acres and No. 324 119¾ acres adjoining the above square. To wife Betsy, four negroes Surry about 35 years of age, Peggy about 45 years of age, Cuty 30 years, Debary about 38 years. Have given unto son Abner Flewellen Holt, three negroes Emily, Hampton and Sam. Gave to son-in-law John B. Ross five negroes. Gave son-in-law Timothy M. Furlow, negro woman and $300. Mentions 310 acres land called the Carter Tract adjoining the land given to my wife, also a tract of land in Gwinnett County which I leave to be sold by my Executors. To son William Simon Holt, in addition to his equal portion, the sum of $200. Son Tarpley Lafayette Holt to receive a collegiate education out of my estate. Daugther Martha S. Holt to receive one bed and furniture extra. Executors: Abner F. Holt, John B. Ross, Timothy M. Furlow. Wit: Simeon Holt, Phillip Thurmond, James Wilson. (p. 75)

HARDY, WHITMILL
January 30, 1837. April 1, 1841. ...of sound mind and memory but knowing the uncertainty of life and the certainty of death. To Eliza Proctor, who is my daughter by my first wife, the sum of $50. To wife Sidney Hardy and my children by her, the balance of my estate. Executors: Robert Collins and wife Sidney Hardy. Wit: Stephen Collins, B. Stebbins, Charles Collins. (p. 78)

WIMBERLY, REBECCA
November 21, 1840. March 1, 1841. I, Rebecca C. Wimberly formerly Rebecca C. Jemison being infirm in health but of sound and disposing mind and memory, do by power reserved to me, in the marriage settlement between myself and present husband James Wimberly, declare this to be my last will and testament. To brother John Jones, the negroes Canada and Sally. To son Ezekiel Wimberly (under 21), the one half of remainder of estate. To brother John Jones, remaining half of estate in trust for daughter Laura P. Fort formerly Laura P. Wimberly. Ezekiel Wimberly when he reaches age 21, he to become Guardian and Trustee for my daughters Caroline H. Jones and Laura P. Fort. Executors: brother John Jones and husband James Wimberly. Wit: John J. Gresham, Jno. R. Boon, Geo. Jones. (p. 79)

DRAKE, FRANCIS
July 23, 1838 Wake County, North Carolina. August 1838 Nash County, North Carolina. I, Francis Drake of the County of Wake and the State of North Carolina being of sound mind and disposing memory...to wife Elizabeth, use of the negroes Fed, Byrd, Perry, Carver, Ally, her three youngest children Say, May, James & Baldy also Caroline and Mary with her two youngest children Maridy and Robert. To wife, two horses that I got of my son W. F. Drake. To daughter Dorothy Drake, the negro girl Siley. Children of deceased son Green, a child's portion of estate. No person to be allowed to bid for negroes in State of North Carolina except my children or son-in-law. Anyone can bid on negroes in State of Georgia. Executors: wife and two sons-in-law Nicholas W. Arrington and Thomas W. Wright. Wit: Wm. Bart, J. A. Drake. (p. 181)

RUTLAND REDDICK
April 1, 1840 Burke County, Georgia. July 6, 1840 Bibb County Georgia...being in weak & inform health but of sound and disposing mind and memory. To nephew Berry Rogers of City of Macon and County of Bibb, all estate real and personal. Having sent for Mrs. Parthenia Cawthron wife of John Cawthron of state of Tennessee to come and nurse me during my illness, I require my Executors to give her the sum of $500 should she arrive in Waynesboro or come to Georgia by the last day of this month. I have many relation to wit. half brothers and sisters and a full brother I know not whether he be dead or alive, and as there is in Tennessee a woman who has been entitled to the appelation of wife by me who has a child married to James Tindal--I declare they are not forgotten but designedly omitted

as legatees. Executor: nephew Berry Rogers. Wit: T. H. Blount, Edward Gaileck, Thos. Moore Berien. (p. 83)

> Note: The will was contested by the daughter, Mrs. James Tindall, on the grounds that her father was not of sound mind and because she had married the man she loved instead of the man of her father's choice. The will was not broken.

THURMOND, PHILLIP

April 15, 1840, Jasper County, Georgia. July 1841 Bibb County Georgia. I Phillip Thurmond late of County of Jasper now of County of Bibb...considering the uncertainty of human existence and being in sound mind and memory. To son Thomas Thurmond, of State of Alabama, all the negroes recently hired to him. To granddaughter Eliza Holt wife of Doctor Abner Holt, a life estate in negroes Raglin and Silva his wife and her children Jordon, Fanny, Aggy and her youngest children whose names not recalled, together with Peterson, Moses, Sam, Fillis, Lewis and negro woman Lucy purchased from Jarrel Beasley. To daughter Parthena Raines wife of Cadwilla Raines of Bibb County, negroes Jaicy, John, Ellick, Coulis, Tilda, Henry and Jordon her children Rhoda and her child Daniel and his wife Lucy and her children Pete, Emily, Caroline, and Bet and her children Jim, Isam, Washington, Levin and Jack. To son John Thurmond, negroes Lydia and her children Graville, Stephen & Lucy, Reuben, Rachael and Stephen A Blacksmith and his wife Diley Jordan and his wife Fanny and her son Sam Israel. To daughter Susan Rivers, negroes Willis, Ben, Reuben, Nancy and Betty and her children Holland, Joe, Dick, Mary, Easter, Frank, Litty, Henrietta. To daughter Eliza Lamar widow of Benjamin B. Lamar, negroes Ben & Bedy of which she is now possessed, also one hundred shares bank stock in the Ocmulgee Bank at Macon, also the sum of $1000. Executors: grandsons Philip F. and Harvey Lamar. Wit: E. Hamilton, William S. Holt, Chas. F. Hamilton. (p. 86)

PITTS, LOUISIANA

April 20, 1841. July 5, 1841. ...of sound disposing mind and memory. To nephew William Thomas Nelson, the negroes Mariah and Sarah, also land in Carroll County, interest in estate of my deceased brother Bazil Pritchard. To nieces Mary Louisa Alden and Louisiana Alden, negroes Jacob and Jubu. My sister Piety Alden to have the possession of the portion of the property devised by me to my said nieces until one or both of them shall marry. Executors: friend Col. Henry G. Lamar and Henry G. Ross. Wit: Piety Alden, Thomas Saulsbury, Benj. E. Myrick. (p. 88)

MINCHEW, PHILLIP

November 8, 1841. January 5, 1842. ...of advanced age and knowing that I must shortly depart from this world. To son NATHAN MINCHEW, my yellow negro woman Sealy about 28, and my boy Giles about 14, Allen 7 years and Henrietta 1 year old. To daughter Melvina Paul wife of William Paul, and to her children, negro Malinda about 20, Edward about 8 years, Martha about 6 years, Mary about 5 years. My friend Freeman Paul to be Trustee for property herein bequeathed. To son George Minchew, negro Levin about 19, Eva about 11, and Simon about 5 years. To son Mottimer Minchew, negro boy Lewis about 16, Adams about 14, Lacy about 13. To son Haywood Minchew, negro Henry about 11, Alford about 9, Lucy about 11. My lands in Houston and Bibb Counties be divided between my three sons George, Mottimer and Haywood. Wit: Aaron Lessel, Lemuel Watson, James B. Johnson. (p. 91)

CALHOUN, ELBERT

May 1, 1840. March 7, 1842. ...of sound mind and memory. To son Aquilla Turner Calhoun, negroes Simon, Ann, Allen, Malinda, Lawrence and Isham alias Reuben. To daughter Elizabeth Smith Bivens, negroes Mariah, Sabrina, Mary, John, Diley. To son Seaborn Augustus Calhoun, negroes Jacob, Caroline, Elizabeth, Andrew, Julia, Isam, Joshua, and lots of land No. 69, No. 84, No. 85 each containing

202½ acres and the east half of No. 83 containing 101½ acres. To
daughter Martha Victoria Calhoun, negroes John, Nancy, Moses, Elvira,
Ester & Bill. To daughter Susan Ella Calhoun, negroes Arnold, Jim,
Wiley, Emeline, Harriet and Benjamin. To son Elbert Calhoun, negroes
Alexander, George, Ephraim, Winey, Susanah, and lots of land No. 347,
No. 340, No. 339, No. 341, No. 349 each containing 202½ acres, also
east half of lot No. 330 and No. 331 each being 101¼ acres all the
above land in 13th District Bibb originally Monroe County. To
beloved wife, negroes Sophia, Caroline, Reuben, Pratt, David, Judy.
Executor: son Aquilla Turner Calhoun and Seaborn Augustus Calhoun.
Wit: Jesse L. Owen, Levi Eckley, C. A. Huggins, J.P. (p. 93)

MARTIN, JOHN
     October 30, 1841. April 14, 1842. ...being indisposed though
of sound mind. To daughter Eliza Mary Martin, negroes Jerry, Patty
and her six children, also Mary and her four or five children that
are in the state of Mississippi. To daughter Martha D. Martin,
negroes Laney and her six children, also Hetty & Mingo and his wife
& her three children. To son Robert Martin, negroes Mary, Griffin,
Janet & child and Eliza & child, little Sam, Daniel, Barnett, Henry,
Candis & Dick. To son John Martin, negroes Betsy Ann & her three
children, Emeline & two children, little Jim, Alfred, Edmond,
Jesse & Mitchell. To daughter Rebecca Frances Martin, negroes
Peggy & her six children. To daughter Elizabeth Leona Griffin Martin,
negroes Peter & Jane & her two children. Title to each daughter's
share to vest in trust to their uncle George Walker. To wife Eliza
Julia Martin, negroes Harriet Ann, Olly, Adeline & Charles, Harry &
his wife Phebe & her son Lumpkin; also my lands in Cherokee, Cass &
other counties in upper part of this State. Executors to dispose
of house and lots in Macon and the lands on Walnut Creek to settle
at discretion with the State Bank. Wife to chose between land in
Macon and my plantation in Houston County. Executors: friends
George Walker and James Smith, also my two sons when they come of
age. Wit: U. L. Wright, Joseph Smith, James Smith. (p. 96)

RYLANDER, JOHN CHRISTOPHER
     October 18, 1842. January 1843. ...of sound mind. To son-in-
law Charles Citeren(?), five dollars. To each of my grandchildren,
each of my daughter's children, five dollars. To my daughter, a
negro woman, also negro man Ben. To sons Mathew E. Rylander and
William J. Rylander, lot of land in Dooly County known as lot No.
97. Wit: Lott Malesly, R. B. Washington, Thos. R. Newton. (p. 99)

HARDIN, MARTIN L.
     December 17, 1842. January 1843. ...of sound mind and memory.
All property real and personal to be equally divided between wife
Sarah Elizabeth and my little daughter (not yet named) except two
colts which to be given to my two nephews James and Henry Wilks.
Executors: John H. Lowe, William G. Macon. Wit: Basil Lamar,
Patrick Cunningham, Alexander I. Raymour. (p. 100)

LONG, LOUISA
     February 14, 1843. June 9, 1843. ...of sound mind and memory.
To daughter Piety Alden, my negro woman Missouri and her two children
named Tyler & Henry, and after her death to her daughter Mary Alden.
Executors to sell boy Providence to best advantage at a year's
credit for notes with undoubted security, and divided said notes
equally between my two grandsons John A. Nelson and James Nelson.
Executors also to sell my present dwelling house in City of Macon in
the corner of Walnut and Bridge Street in like credit of twelve
months for notes with undoubted security, which notes to be divided
as follows, $100 to daughter Lucy Vigal, $100 to daughter Piety
Alden, and residue equally divided between grandsons John A. Nelson
and James Nelson. Executor: son-in-law George Vigal. Wit:
Washington Poe, Fredinand Horne, Eliphalet E. Brown, J.P. (p. 101)

BUSH, ISAAC
     January 19, 1835. February 20, 1835. I, Isaac Bush, of State
of South Carolina and District of Barnwell, being sick but of perfect

mind and memory...sons William and David shall pay all my just debts.
To wife Zilpha Bush, all household and kitchen furniture, and after
her death to my son David. To daughter Sary McElmurray, negroes
Jane, Jack, Tenah, Polly and Lucinda. To son John, if ever should
apply personally or by an agent, our cow and calf. Hereby confirm
all deed and other conveyances heretofore assigned over to William
and David. To grandson Isaac Newman Bush, negro girl Betsey.
Executors: sons David and William. Wit: Samuel Tarver, John B.
Bowers, Sharry Weathusber. (p. 103)

> Note: Certified as copy of original will from Will Book C,
>   page 138, in Barnwell County, South Carolina Court-
>   house. Certified as true copy by Orsamus D. Allen,
>   Judge of the Court of Ordinary for Barnwell District.

DAVIS, REBECCA
     December 1, 1838. October 24, 1844. I Rebecca Davis widow...
body be decently intered at the burying ground of the Baptist Church
at Hone (Hove?) Creek in the County of Twiggs. Son Benjamin Davis
to inherit all my estate real and personal except negro woman Alice
and her children, which are to be sold and proceeds equally divided
among balance of my children. Executors: sons Benjamin Davis and
Elisha Davis. Wit: G. M. Powell, John Powell. (p. 105)

ROSS, LUKE
     Noncupative will September 11, 1844. Joseph Willett, Thomas L.
Ross, and John B. Ross were present on night of sixth day of
September 1844 at residence of Luke Ross, who departed this life
Tuesday morning September 10, 1844. His will that wife Mary G. Ross
possess all of his property. Attest: J. L. Owens, J.P. September
11, 1844. Signed: Jas. Willett, Thomas L. Ross, John B. Ross
(p. 106)

HALL, SELINA P.
     March 4, 1844. July 7, 1845. ...of an advanced age and in
feeble health but of sound and disposing mind. To daughter Susan P.
Howard, all property real and personal, and at her death to go to
her children. Appoint grandson John W. Howard Trustee of my daughter
Susan P. Howard. To granddaughter Isabella A. Howard, negro woman
Caliner. Executrix: daughter Susan P. Howard. Wit: C. Vaughan,
Jos. C. Hunt, James B. Payne. (p. 107)

PERRY, JAMES R.
     July 10, 1845. August 18, 1845. ...being in ill health. Wife
Sarah to have full control of what effects I may die possessed of.
Children be kept and brought up under guidance of their mother.
Executrix: wife Sarah. Wit: J. C. C. Burnett, Rebecca H. King,
James B. Artope. (p. 109)

MOORE, GEORGE W.
     March 23, 1844. January 12, 1846. ...of sound disposing mind
and memory. To wife Polly Moore, negroes Peter, John, Adolphus,
little Peter, America and Caroline. After her death, the negroes
to become property of my grandchildren by my son Joshua G. Moore
late of Bibb County. Also to wife Polly, the negroes Buck and Jenny
and the plantation whereon I now reside containing 202½ acres more
or less. Rest of estate to grandchildren, the children of my son
Joshua G. Moore, deceased. Executors: Daughter-in-law Polly Moore
and grandson Henry E. Moore. Wit: David Reed, Albert B. Ross,
Henry G. Ross (p. 111)

ROSS, MARY G.
     January 1845. January 12, 1846. ...of sound disposing mind and
memory but in feeble health. To daughter-in-law Sarah Ross, wife of
my son Henry G. Ross, and to her children by said son, the negroes
Sam about 27 and Moses about 17. Title to said negroes to vest in
son Thomas L. Ross as Testamentary Trustee of said daughter-in-law
and her children. To John B. Ross in trust for son James L. Ross
and his children, the negroes Letty and Lucy and the sum of $175 in

cash, which has already been paid and advanced to James L. Ross. To
my grandchildren, children of my son John B. Ross, the plantation on
which I formerly resided, being in Bibb County on the East side of the
Ocmulgee river on the read leading from Macon to Clinton, and hereby
appoint Dr. Abner F. Holt as Testamentary Trustee of my grandchildren,
children of John B. Ross. To son Henry G. Ross, in trust for son
Thomas L. Ross and his family, the negro woman Louis, negro girl
Tinsy, also the sum of $300 in cash. To son John B. Ross, negro
woman Chancey about 36. To William C. Redding in trust for son
William A. Ross and his family, a negro woman Pleasant and her child
Mary Ann, also negro man Cyrus and woman Marthy. To John S. Childers
in trust for son Benjamin F. Ross and his family, negro woman Rose
and sum of $300 cash. To John B. Ross in trust for son George W.
Ross, the negroes Emanuel and Pompey and sum $250. To James P.
Holmes of the County of Early in trust for my daughter Maira Wardlaw
wife of George B. Wardlaw and her children, negroes Fanny and her
two children Lucy & Wesley, also negroes Cynthia, Jarrett, Isham To
John B. Ross in trust for my daughter Harriett M. Colquett, negro
Jane and her child Chaney, also sum $1125. To granddaughter Antoinett
E. Griffin, the negroes Sam about 27, Jeney about 22 and George her
child age 1. Title to those negroes to be vested in Joseph Willet
as Trustee and Testamentary Guardian of said Antoinett E. Her
mother Sarah Griffin to have use of said negroes till Antoinette
E. arrives at lawful age or marries. To John B. Ross in trust for
granddaughter Amaretta Ann Ross, $200 to be invested in a negro girl
of that value. Executors: sons Henry G. Ross and Thomas L. Ross.
Wit: William W. Chapman, William S. Holt, James M. Jones. (p. 113)

Codicil to above will dated October 22, 1845. January 12, 1845.
January 12, 1846. Should granddaughter Antoinett E. Griffin depart
this life without leaving a child, the one half property bequeathed
to her shall go to grandson John Thomas Griffin under like trust.
Wit: J. Horne, J. T. Redding, James M. Jones. (p. 116)

BAREFIELD, SAMPSON
    April 27, 1846. July 6, 1846. ...in low state of health but
of sound and sane mind. To my eight children viz. Wm. P., Sampson
W., Robert B., John R., Elsy Maryana, James F., Benjamin R., and
Septimus T., all property real and personal to be equally divided
among them, with exceptions. Son Wm. P. having received $75 said
amount to be deducted from his share. Son Sampson W. having received
a sorrel horse and $40, said amount to be deducted from his share.
Son Robert B. having received a sorrel mare with $40, said amount
to be deducted from his share. To five youngest children viz.
John R., Epsy Maryanna, James F., Benjamin R., and Septimus T., the
sum of $40 each. Executor: brother Richard Barefield. Wit:
J. C. Woodson, John A. Heifer, George G. Miller, J.P. (p. 119)

PATRICK, ABRAM P.
    May 2, 1846. November 2, 1846. ...in delicate health but of
sound mind. To sister Mary Balsly wife of Thomas J. Balsly, property
real and personal. J. R. Gilmer to act as her Trustee. To friend
George M. Logan, one distributive share of estate. To uncle Pleasant
Phillips, one equal share of estate. To uncle James Phillips, one
equal share of estate. To niece Elizabeth J. Lee, one third part
of one equal share of estate to be vested in James T. Morehead as
her Trustee. To niece Jane Elizabeth Patrick daughter of William
Patrick dec'd., one third part of one equal share of estate. To
Nephew Thomas J. D. Patrick son of William Patrick dec'd., one third
part of one equal share of estate. Executors: friends George M.
Logan of Macon, Georgia and James T. Morehead of Greensborough,
North Carolina. Wit: Bennett Bell, Sterling Lanier, Sarah V. Lanier.
(p. 121)

McARTHUR, JOHN N.
    July 22, 1844. November 2, 1846. ...of advanced age. To wife
Harriet, the west half of lot of land No. 155 my present residence
and a negro woman Nancy. Estate to be kept together until children
all become of age. Executors: my three sons Daniel P., Samuel and

John McArthur. Wit: Thomas B. Little, Simon Sikes, Mathew Sikes, William S. Doyle. (p. 123)

MATHEWS, TIMOTHY
     October 14, 1846. November 2, 1846. ...of advanced age and state of affliction though of perfect recollection and sound discretion. To wife Martha Mathews, that portion of my estate which I received from the estate of her father. To Sarah Goode wife of Benjamin Goode and to her children, $600. Nephew Timothy M. Furlow to be Trustee of that bequest. To Margaret Redding wife of Robert Redding and her children, the negroes Isham and his wife Hannah, Watt, Austin, Louisa, Anthony, Emanuel, Harriet, Allen, Tom and George--Timothy M. Furlow to be Trustee of that bequest. Executors: wife Martha and whatever suitable person she may select. Wit: Casey S. Lesusur, Charles T. Hill, James S. Bivens. (p. 125)

FLEWELLEN, ANN
     October 12, 1846. December 28, 1846. ...being weak in body but sound mind and memory. To eldest daughter Patsy Mathews, $500. To second daughter Betsy Lane Holt, $500. To third daughter Nancy Myrick, $500. To youngest daughter Margaret Redding, $500. Remainder to be equally divided among all my children or their legal representatives. Executor: William C. Redding. Wit: Roland Bivans, John G. Hartiman. (p. 127)

ENGLAND, CHARLES T.
     June 26, 1847. July 5, 1847. I Charles T. England of Baltimore, Maryland knowing that I must shortly depart from this world...
G. W. Adams to pay my $50 debt to Edward Tinker. To my sister Mary E. Wyatt, house and lot in Macon. Mr. Charlton has watch and chain valued at $120, returnable and pay said sum to Thomas Purse. Mr. W. Kine has $240 my money and Robt. Munson $150 my money. I am indebted to G. J. Blake. Executor: Geo. W. Adams. Wit: M. C. Williamson, Forney Willis. (p. 128)

     Note: Geo. W. Adams of Chatham County, Georgia refused to
            qualify as Executor.

MCGEE, PERRY
     August 27, 1846. July 24, 1847. ...of advanced age...hope for eternal salvation through the blessed Lord and Savior Jesus Christ, whose religion I have professed and enjoyed 22 years. To wife Mehulday with whom I have lived for 17 years, lot of land No. 16, 4th District originally Houston now Bibb County, containing 202½ acres; also horses, hogs, cows, sheep, household and kitchen furniture two wagons. Lot No. 151 3rd Section 28th District Cherokee and lot No. 102 1st Section 7th District Cherokee to be sold. My children to be educated out of the proceeds. Executors: wife Mahulda and friend William Long. Wit: Milton Rape, E. W. Callihan, Lewis A. Avant. (p. 130)

RANDOLPH, RICHARD H.
     February 24, 1843. September 6, 1847. ...in feeble health but of sound disposing mind and memory. To wife Eliza, my house and lot in City of Macon in which I now reside; also negroes Nancy and Sarah. Balance of estate to be kept together and equally divided between my wife and children Eliza Bullock, Eugenious Wingfield, Richard Henry, Anna Cowles and Thomas Russ, children to receive shares when they reach 21. Eugenius A. Nisbet appointed Guardian for children. Executor: wife Eliza and friend Eugenius A. Nisbet. Wit: B. H. Moulter, E. B. Weed, Thomas R. Lamar. (p. 132)

     Note: Will mentions property in Bibb and Morgan counties,
            Georgia. One set of appraisers appointed for property
            in Bibb and another set of appraisers for the property
            in Morgan.

14

ODOM, SABUD
Undated will. October 23, 1847. ...weak in body but of sound
mind and memory. My mother, as soon as possible after my death, to
take into her care my child George Sabud Odom as Guardian of said
child. My mother Mildred Odom collect debts due me and invest same
in negro property for benefit of said son. In case of the death of
my mother before said son reaches age 21, then my friend Turner Smith
and his wife Elizabeth Smith take said son into their care. For
good causes that are satisfactory to me, I do not wish my wife to
control my child nor do I wish her to share my estate. Wit: Thomas
P. Stubbs, Session Perkins, Robt. B. Lester. (p. 133)

Codicil dated September 24, 1847. If child George Sabud Odom
die before age 21, entire estate to go to mother Mildred Odom,
Sarah Carson & Elizabeth Smith, share and share alike. Wit: Thos.
P. Stubbs, James A. Knight, Leroy J. Kimbrough. (p. 133)

SHOTWELL, HARVEY
January 5, 1848. January 25, 1848. I Harvey Shortwell,
recently residing in the City of Macon but now in Rahway in the State
of New Jersey...being in feeble health but of sound and disposing
mind... Executors may sell property in Georgia and New Jersey for
purpose of paying my just debts. My interest in the drugstore in
City of Macon, conducted by Shotwell and Gilbert, to continue if
partner agrees until the 31st of Decr 1848 when said partnership
by agreement terminates. To wife Louisa Shotwell, rest of estate,
and after her death to my children (unnamed). Executors: friend
and relative Henry P. Shotwell of Rehway, New Jersey and friend James
L. Saulsberry of Macon, Georgia, and wife Louisa Shotwell. Wit:
R. K. Hines, James H. Bishop, John R. Boon (p. 135)

CUTTER, HENRY S.
July 6, 1818. October 15, 1847 Chatham County, Georgia. January
1848, Bibb County, Georgia. I Henry S. Cutter at present of Savannah
in the State of Georgia being of sound and disposing mind, memory
and understanding. To wife Annah, all estate real and personal.
Executrix: wife Annah. Wit: Richd. M. Berrien, Wm. H. Cuyler,
J. Cuyler. (p. 139)

DURRETT, LOUISA B.
February 25, 1848. March 6, 1848. ...of advanced age. To my
daughter Susan G. Cook wife of Henry L. Cook one half my property
real and personal. To son David M. Durrett, other half of property.
Executors: daughter Susan G. Cook and son David M. Durrett. Wit:
Chas. D. Hammond, R. McGoldrick, Saml. F. Goor, Thos. I. Hunt.
(p. 141)

WILDER, WILLIAM L.
April 7, 1848. July 3, 1848. ...being in low state of health,
but of sound and disposing mind. Property to be sold and after
debts are paid, the remainder to be equally divided between my wife
Nancy Wilder, my daughter Susan Ann Rebecca, and my son Charles G.
Wilder. My father Green Wilder and my brother-in-law Isaac F. Herd
appointed as Executors. They also appointed Guardians of my children.
Wit: Elijah D. Tucker, Alexander Jones, George Griggs Miller, J.P.
(p. 143)

PEPPER, DANIEL P.
November 6, 1847. July 3, 1848. ...of sound disposing mind
and memory. To wife Sarah Pepper during her natural life, and in
remainder to my son Jesse George Pepper, my two negro carpenters
James and Richard, also my farm in Randolph County. To wife, my
house and lot in City of Macon, household and kitchen furniture,
horses and carriage, and negroes Shadrack, Charles, Jacob, Henrietta
and Nancy. To son Jesse George Daniel Pepper, the negroes Sandy,
Boney, Will, Harvey, Moses, Emily, May. To son Franklin L. Pepper,
negro Brister and one third part of my cattle, hogs and sheep.
Executors: wife Sarah and son Franklin L. Pepper. Wit: Richard
McGoldrick, Bery Rodgers, George W. Grims. (p. 145)

GROCE, ANN
      October 1, 1848. November 6, 1848. ...of advanced age. To
daughter America Andrews wife of Joseph B. Andrews, a negro girl
about 10 named Amanda, also negro Emeline about 5. To grandchildren,
the children of my son Lewis J. Groce, a negro woman Vina about 28
and her child Harriet. To son Jarrott W. Groce, negro woman Anna
about 25 and negro man Hardy about 50. Lewis J. Groce appointed
Trustee for property given to Jarrott W. Groce. To son Solomon J. B.
Groce, negro boy Harrison about 10, also two lots of land in Cherokee
region of this State. To daughter-in-law, the wife of my son
Solomon, one bay mule. To son Lewis J. Groce and son-in-law Joseph B.
Andrews, each $5. Executors: son-in-law Joseph B. Andrews. Wit:
Chas. P. Hammond, J. R. Clarke, J. P., Richd. McGoldrick. (p. 147)

MACARTHY, WILLIAM HENRY.
      July 17, 1848. November 6, 1848. ...of sound mind and memory.
Wife Ariana to be sole Executrix. She may employ legal advice in the
settlement 'of my business that may be connected with the office I now
hold as Sheriff of Bibb County. Should wife need any assistance in
disposing of any part of my estate, then my brothers to assist her.
My children to receive such an education as means of estate will
allow. Wit: R. McGoldrick, Charlton H. Wells, Chas. T. Quintard,
Albert J. Macarthy, J.P. (p. 149)

ASKEW, JOSIAH F.
      September 19, 1848. December 4, 1848. ...weak in body but of
sound mind and memory. To brother-in-law Green B. Haygood, my
manuscripts either to publish or to deliver my sons when they reach
such an age to appreciate them. If my Library can be retained, it
to be divided between my two sons when they reach an age my
Executor shall think enables them to appreciate it. Remainder of
estate to wife and children, share and share alike. My "Book
Business" be carried on for a time. The Southern Pulpit to be
carried on permanently with my brother Rev'd Jas. R. Thomas of the
W. F. College as editor if his services can be procured. Children
to be strictly governed and brought up in the nurtue and admonition
of the Lord. For this purpose, they to be judiciously scattered
provided friends will take them. I would suggest Betty to my
beloved Sister Paul, D'Arce to Brother Paul as soon as old enough,
Mary to my sister Martha Haygood, and Lovick to any suitable person
who will take him. If my dear mother-in-law can take any of the
family, I beg her to take Emma my own dear wife and her own dear
daughter. Reason for scattering children is that my beloved wife
cannot raiseth children as they ought to be nor manage to provide
for them. Wish my body be interred by Order of the Sons of
Temperance. If not, let it be buried on some cheap plain style by
the side of our dear babes at Sister Calhoun's. If any funeral, let
my beloved Bro. W. R. Branham preach. Executor: brother-in-law
Green B. Haygood. Wit: Thos. Hardeman, Peter Solomon, W. R.
Branham. (p. 151)

TRACY, EDWARD D.
      February 17, 1849. March 5, 1849. ...being infirm and weak of
body, but of sound mind & disposing memory. Executor to sell my
Baker lands, my swamp land, my office. House and lot in which I now
reside to be kept as a residence for the family (children unnamed).
Executors: wife Rebecca Caroline Tracy and friend John J. Gresham.
Wit: J. B. Wiley, T. R. Bloom, Sarah Q. Fluker. (p. 154)

BLAKE, MARY ADALINE
      February 18, 1847. March 19, 1849. All property real and
personal to be vested in a Trustee for benefit of husband Samuel R.
Blake and son Samuel Reese Blake. Absalom H. Chappel of Bibb County
named as said Trustee. The Trusteeship shall cease when son becomes
21. Wit: M. P. Flint, William M. Cromby, Washington Poe. (p. 156)

SOLOMON, HENRY
      February 26, 1845 Twiggs County, Georgia. January 25, 1847
Twiggs County, Georgia. ...of an advanced age. Executor to sell

16

property and pay just debts. Balance of property be divided between wife and lawful children (giving to wife one child's part) except Mary Ann Wiggins wife of William M. Wiggins, to whom I have already given a portion of property. Wife Lucinda Solomon appointed Trustee for daughters until they are old enough to choose for themselves. To son Hartwell Solomon, my gold watch. To son Henry Solomon, $80 in cash or property. Executors: wife Lucinda Solomon and nephew James Land, Peter Solomon and Larkin Griffin. Wit: M. Land, Wm. J. Stephens, Wm. Faulk, Cary Solomon, Abrm. Garbor. (p. 158)

HUDSON, JAMES
January 13, 1849. July 2, 1849. ...of advanced age...professed religion nearly 49 years...an equal division to be made with my wife and children (not named). Executor: son-in-law Henry N. Scarborough. Wit: John Mitchell, John Scott, Joseph Ford. (p. 162)

BURNETT, JEREMIAH
August 8, 1849. November 5, 1849. ...of sound and disposing mind and memory but of feeble health. To wife, the negro woman Hannah and her children. To Narcissa Bailey who has been adopted by me and raised in my family since she was an infant and to my daughter Missouri Ann Rebecca and Ann Eliza, one bed and bedding, bedstead. Youngest children to receive same education as oldest children. Balance of estate be divided among my children, the said Narcissa Bailey and my beloved wife. Executors: son Alexander Burnett and friend John Bailey. Wit: R. K. Hines, Abner Hammon, Ellison Edwards. (p. 164)

Codicil: Dated August 11, 1849. Makes more provision for wife and younger children. Wit: R. K. Hines, G. Parker, Boswell Parker.

RANDOLPH, ELIZA M.
May 30, 1848 Morgan County, Georgia. January 21, 1850 Bibb County, Georgia. To Judge E. A. Nisbet in Trust for my daughter Eliza Bullock Randolph, negro woman Nancy and one fifth part of estate. To Judge E. A. Nisbet in Trust for my daughter Anna Cowles Randolph, negro woman Sarah and her child Judy and one fifth part of estate. To sons Eugenius Wingfield and Richard Henry, each one fifth part of estate. To Judge E. A. Nisbet, one fifth part of estate. Executor: Judge E. A. Nisbet. Wit: E. B. Weed, Martha P. Triplett, Ann R. Williams. (p. 168)

LUNSFORD, ENOCH
January 8, 1850. March 4, 1850. ...weak in body but of sound mind and memory. After payment of just debts, property real and personal be divided between wife, son George J. Lunsford, and grandson McDonald King Brady. Executors: son George J. Lunsford and wife Precilla Lunsford. Wit: Thos. P. Stubbs, M. S. Thomson, Elam Alexander. (p. 170).

CLARKE, MARK D.
October 10, 1850. November 25, 1850. ...of sound and disposing mind and memory. To wife Nancy M. Clarke, all estate real and personal. After her death, estate goes to children Mary V. Clarke and Georgia S. Clarke. Son William F. Clarke already well provided for. Executrix: wife Nancy M. Clarke. Wit: Herman Mead, James M. Green, Washington Poe. (p. 171)

CAUSEY, LEAVIN
November 13, 1850. January 13, 1851. ...in feeble health but of sound mind & memory. To daughter Susan (my most affectionate daughter), nine negroes to wit. Mary, Martha about 17 and child Lucy, Penny about 24 or 25, Collins about 12, Jim about 13, Washington about 14, Solomon 17, Morris about 16, and $2000 cash; also $1000 out of debts due me in Alabama. To wife Nancy, my house and all lands adjoining, being 63 acres more or less, also negro man Tom about 30 or 35. To daughter Jane Beasley (wife of William I. Beasley) and her children, negro woman Mariah and her oldest son John and Lewis. To

17

Julia Manning, two acres more or less off the lot of land I now
reside on. Rest of estate to friend James W. Armstrong. To James
for sons William Causey, Philip Causey and George Causey. To James
W. Armstrong, lot of land on which my son Alexander now lives, being
two acres more or less. Children of Alexander Causey: Charlton
Leavin Causey, William Byron Causey and Polina Causey. Wit:
Washington Poe, Charles Thompson, W. Holmes. (p. 172)

BLACKWELL, RANDOLPH
    March 17, 1850 Madison County, Kentucky. February 24, 1851
Madison County, Kentucky. On February 24, 1851 in the town of Richmond
Madison County, Kentucky, an instrument purporting to be the will of
Randolph Blackwell was brought in--William Rhodes and Robert B.
Cornelison the subscribing witnesses.

    To granddaughter Elizabeth Randolph Winn, negro Jane now in my
possession at James Bogg's, which woman to be held and controlled by
my son John R. Blackwell. Should she die without issue, negro Jane
goes to son John as Trustee for granddaughter's Mary Ann Francis
Pettis' children then living. To grandson William R. Yeddell, negro
child Felix (son of negro woman Jane, mentioned above), boy Bill,
girl Kate. Should he die without issue, then the three negroes
belong to my granddaughter Frances Atkins; and should she die without
issue the negroes go to living children of John McMahan, my grandchildren. To granddaughter Frances Atkins, negro woman Fanny and her
three children. If she die without issue, negroes go to my grandchildren the heirs of John & Polly McMahan. To granddaughter Frances
Atkins, $500. Executors: son John R. Blackwell and friends James
B. Walker and Doctr. Charles J. Walker. Wit: Will Rhodes, R. B.
Cornelison, R. J. Pully. (p. 175)

SCOTT, WILLIAM
    February 21, 1851. March 3, 1851. ...in low state of health but
of sound mind and memory. Family to continue to reside in house in
which I now live and the plantation on Tobesaufkee Creek be kept up
and worked until youngest daughter comes of age or marries. My
interest in Washington Hall and other town property in City of Macon
be sold by Executors. To sister Sarah Gibbons, the notes my brother
John Scott owes me. To daughter Eleanora Scott, negro girl Lucy
about 17, also one fifth interest in estate to be held in trust by
Robert Freeman and William B. Scott. To wife Eliza J. Scott, one
fifth interest in estate. To son William Byron Scott, one fifth
interest in estate remaining, in trust for use of my daughter Harriet
Freeman wife of Robert Freeman. To son-in-law Robert Freeman and
son William B. Scott in trust for use of my daughter Madeline Hamilton
wife of Charles Hamilton, one fifth interest in remainder of estate.
To son William Byron Scott, one fifth interest in remainder of estate.
Executors: son-in-law Robert Freeman and friend John J. Gresham.
Wit: Thos. Hardeman, Simri Rose, Daniel Dustin. (p. 178)

VIGAL, GEORGE
    February 9, 1851. March 3, 1851. ...in low health but of
sound and disposing mind and memory. To Washington Poe in trust for
my daughters Georgianna Lanier, Louisa, Ellen and George, my tavern
house and lot and furniture in East Macon. Negro Lucinda to Georgianna
Lanier, negro Harriet to Ellen Vigal, negro Lewis to George Vigal,
negro Frank to Louisa Vigal, negro Ned to John Vigal, negro Margaret
to my daughter Louisianna Johnson. Remaining negroes Abraham, Malinda,
Winney, Anice and Julia to be sold by Executors and proceeds equally
divided among said children. To son Henry who has treated me in
an unfilial manner, $200, which is his full share of estate. Rest of
property in Georgia and Alabama to children except Henry. Executor:
son John Vigal. Wit: Robt. H. Hardaway, David Flanders, Wm. T.
Lightfoot. (p. 182)

HUNT, ELIZABETH
    January 9, 1851 Monroe County, Georgia. May 5, 1851 Bibb County
Georgia. ...of sound mind and disposing memory. To grandchildren

18

Edward L. Connally, James H. Connally, William F. Connally, and
George A. Connally (children of James and Sarah C. Connally), one
third interest in estate. To daughter Ann F. Keene, one third interest
in estate. At her death, to be divided one third to John W. Walker,
one third to Ann W. Redding wife of W. D. Redding, and one third to
heirs of son Henry W. Tindall. To grandson Henry Brown, the son of
my deceased daughter Nancy M. Brown, one half of the remaining one
third interest in estate. Executor: friend William D. Redding.
Wit: William F. Carrell, Thos. M. Tyler, William C. Redding. (p. 184)

KING, THOMAS
     June 22, 1846. December 12, 1853. ...of sound mind. Payment
of justdebts. Remainder of estate to be divided between wife
Susanna and sons James N. and Thomas H., share and share alike. Have
already given to daughter Ann Mary wife of Charles Campbell. Executors: sons James N. King and Thomas H. King, Charles Campbell. Wit:
B. B. Wharton, William A. Johnson, Thomas Redding. (p. 186)

THOMAS, MICAJAH
     November 17, 1843 Jones County, Georgia. January 11, 1855 Bibb
County, Georgia. ...in good health and of sound mind and memory.
To wife Temperance Thomas, $10. To daughter Adeline Rebecca, negroes
Julia and David, horse valued at $75, two cows and calfs, two feather
beds and furniture. To son Francis A. Thomas, two negroes Tom and
Alonzo. To daughter Susan S. Thomas, negroes Caleb and Caroline. To
daughter Eliza Ann Thomas, negroes John and Charity. To daughter
Francina Rebekah Thomas, negroes William and Ann. Executor to board
out daughter Eliza Ann to some good school for one year and daughter
Francina Rebecca two years. Have already given some property to James
R. Thomas and Sarah Jane Pendleton when they were married. Executors
have $150 for defraying the enclosing and fixing my wife's and several
of my children's graves at Mt. Zion Hancock County. Executors:
sons James R. Thomas and Francis A. Thomas. Wit: Sylvanus Walker,
Robert W. Walker, Seaborn Lawrence, J.P. (p. 187)

The title on spine of Marriage Book A shows the above dates. However, from the typed records here, you can see that an occasional marriage earlier than 1827 is included in this book. Also remember that the very earliest marriages (from 1823) for Bibb County are recorded in Record of Returns Book A.

PAGE	GROOM	BRIDE	DATE
205	Adams, David	Mary Cannon	24 Sep 1835
181	Alden, George W.	Piety Pritchard	27 Jul 1834
279	Alexander, Elam	Ann G. Stone	28 Oct 1838
183	Alexander, William	Mary James	30 Oct 1834
147	Allen, Benjamin	Fanny Burdine	20 Nov 1832
23	Allen, Misu	Rhoda Johnson	16 Jan 1828
280	Altman, David	Nancy Bartlett	31 Oct 1838
133	Altman, William	Mary Rowland	6 Jan 1833
5	Alven, Isaac	Jane Lestley	6 Dec 1827
46	Ammons, Jesse	Lucinda Watson	24 May 1828
199	Ammons, Jesse	Eliza Cannon	5 Aug 1835
59	Anglaw, Jeremiah	Sena Rea	16 Nov 1828
200	Arnold, Giles S.	Delila Flowers	14 Jun 1835
32	Audolf, John	Mary M. Brown	6 Mar 1828
68	Bagby, Thomas W. W.	Elizabeth Patton	31 Dec 1829
88	Baker, Benjamin H.	Martha Oliver	2 Dec 1830
106	Baker, Dempsey	Martha Northworthy	11 Oct 1831
73	Baker, Humphrey	Emily Davis	3 Feb 1830
256	Baker, Milton S.	Cornelia B. Yates	4 Dec 1837
259	Baldwin, Richard C.	Anna Catharine Holt	10 Jul 1837
56	Baley, Samuel T.	Martha D. Strong	29 Apr 1829
51	Barber, Elijah	Sarah Jones	14 Jul 1828
102	Barber, Hircy	Martha Ann Pitts	6 May 1831
58	Barefield, Richard	Epsey Barnett	11 Jan 1829
218	Barnes, Richard J.	Emily Parker	8 May 1836
208	Barret, Jonathan A.	Sarah Pitts	10 Dec 1835
233	Bartlett, John	Ann Moore	3 Apr 1837
113	Bartlett, Myron	Tabitha N. Harvey	20 Jul 1831
234	Bass, Charles L.	Rebecca May Fluker	9 May 1837
194	Bassett, James	Eliza Thompson	5 Feb 1835
203	Bassett, John	Martha A. Corley	21 May 1835
67	Bateman, Micajah	Martha McDonald	16 Dec 1829
65	Bateman, Theophilus	Jemima McDonald	15 Oct 1829
113	Bateman, William	Mary Sikes	18 Dec 1831
81	Bayne, Jamerson A.	Mary M. Fredrick	20 Aug 1830
249	Bazerd, John Adam	Catharine Horse	13 Aug 1837
190	Beall, Thomas M.	Antoinette C. Scott	22 May 1834
237	Beaton, Andrew	Eliza Jane Mackey	9 Mar 1837
266	Bennett, Smith W.	Martha G. Newcomb	25 Mar 1838
64	Berry, James H.	Mary Noles	4 Oct 1829
240	Berry, Matthew	Linda Nobles	19 Jan 1833
91	Berry, Samuel	Mary Smith	24 Apr 1825
115	Berry, Samuel	Mary Smith	24 Apr 1825
55	Bird, Adam	Ellender Folk	22 Dec 1828
283	Blake, Edmund	Eleanor Harris	15 Nov 1838
106	Blancett, Thomas	Nancy Page	26 Dec 1830
36	Blancett, William	Massey Simms (Sims)	6 Jul 1828
39	Blanks, Littlebury	Elizabeth Perdue	29 Jan 1829
249	Blunt, Thomas H.	Sarah Clark	9 Aug 1837
18	Boon, William	Harriett Henson	6 Mar 1827
15	Boon, Willis	Mary Tharp	6 Mar 1827
64	Borin, William E.	Mariah Danelly	24 Sep 1829
242	Bowers, Benjamin A.	Sarah Ann Brown	9 Dec 1836
275	Bowman, John	Martha J. Jones (Mrs)	2 Aug 1838
277	Bowman, Robert	Martha D. Ezzell	23 Sep 1838

PAGE	GROOM	BRIDE	DATE
77	Brady, Alfred	Susan Johnson	13 Jun 1830
38	Brady, John	Marione Colionre	13 May 1827
267	Brantley, John W.	Rhoda Dillard	29 Apr 1838
41	Brasswell, Davis B.	Mary Ann E. Grant	25 Mar 1828
269	Braswell, Duke W.	Caroline S. Beall	6 May 1838
174	Braswell, Jacob G.	Mary Raley	30 Jan 1834
38	Brazell, Timothy	Sophia Killingsworth	13 Jan 1829
160	Bridges, James	Irena Powell	5 Sep 1833
105	Briggs, John	Priscilla Jackson	26 Feb 1831
180	Brinkly, William	Elizabeth Harper	3 Apr 1834
195	Brooks, Daniel B.	Georgia C. Paul	26 Dec 1835
60	Brown, Edward	Narcisey M. Talbot	13 May 1828
228	Brown, Eliphalet E.	Margaret Jane Hollingsworth	3 Nov 1836
258	Brown, George	Sarah Parker	21 Dec 1837
235	Brown, Isham C.	Frances Smith	4 May 1837
257	Brown, Israel F.	Ann Smith	26 Dec 1837
285	Brown, Thomas A.	Eliza Ann Hardin	6 Dec 1838
184	Brown, William G.	Frances S. Jones	16 Sep 1834
125	Bulkley, Edward C.	Harriet J. Hill	1 Sep 1832
142	Bulkley, Edward C.	Harriet J. Hill	1 Sep 1832
8	Bullock, Parton	Duct Smith	2 Oct 1827
266	Burdine, John M.	Mary Ann Jones	20 Mar 1838
111	Burnett, Jeremiah	Susanna Lipsey	27 Oct 1831
119	Burns, James	Sarah McDonald	20 Apr 1832
131	Burns, James	Sarah McDonald	20 Apr 1832
215	Busby, Inman	Penelope Wood	3 Mar 1836
4	Busey, Henry	Axey Turner	26 Aug 1827
104	Bush, Nathan	Elizabeth Butler	27 Oct 1831
78	Butler, David B.	Rebecca A. Campbell	25 Jun 1830
247	Butts, Albert G.	Sarah C. Stovall	11 Jul 1837
80	Byron, Edward	Elizabeth Williams	21 Jul 1830
2	Cain, William	Elizabeth McPowell	27 Sep 1827
1	Calhoun, Thomas M.	Catherine Darrington	27 Aug 1827
94	Calhoun, William H.	Martha Ann Smith	27 Jan 1831
124	Campbell, Archibald M.	Mary W. Willis	19 Apr 1832
136	Campbell, Archibald M.	Mary W. Willis	19 Apr 1832
54	Campbell, James P. H.	Martha Good	26 Jul 1829
11	Campbell, Ransom	Belleyant Smith	27 Aug 1826
148	Dampbell, Ransom B.	Elizabeth Reynolds	27 Aug 1832
287	Capels, Samuel J.	Sarah Ann Wallis	15 Jan 1839
212	Carnes, Peter J.	Emily S. Campbell	21 Jan 1836
273	Carrol, Turner	Saleta Pinckney Glover	12 Jul 1838
210	Carter, David C.	Lucinda M. Hogan	1 Dec 1835
80	Carter, Henry	Martha Cain	25 Jul 1830
50	Carter, Josiah H.	Violater Dyess	5 Feb 1829
228	Carver, Robert	Ann Eliza Hardaway	10 Nov 1836
26	Cousey, Henry	Nancy Wade	8 Nov 1827
183	Chambless, L. G.	Martha E. Russell	15 Sep 1834
90	Champlan, Guy	Mary Ann B. Ellis	16 Dec 1830
239	Chapman, John	Charlotte Flowers	11 Jun 1837
2	Cherry, Abner	Sarah Trent	25 Feb 1828
252	Cherry, Joel T.	Susan C. McCallum	5 Sep 1837
75	Chisholm, Murdock	Amelia G. Barnard	29 Apr 1830
148	Clack, James	Narcissa Brittenham	17 Jan 1833
202	Clark, Berry	Sarah Ammons	7 May 1835
227	Clark, Daniel F.	Eliza Clark	22 Jun 1836
261	Clark, John	Elizabeth Skipper	8 Dec 1838
238	Clark, John C. F.	Adeline Stevens	1 May 1837
67	Clark, William F.	Susan D. Johnston	10 Dec 1829
262	Clarke, Henry	Mary Riley	30 Dec 1838
213	Clarke, John F.	Nancy Ammonds	7 Jan 1836
48	Clements, Gabriel	Sharlott Richardson	27 Mar 1828
189	Clements, Joseph	Patsey Perkins	14 Dec 1834
265B	Cliatt, Alfred M.	Ann Allen	8 Feb 1838
40	Coats, O. S.	Rachael Miller	11 Nov 1829

PAGE	GROOM	BRIDE	DATE
29	Coleman, Robert	Polly Benton Taylor	9 Oct 1827
197	Collins, Charles	Sophia F. Fosseter	1 Jan 1835
283	Collier, John	Patience Lacy	8 Nov 1838
87	Collins, John D.	Martha Bruce	12 Dec 1830
245	Collins, Robert	Eliza C. Smith	27 Apr 1837
270	Collins, William	Letty McLemurray	14 Jun 1838
4	Collum, Absolum	Lucinda Read	21 Jun 1827
128	Cone, William B.	Nancy P. Cook	20 Dec 1832
53	Cook, Hamilton	Keziah McCardle	4 Oct 1827
248	Cooper, George P.	Ellen C. Wilson	20 Jul 1837
61	Corbett, John	Mary H. Watts	23 Sep 1829
254	Corless, William	Faith Grace	29 Oct 1837
102	Council, Jordan T.	Sophia S. Frierson	25 Aug 1831
177A	Covat, James Hamilton	Rebecca Durden	15 Jul 1834
192	Cowfield, John	Tabitha Brumbelow	7 Feb 1835
58	Cox, Drury M.	Zemily E. Hill	5 Feb 1829
82	Craft, Archin	Ellen Bryd	17 Oct 1830
177A	Craft, Jonathan	Martha Burnet	14 May 1834
20	Crawford, Charles	Louiza Boren	5 Jun 1827
267	Creagh, John G.	Lucretia Pratt	29 May 1838
36	Crew, John	Caroline Levingston	25 Mar 1828
172	Damour, John Hyppold	Ann Tobin	10 Feb 1834
30	Danelly, William J.	Ann Eliza Slade	24 Jan 1828
181	Daniel, Amariah	Elizabeth Caroline Pearson	31 Jul 1834
199	Daniel, William	Elizabeth Bone	27 Aug 1835
140	Darnell, Robert	Nancy Frederick	1 Jul 1832
173	Davis, David J.	Mary Ann Hoge	20 Feb 1834
271	Davis, G. L. Mary Chambliss		17 Jun 1838
252	Davis, Harman	Elizabeth McGraw	3 Sep 1837
272	Davis, John	Nancy Bates	20 Jun 1838
54	Davis (Davies), Thomas	Martha Wright	22 Apr 1829
156A	Day, Charles	Mary J. Crocker	22 May 1833
84	Densley, Henry L.	Mary Elliott	14 Sep 1830
236	Denton, James	Emily J. Philips	23 Mar 1837
186	Dickinson, Samuel F.	Susan W. McCook	9 Oct 1834
274	Dickson, Joseph N.	Michel Hamlin	12 Jul 1838
280	Dillard, Colin	Margaret Fish	4 Oct 1838
268	Dillard, Perry	Susan Hambly	6 May 1838
167	Donatre, Frances	Harriet Francisque	21 Dec 1833
196	Doyle, James	Mary Brown	23 Mar 1835
168	Draughon, Thomas J.	Julia A. F. Shell	10 Jan 1834
221	Draughon, William	Martha Shell	19 Oct 1835
265A	Dye, Murphy	Margarett J. Mann	5 Feb 1838
225	Dyer, William	Elizabeth McDaniel	27 Jul 1836
224	Earle, Richard G.	Sarah Kelton	5 Jul 1836
6	Eckless, Clement	Mary Ann Warner	13 Jan 1828
260	Edwards, John	Sarah Sheffield	30 Jul 1837
72	Ellis, George W.	Eliza H. Capers	22 Feb 1830
28	Ellis, Thomas M.	Catherine Wilson	7 May 1827
28	Ellis, Thomas M.	Catherine Wilson	31 Dec 1827
100	Ellis, Thomas M.	Eliza Cunningham	2 Jun 1831
226	Ellison, William H.	Sarah Ann Johnson	1 Sep 1836
156A	Ernest, Asa E.	Julia Kent	16 May 1833
116	Erwin, Dustion	Charlotta Allen	19 Jan 1832
138	Erwin, Dustian	Charlotta Allen	19 Jan 1832
100	Eubanks, James D.	Permelia K. McCook	10 Mar 1831
62	Finch, William	Sarah Audolf	19 Jul 1829
114	Flanders, Henry	Susannah Sandiford	5 May 1831
154	Foard, John	Elizabeth Thomas	17 Feb 1833
120	Folds, Edward	Lucretia Holms	3 Nov 1830
138	Folds, Edward	Lucreta Holmes	3 Nov 1830
65	Folk, Jesse	Lucinda Trawick	4 Dec 1829
162	Fondren, John G.	Nancy Thompson	6 Nov 1833
246	Ford, John	Susan Permenter	5 Jul 1837
220	Ford, William	Dilly Dye	28 Apr 1836

PAGE	GROOM	BRIDE	DATE
257	Fort, Edwin	Mary B. Munson	6 Dec 1837
237	Foster, Alexander H.	Ann M. C. Dewitt	23 Feb 1837
125	Freney, William	Martha Ann C. Colley	17 Jun 1832
135	Freney, William	Martha Ann C. Coolly	17 Jun 1832
10	Fry, John	Maria Stephens	30 Aug 1827
222	Fulkes, Branch	Elizabeth Keller	6 Nov 1836
285	Gamble, James	Bathsheba Beard	25 Dec 1838
11	Gamble, William B.	Mary M. Watkins	3 Nov 1827
151	Gardner, Benjamin	Catharine Collins	14 Feb 1833
57	Garner, Wiley B.	Franceis Finch	7 May 1829
49	Gates, James	Christion Scott	14 Sep 1828
265B	Gatlin, Thomas M.	Martha W. Gatlin	14 Mar 1838
32	Gent, Peter	Aprisnonat Mooney	30 Dec 1827
224	Gernter, Leroy	Mary Ann Courtney	14 Jul 1836
119	Gilbert, Edmond Albert	Elizabeth A. Douglass	3 May 1832
131	Gilbert, Edmond Albert	Elizabeth A. Douglass	3 May 1832
53	Gillis, Angus	Margaret M. Olston	30 Sep 1828
281	Gingainus, George W.	Nancy Brown	24 Oct 1839
42	Glover, Williamson	Florinda Munroe	10 Aug 1828
30	Grayham, Ishmal	Sally Thunderbird	5 Sep 1827
139	Graybill, Jefferson M.	Martha Benton	12 Jul 1832
195	Graybill, Midas L.	Mary Bailey	18 Nov 1834
109	Green, James W.	Ann Bassett	29 Nov 1831
42	Green, John	Elizabeth Killingsworth	29 Jun 1829
272	Green, William A.	Maria L. Jacobs	10 Jun 1838
107	Grice, William	Sarah Doles	4 Oct 1831
210	Griffin, Charles	Emeline Smith	2 Nov 1835
75	Griffin, John	Catherine Hammock	2 May 1830
83	Griffin, Lewis	Delia Melton	24 Jun 1830
21	Griffin, Rial	Martha Langford	14 Oct 1827
84	Griffin, William	Rachael Roberson	13 Dec 1829
44	Grubbs, Benjamin	Claricia Span	22 Jan 1829
44	Grubbs, Thomas	Mary Jackson	24 Jul 1828
137	Hadson, Fielding T.	Elmina Warner	20 Aug 1832
96	Hall, James A.	Elizabeth Cotton	9 Jun 1831
288	Hall, James L.	Kitty Williams	28 Feb 1839
243	Halls, James G.	Margaret Ann Mosely	17 Dec 1837
12	Hamill, Thomas	Barsheba Carson	25 May 1826
74	Hamilton, John C.	Nancy Good	31 Mar 1830
34	Hammock, James	Mary Pollard	2 Aug 1827
74	Hammock, Jeremiah	Martha Dees	27 Mar 1830
204	Hammock, Joshua	Rebecca Smith	2 Apr 1835
241	Hampton, John	Mary Dickson	20 Dec 1835
243	Hancock, Nixon	Sarah Perdue	20 Jun 1836
234	Hancock, William B.	Rachael Whittington	15 Mar 1837
215	Hand, James C.	Martha Smith	30 Jan 1836
187	Harrington, William	Eliza Johnson	25 Sep 1834
86	Harris, Wade	Elizabeth Shivers	13 Oct 1830
191	Harris, Wiley	Maria Shaw	8 Feb 1835
41	Harrold, Joel	Nancy Adams	21 Aug 1828
227	Harrold, Thomas	Mary A. Bullock	8 Dec 1836
116	Harvey, John P.	Charlotta R. Gardner	29 Apr 1832
129	Harvey, John P.	Charlott R. Gardner	29 Apr 1832
19	Head, William J.	Lucy L. Lundy	26 Jun 1827
204	Heard, Isaac F.	Francis Wilder	9 Apr 1835
221	Herrin, Philip	Lucinda Burnett	10 Nov 1836
35	Hickey, Stephen C.	Betsey Raburn	16 Mar 1828
164A	Hightower, Garland	Martha Cumby	17 Nov 1833
219	Hightower, Henry	Rhoda Dillard	24 May 1836
211	Hightower, James	Elizabeth Dillard	18 Oct 1835
97	Hightower, William	Phoeba Dillard	15 Jan 1832
3	Hill, Slaughter	Elizabeth Maulden	31 Jan 1828
182	Hill, Vincent	Maria Davis	30 Jan 1834
121	Hobby, Alfred M.	Ann Eliza Danelly	20 Sep 1832
143	Hobby, Alfred M.	Ann Eliza Danelly	20 Sep 1832
188	Holleman, Joseph J.	Martha Johnson	2 Oct 1834

23

PAGE	GROOM	BRIDE	DATE
163	Hollingsworth, John M.	Euphemia Cunningham	3 Oct 1833
203	Holmes, Frederick	Elizabeth Bagby	22 May 1835
230	Holmes, Isaac	Louisa J. Mott	10 Jan 1837
164	Holmes, John	Caroline E. Bivins	17 Oct 1833
115	Holmes, Julius	Hetty Hatcher	23 Sep 1832
144	Holmes, Julius	Kitty Hatcher	23 Sep 1832
188	Holmes, William	Caroline S. Powell	13 Nov 1834
282	Hopkins, William	Martha Lacy	8 Nov 1838
114	Hoskins, John	Polly Vines	3 Apr 1831
127	Hoskins, Mitchel	Mary Radford	21 Oct 1832
134	Hoskins, Mitchel	Mary Radford	21 Oct 1832
72	Hotsmets, Poldus	Hannah Young	18 Feb 1830
49	Howard, James W.	Martha Rockmore	5 Feb 1829
176	Howard, William J.	Ann Billingslea	24 Apr 1834
184	Howland, Calvin L.	Mary Ann Bradley	28 Sep 1834
14	Huff, Jacob D.	Elizabeth Harris	4 Aug 1825
255	Hughes, William L.	Luicey P. Calhoun	15 Nov 1837
174	Hughes, Willis	Mariann Bagby	20 Feb 1834
173	Humphries, Berry	Jane Carter	4 Mar 1834
9	Humphry, William	Elizabeth Bell	23 Jan 1828
250	Hunt, John	Mary V. Rogers	31 Aug 1837
160	Hunt, Thomas	Ann Eliza Frierson	10 Sep 1833
82	Hunter, Samuel B.	Susanna Jamison	4 Jan 1827
46	Ives, Isaac	Rachael Williams	8 Oct 1828
161	Ives, Isaac	Sarah Chance	2 Oct 1833
47A	Ivey, Anthony	Martha Wood	4 Apr 1830
34	Jackson, Duke	Doty Hood	2 Dec 1827
101	Jackson, George W.	Wilmouth Hatcher	23 May 1831
151	Jackson, Samuel M.	Caroline A. Williamson	6 Mar 1833
158	Jacobs, Philip	Mary Ann Magee	18 Jul 1833
210	Jacobs, William R.	Abbey Dennis	24 Dec 1836
205	James, Absalom G.	Martha Youngblood	23 Oct 1835
126	James, Benjamin	Mary Pitman	1 Jul 1832
144	James, Benjamin	Mary Pitman	1 Jul 1832
95	James, Isaiah	Lucinda Parker	9 Feb 1831
168	James, Joathan	Mary Miles	16 Feb 1834
177B	Jarman, Risdon	Elizabeth Grimes	26 Jun 1834
166	Jenkins, Edward B.	Lodieska Turner	19 Nov 1833
121	Jenkins, Eli	Martha Ross	10 Jun 1832
129	Jenkins, Eli	Martha Ross	10 Jun 1832
94	John, Albert L.	Sally S. Patton	17 Dec 1829
273	Johnson, Alexander	Charlotte McDonald	2 Aug 1838
279	Johnson, Asa A.	Ann Mariah Sledge	28 Oct 1838
198	Johnson, Francis S.	Lucia Griswold	20 Sep 1834
143	Johnson, Henry	Ann Jones	25 Aug 1832
57	Johnson, Josiah	Catherine Carter	12 Mar 1829
164	Johnson, William B.	Caroline B. Bailey	10 Oct 1833
270	Johnson, William J.	Mariah M. Smith	14 Jun 1838
73	Johnston, Allen	Olife L. Calhoun	11 Feb 1830
118	Johnston, Henry	Ann Jones	25 Aug 1832
282	Johnston, William B.	Eleanor Bullock	15 Nov 1838
201	Jones, Alexander	Ruth McCardell	30 Apr 1835
235	Jones, Baldwin	Polly Woodson	21 Mar 1837
240	Jones, Berry	Malinda Shinholster	9 Jul 1834
248	Jones, David H.	Frances C. Lamar	18 Jul 1837
6	Jones, Gabriel	Maria Ann Burton	2 Mar 1828
24	Jones, Gabriel	Martha Jones	31 Dec 1826
79	Jones, Gabriel	Elvia Rowland	1 Jul 1830
157	Jones, George	Eliza B. Rowland	29 May 1833
78	Jones, Isaac	Martha Dailey	29 Jun 1830
208	Jones, Isaac	Nancy Oliver	24 Dec 1835
110	Jones, James	Therza Ann Fitzpatrick	20 Nov 1831
137	Jones, John	Martha Colyer	30 Nov 1832
263	Jones, Samuel W.	Nancy Riley	5 Jan 1839
242	Jones, Seaborn T.	Mary Ann Runnells	25 Oct 1836
16	Jones, William	Elizabeth Rowell	14 Aug 1826

24

PAGE	GROOM	BRIDE	DATE
201	Jones, William M.	Jane Chambliss	15 Feb 1835
258	Jones, Willoughby	Harriet McManus	24 Dec 1837
51	Jordan, Joshua	Elizabeth Hoge	25 Mar 1828
59	Joyner, Middleton	Betsey Montgomery	24 Mar 1829
96	Keller, Samuel	Elizabeth Jones	17 Jan 1832
222	Kelton, Robert	Lucinda Bird	12 Apr 1836
91	Kent, Reubin	Julian Debow	13 Apr 1830
99	Kent, Reubin	Julian Debow	13 Apr 1830
276	Key, Caleb W.	Elizabeth Wimberly	2 Sep 1838
179	Kibbee, John M.	Martha M. Graves	10 Jul 1834
52	Lamar, Jefferson J.	Rebecca Lamar	21 Aug 1828
55	Lamar, Thomas R.	Ann J. Fulwood	25 Sep 1828
219	Lamar, Thomas R.	Eliza M. M. Lamar	14 Apr 1836
176	Lamar, Zackariah	Martha A. Rice	26 Jun 1834
22	Land, Jesse	Tobitha Darby	28 Sep 1826
107	Langford, James	Pherriba Price	10 Mar 1831
71	Langford, Joseph A.	Eliza Herring	7 Feb 1830
150	Langford, William	Mary P. Purdue	30 Dec 1832
193	Lawshe, W. C.	Mary Newsom	19 Dec 1833
40	Leslie, Moses	Nancy Mosley	2 Sep 1828
161	Lesly, John	Martha McNeal	27 Aug 1833
260	Lessell, Henry	Lucinda Martin	12 Sep 1837
9	Lewis, Charles S.	Mahala White	1 May 1827
117	Lewis, Frederick F.	Julia A. Thomas	9 Apr 1832
146	Lewis, Frederick	Julia A. Thomas	9 Apr 1832
86	Lewis, George	Agrapnia Gent	23 Nov 1828
81	Lewis, William L.	Charlotte Peal	17 Oct 1837
262	Lipsey, Gilford	Pheraby Parker	17 Dec 1837
179	Lipsey, Guilford	Lavinia Burnet	26 Feb 1834
256	Lipsey, Hiram	Caroline Bowden	18 Dec 1837
241	Long, Allford	Sarah Dickson	20 Dec 1835
281	Lord, John P.	Mary Ann Flanders	2 Oct 1838
103	Loveing, John	Spicy Ann Johnson	8 Oct 1831
66	Low, Thomas	Eliza A. Lundy	12 Nov 1829
112	Lowe, John H.	Mary F. Hardin	3 Nov 1831
172	Loyd, William	Sarah Killingsworth	23 Mar 1834
111	Lubens, Amos	Julia A. Crawford	17 Mar 1831
25	McCall, Eleazor	Sarah Patton	1 Jul 1827
278	McDonald, Archibald	Lucy Kinsey	4 Oct 1838
47	McDonald, Cade	Elizabeth Harris	11 Sep 1828
29	McGinley, James	Mary Radford	11 Aug 1827
196	McGoldrick, Richard	Martha L. Munson	16 Jul 1835
14	McIntyre, A. C.	Margaret Bozman	24 Jun 1827
288	McKaskell, Murdock	Eliza A. Nixon	15 Jan 1839
99	McKinnee, Joseph	Malinda Baker	19 Oct 1831
142	McKinney, Benjamin	Cynthia Baker	13 Sep 1832
62	McKinney, Caleb	Betsey Smith	23 Aug 1829
159	McKinney, John	Aminta Hamlin	7 Jul 1833
171	McKinney, John	Serena Crane	2 Jan 1834
124	McKinny, Benjamin	Cynthia Baker	13 Sep 1832
112	McNeal, Anderson	Rebecca Rowland	18 Oct 1831
165	McNeil, Fredrick B.	Henrietta J. Pope	12 Dec 1833
238	Maddox, Jesse	Martha E. Jones	4 May 1837
225	Mahan, Charles	Matilda Holly	11 Sep 1836
166	Manpert (Manssenett?), Adolphus	Nelia Anderson	26 Dec 1833
185	Martin, George F.	Mary Ann Smith	4 Sep 1834
169	Martin, James	Elmira Robertson	21 Jan 1834
244	Maxwell, James	Lethe Ann Trent	30 Mar 1837
152	May, William	Martha Smith	4 Apr 1833
85	Meritt, Gilford	Mary Sherry	25 Feb 1830
145	Miles, Druary	Sarah Riley	21 Oct 1832
232	Miller, Elbert	Harriet S. Hamilton	22 Jan 1837
178	Millison, Simeon	Matilda Faircloth	25 Jun 1834
95	Mobley, Joseph	Polly Carter	24 Nov 1831
104	Mobley, William	Levina Clark	28 Jul 1831
263	Molsby, Lott	Mary Turner	4 Dec 1837

PAGE	GROOM	BRIDE	DATE
31	Monckrief, David	Sarah Pollard	5 Sep 1827
163	Montgomery, Benjamin R.	Matilda Hardin	31 Oct 1833
170	Moore, Charles W.	Ann E. Mullally	13 Mar 1834
93	Moore, George W.	Mary Stephens	23 Jan 1831
239	Morrell, Albert	Milly Parks	4 Apr 1833
76	Morrell, William	Martha Pollard	17 Jun 1830
63	Morris, James	Elizabeth Barnes	6 Sep 1829
286	Mulholland, Colin	Adeline Sidney Hunt	24 Dec 1838
50	Munroe, Nathan C.	Tabitha E. Napier	5 Jun 1828
149	Mustian, John L.	Julia Frances Jeter	24 Jan 1833
206	Nance, William L.	Emily Williams	20 Oct 1835
220	Nelms, Allenson	Frances Melvina Williams	31 May 1836
7	Newcomb, Lemuel	Martha Snow	20 Dec 1827
216	Newsom, James	Emily Bickley	17 Jan 1836
89	Newsom, John M.	Catherine McCardle	25 Nov 1830
19	Norman, William S.	Martha Adaline Watts	6 Mar 1827
268	Norris, Thomas	Frances E. A. Myrick	31 May 1838
217	O'Conner, Jerry	Mary Bond	3 May 1836
223	O'Conner, Jerry	Mary Bond	17 Apr 1836
21	Oliver, Isham	Margarett Purkins	7 Jun 1825
155	Oliver, William B.	Sarah M. Bullock	25 Apr 1833
109	O'Pry, Amos	Nancy Robertson	1 Dec 1831
167	Owens, Dennis N.	Elizabeth S. Norman	19 Feb 1834
149	Owens, Franklin	Jane Barker	25 Jan 1833
37	Owing, Aaron	Sarah Phillips	8 May 1828
178	Pace, Thomas	Elizabeth Everett	28 May 1834
20	Parish, Nathan	Jane Bazemore	9 Sep 1827
232	Parker, Burwell	Nancy Jordan	10 Jan 1837
190	Parker, Seth	Eveline Ball	11 Dec 1834
69	Parks, John	Hannah M. M. Allen	31 Dec 1829
198	Parmalee, Abel C.	Catharine McCallum	27 Nov 1835
229	Passmore, Seaborn	Louisa Tharp	29 Dec 1836
48	Patton, David	Perneten J. Pace	17 Jul 1828
284	Patton, James	Almira E. Curry	6 Dec 1838
76	Patton, Robert S.	Rebecca J. Pace	3 Jun 1830
231	Pearce, Theophilus	Martha Pearson	19 Jan 1837
156	Pearson, Shadrack	Elizabeth C. Nichols	21 Mar 1833
47A	Peck, Charles	Jane Ellis	18 Mar 1830
189	Perdue, William W.	Sarah Ann Lyles	9 Dec 1834
194	Perkins, William J.	Nancy Dillard	5 Apr 1835
8	Perry, Ezeakel	Rebecca May	3 Mar 1825
286	Perry, Thomas	Flora Ann Dozier	3 Jan 1839
245	Peyton, William H.	Martha Jones	30 Apr 1837
284	Phillips, Robert	Isabella Curbow	1 Jan 1839
200	Pierce, Mitchel	Elizabeth Hammock	18 Jun 1835
193	Pierce, Rowland	Mary C. Chapman	1 Mar 1835
130	Pitman, Alfred T.	Caroline King	12 Dec 1832
118	Pitman, John	Nancy James	16 Feb 1832
140	Pitman, John	Nancy James	16 Feb 1832
164A	Pitts, George J.	Louisa Maria Howard	18 Dec 1833
39	Pitts, John	Louisanna Troutman	9 Feb 1829
210	Pitts, Richard M.	Mariah Calhoun	13 Jan 1836
45	Pitts, Willis	Bashaby Hammonds	26 Nov 1828
169	Plum, Charles	Martha English	30 Jan 1834
139	Plumb, Charles	Martha Reynolds	7 Jul 1832
122	Plumm, Charles	Martha Reynolds	8 Jul 1832
68	Poe, Washington	Salina S. Norman	24 Dec 1829
244	Pool, E. M.	Teresa Ann Tapley	16 Nov 1836
269	Pope, Juni	Patsey Stuckey	19 May 1838
255	Pope, William M.	Caroline Coleman	7 Nov 1837
218	Powell, J. D. G.	Mary D. Smith	31 May 1836
22	Powledge, Gideon	Susan M. Godfrey	29 Jan 1828
278	Pratt, Thomas	Mary E. Gurganus	28 Oct 1838
207	Price, George W.	Elizabeth C. Grannis	22 Oct 1835
274	Purdue, James	Sarah Hall	3 Jul 1838
47	Radford, Robert	Darien Wiley	5 Apr 1828
233	Raley, James	Elizabeth Reddick	15 Mar 1837

PAGE	GROOM	BRIDE	DATE
77	Ratchals, Wiley	Sarah Summerlin	16 Jun 1830
230	Rawls, J. S.	Sarah M. Anderson	20 Jan 1837
12	Rawls, Moses	Marina Rodes	2 Apr 1826
93	Ray, Henry S.	Mary Jane Smith	6 Jan 1831
155	Reaves, James	Lavinia Loveit	28 Apr 1833
123	Redding, Robert C.	Parizad Watts	28 Jun 1832
141	Redding, Robert C.	Parizad Watts	28 Jun 1832
108	Reid, Hamilton	Anna Johnson	31 Aug 1831
170	Renfro, Alfred E.	Rhoda G. Calhoun	6 Feb 1834
211	Renfro, Campbell	Elizabeth Victory	19 Jul 1835
70	Reynolds (Runnels), Marshall M.	Sarah Allen	10 Jan 1830
192	Reynolds, Nathaniel	Caroline Tharp	10 Dec 1833
162	Rich, James J.	Caroline C. Hollen	31 Oct 1833
16	Richardson, William	Susan Chatfield	15 Nov 1827
56	Rilander, Matthew E.	Nancy Gamble	22 Apr 1829
92	Riley, James	Elizabeth Frost	30 Jan 1831
90	Roberson, Beverly B.	Caroline T. Hoswell	16 Dec 1830
185	Robertson, Robt. P.	Mary Ann Morgan	14 Sep 1834
1	Rockwell, Peter P.	Cynthia Young Simmons	30 May 1827
213	Rodgers, Ascader	Amanda Bassett	3 Jan 1836
165	Rodgers, John	Elizabeth A. Tharp	9 Apr 1833
132	Roland, John	Mary Altman	27 Dec 1832
187	Ross, Thomas L.	Martha Hoge	16 Oct 1834
153	Rountree, William	Amelia M. Robison	17 Apr 1833
264	Rozar, John	Mary M. Powell	21 Jan 1838
253	Rutherford, Josiah	Sarah Honeycutt	26 Sep 1837
153	Rylander, William	Harriet Daves	23 Apr 1833
158	Salsbury, Thomas J.	Elizabeth Grant	30 May 1833
251	Saulsberry, James L.	Mary Ann Curd	7 Sep 1837
175	Scarborough, George W.	Susannah McClendon	16 Feb 1834
23	Scott, Quillah	Lucy Inglett	9 Sep 1827
154	Self, Thomas M.	Mary Bridges	25 Apr 1833
87	Sepker, William	Drucilla Sepker	14 Aug 1830
66	Sharp, James	Catherine Simmons	29 Nov 1829
13	Shaw, Joseph	Lucy Rodgers	4 Oct 1826
83	Shaw, William B.	Lucia H. Moris	18 Aug 1830
236	Sheffield, John C.	Nancy Winslow	26 Feb 1837
247	Shell, Perry	Martha Ann Collier	19 Jul 1837
275	Shotwell, Jacob	Sarah L. Newhall	11 Jul 1838
128	Simmons, Thomas	Sarah A. M. Lanier	27 Oct 1832
175	Skaggs, William	Martha Perdue	17 Apr 1834
214	Skinner, James	Margaret Kicks	10 Mar 1838
197	Skipper, Jacob	Hester B. Baker	17 Sep 1835
17	Sledge, Bryon	Delila Whatley	1 Feb 1826
259	Smith, Benjamin F.	Sarah L. Breithaupt	3 Jan 1838
88	Smith, Caleb	Malinda McKinny	20 Sep 1830
217	Smith, Eli	Frances Hand	22 May 1836
63	Smith, Ezekial	Jane Wardlow	17 Sep 1829
10	Smith, Jeremiah	Milly Bailey	2 Nov 1826
97	Smith, John P.	Eliza R. Benning	5 Jan 1832
	(Bride's name shown as Roenia E. Benning on application)		
117	Smith, Richard	Mary Smith	5 Mar 1832
132	Smith, Richard	Mary Smith	5 Mar 1832
177B	Smith, Richard	Mahala Willoughby	5 Aug 1834
180	Smith, Stephen	Harriett E. Bosworth	18 Jul 1834
146	Smith, Turner	Mary Allen	29 Nov 1832
191	Snelgrove, Starling S.	Susan Wilder	18 Dec 1834
209	Snow, John W. B.	Jane Patton	31 Dec 1835
101	Southall, William L.	Maria Bailey	16 Jun 1831
223	Sowell, Leighton	Lucy Ann Hughes	7 Jul 1836
98	Spears, William	Milley Smith	14 Feb 1831
251	Sperry, John A.	Mary McCallum	26 Sep 1837
27	Stamps, John	Nancy Bulman	8 Aug 1826
105	Steward, Henry	Sophia McKinny	12 May 1831
264	Stokes, Ezekiel C.	Charlotte Honeycutt	5 Jan 1838

27

PAGE	GROOM	BRIDE	DATE
231	Stokes, George	Frances Miller	19 Jan 1837
276	Story, Albert S.	Sarah B. Morgan	20 Sep 1838
287	Strong, Samuel M.	Mary Ella Nixon	15 Jan 1839
206	Stubbs, Thomas P.	Rebecca B. Lundy	12 Nov 1835
182	Sullivan, Alexander	Mary McDonald	31 Aug 1834
120	Swaringin, Edward	Catherine Pitts	16 Feb 1832
15	Swearingin, Edward	Mary Douglass	11 Jun 1827
214	Tabb, Thomas	Hellen Johnson	21 Jan 1836
159	Tarlton, Ransom	Mary Elizabeth Vasser	30 Jul 1833
43	Tarpley, William	Wineford King	5 Mar 1829
70	Teel, Edward	Martha Wheeler	14 Jan 1830
108	Tharp, Jeremiah E.	Narsisia Holmes	6 Sep 1831
122	Thomas, Philip	Mary Roff	2 Aug 1832
136	Thomas, Philip	Mary Roff	2 Aug 1832
253	Thompson, George W.	Amelia B. Wilkinson	1 Oct 1837
226	Tompkins, Stephen W.	Serena Williams	15 Sep 1837
27	Tompkins, William	Elelder Coutch	2 Oct 1827
156	Torres, Francis	Lavinia Brumbelow	9 May 1833
31	Townsend, Cornelius	Eliza T. Beall	27 Dec 1827
45	Tracy, Edward D.	Susan G. Campbell	25 Nov 1828
207	Travis, John S.	Eldetio Parker	6 Dec 1835
277	Trippe, William W.	Ann Eliza Bivins	18 Sep 1838
186	Tucker, Albert	Rebecca Wyche	12 Oct 1834
7	Tucker, Daniel	Sarah Rockmore	14 Jun 1827
89	Tucker, William	Elisabeth Bagby	23 Nov 1830
212	Vickers, James R.	Emeline Daves	17 Jan 1836
135	Victory, Thomas	Elizabeth Patterson	18 Aug 1831
79	Vinson, Larkin	Lucretia Miles	19 Jul 1830
134	Wadsworth, Eli	Betsy McClendon	25 Nov 1832
202	Wadsworth, Melcher	Eveline Strozier	6 May 1835
98	Wagnin, George P.	Louisa B. Danelly	11 Aug 1831
33	Wall, Jesse J.	Sarah Smith	1 Nov 1827
271	Walker, William H.	Mary Ann Smith	3 Jun 1838
25	Wallis, Albert F.	Ann Moore	12 Jul 1827
17	Wallis, Mortimer R.	Sarah Ann Norman	2 Nov 1826
18	Wardsworth, Daniel	Elizabeth Johnston	29 May 1827
133	Warner, Pleasant	Amanda Boice	20 Dec 1832
43	Watson, Lemuel	Eady Pearson	20 Jan 1829
5	Watson, Leroy	Mary M. Brunnet	15 Feb 1827
24	Watson, Thomas	Lenoron Lessell	20 May 1827
85	Wetherby, Abner J.	Mary Ethredge	21 Mar 1830
171	Wheeless, Edmund	Martha Allen	28 Nov 1833
261	White, Benjamin	Elizabeth Miller	12 Nov 1838
61	White, James T.	Claricia Dickson	18 Dec 1828
60	Whitehead, George	Henrietta Finch	4 Jan 1828
103	Whooten, John	Cynthia Rayfield	29 Nov 1831
216	Wiley, John B.	Ann G. Clopton	18 Feb 1836
250	Willbanks, James	Frances Arnold	28 Sep 1837
126	Williams, Green B.	Ester A. Perdue	14 Feb 1832
145	Williams, Green B.	Easter A. Perdue	14 Feb 1833
110	Williams, James	Catherine Arnett	20 Nov 1831
150	Williams, Micajah	Nancy Vickers	17 Feb 1833
3	Williams, Reuben	Mary Ann Green	18 Jun 1826
71	Williams, Whitmill	Mahala Wilcher	7 Feb 1830
37	Willis, William	Betsey Willsheir	14 Aug 1828
35	Wills, Joseph S.	Susan Birdsong	23 Mar 1828
246	Wilson, John	Ailsey Rockmore	12 Jun 1837
229	Wilson, John R.	Elizabeth Melton	29 Dec 1836
157	Wimberly, Henry	Amy Hogans	8 May 1833
92	Wimberly, John	Levina McDonald	27 Jan 1831
26	Wingat, Michael	Rachael Lomeiom	6 May 1827
147	Win, John W.	Sarah Clem	18 Dec 1832
52	Winship, Isaac	Martha A. P. Cook	1 May 1828
152	Wood, Thomas	Matilda E. Graves	28 Mar 1833
69	Worthy, John	Mary Killingsworth	7 Jan 1830

28

PAGE	GROOM	BRIDE	DATE
13	Wright, Edward W.	Elizabeth Morgan	12 Dec 1826
123	Wright, Edward W.	Martha W. Crowell	2 May 1832
141	Wright, Edward W.	Martha W. Crowel	2 May 1832
265A	Wry, William C.	Clarissa Jones	1 Feb 1838
209	Yawn, Nathan W.	Winney Green	19 Dec 1835
33	Young, John W.	Elizabeth Phillips	9 Aug 1827

BUTTS COUNTY, GEORGIA
WILLS, ADMINISTRATIONS OF ESTATES
1826-1841

Pages 1-2: Butts Co., Inventory and Appraisement of Estate of ELISHA BLESSETT, dec'd. given in by ELI CONGER, ROBERT CURRY, ROBERT BROWN... Sworn appraisal May 16, 1826, JAMES BRADY, J.P., ELI CONGER, J.I.C. Total value of estate $1564. 91¼... Recorded July 5, 1826.

Pages 3-4: Will of STEPHEN G. HEARD of Butts County, Ga...."being sick of body but well of mind" ... whole property... 125½ acres adjoining JEREMIAH MULLOY and others my negroes Charlotte and her 6 children, Harriett, Greene, Wilkin, Clark, Warren, Mary... all horses, stock, household and plantation, debts, property and interest of any kind sold and realized in cash and equally divided in halves by my two loving children LOVINA, wife of THOMAS HAMPTON and daughter CAROLINE, reserving and giving to my former wife SARAH, first SARAH WIMPEY 6¼ cents and her two children present living with me named ELIZABETH & OLIVE each 6¼ cents. Appoints THOMAS HAMPTON, WILLIAM GILMORE, Exors. Dated April 19, 1826. Signed STEPHEN G. HEARD... Test. WILLIE B. ECTOR, JEREMIAH MULLOY, WM. H. PARKER. Recorded July 10, 1826... JNO. TARPLEY, C.C.O.

Page 5: Court of Ordinary of Henry Co., Ga. March Term 1825. DAVID LAWSON and SUSANAH LAWSON applied for Letter of Administration on the Estate of ADAM LAWSON, dec'd.

July Term 1825, Henry County Court ordered DAVID LAWSON obtain Letter of Administration of Estate of ADAM LAWSON, dec'd. and ordered DAVID LAWSON have leave to sell negroes and land of deceased estate.

March Term 1826, Henry County, C. O. ordered DAVID LAWSON be required to make title to tract of land in Butts formerly Henry Co., 9th Dist.. Lot #54... 75 3/4 acres as pr bond rendered.

Henry Co. Clerk's office of C. O., July 29, 1826, certified true proceedings, WM. HARDIN, D.C.C.O., Registered July 10, 1826, JNO. TARPLEY, C.C.O. Butts County, Georgia.

Page 6: Butts Co., Ga., An Inventory of property of ADAM LAWSON, dec'd. Amount appraised $1105.25.

Pages 7-8-9: Henry Co., Ga., Appraisers of property of ADAM LAWSON, dec'd. Nov. 10, 1825... WILLIAM GOOLSBEY, WM. B. SMITH, WM. ALLISON, PLEASANT MOORE, ROWLAND WILLIAMS, Registered Sept. 1826, WM. BARKLEY, J.P., JNO. TARPLEY, C.C.O.

Sale of property of ADAM LAWSON Estate, Aug. 25, 1825, DAVID LAWSON, Adm... Buyers at sale: SUSANNAH LAWSON, GEO. W. RIGHT, JOSHUA BOOW, GEO. BRITAIN, JAMES PRIGGINS, JOHN EDWARDS, JAMES CARTER, DAVID LAWSON, ZADOC MARTIN, FERDINAND SMITH... Amount of sale $1113.56½... Registered Sept. 7, 1826, JNO. TARPLEY, C.C.O.

Page 10: Butts Co., Ga., DAVID LAWSON in March 1825 applied to Court of Ordinary of Henry Co. for Letter of Adm. on Estate of ADAM LAWSON, dec'd. Property appraised and sold... now submitted application made to removed administration from County of Henry to County of Butts.. granted after Administrator gave bond in Butts Co. first return in Butts Co... listed were notes payable to DAVID LAWSON by JOHN R. CARGILE, EZEKIEL FEARS, DAVID BEAUCHAMP, JAMES STROUD, THOMAS ROBINSON... Total amt. $288.79.

Page 11: Amount brought forward $288.79, JOHN MALONE, SHETTON LAWSON, JOSEPH POST, JAMES PRIGGINS, WM. B. SMITH, A. BROOKS, BIRD PRUET, SAMUEL JOHNSTON, WM. HARDIN... Total $982.36... Estate DAVID LAWSON, Admr.

Pages 12-13, 14-15:   Inventory of property of ELISHA BLESSETT,
dec'd.   Sold at public sale July 18, 1826. Names of purchasers, NANCY
BLESSETT, SYLVANIE HENDRICK, AARON WOODWARD, JAMES BRADY, CATTETT CAMPBELL,
JOHN WILLINGHAM, JAMES TURNER, JOHN W. COTTON, THOMAS TUCKER, DAWSON
HEATH, JAMES HARKNESS, JOHN BARKLEY, JACOB CLOWER, CLARK HAMMEL, YELVER-
SON THAXTON, JOHN PITTMAN, HUGH HAMMEL, PHINEA KELL, WM. NUTT, JAMES
MORRIS, JAMES C. BANKSTON, NATHANIEL PETERS, STEPHEN BLISSET, HENRY
STORMAN, REASON BLISSIT, WM. HARPER, SAMUEL LOVEJOY, ABEL L. ROBINSON,
JAMES KELLEY, JESSE KELLEY, ELI COOPER, HUGH MORRISON, JAMES H. EDWARDS,
ELI CONGER, BASDELL POTTER.   Total Amt. $1663.49... Registered Nov. 4,
1826... JNO TARPLEY, C.C.O.

Page 15:   Butts Co., Court of Ordinary, March 1, 1826. Present
JOHN MOORE, JOHN HEARD, WOODY DOZIER, ELISHA W. BRAVES, Judges... Ordered
that ELI CONGER, appoint guardian for CINTHIA E. SPEARS, EDGAR SPEARS,
and HENRY SPEARS, orphans of JOSEPH SPEARS, dec'd... JAMES L. BURK and
EZEKIEL WALKER SECURITY... sum of $600 for his guardianship.
     Copy of Bond witnessed March 1, 1824... Signed ELI CONGER, JAMES L.
BURK, EZELIAL WALKER... J. C. GIBSON, C.C.O.

Page 16:   Jasper Co., Ga., J.C. GIBSON, C.C.O. of Jasper Co.
certifies to true copy of bond appointing ELI CONGER guardian of orphans
of JOSEPH G. SPEARS, dec'd.   Dec. 16, 1826... Registered Jan. 2, 1827,
J. C. GIBSON, C.C.O., JNO. TARPLEY, C.C.O., Butts County, Ga.

Pages 16-17-18-19-20:   Inventory of STEPHEN G. HEARD, dec'd...
Appraised by ABNER BANKSTON, STEPHEN HEARD, HUGH H. HEARD, JAMES (X)
BENTLEY, Aug. 11, 1826... Amt. $2733.43.
     Above appraisers oath of fulfillment of their duty... WILLIE B.
ECTOR, J.I.C. Registered March 27, 1827... JNO. TARPLEY, C.C.O.

     Sale of Estate of STEPHEN G. HEARD... Name of purchasers: E. E.
KERKSEY, JAS. BENTLEY, STEPHEN D. HEARD, JEREMIAH MALOY, BENSON JACKSON,
JOHN M. MCMICHAEL, HIRAM GLAZIER, JOHN KIMBRO, JAS. GILMORE, THOMAS
HAMPTON, HUGH H. HEARD, WM. HARTSFIELD, MATTHEW MCMICHAEL, ALLEN MARTIN,
SAMUEL NUTT, JACOB HOLLEY, WEST H. KERKSEY, FERDINAND SMITH, SPIVY CANNON,
BENJ. F. TUCKER, JOHN LASETER, WM. GILMORE, ISAAC NOLEN, CHRISTOPHER
TORCHSTONE, JOEL BALEY, GEORGE BRITON, JOHN CANNON, ZADOC LOVE, PRYOR
EDWARDS, THOMAS RUNNEL, THOMAS MATTHEW, A. REAM, BURWELL JACKSON, BETHANY
CARTER, SIMPSON RUSSEL... Amt. of sale $2833.27½... Reg. Mar. 30, 1827.
JNO. TARPLEY, C.C.O.

Page 21:   ROBERT CURRY, Guardian to HEZEKIAL WHEELER, minors...
Qualified in open court March 29, 1826... JNO. TARPLEY, C.C.O.

     Estate of ELISHA BLESSET dec'd., paid STEPHEN BLESSET, Admr.
$11.43 3/4 December 1826... Registered... JNO TARPLEY C.C.O. March 21,
1827.

     BENJAMIN HAMMOCK Admr. of Estate of JOSEPH G. SPEARS dec'd. for
CYNTHA E., EDGAR C., JOSEPH H. SPEARS, minors, $150.00... December 26,
1825.

     September Term 1823, transferred from Jasper Co., Ga. to Butts Co.,
Ga. for tuition to FURMAN WALTHALL, $6.00... Butts record pr voucher.

Page 22:   January 7, 1826... Cash paid HUGH B. STEWARD for tuition
of JOSEPH H. SPEARS, minor... voucher $2.50. July 16, 1826... 5 3/4
yds. calico for CYNTHA E. SPEARS... voucher $2.31¼, ELI CONGER, guardian.
Reg. May 4, 1827... JNO TARPLEY C.C.O.

     Jasper Co., Ga., Court of Ordinary, May 5, 1823, Present BENNET
CRAWFORD, WOODY DOZIER, JOHN HEARD, JOHN K. SIMMONS, Judges.

     THOMAS LINDSEY, heir of SAMUEL LINDSEY dec'd. 14 yrs., made choice
of GEO. F. SPEAK as Guardian... Granted... LYDIA and SAMUEL LINDSEY
other heirs of SAMUEL LINDSEY under age 14 yrs. and LEROY CURRY and GREEN
B. JACKSON bound for $800 as guardian... These also qualified.

31

January 1st, cash paid NANCY LINDSEY for schooling $8.50. May 5th, cash paid N. WARNER for professional service $4.00. Recorded July, 1823. J. C. GIBSON C.C.O.

Page 23: Returns registered... List of credits paid to orphans of SAMUEL LINDSEY, May 18, 1825.
Returns made to orphans of SAMUEL LINDSEY, June 30, 1826. Register-ed May 10, 1827... J. C. GIBSON C.C.O... JNO TARPLEY C.C.O., Butts Co., Ga.

Pages 24-25: Butts Co., Ga., Dr. to Estate of STEPHEN G. HEARD dec'd. to WM. GILMORE and THOMAS HAMPTON, Exors, Oct. 5, 1826. Note #1 to Eatonton Bank $235.00... Notes #2 to #21 March 10, 1827, Total $1146.75. Note #22, March 10, 1827 to Note #37, July 6, 1826... Total $1648.89... All notes examined and approved... JOHN HENDRICK, J.I.C. Registered May 9, 1827... JNO TARPLEY C.C.O.

Pages 26-27: Will of JOHN SMITH of Putnam Co., Ga. ... "weak of body, sound of memory" ... to beloved wife ANN SMITH all stock and household furniture... to wife for life 2 negroes Charlotte and Molly also 100 acres of land in 1st Dist., Henry Co., Ga., Lot 186($\frac{1}{2}$)... to dau. NANCY C. SMITH one of 1st born children of Molly or Charlotte and 100 acres after death of mother also one bed and furniture... to daus. MARY and MARTHA P. BROWN and NANCY C. SMITH after death of mother Molly and Charlotte equally divided... to my sons THOMAS, JOHN, WYAT, STEPHEN, WILLIAM and MANSEL SMITH and SHERWOOD MASSEY $1.00 each... Appoints wife ANN SMITH and RICHMOND BROWN, Exors... Made July 8, 1823... Signed: JOHN (X) SMITH. Witness: JOHN SMITH, ROBERT HILL, HENRY E. HORN.
Putnam Co., Ga... The Will of JOHN SMITH proven by oath of signed witness March 1, 1824... THAD B. REES, C.C.O., Putnam Co., Ga.

THAD B. REES, C.C.O. of Putnam Co., Ga. certifies this is a true copy of the original will of JOHN SMITH, signed April 27, 1827 by THAD B. REES, Clerk of County Court of Putnam Co., Ga. Reg. May 10, 1827... JNO TARPLEY, C.C.O. Butts Co., Ga.

Page 28: Will of THOMAS RUNNELS of Butts Co., Ga... Made Jan. 12, 1827... Proven Sept. 3, 1872... "being weak in body, sound in mind"... debts paid... wife JANE RUNNELS have all property life time... after wife's death all sold and equally divided between my 4 children, JAMES RUNNELS, WM. RUNNELS, THOMAS P. RUNNELS, GEO. J. RUNNELS... dau. POLLEY COPPEGE to have no part of property as her husband, LEWIS COPPEGE al-ready has her part except one dollar... Appoints ABNER BANKSTON, THOMAS P. RUNNELS, Exors. and wife JANE RUNNELS, Extrix. Signed THOMAS (X) REYNOLDS... Wit: JOHN HEAD, JOHN HEARD, THOMAS (X) HAMPTON.

Page 29: Returns on Estate of JOHN C. PATRICK... Dr. to CORNELIUS ATKINSON, Guardian of orphans of said PATRICK... yearly returns from 1819 to 1825. Returns are for board, schooling, and clothing for SUSAN PATRICK.

Page 30: Record of CORNELIUS ATKINSON, guardian for SUSAN PATRICK, orphan of JOHN PATRICK, dec'd... on Sept. 30, 1826, SUSAN PATRICK now SUSAN MCCUNE, paid in full.

Record 1819-1826... schooling, board, and clothing of MARTHA PATRICK, orphan of JOHN PATRICK... CORNELIUS ATKINS, guardian.

Page 31: CORNELIUS ATKINSON, guardian for MARTHA PATRICK, orphan of JOHN PATRICK, dec'd... Returns for schooling, board, and clothing cont in full account Sept. 30, 1826 to FREEMAN WALTHALL, Dr.

Page 32: CORNELIUS ATKINSON, Dr. to Estate of JOHN C. PATRICK from 1819-1826... hire of negroes account... Jackson Co., Ga... EDWARD ADAMS, C.I.C. Certifies it is a true copy of the records of said court, Jan. 3, 1828... Recorded Jan. 12, 1828... JNO TARPLEY, C.C.O., Butts Co., Ga.

Page 33:   Yearly returns for orphans of JOHN C. PATRICK, dec'd. by guardian CORNELIUS ATKINSON... 1827 for MARTHA PATRICK paid Clerk of Court in Jackson Co., Ga. $4.00... SUSAN MCCUNE now (formerly SUSAN PATRICK) fee to Clerk of Jackson Co., Ga. $4.00... Signed CORNELIUS ATKINSON, guardian... Registered Jan. 14, 1828... JNO TARPLEY, C.C.O., Butts Co., Ga.

Page 34:   Dr. the Estate of STEPHEN G. HEARD to WILLIAM GILMORE one of the Exors... 1827... Vouchers #1 to #16... Total $1086.46½.

Page 35:   Con't Dr. to Estate of STEPHEN G. HEARD... Vouchers #17 and #18, paying out $1253.25... Three vouchers $16, #17, #18 for 20.50 rejected by court,less $20.50. Total paid $1232.75. Reg. Jan. 15, 1828. JNO TARPLEY, C.C.O.

Page 36:   Ga., Butts Co. The estate of STEPHEN G. HEARD, Dr. to THOMAS HAMPTON one of the exors... 1827... Vouchers #1 through #12 money paid to SPENCER HEARD, HUGH H. HEARD, CHARLES HEARD out of his own money. Sworn to JNO. TARPLEY, C.C.O.

Page 37:   Returns of DAVID LAWSON, Adm. of Estate of ADAM LAWSON, dec'd. 1827... Vouchers #1 through #11, Amt. paid $232.28. Registered Jan. 14, 1828... JNO. TARPLEY, C.C.O.

Pages 38-39:   Inventory and Appraisement of Estate of WILLIAM RHODES, dec'd. Items 1 through 65... Total Amt. $1200.12½.

Page 40:   Appraisers' sworn affidavit for certification on estate of WILLIAM RHODES, dec'd... Signed Nov. 1, 1827... GIDEON MATHIS, C. F. KNIGHT, EDWARD WEAVER... SAMUEL BELLAH, J.P. Registered Jan. 15, 1828... JNO. TARPLEY, C.C.O.

Inventory of Personal Property of WILLIAM RHODES, dec'd... sold at public sale Jan. 3, 1828 on a credit till the 25th December next... Purchasers... ABEL BANKSTON, JOHN URQUHART.

Pages 41-42:   List of purchasers con't... RICHARD POUND, WILLIAM THAXTON, THOMAS TUCKER, SAMUEL CLAY, YELVERTON THAXTON, THOMAS MCBURNET, SAMUEL BELLAH, THOMAS POSTER, JAMES PRIGGIN, WM. B. SMITH, GEORGE W. HILL, ABRAHAM MCHATON, ELI COOPER, RICHARD HAMLET, Private sale amt. of whole $473.85. Registered Jan. 15, 1828... JNO. TARPLEY, C.C.O.

Estate of ELISHA BESSET, dec'd... Dr. to STEPHEN BLESSET... March 21, 1827... Voucher Amt. $11.92... Registered Jan. 15, 1828. JNO. TARPLEY, C.C.O.

Page 43:   DAVID LAWSON, Adm. of estate of ADAM LAWSON... To SUSANNAH EDWARDS (formerly SUSANNAH LAWSON) 1825... corn $8.00, pork $5.00, cosser $8.00. Boarding STACY, JOHN, PEGGY, ADAM, DELPHY, and WINRIGHT, children and orphans of ADAM LAWSON, dec'd. one year $180.00... Total $201.00.

Georgia, Butts Co.... Sworn in open court that account is true... March 5, 1828... Signed SUSANNAH (X) EDWARDS... JNO. TARPLEY, C.C.O.

March 3, 1828... Received by a guardian for JAMES SCRUGGS, $194.00. Signed WILLIAM HURST.

1827... Estate of STEPHEN G. HEARD, dec'd... for first, second and third trip expense to and from Milledgeville, Ga. on business for the estate of the deceased... Amt. $21.87½. (No signature given.)

Page 44:   A return to Court of Ordinary of Butts Co., Ga. of real estate of ISABEL MESSER late of Richmond Co., Ga. deceased... 300 acres land in Richmond Co., Ga. granted to ABSALOM RHODES and HENERY MEALING and conveyed from RHODES and MEALING to BENJAMIN DUNN and from DUNN to ISABEL MESSER... 400 acres pine land in Richmond Co., Ga. granted ISABEL MESSER... 202½ acres land in 1st Dist. of Henry Co., Ga. Lot #222 granted ISABEL MESSER.. K. MILLER, Adm. Recorded July 9, 1828, JNO TARPLEY, C.C.O.

Pages 44-45-46:   Inventory and Appraisement of Estate of ABRAHAM
WALDRIP, dec'd.   Items listed and Appraisers signed JOHN ANDREWS, WM.
SMITH, ROBERT ANDREWS.   (No total amount given.)

Pages 46-47:   Sworn by Appraisers of Estate of ABRAHAM WALDROP on
Oct. 17, 1827 before PARHAM LINDSEY, J.P.... Recorded July 9, 1827...
JNO. TARPLEY, C.C.O.

Sale of Estate of ABRAHAM WALDROP, dec'd... POLLEY WALDROP, Admx.
Nov. 3, 1827... Description of articles given and purchasers names...
widow, POLLEY WALDROP, bought most of items... Purchasers: BENJAMIN
HARRISON, JAMES C. DUNSUTH, DRURY COUCH, ROBERT BICKERSTAFF, LARKIN
ADAMS, WM. HIGGINS, JAS. HERRIN, JAS. TERRY, MOSES COUCH, CALVIN GOIN...
Total $395.56¼... Recorded July 9, 1828... JNO. TARPLEY, C.C.O.

Page 48:   Will of JAMES WOOTEN of Butts County, Ga. "in low state
of health sound mind" ... Item 1, sould to God, buried in Christian
manner at discretion of Exor... (2) debts be paid and all property kept
together until oldest child, EDMOND FLEWELLEN WOOTEN comes of age then
equally divided between wife ANNE WOOTEN and EDMOND FLEWELLEN, JAMES
WOOTEN, ADDISON ALMARICIN WOOTEN, SEABORN LAWRENCE WOOTEN, SIMEON
WOOTEN making arrangement so wife has a house and plantation to hold
during life, afterward divided among my children... use of stock for
family to remain... (3) appoint ETHILDRED MCCLENDON and JAMES REEVES,
Exors... Signed JAMES WOOTEN. Witness: FAREWELL JONES, BARTHOLOMEW
HILL, JAMES RANSOME. (No date given.)

Page 49: Before YELVERTON THAXTON, JOHN MCMICHAEL, Justices of
Inf. Court of Butts Co., Ga. on Aug. 3, 1828, FAREWELL JONES, BARTHOLO-
MEW HILL, JAMES RANSOME swore they saw JAMES WOOTEN sign will...
Signed: YELVERTON THAXTON, J.I.C., JOHN MCMICHAEL, J.I.C.   Recorded
Sept. 1, 1828... JNO TARPLEY, C.C.O.

Court of Ordinary, Butts Co., Ga.   January Term 1829... R. H. I.
HOLLEY, Guardian to JOHN M. STRICKLAND, minor... To negro boy received of
WM. STROUD.
July 7, 1828... Signed: R. H. HOLLEY... Schooling of said minor by
hire of said minor $20.00... Negro for 6 months $20.00.

Page 50:   Inventory and Appraisement of Estate of JAMES WALKER,
dec'd. Appraisors JOHN COUGHRAN, JARET BRYANT, JAMES RANSOM were sworn
to perform their duty as appraisors according to law Dec. 3, 1828.
P. PAYNE, J.P.

Page 51:   Estate of ELISHA BLESSET, Adm. Dr... Vouchers paid to
JOHN TARPLEY, WILLIAM HARPER, NEEDHAM LEE, THOMAS R. BARKER, A. C.
MCWHORTER... Approved to JOHN HENDRICK, J.I.C., ELI CONGER J.I.C.,
JOHN MCMICHAEL J.I.C.

Return of SAMUEL BELLAH Adm. of WILLIAM RHODES dec'd... July 1828,
negro sold to SAMUEL BELLAH, negro sold to JOHN URGUHART... 1828 Sept. 2,
negro sold to ELI COOPER... Approved by JOHN HENDRICK, JOHN MCMICHAEL,
ELI CONGER J.I.C.

Pages 52-53:   Butts County, Ga., Inventory of personal property of
JAMES WALKER dec'd. sold at Public Sale Feb. 18, 1829 at ten months
credit. Byrs. CLAYTON M. COODY, JAMES RANSOM, REBECCA COBB. Total
$35.06¼... Recorded March 3, 1829... JNO. MCCORD, C.C.O.

Page 53:   Sale of negro girl, property of JAMES CLAYTON, JR., and
MARY ANN CLAYTON sold at Public Sale Apr. 5, 1828... JAMES CLAYTON, SR.,
Guardian.   Recorded Mar. 4, 1829... JNO. MCCORD C.C.O.

Pages 53-54:   March 2, 1829, Expenses on the Estate of ISABEL
MESSER late of Richmond County dec'd... Expenses for advertisement for
letter of Adm. and sale of lot #222, 1st Dist., Henry County now Butts Co.

going to Columbia County after plats and grants six days at 75 cents per day for self and hors... for income on said estate... rent for year 1827 and 1828 on lot #222... sale of said lot of land Oct. 7, 1828... Recorded March 4, 1829, FRANCES MILLER, Admr... JNO MCCORD, C.C.O.

Pages 54-55: Return of CHARLES BAILEY, Guardian for JOHN M. D. TAYLOR, minor of GEORGE D. TAYLOR, dec'd. Dr. 1827-1828... to hire of negroes Pat, Leroy, Anthony, Rheno, Rose, Alfred to THOMAS B. BAILEY. THOMAS HOWARD, JR., THOMAS B. BAILEY, JOSHUA LOVET, JAMES C. JOHNSON, G. C. WALTON... Vouchers paid to 1826 Nov. 16, CC. ORDINARY, 1827 Feb. 14, JOSHUA LOVER, JOHN HARDEMAN, ISAAC HARDEMAN & Co., June 23, GEORGE SCOT, Dec. 31, SMITH HOMBS... 1828 Jan. 1, SAMUEL THOMPSON, JAMES GILLES-PIE, JOHN JORDAN, BRITON STAMPS, J. MCINTIRE, PARIS PACE, P. PACE Adm. J. M. NELSON, JAMES BUTLER, CHARLES BAILEY, Guardian, CHARLES WHITING. Total paid $333.93½... C. BAILEY, Guardian.

Page 55: Yearly return on estate of JOHN M. D. TAYLOR, minor of GEORGE D. TAYLOR, dec'd. by CHARLES BAILEY, Guardian of JOHN M. D. TAYLOR. 1828 Vouchers paid EDWARD COX, F. D. CUMMINGS, R. FREEMAN, SMITH HOMBS, PAUL CARTER, HCARLES BAILEY, JOHN W. CARDWELL... Total $204.58... Recorded May 6, 1829... JOHN MCCORD C.C.O.

Pages 56-57: Return of CHARLES BAILEY, Guardian for NOAH W. TAYLOR minor of G. D. TAYLOR dec'd. Dr... 1827 hire of Harry and Genny to T. B. BAILEY, Randal to T. B. BAILEY, Milly to BEDFORD CAID, Polly to WILLIAM LESTER, Clarisa to C. BAILEY... Vouchers paid to ORDINARY, BRITION STAMPS, J. MCINTIRE, GEORGE SCOT, JAMES GILLESPIE, SMITH & COMBS, CHARLES WHITING, JOHN HARDEMAN, ISAAC HARDEMAN & CO., PARIS PACE, GEORGE R. GILMORE, JOSHUA LOVET, DR. IRA T. SMITH, JAMES BUTLAR, CHARLES BAILEY, F. D. CUMMINGS, EDWARD COXE, JAMES TO. JORDAN, ROBERT FREEMAN, JOHN F. WALLIS, PAUL CARTER, SMITH & COMBS, B. F. HARDEMAN, JOHN W. CALDWELL. Total $195.64½... Recorded May 6, 1829, JOHN MCCORD, C.C.O.

Pages 57-58-59: Return of CHARLES BAILEY, Guardian for MARY TAYLOR minor of GEORGE D. TAYLOR dec'd., Dr... Hire of negro Lewis to CHARLES BAILEY, 1828. Hire of Sealy to JAMES BULLAR, Sally to JOHN RUPERT, Jerry to WILLIAM LESTER, Mariah to W. W.M. DOWDY, Elijah to WILLIAM R. BROOKS.. Total $190.00.

Returns cont'd. for MARY TAYLOR... Vouchers paid to JAMES GILLISPIE, E. METZLER, SAMUEL THOMPSON, SCOT & HARDEMAN, GEORGE SCOT, ISAAC HARDEMAN & CO., MATHEW RAINEY, JOSHUA LOVET, PARIS PACE, SMITH & COMBS, IRA E. SMITH, JAMES BUTLER, CHARLES BAILEY, Guardian... Total $260.49. 1828 paid THOMAS GOULDING, JOHN D. WALLIS, THOMAS R. ANDREWS, JOHN D. MOSS, JOHN W. CARDWELL... Total $234.37½. Recorded May 6, 1829.

Page 59: Oglethorpe Co., Ga... I, WILLIAM H. SMITH, C.C.O. of Oglethorpe Co. certifies that the returns are true exact from the record of my office of the acting and doings of CHARLES BAILEY, Guardian of JOHN M. D. TAYLOR, NOAH W. TAYLOR and MARY TAYLOR, Minors of GEORGE D. TAYLOR, dec'd. Given under my hand and seal March 13, 1829... WILLIAM H. SMITH C.C.O., Butts Co., Ga.

Return 1828 of WILLIAM HURST, Guardian to JAMES SCRUGGS, Ediot... Total $14.40... JOHN HENDRICK C.C.O.... Recorded May 6, 1829.

Pages 60-61-62-63-64: Inventory and Appraisement of Estate of WATER T. KNIGHT, dec'd. List of personal property valued at $14.37½... List of notes W. TAYLOR, 1818; W. G. FANNINGS Oct. 8, 1818; fi fa J. QUIN vs R. T. PRAITON Feb. 15, 1822; WM. M. HOBBS Jan. 1, 1821; A. J. WHATELY Aug. 12, 1819; BENJAMIN GRUBBS July 17, 1818; HENRY BURDINE Oct. 22, 1821; M. BREWSTER May 28, 1821; July 5, 1821; May 28, 1821; MALINDA FLANAGAN June 2, 1821; ISAAC SIMMONS Mar. 12, 1824; CHARLES C. WEBB Oct. 30, 1821; May 12, 1821; JOHN LEDLOW Jan. 4, 1820; A. BLAKELY Sept. 13, 1824; JOEL CULPEPER Oct. 27. 1821; REP SCOTT Jan. 21, 1822; JOHN PUCKET July 9, 1823; JOSEPH MONTAGUE (no date); AARON OWEN Feb. 27, 1823. Total $462.43.

Page 64: Estate of WALTER T. KNIGHT cont'd. notes and property JAMES MORRIS Jan. 27, 1825; NATH'L. MORRIS June 12, 1826; AARON OWEN May 18, 1821; JAMES FERGUSON receipt for W. F. PHILLIPS Jan. 30, 1828; JAMES SMITH receipt for HENRY BURDINE Oct. 22, 1821; JO. L. SLATTER Feb. 1821; M. HEALY Jan. 11, 1822; W. L. GIBSON Nov. 11, 1821; LUCY LOCKET Oct. 18, 1821; ABNER H. ___ Jan. 1, 1822; WM. MEGILL Nov. 1, 1821; fi fa against GIBSON CLARK Nov. 1, 1825; fi fa ROBERT BALEY Mar. 2, 1827.

List of Asts due Estate of W. T. KNIGHT dec'd. JOHN MCCORD, ABEL L. ROBINSON, MRS. S. BECKS, B. WOOLBRIGHT, NEALY MCCAY, CHARLES ALLEN, JOHN SIMMONS, R. BROWN, H. HATELY, A. MECKLEBERRY, JOHN MCMICHAEL, SAM'L LOVEJOY, GUSTAUVAS HENDRICK, SAM'L CLAY, JAK T. YOUNG... Total $1937.14.

Appraisors CHARLES BAILY, ERMINE CASE, JOHN SIMMONS... Recorded Nov. 18, 1829 JOHN MCCORD C.C.O. Certified HENRY HATELY J.I.C. Nov. 3, 1829.

Pages 64-65-66: Inventory and Appraisement of Estate of JOHN BARKLEY, dec'd. 4 slaves, lot of land No. 216, 1st District, Henry Co., goods and chattels... Value $2108.75... Appraisors JAMES HARKNESS, MORTON BLEDSOE, SAMUEL P. BURFORD... Certified by HENRY J. JACKSON J.P. Oct. 12, 1829... Recorded Dec. 1, 1829, JOHN M. MCCORD C.C.O.

Pages 67-68-69: Will of ARTHUR C. ATKINSON of Clarke Co., Ga. being in sound mind and memory... Item 1. Debts paid... Item 2. Beloved wife ELIZABETH ATKINSON third part of four tracts of land to (viz) one I now live on and Lott No. 220 in Pike Co., Lott No. 203 Butts Co. and Lott in Butts Co. whereon ROBERT BROWN now lives. The land that I now live on to be sold this season and money divided between my wife, son THOMAS, son WASHINGTON. Wife to have all until her death.. Item 3. Land willed to sons THOMAS P. ATKINSON and WASHINGTON G. ATKINSON at mother's death... Item 4. To SUSANNAH GARRETT and her heirs negroes and $200... Item 5. To SARAH GLASS negro and $200... Item 6. To my several children namely, AMOS MCKEE and MARY B. HANCOCK, WINNEFREAD A. FLETCHER, JOSEPH H. ATKINSON property amt. to $200... Item 7. Balance property sold by executors and money equally divided between six children namely WINNE-FREAD, THOMAS, WASHINGTON, MARY, SUSANNAH and SARAH... Item 8. Two sons THOMAS P. ATKINSON and WASHINGTON G. ATKINSON my executors. Signed: A. C. ATKINSON (seal).

Will made 18th May 1828. Wit: BENNETT TUCK, JOHN PATRICK, BENJAMIN ELSBURY.. Wit. oath Oct. 6, 1828 - ASBURY HALL, MILNER ECHOLS, WM. STROUD, JNO. H. LOWE, Clerk, J.I.C. Recorded Nov. 5, 1828.

JNO. H. LOWE, Clk. of Clarke Co. swears will a true copy of will from Clark Co., Ordinary's Office, JNO. H. LOWE, Clk., Nov. 28, 1828... Recorded Dec. 21, 1829, JOHN MCCORD, C.C.O.

Pages 70-71-72: Inventory of Estate of ARTHUR C. ATKINSON dec'd. of Clarke Co., Ga. Nov. 18, 1828... Appraisors appointed Nov. 3, 1828... Slaves, personal property and receipts on JOSEPH H. LUMPKIN for note on JOSEPH B. DILLARD and MARTHA DILLARD 1828, JOSEPH B. DILLARD and MARTHA and MARY D. DILLARD 1825, JOSEPH B. DILLARD and PARKES W. SMITH 1828... Total $3131.82.

Carried forward notes on JOSIAH CHEATHAM and JOSIAH CLARK 1824. Note on JESSE C. BOUSCHELL 1828, ROBERT BROWN 1828, WILLIAM ELSBURY 1828, note on BENJAMIN SANDAY. Due bill on EDWARD JONES. True app. of goods, chattels, credits of the Estate of ARTHUR C. ATKINSON dec'd. Nov. 18, 1828, WM. CRAIG, T. BROWN, BENJAMIN ELSBURY, Appraisors... JOHN H. LOWE, Clk. of Ordinary, Clark Co., Ga. certifies a true copy of record in Clark Co., Ga., Nov. 27, 1828, JOHN H. LOWE, Clk. Recorded Dec. 22, 1829. JOHN MCCORD, C.C.O.

Sale of property of ARTHUR C. ATKINS dec'd. late of Clark Co., Ga., Jan. 8, 1829, Byrs; ALEXANDER HUNTER, WASHINGTON G. ATKINSON, ROBERT BROWN, BENJ. C. GRAVES, THOS. P. ATKINSON, ELIZABETH ATKINS, BENJ. F. TUCKER, ROBERT W. HUNTER, THOS. COXE, BENJ. BLESSETT... THOMAS P. ATKINSON and WASHINGTON G. ATKINSON, Executors... Recorded Dec. 22, 1829, JOHN MCCORD, C.C.O.

Page 73: Return on Estate of ARTHUR C. ATKINSON, dec'd. for year 1828 by THOMAS P. ATKINSON and W. G. ATKINSON, Exr... No. 1 Paid JOHN H.

LOWE, Clk. No. 2 S. THOMAS, No. 3 WILLIAM EDWARDS, Blacksmith, No. 4
JOHN G. MAYNN, No. 5 JAMES JINNINGS, No. 6 W. B. HERRING, No. 7 JOHN B.
GREEN, No. 8 G. D. EDWARDS, N. 9 O. P. SHAW, No. 10 JOHN H. LOWE, No. 11
JOHN TALMADGE, No. 12 BENJ. ELSBURY, No. 13 D. DUPREE, No. 14 THOS. C.
BELLUPS, No. 15 MARY PENSON, No. 16 BOYD PENSON, No. 17 JOHN SHEPHERD,
No. 18 JOHN TALMADGE, No. 19 JOHN GERDINE... Total $251.17 3/4... Negro
sold to WYLEY HILL, Cash received of JOHN FLETCHER... THOS. P. ATKINSON
and WASHINGTON G. ATKINSON, Exr... Recorded Dec. 22, 1829, JOHN MCCORD,
C.C.O.

Pages 74-75-76:   Property sold of Estate of WALTER T. KNIGHT dec'd.
Dec. 23, 1829. Buyrs; HAMLIN FREEMAN, O. P. CHEATHAM, T. R. BARKER,
J. H. STARK, B. F. TUCKER, WILLIS MOORE, J. W. WILLIAMS, R. MASON, W.
MCCAULY, H. MCCOY, B. GRAY, R. MCCORD, JOSH MOORE, J. BANKSTON, E. CASE,
R. W. HARKNESS, W. NIXON, W. LYON, JOHN TARPLEY... Total $118.50...
Recorded Jan. 1, 1830, JOHN MCCORD, C.C.O.

Pages 76-77-78-79:   Inventory and Appraisement of Estate of JAMES
WOOTEN dec'd. 81 items listed at a value of $5533.55½... Notes on CULLIN
ALFORD, JAMES S. MORRIS, JOHN HARDY, THOMAS BULLOCK, MOSES D. WHITE,
JOHN COUGHRAN, JOHN MCELVEN... Appr. certified Jan. 2, 1830 by P. PAYNE,
J. P., R. NOLEN, WM. GILMORE, P. PAYNE, J.P.... Recorded Jan. 12, 1830,
JOHN MCCORD, C.C.O.

Page 80:   Rec'd. Dec. 30, 1829 from CHARLES P. GORDAN late guardian
of LOVEZA C. FLEWELLEN... ELIZA H. ROWLAND and WILLIAM H. FLEWELLEN note
dated 1826... Note FRANCES C. BURT dated 1827... Note LEMMON W. TEATS
dated 1829... Note A. W. ELLINGTON and ANDERSON WORTHYS dated 1828...
Note EATON FLEWELLEN and JAMES BURTS dated 1828. Fi fa in JOSEPH SUMMER-
LIN'S hands against ROBERT HUMBER... JAMES C. DUNSIETH chosen guardian
of LOUIZA C. FLEWELLEN. Total value $452.04... Recorded Jan. 12, 1830,
JOHN MCCORD, C.C.O.

Page 81:   Dr. the Estate of JAMES WALKER to REBECCA COBB, Admx.
paid H. W. KNOLS, JOHN TOWNS, C. M. COODY, RANSON R. COBB, Total $69.10½.
Recorded Jan. 13, 1830, JOHN MCCORD, C.C.O.

Page 82:   Return No. 3, WILLIAM HURST guardian to JAMES SCRUGGS,
Idio, $11.79-$12.50... Recorded Jan. 30, 1830, JOHN MCCORD, C.C.O.
Return No. 2, JNO. M. STRICKLAND, minor, JACOB HOLLY guardian for year
1829, Amt. $33.50, R. H. J. HOLLY. Recorded Jan. 13, 1830, JOHN MCCORD,
C.C.O.

Page 83:   Estate of WALTER T. KNIGHT, dec'd. in account with
AUGUSTIN B. POPE, A dm. from Nov. 2, to Dec. 31, 1830. Vouchers paid
to Ordinary, JOHN HALL for coffin, $7.00, HUBBARD WILLIAMS, CASE and
GOODRICH funeral expenses, $9.56½, HENRY HATELY, KNIGHTS to MCCOY,
SAM'L CLAY, JNO MCCORD... Received from A. L. ROBINSON, N. MCCOY, H.
HATELY, SAM'L CLAY, T. BRONSON, ROBERT BAILEY, JOHN MCMICHAEL... Total
435.97½... Returned Jan. 7, 1830, A. B. POPE, Admr... Recorded Jan. 13,
1830, JOHN MCCORD, C.C.O.

Pages 83-84-85:   Estate of SAMUEL C. STARK, dec'd. in account with
JAMES H. STARK, Adm. from 12th to 31st Dec. 1829... Cash paid in Vouchers
1-17. to HENRY HATELY, Clerk of Ordinary, A. L. ROBINSON, WILLIAM JONES,
L. B. EUBANKS, JOSEPH R. HICKS, WILLIAM HARMON, ALEX LEMON, GEO. THOMAS,
A. B. POPE, HUGH HEARD, LYSANDERS MCLIN, JNO. SIMMONS, MARY CAMPBELL,
SAM'L LOVEJOY, EDWARD BUTLAR, BENJ'M BLESSET.. Cr. Rec. from J. RUSSEL,
JNO. MCMAHAN, HUGH H. HEARD, WM. R. GILMORE, ISAAC SMITH, RICE CLEVELAND,
JOHN PHILLIP, HUGH MORRISON, L. B. EUBANKS, A. L. ROBISON, WM. JONES,
CATLET CAMPBELL, EAEKIEL WALKER, BOSDELL G. POTTER... Total Amount
$110.87½... Return Jan. 4, 1830. JAMES H. STARK, Adm... Recorded Jan.
14, 1830, JOHN MCCORD, C.C.O.

Page 85:   Jan. 7, 1829, Bill of Sale of the Estate of WM. RHODES,
dec'd. sold April 14, 1829 2/3 Lot No. 4, 2nd Dist. of Henry Co. now
Butts Co... Bought by JAMES RHODES for $207.00.

Page 85-86-87:   Return of SAMUEL BELLAH, Adm. of the Estate of WM.
RHODES, dec'd. for 1829... Return for Legetees, JAMES RHODES, HARRIET
RHODES, NANCY RHODES, WILLIAM RHODES, BENJAMIN RHODES, JOSIAH RHODES...
Total amt. $180.36... Recorded Jan. 14, 1830... JOHN MCCORD, C.C.O.

Pages 87-88:   NOAH W. TAYLOR, minor of GEORGE D. TAYLOR, dec'd. to
CHARLES BAILEY Guardian Dr. 1829, Jan. 1... Vouchers 1-25 paid to F. W.
COOK, JOEL G. GLEASON, H. T. DAWSON, J. Y. ALEXANDER, SMITH & COOMBS,
W. V. BURNEY, JAMES BUTLOR, J. W. CARDWELL, HENRY T. DAWSON, ANDREW RHEA,
A. L. ROBINSON, WALTER T. KNIGHT, CASE & GOODRICH STORE, JOHN ROBINSON
STORE, C & S. BAILEY, Physicians, Hire of slaves to F. A. BAILEY, BENJ.
BLESSET, CHARLES BAILEY, C. A. WILLIAMS, O. P. CHEATHAM.

Pages 89-90-91:   Copy of vouchers #1-25... Received of CHARLES
BAILEY, Guardian for NOAH TAYLOR, minor of GEORGE D. TAYLOR, Mar. 9, 1829..
Recorded Jan. 26, 1830... JOHN MCCORD, C.C.O.

Pages 92-93-94-95:   Copy of vouchers #1-19... To CHARLES BAILEY,
guardian of MARY TAYLOR, minor of GEORGE D. TAYLOR, dec'd. Jan. 1829.

Page 95:   Voucher #20, Butts Co., Ga. Received of CHARLES BAILEY,
guardian for my wife MARY FREEMAN formerly MARY TAYLOR a minor of GEORGE
D. TAYLOR dec'd. of the county of Wilkes, Ga. for 5 negroes. Dec. 30,
1829. Signed HAMLIN FREEMAN. CHARLES BAILEY, Guardian for MARY TAYLOR
minor... Recorded Jan. 29, 1830, JOHN MCCORD, C.C.O.

Page 96:   Return of JOHN M. TAYLOR, minor of GEORGE D. TAYLOR,
dec'd. to CHARLES BAILEY, Guardian Dr. 1828-1829... Vouchers 1-16 Amount
$79.53 3/4... Recorded Feb. 2, 1830. JOHN MCCORD, C.C.O.

Page 97:   Butts County, Georgia... Three sworn to distribute the
Estate of SAMUEL C. STARKS (to wit) ERMINE CASE, JNO. SIMMONS and ABEL
L. ROBINSON... Certified Feb. 1, 1830, HENRY HATELY, J.I.C.... Recorded
Feb. 2, 1830, JOHN MCCORD, C.C.O.

Georgia, Butts Co., Court of Ordinary, Jan. 4, 1830... We assign to
ROSANNAH STARK one of the distributees of the estate of SAMUEL C. STARK,
dec'd. one Negro boy worth $500.33 1/3... assign to SAMUEL JAMES H. STARK
the other distributee one negro woman worth $383.33... Assign to SAMUEL
JAMES H. STARK one negro girl worth $150.00... Feb. 1, 1830... Signed
JOHN SIMMONS, ERMINE CASE, ABEL L. ROBINSON... Recorded Feb. 2, 1830,
JOHN MCCORD, C.C.O.

Page 98:   Georgia, Butts Co., Court of Ordinary... to ABEL L.
ROBINSON, JOHN SIMMONS, ERMINE CASE, LAWRENCE GAHAGAN & CATLETT CAMPBELL..
These are to authorize and empower you or any three of you to make
appraisement of Estate of SAMUEL C. STARK late of said county dec'd. and
money produced by JAMES H. STARK the adm. of estate... Wit. the honourable
JOHN MCMICHAEL one of the judges of said court of Ordinary, Dec. 12, 1829.
JOHN MCCORD, C.C.O.

Pages 98-99-100:   Inventory and Appraisement of the Estate of
SAMUEL C. STARK, dec'd. Dec. 15, 1829... Goods and chattel amount
$2242.87 1/2... Certified Jan. 23, 1830 by ABEL L. ROBINSON, ERMINE CASE,
JOHN SIMMONS, Appr.

Pages 100-107:   1830... Cont'd. Inventory and Appraisement of
Estate of SAMUEL C. STARK goods, chattel and credits of the Estate of
SAMUEL C. STARK late of Butts Co., deceased... Value $2429.93 3/4...
Notes 1828-1830 due estate, IGNATIUS RUSSELS, JOHN R. MCMAHAN, WM. R.
GILMORE, JNO. LEMON, ALLEN CLEVELAND, SAM'L. MCLIN, ISAAC LOWE, ISAAC
SMITH, RICE CLEVELAND, JNO. PHILIP, HUGH MORRISON, H. MCLIN, W. GILES,
L. B. EUBANKS, WM. NORRIS, JOS. CAMPBELL, EZEKIEL WALKER, BOSDELL G.
POTTER, GEO. EUBANKS, THOMAS JOHNSON, DAVIS W. MATTOX, WILLIAM ROBERDS,
Mrs. HARTSFIELD, JAS. C. ANDERSON, JNO. G. OWENS, THOS. BEARDIN, JAMES
HUNTS, NEILL STRAHANS, A. L. ROBINSON, SAMUEL (GEX?), EDWARD WEAVER, JAMES
HARKNESS, THOS. ROBINSON, B. F. TUCKER, M. GASTON, ESQR. ALLEN, M. T.

CALDWELL, MAJOR PETTET, JAMES BUNKLEY, HUMPHREY & PRESTON, W. B. NUTT, P. G. CLAY, SAM'L CLAY, SAM'L P. BURFORD, JNO. NUTT, R.R. BRYANT, JNO. HALE, JAMES H. SARK, RUFUS MCCLOUD, WOODY NIGHT, JNO. REEVES, CHARLES BAILEY, N. W. TAYLOR, JNO. M. TAYLOR, SAM'L NUTT, CALVARON KNIGHT, OBEDIAH CHETUM, ROBERT HARKNESS, PERNELLS a/c, MRS. LINDSEY, HUBBARD WILLIAMS, JNO & H. WILLIAM, GEO. OWENS, JNO. ROBINSON, ESQ. ELLIOTT, WILEY THAXTON, MAYS a/c, RICH'D BAILEY, ROBT. HUNTER, MCCLENDON a/c, MAJ. CHAPMAN, RICH'D MASON, ANDERSON a/c, THOS. REBH, JAMES HOGG, W & W BRADLEY, SAM'L CLAY, E. COX, MRS. BECK, DOC SANDERS, MRS. BASKLEY, GEO. W. MARTIN, SAM'L LOVEJOY, NEEDHAM LEE, SAM'L CLARK, JNO. R. CARGILE, JNO NELSON, JAMES REEVES, L. ROAN, JAMES HARDY, BURREL BRIDGES, J. WILLSON, A. CLEVELAND, JNO. SIMMONS, CHARLES W. NIXON, ANDREW a/c, COOPER a/c, JUDGE THAXTON, S. BLISSET, W. HOLLYFIELD, D. MCLIND, COKER DEASON, T. FOSTER, J. T. SPEAKS, DANL PRESSLEY, C. HAMIL, BEAN a/c, JONATHAN BANKSTON, RICH SPEAK, BURTON a/c, JACOB JOLLY, ROBERT SMITH, JNO SHEINREN, JAS. V. HOGG, JNO. WILLIAMS, J. SANDERS, T. FOSTER, WEAVER a/c, CALDWELL a/c, CHILDERS a/c, MATH MCMICHAEL a/c, ANDREW NUTT a/c, GENTRY a/c, HANDS a/c, A. RAMEY, WRAY a/c, JAMES GANEY, R. CASHMAN, RINEY a/c, WALLIS a/c, W. L. MCMAHAN, W. W. KENNON, THOS. B. MCCULLOUGH... Total Amount $3362.84½.

A bond on A. L. ROBINSON to make title N ½ of lot 87, 1st Dist. of Henry now Butts Co. under penalty of $1200.

A bond on JNO R. CARGILE to make title to NW ¼ of Lot 88, 1st Dist. of Henry now Butts Co. under penalty of $1000... LAWRENCE GAHAGAN, ABEL L. ROBINSON, ERMINE CASE, Appr.

Page 108: Georgia Butts Co., Certification that above appraisors performed their duty as appraisors according to law. Jan. 23, 1830, HENRY HATELY, J.I.C.... Recorded Feb. 27, 1830, JHN MCCORD, C.C.O.

Pages 108-110: An inventory of personal property of JOHN BARKLEY, dec'd. sold at public sale on Nov. 27, 1829 on a credit until Dec. 25, 1830. Byr: JANE BARKLEY, R. J. D. BARKLEY, LUKE ROBINSON, WILLIAM B. NUTT, CLARK HAMMEL, WILLIAM MESSER, K. NUTT, LEWIS MOORE, JAMES HARKNESS, WILLIAM GRIMET, ANDREW BARKLEY, STEPHEN W. MILLER, SAMUEL NUTT, THOS. B. BURFORD, C. M. AMOS, R. W. HARKNESS, WILLIAM P. SHERLING, JAMES ANDERSON, MARK POWEL, ELIJAH FULLER, CASPER M. AMOS, MATHEW GASTON, JAMES HARKNESS, JABOS GILBERT, JAMES HOGAN... Total amt. $716.93. Recorded Mar. 1st., 1839, JOHN MCCORD, C.C.O.

Pages 111-112: Dr. the Estate of JOHN BARKLEY, dec'd... to SAMUEL R. NUTT, Adm. paid voucher #1, JAMES WEAKLEY vs JOHN BARKLEY (case in Henry Co. Superior Court), #2, W. J. PEARMON, attorney, #3 ADAM JINKS, #4, Ordinary, #5 paid BLEDSOE for picking out cotton, #6 for bacon for the use of the family, #7 E. FULLER for bacon for the family, #8 HENRY HATELY for coffin $5.00, #9 cash in Central Bank, #10 paid MARTIN for oats for use of family... Total Amt. #395.72½. #11 cash paid for sugar for family use, #12 articles bought for family use, #13 paid HUMERS for 5 pr. shoes $4.75, #14, freight on cotton and rum $2.00, #15 articles for family use, #16 paid JOHN HALE for bacon, #17 expenses to Milledgeville, #18 cash paid CHEATHAM... Total $468.80... Cash on hand $473.08½.. Return this Mar. 23, 1830, SAMUEL R. NUTT, Adm. Recorded Mar. 25, 1830. JOHN MCCORD, C.C.O.

Page 113: Inventory and Appraisement of Estate of JOHN MALONE, dec'd. 5 items listed, value $48.12½... Appraisors: WILLIAM GILES, SPENCER (X) MADDOX, WILLIAM VICKERS, Certified Apr. 13, 1830 by G. T. SPEAKE, J. P. Recorded Apr. 12, 1830, JOHN MCCORD, C.C.O.

Pages 113-114: Inventory and Appraisement of JOHN M. D. TAYLOR, dec'd. 5 negroes valued at $1691.23, Appraisors: ABEL L. ROBINSON, ROBERT BROWN, ERMINE CASE, certified by HENRY HATELY, J.I.C., Jan. 9, 1830.
Two negroes valued $470.00, Appraisors: ABEL L. ROBINSON, ROBERT BROWN, ERMINE CASE, Certified by JOHN HALL, J.I.C., Apr. 18, 1830, Recorded Apr. 19, 1830, JOHN MCCORD, C.C.O.

Page 115:   Inventory of personal property of J. M. D. TAYLOR, dec'd.
Sold at public sale Apr. 6, 1830... Sale of 7 slaves purchased by A. J.
BAILEY, HAMLIN FREEMAN, CHARLES BAILEY, JAS. H. HILL, value $2400.00.
CHARLES BAILEY, Adm... Recorded Apr. 19, 1830, JOHN MCCORD, C.C.O.

Pages 115-120:   Account of Sales for Estate of SAM'L C. STARK,
dec'd. 29th and 30th Jan. 1830... Sold on credit until Dec. 25, 1830...
Byrs: P. G. CLAY, JNO. BLISSET, JAS H. STARK, A. BANKSTON, H. MCCOY,
JNO. ROBINSON, H. WILLIAMS, H. FREEMAN, H. GILBERT, JNO. SIMMONS, H. LEE,
W. HARPER, R. C. MAYS, C. W. NIXON, B. F. TUCKER, R.R. BRYANT, R. ANDREWS,
JOS CARMICHAEL, ROSANNAH STARK, L. MOORE, W. PRIDGEON, R. BAILEY, C.
CAMPBELL, G. W. LOWERY, E. COXE, C. BAILEY, BARNA WISE, R. W. HARKNESS,
THOMAS JOHNSON, J. & H. WILLIAMS, JOS. R. NIX, L. B. EUBANKS, A. L.
ROBINSON, W. BRADLEY, H. HATLEY, C. STARK, B. MCCOY, JOSIAH CHATHAM, D.
TINGLE, M. GAHAGAN, R. D. CANNON, J. R. MCMAHAN, E. CASE, W. ALLISON,
J. W. MASON, R. C. CHAPMAN, J. D. BYARS, J. BUTLER, B. BLESSET, GEO.
THOMAS, W. PRESSLEY, A. CLEVELAND, W. NORRIS, JAS. C. ANDERSON... Total
value $767.82... Recorded May 24, 1830, JOHN MCCORD, C.C.O.

Page 120:   Inventory of Personal Property of JOHN MALONE, JR.,
dec'd. sold May 8, 1830, Byrs: JOHN MALONE, Senr., AUGUSTUS WISE.
Value $37.62½... Return made May 24, 1830, JOHN MALONE, Adm... Recorded
May 25, 1830 JOHN MCCORD, C.C.O.

Page 121:   Return on Estate of ARTHUR C. ATKINSON, dec'd. for
year 1829 by THOS. P. & W. J. ATKINSON, Exrs... Vouchers #1, #2, #3
cash paid JOSIAH C. GARRETT, #4 LAWRENCE GAHAGAN, #5 JOHN ALBERT, #6
LEWIS MCKEE, #7 JONES & HUBBARD, #8 JAMES GILLESPIE, #9, #10, #11
EDWARD COX, #12 STEPHEN THOMAS, #13 HUGH NEISLER, #14 WILLIAM JONES, #15
RICH'D RICHARDSON, #16 WILLIAM ROBERTS, #17 PACK & SMITH, #18 JOHN
MCCORD, #19 LAWRENCE GAHAGAN, Total Amt. $964.96½... Money received in
1829 from JOHN FLETCHER, WILLIAM ELSBERRY, EDWARD JONES, D. C. BALDWIN,
BENJAMIN SANSING, Total Amt. $900.56 3/4, THOS. P. ATKINSON & W. L. ATKIN-
SON, Exrs... Recorded Nov. 9, 1830... JOHN MCCORD, C.C.O.

Pages 122-123:   Estate of LOUISA C. FLEWELLEN a minor 1829... To
JAMES C. DUNSIETH, Guardian... Names mentioned, ROBERT COLEMAN,
WILLIAM SMITH, THOPHILUS FLOWERS the husband of L. C. FLEWELLEN, WILKINS
DESHAZO, ELIZA N. ROWLAND, WILLIAM H. FLEWELLEN, FRANCES SCOTT, LEMON
W. SEAT, ANDERSON WORTHY, A. W. ELLINGTON, THOMAS WARMICK & LORENZO
WALLACE, JOS. SUMMERLIN (Sheffic of Butts) ROBERT HUMBER, LOUISA C.
FLEWELLEN. Amount $735.47 3/4 by JAMES C. DUNSIETH, Guardian of LOUISA
C. FLEWELLEN. Recorded Nov. 10, 1830, JOHN MCCORD, C.C.O.

Pages 123-124-125:   Inventory and Appraisement of Estate of JOHN
BARRON, dec'd. list of goods valued at $730.30, Oct. 29, 1830...
Appraisors, BURREL BRIDGES, JAMES THOMPSON, WM. BARRON, Certified by
HENRY JACKSON, J.P.... Recorded Nov. 13, 1830, JOHN MCCORD, C.C.O.

Pages 125-126, 127-128:   Inventory of personal property of JOHN
BARRON, dec'd. sold at public sale Nov. 26, 1830... Byrs: MORTON BLED-
SOE, SMITH BARRON, OBADIAH HASTY, SUSAN BARRON, R. S. MASON, SAMUEL NUTT,
HENRY BARRON, WILLIAM BARRON, PLEASANT DRAKE, M. POWELL, R. W. HARKNESS,
THOMAS BURFORD, JOSEPH BARRON, JOHN B. REEVES, WILLIAM BRIDGES, JOSIAH
REEVES, JOHN MCDANIEL, WASHINGTON BENNET, SAMUEL P. BURFORD, ISAAC
JINKS, A. WAFFORD... Total $451.76¼... Return Dec. 14, 1830, SMITH
BARRON, Adm... Recorded Dec. 15, 1830, JOHN MCCORD, C.C.O.

Page 128:   GIDEON MATHIS Guardian to CHARLES G. THAXTON...
Inventory of said orphan... Notes due estate by YELVENTON THAXTON, NELSON
COFIELD, WILEY THAXTON, THOMAS BEARDIN, Jan. 1, 1831, GIDEON MATHIS,
Guardian. Recorded Jan. 7, 1831, JOHN MCCORD, C.C.O.

Pages 128-132:   Estate of SAMUEL C. STARK, dec'd. JAMES H. STARK,
Adm... Vouchers paid R. N. MCLIN, JOHN R. CARGILE, CLEVELAND & ANDERSON,
SAMUEL GEE, WHITNAL EASON, DANIEL MARTIN, ROBERT W. SMITH (for use of
SAMUEL C. STARK vs. JEREMIAH MALTON), JAMES HARKNESS, WM. BRADLEY, SAM'L
K. MCLIN, SAM'L CLAY, JNO. HATTON, R. R. BRYANT, JNO. HALL, WM. BLALOCK,

CHARLES STARK, JAS. R. MCCORD, ROSANNAH STARK, CHAS. H. STEPHEN, HENRY LEE, L. GAHAGAN, HUNGERFORD & STODDARD, ELLIS SHOTWELL, AMOS COOPER, GREEN PERNELL, P. PHILLIP, JNO SIMMONS, E. CASE, CASE & GOODRICH, JNO. MCMICHAEL, HENRY HATELY, HEENSON N. JACKSON, A. L. ROBINSON, THOS. R. BARKER, Y. THAXTON, M. M. GILLIAM, S. CLAY, JOSEPH CAMPBELL, W. J. BEANS, JNO. R. CARGILE, M. BARTLETT, B. F. TUCKER, H & J. W. WILLIAMS, JAS. WILLIAM, JAS. H. STARK, Adm. of SAM'L C. STARK, S. C. STARK, DAVID MCLIN, H. FREEMAN, JNO. W. MCCORD, SARAH BEEK, RICH'D BAILEY... Total $1827.49.

Pages 133-136:   Estate of SAMUEL C. STARK, cont'd.... Credits: DAVIS W. MATTOX,   ? ROBERTS, MRS. HARTSFIELD, SAM'L GEES,   ? HOLLY, JNO. G. OWENS, JAMES HUNTS, JAMES C. ANDERSON, A. CLEVELAND, THOS. BEARDIN, JAMES HARKNESS, THOMAS ROBINSON, PLEASANT G. CLAY, SAM'L K. MCLIN, NEEL STRAHAN, JNO. MCMICHAEL, SAM'L CLAY, JNO. NUTT, R. R. BRYANT, WILLIAM HARRIS, JAMES N. STARK, J. R. MCCORD, WOODY KNIGHT, W. B. NUTT, JNO. REEVES, CHAS. BAILEY, N. W. TAYLOR, JNO. M. D. TAYLOR, A. L. ROBINSON, L. ROAN, G. PARNELL, JNO. SIMMON, ROBT. W. HARKNESS, THOS. JOHNSON, RICH'D BAILEY, THOS. R. BARKER, J. R. MCMAHAN, GREEN PERNELL, SAM'L P. BURFORD, R. MCCORD, R. H. CARWELL, Y. THAXTON, O. P. CHEATHAM, JAS. V. HOGGS, EDWARD WEAVER, JOSEPH CAMPBELL, JNO. R. CARGILE, B. F. TUCKER, ISAAC LOWE, JNO. WILLIAMS, HUBBARD WILLIAMS, JAS. BARKLEY, GEO. EUBANKS, C. W. NIXON, JNO. OWEN, JAS. PRIGEON, WILLIAM WOODS, SAM'L NUTT, R. MCCORD, R. W. HUNTER, JNO. ROBINSON, SAM'L CLARK, R. C. CHAPMAN, E. COKE, JAMES WILSON, NEDHAM LEE, CHAS. SHARK, SENR., R. SMITH, RICH'D MASON, THOS. FOSTER, STEPHEN BLESSET, CLARK HAMIL... Total $1827.48½... Returned Jan. 3, 1831, JAMES H. STARK, Adm... Acc for hireing negro $275.06¼. Returned Jan. 3rd 1831... Recorded Jan. 8, 1831, JOHN MCCORD, C.C.O.

Page 137:   R. H. J. HOLLY, Guardian to the Estate of JOHN M. STRICKLAND, minor... heir of negroes $3.06¼... Recorded Jan. 10, 1831, JOHN MCCORD, C.C.O.

WILLIAM HURST, guardian to JAMES SCRUGGS, Idiot... Interest on $75.00 from Jan. 3, 1830 to Dec. 31, 1830... $14.03... Voucher to amount $15.02½. Recorded Jan. 10, 1831, JOHN MCCORD, C.C.O.

Return No. 1, Estate of JOHN BARRON, dec'd. to SMITH BARRON, Adm. Voucher to amount $21.87½... Return Jan. 3. 1831... Recorded Jan. 10, 1831, JOHN MCCORD, C.C.O.

Page 138:   State of Georgia.   Inventory and Appraisement of Estate of JOHN SMITH dec'd., Jan. 4, 1831... 6 negroes $1125.00 bought by NEALY MCCOY, WM. GILMORE, JOHN REEVES, Certified Jan. 4. 1831, LEONARD ROAN, J.P., Recorded Jan. 10, 1831, JOHN MCCORD, C.C.O.

Page 138:   Return made by ELI CONGER, Guardian for the orphans and minors of JOSEPH G. SPEARS, dec'd... Cash paid JOHN TARPLEY, schooling and attention for year 1826, 1827, 1829, 1830 - $64.00. Signed ELI CONGER... Recorded Mar. 9, 1831, JOHN MCCORD, C.C.O.

Page 139:   Return on Estate of ARTHUR C. ATKINSON, dec'd. for year 1830 by THOS. P. & W. G. ATKINSON, Exr... Cash paid STEPHEN THOMAS, BENJ. ELLSBERRY, ROBT. LIGON, N. LEE, JOHN TARPLEY, CHARLES DAUGHERTY, Attorney, JESSE C. BOUSCHELLE, JESSE KERR, Attorney, JOHN TALMADGE, HINES HOLT, Tres., JOHN MCCORD, JACOB BAILEY, STEPHEN THOMAS, JOHN P. SMITH, WM. N. PREYER... Total Amount $1136.45½.

Page 140:   Estate of ARTHUR C. ATKINSON, cont'd.... Monies received 1830, received from WILLIAM ELLSBERRY, CHARLES DAUGHERTY, JESSE C. BOUSCHELLE, $1011.31 ¼, THOMAS P. ATKINSON & WASHINGTON G. ATKINSON, Exr. Recorded Mar. 10, 1831, JOHN MCCORD. C.C.O.

Dr. to Estate of JOHN BARKLEY dec'd. to SAMUEL R.NUTT, Adm. and JANE BARKLEY, Admx... Hire of negroes for year 1830, $488.68 3/4... Cash received of JOHN KIMBROUGH & A. GLENN on execution.

Page 141:   Cont'd - Paid by vouchers, L. GAHAGAN, SAMUEL P. BURFORD, WM. BROOKS, H. LEE, HENRY JACKSON, GEORGE WALL, JAMES H. EDWARDS (for

tuition), JANE ARBELINE orphan of said dec'd., JANE BARKLEY for boarding
and clothing, JENNET A. BARKLEY, ELIZABETH ANN BARKLEY, orphans of said
dec'd., NANCY G. BARKLEY, JOHN N. BARKLEY, SAMUEL R. NUTT, Admr...
Recorded JOHN MCCORD, C.C.O.

Estate of ELISHA BLESSET dec'd. in account with STEPHEN BLESSET one
of Adm... Annual returns, Vouchers, cash paid NANCY BLESSET widow of
dec'd., JOHN BLESSET one of the destributees, WILLIAM HARPER one of the
destributees, WILLIAM HARPER as guardian for minor children... Total
$1213.86... Returned Mar. 7, 1831, STEPHEN BLISSET... Recorded Mar. 18,
1831, JOHN MCCORD, C.C.O.

Page 142:   Estate of JOHN MALONE, JR., dec'd... JOHN MALONE,
Adm., 1830, Apr. 5 ... Vouchers paid 1827 WOODY DOZIER, 1830 S. K. MCLIN,
JOHN GOODMAN, JOHN R. CARGILE, 1831 PERSONS & PHELPS, JOHN R. CARGILE...
JOHN MALONE, Admr... Recorded Apr. 29, 1831, JOHN MCCORD, C.C.O.

Page 143:   Inventory and Appraisement of all goods, chattels and
credits of RICHARD KNIGHT, dec'd... Items listed valued $1067.56½.
App: Mar. 12, 1831, SAMUEL BELLAH, YELVENTON THAXTON, THOS. WILLIAMSON,
WILLIS JARRELL... Certified 26th day of April 1831, C. F. KNIGHT, Admr...
Recorded Apr. 27, 1831, JOHN MCCORD, C.C.O.

Page 144:   Estate of GEORGE BLESSIT minor of ELISHA BLESSIT, dec'd.
to WILLIAM HARPER guardian Dec. 31, 1830... Vouchers paid CASE & GOOD-
RICH, NANCY BLESSET for boarding minor 3 years $352.59½... Returned Mar.
7, 1831... Signed: WILLIAM HARPER, Guardian... Recorded May 3, 1831, JOHN
MCCORD, C.C.O.

Page 144:   Cont'd. Annual Returns of WILLIAM HARPER guardian for
POLLY BLISSIT formerly now POLLY BANKSTON her share of ELISHA BLISSIT
estate... Credit, cash pd ALFRED BANKSTON the husband of the minor
$250.70... Returned Mar. 7, 1831, WILLIAM HARPER guardian... Recorded
May 3, 1831, JOHN MCCORD, C.C.O.

Page 145:   Estate of WILLIAM BLISSIT, minor of ELISHA BLESSIT,
dec'd. to her guardian WILLIAM HARPER in acc current up to 31st Dec. 1830.
1830 Mar. 17th, Voucher #1 paid NANCY BLESSIT for boarding minor 3 yr.
sum and interest $19.30... Credit by minor share of ELISHA BLESSIT'S
Estate, Rec'd. by guardian 15th Jan. 1829.. $234.70 Interest $17.90.
Total returned 7th March 1831. $252.60, WILLIAM HARPER, Guardian...
Recorded May 3, 1831, JOHN MCCORD, C.C.O.

Pages 145-146:   Estate of MARY FREEMAN formerly MARY TAYLOR in
acc. with CHARLES BAILEY her late guardian up to 31st Dec. 1830. Amt.
due guardian on former returns as pr settlement with H. FREEMAN 13th
Dec. 1830 exclusive of vouchers not returned at date as pr voucher #7,
$543.25... 1828, Jan. 4 Cash pd. JOHN HARDMAN for necessarys furnished
minor #8... Nov. 1st pd. SMITH & COMBS a/c voucher #1 $56.93½, 1830 Jan.
1st pd. R. BROWN #2 $6.662/3... Jan. 8 pd. Clk. c.c. Ordinary #3 $1.12½,
pd. JNO. HALL $4 $1.50... Oct. 5, N. LEE taxes for 1829 #5 $2.90½...
Mar. 3, pd. SPENCER & MAYS #6 $1.00... 1830 Dec. 15, pd W. C. DAWSON &
N. C. SAYES for personal services #9 $15.00... Aug. 22 pd. J. H. LUMPKIN
for professional services #10 $5.00... Apr. 22 pd J. H. LUMPKIN for pro-
fessional services #11 $16.66½... 1831 interest on amt. $14.44½ May 5
pd. JOHN MCCORD for final return $1.12½, commission @5% $6.64½ Total
$683.88½ 1830 Dec. 13th Cr. by settlement with H. FREEMAN in which
$619.92½ was liquedated. Balance due CHARLES BAILEY Dec. 31, 1830 $63.96.
Returned Mar. 6, 1831, CHARLES BAILEY late guardian... Recorded May 7,
1831, JOHN MCCORD, C.C.O.

Pages 146-147:   Estate of NOAH W. TAYLOR minor of GEORGE D. TAYLOR,
dec'd. in acc. with CHARLES BAILEY his guardian up to 31st Dec. 1830.
Voucher #1 Dec. 29, 1828 cash paid B. F. HARDEMAN for professional services $3.00, #2 May 6, 1829 cash pd. STEPHEN BAILEY for books $2.75, #3
Dec. 30 pd. JAMES BUTLAR a/c $2.50, #4 1830 Jan. 1st pd. W. W. BRADLEY
a/c $8.00, #5 ROBERT BROWN $6.66½, #6 JAMES H. HILL a/c $30.81½, #7 HENRY
LEE a/c 75¢, #8 Jan. 8, J. MCCORD Clerk of Ordinary $1.12½, #9 Jan. 18,

J. R. MCCORD a/c $1.00, #10 Feb. 2 JAMES H. STARK Adm. of S.C. STARK a/c
$6.50, #11 Apr. 8 pd GREEN MARTIN a/c 50¢, #12 May 22 JAS. H. STARK for
Bible 62½¢, #13 June 29th pd JOHN ROBINSON a/c $18.43, #14 Oct. 4 pd.
NEEDHAM LEE for taxes 1829 $12.90½, #15 Nov. Clk C. Ordinary $2.75, #16
Dec. 1 pd C & S BAILEY Physicians Bill $59.25, #17 Dec. 13, pd HAMLIN
FREEMAN a/c $14.00, #18 Nov. 20 pd CASE & GOODRICH a/c $7.18½, #19
Dec. 31, pd. CHARLES BAILEY Guard. $120.50, #20 Jan. 5 C. P. CHEATHAM
auctioneer $1.00, #21 Dec. 25 JNO. W. WILLIAMS a/c $5.00, #22 Dec. 15 pd.
W. C. DAWSON & G. C. SAYER for professional services $15.00. Total amt.
$326.92¾... Commission on amt. @5%, $16.34½ Total $343.26, CHARLES
BAILEY Guardian... Recorded May 9, 1831, JOHN MCCORD, C.C.O.

Estate of JOHN M.C. TAYLOR minor of GEORGE D. TAYLOR dec'd. In acc.
with CHARLES BAILEY late Guardian vouchers #1, 1830, Dec. 15 cash pd
N. C. SAYER & W. C. LAWSON for professional services, #2 Apr. 22, cash
pd. J. H. LUMPKIN for professional services, #3 1831. May 15, pd. JOHN
MCCORD for final return... Commission @5%, Total $33.90½... Returned Mar.
6, 1831, CHARLES BAILEY, guardian. Recorded May 10, 1831, JOHN MCCORD,
C.C.O.

Pages 148-149:   Estate of JOHN M. D. TAYLOR, dec'd. in acc. with
CHARLES BAILEY, Admr. from Jan. 8th to Dec. 31st, 1830... Vouchers 1-29,
cash paid Clk. C. Ordinardy, R. BROWN, C. & S. BAILEY for medical services
expenses bringing negroes from Lexington to Jackson $5.00, LOEL GLEASON,
FRANCES HATELEY, C. S. COLLIER, JAS. BUTLAR, KIMMY SMITH, JOHN HALL,
funeral expenses $17.00, JAS. B. MCJUNKIN, F. W. COOK, JOHN ROBINSON,
CLERK C. ORDINARY, A. L. ROBINSON, CASE & GOODRICH, O. P. CHEATHAM,
auctioneer, D. J. BAILEY, CHARLES BAILEY, J. R. MCCORD, J. H. STARK Adm.
of S.C. STARK dec'd. B. F. TUCKER auctioneer M. BAETLETT printer, C. &
S. BAILEY medical services, GREEN MARTIN, Clk. C. ORDINARY, H. FREEMAN,
one of the distributees, S. J. BARNETT for walling in grave $15.00,
BURWELL, JINKS for boarding BARNETT while walling grave $4.62½, CHARLES
BAILEY, taxes for year 1829 $2.90⅝, PARIS PACE for expenses of negro man
Leroy while in jail $5.25, Commission @5%. Total $898.28¾.

Account for hireing negroes belonging to the Estate of JOHN M. D.
TAYLOR, dec'd. from the first Tuesday in Jan. to the 6th April 1830.
Alfred hired to JACOB GARDNER $13.25, Pat hired to WM. MCTEAR $6.25,
Anthony hired to WILLARD BRADLEY $13.25, Rhenoe and child to WM. MESSER
$8.25, Rose hired to P. G. CLAY $10.62½... Terms of hireing negroes to
be well clothed and fed and the amt. of the hire to become due 25 Dec.
1830, persons hireing to give notes with Security... Returned 6th March
1831, CHARLES BAILEY, Admr... Recorded 10th May 1831... JOHN MCCORD, C.C.O.

Page 150:   Certification of ERMINE CASE, ABEL L. ROBINSON and
LAWRENCE GAHAGAN as persons appointed to distribute the Estate of SAM'L
C. STARK, May 6, 1831, JOHN HALL, J.I.C.

Georgia, Butts County, Order of Court of Ordinary to assign to
ROSANNAH STARK one of the distributees of the Estate of SAMUEL C. STARK,
a negro boy named Julius worth $450 in cash May 6, 1831. Signed:
LAWRENCE GAHAGAN, ERMINE CASE, ABEL L. ROBINSON... Recorded May 10, 1831.
JOHN MCCORD, C.C.O.

Additional Inventory and Appraisement of the Estate of RICHARD
KNIGHT dec'd. of property which had not come into the hands of C. F.
KNIGHT, Admr. at the time of the former appraisement... 1 horse saddle
and bridle which has been in hands of WILLIAM KNIGHT $40.00, Certified
by appraisers SAM'L BELLAH, YELVENTON THAXTON, CLARK HAMIL, June 10, 1831.
Recorded JOHN MCCORD, C.C.O.

Pages 151-152-153:   Will of ENOCH PEARSON made Apr. 12, 1830,
Butts Co., Georgia. Weak of body but sound of mind and memory... Item
1st, Just debts be paid... Item 2nd, wife DIANNA PEARSON for her support
and maintainance have use and benefit of all negroes, namely Silvery
and her two children Westley and William her son, Mariah and her child

Martha Caroline, Lucey, Sarah, Isbel, Milly and all their increase during her natural life and $100 for note on JOHN M. PEARSON due one year after my death and appoint WILLIAM H. PEARSON & JOHN M. PEARSON.

Guardian to take care of the property and money and apply to wife's needs... Item 3rd, to son WILLIAM H. PEARSON $60 to make him even with my sons JOHN M. PEARSON and DANIEL W. PEARSON who has received land to Amt. of $500... Item 4th, to son JAMES PEARSON $250 to make his land equal to JOHN M. PEARSON & DANIEL W. PEARSON's hundred acres land at $500. Item 5th, to ROBERT POWER my son in law $1.00 balance of his share of estate... Item 6th, to MORDICAR HILL son in law $1.00 balance of his share of my estate. Item 7th, to heirs of my daughter SARAH POWERS $500 in cash or negro property to be applied to use of said daughter SARAH during her lifetime... Appoint JOHN M. PEARSON Guardian of said SARAH and at her death to divide equally among heirs of her body... Item 8th, to JOHN HILL youngest son of my daughter MARY HILL at her death or any time she shall please to give it up... to make him even with her son WILLIAM P. HILL... $400 in cash or negro property... $500 when the negroes is divided to make her $100 up $500... Item 9th, to heirs of my daughter ELIZABETH MCKLEROY $500 in cash on negro property... Item 10th, to my daughter NANCY ADAIR's heirs $500 in cash on negro property but she to have use during her life if she wishes... Item 11th, to my daughter HARRIET HEAD I give negro woman Cate and her son Bill at the price of $500 to make her equal with others... Item 12th, if any remains at death of my wife it shall be equally divided between all the before named except ROBERT POWER and MORDICAL HILL they are to have no part thereof... Item 14, that debts due me and negroes named and their increase at death of my wife be sold and money appropriated as directed in items... Items 14th, WILLIAM H. PEARSON and JOHN M. PEARSON be executors of will... Signed: ENOCH PEARSON (seal)... Test: FRANCES DOUGLAS, MAHALA M. HAYS, WILLIAM P. HILL... Recorded July 7, 1831... JOHN MCCORD, C.C.O.

Page 153: Return of SAMUEL BELLAH Admr. of Estate of WILLIAM RHODES dec'd. for year of 1830... Vouchers paid clerk pr. return 1829, JOHN URQUHART in right of his wife, JAMES M. RHODES, bought for HARRIET RHODES sundries, bought in NANCY RHODES sundries, medicine for BENJAMIN F. RHODES, paid for boarding year 1829 and 1830, for tuition in 1830, one school testament, boarding and clouthing JOSIAH RHODES in 1829 and 1830, Tax for 1829... Total $455.41½. Recorded Sept. 9, 1831, JOHN MCCORD, C.C.O.

Page 154: MARY WALDRUP, Admx. of Estate of ABRAHAM WALDRUP. To amt. of sales as per a/c $219.75 Cr. Feb. 12, 1828... Vouchers #1 paid L. M. ADAMS, #2 ELIJAH MCMICHAEL, J.P. on divers cases comenced against me as admx. at different times in year 1828, 1829, 1830... #3 July 4, 1831 paid Clk. for recording deed... #4 1828 paid fees to C.C.O.... #5 June 22nd paid WM. WIGGINS on note #6 May 5, 1831 paid Clk. of Court of Ordinary... #7 Feb. 12, 1828 paid W. B. ECTOR... Total amt. $153.83½... The Admx. remarks to court that many of her vouchers are incomplete and not regular and prays to court ot allow her until next court ot have them corrected and prepared... C.C.O. Sept. Term 1831, CHARLES BAILEY, J.L.C. Recorded Sept. 9, 1831, JOHN MCCORD, C.C.O.

Page 155: Inventory & Appraisement of the Estate of OVID COWELS dec'd... 12 items listed... MOSELY HOOKER's receipt for ASA STEPHENS note dated July 6, 1827... Total Amt.. $221.37½ Georgia Butts Co., Certification of the appraisement of goods and chattels and credits of the estate of OVID COWLES dec'd., Aug. 30, 1831. App: ABEL L. ROBISON, ROBERT BROWN, HENRY HATELEY.

Georgia Butts Co. Certification of appraisers sworn to perform duty Aug. 30, 1831. HENRY JACKSON, JP. Recorded Sept. 22, 1831, JOHN MCCORD, C.C.O.

Page 156: Sale of property belonging to the Estate of OVID COWLES dec'd. Sept. 6, 1831... Byr.: CARMIN CASE, H. WILLIAMS, C. BAILEY, W. BRADLEY, C. MOORE, J. W. WILLIAMS, B. MCCOY, R. W. HARKNESS. Total $170.87. Recorded Sept. 22, 1831.

Pages 156-157:   Inventory and Appraisement of Estate of SALLEY
PALMER dec'd., taken on Oct. 11, 1831.   The only property presented a
certain boy named ANTHONY which we value at $450... Note on ANN PALMER,
Guardian for JESSE A. PALMER due Jan. 5, 1832... Note on JNO. KELLY,
Guardian for AMASA PALMER due same time $82.80... Note on ANN PALMER,
Guardian for JESSE PALMER due as above $1.20... Total $616.80.

Georgia Butts Co. Certification of true appraisement of goods,
chattels and credits on Estate of SALLY PALMER, dec'd. Oct. 11, 1831...
Appr: SAMUEL NUTT, THOMAS ROBINSON, EZEKIEL WALKER... Appr. sworn to
perform duty Oct. 11, 1831, JOHN HALL, J.I.C.... Recorded Nov. 1, 1831,
JOHN MCCORD, C.C.O.

Pages 157-158:   Butts Co., Ga. Will of JOHN WILLIAMSON, Senr. being
sensible for my advanced age but in usual health and sound in mind and
memory. Commend sould to God... My temporal estate destributed in
following manner (to wit) 1st, give to my beloved children (to wit) SALLY
MOON, POLLY M'CLUSKY, WILLIAM WILLIAMSON, JENNY DOSS, ADAM WILLIAMSON,
ELIZABETH POWERS $1 each as their entire portion of my estate... 2nd, to
my beloved grandson NATHAN WILLIAMSON two lots of land No. 232 and 250,
8th Dist. and lot 250 in 1st Dist. all originally Henry county now Butts
and two negro boys named Jack and Ben and negro woman named Rachel and
her increase... 3rd. to my beloved son JOHN WILLIAMSON all residue of
property both real and personal... 4th, Appoint beloved son JOHN WILLIAM-
SON and beloved grandson NATHAN WILLIAMSON Exrs... Will made Feb. 25,
1831. Signed: JOHN (X) WILLIAMSON, Senr. (Seal)... In presence of JOHN
LOFTON, WILLIAM HARRISON, GUSTAVUS HENDRICK... Sworn in open court Nov.
7, 1831, JOHN MCCORD, C.C.O. Recorded Nov. 7, 1831, JOHN MCCORD, C.C.O.

Pages 159-160-161:   Inventory and Appraisement of the Estate of
JOHN WILLIAMSON, dec'd. List 1-27, list of goods of estate. Notes:
11 on J & H. SUMMERLIN, 4 on JOHN LOFTON & JOHN MCDANIEL, 6 on MILLER &
CLAYTON, 4 on M. J. & W. FERRIL, 1 on P. PRYOR & J. MCBRIDE, 2 on S.
MOORE & J. MCBRIDE & G. WYATT, 1 on W. HARRISON, 1 on J. CRAINE & Z.
ONAIL, 1 on E. STALLWORTH & W. WELCH... Total $5295.86½.

Oath of appraisors JOSEPH SUMMERLIN, WILLIAM HARRISON, ZACHARIAH
ONAIL, WILLIAM BAKER, Nov. 10, 1831.

Certification that appraisors performed duty Nov. 10, 1831, GEORGE L.
THOMPSON, J.P. Recorded Nov. 12, 1831, JOHN MCCORD, C.C.O.

Pages 162-163-164-165:   Stock inventory and appraisement of estate
of WILLIAM REDMAN, dec'd. 51 hogs, 36 sheep, 13 cows, 21 calves, 5
steers, 2 mules, 2 horses, 1 colt... 48 items of goods and chattel...
Total value $1506.25... Notes on JAMES CARTER, JAMES S. MORRIS, THOMAS
THOMAS, JAS. BYARS, DAVID BYARS, E. BUGG, JOSIAH P. STEPHENS... Open acc.
on JOHN REEVES, MR. MOORE, LEONARD ROAN, THOMAS THOMAS, DAVID BYARS,
JAMES BYARS, ANTHONY GILMORE... 5 negroes... Total value of Estate
$3842.25.

Oath of appraisors on Estate of WILLIAM REDMAN, dec'd., JOHN
STEPHENS, J. W. WATKINS, WILLIAM J. STEPHENS, JOHN WHITE. Nov. 2, 1831,
HENRY JACKSON, J.P. Recorded Dec. 27, 1831, JOHN MCCORD, C.C.O.

Pages 165-166-167:   Inventory and appraisement of Estate of JAMES
GRAY, dec'd... 45 items listed at value of $1598.25... Notes on THOMAS
MOTES, JOHN MCCLELAND. Certification of appraisors that this is a true
appraisement as far as was produced by LEWIS H. FARGASON, Admr. Signed:
THOMAS BRANAN, JESSE T. GUNN, THOMAS HULL, Appr. Sept. 15, 1831, JOHN
LOFTON, J.P.

Pages 167-168:   GIDEON MATHIS, Guardian to CHARLES G. THAXTON orphan
Inventory of property of said orphan... Note on YELVENTON THAXTON $204...
Note on WILEY THAXTON $26.68... Total $230.68... Jan. 6, 1832... GIDEON
MATHIS, Guardian.

Page 168:   Return #5 WILLIAM HURST to JAMES SCRUGGS, Idiot $14.14½
Cr.... Paid C.C.O. washing and finding clothing from Jan. 3, 1831 to
Dec. 31, 1831. Total $12.53½.

Annual Return No. 2, Estate of JOHN BARRON, dec'd. to SMITH BARRON,
Admr. 1831... Paid JOHN ROBINSON, tax year 1830, C. & S. BAILEY, HENRY
HATELY... Total money on hand Jan. 1, 1831, $490.26½.

Page 169:   JAMES CLAYTON SENR., Guardian Dr. to JAMES CLAYTON, JR.,
1830. Settled to this date Oct. 6, 1830, $216, JAMES CLAYTON, JR.

Pages 169-170:   Return #1, the Estate of WILLIAM REDMAN, dec'd. in
a/c with JAMES CARTER, adm. from Nov. 7, to Dec. 31, 1831... Names
mentioned, JAMES CARTER, GEORGE W. LOWRY, JOHN REEVES, ANDREW MORRIS,
SAMUEL R. MCLIN, CHARLES MILLER, ROBERT HARKNESS, THOMAS THOMAS, DAVID
BYARS... Total $73.64, Dec. 31, 1831.

Reutrn Jan. 5, 1832, JAMES CARTER, Adm. Estate of SALLY PALMER, dec'd
$254.58... Return Jan. 4, 1832, MATHEW GASTON Admr.

Page 171-172:   Annual return Estate of JOHN M. C. TAYLOR dec'd. in
a/c with CHARLES BAILEY, Admr. to Dec. 31, 1831... Total $8.40.

Annual return of Estate of NOAH W. TAYLOR minor of GEORGE D. TAYLOR,
dec'd. in a/c with CHARLES BAILEY Guardian up to Dec. 31, 1831... Names
mentioned, SAMUEL GEE, L. GAHAGAN, F. HATELY, LOFTON HENDRICK, STEPHEN
BAILEY, HENRY GRAHAM, ELEASE STORE, D. T. DUPREE STORE, CHARLES BAILEY
Guardian... Total $281.00½... Hire of negroes to F. A. BAILEY, CALVERY
F. KNIGHT, JACOB GARDNER, $210.

Page 172:   Return of SAM'L BELLAH, Admr. of Estate of WILLIAM
RHODES dec'd. 1831, Vouchers paid R. STEPHENS for teaching JOSIAH RHODES
one of the heirs, ___? URQUHART for boarding and washing for said JOSIAH
while going to school, ELEASE for clothing HARRIETT RHODES one of heirs,
ELEAN for clothing NANCY RHODES one of the heirs... Total $33.43 3/4.

Returned March 1, 1832 by SAMUEL BELLAH of Estate of OVICE COWLES
dec'd. in acc. with ERMINE CASE Admr. 1831 Vouchers #1 proven pd. C.
BAILEY #2 note pd. R. COWLES & brothers #3, 3 fifas pd. H. COWLES & brothers #4 proven acc. pd. E. CASE #5 proven acc. pd. MACON TELEGRAPH
advertising #6 pd. J. MCCORD Clerk #7 proven acc. pd. H. HATELY burial
expenses ($17.50) #8 E. CASE Admr. #9 ASA STEPHENS insolvent #10 balance
due estate Dec. 31, 1831 Clerk fees for this return - six leggetees, 4
brothers and 2 sisters.

Pages 173-174:   Jan.7, 1832 E. CASE Admr. Estate of RICH'D KNIGHT
dec'd. to C. F. KNIGHT Admr. up to Dec. 31, 1831... Vouchers paid
STARK & PETTITT Attys. for service, S. I. BARNETT for building vault over
grave, paid Y. THAXTON, H. D. KNIGHT for witnesses, to boarding, washing,
lodging and attendance on dec'd. from Jan. 18, 1827 to June 23, 1828,
17 months at four dollars per month. Total $155.88 3/4.

Page 174 Con't.:   Return Jan. 5, 183_ by CALVARY F. KNIGHT Adm...
Acc of sale on Estate of RICHARD KNIGHT dec'd. Feb. 17, 1832... Negro
girl bought by THOMAS WILLIAMSON, horse, saddle & bridle by C. F. KNIGHT,
bed and furniture by ZACHARIAH T. KNIGHT, chest B. H. DERDEN, stone jug
WILLIAM L. WILSON, CHAMBER POT C. F. KNIGHT... Total $383. 3/4.
Rendered March 5, 1832... C. F. KNIGHT Admr.

Page 175:   Estate of WILLIAM BLESSIT minor of ELISHA BLESSIT to
WILLIAM HARPER, Guardian... 1830 Voucher #1 Cash pd. HAMLIN FREEMAN
atty at law... Credits, balance due minor Dec. 31. $243.94.

Annual return, receipt and expenses of the Estate of GEORGE BLESSET
minor of ELISHA BLESSET, dec'd. by WILLIAM HARPER Guardian Apr. 9, 1832..
Balance due $238.06.

Pages 176-177-178-179-180-181: Inventory of the Estate of WILLIAM
REDMAN, dec'd. Dec. 27, 1831. Purchasers: JAMES BYARS, EDWARD BOND, WM.
ALLISON, MARTIN P. DYE, MARY REDMAN, G. W. STUART, CHARLES MILLER,
THOMAS THOMAS, JOSEPH BYARS, HENRY LEE, D. T. DUPREE, TUCKER HIGGINS,
STOKELEY MORGAN, JOHN HENDRICK, JAMES CARTER, JESSE LEVERETT, JOHN SMITH,
HENRY TOLSON, A. L. ROBINSON, WM. HARDY, WM. MESSER, WM. J. STEPHENS,
SAMUEL BELLAH, JOHN STEPHENS, THOMAS WILSON, JAMES ROBERTS, WILLIS JARRELL,
THOMAS MCGOUGH, JOHN ROAN, SAMUEL NUTT, WM. BYARS, JAMES L. MAYO, DAVID
BYARS, ROBERT W. HARKNESS, JOHN M. BROWN, JAMES BAILEY, STEPNA a boy,
ANDREW MORRIS, WASHINGTON POTTER... Total $1119.99 3/4.

Dec. 27, 1831... Inventory of rent of land and hire of negroes of
Estate of WILLIAM REDMAN dec'd. ... Total $283.12½.

Pages 182-183: Annual return #3 Estate of JOHN BARKLEY to SAMUEL
R. NUTT Adm. up to Dec. 31, 1831... Vouchers pd. to H. JACKSON, A. L.
ROBINSON, G. GAHAGAN, JAMES LOVE, P. PHILLIP, JAS. H. STARK Adm. of S.C.
STARK, H. LEES, A. B. POPE, THOMAS B. BURFORD, ELIAS HOUSE, JOHN HALL,
JANE BARKLEY, for boarding 3 children, MATTHEW JINKS... Total $629.78...
Hire of negroes $295.12½. Recorded May 9, 1832 JOHN MCCORD, C.C.O.

Page 183 con't.: Estate of ABRAHAM WALDROP dec'd. to MARY
WALDROP Admrx., Sept. 1831 pd JOHN M. PEARSON for three cases in Justice
Court in favor of SHADRICK MCMICHAEL, A. G. HAYNES & JOHN A. WALKER...
MARY (X) WALDRIP. Recorded July 5, 1832, JOHN MCCORD, C.C.O.

Pages 184-185: FRANCIS DOUGLAS, JOHN M. PEARSON, DAVID WIGGINS,
E. S. KIRKSEY and WILLIAM WIGGINS appointed to appraise estate of GILLIAM
PRESTON dec'd. as produced by ELISHA and JAMES PRESTON Admr. of estate
of said dec'd... July 10, 1832... Inventory included notes on WILSON
CROCKETT, JEREMIAH CANANT, JONATHAN CHILDS, ROBT. SIMMS... Total $430.37½.

Pages 186-187: Inventory & Appraisement of Estate of JEREMIAH
HAMMOCK, dec'd. includes accounts on ROBERT BROWN, ALLEN CLEVELAND,
JOHN PARKER, THOMAS JOHNSON, L. B. EUBANKS, WILLIAM HOOD, JAS. H. STARK,
LAWRENCE GAHAGAN, ABEL L. ROBINSON, P. A. HIGGINS, JAS. W. WATKINS,
JOSEPH W. HARDY (deed)... Total $182.43 3/4... Certified by appraisors
JOHN MCMICHAEL, CHARLES B. LEE, JOHN MCCORD, HENRY HATELEY, B. H. MARTIN,
July 25, 1832, EDWARD WEAVER, J.P.

Page 187 Con't.: Account of sale of estate of SALLY PALMER, dec'd.
1 negro boy ANTHONY to JAMES R. MCCORD Dec. 25, 1832, $495... Returned
Aug. 27, 1832. MATHEW GASTON, Admr.

Page 188: An account of hiring negroes belonging to Estate of
JOHN SMITH, dec'd. late of Alabama, Jan. 1831... JACK MORIAH & SOPHIA
and four children to highest bidder for 12 months... hired by LEVIN
SMITH $200. Aug. 13, 1832, LEAVIN SMITH, Admr.
An account of hire of same negroes of estate of JOHN SMITH dec'd.
Jan. 1832, LEVIN SMITH, Admr.

STEPHEN BLESSIT Admr. of ELISHA BLESSIT dec'd. submits supplement
to last return Jan. 16th 1629... Cash paid WILLIAM HARPER Guardian
$73.00... Returned Sept. 4, 1832 STEPHEN BLESSIT Admr.... Recorded Sept.
10, 1832, JOHN MCCORD, C.C.O.

Page 189: Estate of NOAH W. TAYLOR minor of GEORGE D. TAYLOR,
dec'd... To his guardian CHARLES BAILEY Dr. Vouchers paid to MCDANIEL
GOODMAN, L. GAHAGAN, JOHN HENDRICK, MCDONALD & FRANKLIN, THOMAS HUNT,
J. M. D. BOND, E. CASE, JOHN HARRIS, R. CHAMBERLIN, B. H. MARTIN, F.
HATELEY, JOHN BULLARD, D. MCBEAN, J. H. LUMPKIN, $207.87½... CHARLES
BAILEY Guardian... Recorded Sept. 10, 1832, JOHN MCCORD, C.C.O.

Pages 190-191: No record name given for inventory (perhaps GEORGE
TAYLOR/ minor of Estate of NOAH TAYLOR)... Sept. 4, 1832, List of items
bought by L. B. EUBANKS, YELVINTON THAXTON, O. P. CHEATHAM, SAMUEL
MADDOX, P. H. WHITE, B. H. DARDEN, JOSEPH KEY, STEPHEN BLESSET, SEABORN W.

BOWLES, JOHN W. WILLIAMS, CHARLES B. LEE, JACKSON NEELEY, JOHN MCCORD, JOHN T. YOUNG, ALLEN CLEVELAND... Amt. $57.93 3/4... PEYTON H. WHITE, Adm.

Pages 191-192-193 Cont'd.: Amt. of sale of perishable property of JAMES GRAY, dec'd., Nov. 25, 1831. Purchasers; ALLEN GRAY, ELIZABETH GRAY, GREEN MATTOCKS, HARDY PACE, THOMAS PACE, JAMES CLAYTON, F. S. CARTER, JOHN P. WYATT, JOHN C. BURGESS, RICHARD SHEPHERED, JAMES MILLER, SALLY GRAY, R. R. TARVER... Total $582.78. Recorded Nov. 6, 1832, JOHN MCCORD, C.C.O.

Pages 193-194: Jasper County, Georgia... Will of JOEL WISE being weak and feeble but sound of mind and memory desires my executors reserve for JOHN STEWART a competant maintainance out of my estate during his natural life. All my children except HUGH WISE have in either money or property $150 to make them equal with HUGH. All said children to divide the balance of estate equally including HUGH. AUGUSTUS & BARNEY WISE each have one year schooling in addition to what they heretofore had and all children younger than them in schools in proportion to older children that is a good country school education out of my estate before any division made between them... Desires all stock, present crop, furniture sold and my plantation and ferry to be rented out for one year or more as will be most suitable... Sons HUGH WISE & JACOB WISE Executors. Signed JOEL (X) WISE, Sept. 13, 1825 in presence of JOHN BURGE, BARTON (X) MARTEN, WM. HANCOCK.
Georgia Butts County... Sworn in open court by WM. HANCOCK & JOHN BURGE, Nov. 5, 1832... Recorded Nov. 7, 1832, JOHN MCCORD, C.C.O.

Pages 195-196: Return on Estate of ARTHUR C. ATKINSON, dec'd. by THOMAS P. ATKINSON & WASHINGTON G. ATKINSON for 1831, Exec. of said dec'd. Vouchers paid by exec. to WILLIAM ROBERTS for bond for title given dec'd. for Lot #148 in 1st Dist. originally Henry County now Butts, Jan. 1831... To JOHN MCCORD, J. M. D. BOND, JOHN W. CARDWELL Atty for heirs of FIELDING DILLARD, dec'd., JOSEPH HENRY LUMPKIN, ZELOTUS ADAMS, JOHN LANDRUM, HAMLIN FREEMAN... Total $6600.25... Moneys received from JOSEPH HENRY LUMPKIN, ZELOTUS, WASHINGTON G. ATKINSON, THOMAS P. ATKINSON, HAMLIN FREEMAN, ROBERT BROWN, FOSTER FREEMAN for lot of land No. 220, 8th Dist. originally Monroe now Pile County, ROBERT W. HUNTER $5308.41¼... Balance due exec. $1291.83 3/4. Recorded Nov. 7, 1832, JOHN MCCORD, C.C.O.

Page 197: Furnished the Estate of WILLIAM REDMAN, dec'd. out of stock and crop belonging to sd. estate between time of appraisement and sale $47.90. JAMES CARTER, Adm... Recorded Nov. 12, 1832... JOHN MCCORD, C.C.O.

The orphans of JOSEPH G. SPEAR to ELI CONGER, Guardian, March 7, 1831, paid for tuition and boarding JOSEPH SPEAR one of said minors for year 1831, $4.00... Paid CYNTHIA E. & GOLDSMITH WALKER $10.00... Returned Nov. 5, 1832, ELI CONGER, Guardian. Recorded Nov. 12, 1832, JOHN MCCORD, C.C.O.

Georgia Butts County... CLARK HAMEL, BOSDELL G. POTTER, JAMES E. BANKSTON, NATHAN ELLIS, sworn by law to appraise and equally divide the estate of ELISHA BLESSET dec'd. to each and every Legatee of said dec'd. before WILLIS JARRELL, C.C.O. Oct. 4, 1832.

Pages 198-199-200-201: WILLIAM HARPER, Guardian of GEORGE & WILLIAM BLESSET, JOHN BLESSET, REASON BLESSET, JOHN BLESSET, ALFRED BANKSTON, NANCY (X) BLESSET Widow petition for division of real estate of ELISHA BLESSET and waver the twenty day notice... Sept. term 1832, petition granted... Recorded Sept. 3, 1832, JOHN MCCORD, C.C.O.

Division of property... Northern half of lot #80, 1st Dist. of orig. Henry now Butts to WILLIAM HARPER, $200... Eastern half of lot #65 in 2nd Dist. of formerly Henry now Butts assigned to GEORGE BLESSET at price of $325... Western half of lot #64 in 2nd Dist. formerly Henry now Butts to REASON BLESSET, $400... Northern half of lot #178 in 6th Dist. of Henry County to ALFRED BANKSTON $150... South half of lot #178 in

6th Dist. of Henry County to ALFRED BANKSTON $150... South half of lot #178 in 6th Dist. of Henry County to WILLIAM BLESSET $175 ... Eastern half of lot #64 in 2nd Dist. formerly Henry now Butts County to JOHN BLESSET at the price of $300... South half of lot #80 in 1st Dist. of formerly Henry now Butts County to NANCY BLESSET, the widow of deceased $350... Under our seal Oct. 13, 1832. Signed: CLARK HAMIL (seal), JAMES E. BANKSTON (seal), BOSDELL G. POTTER (seal)... The undersigned acknow-ledged the receipt of the respective sums required so as to make all the shares equal, Oct. 13, 1832, WILLIAM HARPER for myself and guardian for WM. & GEORGE BLESSET, REASON BLESSET, ALFRED BANKSTON, JOHN (X) BLESSET.. Test: J. H. STARK, CLARK HAMIL, J.P.

Page 202: Ordered in Nov. Term 1832 that the proceeding be re-corded... CHARLES BAILEY, J.I.C., JOHN MCMICHAEL J.I.C., JOHN HENDRICK J.I.C. Recorded Jan. 23, 1833, JOHN MCCORD, C.C.O.

Page 202-203: Butts County, Ga. Will of GREEN MCCOY... Sound in mind and memory... It is my will that it be distributed in following manner... To my wife ELIZA my horse and household furniture, a negro boy Shade during her life and then to revert back to my son JAMES H. MCCOY. If son JAMES dies without issue to be equally divided among my father's heirs. To beloved wife ELIZA a negro woman Susan and her child and in-crease during widowhood provided she will support my son JAMES without charge if not without expense or she should marry executors take posses-sion of Susan, child and increase for benefit of son JAMES H. MCCOY... When son JAMES H. MCCOY arrives at age 21 named negroes be delivered to him... Balance of property put at interest for support and education of son JAMES H. MCCOY... Appoints my beloved brother HENRY and BALEY MCCOY my Executors. Signed: GREER MCCOY (SEAL) in presence of ELI BUCKNER, LORENZO G. KENNEDY, JAMES KING... Will recorded Jan. 28, 1833, JOHN MCCORD, C.C.O.

Pages 203-204: Annual Return Estate of JOHN SMITH, dec'd. to LEAVIN SMITH, Adm. 1830 Amt. $121.50... Cr. by hire of JACK, MARIA, SOPHIA, GEORGE, DAVY, LITTLETON & MARY to LEAVIN SMITH for year 1831 and 1832, $32.00. Returned Jan. 7, 1833, LEVIN SMITH, Admr. Recorded Jan. 28, 1833, JOHN MCCORD, C.C.O.

Annual return Estate of RICHARD KNIGHT dec'd. 1832 to C. F. KNIGHT, Admr. paid YELVENTON THAXTON, E. CASE, WILLARD J. HARDEN, HENRY F. HARDEN, PLEDGE W. THOMPSON, JOEL KNIGHT, FREDERICK POLLARD, MCDANIEL GOODMAN, JAMES HARDEN $557.52... Returned Jan. 4, 1833, C. F. KNIGHT, Adm., Recorded Jan. 30, 1833, JOHN MCCORD, C.C.O.

Pages 205-206-207 Con't.: Georgia Butts Co., Inventory & Appraise-ment of estate of JOEL WISE dec'd. Items listed valued at $2008.25... Certified Nov. 9, 1832 by appraisors JOSEPH WRIGHT, PARHAM LINDSEY, RILEY WISE. Appraisors sworn by G. T. SPEAKE, J.P.... Recorded Jan. 30, 1833, JOHN MCCORD, C.C.O.

Pages 207-208: Inventory & Appraisement of Estate of GREER MCCOY, dec'd... Items listed among which were notes on Manly SCROGGIN, ALLEN SIMS, WILLIAM LOW, MARCUS SWINNEY, JAMES M. HILL. Total value $1224.07 3/4... Appraisors JAMES KING, SAMUEL LEE, LORENZO G. KENNEDY... Apprai-sors sworn to perform duty Jan. 12, 1833 before LEONARD ROAN, J.P. Recorded Jan. 31, 1833, JOHN MCCORD, C.C.O.

Pages 209-210-211: Sale Bill for the Estate of GILLIAM PRESTON, Dec. 28, 1832... Buyers: JOHN HALL, JOHN FLOYD, SALLY PRESTON, JAMES M. PRESTON, JAMES THURMAN, STERLING T. HIGGINS, BEDFORD H. DARDEN, POLLARD PAYNE, JACOB T. MAYO, GREEN PENNELL, ELISHA J. PRESTON, WILLIAM HIGGINS, THOMAS THOMAS, JAMES G. MAYO, JOHN F. PRESTON, DAVID HIGGINS, STEPHEN D. MAYO, R. R. MAYO. Total amt. $450.19½... Recorded March 6, 1833, JOHN MCCORD, C.C.O.

Pages 212-213-214-215-216: Inventory of personal property of JOSEL WISE, dec'd. sold at public sale on Dec. 25 & 26, 1832... Buyers:

WILLIAM J. HEAD, JOSIAH WISE, WILLIAM A. MCCUNE, MOSES LUNSFORD, WILLIAM
JOHNSON, PATTRON WISE, WILLIAM VICKERS, GEORGE T. SPEAKE, BARNA WISE,
STERLING T. HIGGINS, JOSEPH HARMON, BEDFORD H. DARDEN, WILLIAM PRYOR,
WILLIAM TEDDLIE, HUGH WISE, NATHAN G. WALLER, JOHN WALKER, DAVID HIGGINS,
WILLIAM GILES, JAMES M. DARDEN, SPENCER MALONE, JAMES PRIDGEN, JOHN MURRY,
JOHN MALONE, BARTON MARTIN, GEORGE W. THOMAS, NICHOLAS JOHNSON, WILLIAM
MORGAN, JOHN FLOYD, JOHN PRICE, ROBERT BIGARSTAFF, RILEY WISE, ALLSEY
DURHAM, CREED WISE, HENRY MURRY, AUGUATUS WISE, JOHN GROSS, WOODY DOZIER,
WILLIAM B. STONE, JOB TAYLOR, MAHALA WISE, GREEN B. JACKSON, JOHN BURGE...
Recorded March 7, 1833, JOHN MCCORD, C.C.O.
     Inventory of notes and accounts not in appraisement... Account for
blacksmith work... Notes on CREED WISE, NICHOLAS JOHNSON, HUGH WISE,
BARNA WISE, DAVID JACKSON, AUGUSTUS WISE... Total Estate, $994... Record-
ed March 7, 1833, JOHN MCCORD, C.C.O.

     Page 217:   NOAH W. TAYLOR minor of GEORGE D. TAYLOR dec'd... To
CHARLES BAILEY his guardian account $53.00... Cr. by hire of negroes to
WILLIAM MESSER, CHARLES BAILEY, DANIEL T. DUPREE, JACOB GARDNER, $213.00.
Balance in favor of estate $160.00, CHARLES BAILEY, Guardian... Returned
Feb. 23, 1833... Recorded March 8, 1833, JOHN MCCORD, C.C.O.

     Estate of ELISHA BLESSET dec'd. in acc. with STEPHEN BLESSET,
Admr. cash paid WILLIAM HARPER, $40.38... Returned March 4, 1833...
Recorded March 8, 1833, JOHN MCCORD, C.C.O.

     Page 218:   Estate of SAMUEL C. STARK in acc. with JAMES H. STARK,
Admr. from Jan. 1 to Dec. 31, 1831... Paid JOHN SANDERS, JOHN BRITTEN,
H. LEE, M. BARTLETT, ROBERT BROWN, S. TAYLOR, WM. HITCHCOCK, JOHN BARTON,
ROBT. C. MAYO, MATHEW MCMICHAEL... Total $422.70.

     Page 219:   Cr. to Estate of SAMUEL C. STARK... JOHN SANDERS,
ISAAC SMITH, JOHN T. YOUNG, JAMES HOGGS, THOS. JOHNSON, W. BEANS, A. L.
ROBINSON, M. F. CALDWELL... $403.03... Returned Jan. 9, 1832, JAMES H.
STARK, Admr... Recorded March 8, 1833, JOHN MCCORD, C.C.O.

     Pages 220-221:   Returns of land and houses belonging to Estate of
S.C. STARK, dec'd. for 1831... Amt. $144.12½... Returned Jan. 9, 1831,
JAMES H. STARK, Admr... Recorded March 8, 1833, JOHN MCCORD, C.C.O.
Return #4 from Dec. 31, 1831 to Dec. 31, 1832... Rent on land and houses
of S.C. STARK by JAMES H. STARK, Adm. March 3, 1833... Recorded March 8,
1833.

     Return by SMITH BARRON, Adm. of JOHN BARRON, dec'd. year ending
Dec. 31, 1832... Paid HENRY BARRON, WM. BARRON, M. BARTLETT, SUSAN
BARRON, one of the distributees in part of her share, CLAYTON HUFF, JOHN
MCCMICHAEL... Cr. rent of land to JOSIAH REEVES $196.94... Returned Jan.
3, 1833, SMITH BARRON, Admr... Recorded March 9, 1833, JOHN MCCORD, C.C.O.

     Page 222:   Return No. 2, Estate of WILLIAM REDMAN, dec'd. in acc.
with JAMES CARTER Admr. from Jan. 1 to Dec. 31, 1832, paid LITTERBERRY
EUBANKS, D. T. DUPREE, LEONARD ROAN, JAMES BYARS, JOHN HALL, JOHN SANDERS,
MARY REDMAN for boarding and taking care of ELIZABETH REDMAN, mother of
WILLIAM REDMAN, dec'd., MARY REDMAN for boarding and clothing MARY RED-
MAN & MARTHA REDMAN, orphans of WILLIAM REDMAN, dec'd.
Total $262.06¼.

     Page 223:   Cr. on Estate of WILLIAM REDMAN dec'd... Rec'd from
notes on JAMES S. MORRIS, JAMES CARTER, LEONARD ROANS, JAMES BYARS, DAVID
BYARS, $262.06¼. Returned March 1, 1833, JAMES CARTER Admr... Recorded
March 9, 1833, JOHN MCCORD, C.C.O.

     JAMES M. & ELISHA J. PRESTON, Admr. of the Estate of GILLIAM PRES-
TON, dec'd... Return Cash $171.68½... Return Feb. 25, 1833... J. M.
PRESTON, Admr... Recorded March 9, 1833, JOHN MCCORD, C.C.O.

     Page 224:   The Admr. of the Estate of JOHN BARKLEY, dec'd... 1831
and 1832... Vouchers on moneys received from SAMUEL NUTT, WM. BROOKS,

E. P. DANIEL, WM. RAY, HENRY JACKSON, T. B. BURFORD, JOHN CARGILE, G. W. HAMIL, SAMUEL NUTT, SR... Total $625.85¼... SAMUEL R. NUTT Admr... Returned March 4, 1833... Recorded Mar. 9, 1833, JOHN MCCORD, C.C.O.

Page 225:   Estate of JOEL WISE, dec'd. to JACOB WISE, Exr. 1832, pd. $15.75. Cr. $360.39 3/4... Returned Mar. 4, 1833, JACOB WISE, Exr... Recorded March 9, 1833, JOHN MCCORD, C.C.O.

Return of SAMUEL BELLAH, Admr. of Estate of WILLIAM RHODES dec'd. for year 1833... Vouchers, pd. to JOHN MCCORD & JOHN HALL for orphans of said estate, MCDANIEL & GOODMAN for HARRIET RHODES one of the heirs of sd. estate her part as a Legatee $130.25, MCDANIEL & GOODMAN for NANCY RHODES one of the heirs, B. H. MARTIN for sd. NANCY, WILSON & MADDOX for sd. NANCY, JOHN URQUHART for BENJAMIN F. RHODES one of the heirs. Total $178.39½... Recorded May 14, 1833, JOHN MCCORD, C.C.O.

Page 226:   Estate of JOHN M. D. TAYLOR dec'd. to CHARLES BAILEY, Admr... Cash paid JOSEPH H. LUMPKIN for professional services rendered in Wilkes Superior Court $50.00... Returned Apr. 16, 1833, CHARLES BAILEY, Adm. of J. M. D. TAYLOR, dec'd... Recorded May 14, 1833, JOHN MCCORD, C.C.O.

Page 226 Con't: Estate of WILLIAM BLESSETT minor of ELISHA BLESSETT dec'd. to WILLIAM HARPER, guardian to Dec. 31, 1832... Credits and amount paid out $332.41½. Recorded May 14, 1833, JOHN MCCORD, C.C.O.

Page 227:   Estate of SALLY alias SARAH PALMER to MATTHEW GASTON, Feb. 7, 1832, paid H. HATELEY for making coffin, Jan. 8, 1833 fee to Clerk of Court Apr. 2, 1832 P. W. WHITE physician, Jan. 8, 1833 C. BAILEY physician, Jan. 10, 1832, JOHN PALMER in part of his share, WILLIAM W. PALMER in part of his share, JOHN KELLEY guardian for AMASA E. PALMER in part of his share, ANN PALMER Guardian for MATTHEW G. PALMER for his share, ASBURY W. PALMER for JESSE A. PALMER and for ROBERT T. PALMER for each of them $25 in part of their share, Apr. 1, 1832 JNO. PALMER in part of his share, WM. W. PALMER Guardian for AMASA E. PALMER in part of his share, ANN PALMER Guardian for MATTHEW G. PALMER, ASBURY W. PALMER, JESSE A. PALMER & ROBERT T. PALMER for part of their share, Jan. 1833, JNO. PALMER in full his share, WM. W. PALMER in full his share, WM. W. PALMER Guardian for AMASA E. PALMER in full his share, ANN PALMER Guardian for above in full... Total $1071.80... Return Mar. 1833, MATTHEW GASTON Admr... Recorded May 14, 1833, JOHN MCCORD, C.C.O.

Page 228:   Account of the Sale of the Estate of JOHN MCMAHAN late of the state of South Carolina dec'd., Sept. 4, 1832, Lot of land #14 in 1st Dist. originally Henry now Butts sold to ROBERT C. MAYS for $25.00. Returned June 5, 1833, J. R. MCMAHAN, Admr. of JOHN MCMAHAN dec'd... Recorded June 5, 1833, JOHN MCCORD, C.C.O.

Annual return estate of JOHN MCMAHAN late of the State of South Carolina, dec'd. to JOHN R. MCMAHAN, Admr... Paid Clerk of Court fee for services. Return June 5, 1833, JOHN R. MCMAHAN, Admr... Recorded June 10, 1833, JOHN MCCORD, C.C.O.

Pages 229-230:   Return on Estate of JOHN BLISSIT minor to WM. HARPER, Guardian to 31st. Dec. 1832... Dr. 1832, Oct. 13th Vouchers #1 cash paid to WILLIAM BLISSIT's share according to return of distributor, #2 paid STARK & PETTIT Atty. for services, #3 April 9th paid Clk. of Ordinary, #4 March 23rd paid C. CAMPBELL for hat for minor $1.50, #5 Nov. 5th paid WM. E. TUCKER for pair of shoes for minor $2.12½, #6 Feb. 24th paid SPENCER & MAY for pair of shoes for minor $1.37½... Cr. balance due minor Dec. 31, 1832 $191.74, WILLIAM HARPER, Guardian... Recorded June 11, 1833, JOHN MCCORD, C.C.O.

JOHN JONES, Admr. with will annexed of Estate of JAMES WOOTEN, dec'd. Vouchers #1 paid Jan. 8, 1830 to C.C.O. for fees due, #2 Sept. 8, 1832 C.C.O., #3 Apr.15, 1832 paid L. L. GRIFFIN for necessaries, to services rendered by myself and wife in various ways in taking care of

51

overseeing lands and attending to family from Nov. 1830 to 31st Dec. 1832, 2 years and upward $433.33. Total $452.98... Cr. 1831 cash made from hands and land, 1832 cash on land, Total $551.00... The above is full return to Dec. 31st. 1832... Recorded June 12, 1833, JOHN JONES, Admr. JOHN MCCORD, C.C.O.

SEABORN L. WOOTEN, minor of JAMES WOOTEN, dec'd. to JOHN JONES... Vouchers #1 paid C.C.O., #2 Dec. 25, 1830 paid A. FULWOOD for tuition $2.75, #3 Dec. 25, 1831 paid A. FULWOOD for tuition $9.45, #4 paid A. FULWOOD for tuition $1.80... Returned as full return to Dec. 31, 1832, JOHN JONES, Guardian... Recorded June 12, 1833, JOHN MCCORD, C.C.O.

ADDISON A. WOOTEN, minor of JAMES WOOTEN, dec'd. to JOHN JONES, Guardian Dr... Vouchers #1-4 paid Dec. 25, 1833, 1831, 1832 to A. FUL-WOOD for tuition... Total $14.68 3/4... Submitted as full return to Dec. 31, 1832, JOHN JONES, Guardian... Recorded June 17, 1833, JOHN MCCORD, C.C.O.

Page 231:   JAMES WOOTEN minor of JAMES WOOTEN, dec'd. to JOHN JONES guardian. Vouchers #1 paid Sept. 8, 1832 to C.C.O., #2 Dec. 25, 1830 paid A. FULWOOD for tuition, #3 paid Dec. 25, 1831 for tuition #4 Jan. 12, 1832 paid A. COLLIER for necessaries... Total $11.02 3/4... above full return to Dec. 1833, JOHN JONES, Guardian. Recorded June 12, 1833, JOHN MCCORD, C.C.O.

SIMEON WOOTEN, minor of JAMES WOOTEN dec'd. to JOHN JONES, Guardian Vouchers #1 paid C.C.O., #2 paid Dec. 25, 1830, A. FULWOOD for tuition, #3 paid for tuition... Submitted full return up to 31st. Dec. 1832. JOHN JONES, Guardian... Recorded June 13, 1833, JOHN MCCORD, C.C.O.

Pages 231-232 Cont'd.:   Will of MATHEW JINKS of State of Georgia, Butts County... in perfect sences and memory... I give to my loving wife PATSEY JINKS all household and kitchen furniture her lifetime or widow-hood and then to my daughters NANCY, ELIZABETH & MARTHA to have loom and dau. NANCY to have red heffer, and all my smith tools to my son MINTION JINKS and 1 gold lot drawn in my name in 2nd section, 3rd. District No. 380 to be divided equally between my three sons ISAAC, ADAM & MINTION. Balance to go to benefit of my family... made June 15, 1833... Signed MATHEW (X) JINKS (SEAL)... Test: NEY (X) PUGH, JOHN S. IRBY, MATHEW GASTON... I appoint ISAAC JINKS & MINTION JINKS as my exors. MATHEW (X) JINKS... Recorded July 1, 1833, JOHN MCCORD, C.C.O.

On July 1, 1833, MATHEW GASTON, NEY (X) PUGH, JOHN IRBY swears before JOHN MCCORD, C.C.O. they saw MATTHEW JINKS sign above will... Recorded July 1, 1833, JOHN MCCORD, C.C.O.

Page 233:   Will of CHARLES HEARD of County of Butts, State of Georgia... being weak in body but perfect sound mind and memory... 1st all debts paid... 2nd all property after debts paid to remain in hands of my beloved companion ELLINOR HEARD for her immediate use during life of widowhood except two negroes Phillis and Betty her child which I wish to be kept together and not seperated but to remain in her possession as above written... 3rd After her death property sold and for Phillis and Betty her child sold togerther, after sale an equal division between my four sons STEPHEN M. HEARD, HUGH H. HEARD, JOHN J. HEARD, GEORGE W. HEARD... 4th, Appoint beloved wife ELLENOR HEARD my executrix... Signed July 22, 1833, CHARLES HEARD (SEAL)... Wit: CLARY BURTON, JOHN (X) BURTON, ROBERT D. CANNON.
Above witnesses swear in open court on July 2, 1833, they saw CHARLES HEARD sign above will, signed CLARY BURTON, JOHN (X) BURTON, ROBT. D. CANNON, JOHN MCCORD, C.C.O... Recorded Sept. 3, 1833, JOHN MCCORD, C.C.O.

Pages 234-235:   A list and inventory of Estate of CHARLES HEARD dec'd. made Sept. 12, 1833... Total amt. $226.12½... A list of debts, note on GEORGE W. HEARD, Acc. against JOHN BURTON, HUGH H. BURTON, 42½ acres of land, negro woman Phillis, $200, negro girl Betty $300... Total $852.64.

Ga., Butts Co., Sept. 12, 1833, Commissioners appointed and sworn as appraisers of estate of CHARLES HEARD dec'd... Com: HUMPHRY GILMORE, ISIAH WISE, RILY WISE, duly sworn by E. S. KIRKSEY, J.P.... Recorded Sept. 23, 1833, JOHN MCCORD, C.C.O.

Page 236:   The estate of MATHEW JINKS, dec'd. Aug. _9, 1833, Appraisors lists to ISAAC JINKS the executor on estate of said dec'd... Total of appraisement $110.12½.

Pages 237-238-239:   Estate of MATHEW JINKS con't... Accounts 1-56 on following: THOMAS MCGOUGH, WILLIAM NUTT, EZEKEL WALKER, JAMES W. WATKINS, WILEY J. BEAN, MICAJAH GANN, ELI CONGER, RISA JINKS, SAMUEL WALKER, LUKE ROBINSON, ROBERT HUNTER, GALES JINKS, WILLIAM HARKNESS, ISAAC JINKS, AMOS A. CONGER, WILLIAM BRIDGES, WILLIS MOORE, WILLIS HOLI-FIELD, ROBERT GRIMMET for 1830. ROBERT GRIMMETT for 1831, SAMUELL NUTT, JOHN JINKS, LEWIS MOORE, JOHN S. IRBY, WILLIAM HAMILTON, THOMAS MCGOUGH, JAMES R. WATKINS, ELI CONGER, MICAJAR GUNN, ALEXANDER HUNTER, JAMES MC-CUNE, WILLIAM CREW, MATHEW GASTON, BROWN LEE, DAVID MCGOUGH, JOSEPH BARRON, GREEN REEVES, EDWARD LAIN, NEY PUGH, SAMUEL P. BURFORD, DORY TAYLOR, WILLIAM BARRON, HENRY BARRON, JOHN DEES, THOMAS ROBINSON, JR., JOSHUA TAYLOR, SAMPSON VICREY, DEABORN HERRIN, ROBERT HUNTER, JAMES ANDERSON, MORTON BLEDSOE... Signed appraisors, THOMAS P. ATKINSON, JOHN S. IRBY, R. H. J. HOLLY.

Appraisors performed duty Aug. 29, 1833... J. R. MCCORD, J.P. Recorded Oct. 2, 1833... JOHN MCCORD, C.C.O.

Pages 239-240:   Georgia, Butts County... Will of RACHEL MAGBY weak in body but sound in mind and memory... All property after paying debts equally divided between lawful heirs and grandchildren... to my son LABAN MAGBEE one share in fee simple forever, son HIRAM MAGBEE one share in fee simple forever... To my dau. TABITHA MAXCY one share during her natural life time and then decend to her children... To my dau. ELIZABETH APPERSON one share during her natural life and then decend to her children... To grandchildren WILLIAM PRYOR, SUSAN PRYOR, MARY PRYOR, one share being heirs of my dau. MARY PRYOR, dec'd... To my grandson-in-law JOHN P. WYATT one good feather bed, furniture and stead... constitute my son LABEN MAGBEE and my friend E. W. LANE my Executors... October 9, 1833. Signed RACHEL (X) MAGBEE (SEAL)... Wit: JAMES THOMPSON, JOSIAH CRAIN, GEORGE L. THOMPSON.
Witnesses sworn in open court Nov. 7, 1833, JOHN MCCORD, C.C.O. Recorded Nov. 9, 1833, JOHN MCCORD, C.C.O.

Page 240:   The Estate of JOSEPH G. SPEAR dec'd. to ELI CONGER, Dr. to schooling JOSEPH H. SPEAR nine months and boarding Dec. 9, 1833. $24.00, ELI CONGER, Guardian... Recorded Dec. 12, 1833... JOHN MCCORD, C.C.O.

Page 241:   Received of ELI CONGER, Guardian of the orphans of JOSEPH G. SPEAR, dec'd. in full of my part of all said estate that came into his hands ($50) 1833... Received by us July 22, 1833... Signed: G. SMITH WALKER and CYNTHIA WALKER... Recorded Dec. 12, 1833, JOHN MCCORD, C.C.O.

Sale of half lot of land belonging to estate of JOHN BARREN dec'd. sold on Dec. 3, 1833 for $325.06¼... HENRY BARREN purchaser... SMITH BARREN, Admr.

Pages 241-242-243:   An inventory and appraisement of Estate of RACHEL MAGBEE, dec'd. Sale of negroes, goods and chattel... Total $4048.25... Appraisers: G. HENDRICK, JAMES THOMPSON, JOSIAH CRAIN, JOSEPH SUMMERLIN, sworn as true appraisement Dec. 23, 1833. GEORGE L. THOMPSON, J.P. Recorded Jan. 22, 1834, JOHN MCCORD, C.C.O.

Pages 244-245-246-247:   Inventory of sale of Estate of RACHEL MAYBEE, dec'd. with hiring and renting of land and negroes on Dec. 27, 1833... Buyers: LABEN MAYBEE, GALES JINKS, ABSOLOM WILLSON, ROBERT WALKINS, HIRAM MAYBEE, JEREMIAH MAXCY, E. W. LANE, ANTHONY GIMORE, C. L.

RAY, WILLIAM H. DAVIS, TRAVEY G. BLEDSOE, EDWARD ONAIL, THOMAS COOK,
RICHARD HARPER, E. B. THORNTON, JESSE SKINNER, JOSIAH CRAIN, J. APPERSON,
J. KING, JOHN EDSON, RICHARD MASON, JOSEPH WILSON, HUGH WILSON, L.
APPERSON, JOHN LOFTON, JOHN W. WILLIAMS, GEOVE HOWARD, WILLIAM T. CREWS,
WILLIAM H. WYATT, THOMAS MCKIBBIN, JOSEPH SUMMERLIN, WILEY C. WELCH,
MASTIN M. EVANS, notes on JOSEPH WILSON, J. KNOWLES, J. LOFTON. Total
$1047.35 3/4. E. W. LANE, LABEN MAGBEE, Exors... Recorded Feb. 3, 1834.
JOHN MCCORD, C.C.O.

Pages 247-248: Yearly return of estate of M. T. BROOKMAN by
Guardian MORTON BLEDSOE, Dec. 4, 1833... Paid for negro hire Jan. 7,
1833 hire of negro by JAMES HARKNESS, Jack by MORTON BLEDSOE, Isaac,
Harriet and Dinah by JOHN ANDERSON. Each said negro to have two summer
and one winter suit of clothes, a hat, blanket and a pare of shoes...
Recorded Feb. 4, 1834, JOHN MCCORD, C.C.O.

Page 248: Return #6 WILLIAM HURST Guardian to JAMES SCRUGGS...
Credit for washing and finding clothing from Jan. 1st to Dec. 31st 1832.
Returned Jan. 2, 1834, WILLIAM HURST... Recorded Feb. 4, 1834, JOHN
MCCORD, C.C.O. Return #7 WILLIAM HURST, Guardian to JAMES SCRUGGS...
same as above for year 1933.

Page 249: The Estate of JOHN BARRON dec'd. to SMITH BARRON, Adm.
Return #1, Vouchers paid SUSAN BARRON, taxes to J. M. D. BOND, JOHN
MCCORD, C.C.O., JOHN HALL... Return Jan. 3, 1834 SMITH BARRON Adm...
Recorded Feb. 4, 1834 JOHN MCCORD, C.C.O.

Estate of MATTHEW JINKS to ISAAC JINKS, Exrs. Jan. 6, 1833...
Paid Vouchers to JOSHUA TAYLOR, JAMES BROWNLEE, JOHN S. IRBYS... Credit:
Jan. 6, 1833 to JOHN S. IRBYS, JOSHUA TAYLOR, JAMES BROWNLEE, ISAAC
JINKS Exrs. Recorded Feb. 4, 1834, JOHN MCCORD, C.C.O.

Pages 249-250-251-252: Estate of JOEL WISE dec'd. to JACOB WISE,
Exrs. 1832-1833... Cost of items for farm listed, Vouchers paid JOHN
MURRY for service rendered at the ferry; paid JOB TYLAR, WIT C. WISE,
RICHARD MCDUFF; taxes; BARNA WISE for blankets; MICHAEL M. WISE for negro
clothing; ELISHA MAYFIELD; WILLIAM HANCOCK; ROBERT MAYFIELD; JOB C.
PATTERSON; HARDY DUKES; JORDAN COMPTON; BLALOCK & SANDERS; WILLIAM B.
STONE; JOHN BURGE, JONATHAN REEVES, WOODY DOZIERS, JAMES H. STARK...
Total $831.67½... Credit: Received from ZACH WISE, A. BICKERSTAFF,
GEORGE HEAD, MOSES LUNCEFORD, F. COMPTON, JACK HEAD, M. BARBER, GEORGE
BARBER, HARDY DUKE, E. MATTOX, JORDAN COMPTON, WARD H. GILES, JAMES
PRIDGEON, CREED T. WISE, DREWRY SAFFOLD, THOMAS SAFFOLD, JOSEPH SLAU-
GHTER, SAMUEL SAFFOLF, PENDLETON SLAUGHTER, ELIZABETH MCCUNE, GREEN
JACKSON, JONATHAN CARTER, GABRIEL SAFFOLD, MORGAN COATS, JOHN COATS, WOODY
DOZIER, C. ATKINSON, F. DOUGLASS, R. BICKERSTAFF, WILLIAM VICKERS,ELISHA
MAYFIELD, ROBERT MAYFIELD, WILLIAM HANCOCK, WILLIAM B. STONE, JOHN BURGE,
JONATHAN REEVES. Total $790.97¾... Returnes Jan. 14. 1834 JACOB WISE.
Recorded Feb. 15, 1834, JOHN MCCORD, C.C.O.

Pages 252-253: Dr. to the Estate of JEREMIAH HAMMOCK dec'd. in
acc. with P. H. WHITE Adm. from Sept. 4 to 31st 1832... Vouchers paid,
Macon Telegraph, Physcians, tax, claim case, postage on 2 letters
(31½¢)... Total $29.30. Credits: Cash from R. N. YOUNG, B. H. DARDEN,
JOHN PARKER, A. CLEVELAND... Total $29.30½... Returnes Jan. 1, 1834
P. H. WHITE, Admr. Recorded Feb. 10, 1834, JOHN MCCORD, C.C.O.

Pages 253-254: Yearly return on Estate of GREER MCCOY dec'd. by
HENRY MCCOY, Exr. Jan. 14, 1834... Butts County, Georgia. Vouchers
paid note principle and interest, C. P. PEARSON, JAMES M. HILL, MCDANIEL
& GOODMAN, B. H. MARTIN, SPENCER & MAYS, P. H. WHITE, L. GAHAGAN, JOHN
MCCORD, ALDEN MICKELBERRY, JOHN W. WILLIAMS, JOHN SAUNDERS, WILLIAM LAW,
SAMUEL J. BARNETT... Credit: JAMES M. HILL, MANLY SCROGGIN, Feb. 8, to
going to Troup County and attending to business for said estate 5 days..
H. MCCOY, Exor... Recorded Feb. 10, 1834, JOHN MCCORD, C.C.O.

Page 254: Estate of RICHARD KNIGHT dec'd. to C. F. KNIGHT, Admr.
Vouchers: Paid taxes for estate of deceased; March 1st, pd. WILLIAM

54

KNIGHT one of the distributees, April 9th, paid ROBERT OREA one of the distributees; Dec. 2nd pd. HILLIARD J. HARDIN his distributive share... Returned Jan. 16, 1834 C. F. KNIGHT, Admr... Recorded Feb. 10, 1834 JOHN MCCORD, C.C.O.

Page 255:   Jones County, Georgia, JOHN DENNIS estate... Court of Ordinary, Sept. adjourned Term 1833... PETER DENNIS vs ELIZABETH CHARLOTT DENNIS... PETER DENNIS wishes to have joint Adm. of said estate instead of ELIZABETH C. DENNIS having sole adm. on ground that he is brother of deceased and will make him equal interest in will. ROBERT & HARDMAN Plffts Atty... Court ordered that will be probated as stated.

Page 256:   ELIZABETH C. DENNIS dissatisfied with decision of the court appeals. DAVID BERRY as security in case paid cost. Signed: ELIZABETH C. DENNIS, DAVID BERRY. Sept. 1833. Test: MATTHEW A. MARSHALL . CHARLES MACARTHY C.C.O.

Court ordered that Letters of Administration with the will annexed be granted to ELIZABETH C. DENNIS upon her giving a bond and security in the sum of $40,000.

Pages 256-257:   Georgia, Talbot County... Will of JOHN DENNIS of Jones County. "being move at my brothers in Talbot County in a state of good health and presence of mind when I left home without any persuation or compulsion to make my will, I wish for there to be a destribution of all property to the three named persons after my death... to sell and divide it in this way after debts and expence is paid... equal division between my wife CHARLOTTE and my brother PETER excepting my brother WILLIAM to have $1000 of my estate." Will made Aug. 16, 1832... Signed: JOHN DENNIS (SEAL)... Wit: LEVI LEE, WILLIAM BATY, HENRY RILEY.

Georgia, Jones County... Court of Ordinary, Sept. 1833... In open court came WILLIAM BATY and HENRY RILEY on oath that the witnessed said will of JOHN DENNIS. Signed: WILLIAM BATY, HENRY RILEY... JAMES GRAY, J.I.C., JOHN R. MOORE, J.I.C., JONATHAN PARISH, J.I.C., Test: CHARLES MCCARTHY, C.C.O.

Page 258:   Georgia, Jones County... ELIZABETH C. DENNIS and DAVID BERRY makes bond for sum of $40,000 and obtained temporary letters of adm. to collect and take care of goods and chattels of JOHN DENNIS dec'd. ELIZABETH C. DENNIS must keep the same without improverishment or waste until legal administration is granted if not then this obligation to be void. Signed: ELIZABETH C. DENNIS, DAVID BERRY, G. W. BATY in presence of C. MACARTHY, C.C.O.

Oct. Court 1833... PETER DENNIS enters appeal.

Pages 259-260:   Jones County, Georgia... PETER DENNIS withdrew appeal and consents that letters of adm. be granted. JAMES SMITH Atty. for CHARLOTTE DENNIS, ROBERT V. HARDEMAN Atty. for PETER DENNIS... The last will of JOHN DENNIS deceased admitted to court and letters of adm. Cum testament Annere granted to ELIZABETH CHARLOTTE DENNIS and ordered that JONATHAN PARISH, PETER CLOWER, SAMUEL GRISWOULD, STERLING W. SMITH, RIDGEWAY HOGAN appointed appraisors.

Appraisors rights granted by court... Witness Jan. 8, 1833 by JOSEPH DAY one of the Judges... CHARLES MACARTHY, C.C.O.

Pages 261-262-263-264-265-266:   An Inventory and Appraisement of estate of JOHN DENNIS, Oct. 14, 1833. Perishable property value $3953.22½... 27 negroes value $13,703.22½, 38 bags gined cotton 13,212 pounds @10½¢... One lot Thompson's medicine and patent right to use the same... 1458 acres of land near Clinton $8000.00... other minor items listed... Total value $23,235.98½... Signed Appraisors: JONATHAN PARRISH, PETER CLOWER, SAMUEL GRESWOULD... Certified Nov. 27, 1833 by WARREN HART, J.P.

Pages 267-276: Amount of Property sold by ELIZABETH C. DENNIS, Admtx. on Estate of JOHN DENNIS, dec'd... Sold on 27th, 28th, 29th, 30th of Nov. 1833. Buyers: JAMES P. LOWE, DANIEL MCCLOUD, JOHN S. WALKER, S. W. NICHOLS, JOHN TAMPLIN, E. C. DENNIS, SAMUEL GRISWOULD, A. COX, M. SULLIVAN, WILLIAM COX, SAMUEL JOHNSTON, WILLIAM FREEMAN, H. CALDWELL, W. WILDER, THOMAS HUNT, J. L. LEWIS, JONATHAN PARRISH, JOHN J. BEASELEY, R. F. SHREWDER, WILLIAM MORGAN, J. C. B. MITCHELL, S. KELLEY, CHESLEY MOORE, PETER DENNIS, JOSEPH JOLLEY, BENJAMIN FINNEY, M. SULLIVAN, HENRY WOOD, LOOTAN BRADY, R. BEASELEY, H. F. WILLIAMS, W. B. STEPHENS, JOHN JEFFERSON, DANIEL TYE, WILLIAM RICHARDSON, WILLIAM JOURDAN, REUBEN JOHN-SON, ROBERT C. PEAK, FRANCIS FICKLING, EPHRIM MOORE, WRIGHT PERMENTER, ABRAM ADAM, SAMUEL LAWTHER, JOHN SIMS, JOSEPH J. COOPER, WILLIAM CALDWELL, PETER OWEN, JAMES TOOLES, JOHN PORTER, WARD WILDER, JAMES GOODWIN, WILLIAM DENNING, GREEN SIMS, NATHANIEL DENNING, J. R. JONES, THOMAS WILLIAMS, NANCY SLATTER, HENRY WOOD, R. E. TAYLOR, ELIZABETH BENNETT, SAMUEL RILEY, M. C. WEST, DANIEL TYE, WILEY PATTERSON, JOHN PERRY, WILLIAM STRIPLING, CHARLES BROOKS, WILLIAM JONES, J. WATSON, SAMUEL FACKLER, N. SOMERS, E. HUTCHINGS, W. KELLEY, GREEN DAVIDSON, THOMAS JONES, JOHN VIN-SON, WILLIAM TOWNSAND, R. DRAWHORN, SAMUEL LOWTHER, THOMAS G. SMITH, JOHN BAKER, S. W. COURSON, D. A. TOUNSON, WILLIAM JORDAN, WILLIAM STEPHENS, H. WOOD, D. BERRY, SARAH TOWNSON. Total Sale $5545.20½. Certified sale on 27th, 28th, 29th, 30th Nov. 1833. E. C. DENNIS, Admx.

Page 277: Memorandum of sale of land and negroes belonging to Estate of JOHN DENNIS dec'd. sold on first Tuesday in Dec. 1833... Land sold to JOHN MARTIN $11,350.00; 19 negroes sold to SAMUEL LOWTHER, PETER DENNIS, RICHARD DRAWHORN, JAMES K. JONES, PETER CLOWER, SAMUEL LOWTHER, THOMAS WILLIAMS, JEREMIAH FICKLING. Total of land and negroes $23,202.00. Certified by E. C. DENNIS, Admrx., Dec. 1833.

Page 278: In account with ELIZABETH DENNIS for 1833... Vouchers 1-14 paid expence of coffin $30.00; Clerk of Court of Ordinary; W. G. POPE, Sunday clothing, expense for walling in grave ($46.12½), JOHN J. BEASELY, ROBERT BEASELY, LOWTHER & LEWIS, BOWIN & STEPHENS, JONATHAN PARRISH, C. MACARTHY, C.C.O.

At term of Court of Ordinary of Butts County held on Jan. 3, 1834 order passed for the removal of the administration of the Estate of JOHN DENNIS late of Jones County to Butts County.

Page 279: Certification of CHARLES MACARTHY, Clerk of Court of Jones County, Georgia certified that the twenty pages contain true Exemplification of JOHN DENNIS' Estate. Given under my hand and seal of the office at Clinton this 18th day of Jan. 1834. CHARLES MACARTHY C.C.O. Recorded March 11, 1834 Butts County. JOHN MCCORD C.C.O.

Pages 279-280: Butts County, Georgia, Will of JOHN R. CARGILE... weak in body but sound mind and memory... Executrix to dispose of such portions necessary to pay debts and funeral expenses... any portion except the plantation and ferry on which I reside. That portion kept for maintainance of herself, children, and for education of latter. Wife MARY CARGILE... Daughter MARY ANN STARK, a town lot in Jackson near the Methodist Church. My other children (names not given) to share in estate. Signed: JOHN R. CARGILE (SEAL)... In presence of JAMES BALEY, EBENEZER MADDOX, SAMUEL R. MCLIN, J.P.

Page 281: Certification of witness JAMES BALEY, EBENEZER MADDOX, SAMUEL R. MCLIN, Feb. 7, 1834... Recorded Mar. 11, 1834, JOHN MCCORD, C.C.O.

Pages 281-282: Inventory and Appraisement of Estate of JAMES M. RHODES dec'd. Feb. 1, 1834, Total $264.90... Certified by appraisors ROBERT ANDREWS, JAMES M. CARMICHAEL. Above appraisors certified Feb. 1, 1834 by YELVENTON THAXTON, J.P. Recorded March 12, 1834, JOHN MCCORD, C.C.O.

Page 283: Return #3 - Estate of WILLIAM REDMAN, dec'd. in account with JAMES CARTER, Adm. Jan. 1, 1833 to Dec. 31, 1833... Vouchers 1-9 paid to WILLIAM ZACHERY and WILLIAM L. GORDON, paid MARY REDMAN, SR., for boarding and taking care of ELIZABETH REDMAN, mother of the dec'd. agreeable to bond given by WILLIAM REDMAN in his life time; Clerk of Court, JAMES CARTER for year 1832. Total $867.28... Credits: A. GILMORE, hireing negroes and payment for land in Columbia County... Total $717.37½. Recorded Mar. 12, 1834 JOHN MCCORD, C.C.O.

Pages 284-285: Account of sale of 340 acres of land in Columbia County as property of WILLIAM REDMAN, dec'd. sold on terms to A. C. ZACHERY for $1000 to be paid in three payments. Returned Jan. 13, 1834 JAMES CARTER, Admr. Recorded Mar. 13, 1834, JOHN MCCORD, C.C.O.

Return: hireing of negroes and renting the plantation of WILLIAM REDMAN, dec'd. for year 1833... To MARY REDMAN, the negroes... To DAVID MCGOUGH, the plantation... To G. MCGRUDER the plantation in Columbia County, Total $314.37½.

Terms for hireing negroes listed. Returned Jan. 13, 1834, JAMES CARTER, Adm. Recorded Mar. 13, 1834, JOHN MCCORD, C.C.O.

Page 285: Return of Estate of JOEL WISE, dec'd. by PARHAM LINDSEY.. Renting and hireing land and negroes to CHARLES TRUSSEE, MAHALEY WISE, WILLIAM JOHNSON, HUGH WISE, BARNA WISE, JAMES P. MCCLUNE, CREED WISE... Total $1022.50... Returned Dec. 26, 1833, PARHAM LINDSEY, Adm. Recorded Mar. 13, 1834, JOHN MCCORD, C.C.O.

Page 286: Return of SAMUEL BELLAH, Adm. Estate of WILLIAM RHODES for year 1833... Vouchers 1-4, paid Clerk of Court, WILSON & MADDOX for NANCY RHODES, one of the heirs of said estate; DR. WHITE, MCDANIEL & GOODMAN. Total $1862½... Returned Feb. 21, 1834, SAMUEL BELLAH... Recorded Mar. 13, 1834, JOHN MCCORD, C.C.O.

Estate of GEORGE BLISSIT minor to WILLIAM HARPER, Guardian to 31st Dec. 1833... Paid MCDANIEL & GOODMAN, Clerk of Court... Total $1.87½... Credit: Balance due minor as pr last return, rent from farm... Total $225.21½. Returned Feb. 28, 1834, WILLIAM HARPER, Guardian... Land rented 7 acres to WILLIAM HARPER, 18 acres to H. B. HAIRSTON, Total $24. Returned Feb. 28, 1834. Recorded Mar. 13, 1834, JOHN MCCORD, C.C.O.

Page 287: Estate of WILLIAM BLISSIT to WILLIAM HARPER, Guardian to 31st Dec. 1833... Paid A. BANKSTON, WHITE & DUPREE, Clerk of Court, MCDANIEL & GOODMAN, C. CAMPBELL. Total $5.12½... Credit: Balance due minor, total $359.00. Returned Feb. 28, 1834, WILLIAM HARPER, Guardian.. Recorded Mar. 13, 1834, JOHN MCCORD, C.C.O.

Pages 287-288: The Estate of GILLIAM PRESTON, dec'd. for year 1833 to JAMES & ELISHA PRESTON, Adm. Vouchers 1-7 May 8, 1833 paid E. S. KIRKSEY for two judgments vs estate, July 12, 1833 paid JAMES C. DUNSIETH for two judgments vs estate in favor of E. MCMICHAEL, July 18, 1833 paid WILLIAM BLALOCK & SAUNDERS, paid J. M. D. BOND for taxes for 1832, Jan. 6, 1834 paid WILLIAM HIGGINS, Feb. 28, 1834, paid WILLIAM POWERS, Oct. 18, 1834 paid J. C. DUNSIETH. Total $72.64½... Credit: notes on B. H. DARDEN, JAMES M. PRESTON, S. T. HIGGINS, JAMES THURMON, Total $72.79½... Returned Mar. 3, 1834 ELISHA J. PRESTON, Adm. Recorded Mar. 14, 1834, JOHN MCCORD, C.C.O.

Page 288: Return on Estate of JOHN BARKLEY, dec'd. by SAMUEL R. NUTT, Adm. 1833. Vouchers 1-8 paid JOHN MCCORD, C.C.O., JANE BARKLEY, R. C. MAYS, SAMUEL NUTT, SENR., DAVID B. GRANT, DAVIS BARKLEY. Total $322.32... Credits: Received from sale of negroes to RICHARD BAILEY $488.68 3/4, SAMUEL R. NUTT, Adm. (No date given.) Recorded Mar. 14, 1834, JOHN MCCORD, C.C.O.

Page 289: Return years 1832 and 1833 for orphans of JOHN BARKLEY dec'd. to viz. ELIZABETH ANN BARKLEY, JANE A. BARKLEY, NANCY G. BARKLEY, JOHN N. BARKLEY minors of said dec'd. by JANE BARKLEY, Guardian... Vouchers 1-13, paid JOHN M.D. BOND taxes, board of ELIZABETH ANN, NANCY G., JOHN N. BARKLEY, paid SPENCER & MAY for ELIZABETH ANN, NANCY and

JANE A BARKLEY, paid THOMAS J. SANDERS for JANE A. BARKLEY, paid JOHN PRICE note: paid MARY MCCLURE for professional service to negro woman, paid JOHN HALL, JAMES WILLIAMS, MORTON BLEDSOE... Total $231.15½... JANE BARKLEY, Guardian... Recorded Mar. 14, 1834, JOHN MCCORD, C.C.O.

Page 290: The Estate of JOHN DENNIS, dec'd. to E. C. DENNIS, Adm. Vouchers 1-7, paid EDWARD T. TAYLOR, SOLOMON HUMPHRIE, T. B. SLADE, J. JOHNSON, J. SMITH, G. W. BATEY... Total $409.24½, E. C. DENNIS, Adm. Recorded Mar. 14, 1834, JOHN MCCORD, C.C.O.

Amount of sale of land and negroes of Estate of JAMES GRAY, dec'd. sold 1st Tuesday, Feb. 1833. Sold to YEARLY STROUD, ELIZABETH GRAY, ALLEN GRAY, Bought land ½ lot of land in 8th Dist. of Henry now Butts County... Total $478.00. LEWIS H. FARGASON, Adm... Recorded Apr. 14, 1834, JOHN MCCORD, C.C.O.

Page 291: JANE JENKINS' property sold by FRANCES DOUGLASS, Guardian on Dec. 24, 1833... Recorded April 28, 1834, JOHN MCCORD, C.C.O.

Return No. 1... The Estate of JAMES GRAY, dec'd. to LEWIS FARGASON, amount to Jan. 1, 1834 Dr.... Vouchers 1-7, cash paid ELIZABETH GRAY, fees, taxes; paid ALLEN GRAY, HARDY PACE, Total $471.36 3/4... LEWIS H. FARGASON, Adm. Recorded May 8, 1834, JOHN MCCORD, C.C.O.

Return of ELIZABETH C. DENNIS, Admx. of JOHN DENNIS, May 5, 1834... Vouchers 1-7, paid H. F. WILLIAMS, J. MCCORD, J. JOHNSON, G. GRISWOULD, L. GRIFFITH, J. PARRISH, J. H. STARK... Total $783.63 3/4, E. C. DENNIS, Admx. Recorded May 8, 1834, JOHN MCCORD, C.C.O.

Pages 292-293-294-295: Court of Ordinary to SAMUEL K. MCLIN, MATTHEW BARBER, JACOB WISE, JAMES BALEY and WILLIAM ALLISON authorise and empower you to make true appraisement of goods and chattels of JOHN R. CARGILE, dec'd. and produced by MARY CARGILE, Extrx. of Estate. Oath witnessed by GEORGE T. SPEAKE, Judge of C.O., Feb.7, 1834, JOHN MCCORD, C.C.O.

Inventory of Estate of JOHN R. CARGILE, dec'd. Items listed valued at $7224.87½. Appraisors: MATTHEW BARBER, SAMUEL K. MCLIN, WILLIAM ALLISON, Apr. 3, 1834.

Pages 296-300: Notes due estate of JOHN R. CARGILE, dec'd... B. A. ROLAND, JOHN BANKSTON, DAVID BYARS, JOS. PORT, SAMUEL TALANT, YOUNG R. HARRIS, S. D. MAYS, BENJAMIN BLESSITT, WILLIAM GROSS. Total $761.60.

The above are considered good. The following notes are insolvent. ROBERT COLLIER, MATTHEW ROUTON, S. GILMORE, JESSE SEAL, JOHN L. BURTON, DANCY MULLIN, PRESSLEY M. COX, R. C. CARGILE, RICHARD SHEARER, W. S. BARTON, ROBERT MCCUNE, NATHAN PHILLIPS, JONATHAN BENTON, L. B. EAVES, GEORGE OGBORN, B. R. WYN, JAMES R. BLANKENSHIP, JOSEPH BENTON, JONATHAN HARKNESS, H. MARABLES, HENRY M. KINZY, WILLIAM LEVERETT, NATHAN HIGGERSON, ANDREW HODGES, ISAAC R. JACKSON, BENJ. WICKER, ROBERT STEWART, ROBERT WILLIAMSON, JAMES SHEARER, HENRY HARRIS, HUGH L. WHITE, JAMES CARGILE, BENJ. JOHNSON, THOMAS RAMSEY, BUCHNER EAVES, HARRIS DUNN, S. PARRISH, J. H. CURRY, ISAAC SIMMONS, WILEY S. ALLISON, DAVID BROGDON, HARRIS GILLIAM, WILLIAM SHEARER, NANCY LINDSEY, WILLIAM PRIDGEON, DENNIS TRAMMEL, PHILLIP THURMAN, JAMES PRIDGEON, WILLIAM GILMORE, LUKE PATRICK, E. T. L. SPENCER, JEREMIAH MCGLOWN, RICHARD COTTON, WALTER FITTS, W. BRADLEY, J. CLEVELAND, SAMUEL NEW, MOSES COX, W. BEAN, O. C. CLEVELAND, JAMES WATSON, JOHN B. DRINKARD, MATTHEW MCMICHAEL, BENJAMIN S. MOORE, JAMES H. EDWARDS, RICHARD SPEAKE, JOHN PITMAN, ROBERT KILCREASE, DANIEL KILCREASE, WILLIAM WORSHAM, THOMAS RAMSEY, MICAJAH THURMON, L. ROBINSON, CHARLES RAMEY, WILLIAM H. UNDERWOOD, THOMAS M. HOGAN, G. W. WILLIAMSON, MORTON L. BURCH in Fayette County, JOHN S. SHEARER, JOSEPH J. CRENSHAW.

All above executions returned no property... Returned May 2, 1834, MARY CARGILE, Extx. Total amount $3660.20... Recorded May 12, 1834, JOHN MCCORD, C.C.O.

Page 301:   Account of sale of Estate of SAMUEL C. STARK, dec'd.
March 1, 1834 Sale of land for $1190.00... Returned June 16, 1834, JAMES
H. STARK, Adm... Vouchers 1-5, paid Taxes, H. HATELEY, C. B. LEE, SPENCER
& MAY,   Total $138.00... Credit: Rent of house to JOHN E. JONES $138.00,
JAMES H. STARK, Adm. June 16, 1834... Recorded June18, 1834, JOHN MCCORD,
C.C.O.

Page 302:   Estate of JOHN SMITH, dec'd. 1833, to L. SMITH, Adm. Dr.
Vouchers 1-3, paid taxes; midwife services $5.87½, Clerk of Court
$104.57. Credits: Hire of slaves to JAMES SMITH, LEAVIN SMITH, ISAAC
SMITH... Returned May 20, 1834 L. SMITH, Adm. Recorded June 18, 1834
JOHN MCCORD, C.C.O.

Pages 303-304:   Estate of JAMES WOOTEN, dec'd... Account with JOHN
JONES, Adm. To services rendered by myself and wife in caring for estate,
overseeing hands and attending to the family... Return July 7, 1834,
JOHN JONES, Admr... Recorded July 8, 1834, JOHN MCCORD, C.C.O.

Estate of SIMEON WOOTEN, SEABORN L. WOOTEN, ADDISON A. WOOTEN,
JAMES WOOTEN, minors to JOHN JONES, Guardian... Paid ANDREW FULWOOD
$5.05 tuition for each minor 1833... Credit: May 27, 1833, JESSE WOOTEN,
Exor. of JAMES WOOTEN, dec'd. received of BENJAMIN PARROT $195.00 for
each minor... Returned July 7, 1834, JOHN JONES, Guardian... Recorded
July 8, 1834, JOHN MCCORD, C.C.O

Pages 305-310:   Inventory and Appraisement of Estate of WILLIAM
LEE, dec'd. List of notes on the following: ALDEN MICKLEBERRY, O. P.
CHEATAM, ISAAC LOW, A. W. H. TWEEDELL, DAVID B. M. MOORE, L. B. EUBANKS,
G. W. LOWERY, W. H. WYATT, H. MAGBY, W. L. MOBLY, CHARLES BAILEY, JAMES
MCLURE, GEORGE EUBANKS, W. J. COLEMAN, WILLIAM MCGLOWN, JOHN V. BERRY,
ASA H. MANN, MATTHEW & SILAS MCMICHAEL, ISAAC HENDRICK, ROBERT BROWN,
A. GOLDSMITH, T. TABB, THOMAS ROBINSON, ELI. PARKS, HENRY BAILEY, JR.,
B. F. TUCKER, JOHN KIMBROUGH, DANIEL OSBORN, GIDEON TANNER, A. H. DAU-
GHERTY, WILEY THAXTON, HENRY HATELY, JAMES R. MCCORD, CHARLES B. LEE,
JOHN WEAVER, SPENCER & MAY, CHRISTOPHER COLLINS, JOHN V. BERRY, R. MASON,
JOHN REEVES, WILLIAM AKIN, JOHN JINKS, SPENCER JINKS, WILLIAM TANNER, DR.
SNODDY, JAMES WILLSON, JACKSON WILLSON, JOHN YOUNG, EDWARD WEAVER, Y.
THAXTON, DAVID HIGGINS, ISAAC PARKS, DANIEL OSBORN, ALLEN J. MANN,
FREDERICK YOUNG, O. C. CLEVELAND, HENDRICK RUNDLE, WILLIAM JARREL, WILLIS
JARREL, ELI PARKS, W. W. GAITHER, J. H. MACKEY, J. GOODMAN, T. J. GRISHAM,
CASWELL ETHRIDGE, NOAH TAYLOR, JACKSON CLEVELAND, J. C. KNIGHT, CATLET
CAMPBELL, JAMES HARKNESS, JAMES STARK, JAMES HIGGINS, TUCKER HIGGINS,
JOHN E. JONES, MICAJAH MCCUNE, LEONARD ROAN, JOHN HALL, SAMUEL SNODDY, R.
B. SANDERS, A. H. DAUGHERTY, CHARLES BAILEY, B. H. DARDEN, JAMES BAILEY,
J. W. WILLIAMS, J. BYARS, JAMES BRADY, JAMES BULLOCK, JAMES TURELL,
DANNIE MARTIN, JAMES THOMPSON... Goods and chattel list... Total value
$861.14½.   Appraisors JOHN H. MCDANIEL, HENRY HATELY, PEYTON H. WHITE...
July 17, 1834... Recorded July 31, 1834, JOHN MCCORD, C.C.O.

Pages 311-315:   A list of articles sold by the administrator of
WILLIAM LEE Estate Aug. 5, 1834. Buyers: HENRY HATELY, EZEKIEL WALKER,
JOHN E. JONES, JAMES W. WATKINS, ASA H. MANN, EDMOND MCDANIEL, YOUNG
R. HARRIS, JOHN MCMICHAEL, ROBERT W. HARKNESS, WILLIS EDISON, JOHN E.
JONES, JAMES W. WATKINS, Y. R. HARRIS, CLARK HAMIL, G. W. BARBER, ROBERT
HARKNESS, E. WALKER, J. J. M. MAPP, JOHN E. JONES, JOHN ANDERSON, JAMES
HARKNESS, GEORGE DAVIS, Y. THAXTON, JOHN W. MCCORD, GUSTAVUS HENDRICK,
SAMUEL SNODDY, J. R. MCCORD, B. A. DARDEN, R. KINDRICK, CLARK HAMIL, J.
W. WATKINS, P. H. WHITE, J. EASON, WILLIAM MCMICHAEL, G. P. BURFORD,
JOHN HENDRICK, JESSE B. ROBINSON, H. W. TAYLOR, J. H. STARK, GEORGE DAVIS,
J. W. ROAN, MRS. LEE, THOMAS MCKIBBEN, ROBERT MCBEES, SAMUEL COLLINS, S.
W. BOWLES, G. W. GUNN, T. C. TAYLOR, C. B. LEE, REUBEN RANSOM, EDMUND
MCDANIEL, J. JESTER, G. W. THOMAS, E. WALKER, JOSHUA TAYLOR, ABSOLOM
WILSON, R. C. MAYS, A. H. DAUGHERTY, Admr. Total Amount $314.48½...
Recorded Aug. 9, 1834, JOHN MCCORD, C.C.O.

Page 316:   Received of HENRY HATELY, Guardian of MARGARET CHISOM
orphan of GATEWOOD CHISOM, dec'd. but now MARGARET THOMAS... all my
Legacy, Aug. 28, 1834, W. S. THOMAS. Signed: MARGARET (X) THOMAS.
Recorded Aug. 28, 1834, JOHN MCCORD, C.C.O.

EDGAR C. SPEAR orphan of JOSEPH G. SPEAR, dec'd. to ELI CONGAR, Guardian Dr... Jan. 16, 1834... Cash paid $50... Returned Nov. 3, 1834, ELI CONGAR, Guardian... Recorded Nov. 11, 1834, JOHN MCCORD, C.C.O.

Page 317:   The Estate of JOHN DENNIS, dec'd... To E. C. DENNIS, Adm. cash paid SAMUEL GRISWOULD, WILLIAM DENNIS, JOHN DENNIS, T. J. & W. H. ATWOOD, SOLOMON HUMPHRIS, H. F. WILLIAM, DANIEL TYES $1238.66½... Credit: received from ABRAM ADAMS, SAMUEL J. JOHNSON, JACK TOMPLIN, WILLIAM COX, BENJAMIN FINNEY, SAMUEL LOWTHERS, WILEY PATTERSON, JOHN MIZZLE, CHRISLEY MOORE, MICHAEL SULLIVAN, JEREMIA FICKLIN, A. MOSSEYS, HENRY WOOD, FRANCES FICKLIN, JOSEPH JOLLEY, JONATHAN PARRISH, RICHARD DRAWHORNS, ROBERT BEASLEY, DANIEL MCCLOUD, WRIGHT PERMENTER, JOHN SIMS, WILLIAM RICHARDSON, PETE CLOWER, THOMAS HUNT, WILLIAM JONES, OLIVER MORTON, WILLIAM JORDAN, JAMES TOOL, L. D. WIMBERLY... Total $2796.40½... Recorded Jan. 14, 1835, JOHN MCCORD, C.C.O.

Page 318:   Estate of JOHN BARREN, dec'd... To SMITH BARREN, Adm. Jan. 6, 1834, cash paid SUSAN BARREN the widow a part of legacy $20.25, paid Jan. 1, 1834 widow for legacy in full $162.56½... SMITH BARREN, Admr... Recorded Jan. 14, 1834, JOHN MCCORD, C.C.O.

Estate of RACHEL MAGBEE, dec'd. in account with E. W. LANE and LABAN MAGBEE Exr. Dec. 31, 1834... Paid JOSEPH WILSON, DR. SNODDY, JOHN LOFTONS, Returned Jan. 5, 1835... Recorded Jan. 14, 1835 JOHN MCCORD, C.C.O.

Page 319:   GIDEON TANNER, Guardian for A. CLEATON. Received Jan. 5, 1835, Recorded Jan. 14, 1835, JOHN MCCORD, C.C.O.

Estate of MATTHEW JINKS... ISAAC JINKS, Excr... Dec. 31, 1834. Vouchers paid 1-15, A. HUNTER, JOSEPH BARRON, E. WALKER, HEY PUGH, R. W. HUNTER, SAMUEL P. BURFORD, W. B. NUTT, JOHN MCCORD, DORY TAYLOR, THOMAS MCGOUGH, ELI CONGER, SAMUEL NUTT, W. B. NUTT, A. A. CONGER, E. CREW. Credit 1834, A. HUNTER, JOSEPH BARRON, E. WALKER, HEY PUGH, R. W. WALKER, SAMUEL P. BURFORD, W. B. NUTT, DORY TAYLOR, THOMAS MCGOUGH, R. CONGER, SAMUEL NUTT, A. A. CONGER, E. CREW, M. GANN, RIAS JINKS, SAMPSON VICKERS, S. J. HERRING, THOMAS ROBINSON, JR., JOHN DEAS, HENRY BARREN, EDWARD LANE, DAVID MCGOUGH, LEWIS MOORE, ISAAC JINKS, Exrs... Recorded Jan. 15, 1835, JOHN MCCORD, C.C.O.

Pages 320-321:   Inventory of Estate of JAMES M. RHODES, dec'd... Sold at public sale Mar. 8, 1834... Buyers: HENRY D. KNIGHT, JAMES R. SMITH, ROBERT ANDERSON, JOHN GLEEN, WOOD KNIGHT, JOHN DUFFY, THOMAS CONNEL, JAMES BRADY, SQUIRE STILLWELL, JOSIAH DRAPER, JAMES DRAPER, IRVIN COLLINS, YELVENTON THAXTON, JAMES R. SMITH, JAMES PRIDGEON, NELSOM DUFFY, JAMES CARMICHAEL, THOMAS FOSTER,   Recorded Jan. 15, 1835, JOHN MCCORD, C.C.O.

Pages 322-323:   Inventory and Appraisement of Estate of JAMES HARRISON, dec'd.   Items listed valued at $265.00... Appraisors, GUSTAVUS HENDRICK, JAMES THOMPSON, J.P... Recorded Jan. 15, 1835, JOHN MCCORD, C.C.O.

Pages 324-325:   Sale of property of Estate of JAMES HARRISON, dec'd. Nov. 27, 1834. WILLIAM HARRISON, Admr. Buyers: JAMES THOMPSON, JOHN HENDRICK, WESLEY C. WELCH, F. M. GRANT, DORY TAYLOR, G. JINKS, E. W. LANE, JOHN B. REEVES, GRAVES HOWARD, GUSTAVUS HENDRICK, WILLIAM H. HERREN, ANN HARRISON, LUCIEN MALIER, JEREMIAH MAXY, WILLIAM H. WYATT, G. T. ROBERTS, W. C. WELCH, C. MASON.   Jan. 5, 1835, WILLIAM HARRISON, Admr. Recorded Jan. 15, 1835, JOHN MCCORD, C.C.O.

Page 326:   Annual Return of Estate of GEORGE M. T. BROCKMAN, a minor for 1834. To his Guardian, MORTON BLEDSOE paid THOMAS R. BLEDSOE for board. Cr.:   hire of negroes to JACK M. BLEDSOE, ISAAC M. BLEDSOE, HARRIETT M. BLEDSOE... THOMAS R. BLEDSOE... Recorded Jan. 19, 1835, JOHN MCCORD, C.C.O.

Pages 327-328:   Dr. the Estate of WILLIAM LEE, dec'd... A. H. DAUGHERTY, Admr. Vouchers 1-8, paid Clerk of Court, A. R. BICKERSTAFF,

for funeral expences $8.25, P. H. WHITE burial expences $24.25, J. W.
WATKINS, burial expences $6.00, taxes, A. H. MANN traveling expences
and postage... Cr. notes JESSE ROBINSON, WILLIAM GARREL, JACKSON CLEVE-
LAND, THOMAS ROBINSON, SR., DANIEL AUSBURN, RICHARD MASON, WILLIAM WYATT,
H. TAYLOR, SPENCER JINKS, JAMES BRADY, B. H. HARDIN, JAMES HARKNESS, JOHN
ANDERSON, A. R. BICKERSTAFF, C. COLLINS, CASWELL ETHRIDGE, CATLETT CAMP-
BELL, JOHN WEAVER, W. L. MOBLEY, WILLIAM AKIN, TUCKER HIGGINS, ALDEN
MICKLEBERRY, JOHN ANDERSON, WILLIAM TANNER, J. W. WATKINS, JAMES THOMPSON,
LEONARD ROAN, GUSTAVUS HENDRICK, JOHN T. YOUNG, JAMES TERRELL, JOHN
HENDRICK, A. W. H. TWEADLE, G. P. BURFORD, J. H. STARK... A. H. DAUGHERTY,
Adm... Recorded Jan. 20, 1835. JOHN MCCORD, C.C.O.

Page 329: MARTIN D. BOWLES to G. HENDRICK his guardian... Vouchers
1-10 paid JESSE BENTON for going to Jackson County, JAMES BYARS, J.
LOFTON, R. GRIER, A. H. DAUGHERTY, STEPHEN BAILEY... G. HENDRICK, Guardian... Cr.: Received from W. C. WELCH, C. BAILEY, J. BYERS, E. S. MANN,
R. GRIER on settlement, W. C. WELCH, MARK CLOE, F. M. GRANT... Jan. 13,
1835 GUSTAVUS HENDRICK, Guardian... Recorded Jan. 21, 1835 JOHN MCCORD,
C.C.O.

Pages 330-331-332: Yearly return of PARHAM LINDSEY Adm. of Estate
of JOEL WISE, dec'd. for 1833-1834... Notes on JAMES DUDLEY, JOHN
LASSITER, W. PHELPS, A. G. HAYNES, taxes, E. L. YOUNG, M. BARTLETT, W.
BLALOCK, Z. ESTES, HENRY KELLUM, C. ATKINSON, Value $551.29½... Credit:
JAMES PRIDGEN, WILLIAM J. HEAD, R. WISE, J. WISE, B. H. & J. M. DARDEN,
J. WRIGHT, B. STONE, D. HIGGINS, W. GILES, JOHN BURGE, G. THOMAS, JOHN
WALKER, S. T. HIGGINS, Y. JOHNSON, W. MCCUNE, JOHN MCCORD, H. JOHNSON,
W. TEALS, W. GILES. Total $829.79½... PARHAM LINDSEY, Adm. Recorded
Jan. 22, 1835, JOHN MCCORD, C.C.O.

Page 333: Yearly return by WILLIAM BLALOCK, Guardian for MARGARET
T. SPEAKE 1834... Cash paid J. R. MCCORD, C.C.O., DAVID J. BAILEY,
Attorney, ten day service rendered in attending to lawsuits for said
minor and finding myself and horse (12.50)... Credit: Cash from RICHARD
SPEAKE, JR., and ANN C. SERROR for hire of Negroes... Recorded Jan. 22,
1835, JOHN MCCORD, C.C.O.

Pages 333-334: List of sale of property of CHARLES HEARD, dec'd.
Oct. 12, 1833. Buyers: HUGH H. HEARD, ERASMUS G. BURTON, C. MOORE, J.
SLONE ISAIAH WISE, W. P. HILL, ELEANOR HEARD, MERIDITH NELSON, WILLIAM
GILMORE, W. TILLERY, G. NOLEN. ELENOR HEARD, Exor. Recorded Mar. 5,
1835, JOHN MCCORD, C.C.O.

Page 335: Estate of RICHARD KNIGHT to C. F. WRIGHT, Adm. 1834.
Vouchers 1-6 paid HENRY F. HARDEN, PLEDGE W. THOMPSON, JAMES HARDIN,
Guardian for HIRAM HARDIN, JOEL KNIGHT, and FREDERICK POLLARD the balance
of their share, ELIJAH F. GREER his distribution share. Returned Feb.
27, 1835, by C. F. WRIGHT, Admr... Recorded Mar. 5, 1835 JOHN MCCORD,
C.C.O.

Pages 335-336: Yearly return for year 1834 on Estate of JOHN
BARKLEY, dec'd. by JANE BARKLEY, Guardian for the minor of said deceased
Mar. 2, 1835. Paid JOHN SAUNDERS medical services of orphan GEORGE
BARKLEY, PAYTON H. WHITE, medical services for orphan NANCY G. BARKLEY,
MCDANIEL & GOODMAN for JANE A. BARKLEY, SPENCER & MAYS for JANE A.
BARKLEY, JOHN MCCORD, Clerk. JOHN M.D. BOND, T. C. ELIZABETH ANN BARKLEY
for board, JOHN N. BARKLEY for board... JANE BARKLEY, Guardian...
Recorded Mar. 5, 1835, JOHN MCCORD, C.C.O.

Page 336: Estate of JOHN M. D. TAYLOR, dec'd., CHARLES BAILEY,
Adm. Dr. Vouchers 1-3 paid taxes for 1832, C. BAILEY, H. FREEMAN...
Returned Feb. 28, 1835, CHARLES BAILEY, Admr... Recorded Mar. 5, 1835,
JOHN MCCORD, C.C.O.

Pages 336-337: Estate of N. W. TAYLOR, 1833 to his guardian
CHARLES BAILEY which was not charged in return of 1833. Vouchers 1-11
paid JOHN MCCORD, WILLARD BRADLEY, CHARLES BAILEY, WHITE & GRESHAM,

MCDANIEL & GOODMAN, THOMAS C. TAYLOR, STEPHEN BAILEY, JOHN M.D. BOND.
Cr.: hire of negroes to WILLIAM MOSSER, JAMES BRADY, CATLETT CAMPBELL,
JACOB GARDNER, ISAAC LOW, WILLIAM BRADLEY, CHARLES BAILEY, Guardian...
Recorded Mar. 5, 1835, JOHN MCCORD, C.C.O.

Page 337: For RACHEL GRAY to ELIZABETH GRAY, Guardian paid
WILLIAM BOYLES for tuition $6.66 2/3 HENRY SUMMERLIN for sundries...
ELIZABETH GRAY, Guardian... Recorded Mar. 7, 1835, JOHN MCCORD, C.C.O.

Pages 337-338-339: Return No. 4, the Estate of WILLIAM REDMAN,
dec'd. JAMES CARTER, Admr. paid Vouchers 1-8, WILLIAM L. GORDON, PRINCE
& REGLAN, printer; Clerk, Tax Collector for 1833, MARY REDMAN for boarding and clothing MARY REDMAN, MARTHA REDMAN, WILLIAM REDMAN, JR., orphans
of WILLIAM REDMAN, dec'd. Paid MARY REDMAN for boarding and clothing
and taking care of ELIZABETH REDMAN, mother of dec'd. agreeable to a
bond given by the dec'd. in his lifetime. Amount $332.42... By amount
charged as per sale of land in Columbia County through mistake on last
return $330.00... By rent of land and hire of Negroes for year 1834...
Home plantation to MARY REDMAN... Lot No. 157 to DANIEL BEAUCHAMP ...
5 negroes hired by MARY REDMAN... Total $279.00... Returned Jan. 21,
1835, JAMES CARTER, Admr... Recorded Mar. 7, 1835, JOHN MCCORD, C.C.O.

Terms for hiring the negroes belonging to the estate of WILLIAM
REDMAN, dec'd. for 1834 and tenting the land, the negroes to have three
suits of cloaths suitable to the seasons, hat, blanket and shoes and
socks, must be well treated, the plantation where the widow lives to
undergo such repares as is needful for a crop, the plantation on Lot No.
157 without repairs Dec. 31, 1833. Signed: JAMES CARTER, Admr., MARY
REDMAN, Admx... Recorded Mar. 7, 1835, JOHN MCCORD, C.C.O.

Pages 339-340-341-342-343: Inventory and Appraisement of Estate
of ENOCH PEARSON dec'd. List of items valued at $4980.39 2/3. Apprai-
sors: JASON GREER, F. DOUGLASS, AMOS GORCE... Certified by J. C. DUN-
SIRTH, J.P. Recorded Mar. 13, 1835, JOHN MCCORD, C.C.O.

List of sale of personal property. Buyers: NANCY PEARSON, JOHN
DAWSON, STEPHEN MILLER, MOSES MOUNCE, F. DOUGLASS, GIDEON KIRKSEY,
WILLIAM HILL, MERIDITH NELSON, LEWIS BENNETT, WILLIAM B. HEAD, JOHN M.
PEARSON, ELIJAH SMITH, D. B. BUTLAR, WILLIAM BENSON, D. MEKLEROY. Total
$158.67¾... 1835 negroes belonging to estate of ENOCH PEARSON, dec'd.
sold to NANCY PEARSON, J. M. PEARSON, REUBEN BRIDGES, JOHN W. HILL, HENRY
HATELY, JAMES PEARSON, 13 negroes valued for $4941.50... WILLIAM H. and
JOHN M. PEARSON, Executors... Recorded Mar. 14, 1835, JOHN MCCORD, C.C.O.

Page 344: Return by executor of Estate of ENOCH PEARSON dec'd.
for the year 1835... Collected notes of J. M. PEARSON $84.25, sale of
cotton $99.96, W. H. & J. M. PEARSON, Exors... Recorded May 11, 1835,
JOHN MCCORD, C.C.O.

Paid out by Executors, Vouchers 1-9 to WILLIAM H. PEARSON, MERIDITH
NELSON, JOHN MCCORD, JAMES PEARSON, F. SMITH, J. M. PEARSON, JOHN
SAUNDERS, Feb. 16, 1835, WILLIAM H. & J. M. PEARSON, Exor... Recorded
May 11, 1835, JOHN MCCORD, C.C.O.

LEAVIN SMITH, Adm. of JOHN SMITH, dec'd... to hire of negroes for
1834, $52.25... Cash paid for taxes, midwife $2.00, Clerk of Court $6.50
Returned Apr. 7, 1835, LEAVIN SMITH, Admr... Recorded May 11, 1835,
JOHN MCCORD, C.C.O.

Page 345: JAMES M. PRESTON & ELISHA J. PRESTON, Admr. on estate
of GILLIAM PRESTON, dec'd... 1835 Vouchers 1-3 paid BENJAMIN CAMERON
on fifa vs GILLIAM PRESTON, JOHN SAUNDERS on account, JOHN M.D. BOND
taxes for 1833. Signed: ELISHA J. PRESTON, Admr... Recorded May 11,
1835 JOHN MCCORD, C.C.O.

Pages 345-346: The Estate of JAMES M. RHODES, dec'd. to JOSHIA
DRAPER, Admr... Vouchers 1-23 paid 1835 WHITE & GRESHAM, GOODMAN &
MCDANIEL, JOHN MCCORD, WILLIAM KNIGHT, DOLPHIN LINDSEY, SAMUEL HAM,

HARDWAY & HAWKIN, CALVERY F. KNIGHT, printer of Telegraph for advertising perishable property, SAMUEL DUFFY, JAMES PIDGEON, JAMES TOLLEY, ROBERT ANDREWS, HENRY D. KNIGHT, JOHN URGUHART, WHITE & GRESHAM, WILSON & MADDOX, PEYTON H. WHITE, JOHN H. DUFFEY, JAMES DRAPER, J. R. & J. W. MCCORD... Signed: JOSIAH (X) DRAPER, Admr... Recorded May 12, 1835, JOHN MCCORD, C.C.O.

Pages 346-347:   The Estate of CHARLES HEARD, dec'd... To Elenor HEARD, Execx... 1833 Vouchers 1-7 paid taxes for 1832, Clerk of Court, L. B. EUBANKS, Ordinary, W. W. PEARSON, JOHN SAUNDERS... 1834 JESSE LOYALL, J. M. MCCLENDON, taxes for 1833. RILEY WISE, ... 1835 JOHN J. HEARD, ELIJAH MCMICHAEL, Clerk. Signed: ELENOR HEARD, Execx... Recorded May 12, 1835, JOHN MCCORD, C.C.O.

Pages 347-352:   Return No. 1... Estate of JOHN R. CARGILE to MARY CARGILE Exerx... 1834. Vouchers 1-62, paid, paid cash for funeral expenses $13.27, SPENCER & MAYS, ANDREW SELLERS, Note in Eatenton Bank, MCDANIEL & GOODMAN, JAMES H. STARK for granting lot of land to THOMAS M. HOGANS, JOHN H. PASKEL, THOMAS J. WHITAKER for tuition of CHARLES and JOHN CARGILE, WILLIAM ALLISON, pocket money for ELIZABETH CARGILE, NICHOLAS JOHNSON for making pair of shoes, JAMES PRIDGEON, W. W. PEARSON, WILLIAM LEE, W. JARRELL, WILLIAM ALLISON, repairing clock, JAMES H. STARK, MCLIN & MADDOX for carpenters work, SAMUEL R. MCLIN, E. MADDOX, SAMUEL R. MCLIN, J.P. PRITCHETT for fodder, JAMES J. CRENSHAW, H. TOMPKINS, A. D. JOHNSON, JOHN H. HENDRICK, S. FULLER, JOB C. PATTERSON, ELI CAPP, PLEASANT POTTER, S. G. JENKINS for FRANCES RHODES, P. H. WHITE, ANDREW SELLERS for tanning and for leather, WILLIAM ALLISON, JOB TYLER, ROBERT N. MCLIN, T. J. SAUNDERS, SAMUEL FULTON, JAMES SHACKELFORD for tuition of children, CHARLES CARGILE, JESSE LOYALL, JAMES D. GILES, SAMUEL FULTON, G. W. SIMONTON, PETER GRINNELL, JEREMIAH PEARSON, WILLIAM S. HURD, H. COOLY, JOHN PRICE, GEORGE T. SEPAKE, RICHARD SPEAKE, JAMES H. STARK, THOMAS TAYLOR, JOHN MCCORD, JOHN E. JONES, shoemaker, JOHN TARPLEY, THOMAS HOUSE, Blacksmith... Total $3749.02½... Credit: 1834 profit on Ferry to this date Feb. 10, 1834, ANDREW SELLERS note; JAMES H. STARK, JOHN BANKSTON note, JESSE HODGES, DAVID BYARS, horses sold to DAVID MERRIWEATHER, WILLIAM HAYES, J. H. STARK, N. JOHNSON, JAMES PRIDGEON, cotton sold; D. J. BAILEY, JOHN HALL, profit from Ferry from Feb. 10 to May 21; JAMES MATTOX, S. MATTOX, E. MATTOX, SAMUEL MCLIN, JAMES J. CRENSHAW, P. POTTER, WILEY STROUD, ANDREW SETTERS, sale of wool, cotton, tobacco, pork, oats; THOMAS SANDERS, keeping cattle, boot in, swapping horses; F. O. CALLAGHAN, GEORGE T. SPEAK, BENJAMIN BLISSITT, RICHARD SPEAKE, JAMES H. STARK, THOMAS HOGAN, J. CLEVELAND. Total $2817.81½... Returned Feb. 13, 1835 by MARY CARGILE, Exerx.

Certification by WADE G. GILES, J.P. that the foregoing six pages contains a true account of her acting as executrix of JOHN R. CARGILE, dec'd. Sworn by MARY CARGILE on Feb. 13, 1835 before WADE H. GILES, J.P. Recorded May 13, 1835, JOHN MCCORD, C.C.O.

Page 352:   Estate of JOHN DENNIS, dec'd. 1834... to ELIZABETH C. DENNIS, Admrx. Vouchers 1-18 paid H. F. WILLIAMS, DANIEL TYE, WILLIAM DENNIS, DANIEL MCCLOUD, SAMUEL GRISWOULD, A. G. & W. H. ATWOOD, DAVID BERRY, JOHN MCCORD, SARAH TOWNSEND, CARTER & BENNETT, PETER DENNIS, SOLO-MON HUMPHRIS, TAX, ELIZABETH C. DENNIS, GIDEON POPE... Total $3538.67¼... DAVID BERRY acting agent for E. C. DENNIS, Admrx. of said dec'd... Recorded May 25, 1835, JOHN MCCORD, C.C.O.

Pages 353-355:   Inventory and Appraisement of Estate of NIEL FERGUSON, dec'd. Items listed valued $3921.75... June 9, 1835, Certifi-cation of Appraisors: JOHN M. PEARSON, JASON GREER, F. DOUGLASS to be true appraisement of goods and chattels of estate of said deceased as furnished by ALFRED W. FERGUSON, Administrator... Recorded June 10, 1835 JOHN MCCORD, C.C.O.

Page 356:   Yearly return on Estate of JOHN BARKLEY, dec'd. by SAMUEL R. NUTT, Admr... 1835 #1 - JANE BARKLEY received on fifa on GEORGE W. MARTIN plus cost of suit... #2 Rec't. continued for effects as the Admrx. and guardian for all the children of JOHN BARKLEY, dec'd. SAMUEL R. NUTT, Admr. Recorded July 8, 1835, JOHN MCCORD, C.C.O.

Estate of JOHN DENNIS dec'd. to E. C. DENNIS, Admx... 1835 Vouchers 1-4 paid PETER DENNIS one of the distributees his part of said estate $2037.33 1/3, D. BERRY, C.C.O. for final returns... DAVID BERRY, Agt for E. C. DENNIS, Admrx... Recorded July 8, 1835, JOHN MCCORD, C.C.O.

Page 357: Estate of GEORGE BLISSITT to WILLIAM HARPER, Guardian.. 1834 Vouchers 1-4 paid TOBY GILBERT for tuition of minor, Clerk of Court, taxes, WHITE & GRESHAM for an arithmetic 50¢, Credit: $243.11½. Returned July 22, 1835, WILLIAM HARPER, Guardian... Recorded Sept. 9, 1835, JOHN MCCORD, C.C.O.

Page 358: Estate of SAMUEL C. STARK in account with JAMES H. STARK, Admr. for year 1834... Vouchers 1-3 paid EZEKIEL TRIBLE in part of his distributive share in right of his wife, DANIEL OSBURN for repairs on house, Clerk of Court... Credit: Received of WILLIAM L. MCMAHAN, MATT MCMICHAEL. Returned July 24, 1835, JAMES H. STARK, Admr... Recorded Sept. 10, 1835, JOHN MCCORD, C.C.O.

Pages 359-360: Return on Estate of ARTHUR C. ATKINSON, dec'd. by THOMAS P. ATKINSON, Exrs. Return made in 1834... 1828 eleven days service attending to business of said estate in Clarke County, twenty-one days business in Clark County, 1829 eleven days business in Oglethrope County, fourteen days in Clarke County, seventeen days in Wilkes County, 1830 nine days in Wilkes County, thirteen days in Clarke County, fifteen days in Clark County, fifteen days in Oglethorpe County, 1831 seventeen days in Taliferro County, twenty-four days going to Appling County, sixteen days in Oglethorpe County, fifteen days in Taliferro County. ($1.00 paid per day)... 1834 cash paid ROBERT BLEDSOE note... 1833 money received NOEL JOHNSON. Returned by THOMAS P. ATKINSON one of the Executors of said dec'd... Recorded Sept. 11, 1835, JOHN MCCORD, C.C.O.

Page 360: Return No. 3, Estate of SEABORN L. WOOTEN a minor to JOHN JONES, Guardian for year 1834... No disbursements... Credits by balance due minor... Received of JESSE WOOTEN Exor of JAMES WOOTEN, dec'd. $263.82... Returned Sept. 5, 1835, JOHN JONES, Guardian... Recorded Sept. 11, 1835 JOHN MCCORD, C.C.O.

Page 361: Return No. 3, Estate of JAMES WOOTEN, a minor to JOHN JONES, Guardian for year 1834... No disbursements. Credits due minor. Received of JESSE WOOTEN, Exor of JAMES WOOTEN, dec'd. $254.52... Returned Sept. 5, 1835 JOHN JONES, Guardian... Recorded Sept. 11, 1835, JOHN MCCORD, C.C.O.

Return No. 3, Estate of ADDISON A. WOOTEN, a minor to JOHN JONES, Guardian for year 1834... No disbursements... Credits due minor... Received of JESSE WOOTEN Exor of JAMES WOOTEN,dec'd. $267.69... Returned Sept. 5, 1835, JOHN JONES, Guardian... Recorded Sept. 11, 1835, JOHN MCCORD, C.C.O.

Return No. 3, Estate of SIMEON WOOTEN a minor to JOHN JONES, Guardian for year 1834... No disbursements... Credits due minor... Received of JESSE WOOTEN, Exor of JAMES WOOTEN, dec'd. $262.85... Returned Sept. 5, 1835. Recorded Sept. 11, 1835, JOHN MCCORD, C.C.O.

Page 362: Property of Estate of JOEL WISE, dec'd. sold by Admr. in town of Jackson, 1st Tuesday Jan. 1835... Negroes sold to JOSEPH WRIGHT & EDWARD B. OXFORD, land Lot #22, 114 acres to ROBERT COLEMAN, frac Lot #33 to HUGH WISE; frac Lot #34 to BARNEY WISE... First Tuesday, Feb. at Monticello, fract Lot #135, fract Lot #130, fract Lot #133 to ROBERT COLEMAN; 50 acres to BURWELL CANNON... Total $8159.18 3/4... PARHAM LINDSEY, Admr.

Pages 362-366: A list of the sale of property NEIL FERGUSON, Oct. 21, 1835... Buyers: ALFRED W. FERGUSON, HENRY M. DUKE, ROBERT MCGRADY, BURWELL B. BREWER, JOB C. PATTERSON, HUBBARD WILLIAMS, DAVID B. BUTLAR, ROBERT LAWSON, E. S. KIRKSEY, JAMES HORTON, MARY WALDRIP, ROBERT MCGRADY, THOMAS DOUGLASS, JOHN POWELL, HENRY HARDING, ALSEY DURHAM, ROBERT BICKER-

STAFF, JAMES S. WALKER, GIDEON KIRKSEY, A. CHATMAN, JOHN M. PEARSON, WASHINGTON HAY, TARPLEY PRICE, WALTER S. ANDREWS, MERIDITH NELSON, IRBIN MOUNTS, BRADY MOORE. Total $565.60 3/4. ALFRED W. FERGUSON, Admr. Recorded Nov. 6, 1835 JOHN MCCORD, C.C.O.

Pages 366-367: Estate of JAMES GRAY, dec'd. 1834... To LEWIS H. FARGASON, Admr. Vouchers 11-23 paid ELIZABETH GRAY, Guardian for RACHEL GRAY, WILLIAM GRAY, JAMES GRAY, JOHNSON AUGUSTER GRAY, ALLEN GRAY... Total $1098.80. Paid HARDY PACE... LEWIS H. FARGASON, Admr... Recorded Nov. 10, 1835 JOHN MCCORD, C.C.O.

Page 367: Estate of RACHEL MAGBEE, dec'd. in acc. with executor... sale of real estate on Jan. 6, 1835 - Lot #218 sold to SAMUEL WYATT: 50 acres on Tussahaw Creek to WILLIAM H. HARPER, negroes to JESSE T. GUNN, MRS. MCCORD, JOHN HENDRICK, JAMES APPERSON, HIRAM MAGBEE, WILLIAM H. WYATT, LABON MAGBEE... Total $4585.81¼... Returned Dec. 7, 1835, E. W. LANE, LABON MAGBEE, Exrs. Recorded Dec. 8, 1835 JOHN MCCORD, C.C.O.

Page 368: Appraisement of property of JANE JENKINS, dec'd. as produced by FRANCIS DOUGLASS, Adm. Two negroes and two notes on WILLIAM BARKLEY and WILLIAM C. JENKINS... Total $850.00... Appraised Dec. 25, 1835 by appraisors JASON GREER, ROBERT BICKERSTAFF, THOMAS DOUGLASS.

Certification of appraisors by JAMES R. MCCORD, J.P., Jan. 4, 1836. Recorded Jan. 7, 1836, JOHN MCCORD, C.C.O.

Estate of JOHN SMITH, dec'd. in account with LEVIN SMITH, Adm. for year 1835... Cash for hire of negroes $45.05½... LEVIN SMITH, Admr.. Recorded Jan. 14, 1836, JOHN MCCORD, C.C.O.

Pages 369-370: Return of the Estate of JOEL WISE dec'd. year 1835. Dr. PATTON WISE, ADNERSON & MARY DUDLEY, BALDWIN & SHORTERY (2 notes). JOHN MCCORD, C.C.O., Editor of Georgia Telegraph, taxes 1834, JAMES BETTS, W. PHILLIPS, M. WHITFIELD, THOMAS BLAIR, JOHN SAUNDERS, C. M. COODY, Editor of Federal Union, G. DAUKINS, HUGH WISE, BARNEY WISE, AUGUSTUS WAIE. Total paid out $2062.95½. Credits: By EDWARD B. OXFORD, JOSEPH WRIGHT, CREED T. WISE, WILLIAM MCCUNE, PATTON WISE, Justice of Peace, JOHN SAUNDERS, THOMAS B. BLAIR, HUGH WISE, BARNEY WISE, AUGUSTUS WISE. Total $1913.51... Returned by PARHAM LINDSEY, Adm. Recorded Jan. 14, 1836 JOHN MCCORD, C.C.O.

Page 370: Estate of SAMUEL C. STARK in account with JAMES H. STARK, Admr. Year 1835... Vouchers 1-3 paid EZEKIEL TRIBLE in part of distributive share in right of his wife, taxes, J. W. & H. WILLIAMS for work and material for house. Credit: Sale of land $1190.00... Returned Jan. 2, 1836, JAMES H. STARK, Admr... Recorded Jan. 14, 1836, JOHN MCCORD, C.C.O.

Page 371: Return of SAMUEL BELLAH, Adm. of estate of WILLIAM RHODES dec'd. year 1835... Vouchers 1-3 paid Clerk, JOHN URQUEHART for clothing for NANCY RHODES one of the heirs of said estate, JOHN SINGLETON in right of his wife NANCY J. RHODES now NANCY J. SINGLETON... SAMUEL BELLAH, Adm. Recorded Jan. 14, 1836.

Estate of ELI KNIGHT minor of C. F. KNIGHT, Guardian... Paid JAMES H. STARK... Credit: Sale of land $79.00... Returned Jan. 8, 1836 by CALVERY (X) KNIGHT, Guardian... Recorded Jan. 14, 1836 JOHN MCCORD, C.C.O.

Pages 371-372: Estate of JAMES HARRISON to WILLIAM HARRISON, Adm. Vouchers 1-19 1835, Paid SAMUEL SNODDY medical bill, JOHN M. D. BOND taxes, JOHN HENDRICK, WESLEY C. WELCH, Clerk of Court, MCDANIEL & GOODMAN, Cost in case vs JAMES LUMMAS, RACHEL ANN HARRISON one of the distributees in part of her share STEPHEN BAILEY, JOHN LOFTON, WILLIAM HARRISON, RACHEL A. HARRISON one of the distributees, TRAVY G. BLEDSOE. 1836 - Paid RACHEL ANN HARRISON part of share, JOHN HENDRICK, J.P., JAMES H. STARK, Attorney, RACHEL ANN HARRISON balance of her share $582.38 3/4... Credit: Sale bill purchased by JOHN B. REEVES & WILLIAM H. HARRISON, rent collected for lot in Cherokee $1167.25... Returned Jan. 8, 1836, WILLIAM HARRISON Adm. Recorded Jan. 14, 1836 JOHN MCCORD, C.C.O.

Page 373:   Return on estate of GREER MCCOY, dec'd. by HENRY MCCOY Executor 1836. Cash paid 1834 WILLIAM LOW, PEYTON H. WHITE, JOHN MC-CORD, NEALY MCCOY, JOHN WILLIAMS, MARY E. TORBET, J. M. D. BOND, 1835 - JAMES M. HILL, N. W. PERSONS, GRIEVE & ORME - Cash received from JAMES M. HILL, WILLIAM LOW, MARCUS SWINNG, YELVENTON THAXTON. Returned HENRY MC-COY, Exor... Recorded Jan. 15, 1836 JOHN MCCORD, C.C.O.

Page 374:   MARTIN & BOWLS to G. HENDRICK, Guardian. Vouchers 1-10, paid R. S. MANN, J. MCCORD, MCDANIEL & GOODMAN, ABNER NOLEN, BARTLETT PRINTER, G. HENDRICK, J. H. STARK... Signed GUSTARVUS HENDRICK, Guardian. Recorded Jan. 15, 1836, JOHN MCCORD, C.C.O.

Estate of MATTHEW JINKS to ISAAC JINKS, Exor. 1835 - Vouchers 1-6 paid HENRY BARRON, J. W. WATKINS, WILLIAM HAMILTON, JAMES A. MCCUNE, MATTHEW GASTON. Returned Jan. 11, 1836 ISAAC JINKS, Exr. of MATTHEW JINKS... Recorded Jan. 15, 1836 JOHN MCCORD C.C.O.

Page 375:   Yearly return of Estate of NOAH W. TAYLOR by his guardian CHARLES BAILEY for year 1835.   Vouchers 1-13 paid 1834 JAMES H. STARK, 1835 paid JOHN MCCORD, A. C. VAIL, JOHN GOODMAN, J. H. STARK, A. R. BICKERSTAFF, SPENCER & MAYS, WILSON & MADDOX, P. H. WHITE, STEPHEN BAILEY, HENDRICK & GOODMAN, WILLIAM E. TUCKER... Credit: by hire of negroes to JAMES BYARS, HAMLIN FREEMAN, J. B CARMICHAEL, CATLETT CAMPBELL... Returned Jan. 11, 1836 CHARLES BAILEY, Guardian for N. W. TAYLOR... Recorded Jan. 16, 1836 JOHN MCCORD, C.C.O.

Page 376:   Annual return of DAVID SMITH, Guardian for the minor of FRANCIS TORBET, dec'd. for year 1835... Estate of minors HUGH S., SARAH M., ROBERT W., ROSANNA S., FRANCIS T. of FRANCIS TORBET dec'd. in account with DAVID SMITH, Guardian... Vouchers 1-4 paid DAVID L. BAILEY, JOHN MCCORD, JOHN P. BUCKAMAN, Expenses traveling to and from S.C. on business of estate... Credit: Received from JOSEPH CALDWELL, Adm. of estate of FRACNIS TORBET, dec'd... Recorded Jan. 18, 1836 JOHN MCCORD, C.C.O.

Page 377:   Return No. 5, estate of WILLIAM REDMAN, dec'd. Acc with JAMES CARTER, Adm... 1835 Vouchers 1-7 paid tax collector, Clerk of Court, HUGH B. STEWART for tuition of MARY REDMAN orphan of WILLIAM RED-MAN, dec'd. Paid MARY REDMAN for boarding and cloathing of MARY REDMAN, MARTHA REDMAN, WILLIAM REDMAN orphans of WILLIAM REDMAN, dec'd., paid MARY REDMAN for taking care of ELIZABETH REDMAN mother of dec'd... Credit renting land and hire of negroes. Returned Jan. 11. 1836 JAMES CARTER Admr... Recorded Jan. 18, 1836 JOHN MCCORD, C.C.O.

Page 378:   Account of hiring and renting land belonging to estate of WILLIAM REDMAN, dec'd. for year 1835... 5 negroes to MARY REDMAN and rented plantation whereon she lives. Rent plantation on Lot No. 157 to DANIEL BEAUCHAMP, JAMES CARTER, Adm... Recorded Jan. 18, 1836... JOHN MCCORD, C.C.O.

Pages 378-381:   Return No. 2... Estate of WILLIAM LEE, dec'd... To A. H. DAUGHERTY, Admr... Vouchers 1-18, paid JAMES W. WATKINS, J. W. WILLIAMS, R. ROBERT GREER, J. & T. WINSHIP, CHARLES BAILEY, JOHN HALL, Macon Telegraph, R. C. MAYS, CORNELIAS SLATEN... Credit: 1835 SAMUEL SNODDY, M. F. MCCUNE, C. B. LEE, ISAAC LOW, WILLIS JARRELL, J. C. KNIGHT, A. WILSON, D. MARTIN, R. RANSOM, JAMES MCCUNE, F. YOUNG, CHARLES BAILEY, A. L. ROBINSON, J. BERRY, JASON H. MACKEY, A. H. MANN, JOHN REEVES, JOSEPH BYARS, EDWARD WEAVER, D. B. M. MOORE, N. W. TAYLOR, J. J. M. MAPP, JAMES BAILEY, O. P. CHEATHAM, H. HATELY, G. W. LOWERY, JOHN HALL, W. W. GAITHER, HIRAM MAGBEE, JAMES WILSON, WILLIAM J. COLEMAN, HENDRICK RANDLE, GIDEON TANNER, RICHARD MASON, JAMES HARKNESS, JAMES HIGGINS, JOHN E. JONES, R. B. SANDERS, B. H. D. DARDEN, JAMES BRADY, JAMES BULLARD, THOMAS ROBINSON, DANIEL OSBORN, H. HATELY, J. R. MCCORD, W. J. COLEMAN, HENRY BAILEY. Total $431.85¼... A. H. DAUGHERTY, Adm. Recorded Jan. 20, 1836, JOHN MCCORD, C.C.O.

Pages 381-382-383:   ELIZABETH TORBET, Admx. and JOSEPH CALDWELL, Adm. of estate of FRANCIS TORBET, dec'd. in acc. with ordinary of Fair-field District charged with amount of interest of cash received up to

1830. Listed was all cash received through 1835 on estate from the com-
plete appraisal made on July 28, 1829. All cash subject to distribution
on Jan. 1, 1835 to ELIZABETH TORBET, the widow one third, HUGH S. TORBET,
SARAH MCCRORY TORBET, ROBERT W. TORBET, ROSANNAH S. TORBET, FRANCES J.
TORBET... Signed JOSEPH CALDWELL... Examined and approved July 20, 1835.
JOHN R. BUCHANAN as Federal District Ordinary... Recorded Jan. 20, 1836
JOHN MCCORD, C.C.O.

    Page 383:   Administration on estate of JAMES M. RHODES, dec'd...
Jan. 6, 1835 by sale of lot of land 150 acres belonging to estate sold
to JAMES DRAPER... JOSIAH (X) DRAPER, Adm... Recorded Feb. 1, 1836
JOHN MCCORD, C.C.O

    Page 384:   Estate of JAMES WOOTEN, dec'd. to JOHN JONES, Adm...
Year 1834 Return No. 3, Vouchers 1-2 paid J. M. MCCLENDON, G. L. & J. P.
SMITH, Credit: crop of cotton $601.31... Returned Sept. 6, 1835 JOHN
JONES, Adm. Recorded March 8, 1836, JOHN MCCORD, C.C.O.

    Pages 384-385:   The Estate of RACHEL MAGBEE, dec'd. in acc. with
E. W. LANE & LABEN MAGBEE, Exrs. for year 1835 up to Jan. 2, 1836 when
we came to a final settlement with Legatees... Vouchers 1-18 paid JAMES
STARK, Tax 1834, Painters, JOHN H. MCDANIEL, HENRY SUMMERLIN, G. HENDRICK,
DR. SNODDY, Clerks, award of arbitrators, Superior Clerk, JAMES H. ROBERTS
Pasting in the grave, recording deed, letters dismissary of estate,
finding burying charges for boy DANIEL BLEDSOE receipt for coffin,
services and expenses in going to Paulding City to view and sell estate
land their pr. L. MAGBEE, E. W. LANE services and expences in going to
Gilmer County for the above purpose... Total $4673.80... Each legatees
part of said estate $934.76 which they have received... Jan. 2, 1836
E. W. LANE and LABEN MAGBEE, Exrs... Recorded March 8, 1836, JOHN MCCORD,
C.C.O.

    Page 386:   Return of sale of land and negroes of estate of NEIL
FERGUSON, dec'd. One lot in 14th District formerly Monroe now Butts sold
to PARHAM LINDSEY $1000.00. (11) Negroes sold to WILLIAM JINKS, H. M.
DUKE, T. H. TUGGLE, A. W. FERGUSON... Returned Feb. 2, 1836, A. W.
FERGUSON, Adm... Recorded Mar. 19, 1836 JOHN MCCORD, CCO.

    Pages 386-388:   Will of NATHAN WILLIAMS of Butts County, Georgia
made Mar. 14, 1836. Proven Apr. 2, 1836... NATHAN WILLIAMS sound in
mind and memory... just debts paid... Bequeaths 1st to my beloved wife
ELIZABETH WILLIAMS one negro woman during her natural life then to go to
her two children MARTHA and MARY and also PETER until they become of age
or marry also $250 cash, household goods she brought with her... 2nd
to my dau. LYDIA CARTER $200... 3rd my dau. AGNES R. EVANS negro boy Tom.
4th to CLINTON A. WILLIAMS my son 1/2 lot of land No. 181, 2nd Dist.
of Wayne County and $150... 5th to my dau. THURZY H. WILLIAMS $200... 6th
to ROLAND WILLIAMS my son $300... 7th to my dau. NANCY O. WILLIAMS $350..
8th to JAMES M. WILLIAMS my son 1/2 lot of land No. 181 in Wayne County,
2nd District also $10... 9th to WILLIAM WILLIAMS my son $400... 10th
to NATHAN H. WILLIAMS my son $200... 11th to my dau. MARTHA T. WILLIAMS
$300 also to MARY ANN WILLIAMS the like sum and a good bed and funiture
a piece... 12th at completion of present crop to be sold and after distribution all money equally divided among the legatees with exception of
decent suppery of my wife and little ones for the next year... lastly
appoint my nephew STEPHEN W. PRICE and my son NATHAN H. WILLIAMS Executors... Signed: NATHAN WILLIAMS (SEAL). Wit: JOHN PRICE, E. W. LANE,
SILAS ELLIOTT J.P... Probated April 2, 1836 before EZEKIEL WALKER,
THOMAS P. ATKINSON, JOHN HALL... Recorded April 4, 1836, JOHN MCCORD,
C.C.O.

    Pages 389-401:   Inventory and Appraisement of Estate of ALLEN
MCCLENDON late of Butts County taken on Dec. 23, 1835... Items listed
first names of 72 negroes valued at $30,400, goods and chattels, notes
on ISAAC C. PARKS, ARCHIBALD SMITH, WILLIAM HILLOWAY, ADAM BLAIR, WILLIAM
JONES, CHARLES HOBBS, HIRAL LESTER, TURNER MCGLAUN, AUSTINE COOK, JOHN B.
RUSSELL, WILLIAM R. ANDERSON, SARAH & PEUREFOY TINGLE, WILLIAM F. MCTYRE,

WILLIAM RUSSELL, WILLIAM HADEN, JOHN JONES, ELI PARKS, JESSE TOLLESON, ARTHUR HAMILTON, JAMES G. NORRIS, AMOS EDMONDS, HEATH & CLEMANS, JOSEPH CAMPBELL, PETER W. WALKER endorsed by HENRY C. GILLS, JOHN WEAVER, R. BICKERSTAFF, POUNCEY MAXCY, E. L. YOUNG & CO., WILLIAM BENSON, THOMAS J. FERGUSON, JOHN GOLDSMITH, WILLIAM MCWHORTER, FERGASON & EVANS, JOHN TILLERY, DANIEL T. DUPREE, ISAAC HENDRICK, GEORGE EUBANKS, EDWARD WEAVER, JOHN M. PHILLIPS, HUGH WISE, DAVID EVANS, THOMAS BEARDEN, JOEL MCCLENDON, DANIEL OSBORN, KIRKSEY & HENDRICK, POWER & POWERS, WILLIAM B. DICKERSON, LOW & MICKELBERRY, JOHN H. WEAVER, WILLIAM F. MAPP, ZION R. BALLARD, DAVID MADDEN, JAMES HAGEN, L. LONG, WILLIAM DUFFIE, JOHN AKINS, NATHAN JORDAN, WILLIAM PRYOR, J. R. MARTIN, MARTIN & ANDREWS, JOHN PARHAM, JORDAN MILAM, DAVID MONTGOMERY, BAZEL SMITH, JEFFERSON HICKS, JOHN W. NEWMAN, COOK & GRAY, MATTHEW ORR, WILLIAM AKIN, DUDLEY COOK, LEMMON ROGERS, JOHN REED, BOLIN BROWN, GILLIS WRIGHT, WILLIAM MCCULLOCH, VANBIBER LEEK & CUNNINGHAM, EDMOND HEAD, JOSEPH SENTELL, THOMAS COKER, WILLIAM HARDY, RAINEY NEIL & CUNNINGHAM, THOMAS FINCHER, WILLIAM MILES & CO., FRANCES MILLER, LOVEJOY & MARTIN, WALLER & WALLER, ALFRED ANDERSON, S. H. HORN, WASHINGTON C. CLEVELAND, NICHOLAS PEUREFOY, ISAAC PARKS, MCCLENDON & MARTIN, ALLEN W. PRIOR rec'd. for collection 4 notes on NICHOLAS & CAS-WELL PEURIFOY and one note on JEPTHA MCCLENDON, ANDREW TENANT, JAMES H. EDWARDS,... Listed were 15 farm items in Pike County... Total of estate $40,758.96½. Certification by Appraisors JAMES H. CAMPBELL, J. M. MC-CLENDON, JOHN GOODMAN of true appraisement of goods, chattels and credits of estate of ALLEN MCCLENDON, dec'd. as furnished by WILLIAM F. MAPP, Admr... Sworn before CHARLES R. WALLER, J.P. Mar. 14, 1836... Recorded Apr. 16,1836 JOHN MCCORD C.C.O.

Pages 401-402: A list of property of JAMES ANDERSON, dec'd... goods and chattel... notes on WAITMAN GASDEN, EZEKIEL GASDEN, MATTHEW ANDERSON, ALEXANDER & LUKE PATRICK, SILAS PLUCKETT, JAMES ANDERSON. Total value $1767.36¼.

Certification by appraisors WILLIAM BENCE, REASON BLISSITT, WILLIAM HARPER of JAMES ANDERSON, dec'd. sworn by YELVENTON THAXTON, J.P., Feb. 29, 1836. Recorded May 4, 1836 JOHN MCCORD, C.C.O.

Pages 403-404-405: Inventory and Appraisement of estate of NATHAN WILLIAMS, dec'd... Apr. 13, 1836... List of goods and chattels, 10 negroes, notes on Z. & J. FALKNER, J. W. & Z. FALKNER, H. B. STEWART, H. B. WHITE & G. W. H. STEWART, WILLIAM W. KENNON... Total $6096.18.

Certification of appraisors E. W. LANE, JAMES CARTER, WILLIAM ALLISON of true appraisement of estate of NATHAN WILLIAMS, dec'd. sworn before SILAS ELLIOTT J.P... Apr. 13, 1836... Recorded Apr. 16, 1836 JOHN MCCORD, C.C.O.

Pages 406-407: Estate of JAMES WOOTEN to JOHN JONES, Admr. for year 1835... Vouchers 1-5 paid SANFORD & MARTIN, NICHOLAS A. PEURIFOY, A. F. THOMPSON, JAMES B. HOGAN & THOMAS HOGAN blacksmith, ALLEN MCCLENDON. Total $522.55 3/4... Credit: April 1835, cotton sold to W. J. RICE, cotton sold to J. ROGERS $825.18... Returned May 23, 1836 by JOHN JONES, Admr... Recorded June 1, 1836 JOHN MCCORD, C.C.O.

Estate of ADDISON A. WOOTEN to JOHN JONES, Guardian year 1835.. Return No. 4 paid Sept. 3, 1835 GEORGE W. VARNER for tuition, Clerk of Court. Total $11.12½... Credit: Balance due minor as per last return with interest, received of JESSE WOOTEN, Exor. of JAMES WOOTEN, balance due minor $302.97½... Returned May 23, 1836 JOHN JONES, Guardian... Recorded June 1, 1836 JOHN MCCORD, C.C.O.

Page 407: Estate of JAMES WOOTEN minor to JOHN JONES, Guardian 1835 No. disbursement... Credit: Received of JESSE WOOTEN, Exor. of JAMES WOOTEN and balance due minor since last return $298.75½... Returned May 23, 1836 JOHN JONES, Guardian... Recorded June 1, 1836 JOHN MCCORD, C.C.O.

Estate of SEABORN L. WOOTEN minor to JOHN JONES, Guardian 1835. Return No. 4, Vouchers 1-2 paid JOHN BOSTOCK for tuition $14.00, Clerk

of Court $15.12½... Credit: $308.84... Balance due minor $293.71½...
Returned May 23, 1836 JOHN JONES, Guardian... Recorded June 2, 1836
JOHN MCCORD, C.C.O.

Page 408:   Estate of SIMEON WOOTEN minor to JOHN JONES, Guardian
1835... Return No. 4, Vouchers 1-2 paid JOHN BOSTOCK for tuition, Clerk
of Court $15.12½... Credits: $308.87... Balance due minor $293.74...
Returned May 23, 1836 JOHN JONES, Guardian... Recorded June 2, 1836 JOHN
MCCORD, C.C.O.

Pages 408-409-410:   Inventory and Appraisement of estate of ISAIAH
WISE of Butts County, dec'd... List of goods and chattels, 2 negroes, 5
notes made by ROBERT SMITH, ISAIAH WISE & H. DUNSIETH dated Dec. 30, 1833,
7 notes made by LEWIS BENNETT & THOMAS LOVORN dated Feb. 19, 1835, 2 notes
by JOSEPH DAWSON Dec. 25, 1835, note by WILLIAM SMITH, JR., Feb. 26,
1834, note by JAMES B. SMITH Jan. 21, 1835... Total $1698.00.

Certification of appraisors DAVID HIGGINS, ROBERT MAYFIELD, LEWIS
BENNETT, HUGH H. HEARD of true appraisement of goods, chattels, and
credits of estate of ISAIAH WISE and sworn before JAMES C. DUNSIETH, J.P.
May 18, 1836. Recorded June 22, 1836 JOHN MCCORD C.C.O.

Pages 411-418:   Inventory of all property and personal of estate
of STERLING CAMP, dec'd.   July 7, 1836. Listed 20 negroes, goods and
chattels, notes on REUBEN PAIN and R. H. GROCE due Dec. 25, 1826, H. B.
HURSTON and L. L. HURSTON due Dec. 25, 1836, R. MEEK JR. & R. MEEK SR.
dated Dec. 25, 1834, WILLIAM ADAIR dated Dec. 12, 1835; LOIS DEES, C. D.
HEFLIN, BENJAMIN SANGSING Dec. 30, 1835; STEPHEN SANDERS Dec. 24, 1832;
EZEKIEL W. GOSDEN & PARKS W. SMITH Dec. 15, 1835; SAMUEL BENTON Oct. 23,
1835; GEORGE W. THOMAS Oct. 8, 1835; WILLIAM BISHOP, ELISHA COKER, ROBERT
MEEK Jan. 6, 1835; JAMES R. SMITH Aug. 7, 1835; B. CHEEK June 29, 1835;
H. B. HURSTON Jan. 12, 1836; JOAB WILLIS May 23, 1835; EZEKIEL GASDEN
Feb. 6, 1835; JAMES HENDERSON Jan. 2, 1835; BARTIN MARTIN & JAMES HENDER-
SON July 6, 1835; WILLIAM W. GILMAN & ELISHA COKER Feb. 16, 1836; HENRY
HATELY May 30, 1835; OLIVER CLEVELAND Dec. 11, 1835; WILLIAM BISHOP by
J. ANDERSON Aug. 11, 1835; H. B. HURSTON & J. L. HURSTON July 1, 1835;
SHARRACK BULLOCK Nov. 25, 1834; WATERMAN GASDEN Jan. 4, 1835; SHADRICK
BULLOCK May 23, 1835; HENRY HATELY May 30, 1835; JACOB CAPE & BRINK CAPE
Mar. 11, 1835; E. A. HILL Aug. 5, 1835; JAMES WILLIS & JACOB WILLIS July
15, 1835; E. A. WISE & W. H. MILLER Sept. 30, 1835; WILLIAM G. SHEARER
July 7, 1835; W. GRAY & T. GRAY Dec. 9, 1831; LUKE PATRICK Feb. 10, 1829;
BRANTLEY A. ROWLAND Dec. 22, 1835; ISAAC COKER Jan. 21, 1831; REUBEN
BANKSTON Oct. 22, 1835; JOHN W. WILLIAMS & WILLIAM W. WILLIAMS Jan. 1,
1836; SHADRICK HUMPHREY & JAMES HUMPHREY Dec. 25, 1835; JAMES HUMPHREY &
STEPHEN HUMPHREY Jan. 16, 1836; SHADRICK HUMPHREY & JAMES HUMPHREY Dec.
25, 1835... Cash found in hands of deceased that JOHN CAMP, the first
administrator took and lent out, which is to be returned at Christmas
next... Total $15,310.75 3/4.

Page 418 Con't.:   Certification of appraisors CLARK HAMEL J.P.,
YELVENTON THAXTON J.P., DAVID KIMBREE, NATHANIEL ANDERSON of true appraise-
ment of estate of deceased sworn before CLARK HAMIL J.P. July 7, 1836...
Recorded July 18, 1836 JOHN MCCORD, C.C.O.

Page 419:   Estate of WILLIAM BLESSET to WILLIAM HARPER, Guardian
Dec. 31, 1835... Vouchers 1-2 Paid taxes, Clerk of Court... Credits;
Value of estate $408.74½... Returned July 8, 1836 WILLIAM HARPER, Guar-
dian... Recorded July 20, 1836 JOHN MCCORD, C.C.O.

MORTON BLEDSOE, Guardian 1836 to estate of GEORGE M. T. BROCKMAN,
minor... hire of negroes to JAMES WILLIS, MORTON BLEDSOE, THOMAS R.
RUSSELL... Total $199.87½... Vouchers 1-6 paid Clerk, THOMAS R. RUSSELL,
ELIJAH HOTZCLAW, GEORGE R. GILMER, JOHN M. D. BOND... Total $79.00...
Returned MORTON BLEDSOE, Guardian... Recorded July 26, 1836 JOHN MCCORD,
C.C.O.

Pages 420-422:   Estate of JOHN R. CARGILE dec'd. in acc. with MARY
CARGILE, Extx. 1835... Return No. 2, Vouchers 1-48 paid E. A. BRODDUX,

GEORGE THOMAS, WILLIAM H. CRANE, CHARLES CARGILE, SAMUEL FULTON, WILLIAM TANNER, GEORGE SUTTEN, JOHN HENDRICK overseers wages, WHITE & GRESHAM, SPENCER & MAYS, HAMLIN FREEMAN, JOHN MCLURE, JOHN SAUNDERS, THOMAS J. GILES, Clerk of Court, JAMES H.STARK, CHARLES CARGILE, Grant fee on 5 lots of land, ZACHAREAH WHITE, GREEN H. WALKER, JOHN HINTON, W. F. WAGEN-CROFT, W. G. BARTON, JOHN PRICE, F. & J. MCLENDON, THOMAS HOUSE, MCLIN & MADDUX, T. & J. SAUNDERS, ARCH FINCHER, ALEX CROWDER, WILL A. MOORE city surveyor, T. & J. MCLENDON for damages done to their goods by accident at the ferry ($27.34), H. WALLER, HOLLIS COOLY, J. WAKEMAN, JAMES H. STARK, JOSIAH HARKNESS, W. C. PENN, DAVID MERRIWETHER, Credit received of W. GAMMAGE for sale of lot of land in Monroe County, received for entertaining travellers ($18.98), received of GEORGE THOMAS, sundries, cotton sold to SMITH & ROGERS, note vs BLANKENSHIP, JOHN HENDRICK, YOUNG R. HARRIS note, entertaining travellers 7 Co. $23.68 3/4, Claims vs WILLIAM T. BURTON, Claim vs THOMAS HOUSE, travellers $25.50, cart sold to JESSE HODGE, trade for a yoke of steers taken in part for a bad debt on JOHN S. SHEARER... Total $1,194.20 3/4... Returned June 14, 1836, MARY CARGILE, Extx.

Certification of true return by MARY CARGILE sworn before WADE H. GILES, J.P. June 14, 1836... Recorded July 26, 1836, JOHN MCCORD, C.C.O.

Pages 423-424: A list of hireing the negroes and renting the land belonging to estate of ALLEN MCCLENDON, dec'd... Jan. 4, 1836 on a credit til Dec. 25, 1836 WILLIAM F. MAPP, Adm. Plantation whereon dec'd. lived to MARY S. MCCLENDON; mill and 30 acres to J. M. MCCLENDON: J. J. MAPP the Towaliga plantation; S. W. THAXTON 20 A of land; WILLIAM POWERS 35A tennant place; H. J. SMITH store house; GEORGE JORDAN workshop; Negroes hired to SAMUEL MITCHEL, J. J. MAPP, JAMES H. STARK, G. M. HARTSFIELD, WILLIAM F. TYRE, WILLIAM W. FORD, MARY S. MCCLENDON, GEORGE JORDAN, DAVID ANDREWS, HOWEL ANDREWS, D. S. PATTERSON, LEWIS BENNETT, ISAAC NOLAN, WILLIAM F. MCTYRE, J. M. MCCLENDON, JOHN HIGGINS, THOMAS G. GILES, MOSS MOUNTS, A. F. THOMPSON... Total $2484.00... WILLIAM F. MAPP, Admr. Recorded Aug. 31, 1836 JOHN MCCORD, C.C.O.

A list of renting lands and town property belonging to estate of ALLEN MCCLENDON, dec'd. in Zebulon, Pike County... On Dec. 30, 1835 rented to WILEY F. MARTIN one house and lot in Zebulon; TILMAN LEAK one do do do; G. W. REEVES do do; JEFFERSON HICKS do do; JESSE B. REEVES one stable and lot; MARY S. MCCLENDON one brick yard lot; JESSE B. REEVES one half acre; MARY S. MCCLENDON one house and plantation; THOMAS FLETCHER one house and plantation; ALLEN W. PRYOR do do; DAVID ANDREWS do do; WILEY F. MARTIN one two acre lot.. Total $484.50... WILLIAM F. MAPP, Admr... Recorded Aug. 31, 1836 JOHN MCCORD, C.C.O.

Page 425: Hiring and renting property of ALLEN MCCLENDON, dec'd. in Jasper County on Jan. 8, 1836... JOHN DINGER one house and plantation; E. S. KIRKSEY do do; HENRY HARDIN do do; JOHN WOOD do do; JAMES DARDIN do do; Negroes rented to JOHN A. RAGLAND, JOHN WOOD, MARY S. MCCLENDON, W. S. ANDREWS, POUNCY MAXCEY, WILLIAM F. MAPP. Store house in Zebulon rented. Total $1,093.50... WILLIAM F. MAPP, Adm... Recorded Aug. 31, 1836 JOHN MCCORD, C.C.O.

ELISHA J. PRESTON, Admr. of estate of GILLIAM PRESTON, dec'd. Jan. 12, 1835 cash received for rent of land $26.00; 1836 Mar. 27 paid JAMES H. STARK $5.14; Balance due estate $20.86... ELISHA J. PRESTON, Adm... Recorded Sept. 6, 1836 JOHN MCCORD, C.C.O.

Pages 426-428: Inventory and appraisement of estate of ARISTOTLE G. DUKE, dec'd. Listed no cash on hand, one part lot of land in Butts County, No. 202, 5 Negroes, goods and chattels, notes on TOPLY DUKE, Aug. 19, 1933; SPENCER & MAY due Dec. 25, 1836, THOMAS BURFORD and DORY TAYLOR due Dec. 25, 1836; DORY TAYLOR due Dec. 25, 1836. Total value of estate $5,324.32½.

Certification by oath of appraisors ROBERT (X) GRIMMETT, JOHN (X) JINKS, DORY (X) TAYLOR, SAMUEL P. BURFORD, WASHINGTON G. ATKINSON as containing a true appraisement of estate of ARISTOTLE G. DUKE dec'd. as was produced by Admr. CHARLES A. KILLGORE before ELI CONGER this Sept. 6, 1836... Recorded Sept. 9, 1836. JOHN MCCORD, C.C.O.

Page 428:   A list of notes and other evidences of debt received of
JACOB WISE, Exr. of JOEL WISE, dec'd. by PARHAM LINDSEY, Adm. of JOEL
WISE, dec'd. No. 1-94 Principle and Securities:

William J. Head & James D. Head
Riley Wise & Isaiah Wise
  Do   Do   Do   Do
Isaiah Wise & Riley Wise
  Do   Do   Do   Do
William Vickery & G.T. Speake
John Walker & Willis Giles
James M. Darden & B. H. Darden
Patton Wise & Augustus Wise
Barton Martin & Mahaly Wise
Joseph Wright & Richard Mayo
N. G. Waller & Zachariah Williams
Barney Wise, Wm. Johnson, A. Wise
Barney & Henry Murry
John Murry & William B. Stone
William Giles & Creed T. Wise
Augustus Wise & Barney Wise
B. H. Darden & James M. Darden
William A. McClune & Wm. Giles
John Berge & William Vickers
Henry Murry & John Murry
G. T. Speake & Jesse Jolly
William Teddle & George Dawkins
Nicholas Johnson
Richard Speake, Sr.

Henry Murry & Hugh Wise
Nicholas Johnson & Henry Murry
Nicholas Johnson & William Johnson
William B. Stone & John Berge
George W. Thomas & John Berge
N. G. Waller & Zachariah Williams
Joseph W. Slaughter & Henry P.
  Slaughter
S. G. Higgins & W. A. McCune
David Higgins & James Higgins
Joseph Harmon & William Vickers
Joseph Harmon, Solomon Fetts,
  G. T. Speake
Hugh Wise & Henry Murry
Barney & William Johnson
Barney & Augustus Wise
John Murry & Thomas House
William Giles & William A. McCune
Thomas House & John Murry
William Johnson & Agustus Wise
James Pridgeon & Barney Wise
Mahaly Wise & William B. Stowe
G. T. Speake & Spencer Malone
Richard Speake, Sr. & Richard
  Speake, Jr.
Joseph W. Salughter & John Murry
Richard Speake, Jr. & G. T. Speake

Total Value $2,018.68. All the above notes given to the executor of
JOEL WISE, dec'd. and all due the 25th of Dec. 1833. All dated before the
decease of JOEL WISE.

Notes No. 1-8 on N. JOHNSON, PASCHAL TRAYLOR & WILLIAM CHEEK,
THOMAS HOUSE & BARNEY WISE, BARNEY WISE, AUGUSTUS WISE, GEORGE M. WILLIAM-
SON. Total value $537.62½.

Received of JOHN MCCORD, C.C.O. all foregoing notes belonging to
the estate of JOEL WISE, dec'd. which was deposited in his hands by
JACOB WISE. Amount $2,555.30½... Received this 14th Dec. 1833 by me.
PARHAM LINDSEY, Admr. Recorded Jan. 26, 1841 JOHN MCCORD, C.C.O.

BUTTS COUNTY, GEORGIA - DEED BOOK A

Butts County, in upper central Georgia, was created from parts of
Henry and Monroe Counties in 1825, making it the 64th. in order of or-
ganization. It was named for Capt. SAMUEL BUTTS, an outstanding militia
soldier in the War of 1812, who was killed while fighting the Creeks in
1814. Butts Countians cannot agree as to whether Jackson, the county
seat, was named for Gen. ANDREW JACKSON, or JAMES JACKSON, Governor of
Ga. in 1798. Both men were popular through here at this time.

Butts County in geographical location is situated next to and due
East of Spalding Co., Southeast of Henry Co., due South of Newton Co.,
due West of Jasper Co., and adjoining Butts Co. and due South of it
are Monroe and Lamar Counties.

Page 1: JOHN PRESCOTT, SR. of Burke Co. sold to JACOB LAMB of the
same place, for $40. 1st Dist. of Henry County, Georgia. Lot #84,
202 1/2 acres. L. F. POWELL, J.P. February 7, 1826 - A. L. ROBINSON,
Clerk - JOHN B. BECK, Witness.

Page 2: January 25, 1822 - ISRAEL WATSON of Laurens Co., Georgia
to URIAH KINCHEN, same address, for $250. Lot #40, 9th Dist. of Henry
Co., drawn by ISRAEL WATSON in Land Lottery, January 12 - 202 1/2 acres.
Wit. WM. MARLIN, APPLETON ROSSETER, J.I.C.

Page 3: February 7, 1826 - URIAH KINCHEN, Laurens Co., Georgia to
NEIL MONROE, same place. $160.00 202 1/2 acres. 9th Dist. of Henry Co.
Lot 40 drawn by ISRAEL WATSON in the recent Lottery. Witt. GEORGE
MATHER (MATHIS), THOS. MOORE, J.P.

Page 4: January 16, 1826 - NEILL MONROE, Laurens Co. Georgia to
MATTHEW BARBER, Butts Co. for $250 9th Dist. Henry County, formerly
Butts Co., Dist. 40 202 1/2 acres was drawn and granted to ISRAEL WATSON,
of Laurens Co., Georgia McLendons Dist. JOHN WORD, Witt. and A. L.
ROBINSON, J.P.

Page 5: January 25, 1826, ISAAC NOLAND, Sheriff, RICHARD NOLAND,
JOHN MCBRIDE, ROBERT W. HARKNESS, are held and firmly bound unto his
Excellency GEORGE M. TROOP, Governor and Commander in chief of the Army
and Navy of this State and of the Militia thereof, in the full sum of
$20,000 to be paid to the said G. M. TROUP, Governor of the said state
for the time being.
     Whereas the above bound ISAAC NOLAND, Sheriff, was on the 16th day
of January 1826 elected Sheriff of the County of Butts in said State
     Sealed and delivered in the presence of JOHN R. CARGILL, J.I.C.,
WILLIE B. ECTOR, J.I.C., ZELVENTON THAXTON, L. B. and A. L. ROBINSON,
Clerk.

Page 6: Following ISAAC NOLAND'S Oath to faithfully execute office
to Sheriff.

Page 7: Following ROBERT W. HARKNESS'S Oath to execute office of
Deputy Sheriff.

The above two signed by JOHN HENDRICK, WILLIE B. ECTOR, JOHN R.
CARGILE.

Page 7: Hancock County, Georgia December 14, 1822, between HENRY
KINDALL, JR. and THOS. H. KINDALL of Hancock Co., Georgia and HENRY
KINDALL, SR. of Warren County, Georgia $100. 1st. Dist. Henry County,
Georgia Lot #108, 202 1/2 acres, granted to DAVID MARTIN. Witt: CLS
RANSOM - THOS. L. LATIMORE, J.P.

Page 8: Butts County, Georgia February 10, 1826. ARISTOTTLE G.
DUKE, same County and WILLIAM P. HOLIFIELD, same place, $600. 1st Dist.
of Henry Co. #55 Dist. 202 1/2 acres. Witt. B. F. TUCKER and ROBT.
BROWN.

Page 9: Indian Springs, January 26, 1826, Butts County, Georgia
JOEL and SARAH BAILEY to JOHN HUMPHRIES, a negro girl, named Minta, 16
years old, for $400. Witt. SAMUEL F. SANDERS.

Page 10: Laurens County, Georgia March 1, 1824. ISAAC BROOKING of
Laurens Co. and to THOMAS P. CHAIRS, same address. 1st Dist. of Henry
Co., Dist. 172, $250. Witt. ENOCH ROE and NANCY ROE.

Page 11: Laurens County January 3, 1826, THOMAS P. CHAIRS and
THOMAS ROBINSON of Jasper County, Georgia $160. Dist. 1, Henry Co.,
Georgia Lot 172. Witt. THOS. GREEN.

Page 12: Laurens Co., Georgia March 4, 1820. ANGELINE G. CHAIRS,
wife of THOS. P. CHAIRS, a separation, he relinquishing all her rights
of Dowry.

Page 12: Henry County, Georgia 12-18-1825, ARISTOTTLE DUKE and
A. L. ROBINSON, $700. 202 1/2 acres, 5th Dist. Lot 182. Witt. STEPHEN
G. HEARDS, W. C. PARKER, J.P.

Page 13: Jasper County, Georgia 1826 (Feb. 9) FRANCIS IRWIN of
Jasper Co. and CHARLES RAMY, Butts County, Georgia $500. 1st. Dist. Lot
#88. Witt. WILSON RAMEY, D. TREADWELL, J.P.

Page 14: December 2, 1823, EMANUEL SHEAROUSE of Effingham Co., Ga.
and LYDIA his wife, and JONATHAN MILLER $100. 1st. Dist. of Henry
County, 202 1/2 acres, Dist. 73. Witt. MATTHEW HIATT, FURNEY WELL,
J.I.C.

Page 15: Jones County, Georgia, February 17, 1826. JONATHAN MILLER
Jones Co. and JOHN SIMMONS of Butts County, $600. Originally Henry Co.,
Lott 73, 1st. Dist. 202 1/2 acres. Witt. WILLIAM H. INGRAM and THOMAS
MAFETUR (?).

Page 16: Hancock County, Georgia, December 22, 1821 DAVID MARTIN,
Warren County, Georgia. HENRY and THOS. H. KINDALL, Hancock County,
Merchants $40. 1st. Dist. Henry County #108, 202 1/2 acres. Witt.
JOHN MITCHELL.

Page 17: March 4, 1825, Warren County, Georgia. SAMUEL TORRENCE
and the justices of the Hon. Inferior Court, Co. of Butts - JOHN HEN-
DRICKS, YELVENTON THAXTON, ELIE CONGAR and WILEE B. ECTOR of the other
part. Dist. 89, Drawn in Land Lottery by SAMUEL TORRANCE, 202 1/2
acres, Witt. JOHN J. JOHNSON and GERALD CAMP, J.P.

Page 19: Warren County, Georgia MATILDA TORRENCE separates from
SAMUEL TORRENCE March 4, 1826 - GERALD CAMP, J.P.

Page 19: Butts County, Georgia, March 7, 1826. CHARLES RAINEY
and JNO. R. CARGILE $400. Lott 88, orig. Henry Co., now Butts 104 1/4
acres. Wit. JOHN MCGINTY, HENRY LEE and ABSALOM RAINEY.

Page 21: Butts County, Georgia, March 16, 1826, CHARLES RAMEY
and JOHN R. CARGILE, $600. West half of Lot 88, formerly the 1st. Dist.
of Henry Co., now 6th Dist. of Butts, 101 1/4 acres, orig. granted to
ALLEN ROBINETT, 2-22-1823. Witt. STEPHEN RIGHT, WILLIE B. ECTOR, J.I.C.

Page 22: December 31, 1825, EMANUEL SMITH and wife, CATHERINE
SMITH, Henry Co., Georgia and JOHN SMITH of Morgan County, Georgia
$250. 9th Dist. part of Lot 73, Witt. JESSE BRIANT & JOS. KEY.

Page 23: August 24, 1825 - Henry County, BENJ. F. TUCKER and ELIE
CONGAR both of Henry County, Georgia $175. Lot 181 1st. Dist. 50 acres.
Witt. WALTER BEAN, A. L. ROBINSON, J.P.

Page 24: Habersham County, Georgia JAMES HENDERSON, same Co., appt.
ARTHUR ALEXANDER, his atty. to obtain grant of land, 1st. Dist. Henry
County, drawn by CYNTHA HANEY, widow of Capt. TRAMILS Dist. Habersham
Co., Ga. being in Dist. 60 - May 20, 1822. Signed: JOSEPH HENDERSON.
Wit. MILES DAVIS.

Page 25: Habersham County, Ga. I do hereby certify that I did join in lawful wedlock, JAMES HENDERSON of said County to CINTHIA HENY, late widow of MOSSES HANEY, deceased. Certified by me this 21st. April 1822. JAMES HUDGINS J.I.S. March 30, 1826.

Page 25: Pulaski Co., Ga. March 23, 1822. WM. KEEN, same Co. - DAVID THOMPSON and THOMAS BRODDAS, county of Jasper, Ga. $500. 202 1/2 acres Lot 72 1st. Dist. of Henry Co. Wit. CHAPEL BOUTWELL and JAMES BROWN of Pulaski County, Ga. JAMES BROWN and WM. KEEN, also CHAPPEL BARTWELL, April 13, 1822.

Page 26: Monroe County, Ga., December 10, 1825, JOSEPH SENTELL, Monroe County and HUGH M. ECTOR, for $834. #45 in Dist. 14th 202 1/2 acres. Wit. WILSER BROCHER, and C. M. COODY, J.P.

DOLLY ECTOR, wife of HUGH W. ECTOR, Butts County, relinquishes her claim. April 12, 1826.

Page 27: January 24, 1825, PHILLIPS BIRD, Hall County, Ga. and JOSEPH SENTELL, Monroe County, Georgia $140 202 1/2 acres, 14th. Dist. Monroe County #94 Wit. Levi M. ADAMS and JAMES WILLIN, J.P.

Page 28: April 15, 1825, between ELIJAH TWILLEY, DeKalb County and JOSEPH SENTELL, Monroe Co., $200 104 1/4 acres. Wit. RAILEY TURNER & THOS. ANDERSON.

Page 29: September 6, 1824, RICHARD LAWRENCE, Monroe Co., Ga. and JOS. SENTELL $500, 202 1/2, 14th. Dist. of Monroe Co. Dist. 61. Wit. LEVI M. ADAMS, wife of RICHARD LAWRENCE, DIEDAMA LAWRENS

Page 30: December 16, 1824, Jasper Co., JOSEPH BUCK, Newton County, Ga. and JOHN REEAVES of Jasper County - Witnesseth that JOSEPH BUCHANAN, for $500. 1st. Dist. Co. of Henry, 202 1/2 acres Lot #27. Wit. JOEL FLANAGAN, EDWARDS FLANAGIN, J.P.

Page 31: April 6, 1826, WOODY DOZIER, Jasper Co., Ga. and ISHAM FREEMAN, Butts $200. Lot 95, 1st. Dist. orig. Henry, now Butts. Wit. JOHN HOLMES and JAMES PRIDGEIN. WM. BARKLEY, J.P.

Page 32: April 11, 1826, JONATHAN HARKNESS and JAMES MCLIN, $143. 1st Dist. #99, Witt. GEORGE S. HARKNESS and JOHN R. CARGILE, J.I.S.

Page 33: January 9, 1826, JAMES ATWELL of Richmond County, Ga. and THOMAS ROBINSON of Jasper Co., Ga. $150 1st. Dist. Henry Co. Lot 170, Wit. GEO. M. WALKER & W. B. THOMAS, J.P.

Page 34: Jasper County, Georgia, January 23, 1836, THOS. ROBINSON, Jasper Co. and WM. C. PARKER, Butts Co., Georgia $150 5th Dist. Lot #170, 202 1/2 acres. Wit. ADOLPHUS SLAY & HENRY JACKSON, J.P. Wife: SARAH ROBINSON.

Page 35: Chatham County, Ga. VALENTIME CREVENT (?) $100. ADDAM G. SAFFOLD bought in Henry Co. Lot #34 202 1/2 acres 2nd Dist., July 10, 1822. Wit. C. C. GRIMOLD (GRISWOLD?), JAMES MORRISON, MAYOR of Savannah.

Page 37: Morgan County, Ga. ADAM G. SAFFOLD to ADDISON MANDALL and THOS. CAMPBELL, County of Bibb Lott 34, Dist. 2nd of Henry Co., obtained from VALENTINE CREVEN, April 22, 1828. Wit. SEABORN JOHNSON & SIMEON WALKER, J.P.

Page 38: June 25, 1823, JACOB WILLCOX and ADAM G. SAFFOLD both of Georgia $100. Lot 66 Co. of Henry 202 1/2 acres, was drawn by WM. W. HALL in Lottery May 16, (1823) (Co. of Chatham) W. W. GORDON, N.P. and CHAS. WATSON.

Page 40: A. PORTER - Georgie-Morgan Co. ADDISON MADDEL, (MANDAL) Lot 66, 1st. Dist. of Henry Co., obtained from JACOB WILCOX, is moving, and now resells to ADISON MANDEL and THOMAS CAMPBELL. May 12, 1828.

74

Page 41: Butts County, BENJAMIN MAGAUICK has given and bequeathed to my son-in-law and daughter, THOS. BLAIR and wife MARY BLAIR. Stock and house furniture, guns, etc. May 12, 1828.

Page 42: July 11, 1825, between JAMES MOORE of the County of Richmond, and BENJAMIN REDMAN, same County, for $60. County of Henry 202 1/2 acres, 9th Dist. Lot 51, from the Grant dated June 10th, 1825. WILL MOORE, ROBERT THOMAS, J.P. & WILLIAM MOORE. May 16, 1828. A. L. ROBINSON, Clerk.

Page 43: Henry Co., Ga., September 17, 1824, between CLAYTON DOSS and FRANCES MILLEN (MILLER) $500. Lot #254, 8th Dist. Wit. R. E. MABRY, JOHN MCBRIDE, J.P. Wife, MARY.

Page 44: Butts County, January 9, 1826, between ROBERT WATSON and FRANCIS MILLER $500. Between Lots 253 and 254. Wit. GUSTAVUS HENDRICKS and WM. MERCER.

Page 45: Jasper County, Ga. January 28, 1822 between LUKE LASITER of the County of Laurens and THOS. ROBINSON, Jasper Co., Ga. $150. 200 1/2 acres in the County of Monroe, Dist. 4th, Lot 34. Wit. JOS. TAYLOR, LUKE ROBINSON & JAMES WYNN. May 18, 1828.

Page 47: Jasper Co., October 5, 1822, JOHN CAMPBELL of Newton Co., Ga., and LUKE ROBINSON Jasper Co., Ga. $200. 202 1/2 acres 1st. Dist. Lot 154. Wit. GUY W. SMITH and SAM FEARS, J.P.

Page 47: Henry County, Ga., August 22, 1825 between LUKE ROBINSON and JESSE CLAY of Jasper, $470. Lot #206, 1st. Dist. of Henry Co. B. F. TUCKER, 1828.

Page 48: Upson County, Ga., May 21, 1826. JOHN KEENAN and BURWELL JINKS of Butts Co. $100. 1st. Dist. of Henry Co. Lot 150, which lot of land was drawn by JOHN HENSON and TWIGGS KEENAN buying 99 9/10 acres for himself. Wit. SILMON KEENAN & WM. BARRON, J.P.

Page 50: February 19, 1824. DREWRY DUKE, of Burke County, Ga. and BURWELL JINKS of Henry Co. $200. 1st Dist. of Henry, Lot 151. Wit. JAMES DUKE and AZARIAH DUKE, J.P.

Page 50: On or before the first day of January 1826, I Promise to pay JOSEPH SUMMERLIN the sum of $500 - December 18, 1824. WM. MCNEES.

Page 50: Clarke County, Ga., December 18, 1824, between WM. MCNEES and JOSEPH SUMMERLIN, Henry County, promised to pay before January 1, 1826. Also involves negro man, Nedd. Wit. ROBERT LIGON & A. W. BROWN, J.P.

Page 52: February 25, 1826, between PRUDENCE PHILLIPS, widow of Pulaski County, Ga. and THOMAS ROBINSON, Jasper Co., $200. Butts Co., Lot 153 - 202 1/2 acres. Wit. ROBERT HODGE and THOS. ROWLING. JAMES F. BURKE, J.P.

Page 53: Butts County, DAVID LAWSON, WILLIAM BARKLEY and JONATHAN NUTT for $2500 March 6, 1826. DAVID LAWSON, adm. of the late ADAM LAWSON.

Page 54: December 16, 1825. DANIEL NOLLEY & CO., County of Wilkinson, Ga. and ROBERT C. CHAPMAN, Twiggs County, Ga. $500. 1st. Dist. of Henry Co., Lot 9, 202 1/4 acres, lot originally granted to TIMOTHY GRANS of Effingham Co., Ga. Wit. THOMAS JACKSON and ROBERT GILES, J.P.

Page 55: June 5, 1826 between ALEXANDER MCCREE, Clarke Co., Ga. and RICHARD POUNDS, Butts County, $120 on Yellow Water Creek, 202 1/2 acres Lot 128, in 1st. Dist. of Henry Co. Wit. WM. MCCREE and F. M. MCCREE.

Page 57: Monroe Co., Ga. October 15, 1825. Between WM. LOVEJOY and WM. WILLSON and S. LOVEJOY, county of Monroe $600. Lot, 69, JOHN B. LOVEJOY and BEN A. BROWN.

Page 57: Monroe Co., Ga., October 29, 1823, WM. CARPENTER & WM. L. WILSON & SIM LOVEJOY $235. 4th Dist. of Monroe, Lot 16, 101 1/4 acres. Wit. JOHN B. LOVEJOY & R. L. CARGILE.

Page 58: Screven County, Ga., March 3, 1826, STEPHEN BUTLER - WM. L. WILSON & SIMEON LOVEJOY, Butts County, Ga. $400. 4th Dist. of orig. Monroe Co. now Butts. Lot 49. Witt. J. ANDREWS & JAMES H. WADE, J.P.

Page 59: September 6, 1825, Jones County, Ga., between HENRY W. GRIFFETH, of Jones Co. and WILSON & LOVEJOY of Monroe Co. $300. Lot 70, 4 Dist. of Monroe. Wit. THOMAS COKER and JOHN B. LOVEJOY.

Page 60: November 3, 1825, Henry Co. BURWELL JINKS and HUGH HAMIL, Henry Co. 75 A of land, $250. 1st. Dist., part of Lot 77 - Wit. RICHARD COTTON, SAML. CLAY.

Page 61: Butts Co., STEPHEN BLESSETT, REASON BLESSIT, JOHN MC-MICHAEL and WM. MULKEY, sum of $5000. adm. of ELISHA BLESSITT, May 8, 1826.

Page 62: Elbert County, June 1, 1826, SINGLETON W. ALLEN and ROBT. G. TURMAN $300. Henry Co. 9th Dist., not Butts Co. 202 1/2 acres, originally granted to HENRY CABINESS. Wit. E. N. CALHOUN, BEVERLY ALLEN, J.I.C. Wife, JANE L. ALLEN. Signed: SINGLETON W. ALLEN.

Page 63: Elbert County, Ga., December 19, 1825. HENRY P. BROWN, same County and JAMES BROWN, of Morgan County, Ga. for $600. 8th Dist. Henry County, Ga. 202 1/2 acres #255 Lot, BENJAMIN HOUSTON, Witt. ISHAM G. ROGERS, DAVID P. JAMES, J.P., HENRY P. BROWN also, ISAAC ALMAND, J.P. CHERRY BROWN, wife.

Page 64: Morgan County, Ga., June 16, 1826, between JAMES N. BROWN, and JOHN HENDRICK, of Butts County, Ga. $800 8th Dist., formerly Henry, now Butts Co. 202 1/2 A, #255. Witt. THOS. MACKEY, JAMES KEELAN, & JOHN MCCOY. Signed: JAMES N. BROWN; Wife, MARTHA BROWN.

Page 66: Henry County, October 24, 1825, WILLIAM REEVE and HENRY D. KNIGHT of Monroe County, Ga. $400. 2nd. Dist. on the water of Towliaga Creek #5 Dist. granted to JONATHAN WALKER 202 1/2 acres. Witt. C. F. KNIGHT, SAMUEL BELLAH, J.P.. Signed: WILLIAM REEVE; Wife: LUCY REEVES.

Page 67: Georgia, September 15, 1824 between FERIBEE TOOTLE, Washington Co., Ga., and SAMUEL KIGHTS of Monroe County, Ga. $100. 4th Dist. of Monroe Co. No. 198 Lot, Witt. DAVID SHEFFIELD & ENOCH TOOTLE. Signed: ENOCH TOOTLE. Also FERIBEE TOOTLE and DANIEL B. SHEFFIELD. WINIFIELD WRIGHT, J.P.

Page 68: Butts County, Ga., Chatham County, Ga. W. & WM. MARSH, suit against J. R. WAINTER, July 24, 1826 for $72. ISAAC NOLEN, Sheriff, highest bidder, I Love - 1st. Dist. of Butts Co. Lot 212 containing 202 1/2 acres. Witness. JOHN TARPLEY, JOHN R. CARGILE, J.P. & ISAAC NOLEN, Sheriff.

Page 69: Monroe County, Ga., October 17, 1825, JOHN BRITTON & RICHARD NOLEN both of Monroe Co. $1400. 202 1/2 acres 4th Dist. of Monroe, SANDFORD BRITTON. Witt. Signed: JOHN BRITTON; wife, MARY - JOHN MCBRIDE, ISAAC NOLEN.

Page 69: Butts County, Ga., March 4, 1826, JOHN BULL of Chatham County, Ga. $100 and JAMES WASHINGTON - 4th Dist. of Monroe County, Ga. Lot 83, 202 1/2 acres. Witt. B. LATHROP, WM. C. MILLS, Savannah, March 4, 1826.

Page 70: Butts County, Ga., January 30, 1826, between ELISHA ED-WARDS and WM. VICKERS, $150. 30 acres, Lot #31 in the 9th Dist. of formerly Henry Co., now Butts GEORGE BRITTON and WM. BARKLEY, Witt. Signed: JOHN EDWARDS - ELISHA EDWARDS.

Page 71: Putnam County, Ga., February 11, 1826. SAMUEL BREEDLOVE & WM. GILMORE of Butts County, $700. 202 1/2 acres, 4th Dist. of formerly Monroe Co., now Butts Lot #158, survey of Monroe County, drawn by PEYTON CLEMENTS, JR. of CAPT. SAMUEL JOHNSTON'S Dist. of Putnam Co., Ga. Witt. WM. GARRARD & HENRY C. LANE, J.P. Signed: SAMUEL BREEDLOVE.

Page 72: Henry County, Ga., January 18, 1826 GEORGE W. KEY, of Jackson Co., Ga. and GEORGE BRITTON of Henry Co., $200. 9th Dist. of Henry Co. Lot #36 granted to GEO. W. KEY, October 27, 1824, 80 acres. Signed: GEORGE W. KEY. Witt. JOHN R. CARGILE & STEPHEN KIGHT. JOSEPH KEY, J.P.

Page 72: Putnam County, Ga., March 17, 1824 between PEYTON CLEMENT and SAMUEL BREEDLOVE $500. 4th Dist. of Monroe Co., Ga. Lot #58 of 202 1/2 acres. Signed: PEYTON CLEMENTS - Witt. WILLIAM COOK, B. VAN WAGENER & WM. J. ROLEY, J.P.

Page 73: Newton Co., Ga., March 7, 1823. WILEY HOWELL (WILIE HOWELL) and NEEDHAM LEE of Monroe Co., Ga. $300. Plot #16 in the 4th Dist. of Monroe Co. 202 1/2 acres. Signed: WILEY HOWELL Witt. JOHN H. TRIMBLE and BURRELL MATTHEWS, J.P.

Page 74: Washington County, Ga., April 1825, between MIDDLETON POOL and NEALEY MCCOY of Henry County, Ga. for $400. 202 1/2 acres, 1st. Dist. of Henry, Lot #38, drawn by ZABEL ARNET of Travis' District. Warren County, GABRIEL JONES, surveyor. Signed: MIDDLETON POOW. Witt. THOS. BATEMAN & JOHN RUSH, J.P.

Page 75: Same people involved, buying for $160. for 202 1/2 acres. Signed: ZABEL ARNEL - Witt. RUTHY WILCHAR & HEREMIAH WILCHAR, J.P.

Page 76: Jasper County, Ga., December 28, 1825. LUKE WILLIAMS and HENRY JACKSON both of Jasper Co. $400. 1st. Dist. of Henry Co., Lot #188, 202 1/2 acres. Signed: LUKE WILLIAMS. Witt: NATHAN WILLIAMS. WM. C. PARKER, J.P. Wife: ANNA WILLIAMS.

Page 77: Newton County, Ga., August 2, 1824, between JOSEPH LANE and LEVIN SMITH of Morgan County, Ga., for $500. (Lot of land drawn by NIMROD SMITH, Cobbs Dist. Walton Co.) 4th Dist. of Monroe, 202 1/2 acres Lot #9, Witt: ANN LANE, LEONARD CARDIN, RICHARD SMITH, J.P. Signed: JOSEPH LANE, Wife: ELIZABETH LANE.

Page 78: State of Georgia, April 29, 1826. BENJAMIN REDMAN, Richmond County, Ga. and WILLIAM REDMAN for $170 in the County of Henry, now Butts 202 1/2 acres, 9th Dist. of Henry, Lot 51. Grant from the state dated June 4, 1825. Signed: BENJ. REDMAN _ Witt: A. J. MURPHY, JAMES MURPHY, J.P.

Page 80: Jasper County, Ga., June 22, 1825. NANCY CARPENTER of Jasper Co. and CLARKE HAMIL of Henry Co., Ga. $212.50, Lot #48. Signed JANCY CARPENTER Witt: B. C. JOHNSON & WM. JOHNSON, J.P.

Page 81: Butts County, Ga., ROBERT CURRY and ROBERT BROWN for $500. March 6, 1826 ROBERT CURRY is this day appointed Guardian to HEZIKIAH WHEELER and GIDEON WHEELER, Orphans of HEZEKIAH WHEELER, decd. JOHN TARPLEY, C.C.O.

Page 81: Butts County, GEORGE T. SPEAK, PHILIP CAUSEY and STEPHEN KIGHT appointed guardians of THOMAS, JAMEY, LYDIA & SAMUEL LINDSAY, orphans of SAMUEL LINDSAY, paid $1000, July 3, 1826, JOHN TARPLEY, C.C.O.

Page 82: Screven County, Ga., November 1, 1825 - B. W. GRINER appoints his attorney CHARLES N. MCCALL to buy land in County of Henry, 8th Dist. B. M. GRINER Witt: FRANCIS MCCALL & M. N. MCCALL, J.P.

Page 82: Jasper Co., Ga., BENJ. W. GRINER of Screven Co., Ga., for 2&12 dollars, paid by CHURCHILL MASON of Henry Co., Ga. 8th Dist. of Henry Co. Dist. or Lot #231, December 20, 1825. Signed: BENJAMIN GRINER by CHARLES H. MCCALL, his attorney - Witt: SILAS B. BUCHANAN and WM. WOODARD, J.P.

Page 83: August 15, 1825 - BENJ. F. TUCKER for $351. for a negro woman named Charlotte, age 31 years. Signed: WILLIAM GILMORE & THOS. HAMPTON TEST: JAMES KING & WILLIAM BARKLEY, J.P.

Page 83: April 3, 1826, ABNER WELBORN of Wilkes Co., Ga. and WILLIAM (WILLIAMSON) ROBY of Jasper County, Ga., $300 for 202 1/2 acres of Lot 2 in the 9th Dist. of Henry Co. now Butts County, Ga. drawn by POLLY BESS, (widow) January 7, 1822. Signed: ABNER WELBORN - Witt: THOMAS WRIGHT and A. LUMMUS.

Page 85: April 3, 1826 between WILLIAMSON ROBY of Jasper Co., Ga. and JOHN N. ROBY of Butts Co., Ga. $200. 202 1/2 acres Lot 2 in 9th Dist. of Henry now Butts County. Signed: WMSON ROBY - Witt: L. M. ADAMS, J. M. PEARSON, J.P.

Page 86: Jasper County, August 12, 1826 between WM. M. COCHRAN Newton Co., Ga. and BENJAMIN BLISSET Lot #73 in 4th Dist. of formerly Monroe Co., Ga. and Butts Co., Ga. 202 1/2 acres. Signed WM. M. COCHRAN Witt: T. W. WRIGHT & JAMES BETTS, J.P.

Page 87: Wilkes County, Ga., WILLIAM A. PICKETT to WILLIAM KNIGHT Monroe Co., Ga. now in the Co. of Butts Lott #177, 3rd Dist. (drawn by ABNER PIGGOT of Wilkes Co. and Willis' Dist.) 202 1/2 acres, June 18, 1826. WILLIAM PICKETT, JOHN HOLIDAY, Witt: and CONSTATINE CHURCH, J.P.

Page 88: Wilkes County, Ga., WILLIAM A. & GEORGE P. PICKETT & REBECCA HENLY formerly REBECCA RICKETT, heirs of ABNER RICKETT, dec'd., otherwise called ABNER PIGGOT. and I. LENOV (?) PICKETT, widow and relict of said ABNER, representing the above lot of land, with GEORGE P. PICKETT our true and lawful attorney, given authority to dispose of it. December 1, 1825. SUSAN PIGGOTT - REBECCA HENLY & WM. P. PEGGOT. Witt: ALLEN P. RICE, WILLIAM L. WILKINS, & NATH BURGAMY. CONSTATINE CHURCH, J.P.

Page 89: Baldwin County, Ga., December 6, 1825. The above family of ABNER PICKETT & WILLIAM KNIGHT still involved with Lot #177.

Page 91: Butts County, Ga., July 11, 1826 between PLEASANT DRAKE and BURWELL BRIDGES of Butts County, Ga. $50. Lot #185 of 5th Dist. formerly Henry now Butts Co., Signed: PLEASANT DRAKE. Wit: WYLIE FOSSILL & JOHN LLOYD, J.P.

Page 92: Butts Co., Ga. March 18, 1826 between ELIJAH MCMICHAEL and the Trustees of the Baptist Church at Sandy Creek for $10. for 2 1/2 acres Lot #31 in the 14th Dist. Signed: ELIJAH MCMICHAEL - Wit: BRITTON ADAMS & L. M. ADAMS, J.P.

Page 93: Butts County, Ga., August 24, 1826. REASON E. MABRY & JOHN HENDRICK. $110. Lot $225 and 256 of 27 1/2 acres, 8th Dist. of orig. Henry, now Butts. Signed: REZIN E. MABRY - Wit: JOHN GOODMAN and SAMUEL LOVEJOY.

Page 94: Laurens Co., Ga. March 3, 1824. JACKSON HAMMOCK and SAMUEL G. BROWN, county of Jefferson, Ga. $200. 202 1/2 acres Dist. #1. Signed: JACKSON HAMMOCK Witt: JACOB W. GOODOWN (GOAWDOWN?) and JOHN B. HUDSON. JOHN JORDON, J.P., September 2, 1826.

Page 95: Wilkes Co., Ga., September 5, 1826 between ARCHIBALD BRYANT and ABRAM M. JACKSON, Clark County, Lot #105, $600 1st. Dist. of Henry now Butts County. Witt: JAMES BLAKELY & HARTWELL JACKSON, JR. - M. S. DENT, J.P. Signed: ARCHIBALD BRYANT.

Page 95: September 20, 1824 between WILLIAM HOLIFIELD and REBECCA HOLIFIELD, his wife for $600 unto JOSEPH CAMPBELL 3rd. Dist. County of Monroe, Ga. Lot 244, containing 202 1/2 acres. Witt: YELVERTON THAXTON and ARCHIBALD JOHNSON, J.P. Signed: WILLIAM HOLIFIELD & REBECCA HOLI-FIELD.

Page 98: Henry County, Ga., ANN C. SPEAKE, same Co. to her daughter MARGARET TATE SPEAKE, a negro woman Dolly, and her boy Claborn, never

to be sold out of MARGARET SPEAKE'S Family, December 28, 1824. Signed:
ANN C. SPEAKE Witt: JESSE JOLLY & GEORGE T. SPEAKE. WILLIAM BARKLEY,
J.P.

Page 99: Jasper County - January 19, 1826, between GEORGE W. KEY
of Jackson Co., Ga. and WILLIAM BARKLEY, Butts formerly Henry County,
$200. 9th Dist. Lot #36 75 3/4 acres. Signed: GEORGE W. KEYES. Witt:
WM. ASKEW, LUKE JOHNSON. Butts Co., Ga.

Page 100: Hall County, Ga. WILLIAM HODGE same Co. his atty.
ALEXANDER HODGE, Lot #12, 4th Dist. of Monroe Co., Ga. Feb. 16, 1825.
Signed: WM. HODGE Witt: JOHN COTTON & JOHN MCELHANON. Jas. K. OLIVER,
J.P. April 19, 1825

Page 100: Hall Co. April 19, 1825 between WILLIAM HODGE and JOSEPH
T. CUNNINGHAM County of Jackson, $92. Land in the Co. of Monroe, 4th
Dist. Lot #12, (drawn by WM. HODGE of Scotts Dist. of Jackson Co.).
Signed: WILLIAM HODGE & ALEXANDER HODGE, Atty. and Witt: SAM'L K.
OLIVER and ISAAC WHORTON, J.P.

Page 102: Wilkes County, Ga., Feb. 25, 1822, JAMES ECHOLS, Agent
for BENJ. ECHOLS and WILLIAM WILLINGHAM, Lincoln Co., Ga. $400. 202 1/2
acres Henry Co. 5th Dist. Lot #40. Signed: JAMES ECHOLS, Agt. for
BENJ. ECHOLS. Witt: B. W. HUBBARD & P. M. COLLIER, J.P.

Page 103: July 11, 1826 Butts County, Ga. between PLEASANT DRAKE
and SMITH BARREN Butts Co. for $120. Lot #185, 1st. Dist. orig. Henry
now Butts County. Signed: PLEASANT DRAKE - Witt: WYLIE FERRILL & JOHN
LLOYD, J.P.

Page 104: Henry County, Dec. 21, 1824 between THOS. ROBINSON &
JAMES REEVES, the former of Henry Co., and the latter of Jasper County.
$1500. 1st Dist. Lot #199, 202 1/2 acres (granted to AQUILLA PHELPS
and from PHELPS to ROBINSON). Witt: JESSE CLAY, A. L. ROBINSON, J.P.
THOS. ROBINSON. Signed. Akn in presence of HENRY JACKSON, J.P.
9-25-1826 SARAH ROBINSON, Wife.

Page 105: January 26, 1825, between THOMAS PERSONS and WILLIAM
ALLISON both of Henry County, Ga. for $250. 202 1/2 acres, 9th Dist. of
Henry, Lot #591. Signed: THOS. PERSONS. Witt: ALEX. ALLISON & WM.
KITCHEN, JOS. KEY, J.P., Dec. 10, 1825

Page 106: Putnam County, Ga. April 17, 1824 between WM. T. PARKER,
Putnam Co. and JAMES MCLEROY, Jasper Co., for $100 in Henry Co. 1st.
Dist. Lot #175 202 1/2 acres. Signed: WILLIAM T. PARK. Witt: THOS.
HARDIMAN, JOE M. DUNN, J.P.

Page 107: January 12, 1826 between JAMES MCLEROY Jasper Co. and
THOMAS S. PEARSON, $300.50, in Henry Co. 1st. Dist. Lot 175, 202 1/2
acres. Signed: JAS. MCLEROY. Witt: J. M. PEARSON and JAMES BETTS,
J.J.C. Wife: SARAH MCLEROY.

Page 109: Butts Co., Ga. September 30, 1826 between THOS. G. PER-
SONS (PEARSON) and GREEN L. HOLLY of Walton County, Ga. $612.50, orig.
Henry now Butts 1st. Dist. Lot 175. Signed: THOMAS G. PEARSON - Witt:
MORTON BLEDSOLL & ABEL L. ROBINSON, Clk.

Page 110: Montgomery County, Ga., JOHN FREVASK of Tatnall County,
Ga. son SION FREVEASK same Co. his Atty, for land in Monroe Co. 14th
Dist. Lot #74, Jan. 10, 1826. Signed: JOHN TREVASK - Witt: JACOB
TAYLOR, J. G. CONNOR, J.J.C.

Page 110: Monroe County, Ga., January 18, 1826 between JOHN FIVEASH
and son SION FIVEASH (your guess is as good as mine) of Montgomery Co,
SION acting as agent for JOHN FIVASH and GIDEON TANNER for $400. Lot
#74 in 14th Dist. of Monroe Co. Signed: SION FIVEASH & JOHN FIVEASH.
Witt: JOHN TOWNS & ROLLINS SMITH, J.P.

Page 111: Putnam County, Ga., May 11, 1826 between JAMES BRYANT and JOHN CAPPS of Henry Co. $300. Dist. #9 Henry Co., on the Ocmulgee River, bounded by land belonging to ELLIS, ARCHOLS, MOONEY, LEMON & STROUD 152 1/2 acres, Lot 75 except 50 acres granted to MCCALL. Signed: JAMES BRYANT. Wife: MARY BRYANT. Witt: C. BUSTIAN, JOHN D. STEVENS & NATH. HARRISON, J.P.

Page 113: Monroe County, Ga., Sept. 1, 1826 between WILLIAM B. CLARK of Butts Co. and ZADOCK LOVE (or Lane, diff. to read) Lot #23 in Dist. 4 of Butts Co., formerly Monroe Co., 200 acres for $200. Signed: WM. B. CLARK. Wit: EZRA MORRISON, JOHN HAYNES, J.P.

Page 114: Butts County, Ga., Jan. 20, 1826 between BENJAMIN F. CHIN (?) of Richmond Co. and SAMUEL L. BRYANS of Henry County, Lot #47 cont. 202 1/2 acres in 9th District. Witness: HENRY PORTER.

Page 115: December 22, 1825, ALLEN B. POWELL of McIntosh Co., Ga. and CHARLEY J. MCDONALD of Bibb County, Ga. for $200, Lot No. 80 in 1st District of Henry County. Wit: FRANCIS M. SCARLETT (or Scostett) and JAMES M. D. KING.

Page 116: Henry County, Ga., Oct. 7, 1825 bet. ROLAND WILLIAMS and URIAH TYALOR of same county for $1200 Lot #50 in 9th. Dist. Wit: JOHN R. CARGILE, JOHN BANKSTON, JOS. KEY, J.P. and also JOSIAH HARDY, JOSEPH BENTON.

Page 118: Butts County, Ga., Oct. 13, 1825 bet. JOHN BANKSTON and URIAH TAYLOR for $200, 50 acres being Lot #50 in the 9th District. Signed: JOHN BANKSTON. Wit: JOHN R. CARGILE, JOSIAH HARDY, JOSEPH BENTON, SR., JOS. KEY, J.P.

Page 119: Sept. 15, 1824 between ROLAND WILLIAMS of Henry County and JOHN BANKSTON for $100, 50 acres in 9th District, Lot #50. Wit. WM. SPEER, JOHN G. WILLIAMS, WILLIAM BARKLEY, J.P.

Page 120: Butts County, July 8, 1826 between URIAH TAYLOR and JOSIAH HARDY for $1500, Lot #50 cont. 202 1/2 acres in 9th Disttrict of Butts, formerly Henry Co. Wit. E. T. SPEAKE, ISHAM FREEMAN.

Page 121: May 21, 1820 between IRVIN H. DAVIS of Wilkes County and ROWLAND WILLIAMS of Jasper County, Ga., Lot #50 in 9th Dist. of Henry Co. Wit: M. HENDERSON, ELIJAH PHILIPPS, J.P.

Page 122: Bibb County, Ga., June 21, 1826 between MARTIN WHITE-HEAD & ROBERT SHARP for $150 Lot #53 in 9th District of Butts Co. cont. 202 1/2 acres. Wit: JOHN MCALLISTER, DANIEL WADSWORTH, J.P.: SARAH WHITEHEAD, wife of MARTIN WHITEHEAD.

Page 123: Monroe County, Ga., June 22, 1825 bet. JOHN M. PEARSON and DANIEL M. PEARSON of Jasper County for $250, 185 acres being Lot 80 in 14th District of Monroe County. Wit: POLLY HILL, ENOCH PEARSON.

Page 125: Butts County, THOS. NAPIER, WILES B. ECTOR of Eatonton, Putnam Co., Ga. (firm of NAPIER & ECTOR) 1821, ECTOR indebted to the firm for $4000, son and Agent, THOS. T. NAPIER. Paid in full August 12, 1820. Signed: NAPIER. (Editor's note: see Meriwether Co., Ga. records for a WILEY B. ECTOR.)

Page 126: Jasper County, November 3, 1825 bet. JOSEPH MARSHBURN of Jasper County and ISHAM HUCKABY of Jasper Co., for $300 in Monroe County, Ga., 202 1/2 acres drawn by DAVID OWENS of Knoxes Dist. in Jackson Co., Ga. Wit: HOLLIS COOLEY, THOS. BEALL, J.P. Signed: JOSEPH MARSHBURN.

Page 127: Butts County, Dec. 20, 1824 between CHLOE FANNIN of Morgan Co., Ga. and THOMAS BLOODWORTH for $32, County of Monroe, Ga. and 14th Dist. Lot No. 17 cont. 202 acres. Wit: ROBT. GUTHRIE, WM. W. CARLISLE.

Page 128: April 18, 1826 Butts County, GEORGE BUTTON, $150 on Little Sandy Creek half Lot 78. AMOS GAREY, PRYOR EDWARDS, JOHN W. PEARSON. Signed: GEORGE BRITTON.

Page 129: Butts County, March 9, 1826 between SAMUEL J. BRYANT of Newton Co., Ga. and WILLIAM BARKLEY of Butts Co., for $300, Lot #47 in 9th District originally Henry County, now Butts cont. 202 acres, drawn by B. F. CHEWS of Chatham Co., Ga. and transferred to S. J. BRYAN. Wit: JOHN SIMMONS, FERNINAND SMITH, JOSEPH KEY, J.P.

Page 130: Butts Co., June 2, 1820 between JOHN CANNON and WILSON BRACKET for $350 Lot #29 cont. 202 1/2 acres on Sandy Creek originally Monroe County, Ga. but now Butts Co. and 14th District, granted to THOS. CUTHBERT of Columbia City, Ga. Wit: AVINGTON WILLIAMS.

Page 131: Butts Co., Ga., BETHENA CANNON, wife of JOHN CANNON, relinquishes her claim of power on June 3, 1826.

Page 131: Butts County, Ga. Jan. 4, 1826 between PLEASANT MOORE of formerly Henry County, now Butts and ROBERT SHARP of Jasper County for $1075, Lot #52 in 9th. District cont. 202 1/2 acres. Wit: JAS. KING, THOS. BENTON, JNO. R. CARLISLE, J.J.C. Signed: PLEASANT MOOR.

Page 133: Butts Co., ELIZ MOORE, wife of PLEASANT MOORE renounced all claim of power on the death of her husband, this 24 January 1826.

Page 133: Monroe County, Ga., Court of the Co. of Baldwin, Ga. at the suit of Administrators of JOHN TROUTMAN, deed against F. M. BUTLER and WM. O. PRATT, Sheriff 1824, a public sale in Monroe Co. Highest bidder was PETER STUBBS for $235, July 6, 1824.

Page 135: Georgia, Baldwin Co., March 9, 1825 between PETER STUBBS and BENJAMIN GACHET of Jones County, for $235 for 202 1/2 acres in Dist. of Monroe Co., Lot # 206. Signed: P. STUBBS, wife ANN. Wit. JAS. E. GATCHET, H. ALLEN, J.J.C.

Page 136: September 3, 1825 between LEWIS JONES of Franklin Co., Ga. and BOLIN SMITH of Monroe Co. for $800, 202 1/2 acres in 4th Dist. of Monroe, Ga. Lot #200. Nov. 24, 1823. Wit: JAMES RAMSEY, JONATHAN L. RAMSEY. Signed: LEWIS JONES.

Page 136: Franklin Co., Ga., SARAH JONES relinquishes her dowry.

Page 137: Jan. 4, 1826 between JAMES ANDERSON of Columbia Co., Ga. and WM. HUGHS of Wilkes County for $110 for 202 1/2 acres in 1st. Dist. of Henry now Butts Co. Ga., Lot #91. Wit: PATRICK J. BARNETT, THOS. LASLEY, J.P. Signed: JAMES ANDERSON.

Page 139: January 4, 1820 between WM. HUGHS of Wilkes Co. and JOS. SUMMERLIN of Butts County for $110, 202 1/2 acres in 1st. District of Henry Co. Wit: JAS. HEARD, G. H. HUGHES, J.P.

Page 140: Butts County, Oct. 27, 1826 between PLEASANT DRAKE and LUKE ROBINSON, both of Henry County, for $380, Lot 185 in 1st. Dist. of Henry now Butts Co. cont. 127 1/2 acres.

Page 141 & 142: Building a jail, approved by JOHN R. CARGILE, JOHN HENDRICK, YELVERTON THAXTON, ELI CONGAR and WILIE B. ECTOR. Page 143: Still about Jail, with WM. HITCHCOCK and STOCKBY MORGAN, Oct. 9, 1826. GEO. BARBER, W. H. CAY.

Page 144: Oglethorpe Co., Ga., Nov. 4, 1825 bet. BENNETT MARTIN and JOEL TARPLEY, both of the county, for $100, land drawn in the Co. of Hneyr by JAMES TYE in Land Lottery, Lot 122 in 1st District of Henry Co. Wit: ROBT. W. TARPLEY, JAMES TARPLEY, J.P. Signed: BENNETT MARTIN.

Page 143: Dec. 20, 1825. WM. C. PARKER and JONATHAN NUTT for $500 in Henry Co. Lot #116 in 1st. District on Yellow Water Creek, 202 1/2 acres to JOHN WHITTAKER. WIT: SAM. R. NUTT, ROBT. BROWN. Signed: WM. C. PARKER, wife NANCY PARKER of Morgan Co.

Page 144: Butts Co., Ga., Nov. 20, 1825 between JONATHAN NUTT and WM. HAMILTON for $600, Lot 117 granted to JOHN WHITTAKER cont. 202 1/2 acres. Wit: JOS. CARMICHAEL, JAMES HARKNESS. Signed: JONATHAN NUTT, wife ELINOR.

Page 146: Oct. 25, 1825 between JAMES FARLEY of Jasper County and BLANY MEEKS of Gwinett Co., for $300, Lot #26 in 4th Dist. Monroe Co., drawn by BLANEY MEEKS. Wit. HENRY D. PAIN, I. SIMMS.

Page 148: Chatham Co., Ga., 1822, ELISA ANN TUTHILL sells to GEORGE SCHLEY of City of Savannah for $300, Lot #71 in 4th Dist. of Monroe Co. cont. 102 1/2 acres. Wit: ISABEL HARVE, DAVID PALACK. Signed ELIZA ANN TUTHILL.

Page 150: Monroe Co., May 19, 1826 between GEORGE SCHLEY of City of Savannah and County of Chatham, Ga. to WM. HADEN of Butts Co., Lot 71 in 4th Dist. of Monroe Co., Ga. cont. 202 1/2 acres drawn by the widow ELIZA ANN TUTHILL of Savannah, widow of MILLS, and conveyed to GEORGE SCHLEY.

Page 152: Butts Co., Ga., Nov. 25, 1823 between JAMES SMYTH and PHINEAS KELL of Henry Co. for $200, Lot #166 cont. 202 1/2 acres in 8th. Dist., in the same lot drawn by JAMES SMITH KITTLE. Wit: JAMES HOLLOWAY, DAVIS SMITH, J.J.C. Signed: JAMES SMITH.

Page 153: May 12, 1802 between JOHN F. SMITH of Chatham Co. by his Atty. SAMUEL J. BRYAN and JESSE LANE, Lot 82 in 4th Dist. Monroe Co. cont. 202 1/2 acres, drawn in Lottery by JOHN F. SMITH. CHAS. KENNAN, JOHN T. SMITH by Atty. SAML. J. BRYAN, JOHN SMITH, J.P.

Page 155: Newton County, Ga. Oct. 20, 1826 between SAMUEL J. BRYAN and ZEKE LAW (Might be JESSE) for $200, Lots 81 & 82 in 4th Dist. of Monroe Co. and covers 202 1/2 acres. Wit: CHAS. KINMON, JOHN SMITH, J.P. Signed: SAMUEL J. BRYAN.

Page 156: Newton County, Oct. 12, 1826, MRS. ELIZABETH BRYAN, wife of SAMUEL J. BRYAN relinquishes her dowry in the 2 lots sold to ZEKE LAW.

Page 156: Monroe Co., Ga. July 16, 1824 between SAMUEL BRADY, formerly of Wilkinson County, but now of Bibb Co., Ga. and SAMUEL J. BRYAN for $200 for 202 1/2 acres in the 4th Dist. of Monroe Co., drawn in Land Lottery held 1821 in Milledgeville, Ga. by SAMUEL BRADY. Wit: EDWARD HICKS, THOMAS GASTON, J.P. Signed: SAMUEL BRADY.

Page 158: Monroe Co., Ga., Dec. 29, 1823, between JOHN C. WILLS and NATHAN ELLIS of Henry County for $250 for the South half of the parcel of land or 1st. Dist. of Henry Co. Lot #50. Wit: STEPHEN BARKWELL, ELIJAH PHILLIPS, J.J.C. Signed: JOHN C. WILLIS.

Page 158: Butts Co., Ga. Feb. 20, 1826 between JACOB ENGTEL (or ENGLUT) of Richmond Co., Ga. and NATHANIEL ELLIS of Butts Co., for $300, half of Lot #50 in 1st. formerly Henry, now Butts County (being the North half of South Lot) adj. HARPER and BLISSIT. Wit: JAMES BRADY, ELI CONGER, J.J.C. Signed: JACON ENGLUT.

Page 159: Butts County, Ga., March 28, 1826 between THOMAS KENNY and HENRY J. BAILEY for $350 for 100 acres in Butts Co., formerly Monroe Co., West side of Cobbin Creek, part of Lot 211, 3rd. Dist., land bring drawn by THOMAS KENNY form Gov. GEORGE M. TROOP. Wit: BECK BAILEY, ZELVERTON THAXTON, J.J.C. MARY KENNY, wife of THOMAS KENNY renounces and relinquishes her claim on the land. Signed: MARY KENNY.

Page 161: Morgan County, Ga., SAMUEL WILKERSON - $300. Full payment for land in the 4th Dist. of Monroe Co., now Butts, part of the Dist. Lot #72, bounded North by Lot #47, South by #77, East by #71 and West by #73. (Note: The Lottery book shows it should be bounded North by 37, South by 73, West by 71), Jan. 4, 1826. Wit: MATTHEW CAMPBELL, BOOKER LAWSON, J.P. Signed by ABSALOM BARNES.

Page 162:   Warren Co., Ga. JOSEPH LEONARD, Administrator of JOHN WILLSON, dec'd. late of sd. Co., first Tuesday in October 1825, at Court House, County of Henry, Georgia. Lot 35, 2nd Dist., cont. 202 1/2 acres were knocked off to ALBERT G. BUNKLEY for $354. Oct. 28, 1825 between JOSEPH LEONARD, Admn. and CELIA WILLSON, wife of JOHN WILLSON. WILLIAM SELL, J.P.

Page 164:   Butts Co., Ga. Suit of A & E MCCLENDON, Executor of ISAAC MCLEONDON, dec'd. agst. DAVID LAWSON, admn. of ADAM LAWSON, decd. ISAAC NOLEN, Sheriff did seize the fraction of land deserted, as the property of ADAM LAWSON (dec'd.) Dec. 5, 1826 and sold at public sale, WILLIAM BARKLEY, highest bidder, bought at the sum of $70, the parcel of land in Butts Co., North Dist. of formerly Henry, now Butts Co., Ga. Lot #55 cont. 83 acres. Signed: A. L. ROBINSON, Clk. of Superior Ct. Butts Co.   Signed: ISAAC NOLEN, Sheriff.
   Also - GEORGE T. SPEAKE buys at public outcry, land in 9th Dist. of Cutts Co. Wit: WILLIAM BLAYLOCK, WILLIAM BARKLEY, J.P.

Page 167:   Butts County, Ga., WILLIAM BLAYLOCK bought more of the land Dec. 5, 1826. Wit: GEORGE T. BLAYLOCK, GEORGE T. SPEAKE.

Page 168:   Butts Co., Ga., June 29, 1826 between PHINEAS KELL and MAJOR STANLEY of same Co. for $400, 202 1/2 acres in 8th Dist. formerly Henry, now Butts Co., Dist/ 166, drawn in Lottery in name of JAMES SMITH, of Killery Dist., Wilkinson Co. Wit: JOHN HARPER, HUGH HAMIL, JAMES BRADY, J.P. Signed: PHINEAS KELL.

Page 169:   Walton County, Ga., Jan. 19, 1824 between JOSEPH BROOKS, WALTON County and SAMUEL BELLAH of Monroe Co. for $100, Lot 242 lying in 3rd. Dist. of Monroe Co., Ga., drawn by MARTIN DANIEL, lying in the waters of Towaliga Creek cont. 202 1/2 acres. Wit: ALLEN ROBERTS, ROBT. MCECHOLS, J.P.

Page 170:   Henry Co., Ga., Jan. 21, 1826 between CHAS. HULSEY and JAMES CLAYTON for $350, one half of land in 8th. Dist. of Henry Co., now Butts Co., part of Lot #221 cont. 101 1/4 acres bounded by MASONS. Wit: JAMES FLETCHER, WILLIAM PATE, JAMES KIMBROUGH, J.P. Signed: JAMES HULSEY.

Page 171:   Butts Co., Dec. 12, 1826 bet. STEPHEN KIGHT and JOHN BROWN, JR., both of Butts Co., formerly Henry Co. for $200, 103 acres in 9th Dist. Lot #39 to JOHN BROWN, JR. Wit: RICHARD SPEAKE, WM. BARKLEY, J.P. Signed: STEPHEN KIGHT.

Page 172:   March 19, 1826 between SAMUEL LEE of Gwinnett Co., Ga. and HENRY LEE of Henry Co., Ga. $200 for 202 1/2 acres in 1st. Dist. of Henry Co., Lot #161. Wit: EDWARD LEE, JESSE CORBET. Signed: SAMUEL LEE.
   JANE G. LEE, wife of SAMUEL LEE, does declare she voluntarily release unto the sd. HENRY LEE, her claim of dower in the land sold March 19, 1826.

Page 174:   Butts Co., Ga., March 10, 1826, between JAMES GRAY, JR. of Newton Co., Ga. and MICAJAH FERRELL of Henry Co., originally, now Butts Co., $200 for 202 1/2 acres in 1st. Dist., Lot #131. Wit: WM. M. THOMPSON, SHELBY DAWNS, J.P. Signed: JAMES GRAY, JR., wife ELIZABETH GRAY.

Page 175:   Jasper Co., Ga., Dec. 18, 1826 between ZACHARIAH WILLIAMS and THOMAS ROBINSON both of the 1st. Dist. of Henry Co., Lot #206 and 202 1/2 acres. Wit: LUKE WILLIAMS, ABEL L. ROBINSON, Clk. Ct. of Butts Co. Signed: ZECHARIAH WILLIAMS.

Page 176:   Butts Co., Ga. Oct. 3, 1826, SAMUEL NUTT, SR. to WM. B. NUTT for $200, 1/2 of Lot #136 in 1st. Dist. of Henry Co., now Butts Co. Wit: JOHN BARKLEY, SAMUEL NUTT, JR. and EZEKIEL WALKER, J.P. Signed: SAML. NUTT, SR.

Page 177:   Dec. 16, 1822 between JOHN GLENN of Monroe Co., Ga.

and WILLIAM MCWHORTER of same Co., $114 for Lot #240 in Dist. 3 cont. 67 1/2 acres. Wit: SAMUEL BELLAH, DOLPHIN LINSEY, NEEDHAM LEE, J.P.

Page 178: Morgan Co., Ga., 1826 between SAMUEL WILKERSON and MATTHEW CAMPBELL for $100, Lot #72 in 4th Dist. formerly Monroe Co., now Butts Co., adjacent to Lot #67. Wit: WILLIAM BLAYLOCK, BOOKER LAWSON, J.P. Signed: SAMUEL WILKERSON.

Page 180: Jan. 1, 1824 between JEPHTHAR BRAMLEY and MCWHORTER both of Georgia and MCWHORTER of Monroe Co., for $220, dated Dec. 8, 1821 for 202 1/2 acres. Test: MICAJAH PERRY, GEORGE B. WAGGONER, HENRY HIGHT, J.J.C. Signed: JEPHTHAT BRAMLEY.

Page 180: August 5, 1823 between THOMAS ROBINSON of Jasper Co., Ga. and SAMUEL NUTT of Henry Co., Ga., for $400 for Lot 136 on Yellow Water Creek. Signed: THOS. ROBINSON. Wit: JOHN PRICE, ELI CONGOR, J.J.C.

Page 181: Butts Co., Ga., Jan. 2, 1827, SAMUEL R. NUTT and JOHN MCMICHAEL of Butts Co. for $510 paid by MCMICHAEL, for 1/2 of Lot 136 South side of Lot 121, cont. 104 1/4 acres in 1st. Dist. of Henry now Butts Co. Wit: ABEL L. ROBINSON, JOHN R. CARGILE, J.J.C. Signed: SAMUEL R. NUTT.

Page 182: Butts Co., Ga., Dec. 24, 1826 between JOHN M. FAULKNER and LUKE ROBINSON of Butts Co., for $312 for Lot #86 cont. 202 1/2 acres in Dist. ___. Signed: JOHN M. FAULKNER. Wit: JOHN FAULKNER, JAMES BETTS, J.P.

Page 183: Aug. 5, 1823 between LUKE ROBINSON of Henry Co., Ga. and SAMUEL NUTT of Jasper Co., Ga. for $600 for Lot #54 on Waters of Yellow Water Creek in 1st. Dist. of Henry Co. Wit: JOHN PRICE, ELI CONGER, J.J.P. Signed: LUKE ROBINSON.

Page 184: Butts Co., Ga., Dec. 26, 1826 between THOS. ROBINSON and MATTHEW GASTON for $550, lot #153 in 1st. Dist. of Henry Co. now Butts Co., granted to PRUDENCE PHILLIPS of Pulaski Co., Ga. Wit: JOHN ROBINSON, ABEL L. ROBINSON, Clk. Sup. Ct. Butts Co. Signed: THOMAS ROBINSON (Note, lot cont. 202 1/2 acres).

Page 185: May 5, 1826, between FREDERICK HERB, City of Savannah, Ga. and LEGGIT ROBINSON for $600 in the 1st. Dist. of Henry Co., Ga. 202 1/2 acres Dist. #137. Witt: JOB W. BOLLS and JAMES EFFINGER JP. Signed: FREDERICK HERB.

Page 186: Chatham Co., Ga. Before JAMES EFFINGER, Esq. appeared Mrs. MARGARET HERB and relinquished her claim on the above land.

Page 187: Emanuel County, Ga. Dec. 9, 1823 between JANE HICKS and SAMUEL HICKS, both of Emanuel County, for $100 in the 14th Dist. of Monroe Co., Ga. Lot 45 of 202 1/2 acres drawn by JANE HICKS in Land Lottery of this state. Witt: MARTHA HICKS, WM. RANELAND, CHAS. C. JANKINS, J.P., JANE (her mark) HICKS - A. L. ROBINSON, C.J.C.

Page 188-189-190: July 11, 1823 between GEORGE HERBY of Liberty Stand, Chatham County, Ga. and FREDERICK HERB of Savannah, Ga. Chatham Co. for $250 in Henry Co., 202 1/2 acres in 1st Dist. Lot #137 drawn in the Land Lottery of 1821 by GEORGE HERB. Witt: JOHN DILLON, MOSES CLELAND and PETER BLAKS. Signed: GEORGE HERB & MARY HERB, Wife.

Page 191: Butts Co., Ga. Dec. 26, 1826 between LEGGIT ROBINSON and THOS. ROBINSON, for $1200 1st Dist. of Henry Co., Ga. not Butts Co. Lot #137 of 202 1/2 and granted to HERB (GEO) of Chatham Co., Ga. Witt: ABEL L. ROBINSON, Clk. of Superior Crt., Butts Co. Signed: LEGGET ROBINSON.

Page 192: Butts County, Ga. Jan. 11, 1827 between LUKE ROBINSON and JAMES HARKNESS both Butts Co. for $400. 1st. Dist. of Henry Co. now Butts County, Ga. Lot #86. Witt: ABEL L. ROBINSON, JAMES H. EDWARDS, J.P. Signed: LUKE ROBINSON.

Page 193: Monroe Co., Ga. Mar. 25, 1825 between RICHARD CHESHIRE and DANIEL M. PEARSON, both of Jasper County, Ga. for $135 for 50 acres part of Lot 63 in Dist. of Monroe County, Ga.

Page 194: Jan. 1, 1827 ABEL L. ROBINSON and URIAH TYALOR both of Butts County, Ga. 1st Dist. of orig. Henry now Butts Co., Lot 182 was bought for $1000, containing 202 1/2 acres. Witt: THOS. THORNTON and NEEDHAM LEE J.P.

Page 195: Jasper County, Ga. July 18, 1823 between BENJ. KING and BASDELL POTTER, both from Jasper Co., Lot #81 in 1st. Dist. of Henry Co. containing 202 1/2 acres was sold for $300. Witt: P. L. WEEKS and LEVI DANIEL.

Page 196: Butts County, Ga. Jan. 25, 1827, between JONATHAN NUTT and HUGH MCLINN, for $900 in Henry County at time of survey, 1st Dist. Lot 97, containing 202 1/2 acres granted to ZACH COWARD, Sept. 8, 1823. Witt: J. W. PETTIT, WM. BARKLEY, J.P.

Page 197: Butts County, Ga. Jan. 22, 1827 between ISAAC MCWHORTER and DAVID MCLIN for $250 - 50 acres, Lot #241 in 3rd Dist. formerly Monroe County now Butts County, Ga. Granted to ZEPH PSERNLEY (?). Witt: JNO. V. DUNN.

Page 198: Butts County, Ga. Jan. 24, 1827, between DANIEL TINGLE and ISAAC SMITH for $50, in Henry County when surveyed. Lot #7, 1st Dist. of Henry, now Butts Co. Orig. granted to BETHANY HATCHER. Witt: R. E. CHAPMAN, NEEDHAM LEE, J.P.

Page 199: Newton County, Ga. Feb. 7, 1826 between RICHARD LOSELL and ARMISTEAD BRANCH. Paid $1600 for Lot #207 in the 3rd Dist. of Monroe Co. containing 202 1/2 acres each. Witt: JOHN V. DUNN, JOHN SMITH, J.P.

Page 200: Henry County, HANNAH MATTHEWS, wife of GIDEON MATTHEWS, concerns Lot #76 in 1st Dist. of Henry County. Witt: SAML. BELLAH. Signed: HANNAH.

Page 201: Jasper Co., Ga. Feb. 1, 1827 between THOMAS and ARCHI- BALD SEALS of Warren County, Ga. in Henry County at time of survey, 202 1/2 acres on Lot #109. Witt: SOLOMON GRASS and JESSE LOYALL.

Page 202: Oct. 7, 1822 between ENOCH ROGERS and JOSEPH WASHBURN former of Jackson Co., Ga. latter of Jasper Co., Ga. pays $500 for Lot #41 in the 4th Dist. of Monroe Co., Ga. containing 202 1/2 acres. Witt: BEVERLEY DANIEL with ZEPHPAH WATKINS, J.P.

Page 203: Jasper Co., Ga. Feb. 17, 1826 between ISHAM HICKABY of Jasper Co. and ELI GLOVER who buys 50 acres in the 17th Dist. of Jasper Co., Ga. part of Lot 91, also in the 4th Dist. County of Monroe, Lots 41 containing 202 1/2 acres drawn by DAVID EVANS, of Knox Dist. Jackson County, Witt: JAMES T. HOLMS, JAMES E. BROWN and ISAAC BARLING, J.J.C.

Page 204: DeKalb County, Ga. Jan. 1822, between AARON CLIFTON and GEORGE W. MCGEE of Butts County, Ga. for $200. parcel of land in the County of Henry, now Butts County 1st Dist. CLEMMY F. CLIFTON and GEO. CLIFTON, J.P.

Page 205: Baldwin County, Ga. Nov. 8, 1825 between JAMES HICKS of Emanuel Co., Ga. and HUGH W. ECTOR of Monroe Co., Ga. for the sum of $200. purchased Lot 45, in the 14th Dist. containing 202 1/2 acres, drawn in the late Land Lottery by JAMES HICKS. Witt: JAMES SMITH, R. G. CRIT- TENDON, J.P.

Page 206: Butts County, Ga. Jan. 14, 1826 between WM. W. BOYD and HUGH W. ECTOR both of Butts Co., for $553.75 bought land on the waters of Little Sandy Creek, formerly in Monroe County, 14th Dist. Lot 60 containing 101 1/4 acres, West half of lot. Witt: JAMES CARGILE, WILLIE B. ECTOR & WM. W. BOYT.

Pages 209/210: Butts County, Ga. Dec. 10, (1829?) between ABEL D.
ROBINSON and LUKE ROBINSON both of Butts County. $1200 for negroes,
2 negro women with 2 children each. Witt: JOHN ROBINSON and SAMUEL
STRATHAN.

Page 211: Butts County, Ga. Feb. 20, 1827 between WILSON CROCKETT
and ROBERT SMITH for $300 will purchase the land in the Late Land Lottery
#29 in the 14th Dist. of Monroe Co., Ga., now Butts County bu survey
202 1/2 acres, lying on waters of Sandy Creek. Witt: ELIJAH MCMICHAEL
and HUGH W. ECTOR.

Page 212: Butts Co., March 1, 1826 between JOSEPH SENTELL and
WILLIAM SMITH, State of South Carolina. For $1000, he purchased 202 1/2
acres of land in the 14th Dist. of formerly Monroe County, now Butts Co.,
Lot #45. Witt: LEVI M. ADAMS and ROBERT SMITH.

Page 213: April 20, 1826 between WM. REIMES of Bullock Co., Ga. and
JAMES COBB of Tattnall County, Ga. in Dist. 92 formerly 1st District of
Henry County, for $175. 202 1/2 acres were purchased. This had been
granted to said WILLIAM REIMES January 31, 1824. Witt: JOHN REIMES and
R. T. STANDARD.

Page 214: August 3, 1826 between JAMES COBB, Tattnall County, Ga.
and NATHAN FISH of Jasper County, Ga. for $150. Lot #92 in the 1st
Dist. now Butts County, made to WM. REAMS of Denmark, Ga. Dist. in Bulloch
Co., Ga. January 31, 1824 in Book of Henry County, 1st Dist. page 141,
202 1/2 acres sold by REIMS to JAMES COBB on April 20, 1826. Witt:
HUGH MCDONALD, CALVIN FISH, and BENT CRAWFORD, J.J.C.

Page 215: Butts County, once Monroe County, Ga. Suit of JOHN
ANDREWS and MARTIN HOLLOWAY against JOHN and RICHARD CHESHIRE with ISAAC
NOLEN, Sheriff, adv. and sold publicly April 4, 1826 in Butts County,
Ga. for $54.00 sold to JOHN M. PEARSON. Witt: ELIJAH MCMICHAEL &
JOHN MCBRIDE J.P.

Page 217: Butts County August 25, 1826 between JOHN W. PEARSON and
OBED PERRY. $150. purchased 50 acres (1/4 Lot #63) 14th Dist. formerly
Monroe County, now Butts Co., Ga. Witt: JOHN CHESHIRE, L. M. ADAMS, J.P.

Page 218: Butts County, Ga. Oct. 14, 1826. REAGIN (or REZIN) E.
MABRY and JOHN HENDRICK purchased for $600 in the 8th Dist. of Henry
County, Ga. now Butts County, Ga. the So. half of Lot #254 of 101 1/2
acres. Witt: JOHN GOODMAN, MARY HENDRICK and FRANCIS MILLER, J.P.
(March 13, 1827)

Page 219: Jan. 31, 1827 between JOHN SIMMONS of Butts Co., Ga.
and JOHN SANDERS, Jasper Co., Ga. $1200. 202 1/2 acres of land was sold,
on Lot 63 in the 1st Dist. of orig. Henry Co., now Butts dated Nov. 6,
1823. Witt: MARCUS ROBY and JOHN N. ROBY.

Page 220: Butts County, Ga. JOHN R. CARGYLE, YELVERTON THAXTON.
ELI CONGER, and JOHN HENDRICKS, Justices of Inferior Court, 1826, do
convey to the town of Jackson and the Trustees of the Presbyterian
Church: JOSEPH CARMICHAEL, GEORGE HARKNESS and CHARLES ALLEN, a lot of
land containing 2 acres, Lot No. B. for erecting a Church.

Page 222: Butts County, Ga. March 5, 1827 between JOEL TARPLEY of
Oglethorpe County, Ga. and THOMAS ROBINSON of Butts County, Ga. for $600
sold land drawn by JAMES PYE in the Late Lottery, Lot 122 in Dist. 1
Witt: STARLING CAMP and SAMUEL BELLAH, J.P.

Page 223: Monroe County, Ga. WILLIAM MCWHORTER and SAMUEL BELLAH
of Monroe Co. sell to Baptist Church of Christ at Towilaga, 4 acres of
land Lots 241 and 242 in the 3rd Dist. of Monroe (now Butts Co., Ga)
Oct. 5, 1825. Witt: YELVERTON THAXTON, HUGH HAMIL and GEORGE OWENS.
Signed: WILLIAM MCWHORTER and SAMUEL BELLAH.

Page 225: Butts County, Ga. THOMAS ROBINSON gives to his son ABEL
ROBINSON, several negroes to claim until the death of his wife, SARAH,
SILAS ELLIOTT, J.P.

Page 226: July 31, 1826 between REAGIN E. MABRY, Butts County and JAMES H. ROBERTS, Morgan County, Ga. sold for $450 in the 1st Dist. of originally Henry now Butts County, part of Lot 250. Witt: JOHN MC-CLELLAND, JOHN HENDRICKS, J.J.C.

Page 227: Walton County, Ga. Oct. 8, 1823 between MASON DOROTHY and ROBERT H. WESTON for $100 bought land in Henry Co., Dist. 42. Witt: JAMES BLASINGAME and ROBERT MULLINS. Signed: MASON DOROTHY.

Page 228: Walton Co., Ga. Oct. 8, 1823 between ROBERT H. WESTON and JOHN H. BEARDEN, Walton County, Ga. for $500 sold in the County of Henry Lot 42. Witt: JAMES BLASENGAME and ROBERT MULLINS.

Page 229: DeKalb Co., Ga. 1825 between MASON DOUGHERTY and THOMAS HOUNS of DeKalb County, 50 acres for $50. in the 1st Dist. of Henry County, Ga. (Note: name could be HOUSE, HOUR or HOUN). Witt: JOHN REID and GEORGE CLIFTON, J.J.C.

Page 230: Jasper County, Ga. Dec. 10, 1826 between THOS. "HOUSE, HOUR or HOUN" (see 229) of Henry County and BASTIN or BARTTIN MARTIN, Jasper Co. for $50, for 50 acres in Dist. 42. 1st Dist. of Henry WILLIAM SCOTT, HENRY MURRY and THOMAS HOUSE.

Page 231: Liberty County, Ga. Jan. 7, 1824 between WILLIAM BAKER and CLEMENT MOORE, of Baldwin County, Ga. paid $250, for land in Henry County, Ga. lot 3, 9th Dist. Witt: URIAH WILCOX and THOS. J. SHEPARD, LEWIS HINDS J.P.

Page 232: Monroe County, Ga. Nov. 19, (1825?) between JAMES ANDREWS Paid $75 for 50 acres, located in the 4th Dist. Lot 30, bounded by ROBERT HUMBER, ELIJAH MCMICHAEL and JAMES ANDREWS, JOHN BEDINGFIELD & W. W. BOYT.

Page 233: Butts Co., Feb. 16, 1827 between JAMES HUNT and SARDIS Baptist Church in cosnideration of good will and regard for religion, has given 2 acres of land, part of Lot 230. Witt: RICHARD W. MASON and DANIEL CARTER, FRANCIS MILLER, J.P.

Page 234: Henry County, Ga. Oct. 18, 1824 between WILLIAM L. SMITH, Habersham County, Ga. and THOMAS COOK, Henry County in 1st Dist. Lot 194. Witt: PEGGY FERRILL, JOHN FERRILL, J.P.

Page 235: Henry County, Oct. 17, 1825 between URIAH TAYLOR and ROLAND WILLIAMS, $200 for 202 1/2 acres in the 1st Dist. of Henry Co., Lot 157 and 164. Witt: JOHN CARGILE and JOHN BANKSTON, SILAS ELLIOTT and JOSEPH KEY, J.J.P.

Page 236: Henry County, Feb. 16, 1827 between ROLAND WILLIAMS and BENJAMIN REDMAN, Richmond Co., Ga. bought in Butts Co., originally Henry Co., Ga. 202 1/2 acres in the 1st Dist. of Henry, now Butts County #157, grant dated July 29, 1824. Presence of WILLIAM REDMAN. Signed: ROLAND WILLIAMS with MOSES CASE, J.P.

Page 239: Butts County, Ga. Jan. 24, 1827 between GEORGE WILLIAMSON and JOHN ROBINSON, for $220, buys 1 road wagon and four horses. EZEKIEL WALKER, J.P.

Page 240: Baldwin County, Ga. March 5, 1827 between SEABORN JONES and ALLEN MCCLENDON in Butts County, Ga. 202 1/2 acres in 4th Dist. Lot. #75 originally granted to ISAAC FLUSHING on Towilage River. WILLIAM RUTHERFORD, J.J.C.

Page 242: November 22, 1824 between BENJAMIN MAY and JAMES BUNKLEY $700. Located in 1st Dist. of Henry County, Ga. Signed: BENJAMIN MAYS. Witt: JOHN HENDRICKS & WM. TOOLEY, J.P.

Page 243: Butts County, Nov. 10, 1826 between JOHN WYATT and JOHN WILLIAMSON, for $250 located in 8th Dist. of Henry County, now Butts County, #232, granted to DANIEL MCREES. Witt: JAMES HUNT and WM. HARRISON.

Page 244: Butts County, Ga. between JORDAN McCULERS and JOHN WIL-
LIAMSON, Paid $700 for 202 1/2 acres in the 1st Dist. of formerly Henry
Co. now Butts Co. #250 grant to JOURDAN MCCULERS of Warren County, Ga.
Witt: ELIZABETH HALE and JOHN MOORE, J.P.

Page 245: Butts County, Ga. for love and affection whic I have for
to LORENA MCMICHAEL-a certain red and white cow; the first heifer calf
to SILAS MCMICHAEL, her brother and to MINESA MCMICHAEL, a red heifer
calif with a red face; and the next calf to a son of MATHEWS MCMICHAEL.
July 3, 1826. Signed: MARTHA STEPHENS. Witt: C. C. MONTGOMERY, YEL-
VERTON THAXTON, J.J.C.

Page 246: Butts County, Ga. Dec. 15, 1825. A. L. and L. ROBINSON
of one part, and ARISTOTLE G. DUKE of the other same County $300 for
202 1/2 acres in the 1st Dist. Lot 55. Witt: STEPHEN G. HEARD, WM.
C. PARKER, J.P.

Page 247: Lincoln County, Ga. Feb. 8, 1827 between ALLEN RAMSEY
and ELIZA RAMSEY, his wife and ARISTOTLE DUKE, Butts Co. $300 for 202
1/2 acres, in the 1st. Dist. of Henry Co. now Butts Co., Ga. in Dist.
202. Witt: WESLEY GETER, MARY N. RAMSEY and JOHN KILGORE.

Page 248: Putnam Co., Ga. Nov. 29, 1826 between HUGH FREEMAN and
NEALY MCCOY, of Butts County, Ga. for $400, receives 202 1/2 acres on
Lot 54. 1st Dist. of formerly Henry County, now Butts County, Ga. Witt.
HENRY COATES and LAWRENCE ALLEN, J.P.

Page 249: Butts Co., Feb. 15, 1827 between SAMUEL KIGHT and WILSON
L. LOVEJOY, for $100 for 202 1/2 acres in the 4th Dist. of formerly
Monroe Co., and Butts County, Ga. #79. Witt: R. MOORE and RICHARD
PARKER.

Page 251: Feb. 1, 1827 between JESSE SIMMONS, Hancock Co., Ga. and
ROBERT W. HUNTER, Butts County for $350 for land on Tussahaw Creek,
Butts Co., Ga. 202 1/2 acres, lot 184. Witt: PHILIP TURNER, ROBT.
LUCAS & JESSE LOCKHART, J.J.C.

Page 252: June 2, 1826 between ROBERT BICKERSTAFF, Jasper Co. and
LARKIN TURNER of Butts County, Ga. for $300. for 202 1/2 acres in the
14 Dist. of formerly Monroe Co. now Butts Co., Ga. Dist. 442. Witt:
SARAH BICKERSTAFF, ROBT. BICKERSTAFF, wife NANCY. WM. HANDCOCK, J.P.

Page 254: Jasper Co., Ga. Dec. 14, 1826 between THOMAS MORRIS of
Jasper Co. and GEORGE MCCLAIN of Pike Co., Ga. in the 3rd Dist. of ori-
ginal Monroe Co. now Butts Co., Ga. Dist. 144, $130 for 202 1/2 acres.
Drawn by THOMAS MORRIS and granted Nov. 28, 1826. Witt: WILLIAM HOLT.

Page 255: Pike County, Ga. Dec. 22, 1826 between GEORGE MCCLAIN
and WILLIAM REAVES of Butts Co., Ga. $500 in the 3rd Dist., formerly
Monroe Co., Ga. now Butts Co. Lot 144 containing 101 1/4 acres (So. side)
wife HESTER. Witt: BENJAMIN BROWN and LEVI MARTIN, J.J.C.

Page 256: Jasper Co., Ga. April 12, 1827 between BENJAMIN ELLIS
and ISAAC SMITH of Butts Co. for $650 - 202 1/2 acres in Butts County
orig. 4th Dist. of Monroe, Distinguished by No. 6, originally granted
to BENJ. ELLIS. Witt: HENRY ELLIS and R. WALKER, J.P.

Page 257: Butts County, Ga. May 23, 1826 between ISHAM FREEMAN of
Butts Co. and CHARLES ALLEN $200 for #75 in the Dist of former Henry Co.
now Butts in the presence of WILLIAM LANIER and NANCY SHADRACK and
WILLIAM SHIELDS. WILLIAM BARKLEY, J.P.

Page 258: Butts Co. Feb. 28, 1827 between WILSON & LOVEJOY and
SAMUEL MADDOX of Monroe Co. $414 in the 4th Dist. of orig. Monroe Co.,
now Butts Co. Lot 49. Sgd: WM. L. WILLSON and SIMEON LOVEJOY. Witt:
R. MOORE and HUBBARD WILLIAMS.

Page 259: August 29, 1826 between WILLIAM HADEN of Butts Co. and
SAMUEL MADDOX of Monroe Co., for $600. 102 1/2 acres in the 4th Dist.

of Monroe, last part of No. 77, adj. Lot #78 on the East. Wit: CHAS.
P. WALLER and NEEDHAM LEE, J.P.. MARY S. HADEN, wife of WILLIAM HADEN.

Page 260: Butts Co. May 15, 1827 between JACON LAMB of Monroe Co.,
Ga. and JAMES HARKNESS, 1st Dist. of Henry Co. Drawn and granted to
JOHN PRESCOTT Lot #84 cont. 202 1/2 acres - no amount given: Witt:
R. W. HARKNESS, A. L. ROBINSON, Clk of Court. Sgd. JACOB LAMB.

Page 261: Butts County, Ga. June 10, 1826 between JOSEPH SENTELL
and D. DAVID WALDROP of Jasper Co., Ga. $175 S. half of Lot #94 cont.
101 1/4 acres in originally Monroe Co. now Butts Co., Ga. and 14th Dist.
on the Ocmulgee River. Witt: ROBERT ANDREWS, CURTIS B. ECTOR, J.J.C.
Sgd: JOSEPH SENTELL.

Page 262: Jan. 1. 1827 between JOHN CANNON and BYTHENY CANNON, his
wife and ROBBERT HUMLER, all of Butts Co. for $1000 in the 14th Dist.
formerly Monroe Co., now Butts, Lot #46. Witt: GEORGE PARKER, JOHN
M. PEARSON, JP.

Page 263: Butts Co., Ga. July 12, 1826, ABRAHAM WALDROP and BENJ.
HARELSON both of Butts Co. - for $275 - 87 acres, Lot #94 in 14th Dist.,
formerly Monroe now Butts Co. DAVID WALDROP. Witt: SOLOMON N. RICHARD-
SON. Sgd: ABRAHAM WALDROP.

Page 264: Butts Co., Ga. May 15, 1827 between JACOB LAMB, Monroe
Co. and JAMES HARKNESS of Butts Co., for $200 in the 1st Dist. of
Henry, granted to JOHN PRESCOTT of Henry Co. Lot #84 containing 202 1/2
acres. Witt: R. W. HARKNESS, A. L. ROBINSON, Clk. Sgd: JACOB LAMB.

Page 264: (Lower half) Jasper Co. June 27, 1826 between DAVID
SCARBOROUGH of DOOLY County, Ga. and JOSEPH MCMICHAEL, Jasper Co., Ga.
for $200, in Monroe Co., now Butts Co., Lot #175 and 3rd Dist., 202
1/2 acres. Witt: JUDITH HANCOCK, WM. HANCOCK, J.P.

Page 265: (2 pages) fifas issued out of the Inferior Court of
Walton Co., Ga. at the suit of NELSON RIDGEWAY, against DICKSON PARHAM,
J. ISAAC NOLAN, Sheriff of Butts Co., did lately sieze the lot of land
described as property of DICKSON PARHAM, June 5, 1827, JAMES RIDGEWAY,
highest bidder for $44.75, Dist. 3, formerly Monroe, now Butts Co.
Test: ROBT. W. HARKNESS, A. L. ROBINSON, Clk, Superior Court, ISAAC
NOLAN Sheriff

Page 268: Butts Co., June 2, 1827 between LARKIN TURNER and WM.
SMITH, SR. for $900 in Monroe County at time of survey on Big Sandy Creek
Lot #44 in 1st. Dist. cont. 202 1/2 acres. Witt: J. C. DUNSEITH, LARKIN
ADAMS, JM PEARSON, J.P.

Page 269: May 11, 1827 between JAMES M. DUNN, ADM for GEORGE MADDOX
(decd) and RICHARD LANGFORD, land #59 in 14th Dist. of orig. Monroe Co.
now Butts for $500 (both MEDOWS and MADDOX were used). Witt: BURWELL
KINDRICK, JAMES A. DUNN, ADM and JOHN MCBRIDE.

Page 270: Butts Co. June 15, 1826 between ROLAND WILLIAMS and
CHAS MILLEN Newton Co. for $250, Lot 164, 1st Dist. Henry Co. now Butts
202 1/2 acres. Witt: JESSE GOODWIN, GEORGE WILLIAMSON and E. WALKER,
J.P.

Page 271: For the good will and affection for Dau. HARRIETT BYARS,
I have given one negro girl named MARGIT, 5 yrs. old, Jan. 4, 1827.
Sgd: JOSHUA RICHARDS. Test JOSEPH BYARS and HENRY BYARS. JOSEPH
KEY, J.P.

Page 272: July 3, 1827, Lot 126 against JOSEPH HENDERSON, owner,
sold at public outcry, ZECHARIAH DEASON, being the highest bidder at
$135, by JESSE NOLAN, Sheriff, cont. 126 1/2 acres. 1st Dist. of for-
merly Henry Co. now Butts, lot #126. Witt: AUGUSTIN B. RAPE, ABEL L.
ROBINSON, Clk. I. NOLAN.

Page 273: Henry Co., Ga. Mar. 16, 1825 between SAMUEL STRAHAN and

89

THOMAS ROBINSON for $275 in Monroe Co., Ga. 4th Dist. leading from the Mineral Springs to the High Shoals on the Tolilaga River containing 202 1/2 acres. Lot #34 ABEL L. ROBINSON, ANDREW NUTT, J.P. Sgd: THOS. ROBINSON.

Page 274: Monroe Co., Ga. Sept. 26, 1823 (right) between GEORGE EUBANKS of Monroe Co. for $200 to HENRY EUBANKS - 100 So-half of Lot 21 of the 4th Dist. BERRY EUBANKS. Witt: LEMUEL (or SAMUEL) PARKER, SANDER PARKER, ALFRED WHITE, Aug. 7, 1829.

Page 275: Morgan Co., Ga. July 31, 1826 between JOHN M. DAVENPORT and AMBROS EDWARDS of Abbeville Dist. of S. C. 1st Dist. #75 in Co. of orig. Henry, now Butts Co. 202 1/2 acres for $560. (This deed used 2 whole pages describing notes.) Witt: FRANCIS CONNER, JOHN RICE, RICHARD SMITH, JOHN M. DAVENPORT.

Page 277: Henry Co. Jan. 18, 1826 between GEORGE W. KEY of Jackson Co., Ga. and LEDFORD EDWARDS of Henry Co., for $100 in the 9th Dist. of Henry, Lot 36 granted to GEO. W. KEY, Oct. 27, 1824, containing 56 acres. Witt: JOHN R. CARGILE, STEPHEN KIGHT, and JOSEPH KAY, J.P. Sgd: GEO. W. KEY.

Page 277: (2) Butts Co., July 16, 1827 between LEDFORD EDWARDS and WILLIAM VIKERS for $250, 9th Dist. formerly Henry Co., now Butts Co., Lot 36 cont. 56 acres. Granted to GEORGE W. KEY Oct. 27, 1824. Witt: GEORGE T. SPEAKE, WALLACE W. LEMMONS, JOHN R. CARGILE. Sgd: LEDFORD EDWARDS.

Page 278: Muscogee Co., Ga. June 9th. 1827 between PLEASANT MACON of Muscogee Co and ALLADON WILKINS of Jasper Co. for $250 in the 1st Dist. of Henry, now Butts Co., Dist. 134 cont. 202 1/2 acres. Witt: STEPHEN STEPHENS, ROBERT SHERMAN, J.P. Sgd: PLEASANT MACON.

Page 279: Jefferson Co., Ga. July 16, 1827 between GEORGE EUBANKS SR. of Jefferson Co. for $300 in the County of Butts, 101 1/4 acres, Lot #21 in the 4th Dist. of Monroe Co., now Butts Co. Drawn by LEVI MORTON of Halls Dist. in Jefferson Co. (This was left unfinished in the Deed Book) P. 280.

Page 281: Butts Co., Ga. Richmond Brown, ANDERSON BROWN and CHARLEY RAMEY, May 7, 1827 apply for administration of property of JOHN SMITH, late of Putnam County, Ga.

Page 282: Butts Co., Ga. Oct. 3, 1826 between WILLIAM MOORE and RILEY WISE for $1200. in Monroe Co., Ga. now Butts Co., 202 1/2 acres, granted to GEORGE NEWTON of Screven Co., Lot 3. Witt: P. LINDSEY, E. S. KIRKSEY, P. G. BROGDON and PARHAM LINDSEY J.P.

Page 283: Butts Co., August 16, 1827 between JOHN BROWN, SR. and JOSIAH W. BARBER, $400 for 103 acres, Lot #39 in the 9th Dist. formerly Henry Co. now Butts Co. RICHARD BAILEY, ABEL L. ROBINSON, Clerk of Court.

Page 284: Butts Co., March 5, 1827 between JAMES BLAIR, SR. of Habersham Co., Ga. and ALFRED W. FERGUSON of Butts Co., in the 14th District of Monroe Co., now Butts #77, 202 1/2 acres. JOHN HARKNESS, affirmed by JOHN HAIRSTON and JOHN M. PEARSON, J.P. and LUCINDA FERGUSON.

Page 285: Butts Co. from the Superior Court of Baldwin Co., Ga. a suit by DAVID CRAWFORD against TIMOTHY BREWIN for land, Sept. 1, 1827 at a public sale, Sheriff NOLAN sold to WILLIAM J. HANSELL, highest bidder, for $288. Lot 196, 1st Dist. originally Henry now Butts Co., containing 202 1/2 acres. Sold by SAMUEL CLAY, Sheriff. Witt: JOHN W. A. PETTIT, JOHN HENDRICKS, J.J.C.

Page 286: Butts Co., July 27, 1827 between RICHARD POUNDS and THOMAS ROBINSON, SR., for $700, 101 1/4 acres. Lot 123 in 1st Henry Co. now Butts Co., 1st. Dist. on Yellow Water Creek, originally granted to ALEXANDER MCCLURE. Witt: JAMES H. EDWARDS, BENJAMIN F. TUCKER, J.P. (bottom of page 287).

Page 288: Butts Co., Aug. 3, 1827 between JESSE JOHNSON of Henry
Co. and ALISON MOSELEY of Butts Co. for $300, Lot #198, 8th Dist., orig.
Henry Co. now Butts, 202 1/2 acres. Witt: HENRY SUMMERLIN, TRACY BLAD-
SOE, FRANCIS MILLER, J.P. (Note: The above JESSE JOHNSON is the ancestor
of Pres. Johnson.)

Page 289: Butts Co. Aug. 16, 1827, JOHN BROWN, JR. and JOSEPH W.
BARBER for $400 102 acres, Lot #39 - 9th Dist., formerly Henry Co., now
Butts Co. Test: RICHARD BAILEY, A. L. ROBINSON, Clerk of Court. Sgd.:
JOHN BROWN X.

Page 290: Butts Co. Sept. 8, 1826 between JOHN ROOKS of Putnam Co.,
and WILLIAM PLAYLOCK of Butts Co., for $550, in the 9th Dist. formerly
Henry Co. now Butts Co. #27. Witt: JONATHAN HARKAMP, JOHN R. CARGILE,
JOHN ROOKS, wife WINNEY ROOKS.

Page 291: Nov. 1826, GEO. W. WRIGHT, Jasper Co. and JOEL WISE, for
consideration of $300 for 54 1/4 acres, #33 in 9th Dist., orig. HENRY,
now Butts on the Ocmulgee River. Witt: JOHN MALONE, JOHN HOLMES &
JOHN MALCOM.

Page 292: Butts County, Ga. Aug. 18, 1827 between JOHN K. CAUSEY
and THOMAS COOK, for $124, in the 1st Dist. of orig. Henry Co. now Butts
Co., part of Lot 227 of 101 1/2 acres by Tussahaw Creek. Witt: Henry
JACKSON, WILLIAM ROLLANS.

Page 293: Butts Co., Ga. Aug. 18, 1827 between JAMES HUNT and
RICHARD HARPER of Elbert Co., Ga. for $162 in County of Henry, now Butts
Co., Ga. Granted to WM. W. JORDAN, #217, 8th Dist. of orig. Henry Co.
now Butts Co. 202 1/2 acres. Witt: SAMUEL MOORE, WM. ROLLANS, J.P.

Page 294: Charlton Co., Ga. WILLIAM A. BLACK, have appointed
AZARIAS DOSS of Walton Co., Ga. as my true and lawful attorney for me,
to purchase a certain tract of land in Henry County, Ga. Lot #51, 1st
Dist. this 10th day of Dec. 1822. Witt: W. W. BLACK, and GEORGE L.
COPE, J.J.C.C.C.

Page 294: #2 Butts Co., Ga. at the suit of WILLIAM RAMSEY vs
GEORGE T. SPEAKE, I, ISAAC NOLEN, Sheriff, did lately sieze after being
duly and publicly advertised agreeably to law, August 7th, 1827, did by
public sale, in Butts County, when WILLIAM BLALOCK, being the highest
bidder, bought for $143.75, land situated in the County of Butts formerly
Henry Lot #96, in the 7th Dist. Sgd: ISAAC NOLAN, Sheriff, SAMUEL K.
MCLIN, ABEL L. ROBINSON, Clerk.

Page 296: Monroe Co., Ga. JAMES GRESHAM for $125. Paid by GIDEON
WHITLOCK of S. C. and District of Chester, do sell all that plantation,
and part of the land containing 100 1/4 acres being the S. side of Lot
#5, in the 4th Dist. of Monroe County, Lot 54, Dec. 1825. Witt: HENRY
HEAD & WILLIAM WHITTED. Sgd: JAMES GRESHAM.

Page 297: Butts County, Ga. Sept. 7, 1827, between SAMUEL CLAY
and WILLIS HOLEYFIELD (HOLIFIELD) both of Butts Co., for $350 in orig.
Henry now Butts Co., Ga. 1st. Dist. Lot #76 cont. 101 1/4 acres, East
half of Lot. Witt: ABEL L. ROBINSON, JOHN MCMICHAEL, J.J.C. Sgd:
SAMUEL CLAY.

Page 298: Butts County, Ga. Sept. 7, 1827 between SAMUEL CLAY and
SAMUEL R. NUTT, for $250 in Butts Co., orig. Henry Co., Ga. in the
1st Dist. 1/2 Lot 76 cont. 101 1/2 acres. Witt: ABEL L. ROBINSON and
JOHN MCMICHAEL.

Page 299: #2 Butts Co., Ga. Sept. 8, 1827 between JOHN J. SMITH
& WILLIAM A. MCCUNE both of Butts Co., for $525 in orig. Henry Co. now
Butts, in the 9th Dist. Lot #25 cont. 202 1/2 acres. Witt: J. M. PEARSON
J.P., GULLUM PRESTON & WILLIAM C. FERRILL.

Page 299: (1) Henry Co., Ga. Dec. 27, 1824 between GEORGE AUSBUM
(GEO. ORSBUM) I believe if it was really spelled correctly, it would
be "OZBURN" of Newton Co., Ga. and JOHN J. SMITH for $450, in the 9th

Dist. #25 Lot, cont. 202 1/2 acres. Witt: ROBERT C. GRAVES, WILLIAM BARKLEY.

Page 301: June 13, 1827 between DAVID LOCKHART of Jones Co., Ga. and THOMAS and CHARLES EVINS, administrators of Henry Pope, decd of Monroe Co. for $125. Paid by HENRY POPE, dec'd in the 8th Dist. of Henry Co. Ga. #129. Witt: CHARLES B. MARSHALL, WILLIAM CANDLER, J.P. Sgd: DAVID LOCKHART.

Page 302: Butts County, Ga. I, GEORGE OWENS of Butts County, do appoint my trusty friend KENNON of Caswell Co., N. C., as my attorney to collect any money coming to me as administrator of THOMAS OWEN, Decd. from the estate of JOHN GLYNN (Dec?) of Hanover Co., Va., and to receipt these in my name and whatever for the said WM. KENNON. This 26th day of Sept. 1827. Sgd. GEORGE OWENS. Signed, sealed and ackn. in Open Court in presence of CHAS. J. MCDONALD, Judge S. C.

Page 303: Butts County for the goodwill and affection that I have for my niece, MARTHA E. MANN, I have given to her one cow and the increase and calf. This 12th day of July 1827. Sgd. WILLIAM MILLS. Witt: GRACE MCWHORTER, NEEDHAM LEE, J.P.

Page 304: Morgan Co., Ga. Sept. 25, 1825 between LOUISA LEACH, Adms on the estate of ROBERT LEACH, dec'd of Morgan County and ROBERT CURRY for $310 for land in Henry Co., Ga. #37 in the 2nd Dist. Witt: HENRY RICHARD RUPELL (NB it just occurred to me that name should be RUSSELL I never heard of RUPEL and this could be one 'S' and one 'l' and be RUSSELL. I remember it from before.) and JAMES ROBSON, J.P., LOUISA LEACH.

Page 304: (2) Butts County, Ga. Oct. 15, 1825 between JOHN R. LEACH Adms attorney for Louisa Leach, Adms for ROBERT LEACH and ROBERT CURRY for #310 in the 2nd Dist. of Henry Co. #37. Witt: WILLIS DAVIS, MICHAEL M. CLARK. Sgd. J. R. LEACH.

Page 305: Butts Co., Ga. MICHAEL M. CLARK, together with WILEY JONES were witness to the above, this 17 day of Jan. 1826. SAMUEL BELLAH, J.P.

Page 306: Nov. 27, 1826 between WOODY DOZIER of Jasper Co., Ga. and PLEASANT POTTER, same county, for $300 in the 9th Dist. of orig. Henry now Butts Co. #57 cont. 170 acres. Witt: DAVID LAWSON, ANDERSON BROWN, G. W. WRIGHT, WOODY DOZIER and wife, ELIZABETH DOZIER. JOSEPH KEY, J.P.

Page 307: Nov. 27, 1826 between DAVID LAWSON of Butts Co. and PLEASANT POTTER of Jasper Co., Ga. for $200 for 101 1/4 acres in the N. half Dist. of Lot #54. Witt: W. WRIGHT, WOODY DOZIER J.J.C. Sgd. DAVID LAWSON.

Page 308: Butts Co., Ga. that we, MARY WALDRIP, ROBERT SMITH and BENJAMIN HARRISON are held unto the Judges of the Court of Ordinary in the sum of $3000 for payment this 3rd day of Sept. 1827 the above bound admstr. of ABRAHAM WALDRIP, late of Butts Co. Sgd. MARY WALDRIP, ROBT SMITH & BENJAMIN HARRISON, JOHN TARPLEY, C.C.O.

Page 309: Butts Co., Jan. 1, 1827 between DOBIE DAVIS and LEVI LESTER of Edgefield Dist. of S. C. for $600 for land cont. 202 1/2 acres. Lot #235 in the 3rd Dist. of Monroe Co. now Butts County. Witt: ALEX-ANDER HALL, CHARLES HAMMOND sworn to before me this 10th day of Oct. 1827 JOHN HENDRICKS, JJC.

Page 310: Butts Co., Sept. 28, 1827, between ROBERT SHARP for $75 and PLEASANT POTTER in formerly Henry Co., now Butts Co., Ga. 9th Dist. #53 cont. 101 1/4 acres, East side of Lot. Witt: JAMES P. SHARP, WOODY DOZIER JJC.

Page 311: Sept. 7, 1827 between WILLIAM G. CONEY (?) and WILLIAM SMITH for $800. in the 14th Dist., Lot 28 of Monroe Co., Ga. but now in the 1st Dist. of Butts Co., cont. 202 1/4 acres (Originally granted to

LYDIA SILLIAMSON, Jan. 8, 1822). Witt: A. R. BICKENDORF, J. C. DUN-
SEATH. Sgd. WM. G. CONEY, JOHN M. PEARSON, JP.

Page 312: Butts County, Ga. That we, JOEL BAILEY, ABNER BANKSTON
and JONATHAN NUTT are held and firmly bound by the Judges of the Court
for the sum of $1000, we bind ourselves as Administrators, dated July
2nd 1827, JOEL BAILEY appointed guardian to STEPHEN BAILEY, Orphan of
SIMON BAILEY. Sgd. in open Court, JOHN TARPLEY, CCO.

Page 313: Jasper Co., Ga. March 18, 1827 between REUBEN C. SHORTER
of Jasper Co. and JOEL BAILEY of Butts Co. for $50 in the 4th Dist. of
Monroe, Ga. now Butts Co. Lot 31 leading from Scotts Ferry to the Mineral
Spg. adj. land of ABNER BANKSTON cont. 12 1/2 acres. Sgd. REUBEN C.
SHORTER. Witt: WM. BARKER and JESSE LOYALL, JP.

Page 314: Putnam Co., Ga. Sept. 11, 1827 between THADDEUS B. REESE,
of Putnam Co., Ga. and SAMUEL JONES of Wilkes Co., Ga. for $300 for 202
1/2 acres in Henry Co. 5th Dist., Lot 132 now in Butts Co. Witt: WYLIE
NELSON, L. HUDSON JJC.

Page 315: Putnam Co., Ga. received of SAMUEL JONES of Wilkes Co.,
Ga. $600 complete payment of 4 negroes, NANCY a woman, and SARY a girl,
LUCY a girl, and JIM a boy child. This 11th of Sept. 1827. COLEMAN
PENDLETON.

Page 315b: Putnam Co., Ga. Feb. 16, 1824 between IRBY HUDSON and
THOMAS BEARDING, Monroe Co., Ga. for $1010 for 202 1/2 acres Lot 13,
4th Dist. of Monroe Co. Witt: GRAY COLE, MATTHEW FARLEY, JP. Sgd.
IRBY HUDSON.

Page 316: March 18, 1827 between REUBEN C. SHORTER, Jasper Co.,
and JOEL BAILEY Butts Co., Ga. for $50, 4th Dist. of Monroe now Butts
Co., Lot 3. Sgd. REUBEN C. SHORTER. Witt: WM. PARKER and JESSE LOYALL,
JP.

Page 317: June 13, 1827 between BOLLIN SMITH of Butts Co., Ga and
JOEL BAILEY for $820, not finished in Deed Book (see page 321).

Page 318: Monroe Co., Ga. Aug. 23, 1825 between RICHARD CHESHIRE
and WEST H. KIRKSEY for $400 for 101 1/4 acres, Lot 63 in the 14th Dist.
of Monroe, SE half. Witt: JOHN M. PEARSON, FRANKLIN KIRKSEY and
W. W. BOYT, JP. Sgd. RICHARD CHESHIRE

Page 319: Butts Co., Nov. 13, 1827 between WEST H. KIRKSEY and
ELIJAH MCMICHAEL for $300 in the 14th Dist. of formerly Monroe now Butts
Co., 101 1/2 acres. Witt: ISHAM NELSON, DANIEL W. PEARSON, JOHN M.
PEARSON, JP. Sgd. ELIJAH MCMICHAEL.

Page 320: Butts Co., Ga. Feb. 27, 1827 between DOLPHIN LINDSEY
Butts Co. and JOHN SIMS of Oglethorpe Co., Ga. for $800. Lot 32 2nd.
Dist. of Henry Co. when surveyed now Butts Co. cont. 202 1/2 acres.
(Drawn and granted to WM. HAMMOND) Witt: JOSEPH LINDSEY, WM. KNIGHT,
SAM'L BELLAH. Sgd. DOLPHIN LINDSEY.

Page 321: June 30, 1827 between BOLIN SMITH of Butts Co. and JOEL
BAILEY for $820 containing 202 1/2 acres in 4th Dist. originally Monroe
now Butts Co. No. 2. Witt: LEVI COBB, STEPHEN P. BAILEY. Sgd. BOLIN
SMITH, SAMUEL BELLAH, JP.

Page 322: Butts Co., Ga. Nov. 27, 1827 between HENRY D. KNIGHT and
GEORGE WILLIAMS of Oglethorpe Co., Ga. for $500 in Henry Co. 2nd Dist.
at time of survey No. 5, cont. 202 1/2 acres. Witt: EZEKIAL STRICKLAND,
ABEL L. ROBINSON, Clk.

Page 323: Richmond Co., Ga. I, HINMAN MATTHEWS, for good cause
and consideration do appoint BENJAMIN F. TUCKER of Butts Co., as my
attorney to ask demand for and to receive of the firm of SPENCER and
ROGERS of Butts Co. and collect claims in my name. Nov. 8, 1827. A. G.
RAYFOLD, JP, HERMAN MATTHEWS.

Page 324: Sept. 22, 1825 between BENJAMIN MARONEY of Monroe Co., Ga. and JOEL BAILEY for $600 cont. 101 1/4 acres 4th Dist. of Monroe Co., Ga. now Butts NW part of #62, adj. THOMAS MATTHEW'S land and JAMES WOOTEN, owning the other half. Witt: J. W. FOSTER, C. M. COODY, JP.

Page 325: Butts Co., Ga. Dec. 26, 1826 between JAMES GRESHAM and JOEL BAILEY both Butts Co, 202 1/2 acres, 4th Dist. Lot 33 orig. Monroe now Butts Co. Granted dated Dec. 8, 1823. Wit: GIDEON WHITTED, BOLIN SMITH, JAMES & JOEL BAILEY. P. 395 Dec. 27, 1826, C. M. COODY, JP., Sgd. BOLIN SMITH.

Pages 326 & 327: Butts Co., Ga. in obedience to a writ of fifas issued out of the Superior Court, county of Elbert, Ga. at the suit of the Justice of the Inferior Court, by their attorney HEARD and HEARD, for the use of MARTIN DETWYLER, guardian of PHILLIPS WILLWHITE against MICHAEL T. WILLWHITE, guardian of JOHN WILLWHITE, DRURY OGLESBY by WM. W. WILLIFORD, Sheriff of the County of Elbert, did lately sieze the tract of land described as the property of JOHN WILLWHITE and on Dec. 4, 1827 at public sale in Butts Co., when LINDSEY OGLESBY the highest bidder paid $165. bwtween SAMUEL CLAY, Sheriff in formerly Henry not Butts Co., Ga. Lot 85 cont. 292 1/2 acres. Witt: CHAS. ALLEN, ABEL L. ROBINSON, Clerk.

Page 328: DeKalb County, Ga. I, JOHN S. WELCH of DeKalb Co., Ga. do appoint GEORGE OWENS of Butts Co., Ga. as my lawful attorney to deliver to THOMAS OWENS, a lawful title to ascertain lot or tract of land drawn by me in my name in the late land lottery in the 14th Dist. of Muscogee County, Ga. Lot 196 and the said THOMAS OWEN is to grant the said land to GEORGE OWEN, my lawful attorney to do the same as myself would do. Sept. 3, 1827. JAMES H. KIDD, PANDSOM HAMPTON, J.P. Sgd. JOHN S. WELCH.

Page 328: (Bottom) Butts Co., Jan. 14, 1826 between ZACHARIAH PHILLIP and DOUG WATSON of Morgan Co., Ga. for $700 for Lot No. 104 in the 14th Dist. formerly Monroe not Butts County, Ga. containing 70 acres. Witt: DAVID WRIGHT, JOHN A. HAIGWOOD.

Page 329: Fayette Co., Ga. MARY PHILLIPS wife of ZACHARIAH PHILLIPS a quit claim. JAMES MCBRIDE, JP.

Page 330: Monroe Co., Ga. DAVID WRIGHT being duly sworn says he saw ZACHARIAH PHILLIPS sign, seal and deliver this deed to JOHN A. HAIGWOOD, this 15th day of May 1827. ARDIN S. RUCKER, JP.

Page 331: Butts Co., Ga. Sept. 15, 1827 between THOS. MATTHEWS and JOEL BAILEY both of Butts Co., for $1000 for Lot 57, 4th Dist., in orig. Monroe now Butts Co., Ga. containing 202 1/2 acres and drawn by ASA LANGTON of Harris Dist., Franklin Co., Ga. on Feb. 28, 1823. Witt: JEPTHA FOOSHA (FOUSHE'). Witt: STEPHEN P. BAILEY, C. M. COODY, J.P. Sgd. THOS. MATTHEWS.

Page 331: Butts Co., Ga. URIAH TAYLOR gives to his grandson, URIAH TAYLOR PORTWOOD, son of HOWARD PORTWOOD, one milk cow and calf, and one-year old bull, for the love and affection I bear my grandson. This Dec. 11, 1827. SILAS TAYLOR, ELI CONGAR, JJC. Signed URIAH TAYLOR.

Page 332: Butts Co. RICHARD R. WILLIAMS makes deed of a lot of land known as lot 248 in the 5th Dist., Coweta County, Ga. from SAMUEL BENTON last November or December 28, 1827. Witt: B. F. TUCKER, JP, RICHARD R. WILLIAMS.

Page 333: Butts Co., Dec. 26, 1826 between JAMES GRESHAM and JOEL BAILEY for $500 for 202 1/2 acres in the 4th Dist. Lot #33 of Monroe County now in Butts County. Dec. 8, 1826. Witt: GIDWON WHITEHEAD, BOLIN SMITH, C. M. COODY, JP.

Page 334: Butts Co., March 7, 1827 between JOHN TRAMMEL of Habersham Co., Ga. and IGNATIUS RUSSELL for $200, Lot 7, 1st Dist. in Henry Co., now Butts Co. Witt: WILLIAM I. RUSSELL, TINSLEY HEATH & JOHN TRAMMEL, JP.

Page 335: Jan. 15, 1826 between JOHN VINES of Walton Co., Ga. and FRANCIS DOUGLASS for $200 for 202 1/2 A in the 9th Dist. of Henry Co., now #4 of Butts Co. Witt: STEPHEN KNIGHT, THOS. THORNTON & HIRAM GLAZIER.

Page 336: Butts Co. July 23, 1827 between ISHAM FREEMAN and WM. BLALOCK for $300, for 101 1/4 acres in the 1st. Dist. of Henry Co. formerly now Butts Co. on the Yellow Water Creek, Lot 95 adj. 96. H. MCLIN, SILAS ELLIOTT, JP.

Page 337: Baldwin Co., Ga. that I, JAMES M. WALLACE of Savannah, Ga. do appoint THOMAS KENAN as my lawful attorney in fact and in deed, as he sees proper in buying a tract of land containing 202 1/2 acres in the 1st. Dist. of formerly Henry now Butts County, Lot 163 in the vicinity of Indian Springs, this 7th. of Oct. 1826. JAMES M. WALLACE.

Page 337: -2- This indenture made this 30th day of November 1826 between THOS. H. KENAN of Baldwin Co., Ga. and JOEL BAILEY of Butts Co., THOMAS H. KENAN acting as power of Attorney for JAMES H. WALLACE land in 1st Dist. of formerly Henry now Butts Co. Lot 163 for $53. Sgd: THOMAS S. KENAN. Witt: ROBERT MICKELJOHN, J. T. CUSHING.

Page 338: Butts Co., Ga. Feb. 22, 1827 between WILLIAM BLALOCK and JOEL BAILEY for $40 for part of Lot 54 in the 9th Dist. of formerly Henry now Butts Co., the South part of the lot adjacent BAILEY, BARKLEY and POLLEN land containing 25 acres. Witt: BOLIN SMITH, STEPHEN P. BAILEY. Sgd: BLALOCK.

Page 339: Butts Co. Jan. 30, 1826 between WILLIAM H. FIGGS of Green Co. sold to RANDALL ROBINSON of Butts Co., Lot #31 in 2nd Dist. of orig. Henry drawn by and granted to Figgs by Gov. TROUP. Sold for $700. Witt: ALEX HALL and JOHN E. ROBINSON, SAMUEL BELLAH JP.

Page 340 & 341: Butts Co., Ga. April 29, 1826 between DAVID LAWSON acting as Administrator for ADAM LAWSON, dec'd. and ABEL BAILEY as the other part. ADAM LAWSON did in this lifetime obligate to make titles to WILLIAM B. SMITH for 75 3/4 acres known as Lot 54 in the 9th Dist. of formerly Henry now Butts Co., and in the March term of said Court 1826 ordered that the Administration of the said DAVID LAWSON make title on the receipt of $151.50 from JOEL BAILEY. Witt: J. H. CURRY, HENRY BLANKENSHIP, JOSEPH KEY JP.

Page 342: Monroe Co., Ga. Jan. 16, 1824 between DANIEL MABRY for $20 to JOHN GLENN for land in the 2nd Dist. of Henry Co., Lot 127 in 2nd Dist. Witt: RICHARD HOLLOWAY, SAMUEL BROOKS, J.P.

Page 343: Butts Co., Ga. Feb. 20, 1827 between JOHN SIMS, Oglethorpe Co., Ga. and DOLPHIN LINDSEY of Butts Co. for $800 on Lot 2 in the 2nd Dist. of formerly Henry now Butts Co., containing 202 1/2 acres being drawn by and granted to THOMAS COOKSEY. Witt: ALEX HALL, SAMUEL BELLAH, JP. Sgd: JOHN SIMS.

Page 343: 2 Feb. 1822 between JOHN DENNIS of Hancock Co., Ga. and JOHN GLENN of Monroe Co., Ga. Lot $240 in the 3rd Dist. of Monroe Co., for $400. Witt: JOHNSON DENNIS, ASHETON ROSSETER, JP.

Page 344: Butts Co. Feb. 4, 1822 between WILLIAM HANNA and DOLPHIN LINDSEY, HENRY Co. for $559 on Lot 32. Witt: WM. MCWHORTER, DAVID EVANS, JP.

Page 345: Butts Co. Jan. 4, 1828 between JOHN R. CAWSEY and GUSTAVUS HENDRICKS of Jones Co. for $1500. in 1st. Dist. orig. Henry now Butts Co., Lot #127 (except so much as has been sold and conveyed to THOMAS COOK, not exceeding 11 1/4 acres) containing 191 1/4 acres. Witt: ABEL L. ROBINSON, JOHN HENDRICKS, JJC.

Page 346: Butts Co., Jan. 29, 1827 between Lot HEARN and DOLPHIN FOR $500. Lot #239, 3rd. Dist. of formerly Monroe Co., now Butts Co., Ga. containing 202 1/2 acres. Witt: WM. COUSINS, JOHN PHILLIPS, JP.

Page 346: (2) Butts Co., April 12, 1827 between WILLIAMSON BIRD of Taliaferro Co., Ga. and ISAAC MOONY for $200. Lot 81 in the 9th Dist. orig. Henry now Butts Co., orig. drawn by WM. BIRD which lot contains 202 1/2 acres. No signers.

Page 347: Butts Co. LEVI STEVENS said a certain deed of land executed by BANKSTON & ROBERTS unto GEORGE N. FONNILY of formerly Henry now Butts Co., that he is one of the subscribing witnesses of said deed and further states deed was executed in Feb. 1823 and was a mistake in its being dated 1822. Signed: LEVI STEVENS, JOHN R. CARGILE JJC.

Page 348: May 7, 1823 between JAMES OLIVER of Laurens Co., Ga. and BENJAMIN MAY of Jones Co., Ga. for $200 in Monroe Co. 3rd Dist. Lot 122 containing 202 1/2 acres. Wit: JONAH HAM, AMOS LOVE, JJC.

Page 349: ROBERT W. HARKNESS, JOSEPH SUMMERLIN, SAMUEL CLAY and JOHN ROBINSON are held and firmly bound unto his Excellency, JOHN FORSYTH Gov. of Georgia and Commander in Chief of the Army for $20,000 - whereas ROBERT W. HARKNESS, on Jan. 7, 1828, is elected Sheriff of the County of Butts, in Georgia and that he shall perform all duties expected of him. Signed in the presence of: ZELVERTON THAXTON, JJC, JOHN MCMICHAEL, JJC, JOHN R. CARGILE, JJC, ROBERT W. HARKNESS, JJC., SAMUEL J. CLAY, JJC., JOHN ROBINSON, JJC.

Page 350: Butts Co. Dec. 12, 1827 between URIAH TAYLOR and LEWIS and WILLIS MOORE, all of Butts Co. for $1000, in the 1st. Dist. or originally Henry Co. now Butts, Lot 182 of 202 1/2 acres. Witt: JOHN TARPLEY, ZELVERTON THAXTON, JJC.

Page 351: Bibb Co., Jan. 7, 1828 between ADDISON MANDALL and THOMAS CAMPBELL Bibb Co., and JOSEPH CAMPBELL of Butts Co., for $550 for a lot of land in formerly Henry now Butts Co., containing 202 1/2 acres, lot was drawn by VALENTINE CRANE of Chatham Co., Ga. Witt: EDW. W. WRIGHT, J. A. MANDALL, M. ROBERTSON JJC, THOMAS CAMPBELL.

Page 352: Jan. 18, 1828 between WILLIAM Y. HANSELL of Baldwin Co., Ga. and GUSTAVUS HENDRICK, Jones Co., Ga. for $700, land formerly in Henry now Butts Co. Lot 196, in 1st Dist. (drawn by TIMOTHY BRUEN of Baldwin) of 202 1/2 acres. JAMES SMITH, Notary Public, Clinton, Ga. SOL HOGO, JP.

Page 353: Butts Co. Jan. 14, 1828 between URIAH TAYLOR and ABEL L. ROBINSON for $200 in 1st. Dist. orig. Henry now Butts Co. Lot 91 containing 202 1/2 acres BENJ. F. TUCKER, THOS. W. COLLIER and Sgd: URIAH TAYLOR.

Page 353 and 354: Butts Co. in obedience to a writ of fi fas from Court on the suit of WILLIAM ASKEW against BENJAMIN S. MOON, I, ROBERT W. HARKNESS, Sheriff, did sieze the tract of land, and publicly advertise and on June 3, 1828 at public sale sold to highest bidder, A. L. ROBINSON for $2.50 for Lot 39, in the 1st Dist. of formerly Henry now Butts containing 202 1/2 acres lost by BENJ. S. MOON. Witt: JAMES W. HOGG, JOHN HENDRICK, JJC, HARKNESS, Sheriff.

Page 355: Butts Co. Nov. 27, 1827 between THOMAS KENNY and ARMSTEAD BRANCH for $250 in formerly Monroe now Butts Co. 3rd Dist. Lot 211 on Cabin Creek containing 50 acres. WILEY THAXTON, YELVERTON THAXTON JJC.

Page 356: Butts Co. Dec. 24, 1827 between DAVID LAWSON and Justice of Inferior Court for $30 in 9th Dist. of formerly Henry now Butts Co. Lot 64 containing 17 acres, the said fraction of land to be used by ELI CAPP QUINN for his actual life and at his death to be for the use of the poor of Butts County forever. Signed: DAVID LAWSON, GEORGE W. BARBER and JOSEPH KEY JP.

Page 356: (2) Butts Co., Nov. 8, 1827 between ROBERT W. HUNTER and LUKE ROBINSON in 1st Dist. of Henry now Butts Co., Lot 184 for $700. JOHN TARPLEY, ABEL L. ROBINSON Clerk of Superior Court, Butts Co.

Page 357: Jan. 1, 1828 between WADE H. TURNER of Henry Co., and WILLIAM HARRISON of Butts Co., for $600. Lot 250 cont. 202 1/2 acres, 8th dist. formerly Henry, now Butts Co. (granted to SAMUEL G. NORMAN of Emanuel Co., Ga. Witt: JAMES G. LYLE, ANDREW R. MOORE & THOMAS D. JOHNSON, JP.

Page 358: Butts Co. Jan. 14, 1828 between WM. GILMORE and THOMAS HAMPTON Exec. of STEPHEN G. HEARD, dec'd both of Butts Co., and LEWIS SMITH for $1133.50 in 1st Dist. cont. 125 1/2 acres, Dist. 5. BENJ. F. TUCKER, Clk of Super Court of Butts Co. Jan. 1828. WILLIAM GILMORE and THOS. HAMPTON.

Page 359: Jasper Co., Ga. Feb. 6, 1828 between MISBACH LOWERY on the one part and ELISHA LOWERY of Jasper Co., for $100 for the N. half of Lot in the 1st. Dist. of Orig. Henry Co., now Butts in the Dist. 57 Cont. 101 1/4 acres. JOHN TARPLEY and ABEL L. ROBINSON.

Page 360: Butts Co. Jan. 23, 1828 between ABEL L. ROBINSON and JOHN TARPLEY for N. half of Lot 91 in 1st Dist. of orig. Henry, now Butts Co. cont. 101 1/4 acres for $90. Wit: JOHN ROBINSON, YELVERTON THAXTON, JJC.

Page 361: Butts Co., Ga. Dec. 14, 1827 between GEORGE W. LOWERY and CHAS. M. and JAMES BERRY of Newton Co., Ga. for $225 a certain lot containing 202 1/2 acres in the 1st dist. of formerly Henry, now Butts Co. #58 adj. PRESLEY and others. Witt: J. A. MALONE, EZEKIEL WALKER, CHAS. M. BERRY and JAMES BERRY.

Page 362: Jan. 17, 1828 between WILLIAM STROUD and HENRY VAN BIBER for $400 for 111 acres in 9th Dist. of formerly Henry now Butts Co. Dist. 72 ABEL L. ROBINSON, JOHN R. CARGILE and WILLIAM STROUD.

Page 362: (2) Butts Co. Dec. 20, 1826 between THOMAS GARRETT and NANCY GARRETT of DeKalb Co., Ga. and JAMES GIBSON for $150 in the 4th Dist. of formerly Henry now Butts Co., Ga. containing 202 1/2 acres. Wit: AVINGTON T. WILLIAMS JP, JOHN TILLER, THOS. and NANCY GARRETT.

Page 363: Butts County, Ga. May 8, 1827 between ZACHARIAH DEASON, AMBROSE DEASON and BENJAMIN DEASON and JOHN P. SWIFT for $800 for land Lot 200 cont. 202 1/2 acres in the 1st. Dist. of formerly Henry now Butts Co. (originally granted to NATHANIEL BOND) JOHN MCMICHAEL JJC. (Signed by 3 DEASON men.)

Page 364: Butts Co., Nov. 22, 1827 between WILLIAM BLAIR, Monroe Co., Ga. and WILLIAM AIKEN for $800 in the 4th Dist. in formerly Monroe Co. now Butts Co. Lot 85, drawn by ELIZABETH JONES. Wit: JOEL HARDEN, PARHAM LINDSEY, JJP.

Page 365: Butts Co., Ga. Feb. 6, 1828 GEORGE W. LOWERY for $100 sells to KIRBA D. LOWERY the W. half of a Lot #58 cont. 101 1/4 acres in the 1st Dist. formerly Henry now Butts Co. JOHN TARPLEY, ABEL ROBINSON, Clk.

Page 366: Butts Co., Ga. Dec. 12, 1827 between JOSEPH SUMMERLIN and URIAH TAYLOR for $400 in the 1st Dist. of formerly Henry now Butts Co., Lot #91 cont. 202 1/2 acres. Sgd: JOHN TARPLEY.

Page 367: Butts Co. In obedience to a writ of fi fa issued by Court of Capt. COMPTON'S Dist. in Jasper County, Ga. at the suit of JOHN S. PORTER against BARTIN MARTIN, SAMUEL CLAY, Sheriff of County siezed 50 acres of land and after advertising did Jan. 1, 1828 sell by public sale to the highest bidder HAMLIN FREEMAN for $24, the 50 acres in the NE corner of Lot 42 in the 1st. Dist. of formerly Henry, now Butts Co. P. G. CLAY, ABEL ROBINSON, Clk. SAM'L CLAY, Sheriff.

Page 368: Butts Co. Mar. 12, 1827 between JOHN R. LEACH, Twiggs Co., Ga. and GEORGE W. BARBER for $200. Lot 102, 1st Dist. formerly Henry Co. now Butts Co. RICHARD BAILEY, B. F. TUCKER, JP and JOHN R. LEACH.

Page 369 and 370: Butts Co,, Ga. April 12, 1827 between WILLIAMSON BIRD of Taliaferro County, Ga. and ISAAC MOONEY for $200, for Lot 81 in 9th Dist. formerly Henry now Butts Co., (Drawn by PHILAMON BIRD) containing 202 1/2 acres. Witt: WILLIS BENTON, HENRY SUMMERLIN and WILLIAM BIRD.

Page 371 and 372: Butts Co obtained a writ from Justice of Butts Co., suit of YOUNG R. NORRIS against JAMES MORRIS and SAMUEL CLAY, Sheriff of County did sieze Lot of Land #21 property of JAMES MORRIS, did advertize and on Jan. 1st. 1828 sell at public sale and YOUNG R. NORRIS, highest bidder at $26 bought in the 1st Dist. formerly Henry now Butts Co. Lot 21 of 202 1/2 acres. SAMUEL CLAY, Sheriff, BRYANT U. HAMIL, and SAMUEL P. BURFORD, JP.

Page 372 and 373: Butts Co., August 27, 1827 between JOHN SMITH, Morgan Co., Ga. and AMANUEL SMITH Butts Co. for $25 for 50 acres of the district known by 9th Dist. of Henry Co. Dist. 73 NW corner (perhaps Lot 73) RICHARDSON PENNINGTON and HENRY PENNINGTON.

Page 374: We, SAMUEL BELLAH, NEEDHAM LEE and CALVERY KNIGHT this 5th day of November 1827 for $2000 they bound themselves administrators of WILLIAM RHODY dec'd. to make a true inventory of the property of deceased, and if later find the deceased had made a will, all obligations will be void. WM. TARPLEY CCO, SAM'L BELLAH, NEEDHAM LEE, and C. F. KNIGHT.

Page 375: Butts County, Ga. Feb. 26, 1828 between BOLIN BRIANT and AUGUSTUS BINNS, for $200 for 101 1/4 acres, Lot #105 in the 1st District orig. Henry Co. now Butts Co., drawn by ARCHIBALE and BOLIN BRYANT of ALEXANDER S. MIM'S Dist. Wit: WM. SAFFOLD and M. S. DENT, JP. Sgd. BOLIN S. BRYANT.

Page 376: Newton Co., Ga. Jan. 12, 1828 between JOHN PERKINS of Toliver (Taliferro County, Ga. and THOMAS HULL of Butts Co., for $224.64 on lot 194 West of the Okmulgee River in the 8th Dist. orig. granted to ALFORD PERKINS dated May 28, 1824. Wit: JOHN MCCLELLAND, WM. CLARK, JP. Signed: JOHN PERKINS.

Page 377: Butts Co., Ga. March 20, 1828 between BENJAMIN BLISSIT and ALLEN MCCLENDON of Jasper Co., Ga. for $200. 4th Dist. orig. Monroe Co. now Butts Co. 73rd Lot. Wit: STEPHEN BLISSIT, YELVERTON THAXTON. Sgd. BENJ. BLISSIT.

Page 378: BENJAMIN MARONEY for $1000 paid by BARTHOLOMEW STILL, 202 1/2 acres on Lot #13 4th Dist. of formerly Monroe Co. now Butts Co. Witt: JOHN COUGHRAN, C. M. COOLEYT, JP.

Page 379: Butts Co, Ga. Feb. 22, 1828 between JOHN COUGHRAN and BARTHOLOMEW STILL for $350 for 30 acres on Sandy Creek, Lot #64 in the 4th Dist. of Monroe Co. formerly, now Butts Co. Witt: JAMES RANSOM, C. M. COODY, JP.

Page 380 and 381: Dooly County, Ga. Nov. 23, 1825 between JESSE VICKERS by his Atty. WM. H. GOLDSMITH of Twiggs Co., Ga. and WM. PRESSLY Henry Co., Ga. for $60. 202 1/2 acres in the 1st Dist. of Henry.

Page 382: Butts Co. Mar. 12, 1828 between JAMES HARKNESS & JOHN PHILLIPS and ROBERT WHITE sold 202 1/2 acres on Lot 84 in orig. Henry now Butts Co. for $600. Witt: WILLIAM HAMILTON, ABEL ROBINSON, Clerk.

Page 382-2: Butts Co. Oct. 30, 1827 between NATHANIEL RAMEY and THOS. R. BARKER both Butts Co., sold for $1000 in Monroe Co., Ga. at time of survey, 3rd Dist. Lot 172 cont. 202 1/2 acres. Witt: JAMES P. SHARP, JOHN MCCARGILE, JJC (N. RAMEY)

Page 383: Henry Co., Ga. April 2, 1825 between A. S. ROBINSON and ALEXANDER NORTHCUTT of Henry Co. for $200 for 50 acres, the N & S Line of #147 in the 1st Dist. of Henry Co. on Wolf Creek, granted to WM. L. JOHNS. Wit: CHAS. BECOBY, CARTER CREW.

Page 384: Oct. 6, 1826 between JOHN LASSITER, Butts Co. and WILLIAM HARPER of Pike County, Ga. (NB The Book had WM. HARPER then a WILKINS and the one that signed it was WILKINS HARPER. Guess he forgot to put WILKINS where it belonged) sold for $225 for 101 1/4 acres, W. half of Lot 35, 1st Dist. of formerly Henry now Butts Co. Witt: JAMES KING, B. F. TUCKER and HIRAM GLAZIER, EZEKIEL WALKER, JP. Signed: WILKINS HARPER.

Page 385: Richmond Co., Ga. April 5, 1826 between JOB S. BARNEY and JOSEPH C. ADKINS of Greene Co. for $200. 1st Dist. orig. Henry now Butts County, originally granted to MORDECAI EVANS. Wit: JANE R. EVANS, J. W. MEREDITH, JP.

Page 386: Richmond Co., Ga. MARGARET BARNEY, wife of JOB BARNEY relinquishes her claim of land unto JOSEPH C. ADKINS, Apr. 5, 1826. Wit: J. W. MEREDITH, JP.

Page 387: Butts Co., Ga. March 28, 1827. Rec'd of ALEX HUNTER, $225 in full payment for a certain mulatto boy named WARREN about 8 years old. Wit: SANDERS THOMAS, BENJAMIN F. TUCKER, JP. Sgd. THOMAS HAMPTON.

Page 387: Butts Co., Ga. March 31, 1828 between WILLIAM MCWHORTER and SAMUEL MADDOX of Monroe Co., Ga. for $600, the land whereon I now live, it being part of 2 lots in 3rd Dist. of formerly Monroe now Butts Co., first granted to ZEPHTHAH BRANTLEY 2 other acres excepted, which is deeded to the Baptist Church at Towilage. Wit: HUGH HAMIL, SAM'L BELLAH, JP., W. A. MCWHORTER.

Page 388: Clark Co., Ga. March 26, 1828 between JOHN NANCE and WILLIAM L. WILSON, for $150 in Monroe Co. when surveyed now Butts Co., cont. 202 1/2 acres in the 4th Dist. Lot #39 orig. granted to JOHN NANCE, AUGUSTUS REED, A. BROWN, J.P.

Page 389: Butts Co., April 2, 1828 between JAMES H. ROBERTS and GILES T. ROBERTS for $238 in the 1st Dist. of formerly Henry now Butts Co. Lot 254 bounded by land of JAMES BROWN and WM. MESSERS, cont. 54 1/4 acres. Wit: JOHN GOODMAN and JOHN HENDRICK, JJC. Sgd: JAMES H. HENDRICK.

Page 390: Used in boundaries of the above purchase.

Page 391: Butts Co., Ga. March 20, 1828 between THOMAS TUCKER and JAMES BRADY both Butts Co., buying for $225. Lot #12 in the 1st. Dist. of formerly Henry now Butts Co., granted to JONATHAN BARNES. Wit: BRYANT HAMIL, W. H. CHAPMAN and WM. GARDNER. Signed THOMAS TUCKER. (The above transaction was paid for with promissory notes due Dec. 25, 1828 and dated Oct. 5, 1827 rec'd from JAMES MCCALLEY and JAMES BENTLEY.)

Page 392: Carried the signatures of JAMES BELLAH, April 19, 1828 to above.

Page 393: Butts Co., Ga. March 29, 1827 between HUGH B. STEWART & PLEASANT POTTER, both of Butts Co. for $400 for Lot 50 cont. 29 3/4 acres in the 9th Dist. of formerly Henry now Butts Co. Wit: JAMES MADDUX and JNO. R. CARGILE. Sgd. HUGH B. STUART.

Page 394: Butts Co. April 22, 1828 between JOHN R. CARGILE, JOHN HENDRICKS and JOHN MCMICHAEL, Justice of Inferior Crt. Butts Co. and AMASA SPENCER, Henry lo. for $25, in Town of Jackson, Lot 3 in Square 9. Witt: ISIAH HARDY, WILLIAM BARKLEY, JP. Sgd. by the 3 above named.

Page 395: Henry Co. Oct. 13, 1826 between AARON BROOKS and WILLIAM STROUD for $350. in 1st. Dist. of formerly Henry now Butts Co., Lot 11 Wit: SOLOMON STRICKLAND, G. GRIER, JJC. Sgd. AARON BROOKS.

Page 396: Butts Co., Ga. Feb. 13, 1828. ALANSON MOSELEY and WILLIS R. HEATH of Newton Co., Ga. for $225 Lot 198 in 8th Dist. in formerly Henry now Butts Co., Witt: HENRY SUMMERLIN, JOHN W. MASON, WM. ROLLINS, JP. Sgd. ALANSON MOSELEY.

Page 397: Butts Co. March 13, 1828 between WILLIAM HARPER of Pike Co., Ga. and JOHN BROWNING FULLER, Butts Co., for $275 containing 101 1/4 acres, 1st. Dist. of formerly Henry now Butts Co., East half of Lot 35. Wit: TIMOTHY FORD, N. FORD, JP. Sgd. WILLIAM HARPER.

Page 398: Butts Co., May 13, 1828 between ARISTOTLE G. DUKE and WILLIAM HOLIFIELD Lot 55 in the 1st. Dist. formerly Henry now Butts Co., 202 1/2 acres at $600. Wit: A. L. ROBINSON, YELVERTON THAXTON, JJC. Sgd. ARISTOTLE G. DUKE.

Page 399: Burke Co., Ga. Oct. 5, 1827 between JOHN FRYER Burke Co. and ALEXANDER HUNTER for $212 for 202 1/2 acres, Lot 169 1st. Dist. formerly Henry now Butts Co. Wit: ANGUS ROE, WILL COLTON, JP and R. W. HUNTER.

Page 400: April 9, 1828 between ROBERT TUCKER, Fayette Co., Ga. and ROBERT W. HUNTER, Butts Co., trustees for the heirs of BENJ. F. TUCKER for the love and affection ROBT. TUCKER has for his son, he gives him a negro slave, a girl about 16, named MELINDA. Then ROBT. W. HUNTER gives BENJ. F. TUCKER, the son $10 for the slave. Wit: DOBIA HUDDLE, BENJ. HUDDLE, LEWALLEN MORGAN, JP.

Page 401: April 9, 1828 FRANCIS MILLER and JOSEPH SUMMERLIN are bound to their Honor the Judges of the Crt. of Butts Co. for $2500, Jan. 10, 1828 to make a true account of the inventory of ISABEL ___? of Richmond Co., Ga. Sgd. FRANCIS MILLER, JOSEPH SUMMERLIN, JOHN TARPLEY, CCO.

Page 403: Butts Co., MANSEL SMITH, ELI CONGER and CHARLEY RAMEY pays $500 and are bound to the Court, to make a true account of the Administration of JOHN SMITH, late of Putnam County, Ga. This was May 5, 1828. WM. TARPLEY, CCO. Signed: M. J. SMITH, ELI CONGER and CHARLEY RAMEY.

Page 404-405: Butts Co., April 4, 1828 between ALEXANDER HUNTER and ROBERT W. HUNTER both of Butts Co. Trustee for heir of JANE TUCKER and BENJAMIN F. TUCKER and for the affection which ALEXANDER HUNTER beareth his daughter JANE TUCKER and her husband BENJAMIN F. TUCKER and for the sum of $10 have delivered two slaves, one a girl, ANN 11 years old and a boy WORIN 9 years old, during the term of their natural life. Wit: THOS. B. BURFORD, J. H. GARNET, SAMUEL P. BURFORD. Sgd: A. HUNTER, R. W. HUNTER.

Page 406: Newton Co., Ga. Sept. 1, 1825 between ALEXANDER HALL of Monroe Co., Ga. for $300 for part of Lot 236, 3rd Dist. of Monroe Co. on the Towilaga River. Witt: ZELVERTON THAXTON, SAMUEL WARD. Sgd. D. ECHOLS.

Page 407: Butts Co. June 8, 1827 between ROLAND WILLIAMS, Henry Co., Ga. and GREENLEE HOLLY, for $300 for 101 1/4 acres in the 1st. Dist. of Henry Co. Lot #177 (n. side). Wit: RICHARD H. HOLLY, EZEKIEL STRICKLAND. Sgd. ROLAND WMS.

Page 408: Butts Co. This is to certify that I have this day appointed JAMES S. MEEK my true and lawful attorney to transact my business with R. BROWN. Witt: ROBERT BROWN, THOMAS ROBINSON. Sgd. JAMES L. BURKS. June 3, 1828.

Page 409: Jasper Co., Ga. Feb. 25, 1823 between WILLIAM LUCROY Henry Co., Ga. and JAMES S. BROWN for $300 for up to 50 acres in the 1st Dist. part of Lot 254 in Henry Co. Wit: ELISHA BROOKS, TANDY W. KEY. Sgd. WM. LUCROY.

Page 410 and 411: JOSEPH SUMMERLIN, Dep. Sheriff, seized the land of SUSANNAH PERMENTER on June 3, 1828 after publicly advertising, and was sold at public sale, bought by RICHARD P. BAILEY, as highest bidder for $27 now between ROBERT W. HARKNESS, Sheriff of Butts Co. and RICHARD BAILEY becomes the owner of the S. half of Lot #58 in the 4th Dist. and cont. 101 1/4 acres. Witt: CYRUS PHILLIPS, A. L. ROBINSON, Clk. of Court ROBT. W. HARKNESS, Sheriff.

Page 412 and 413: Henry County, Apr. 7, 1828 between AUGUSTUS
B. POPE and WM. A. CALLAWAY of Henry Co., Ga. CALLAWAY holds notes of
POPE (promissory notes dated Jan. 1, 1827 which have become due. Sgd:
AUGUSTUS B. POPE. Witt: BENJAMIN COOK and THOS. D. JOHNSON, JP.

Page 414 and 415: Oct. 11, 1825 between GEORGE SHINHOLSER, Wilkinson Co., Ga. and THOMAS SHINHOLSER of Baldwin Co., Ga. for $500 for 202
1/2 acres, located in the 1st Dist. of Henry Co. Lot 219. Wit: PETER
GREEN, JR. and JOHN BOZEMAN, JP. Sgd. GEORGE SHINHOLSER.

Page 416: Nov. 4, 1825 between THOS. L. SHINHOLZER of Baldwin Co.,
Ga. and EZRA B. JONES of Baldwin Co. for $500 for 202 1/2 acres in the
1st. Dist. of Henry Co., Lot 219. Sgd. GEORGE SHINHOLSER. Wit: H.
ALLEN and JOHN BOZEMAN.

Page 417: Dec. 14, 1825 between EZRA B. JONES, Baldwin Co. and
GUSTAVUS HENDRICKS Jones Co. for $500 for 202 1/2 acres in the 1st Dist.
of Henry, Lot 219. Signed: J. S. JORDAN, JOS. DAY, JJC. Sgd: E. B.
JONES.

Page 418: Cancelled.

Page 419: Jones Co., Ga. I, THOS. W. COLLINS of Houston Co., Ga.
appoints G. H. BRYAN of Jones Co., Ga. for my attorney to take possession
of any lands of any fortunate drawings I may make in the Lottery to sell
same for me. This Nov. 13, AD 1821, HIRAM ADAIR, JOHN JENKINS, JP.
Sgd. T. W. COLLINS.

Page 420: Bibb Co., Ga. Jan. 27, 1824 between GEO. H. BRYAN,
Atty. for THOS. W. COLLINS and JAMES HOLDERNESS, for $25 for land drawn
in Lottery in the 1st. Dist. of Henry Co. #29. Wit: JOHN P. BOOTH,
JOHN P. GRACE, JP., GEO. H. BRYANS.

Page 420-2: Feb. 17, 1824 between JAMES HOLDERNESS and DAVID T.
BOOTH, Bibb Co., Ga. for $200 in the 1st. Dist. of Henry, Lot 29, drawn
by THOS. W. COLLINS, Jones Co. cont. 202 1/2 acres, this Feb. 6, 1828.
Wit: JOHN P. BOOTH, P. GRACE, JP., ISAAC HOLDERNESS.

Page 422: July 18, 1825 between DAVID S. BOOTH, Bibb Co. and
SHADRACH F. SLATTER, Jones Co., for $120 in the 1st. Dist. of Henry Co.
Lot 29, cont. 202 1/2 acres, granted to THOS. W. COLLINS Jones Co. Sgd:
DAVID S. BOOTH, HOPE H. SLATTER, T. MILLER, JP.

Page 423-2: Jones Co., Ga. March 12, 1827 between SHAD. S. SLATTER
and GUSTAVUS HENDRICK both Jones Co. for $200 in the 1st Dist. of
formerly Henry not Butts Co. Lot #29 cont. 202 1/2 acres, granted to TOM
COLLINS of Jones Co., Ga. Dist. 2. Wit: D. S. SPARKS, JAMES GRAY JJC.
Sgd: SHADRACK SLATTER, PERMENTER'S Dist.

Page 425: Jasper Co., Nov. 3, 1827 between L. WILSON & SIMEON LOVE-
JOY of Butts Co., Ga. and ALLEN MCLENDON of Jasper Co., Ga. & JERIMIAH
McLENDON of Butts Co., Ga. for $23 in the 4th Dist. of Monroe Co., Ga.
Nos. 69 and 90 at time of survey but now of Butts Co. 405 acres. Wit:
J. LEMMON, WM. HANCOCK and W. L. WILSON.

Page 426: Butts Co., Ga. July 8, 1828 between JOHN R. CARGILE,
JOHN MCMICHAEL and YELVERTON THAXTON, Justices of Inferior Court of
Butts Co., of one part and HOWELL HOLLY of Walton Co., Ga. for $400.32
in the town of Jackson, Butts Co. No. 1 in the square #13. Wit: JOHN
TARPLEY, ABEL L. ROBINSON, Clk. JOHN R. CARGILE, JJC. JOHN MCMICHAEL
and YELVERTON THAXTON.

Page 427: Butts Co., Ga. JOHN H. ROBY and FRANCIS DOUGLAS for $1000
July 8, 1828 are appointed administrators for MARCEY ROBY, dec'd made
inventory of the dec'd and do make a true and just account of his belong-
ings. Wit: JOHN TARPLEY, Clk. JOHN N. ROBY. FRANCIS ROBY.

Page 428: Butts Co., Ga. Feb. 2, 1828 between SYLVANUS KINDRICK,
Monroe Co., Ga. and SAMUEL RIDGEWAY of Elbert Co., Ga. for $350 for the

W. half of Lot 212, cont. 101 1/4 acres in the 3rd. Dist., formerly
Monroe now Butts Co., being drawn and granted to JOHN KINDRICK or
SLYVANUS KINDRICK, ALEXANDER HALL, LEMUEL TENNISON.

Page 429: Butts Co., Ga. Feb. 7, 1828 between JOSEPH HALE and JOHN
HARPER, Butts Co. for $336 land in the 1st. Dist. of formerly Henry now
Butts Co. Lot #51. JOHN DAVIS and JAMES ROGERS. Sgd: JOSEPH HALE,
DAVID MALCOLM, JP.

Page 429-2: Butts Co. In obedience to a fi fa from the Court of
McIntosh County, Ga. at the suit of WM. ROBERTS vs JOHN COLWELL, SAMUEL
CLAY Sheriff siezed the land, advertised and at public sale sold to
JAMES WEST and BARRINGTON KING, Exec. of Est. of LANCE NEPHEW, the highest
bidder at $54 in the County of Butts, 14th Dist., 202 1/2 acres. Jan. 1,
1828. JAMES N. HOGG, JOHN BULLARD and A. L. ROBINSON, Clk. of Ct.
Witnesses. Signed: SAMUEL CLAY, Sheriff.

Page 431: Butts Co., Ga. Feb. 18, 1828 between ABEL & LUKE ROBINSON
and MORTON BLEDSOE in the 1st. Dist. of formerly Henry now Butts County
cont. 202 1/2 acres Lot 146 also 50 acres, part of Lot 147. Wit: R. W.
HARKNESS, JAMES HOGG, JOSEPH KEY, JC.

Page 432: Feb. 2, 1828 between HIRAM B. BLOODWORTH of Monroe Co.,
Ga. and JOHN COCHRAN of Butts Co. for $600 in the 4th Dist. formerly
now Butts Co. 202 1/2 acres on Lot 64 surveyed on Sept. 22, 1824 by
BEVERLEY ALLEN and granted to BLOODWORTH, Oct. 18, 1824 JOEL BAILEY,
POLLARD PAYNE, HIRAM B. BLOODWORTH and C. M. COODY, J.P.

Page 433: March 8, 1828 between BENJAMIN HARRISON and JOHN ANDREWS
both Butts Co. for $100. Lot 94, 14th Dist. formerly Monroe now Butts
Co. being a 50 acre half of Lot 94. Wit: ROBT. ANDREWS (JOE RHED?)
WM. C. TENNELL & JULE PEARSON.

Page 434: Butts Co., I, THOMAS STONE of Butts Co., Ga. do mortgage
in trust unto NANCY DENT (or DART or DERST) Jones Co., Ga. certain
negroes to wit: a negro woman named ANN about 25 years old and her child,
a boy named SAM, about 7, to better secure the payment of $450 which
WILLIAM SIMPSON and myself have given our notes this day unto NANCY DENT
to be paid by the 25th day of December next, then this mortgage will
become null and void. Wit: DAVID WRIGHT, ROLLIN SMITH, JP and signed:
THOMAS STONE, Feb. 20, 1828 for value received and assign the written
mortgage to ROGER MCCARTHY. NANCY DENT, JOHN by H. LAWSON.

Page 435: Butts Co. Dec. 24, 1827 between FRANCIS MILLER, Henry Co.,
Ga. and JAMES SAYER (or LOYERS) of Greene Co., Ga. for $20 in 8th Dist.
of formerly Henry now Butts Co. for SW corner of 2153 (?) Dist. HENRY
SUMMERLIN, JAMES MORRISON and Signed: FRANCIS MILLER.

Page 436: Butts Co. July 9, 1828 between ALEXANDER URQUHARDT and
CALVARY F. KNIGHT for $200 on or before Dec. 25 in the 3rd Dist. of
formerly Monroe now Henry Co. Lot #176 in the 2nd Dist. of Early Co.
Lot 225 and a white bay mare with white streaks in her face for the sum
of $200. Wit: JAMES V. HOGG, JOHN TARPLEY, SAMUEL P. BURFORD, and
Signed ALEXANDER URQUARTDT.

Page 437-2: Butts Co., Ga. August 24, 1828 between EVAN RAGLAND,
Newton Co., Ga. and ELEAZER MOBLEY, Butts Co. for $600 formerly Henry
now Butts Co. 1st. Dist. #52-202 1/2 acres. Wit: C. D. PACE, MCCORMACK
NEAL, JP and Sgd. EVAN RAGLAND.

Page 438: Butts Co., Ga. August 5, 1828 between WILLIAM PRESSLEY
and LEVIN SMITH for $150 in the 1st. Dist. 100 acres, N. half of Lot
6 on Little Sandy Creek. Wit: JAS. N. HOGG, EDW. WEAVER, WM. PRESSLEY.

Page 439: Butts Co., August 5, 1828 between PRESSLEY and WILLIAM
KIMBROUGH for $350 in the 1st. Dist. formerly Henry now Butts Co. 100
acres in Lot 6 half separated by Little Sandy Creek. Wit: JAMES V.
HOGG, EDW. WEAVER, WM. PRESSLEY.

Page 440: July 1, 1828 between GEORGE BRITTAIN and RICHARD POUND, 9th Dist. formerly Henry now Butts Co. cont. 80 acres part 8, 36th Dist. for $335. JOHN TARPLEY, ABEL ROBINSON, Clk. Sgd. GEORGE BRITTAIN.

Page 440-2: Butts Co. Feb. 28, 1827 between HUGH HAMIL and CLARK HAMIL for $200 1st. Dist. formerly Henry now Butts Co. Lot 17, cont. 101 1/4 acres. JAMES V. HOGG, ABEL ROBINSON, Clk., HUGH HAMIL. Sgd.

Page 441: Feb. 12, 1827 between DAVID F. EVANS and LEVI MARTIN, Pike Co., Ga. in 3rd Dist. of formerly Monroe now Butts Co. #144, 101 1/2 acres N. half for $500. FORT WM. REEVES, PRIER REEVES and Sgd. DAVID F. EVANS (his mark).

Page 443: Butts Co., Ga. Feb. 6, 1827 between BENJAMIN F. TUCKER and ABEL L. ROBINSON and SAMUEL STRAHAM for $500 #147 in the 1st Dist. formerly Henry now Butts Co. Witt: JAMES L. BURKS, JOHN CARGILE JJC. Sgd. B. F. TUCKER and A. L. ROBINSON.

Page 444: Butts Co. ELIJAH FULLER for $400 to ROBERT W. HUNTER, a negro STOVER sound in body and mind, BETTA a woman about 35 years old, HIRAM 4 years old, ASA about 10 months old, June 3, 1828. Wit: ISHMAEL STEWART, ALEX HUNTER. Sgd. ELIJAH FULLER.

Page 444-2: Butts Co., Rec'd of ROBERT W. HUNTER $75.25 being the full amount of purchase money rec'd from sale of a negro woman named HAGAR, 40 yrs. old, which was levied on as the property of BENJAMIN F. TUCKER to satisfy a fi fa in favor of ADNA ROE and the said HUMBER L. GAHAGAN, this 2nd of September 1828. R. N. HARKNESS, Sheriff.

Page 445: Jones Co., Ga. I, JOHN KING, in consideration of $600 paid by DAVID BERRY for Lot 174 in the 1st. Dist. of Henry Co., becomes the owner, drawn by JOHN KING this 9th day of Dec. 1825. Sgd. JOHN KING, wife PRISCILLA.

Page 446: Jasper Co., Ga. Aug. 30, 1828 between ROBERT TUGGLE and THOMAS G. JONES Exec. on estate of WILLIAM JONES, dec'd of Greene Co., Ga. for $300. Lot 187 8th Dist. of formerly Henry now Butts Co. cont. 202 1/2 acres; that the TUGGLES (ROBERT LEE and THOMAS) shall pay notes when due, otherwise it remains in full force in hand. Witt: HOLLIS COODY, JESSE LAYAL, JP. Sgd. ROBERT TUGGLE.

Page 447: Wilkinson Co., Ga. JAMES LINDSEY Sheriff, has "lines" on a certain negro woman named PHOEBE by virtue of a fi fa from a Court of Lawrence County when WILLIE ANN EASTERS was plaintiff and DUNCAN MCNEAR defendant. Sold for $300, highest bidder, JAMES LINDLEY, Sheriff.

Page 448: Butts County, Ga. March 4, 1828 in obedience to a fi fa suit of JOSEPH MOSS against BRIDGETT PAM (or POW) sold at public sale for $70, highest bidder to WM. P. FOSTER, in the 3rd Dist. in formerly Monroe, now Butts Co. 202 1/2 acres. Lot number not known. Wit: BENJAMIN F. TUCKER, A. L. ROBINSON, Clk. of Court and R. W. HARKNESS, Sheriff.

Page 449: Pike Co., Ga. Oct. 24, 1828 between LEVI MARTIN and GEORGE WILLIAMSON of Oglethorpe Co., Ga. for $500 formerly Monroe now Butts Co., Dist. 104 granted to ZEKE MARTIN, March 9, 1824, HENRY P. JONES, 101 1/4 acres. Wit: LEVI EVANS, WM. MARTIN and JOHN SESSIONS, JP.

Page 450: Butts Co., Mar. 13, 1824 between JESSE MARTIN and HENRY P. JONES for $100, 202 1/2 acres in the 1st. Dist. Lot 191. Granted to JESSE MARTIN dated March 1824. Wit: FEENEY HOLLIDAY, JAMES LAIN, SR. (JESSE MARTIN), JAMES TASSANEE, JJC.

Page 451: Burke Co., Ga. Jan. 10, 1828 between HENRY P. JONES and LEASTON SNEEDE, for $200 in Henry Co., Ga. at the time of survey 202 1/2 acres in the 1st. Dist. Lot 191, granted to JESSE MARTIN Mar. 9, 1824 bounded by lots 194, 162, 192, 190. Wit: MARTHA SLADES, JOHN H. HENRY. Sgd: HENRY P. JONES.

Page 452 and 453: Jan. 22, 1828 between LEASTON SNEED of Burke
Co., Ga. and JOHN GOODMAN of the Co. of Butts 1st. Dist. of Henry
formerly, now Butts Co. Lot 191 202 1/2 acres. Sgd: LEASTON SNEED, ALAN-
SON MOSTEY & JOHN HENDRICK.

Page 454: Butts Co., We, REBECCA WALKER, WM. H. GOLDSMITH, JAMES S.
MORRIS and BARTHOLOMEW STILL pays $2500 and are bound Nov. 3, 1828 as
administrators of JAMES WALKER, decd., and will make a true and just
account of his property unless a later last will and testament is found.
Signed: R. WALKER, W. H. GOLDSMITH, JAMES S. MORRIS & BARTHOLOMEW STILL.

Page 455: Butts Co., Ga. ABRAM M. JACKSON of Jackson Co., Ga. and
AUGUSTUS BINNS of Wilkes Co., Ga. have divided a lot of land in the
1st Dist. formerly Henry now Butts County #105 cont. 202 1/2 acres, A. M.
JACKSON the East side and A. BINNS the west, Nov. 16, 1828. A. L.
ROBINSON, JOHN MCMICHAEL JJC. Sgd: JACKSON & BINNS.

Page 455-2: Wilkes Co., Ga. Bolin BRYANT, 21 yrs of age last June
has made no other conveyance of a certain half of a Lot drawn by ARCHI-
BALD BRYANT in formerly Henry now Butts Co. Lot #105, Sept. 16, 1826.
JOHN HEAD, JP., BOHLING X BRYANT.

Page 456: Wilkes Co., Ga. Sept. 16, 1828 between BOLING BRIANT and
AUGUSTUS BINNS for $200, 101 1/4 acres 1/2 lot of #105 of formerly Henry
now Butts Co., drawn by ARCHIBALD and BRIANT (BOLING) of ALEXANDER S.
MYER'S Dist. of Wilkes Co. Wit: AMOS CHUMS, JOHN HEAD, JP and sgd:
BOLING BRYANT X his mark.

Page 457: Butts Co., Ga. J. RICHARD BAILEY in consideration of
the low I bear my daughter, HENRY MEDORA BAILEY, my only child, I hereby
bequeath the following property: HENRY, a negro man about 35 years of
age and HARRIETT age 17. I set my hand and seal this 20 of June 1830.
Sgd: RICHARD BAILEY. Wit: RALPH CUSHMAN, JOHN ROBINSON.

Page 458: Butts Co., Ga. July 24, 1828 between WILLIAM BYARS and
DAVID BYARS for $150 for land where DAVID lives, NE qtr. of Lot 129,
1st Dist. formerly Henry, now Butts Co., cont. 50 acres. THOMAS THOMAS,
JOSEPH KEY, JP., WM. BYARS. Sgd.

Page 458-2: Oglethorpe Co., Ga. HENRY BAILEY of Oglethorpe Co. for
the paternal love I bear toward my son, WILLIAM W. BAILEY, my youngest
child, I give one negro girl MARTHA, a yellow boy and complected, this
Jan. 8, 1827. Wit: RICHARD P. BAILEY. Sgd: HENRY BAILEY.

Page 459: Received of STEPHEN BLESSIT $232.50 in full payment for
a certain negro Girl named FENBY, 14 years old. Sgd: JACOB CLOWERS (?)
Wit: ROBERT BROWN and THOS. R. BARKER.

Page 459-2: Butts Co. November 13, 1824 between WM. BYARS and NATHAN
BYERS of Spartanburg Dist. S. C. for $260 in Dist. of formerly Henry now
Butts Co. 1/2 lot of 129 in S. Dist. adj. REDMAN, drawn by JOHN JONES
(or JOSEY) of FRAZIER'S District Liberty Co. conveyed to ENOCH DANIEL
and from him to RONERT HENDRY and from him to WILLIAM BYARS by deed
dated Jan. 28, 1827 signed, sealed and delivered. Sgd.: WM. BYARS.
(Note: I don't know if Liberty Co. is Ga. or S. C. since S. C. is involved)

Page 460: Butts Co. Nov. 17, 1828 between ABRAM M. JACKSON Jackson
Co., Ga. and JOHN MCMICHAEL, Butts Co. 1st Dist. formerly Henry now
Butts Co. part of Lot 105 cont. 50 acres in N corner of the lot for
$300. Test JOHN ROBINSON, A. L. ROBINSON, Clerk. Sgd: ABRAM M. JACKSON.

Page 461: Butts Co. in obedience to a fi fa from Butts Co., Ga.
Court, CHARLES RAMEY against JOHN KIMBROUGH, NEIL STRAHAN, the constable
siezed Lot 6, 1st. Dist. of Henry formerly now Butts 202 1/2 acres, after
advertising ROBT. W. HARKNESS, Sheriff, Nov. 1, 1828 and at public sale
sold to HAMLIN FREEMAN and WILLIAM V. BEENEY highest bidders for $38.50.
Wit: JAMES H. STARK, ERMINE CASE. Sgd: R. W. HARKNESS.

Page 462-3: Butts Co. in obedience fi fas issued from Court from
McIntosh Co. WILLIAM ROBERTS against JOHN CALDWELL, I SAMUEL CLAY, Sheriff
seized Lot 47 in the 14th Dist. of formerly Monroe now Butts Co., Ga.
cont. 202 1/2 acres Jan. 1, 1828 after advertising did sell at public
outcry to CHARLES WEST and BENNINGTON KING, highest bidders, the estate
of JAMES NEPHEW, decd. for $50. Jan. 5, 1828. Wit: WM. W. BINNS (or
BROWN), AUGUSTUS B. POPE, A. R. ROBINSON, & SAMUEL CLAY, Sheriff.

Page 464: Pike Co., Ga. Sept. 15, 1828 between THOS. BLOODWORTH,
Pike Co. for $200 paid by WM. M. BLAYLOCK in 4th Dist. Lot #17 formerly
Monroe now Butts Co. drawn by CHLOE SAVENEN of Morgan Co., Ga. Oct. 18,
1824, 202 1/2 acres, Sgd: THOS. BLOODWORTH. Wit: HIRAM B. BLOODWORTH,
SOLOMON BLOODWORTH and ISAAC BURNETT, C. M. COODY, J.P.

Page 465: Butts Co. Dec. 5, 1828 between WILLIAM L. PARKER and
DRONNA NUTT in the 1st Dist. of formerly Henry now Butts, Lot 170 granted
to JAMES ATWELL cont. 202 1/2 acres. Sgd: WM. C. PARKER, R. W. HARKNESS,
JOHN MCMICHAEL, JJC.

Page 467: Butts Co., Ga. Feb. 16, 1827 between ROBERT KIMBELL and
BENJAMIN KIMBELL for $200, #94 in 2nd Dist. of formerly Henry now Butts.
Co., Ga. NE part of tract. Wit: WM. KIMBELL. Sgd. ROBERT KIMBELL,
WM. MCCALLEY, A. L. ROBINSON, Clk.

Page 468: Butts Co., Ga. Dec. 15, 1828 between WM. KIMBELL and
BENJ. KIMBELL sold to WM. MCCALLEY for $150. 75 acres of land Lot #94
in 2nd Dist. of formerly Henry now Butts Co., Ga. STERLING KEMP, A. L.
ROBINSON, Clk. of Court. Sgd. WILLIAM KIMBELL and BENJAMIN KIMBELL.

Page 469: Oct. 13, 1823 between WM. PHELPS, JONES B. and HUGH H.
HEARD of Jasper Co., Ga. for $250, 202 1/2 acres in the 14th Dist. Monroe
Co., Ga. Sgd: WM. PHELPS. Wit: AQUILLA PHELPS and JOHN HEARD, JJC.

Page 470: Butts Co. July 3, 1827 between SAMUEL KIGHT and RICHARD
PARKER for $400 for 202 1/2 acres, formerly Monroe now Butts Co., Ga.
Lot 80, 4th Dist. WM. L. WILSON, SIMEON LOVEJOY. Sgd: SAMUEL KIGHT.

Page 471: Butts Co. Nov. 19, 1828 between JOHN and WM. F. STEPHENS
and SAMUEL LEAK, Lot #s 63 and 65 in 9th Dist. formerly Henry now Butts
Co. on the Ocmulgee River adj. they and LAWSON, 225 acres and one parcel
in Jasper Co. cont. 18 acres adj. RAY and BURTON and the River. Sgd:
JOHN STEPHENS. Wit: THOMAS KEY and JOSEPH KEY, JP and WM. STEPHENS.

Page 472: Jasper Co., Ga. JACOB WISE for the love he bears toward
his daughter ANNA N. VICKERS, I give the negro woman CYNTHIA and her
son WASHINGTON, this July the 24th 1828. Sgd: JACOB WISE. Wit: CREED
WISE, WM. HANCOCK.

Page 472-2: Butts Co. Dec. 23, 1828 between BENJ. TURNER of Henry
Co. and WM. BYARS, $300 in the 1st Dist. form. Henry now Butts Co. Lot
127 in plan of S's Dist. drawn by S. BENJ. TURNER. Wit: WM. BYARS,
THOS. THOMAS. Sgd: S. BENJ. TURNER and EDW. WEAVER, JP.

Page 473: Butts Co., Ga. Aug. 20, 1827 between ROBT. KIMBELL and
WM. MCCOLLEY for $110 part of Lot 94, 2nd Dist. of formerly Henry now
Butts Co. NW corner of lot Cont. 40 acres, bordering on D and BENJ.
KIMBELL. Wit: WM. KIMBELL & JAS. TURNER.

Page 474: Butts Co., Ga. Feb. 18, 1828 between JEREMIAH MULLOY
and WM. BYARS for $120 in the 1st. Dist. of formerly Henry now Butts Co.
the W. half of Lot 28, drawn by NORDICA HOWARD and from him conveyed to
MULLOY, Dec. 31, 1827. Wit: LEONARD ROAN, JOHN REEVES. Sgd: JEREMIAH
MULLOY.

Page 475: Butts Co., Ga. Jan. 28, 1826 between ROBERT HENDRY and
WM. BYARS for $200 in the 1st Dist. formerly Henry now Butts Co. Lot
3129, drawn in last Lottery by JOHN LOSEY ? of Frasers Dist. Liberty Co.
and by him conveyed to ENOCH DANIEL and then to ROBERT HENRY, Nov. 20,
1824. Wit: WM. PRESSLEY and WM. HERST. Sgd: ROBERT HENDRY.

Page 476: Butts Co., March 20, 1828 between ALDEN MICKELBERRY and CATLETT CAMPBELL for $600, 202 1/2 acres in 1st. Dist., Lot 44 in formerly Henry Co. now Butts Co. Sgd: ALDEN MICHELBERRY. Wit: WM. C. PARKER and JAMES MEEK, JC.

Page 1

Harper, William	Blisit, Nancy	April 6, 1826
Freeman, William	Kendrick, Adeline I.	May 17, 1826
Goldsmith, Allen	Campbell, Emily	May 7, 1826
Lee, John	Henderson, Elizabeth	June 20, 1826
McClure, William A.	Patrick, Susan	July 9, 1826
Rogers, John	Chapman, Mary Ann	July 4, 1826
Smith, Ferdinand	Smith, Martha	Aug. 8, 1826

Page 2

Bean(?), Willie	Crew,	July 27, 1826
Hartsfield, William T.	Spam (Ham?), Sophia	March 21, 1826
Brogdon, Peterson G.	Turner, Telletha	July 23, 1826
Mitchell, Peter	Collins, Sarah	Aug. 17, 1826
O'Neal, Aaron	Ray, Frances	July 20, 1826

Page 3

Hunt, Josiah	Tummerlin, Mary	Oct. 5, 1826
Higgiry, John	Bankston, Sophia	Oct. 5, 1826
Shepherd, Thomas I.	Look, Susan	Oct. 18, 1826
Hibler, Eldred N.	Brown, Nancy K.	Nov. 30, 1826
Barber, George W.	Lovejoy, Louisa N.	Jan. 28, 1827
Reynolds, Thos. O.	Cradic, Eliz.	Sept. 10, 1826
Hinkney (Kinksey), Wm.	White, Martha	Jan. 10, 1827
White, Henry B.	Phillips, Sarah	Feb. 6, 1827
Price, Robert	Harkness, N. N.	Mar. 8, 1827
Higgenbotham, A. B.	Benton, Mary	Mar. 16, 1827
Phillips, Nathan	Brown, Lucinda	Mar. 8, 1827

Page 5

Meck-(?), James B.	Phillips, Rebecca	May 9, 1827
Edwards, Ledford	Lawson, Stacey	Apr. 19, 1827
Paye (Payne), John	Hooten, Jessafy	Aug. 3, 1827
Mays, Jacob T.	Preston, Nancy	Aug. 23, 1827
Hardigue, Hiram	Coleman, Mary	Sept. 27, 1827

Page 6

Murray, Henry	Wise, Jane	Sept. 8, 1827
Knight, Woody K.	Kelly, Martha	Nov. 22, 1827
Smith, James	Lin, Martha W.	Nov. 28, 1827
Robert, James H.	Summerlin Louisa	Nov. 29, 1827
Cox, Willis	Davis, Mary	Dec. 6, 1827

Page 7

Coatty, William A.	Wall, Mary	July 10, 1827
Reeves, James	Phillips, Nancy	Dec. 18, 1827
Clayton, James	McBride, Mary	Jan. 14, 1828
Rollins, Williams	Welch, Lucy A.	Jan. 12, 1828
Wise, Augustus	Wise, Mecca	Dec. 16, 1827

Page 8

Wise, Barna	Wise, Aney	Jan. 6, 1828
Heard, Hugh H.	Gilmore, Jane	Dec. 23, 1827
Williams, John	McCord, Martha E.	Jan. 24, 1828
Maddox, Ira	Atkinson, Eliz. S.	Dec. 20, 1827
Welsh, Willey	Welsh, Lydia	Mar. 9, 1828

Page 9

Williams, C. A.	Clower, Mary	Mar. 18, 1828
Atkinson, Thos. F.	Hunter, Elmira	Mar. 25, 1828
Amos, Wm. C.	Harper, Sarah	May 29, 1828
Nickson, Wm. H.	Lawson, Margaret	May 22, 1828
Barber, Isiah W.	Patrick, Martha	July 3, 1828

Page 10

Williams, Robert	Eason, Ann E.	Aug. 20, 1828
Floyd, Sammie	McCun, Mary	Aug. 5, 1828
Bradley, Wm.	Reta, Ann Eliza	Aug. 21, 1828
Hogg, James V.	Medley, Tabitha	Aug. 21, 1828
Brown, John H.	Johnson, Nancy	Aug. 28, 1828

Page 11

Cox, Sammie	Wall, Eliz.	July 6, 1828
Kinnon, H. I. M.	Flewellen, Nancy	Sept. 16, 1828
Britton, Emanuel	Smith, Jane	July 13, 1828
Byars, Henry	Presley, Eliza	Oct. 2, 1828
Strickland, Ezekial H.	Bledson(e?), Eliza Ann	Nov. 6, 1828
Striplin, David	Dunn, Ann	Nov. 23, 1828

Page 12

Oliver, John I.	Pendleton, Louisa Emily	Dec. 4, 1828
Leseur, Carry	Sharp, Eliz. Ann	Dec. 18, 1828
Pearson, Daniel W.	Nolen, Nancy	Dec. 16, 1828
Ridgeway, Boyle	Brown, Eliz. W.	Dec. 25, 1828
Quimmet, James H.	Strickland, Elizer	Jan. 8, 1829

Page 13

Rice, Stephen W.	Berry, Julia M.	Jan. 15, 1829
Quincy, Calvin	Waldrop, Dorcas	Dec. 28, 1828
Amos, O. M.	Robinson, Christian	Jan. 15, 1829
Smith, Huting	Springfield, Rebecca	Jan. 15, 1829
Couch, Dury	Coating, Nancy	Jan. 6, 1829

Page 14

Crum, Robert M.	Edwards, Milley	Nov. 2, 1829
Hasty, Obidiah A.	Bridges, Roena	Jan. 27, 1829
Conger, Amos A.	Jinks, Rosannah	Dec. 22, 1828
Bradley, Wm.	Rhea, Susan S.	Dec. 21, 1828
Etheridge, Caswell	Bond, Deanna	Feb. 4, 1829
Flewellen, Wm. H.	Mason, Luraney	Feb. 5, 1829
Jackson, Hinson H.	Faulkner, Oliva	Feb. 10, 1829
Bearding, Elijah	Wright, Harriett	Feb. 12, 1829
Gahagin, Lawrence	Mobley, Eley F.	Feb. 17, 1829
Springfield, Moses	Andrews, Margaret	Feb. 19, 1829
Cobb, Levi	Walker, Rebecher	Nov. 18, 1829

Page 15

Omon, John G.	Crain, Eliza A.	Mar. 11, 1829
Kennady, James	Crain, Harriett	Mar. 25, 1829
Edwards, John	Lawson, Susannah	30, 1827
Reeves, Green B.	Thompson, Nancy	Dec. 5, 1827
Mason, John	Holmes, Nancy	Dec. 23, 1827
Bledsoe, Harvey G.	Hall, Julia	Oct. 26, 1828
Capps, John	Wilkerson, Sarah	Mar. 3, 1829

Page 16

Williams, Hubbard	Moore, Emily	Mar. 10, 1829

Page 17

Adams, Britain	Cheek, Frances	July 20, 1826
Bankston, Alfred	Blessit, Polly	Apr. 30, 1829
Bailey, Richard	Watts, Emily B.	Apr. 28, 1829
Deason, John	McClure, Mary	Jan. 15, 1829
Andrews, James	Muckelroy, Seny	Apr. 2, 1829
Nicks, Joseph R.	Clay, Mahala	June 9, 1829

Page 18

Summerlin, Joseph	McGee, Seletha W.	June 11, 1829
Jones, Wm. C.	Smiley, Caroline M.	July 10, 1829
Falkner, James N.	Gaston, Emily	July 30, 1829
White, Christopher	Lee, Jane	July 9, 1829
McCoy, Henry	McMichael, Nancy	Aug. 25, 1829
Lee, Henry	Clay, Eliz B.	Sept. 17, 1829

Page 19

Smith, Robert	Pope, Pheriby	Sept. 2, 1829
Bally, James	Higgins, Eliza	Sept. 22, 1829
Anderson, James	Harris, Sally	Oct. 15, 1829
Bridges, William	Jinks, Mary	Oct. 29, 1829
Weathers, Joel	Hartsfield, Mary	Nov. 15, 1829
Blessit, John	Collins, Frances	Nov. 26, 1829
Smith, George W.	Raon, Frances M.	Nov. 24, 1829

Page 20

Freeman, Hamblin	Taylor, Mary	Dec. 6, 1829
Ransom, James	Holloway, Julia	Dec. 10, 1829
Hardman, Uriah	Oats, Charlotte	Oct. 15, 1829
Head, Willis	Harper, Eliz. D.	Nov. 12, 1829
Buchanan, Thos. E.	Edmondson, Sarah Ann	Dec. 24, 1829
Collier, Benj. F.	Kennon, Louise	Dec. 25, 1829

Page 21

Watson, Robert	Wooten, Eliz	Dec. 20, 1829
Harrison, James	Brown, Richanry	Jan. 3, 1830
Martin, Daniel	Eason, Lydia	Feb. 23, 1830
Dawson, John	Smith, Keziah	Feb. 18, 1830
Moore, Willis	Conger, Rebecca	Feb. 28, 1830
Lindsey, Joseph	Branham, Hansy	Mar. 3, 1830

Page 22

Penn, John T.	Hood, Rebecca	Dec. 21, 1829
Hardin, Henry	Coatney, Lucinda	Dec. 28, 1829
Moore, Lewis	Hunter, Nancy	Feb. 25, 1830
Wise, Isiah	Smith, Rosannah	Mar. 18, 1830
McCord, Greer	Mickelberry, Maryann C.	Apr. 4, 1830
Gray, William	Woodward, Rebecca	Apr. 4, 1830

Page 23

Ingram, John S.	Warlick, Mary Jinks (widow)	Apr. 8, 1830
Roberts, Isaac	Cockrie, Davces	Apr. 18, 1830
Laddon, Jepe	Smith, Louisa	Apr. 14, 1830
Burk, Littleton L.	McCune, Nancy	June 15, 1830
Morris, Andrew	Hancock, Nancy	June 17, 1830
Brown, William	Boice, Sarah	June 27, 1830

Page 24

Kirksey, Gideon	Kirksey, Nancy	July 8, 1830
King, John G.	Whitehead, Sarah L.	July 8, 1830
Bennett, Washington	Jinks, Gary	July 15, 1830
Mixon, Chas. W.	Williams, Eliz	July 28, 1830
Rhodes, James	Draper, Nancy	Aug. 5, 1830
Wright, Chas.	Alexander, Lucinda	June 2, 1830

Page 25

Head, Richard C.	Bowling, Harriet	June 3, 1830
Speaks, Geo. T.	Giles, Martha F.	Oct. 10, 1830
Eubanks, Wm. Geo.	Owen, Rebecca	Oct. 17, 1830
Harp. Sam'l	Jinks, Molly	June 17, 1830
Hasty, Thos. P.	Powell, Eliza	Oct. 17, 1830
Sanders, Robert B.	Mickleborough, Martha	Nov. 7, 1830
Floyd, Thompson	Mayfield, Galaza	Sept. 23, 1830

Page 26

Flowers, Theophilus	Flewellen, Louisa C.	Jan. 18, 1830
McDaniel, John H.	Lofton, Mary Ann C.	Nov. 25, 1830
Harkness, Josiah	Shadrick, Mary Ann	Sept. 3, 1830
Maddux, David	Pace, Malinda	Aug. 16, 1830
Bates, Horace Julius	Hendrick, Mary Ann	Jan. 3, 1831

Page 27

Basnadore, Matthew	Killeress, Eliz.	Feb. 24, 1831
Mayo, Stephen D.	Brown, Margaret	Feb. 15, 1831
Bailey, Charles	Hendrick, Eliz	Mar. 15, 1831

Riddle, Bennett S.	Phelps, Emily	Mar. 30, 1831
McClane, Sehiel James	Baird, Louisa	Mar. 8, 1831
Malone, Spencer	Parker, Eveline	Apr. 10, 1831

Page 28

Wise, Joel	Martin, Mahala	Apr. 24, 1831
Hearst, Washing W.	Presly, Marthy	Apr. 21, 1831
Parker, John	Owen, Eliz	May 17, 1831
Coatney, John B.	Trash, Luraney	June 24, 1831
Miller, Elijah	Springfield, Isabella	July 31, 1831
Marchman, John	Thomas, Mary Ann	Sept. 23, 1831
Walker, Thos.	Goin, Nancy	Sept. 29, 1831

Page 29

Woolf, George	Goin, Eliza	Oct. 5, 1831
Pike, Zion	Norris, Nancy	Jan. 23, 1831
McClure, John	Beauchamp, Anne	Jan. 14, 1830
Lee, Stewart	Barnett, Julia S.	Nov. 27, 1831
Ferguson, Alfred W.	Williams, Martha	Dec. 20, 1831
Heard, George W.	Heard, Caroline	Dec. 18, 1831

Page 30

Smith, William	Whitehead, Julia	Jan. 5, 1832
Nelson, Meredith	Mackleroy, Sarah	Jan. 28, 1832
Deason, Benjamin	McClower, James	Feb. 16, 1832
Ivy, (Ivey), Edwin	Bridges, Arreny	Feb. 23, 1832
Coalman, Robt. P.	Smith, Margaret	Mar. 1, 1832
Harmon, Joseph	Felts, Anne Mariah	Mar. 3, 1832
Daughtry, Alexander H.	Grier, Jane	Jan. 10, 1832

Page 31

Blalock, Wm.	McLin, Matilda F.	Feb. 17, 1832
Cann, Wm.	Tomlinson, Harriet	Mar. 15, 1832
Owens, Alfred	King, Sobrina	Dec. 28, 1831
Cochran, Thomas Y.	Cawthon, Mary Ann	Apr. 12, 1832
Buttrill, Wm.	Brooks, Charity	Apr. 24, 1832
Key, Joseph	Delmar, Eliz	Dec. 1, 1831
Die, James	Hardman, Martha	Jan. 5, 1832

Page 32

Robey, Robert	Robey, Nancy	May 13, 1832
Dicken, John	Kimbole, Margaret	Apr. 25, 1832
Thomas, Wm. S.	Chisom, Margaret	July 1, 1832
McCord, James R.	Carter, Mary Ann	Mar. 8, 1832
Willinham, Harvey	Hardman, Mary	Sept. 11, 1832
Williamson, Nathan C.	Summerlin, Irean	Oct. 21, 1832
Moore, George A.	Fletcher, Ann M.	Oct. 18, 1832

Page 33

Preston, Eliza I.	Mays, Lucy W.	Nov. 30, 1832
Gray, Allen	O'Nail, Palantine	Nov. 11, 1832
McMichael, Wm. G.	Gaston, Emily J.	Dec. 20, 1832
Nelson, Hiram	Lindsey, Anna	Dec. 24, 1832
Duke, Robert Y.	Douglas, Martha	Dec. 25, 1832

Page 34

Mobley, Marvin L.	Robinson, Mary A.	Dec. 28, 1832
Power, Enoch L.	Power, Eliz	Dec. 30, 1832
Thompson, Edward	Griffin, Sarah	Jan. 3, 1833
McGlown, Turner	Boswell, Lucinda	Jan. 26, 1833
Gardner, Wm. A.	Hogg, Sarah	Jan. 4, 1833

Page 35

Amos, John K.	Byars, Lucy	Jan. 27, 1833
Cox, David	Pittman, Mary	Jan. 24, 1833
Ray, Washington	Waldrip, Eliz	Mar. 11, 1833
Robinson, Thomas	McClendon, Eliza	Mar. 21, 1833
Moody, John M.	Tillery, Temperance Ann	Mar. 27, 1833
McLin, Robert H.	Potter, Exor	Apr. 20, 1833

Page 36
Blept (Bless), John M.   Moore, Eliz   Apr. 16, 1833
Duffey, David L.   Maddox, Mary   Dec. 27, 1833
Cotter, Wm. M.   Davis, Martha   June 9, 1833
Bledsoe, N. James   Berry, Mary   June 13, 1833
Giles, Thos. J.   Maddux, Mary   July 21, 1833
McCord, John   Alexander, Sarah   May 2, 1833

Page 37
Anderson, Nathaniel   Chatham, Eunice B.   July 18, 1833
Urguhart, Alexander   Knight, Aleatha   Jan. 17, 1832
Surer, Wm. G.   Rowlin, Sarah   Dec. 18, 1832
Carmichael, John B.   Andrews, Mary A.   Aug. 8, 1833
Jones, John E.   Thompson, Thozza   Oct. 19, 1833
Maxcey, John   Heard, Olivia   Oct. 24, 1833

Page 38
Mercer, Joysy   Stroud, Emily Caroline   Oct. 31, 1833
Hall, W. John   Rhea, Mary H.   Nov. 17, 1833
Torbet, Benj. F.   McCord, Mary E.   Nov. 19, 1833
Phillips. Reuben   Greer, Martha   Nov. 21, 1833
Hogue, Cunningham   Hamilton, Nancy   Dec. 6, 1833
Bailey, Charles   Smartt, Amanda M. F.   Dec. 5, 1833

Page 39
Gilmore, Humphries J. W.   Coleman, Sarah H.   Dec. 8, 1833
McCune, Alexander   Payne, Malinda   Oct. 26, 1833
Skinner, James G.   Maddox, Eliz   Dec. 20, 1833
Byars, Richard   Kimbrough, Elvira   Dec. 22, 1833
Price, Tapley   Tomlinson, Suffana   Nov. 13, 1833
Sanders, Thos. J.   Atkinson, Lucy   Jan. 2, 1834
Collins, Irben   Carmichael, Matilda   Jan. 16, 1834

Page 40
McClure, Thomas   Hardy, Sarah   Dec. 19, 1833
Davis, Chrispin   Bray, Martha   Nov. 28, 1833
Norris, George   Payne, Olive   Feb. 16, 1834
Ware, John S.   Gates, Jane   Feb. 27, 1834
White, Peyton H.   Lee, Sarah H.   Feb. 20, 1834
Miller, Wm. H.   Ray, Eliza   Feb. 27, 1834
Sanders, Alex.   Broughton, Mary Ann   Jan. 9, 1834

Page 41
Meddon (Madden?) Tolever   Johnson, Martha   Feb. 6, 1834
Spencer, David   Lemon, Jane   Apr. 3, 1834
Cleveland, Wm. J.   Blipit (Blisit) Lavina   Mar. 27, 1834
McCord, John W.   Cook, Mary   Mar. 29, 1834

Page 41
Capps, Moyes T.   Garrison, Mary   June 17, 1834
Hurst, Billington S.   McCallum, Eliz   Aug. 1, 1834
Parker, Mile   Taylor, Charity   July 20, 1834

Page 42
Whitt (White), John W.   Kilerease, Rilzy Ann   July 27, 1834
Herrin, Wm. H.   Stephens, Nancy   Sept. 2, 1834
Still-Well, Square   Foster, Ann   Sept. 7, 1834
McGlown, Wm.   Henningan, Louisa   Aug. 16, 1834
Gerguson, Thos. J.   McCullough, Hannah   Aug. 28, 1834
Taxton, Green C.   Weaver, Marthy J.   Sept. 11, 1834
McMichael, Griffin C.   Price, Ann   Oct. 16, 1834

Page 43
Robert, Giles T.   Warsack, Martha   Oct. 21, 1834
Jackson, Paskel H.   Crawford, Sarah   Oct. 16, 1834
Mayo, John M.   Mickelberry,
                                  Sarah Ann Rebecca   June 5, 1834
Bagwell, James W.   Norris, Mary Ann   Nov. 5, 1834
Tweedell,
  Alex Washington Holbert   Moore, Sarah   Nov. 27, 1834

111

Mann, Asa M.	Tazewell, Eliza	Nov. 26, 1832

Page 44

Head, William	Smith, Lemima	Oct. 28, 1834
Mason, Leonard	Lofton, Jane Diana	Oct. 20, 1833
Mason, Larkin	Price, Rachel H.	May 11, 1834
Lindsey, John	Bellah, Lummina	Dec. 28, 1834
Weaver, John H.	Nixon, Carolina	Dec. 31, 1834
Williams, Nathan H.	Potter, Armintha	Jan. 1, 1835
Faulkner, James W.	McMichael, Lourany	Jan. 8, 1835
Moore, David B. M.	Davis, Elmira	Jan. 8, 1835

Page 45

Henderson, John	Pridgen, Marjorie	Jan. 9, 1835
Wheatley, Joseph	Prince, Lucy	Jan. 20, 1835
Low, Isaac	Brittain, Susan	July 10, 1834
Higgins, Joseph	Kay, Judith W.	Oct. 16, 1834
Stringfellow, Richard	Pridgen, Lucy Ann	Dec. 8, 1834
Duke, Henry M.	Ferguson, Elmira	Dec. 10, 1834
Jinks, Spencer	Kimbrough, Louisa	Jan. 8, 1835

Page 46

Draper, James	Connel, Rebecca	Feb. 4, 1835
Mason, Richard G.	Wood, Louise E.	Feb. 13, 1835
Tomlinson, Daniel	Robinson, Catherine Jane	Nov. 20, 1834
McNair, Samuel	Tyson, Mary	Feb. 17, 1835

Page 46

Smith, Richard	Watkins, Eliz. Adeline	Apr. 16, 1835
Andrews, Wm. Walters S.	Harrison, Jane	Oct. 26, 1833
Duffy, W. Samuel L.	Carmichael, Eliz.	Nov. 25, 1834

Page 47

Brawner, Wm. Henry J.	Duffey, Jane	Nov. 25, 1834
Harkness, James W.	Boyd, Martha	Apr. 20, 1835
Payne, Asa	Tyson, Eliza	Apr. 29, 1835
Goodwyn, Mack	Waller, Nancy M.	May 24, 1835
Wing, Andrew J.	Stratton, Martha	May 29, 1835
Britton, James	Holloway, Seleta	Mar. 26, 1835

Page 48

Harky, Uriah	Duffey, Rachel	Sept. 1, 1835
Harmon, Sherwood B.	McCoy, Eliz.	Sept. 4, 1835
Thaxton, Wm.	Clark, Martha R.	Sept. 17, 1835
Campbell, Simeon	Weaver, Nancy H.	Sept. 17, 1835
Bankston, Boling K.	Rogers, Eliz.	Dec. 28, 1834
Wright, Wm. P.	Griffin, Mazilla Ann	Sept. 20, 1835
Frasher (Thrasher), Samuel G.	Draper, Kiziah	Sept. 24, 1835

Page 49

Wakefield, Samuel	Lee, Sarah	Sept. 27, 1835
Harper, William	Clayton, Harriett	Feb. 3, 1835
McLin, Robert	Fowler, Cynthia	Sept. 22, 1835
Taylor, Noah W.	Michleberry, Frances Jane	Nov. 1, 1835
Hill, John W.	Mounts, Martha A.	Oct. 20, 1835
Gilmore, Robt.	Smith, Julia	Dec. 8, 1835
O'Neal, Edward W.	Gray, Sara	Dec. 10, 1835

Page 50

Spears, Harvey	Wayne, Margaret J.	Dec. 17, 1836
Tomlinson, Wm.	Wallace, Susan	Dec. 17, 1835
Harkness, W. Wm. S. B.	Faulkner, Emily A.	Dec. 24, 1835
Preston, James M.	Smith, Permella W.	Dec. 28, 1835
Coen, Wm. A.	Kirksey, Margaret	Dec. 31, 1835
Vineson, Henry J.	Donaldson, Mary N.	Jan. 3, 1836
Slaughter, Robt. W.	Speake, Margaret	Jan. 6, 1836

Page 51

Wheeler, Gideon R.	Connell, Mary	Jan. 12, 1836

Lisles, John	Head, Catherine	Jan. 19, 1836
Johnson, John W.	Miller, Lydia A.	Jan. 28, 1836
Wilson, John R.	McCord, Mary A.	Mar. 14, 1836
Smith, David	Lovern, Eliza	Feb. 18, 1836
Maddux, Benj.	Hadin, Judy A.	Feb. 25, 1836
Chapin, Buford	Bankston, Nancy C.	Mar. 29, 1836

Page 52
Preston, John F.	Crawford, Louise Ann	Mar. 10, 1836
Goodwin, Stith	Hutto, Mariah	Mar. 17, 1836
Mayo, Robert P.	Preston, Elizabeth Ann	Nov. 29, 1835
Carmichael, Hugh W.	Thompson, Nancy	Apr. 17, 1836
Bence, Wm.	Tison, Jane	Apr. 19, 1836
Bankston, Abner	Turner, Sarah	Apr. 19, 1836

Page 53
?, John B.	Scott, Kesiah Ann G.	Dec. 22, 1831
Blank, Thomas	Duke, Ally	Apr. 17, 1836
Tennant, Andrew	Waller, Elizabeth	May 15, 1836
Hardman, Benjamin J.	Key, Demaris	Oct. 8, 1833
Wyatt, Z.	Delamar, Joanna	Nov. 19, 1835
Russell, Timothy J.	Bledsole, Emily J.	Aug. 14, 1836
Gresham, Thos. J.	Lee, Susan A.	Aug. 30, 1836

Page 54
Ross, Elias	Philips, Martha	Aug. 2, 1836
Ross, James	Morris, Mary Ann	Sept. 20, 1836
McKnight, John B.	Camp, Emilina	Oct. 13, 1836
Taylor, Wiley B.	Maddux, Mary	Oct. 24, 1836
Henderson, Green	Holloway, Martha	Dec. 20, 1836
Rowe, David	Springfield, Margaret	Dec. 15, 1836

Page 55
Thaxton, John	Weaver, Eliz.	Dec. 29, 1836
Golding, Jeremiah	Bray, Jane	June 16, 1836
Gallahar, Thos. F.	Golden, Mary	Dec. 22, 1836
Bellah, Reuben J.	Woodruff, Tabitha	Jan. 8, 1837
Simmons, Mitchell T.	Davis, Eliz.	Jan. 11, 1837
Smith, John	Harrison, Mary	Jan. 12, 1837
Mobley, Jackson	Watson, Mary	Jan. 20, 1837

Page 56
Moody, Benj.	Tennant, Sarah	Jan. 10, 1837
Hammond, John	Davis, Emily	Sept. 21, 1836
McClain, W. George	Callen, Eliz.	Mar. 1, 1837
Pye, Griffin F.	Johnson, Sarah R.	Mar. 2, 1837
Ferguson, Jonathan H.	McCallum, Rebecca	Mar. 12, 1837
Mays, Henry G.	Stroud, Matilda R.	Mar. 23, 1837

Page 57
Berry, John V.	McCune, Eliz. A.	Oct. 15, 1835
Anderson, Isham	Wright, Mary Ann	May 14, 1837
Rich, Jackson	Collins, Louisa	Dec. 3, 1835
Kendrick, Samuel	Hamie, Eliz.	May 15, 1836
Martin, Bartin	Woodruff, Malinda	Mar. 28, 1837
Cochran, Thomas G.	Boyd, Lucy A.	Jan. 8, 1837
Hurst, George	Shaddock, Rebecca	June 4, 1837

Page 58
McCune, Micajah	Atkinson, Nancy	Sept. 27, 1836
Higgins, Sterling	Beavers, Harriet B.	Oct. 20, 1836
Giles, James D.	Holloway, Gerona	July 13, 1837
Wright, John J.	Martin, Rebecca	July 13, 1837
Stodghill, Wm. F.	Adeline, Justine	June 5, 1837
McLane, George W.	Beard, Eliz Ann	July 17, 1837
Pearce, James	Prince, Sarah	July 23, 1837

Page 59
| Snoddy, Samuel | McClendon, Mary | Aug. 16, 1837 |

Haynes, Robt. H.	O'Neal, Eveline	Aug. 17, 1837
Mayo, Robt. T.	Lassiter, Lucy	Sept. 5, 1837
Carter, John	Mayo, Nancy J.	Sept. 14, 1837
Cothran, Jordan	Gilmore, Nancy G.	Sept. 28,1837
Byars, Obidiah	Teddars, Malinda	Sept. 28, 1837
Carter, Bradford	Byars, Lucretia	Oct. 18, 1837

Page 60

Bankston, Wm. R.	Collins, Mahaley	Oct. 5, 1837
Vinson, Andrew J.	Thaxton, Mary C.	Oct. 12, 1837
Johnson, Samuel	Bence, Sarah	Oct. 18, 1837
Herrall, George	Smith, Martha	Sept. 26, 1837
Hail, John	McClendon, Mary	Sept. 27, 1837
Wise, Frances M.	Kinard, Serena	Oct. 19, 1837
Gwinnett, A. J.	Tanner, O. Eliz. J.	Oct. 26, 1837

Page 61

Burkhart, Irvin (Ivan) Jacob	Harrison, Rachel Ann	Oct. 30, 1837
Harper, Wm.	Bankston, Jimima	Nov. 8, 1837
Wyatt, Wm.	Thompson, Catherine	Oct. 15, 1837
Rabun, Henry	Alred, Harriett	Nov. 24, 1837
Sims, Mark	Gunn, Mary W.	Nov. 24, 1837
Lindsey, Caleb A.	Dodd, Julia	Dec. 31, 1837
Simmons, James M.	Davis, Nancy	Jan. 3, 1838

Page 62

Maddox, James T.	Hancock, Harriet H.	Nov. 30, 1837
Woodfin, Moses	Hutto, Mary Ann	Jan. 4, 1838
Hutto, Hamilton	McDuff, Cynthia	Jan. 11, 1838
Stone, Hezekiah	Waller, Talitha	Dec. 21, 1837
Cook, William	Key, Amelia C.	Jan. 4, 1838
Oxford, Edward B.	McDowell, Eliz. G.	Dec. 28, 1837

Page 63

Maddux, Ebinezar	Kinard, Terisa	Jan. 28, 1838
Burford, Samuel P.	Powell, Louisa	Feb. 4, 1838
Bickerstall, A. H.	Compton, Susan C.	Jan. 16, 1838
Lee, James	Wright, Matilda	Feb. 15, 1838
Findley, Thomas P.	McClure, Mary A.	Feb. 4, 1838
Phillips, Elijah	Britton, Henry	Mar. 8, 1838

Page 64

Pierce, Andrew	Franklin, Elizabeth	Mar. 18, 1838
Ramsey, Hiram	Gwinnett, Nancy	July 20, 1837
Compton, P. M.	Deveaux, Lydia	Apr. 8, 1838
Jarrell, William	Camp, Mary	Feb. 6, 1838
Phillips, Jefferson	Britton, Lucy Ann	Mar. 29, 1838
Adams, Seth K.	McClendon, Mary G.	Apr. 15, 1838
King, Alfred H.	Jinks, Narcissa	May 27, 1838

Page 65

Connell, Thomas	Andres (orW), Margaret	July 26, 1838
Dicken, Hampton T.	Bird, Ellen D.	Aug. 5, 1838
Brewer, Alfred	Coleman, Mary A.	June 5, 1838
Sanders, Thos. J.	Patterson, Eliz.	June 14, 1838
Douglas, Robert F.	Douglas, Sara Jane	July 19, 1838
Hand, Willis	Cawthon, Nancy	Aug. 10, 1837
Willard, Henry	Powell, Lucinda	Aug. 26, 1838

Page 66

Dye, William	Hardman, Athy	Sept. 13, 1838
Mann, James W.	Smith, Elizabeth	Sept. 18, 1838
Moore, Wm. J.	Thrash, Milly Ann	Sept. 25, 1838
Jester, Abner	Foster, Anjuline	Sept. 26, 1838
Jones, Wiley	Hardy, Mary	Oct. 25, 1838

Page 67

| Hamil, Willis J. | Phillips, Julia Ann | Nov. 1, 1838 |

Phillips, John	Wilson, Eliza Ann	Nov. 15, 1838
Shadrick, Wm.	Maddox, Ava	Nov. 22, 1838
McMichael, LeRoy	McCune, Mary T.	Sept. 26, 1838
Hendrick, Mastin D.	Douglas, Martha	Nov. 1, 1838
Thurman, John B.	Glass, Mary E.	Dec. 5, 1838
Norris, Yancey R.	Berry, Martha	Dec. 18, 1838
Johnson, Benj. J.	McLin, Kathryn	Jan. 1, 1839
Buttrill, Britton	Hudson, Louisa A.	Dec. 18, 1838

Page 68
Andrews, Samuel W.	Johnson, Ann	Jan. 6, 1839
McClendon, James W.	Anderson, Mary Ann	Jan. 27, 1839
Tomlinson, Leonard F.	Moore, Martha	Feb. 17, 1839
Woodruff, Erwin	Bellah, Mary	Mar. 18, 1838
Key, Richard	Smith, Mariah	Apr. 7, 1839
Barber, Josiah W.	Smith, Adaline	Apr. 19, 1838

Page 69
Huddleston, John F.	Phillips, Eliza A.	July 3, 1839
Strickland, Solomon	Harwick, Hulda A.	June 5, 1839
Pettigrew, John E.	Harkness, Mary H.	July 18, 1839
Ragland, Williamson	Ragland, Eliza	July 13, 1838
Smith, James M.	Freeman, Jimmina	Aug. 11, 1838
Bickerstaff, Wm. J.	Humber, Martha C.	Sept. 13, 1838

Page 70
Harris, Thomas	Kimbrough, Adaline	Aug. 26, 1839
Standard, Fleming J.	Head, Caroline	Oct. 3, 1838
Pearce, Thomas	Moody, Martha	Sept. 1, 1838
Kimbrough, John	Wright, Edey	Oct. 15, 1838
Andrews, John	Loyal, Sarah A. H.	Nov. 7, 1838
Gaston, Matthew	Curry, Agnes	Dec. 8, 1838

Page 71
Bigbie, Archibald	Smith, Martha Ann	Dec. 11, 1839
Cretinden, James	Mayfield, Nancy	May 7, 1839
Cleaton, Austin	Bentley, Sarah	Nov. 7, 1839
McEnin, Alexander	Payne, Roda	Dec. 5, 1839
Jones, Wm. E.	Duke, Jane Rebecca	Jan. 3, 1840
Woodward, Wm.	Andrews, Nancy	Dec. 19, 1839

Page 72
Harkness, Thos. M.	Berry, Harriett C.	Dec. 18, 1839
Bickerstaff, Tollard B.	Hancock, Sophia	July 11, 1839
Grimmet, Thos. L.	Magbie, Sarah A. R.	Nov. 28, 1839
Bailey, Stephen	Pearman, Martha Susan	Dec. 6, 1838
Foster, William J.	Jester, Mary	Dec. 14, 1838
Standard, George H.	Goggins, Mary	Jan. 7, 1840
Robert, Humber	Anderson, Eldora	Jan. 21, 1840

Page 73
Lee, Larkin	Jolly, Eliz. Jane	Jan. 21, 1840
Bailey, Thos. R.	Greer, Mary	Jan. 23, 1840
Wood, Richard N.	Kimbrough, Mary Ann	Dec. 22, 1839
Hardy, Elbert	Woodfin, Sarah	Feb. 27, 1840
Torbet, Hugh S.	Bently, Mary Ann	Feb. 13, 1840
Beauchamp, John	McClure, Elizabeth	Mar. 5, 1840

Page 74
Mayo, Wm. J. D.	Mayo, Nancy T.	Mar. 12, 1840
Head, Wm. H.	Delemar, Amanda	Mar. 13, 1840
Davis, Wm.	McCormit, Leah (McCormick)	Mar. 18, 1840
Harris, Thos.	Byars, Artomissa	Mar. 12, 1840
Morris, John C.	Watkins, Nancy	Jan. 23, 1840
Williamson, Nathan C.	Thompson, Agnes	June 25, 1840
Hamilton, Tyre D.	Ellis, Elizabeth Ann	Aug. 26, 1840

Page 75
Middlebrooks, James W.   Anderson, Elizabeth   Sept. 24, 1840
Bowles, Jesse H.   Chafin, Elizabeth   Oct. 8, 1840
Draper, John   Davis, Telitha G.   Aug. 11, 1840
O'Neal, Zachariah   Taylor, Parmela   Oct. 16, 1840
Mills, Thomas   Gainey, Sarah   Oct. 19, 1840

Page 76
Clark, Wm. F.   Holloway, Sophronia   Oct. 29, 1840
Kilcrease, Jackson   Payne, Elizabeth   Oct. 29, 1840
Madden, Richard C.   Hately, Sarah   Oct. 21, 1840
Underwood, Lawson   Preston, Patsy P.   Nov. 8, 1840
McCord, James R.   Watts, Nancy   Nov. 17, 1840
Greer, David   Robinson, Matilda Ann   Oct. 8, 1840
Watkins, Alfred M.   Byars, Martha Jane   Nov. 26, 1840

Page 77
Gossett, John   Campbell, Eliza   Nov. 26, 1840
Preston, Wm. G.   Smith, Delia   Dec. 20, 1840
Barnett, John L.   Duncan, Pheba A.   Dec. 8, 1840
Cole, John B.   McCoy, Susanna H.   Dec. 22, 1840
Tredwell, Seborn N.   Willard, Sarah E.   Jan. 22, 1835
Foster, Claiborn   Connell, Catherine   Dec. 30, 1840
Harkness, John B.   Tucker, Elizabeth Ann   Jan. 3, 1841

Page 78
Fuller (Paller), Waldrop Goin, Mary   Dec. 27, 1840
Buttrill, Asa   Manley, Lucy J.   Jan. 14, 1841
Bledsoe, Elijah M.   Carter, Susan   Feb. 9, 1841
Boyd, James   Smith, Ailsey   Jan. __, 1841
Shilds (Shields), Wm. B. Lyon, Adaline H.   Mar. 4, 1841

Page 79
Thompson, Vincent T.   Mayo, Morning L.   Apr. 1, 1841
McCallum, Ignatius F.   Benson, Mary M.   Mar. 25, 1841
Floyd, William   Moody, Elizabeth   Mar. 12, 1840
Mays, Robert   McCune, Nancy   Dec. 15, 1840
Daughtery, Alexander J.   Key, Margaret   May 16, 1841
Bailey, David J.   Grandland, Susan Mary   May 25, 1841

Page 80
McMichael, Levi   Redman, Mary C.   July 1, 1841
Harkness, James   Hendrick, Mary   June 8, 1841
Plymale, Michael   Moore, Sarah H.   Aug. 1, 1841
Williams, Joseph   Draper, Mary Ann Rebecca   June 13, 1841
Higgins, Wm. H.   Clark, Adaline C.   July 30, 1841
Fullerton, Wm. R.   Hammond, Sarah R.   Aug. 18, 1841
Forrester, George   Gresham, Mary F.   Sept. 7, 1841

Page 81
Mayo, James C. T.   Powell, Mary   Sept. 19, 1841
McDaniel, John H.   Hunter, Margaret   Oct. 13, 1841
Elder, Wm. A.   Barlow, Cyntha   Oct. 21, 1841
Harper, Reuben J.   Carter, Martha A.   Nov. 1, 1841
Harper, Benjamin L.   Tarpley, Eliz. H.   Nov. 2, 1841
Watkins, Albert A.   Nolen, Sarah R.   Nov. 4, 1841
Irby, Samuel   Gilbert, Elizabeth   Nov. 18, 1841

Page 82
Smith, Wm. H.   Lyon, Frances A. G.   Oct. 6, 1841
Hodges, Wm.   Andrews or (Anderson), Elizabeth Nov. 25, 1841
Nolen, Morda   Lasiter, Martha T.   Nov. 30, 1841
Bankston, Henry M.   Davis, Permelia B.   Dec. 31, 1841
Barnett, George W.   Walker, Elizabeth   Dec. 19, 1841
Smith, Austin G.   Lumsden, Mary   Jan. 6, 1842
Mounee, Urbin D.   Gilmore, Martha   Jan. 23, 1842

Page 83
Payne, Henry   Mires, Sarah   Nov. 14, 1841

116

Shields, James M.	Smith, Mary C.	Dec. 30, 1841
Henderson, Jacob J.	Powell, Caroline	Dec. 30, 1841
Chafin, Nathan Perry	Loving, Mable	Dec. 16, 1841
Smith, Samuel F.	Lindsey, Amy	Jan. 9, 1842
Smith, Wm. S.	Hughs, Mary	Jan. 19, 1842

Page 84

Duffey, Samuel J.	Burford, Elizabeth	Jan. 27, 1842
Marshall, Ira	Cole, Elizabeth	Dec. 7, 1841
Waller, Jeremiah P.	Lindsey, Lydia	Dec. 19, 1842
Bennett, Benjamine J.	Harrison, Margaret	Mar. 29, 1842
Holloway, Simpson, J.	Crabtree, Martha	Mar. 29, 1842

Page 85

Crawford, Richard	Cargile, E. M.	Apr. 21, 1842
Glass, Pleasant M.	Miller, Margaret H.	June 22, 1843
Butts, Noah	Jenkins, Martha G.	Feb. 24, 1842
Kitchens, Henry	Prince, Mary	Dec. 12, 1841
McBride, John W.	Loften, Frances A.	May 3, 1842
Wise, Francis M.	Kinard, Martha	June 12, 1842

Page 86

McWorther, Wm. C. D.	Mangham, Cathrine F.	July 11, 1842
Smith, Francis A.	Brady, Mary	Sept. 16, 1842
Jackson, Milton H.	Bankston, Mary A.	Sept. 28, 1842
Stockbridge, Ebenezer	Fellows, Sarah	Oct. 13, 1842
Gamble, James A.	Gamble, Nancy H.	Nov. 30, 1842
Gilmore, Roburtus F.	Bond, Jane	Dec. 7, 1842
Johnson, Arnold	Thaxton, Elizabeth	July 4, 1842

Page 87

Kimbell, James G.	Anderson, Martha	July 30, 1843
Gilmore, Robert F.	Bond, Sara Jane	Dec. 1, 1842
Payne, Wm. J.	Wallace, Mary	Dec. 24, 1842
McCurdy, John W.	Tiddards, Ann	Dec. 22, 1842
McKelroy, Dawson	Mayo, Margaret	Dec. 29, 1842
Higgins, John H.	Beavers, Sarah C.	Jan. 24, 1843
Duke, Weakley W.	Jenkins, Penelope	Dec. 27, 1842

Page 88

Lowery, Jackson	Cawthon, Martha	Dec. 22, 1842
Delemer, James C.	Smith, Cathrine	Jan. 3, 1843
Bowlin, Wm.	Stodghill, Malvana	Jan. 24, 1843
Cape, John	Wilson, Louisa	Mar. 23, 1843
Lee, Harny S.	Malone, Mary A.	Apr. 2, 1843
Jester, Henry	Lindsey, Mary Ann	June 15, 1842

Page 89

Jinks, Wiley	Hancock, Permelia	Aug. 17, 1842
Johnson, Joel T.	Allen, Susan A.	Mar. 8, 1843
Duke, Wm. M.	Wilkerson, Nancy C.	July 5, 1843
Jinks, Burrell	Maxey, Mary	July 19, 1843
Lasseter, Perry	Robertson, Haney	Oct. 12, 1843
Bellah, Samuel	Lindsey, Lucinda	Nov. 6, 1843
Barron, Henry	Eidson, Penelope	Nov. 19, 1843

Page 90

Johnson, Burrell	Collons, Jane	July 20, 1843
Byars, Harold	Nutt, Eliza	Nov. 23, 1843
Lawshee, Lewis	Atkinson, Eliza	Dec. 7, 1843
Wilson, John E.	Davis, Amanda Ann	April 22, 1843
Folds, William	Goldwin, Frances G.	Nov. 29, 1843
Bledsoe, James H.	Curry, Mary Ann	Dec. 24, 1843
Scandrett, Wm. A.	McClendon, Harriett C.	Nov. 15, 1843

Page 91

Latson, George J.	Martin, Nancy	Dec. 21, 1843
Hardy, Josiah	Andrews, Diannah	Jan. 26, 1843
Sherry, Wm.	Lewis, Eliz. H.	Jan. 2, 1844

Henderson, Jacob J.	Beauchamp. Eliz.	Jan. 3, 1844
Bettenton, Leroy	Duke, Martha Ann	Jan. 7, 1844
Malone, Charles B.	Burford, Harriett E.	Jan. 11, 1844
Lindsey, John G.	Mangham, Eleanor	Dec. 19, 1843

Page 92
Ray, Mark	Mason, Nancy	Dec. 28, 1843
Lindsey, Jonathon	Waldrip, Rebecca	Jan. 13, 1842
Lawson, Robert	Hendrick, Lucy E.	Dec. 1, 1842
Dicken, Marion M.	Freeman, Eliz A.	Jan. 11, 1844
Henderson, James	Rhodes, Nancy	Mar. 4, 1844
Giles, Wm. J.	Lunsden, Mary Ann	May 5, 1844

Page 93
Hungerford, Charles	Hendricks, Lucy E.	June 20, 1844
Pool, Wm.	Nelson, Jane	June 30, 1844
Collins, Samuel	Folds, Sarah Ann Preston	July 8, 1844
Duke, Henry	Stodghill, Catherine	Oct. 19, 1843
Dempsey, Harry W.	Hand, Rebecca	Dec. 30, 1843
Latson, David W. T.	Martin, Susan	Jan. 1, 1844

Page 94
Giles, Wm. H.	Meredith, Nancy	May 16, 1844
Heath, Chappell	Weaver, Elizabeth	Oct. 3, 1842
Carr, David S.	Hartsfield, Eliz.	Oct. 8, 1842
McElhanney, Wm. L.	Johnson, Matilda A. C.	Nov. 19, 1842
Moore, Stephen	Vickers, Eliz.	Oct. 15, 1843
Saunders, Simon H.	Lyons, Loxina Luckie	Feb. 22, 1844

Page 95
Thompson, John H.	Key, Mary L.	Sept. 6, 1844
Davis, Jonathan	Bledsoe, Mary Ann	Oct. 4, 1844
Funderburk, Joseph S.	Kell, Sarah E.	Nov. 6, 1844
Broughan, James	Jinks, Mary Ann	Nov. 24, 1844
Slaughter, Wm. A.	Wise, Sarah Jane	May 9, 1844
Holifield, James B.	Barnett, Caroline B.	Nov. 15, 1844

Page 96
Lummus, Cornelius	Gunn, Emmeline	Oct. 13, 1844
Sparks, Wm.	Evens, Eliz. W.	Dec. 10, 1844
Fielder, Joseph	McMichael, Eliz. A.	Dec. 17, 1844
Gregory, Robert	Hughs, Rebecca	Dec. 2, 1844
Meredith, Wm.	Aiken, Mary Ann	Dec. 26, 1844
Burford, Wm. H.	Burford, Eliza C.	Dec. 29, 1844

Page 97
Andrews, Walter S.	Phillips, Mary	Oct. 30, 1844
Thomason, Jefferson C.	McKibben, Margaret	Dec. 31, 1844
Payne, Francis P.	Payne, Jane	Dec. 12, 1844
Franklin, Wm.	Payne, Nancy	Jan. 15, 1845
Thompson, Wm. J.	Prior, Signey G.	Jan. 9, 1845
Higgins, Pattillo	Gregory, Mary A. Y.	Dec. 15, 1844
Byars, Andrew F.	Weaver, Lucy Ann	Jan. 15, 1845

Page 98
Lunceford, Cornelius S.	Evens, Mary Ann	Jan. 23, 1845
Stark, James C.	Anderson, Minerva E.	Feb. 5, 1845
Maddux, David	Kinard, Christinia	Feb. 6, 1845
Atkinson, Abner	McDaniel, Henrietta	Mar. 6, 1845
Hixon, Eldred S.	Kinard, Miley A.	Dec. 2, 1835
Griffin, Robert	Hixon, Mary H.	Dec. 3, 1835

Page 99
English, Wm. W.	Donaldson, Lavinia	Jan. 23, 1840
Latson, Robert	Payne, Martha	July 6, 1840
Folds, Thomas	Cornell, Eliz.	May 10, 1840
Williams, Augustine	Phillips, Lalitha Jane	Sept. 11, 1843
Donelson, Wm. H.	Collens, Nancy E.	Nov. 3, 1842
Hall, David	Shockly, Leander A.	Oct. 1, 1844
Singley, John L.	Cole, Emily	Jan. 26, 1845

Benton, Jessie	Sellers, Ellender	Mar. 15, 1845
Gregory, Thomas Y.	Bryant, Malinda	May 8, 1845
Mangum, James M.	McCoy, Jane	May 21, 1845
Sutton, Stephen	Lovett, Harriet S.	Aug. 29, 1844
Mayo, Anderson	Mayfield, Sally	May 8, 1845
Maddux, Green B.	Thomas, Elizabeth	Feb. 27, 1845
Upchurch, Wm. J.	Kelly, Catherine	June 12, 1845

Page 101
Smith, John A.	Tourrell, Ellen Ann	June 29, 1845
Marshall, Ira J.	Tingle, Winney	Feb. 13, 1845
Greer, Wm. H.	Torbet, Rosannah	May 29, 1845
Bowman, John	Reeves, Sara W.	July 10, 1845
Hunter, Samuel S.	Smith, Martha	Sept. 12, 1845
Sparks, John S.	Goodwin, Mary	Oct. 1, 1845
Hughs, Wm. B.	Britton, Mary	Oct. 2, 1845

Page 102
Bartlett, George T.	Saunders, Virginia L.	Oct. 16, 1845
Weaver, Wm. L.	Andrews, Emily L.	Oct. 19, 1845
Woodruff, Wm. B.	Tillery, Margaret	Oct. 27, 1845
Morris, James M.	Jarrell, Annis	Oct. 30, 1845
Murdock, Henry F.	Reeves, Emily	Nov. 12, 1845
Goddard, Lucius	Redman, Martha	Nov. 13, 1845
Waldrop, Edmund	Dearing, Lucy Ann	Nov. 16, 1845

Page 103
Hughes, E. D.	Philips, Mary	Nov. 20, 1845
Blanks, John	Dorton, Emeline	Dec. 17, 1845
Alleson, Robt. W.	Barber, Susan A.	Dec. 18, 1845
Kendrick, Burwell Jones	Bond, Margaret Dianna	Dec. 28, 1845
Byars, Benjamin M.	Meredith, Eliza Jane	Jan. 1, 1846
Barron, Wm. J.	Cleveland, Eliz M.	Dec. 4, 1845
Weaver, Wm. R.	Thomas, Malinda	Jan. 20, 1846

Page 104
Hardy, Jesse	Henderson, Mahala	Jan. 1, 1846
Reeves, Milton	Murdock, Ally	Feb. 4, 1846
Powell, Enoch	Freeman, Harriett	Feb. 8, 1846
Woodward, Aaron	McKay, Martha E.	Sept. 3, 1845
Manley, T. Geo. W.	McClendon, Mary	Feb. 26, 1846
Goddard, Lorain P.	Wilkerson, Martha S.	Mar. 5, 1846

Page 105
Bryan, Alsa B.	Bishop, Rebecca M. A.	Jan. 15, 1846
Martin, Wm.	Latson, Hester Eliza	Feb. 13, 1846
Bellah, Hiram	Moody, Catherine	Mar. 17, 1846
Moody, Greenberry	Lindsey, Adaline	Apr. 1, 1846
Brown, Wm.	Futral, Rebecca	Apr. 12, 1846
Britton, Henry	Harris, Mary H.	Dec. 18, 1845
Mickelberry, Wm. H. C.	Mobley, Emily	Nov. 19, 1845

Page 106
Davis, James M.	Thomas, Susan Elisabeth	July 5, 1846
Byars, George W.	Meredith, Martha	Aug. 6, 1846
Folds, John L.	Patrick, Chloe Ann	Aug. 14, 1846
Beaver, Green B. W.	Mayo, Cecily T.	Sept. 17, 1846
Woodward, Robert	Andrews, Martha E.	Sept. 24, 1846
Meredith, James	Byars, Ann	Sept. 24, 1846
Warlick, Jefferson	Burford, Nancy	Oct. 29, 1846

Page 107
Jarrell, Henry J.	Buckner, Martha M.	Nov. 1, 1846
McMichael, Thos. J.	Sheppard, Mary P.	Nov. 22, 1846
Pryor, Phillip H.	Head, Mary E.	Nov. 19, 1846
Mann, Richard P.	Cox, Mary Amanda	Nov. 29, 1846
Crain, Nathan E.	Cox, Nancy L.	Dec. 10, 1846
McMichael, John G.	McCune, Caroline M.	Dec. 10, 1846

Page 108

White (Whitt), David	Cole, Clarissa A.	Dec. 13, 1846
Webb, Chas.	Bailey, Margaret	Dec. 17, 1846
Tennant, Geo. A.	Dodd, Isabella	Jan. 3, 1847
Key, Aaron J.	Davidson, E. H. M.	Jan. 7, 1847
Lofton, John H.	Gunn, N.	Jan. 24, 1847
Gunn, Franklin	Barnes, Martha Ann	Dec. 31, 1846
McClendon, Jeremiah P.	Dillon, Sarah M.	Jan. 27, 1847

Page 109

Boughan, Joseph A.	Barber, Terese A.	Feb. 18, 1847
Blythe, Wm.	Liles, Abigail	Dec. 31, 1846
Hardy, Jacob	Beauchamp, Mary	Feb. 4, 1847
Holloway, Wm. K.	Clark, Sarah Ann	Feb. 7, 1847
Washington, Robt. M.	Casting, Mary J.	Feb. 9, 1847

Page 110

Giles, John F.	Lemon, Mary Ann	Feb. 18, 1847
Greer, Samuel	Crocket, Mineva A. R.	Feb. 25, 1847
Gilmore, Geo. W.	McEven, Caroline	Feb. 26, 1847
Skipper, John	Pace, Adeline F.	Mar. 14, 1847
Washington, George H.	Lewis, Catherine M.	Mar. 16, 1847
Jackson, Henry M.	Lewis, Susan Eliz.	Mar. 21, 1847
Chapman, Wm.	Dosett, Eliz. Ann	Apr. 1, 1847

Page 111

Pittman, Joseph	Cargile, Susan T.	May 11, 1847
Newton, Oliver H. P.	Bryon, Susan J.	June 8, 1847
Miles, James	Bankston, Margaret	July 8, 1847
Cash, Joel F.	Hunter, Eliza	July 1, 1846
Giles, Wm. Powell	Spinks, Sarah	Aug. 29, 1847
Edge, Reuben G.	Beardin, Rena	Sept. 23, 1847
Lavenier, Daniel G.	Savage, Eliz.	Mar. 28, 1847

Page 112

Nelson, Wm. H.	McGough, Martha Ann	Oct. 31, 1847
Thaxton, Yelverton	Washington, Mary A.	Mar. 4, 1847
Carter, Joseph	Benson, Marthena Caroline	Dec. 4, 1847
Henry, Hendrick or Henry Hendrick?		
Pricket, Jesse H.	LeSueur, Eliza	Dec. 2, 1847
Mayo, David W.	Edison, Harriett Ann	Dec. 26, 1847
Rooks, G. B.	Pricket, Eliz H.	Dec. 23, 1847
	Wallace, Eliz.	Jan. 6, 1848

Page 113

Stodghill, John T.	Brooks, Sarah L. J.	Dec. 30, 1847
Ross, Robt. H.	Standard, Martha Ann	Nov. 30, 1847
Kitchens, Nelson	Martin, Frances	Nov. 28, 1847
Phillips, Green M.	Derdin, Frances	Feb. 10, 1848
Pelt, T. W.	Bankston, Sarah Eliz.	Feb. 3, 1848
Camp, Nathan F.	Andrews, Sarah N.	Mar. 2, 1848
Prickett, Geo. W.	Cole, Mary Jane	Apr. 19, 1848

Page 114

Harkness, James W.	Spencer, James	June 15, 1848
Pratt, John W.	Allison, Martha A.	Mar. 30, 1848
Acres, J. T.	Stone, Charlotte	May 11, 1848
Collins, James A.	Foster, Mary J.	June 19, 1848
Hammonds, Russell	Murdock, Mary Ann	May 14, 1848
Forgarty, W. James	Hughes, Mary Ann Rebecca	Aug. 17, 1848
Butner, Julius T.	Funderburk, Sarah Eliz.	Sept. 14, 1848

Page 115

Milner, W. A. R.	Johnson, Frances M.	Sept. 10, 1848
Smith, Green	Morris, Nancy J.	Oct. 22, 1848
Burford, Samuel H.	Ingram, Nancy M.	Oct. 12, 1848
Ball, John	Hunter, Eliz.	Nov. 15, 1848
Lynch, James L.	Weaver, Nancy S.	Dec. 3, 1848
Clark, James B.	Hoard, Mary	Dec. 14, 1848

| Amos, John K. | Brownlee, Jane | Dec. 14, 1848 |

Page 116

Andrews, Robt. D.	Hardwick, Julia	Jan. 14, 1848
Evans, Wm. H.	Jinks, Mary E.	Dec. 23, 1848
Barnes, Corday	Hardy, Margaret	Jan. 22, 1849
Dunseith, Wm. J.	Payne, Rhoda	Feb. 1, 1849
Seaver, Jarrette P.	Thomas, Arty	Dec. 14, 1848
Maddox, Dennis	Carter, Lutecia	Jan. 14, 1849
Carroll, Elbert	Harrison, Eliz.	Jan. 24, 1849

Page 117

Maddox, Spencer	Carter, Lodissa Malinda	Feb. 6, 1849
Hardy, John	Henderson, Sarah	Feb. 19, 1849
Ellis, Daniel R.	Miles, Eliz.	Feb. 13, 1849
Martin, Wm.	Lewis, Cecelia	Aug. 17, 1848
Dick, Wm. L.	Lee, Martha	Mar. 4, 1849
Lumsden, Jesse M.	Smith, Mary	Feb. 18, 1849

Page 118

Woodward, Newdigate	McKibben, Sarah Ann Jane	Mar. 15, 1849
Melton, Richard	Moore, Nancy L.	July 8, 1848
Norris, Nathaniel	Curington, Katherine	Dec. 28, 1848
Smith, John G.	Elliott, Harriett C.	Jan. 1, 1849
Kimbell, Finney M.	McGough, Margaret J.	Feb. 11, 1849
Dougherty, W. D.	Barlow, Sarah Ann	Mar. 26, 1849
Barber, Matthew T.	Sheppard, Eliz J.	Apr. 25, 1849

Page 119

Crawford, R. A.	Lee, Ann E.	May 14, 1849
Maddox, Wm. S.	Atkinson, Eliz. S.	June 8, 1849
Bankston, Creed T.	Hughs, Lydia Ann	July 14, 1849
Foster, Samuel	Barnett, Lucinda	July 26, 1849
McClendon, Jeremiah P.	Carson, Sarah E.	Aug. 2, 1849
Freeman, Alexander	Millon, Eliz. D.	Aug. 5, 1849
Heath, James H.	Curry, Eliz. A.	Aug. 9, 1849

Page 120

Gresham, Wm.	Elder, Sarah Anna	Aug. 13, 1849
Clower, James M.	McCune, Olive J.	Aug. 13, 1849
Weaver, Edw. G.	Andrews, Cathering J.	Oct. 11, 1849
Cane, John W.	Key, Sarah J.	Oct. 4, 1849
Lemon, Wm. A.	Giles, Martha A. M.	Oct. 14, 1849
Moore, James T.	Smith, Sarah	Oct. 28, 1849

Page 121

Hansford, Robert B.	McCune, Eliz. A.	Nov. 4, 1849
Wright, Wiley S.	Thornton, Martha Ann	Nov. 13, 1849
McCune, Rufus W.	Alexander, Mary S.	Nov. 14, 1849
Morris, John S.	Hoard, Nancy F.	Nov. 22, 1849
Phelps, Joel Jacob	Gruble, Amanda Eliz.	Nov. 28, 1849
Curry, Wiley G.	Mosely, E. C.	Nov. 27, 1849

Page 122

Mayfield, Archibald	Andrews, Mary	Dec. 2, 1849
Banks, Starke W.	Barber, Sophirah M.	Dec. 4, 1849
Duke, Pinckney C.	Malone, Martha	Dec. 6, 1849
Swan, Wm. T.	Tennant, Sisley	Dec. 12, 1849
Nutt, John G.	Strickland, Mary Ann	Dec. 13, 1849
Elder, Wm. W.	Neal, Julia	June 3, 1849

Page 123

Kendrick, John D.	Carmichael, Margaret M.	Aug. 14, 1849
Tennant, A. J.	Dodd, Marcella	Dec. 18, 1849
Shire, Newman	Lewis, Susan E.	Dec. 20, 1849
Barkley, John H.	Moore, Mary	Jan. 10, 1850
Nutt, James B.	Isabellah, Mary	Jan. 10, 1850
Spinks, George W.	Deason, Matilda	July 10, 1850

Hudgins, Noel Z.	Wages, Sarah A.	Sept. 28, 1847
Dennis, John M.	Holifield, Sarah	Jan. 27, 1850
Tucker, Robt. Henry	Benson, Sarah A. Eliz.	Jan. 17, 1850
Umphy (Humphrey?), Wm.	Edison, Sarah	Feb. 10, 1850
Carpenter, Alexander	Cook, Sarah	Feb. 14, 1850
Bailey, Stephen	Harrington, Caroline	Feb. 14, 1850
Coghorn, Andrew J.	Coody, Amanda M. J.	Feb. 24, 1850

Simmons, James H.	Crum, Eliz. C.	May 10, 1840
Dodson, Charles	Byars, Martha	Apr. 4, 1850
Blackburn, Wm.	Dickerson, Martha	Mar. 23, 1849
Mayfield, John	Duke, Eliz. Ann	Feb. 21, 1850
Mahaffey, David G.	Brown, Susan	Mar. 10, 1850
Moore, Lewis	Edwards, Lydia D.	May 26, 1850

Carter, Leonidas	Harper, Eliz. F.	June 6, 1850
Andrews, John	Nelson, Mary K.	July 21, 1850
Duke, Micajah C.	Holifield, Mary	Aug. 1, 1850
Camp, James P.	Dillon, Mary A.	Aug. 7, 1850
Harris, Seaborn J.	Britten, Mahoney H.	Dec. 16, 1849
Minter, W. Jefferson	Kelly, Mary Ann	May 12, 1850

Kelly, George W.	Stapels, Angeline	May 12, 1850
Rooks, Wm. J.	Stapels, Minerva H.	July 28, 1850
Britten, Marion F.	Kelly, Alean	July 4, 1850
Buchanan, Charles G. J.	Moore, Peggy	July 1, 1850
Prickett, Israel	Milburn, Martha	Aug. 13, 1850

Herrin, James	Crain, Caroline	Sept. 8, 1850
Hodges, Jackson	Hillman, Margaret	Sept. 11, 1850
House, Daniel J.	Arnold, Nancy A.	Sept. 15, 1850
Bence, Wm. F.	Miles, Eliza E.	Sept. 23, 1850
Coker, Wm.	Bankston, Elizabeth	Oct. 3, 1850
Treadwell, Abram	Bankston, Lavica	Aug. 26, 1850

Bishop, Chas. H.	Jackson, Mary Jane	Sept. 26, 1850
Ham, John G. S.	Wilkerson, Mary	Nov. 5, 1850
Evans, John J.	English, Sarah K.	Dec. 3, 1850
Hoard, Harrison J.	Brady, Sarah M.	Dec. 5, 1850
Siles, Thomas J.	Spinks, Mary Ann	Dec. 25, 1850

Young, Wm. S.	Fuller, Susan L.	Dec. 25, 1850
Benton, Samuel M.	Brewer, Eliz. J.	Oct. 16, 1850
Still, Henry R.	Crenshaw, Susan P.	Oct. 25, 1851
Benson, Richard A.	Brewer, Margaret B.	Nov. 15, 1849
Preston, Gilliam H.	Smith, Eliz.	July 12, 1849
Thaxton, James M.	Akins, Sarah Jane	Jan. 3, 1850

Johnson, Seaborn H.	King, Mary F.	Oct. 17, 1850
McElroy, J. L. W.	Duffey, Martha E.	Jan. 16, 1851
Tingle, Thos. W.	Coughran, Eliz.	Jan. 9, 1851
Preston, James M.	Smith, Jane W.	Dec. 24, 1850
Gunn, Columbus	Barnes, Mary Jane	Dec. 26, 1850
Stodghill, Henry S.	Gunn, Adeline	Dec. 31, 1850

Brazim, Lansen	Smith, Martha	Jan. 5, 1851
Jinks, Burton	Wells, Eliza	Jan. 19, 1851
Barnes, Henry	Giles, Eliza	Jan. 7, 1851
Connell, Wm.	Fielder, Sarah	Jan. 14, 1851
Haislip, Thos. J.	Andrews, Martha J.	Jan. 23, 1851
Coody, Wm. J.	Durham, Ann	Jan. 26, 1851

Page 133

Draper, James	Beard, Rebecca	Jan. 13, 1851
Mayo, Wm. T.	Brooks, Nancy P.	Feb. 16, 1851
Holifield, Wiley	Mayo, L. J.	Mar. 14, 1851
McNeely, Wm.	Ray, Sarah F.	Sept. 20, 1851

Page 134

Bird, R. W.	Tennant, Rachel	Oct. 8, 1850
Kicker, W. G.	Parker, Mary S.	Nov. 24, 1851
Ridgeway, John H.	McKibben, Matilda	Feb. 6, 1851
Cargile, Augustus	Dyson, Mary Elizabeth	Apr. 3, 1851
Stodghill, John Thomas	Wilkerson, Elizabeth A.	Jan. 27, 1849
McClendon, Wm.	Cox, Rachel A.	Apr. 21, 1842

Page 135

Kelly, Wm.	Britton, Mary M.	Sept. 26, 1851
Fogarty, Andrew J.	Hodgins, Rebecca	Sept. 8, 1851
Norris, John A.	Maddox, Elizabeth	Apr. 20, 1851
Greer, John	Moore, Mary L.	Mar. 25, 1851
Mayo, A. G.	Brooks, Hannah R.	Apr. 20, 1851
Stroud, James	Burford, Judith	Dec. 19, 1850

Page 136

Gilpin, Joseph M.	Dickinson, Eliza	May 4, 1851
Lunsden, James	Pernell, Margaret A.	May 27, 1851
Weaver, John I.	Pace, Mary T.	Sept. 4, 1851
Gaston, Matthew	Delamar, Sally	Sept. 11, 1851
Barlow, Richard	King, Frances	Sept. 18, 1851
Saunders, Simon H.	Newton, Susan F.	Sept. 23, 1851
Preston, Thos. J.	Edison, Eliz.	June 19, 1851

Page 137

Kelly, J. T.	Crowder, Vianna	Oct. 1, 1851
Welsh, James H.	Curry, Mary	Nov. 13, 1851
Moore, John L.	Strickland, Mary Jane	Nov. 16, 1851
Lumsden, Jerimiah T.	Malone, Emily	Nov. 27, 1851
Kimbell, Benjamin F.	Booles, Frances A.	Dec. 21, 1851
Cargile, Frederick	Phillips, Susan	Dec. 25, 1851
Walker, Gus Davis C.	Henderson, Lucy Frances	April 29, 1851

Page 138

Jobson, Joseph S.	Key, Elizabeth	Dec. 25, 1851
Robinson, Wm. G.	Lofton, Rosannah L. H.	Dec. 25, 1851
Buttrill, Britton	McCord, Martha Emeline	Jan. 1, 1852
Bankston, James R.	Philips, Eliza.	Jan. 5, 1852
Hendrick, Wm. H. L.	Lee, Susan G.	Jan. 24, 1852
Lee, Wm. J.	Hendrick, Caroline R.	Feb. 17, 1852
Foster, Chas.	Thaxton, Hammet	Mar. 18, 1852

Page 139

McKibben, Samuel	Harkness, Mary Ann	Apr. 4, 1852
Mayfield, Elisha	Gilmore, Sarah	Feb. 12, 1852
Chenoworth, John	Armstrong, Jane	Apr. 10, 1852
Rowland, James	Kimbell, Mary W.	May 20, 1852
Thornton, Wm. B.	Bennett, Jane	June 27, 1852
Polk, Chas.	Hodges, Susan	June 17, 1852

Page 140

Thomas, Noah	Pernell, Sarah J.	July 5, 1852
Moore, Wm. J.	Lewis, Eliz. C.	Oct. 5, 1852
Godsey, Saml. G.	Allison, Susan A.	Oct. 24, 1852
Evans, Wm. H.	Health, Samantha	Nov. 25, 1852
Woolcott, Winthrop W.	Hays, Lucia A.	Nov. 10, 1852
Godsey, Madison M.	Barnes, Louisa H.	Nov. 9, 1852

Page 141

| Carter, Leonidas | Nelms, Pencillar | Dec. 21, 1852 |
| Dennis, Richard G. | Meredith, Mary B. | Dec. 26, 1852 |

Williamson, Thos. J.	Ingram, Elisha Ann	Dec. 23, 1852
Smith, Henry P.	James, Sally W.	Jan. 6, 1853
Maddux, A. G.	Beauchamp, Martha C.	Jan. 27, 1853
Tillery, John	Coal, Avena	July 25, 1852

Page 142

Lee, Wm. J.	Hendricks, Caroline R.	Feb. 17, 1852
Foster, Charles	Thaxton, Harriett	Mar. 18, 1852
Head, Wm. R. S.	Lewis, Sarah M. A.	Feb. 25, 1853
Stroud, Manson	Duke, Eliz.	Aug. 4, 1851
Payne, T. J.	Horton, Martha	Jan. 1. 1853
Wright, Benjamin A.	Brady, Martha	Feb. 7, 1853

Page 143

Smith, Isaac	Bond, Lucy T.	Apr. 22, 1852
Heard, Thos. C.	Allison, Mary T.	Feb. 26, 1852
Fincher, James	Freeman, Cynthia	Apr. 17, 1852
Lewis, Francis H.	Brown, Nancy	Sept. 15, 1851
Harkness, John B.	Hunter, Eliz.	Sept. 18, 1853
Kellog, Uriah	Wilkerson, Arline V.	Feb. 26, 1853

Page 144

Morris, Wm. F.	Tillery, Martha J.	Jan. 17, 1852
Latlon, Jacob H.	Hamil, Margaret Jane	Feb. 26, 1853
Bryan, James H.	Daugherty, Margaret E.	Feb. 27, 1853
Giles, Wm. F.	Meredith, Elizabeth M.	Feb. 1, 1853
Bray, A. J.	Thomas, Permilia	Jan. 3, 1854
Pitts, Francis M.	Ward, Rebecca J.	Nov. 6, 1853
Walker, Jeptha F.	Hudson, Sarah	Dec. 11, 1853

Page 145

Dodson, James	Wise, Nancy	Nov. 29, 1853
Wise, Creed T.	Maddox, Matilda	Nov. 19, 1853
Wallace, John	Philips, Bertha	Feb. 2, 1854
Duke, James H.	Mayo, Martha	Nov. 20, 1853
Tood, Benj. A.	Askew, Eliz.	Apr. 19, 1853
Williams, A. J.	Wilson, Eliz.	Dec. 15, 1853

Page 146

Price, M.	McDaniels, Julia C.	Feb. 14, 1854
Osburn, Alexander	Lee, Mary A.	Dec. 15, 1853
Walthall, Thurman	Price, Martha E.	Oct. 2, 1853
Philip, Frederick L.	Hardy, Susa	Mar. 15, 1853
Bond, Wm. A.	Curry, Harriett A. D.	May 19, 1853

Page 147

McCord, James R.	Kenny, Louisa M.	Sept. 1, 1853
Shaw, Saml. P.	Jackson, Martha W.	Sept. 13, 1853
Walker, Jeptha F.	Hudson, Sarah	Dec. 15, 1853

Page 148

Logan, John	Standford, Eliz.	Apr. 16, 1854
Lummus, John W.	Carter, Nancy C.	Jan. 4, 1854
Ham, Cicero	Maddox, Mary E.	Dec. 4, 1853
Watson, Benj. F.	Fears, Georgia Ann	May 11, 1854
Ingram, Wm. B.	Burford, Ann	June 19, 1854

Page 149

Smith, John G.	Jinks, Nancy	July 6, 1854
Burns, George	Fossette, Drusilla	May 18, 1854
Freeman, Wm. H.	Garr, Susan F.	Apr. 25, 1854
Vickers, Jacob	Nelson, Rosannah	Feb. 19, 1854
Duke, Silas M.	Logan, Mary F.	June 4, 1854
Burford, John B.	Ferrell, Mary	June 8, 1854

Page 150

Stallsworth, Thos. H.	Williamson, Minny A.	Dec. 20, 1853
Washington, John W.	Moore, Sarah E.	Feb. 20, 1854
McMichael, James M.	Gaston, Amanda	Feb. 23, 1854

Andrews, Allen M.	Ingram, Mary Jane	Feb. 8, 1855
Duke, P. C.	Glazer, Mary	Sept. 28, 1854
Maddox, Henry R.	Cole, Selina R.	July 13, 1854

Page 151

Morris, Monroe	Nolen, E. R.	Sept. 25, 1854
E'Dalgo, Francisco	Freeman, Martha	June 12, 1854
Slaton, Samuel	Nutt, Nancy G.	Nov. 9, 1854
Thaxton, Richmond R.	Ferguson, Margaret J.	Nov. 9, 1854
Kimbrough, W. C.	Kilgore, Henrietta	Apr. 17, 1853

Page 152

Collins, John C.	Bird, Mary	Oct. 14, 1854
Etheridge, John D.	Alexander, Catherine	Dec. 21, 1854
Nutting, Chas. A.	Merrit, Eliz. A.	Feb. 20, 1853
Varner, Clinton L.	Gray, Ann	Mar. 13, 1853
Gelleland, Franklin	Willis, Catherine	July 2, 1854
Gilleland, Dempsey	Turner, Sarah	Mar. 13, 1854

Page 154

McMichael, James M.	Gaston, Amanda B.	
McElhenny, George W.	Johnson, Susan J.	Aug. 18, 1853
Baslow, E.	Crane, Amanda H.	Nov. 25, 1854
Hodge, Bluford	Phillips, Spaey	Oct. 5, 1854
Andrews, Allen M.	Ingram, Jane	Feb. 8, 1852
Turner, Marcey	Pearman, Imoline	July 6, 1854
Greer, Thos. T.	Hartsfield, Frances E.	Jan. 8, 1854
Patrick, John J. Kirk	Smith, Rosannah J.	May 6, 1853
Banks, Wm.	Moore, Jane R.	Apr. 4, 1853
Mayo, John W.	Weldon, Frances	Jan. 10, 1856
Mayo, Wm. J.	Turner, Mary A.	Jan. 13, 1856
Cook, Zeno	Gunn, Miriam	Nov. 27, 1855
Mangum, Wyley P.	Heath, Mary A.	Oct. 4, 1855

Page 155

Fretwell, A. J.	Barber, Joanna E.	Apr. 10, 1855
Lewis, Jesse C.	Head, Emily F.	Nov. 25, 1853
Gilleland, Dempsey	Walden, Ellen	May 4, 1856
Goodman, Jesse W.	Andrews, Martha A.	Jan. 10, 1856
Giles, Edward P.	Wise, Cyrena	May 10, 1856
Byars, Lafayette	Preston, Virginia F.	Jan. 9, 1856

Page 156

McDaniel, John G.	McCune, Lucy C.	July 24, 1856
Duke, Green H.	Mayo, Nancy E.	Aug. 4, 1856
Saunders, Wm.	White, Mary	Aug. 31, 1856
Brown, W. T.	Jackson, Minerva A.	Nov. 16, 1856
Slaton, Oliver H. F.	Lyons, Sarah Jane	Nov. 9, 1856
Stewart, James P.	Deason, Nancy Jane	Dec. 7, 1856

Page 157

Mayo, Richard J.	Andrews, Mary Ann	Dec. 11, 1856
Lumsden, Bolin T.	Campbell, Eliz.	Dec. 11, 1856
Carter, Thos. J.	Barnett, Sarah M.	Dec. 14, 1856
Mayo, John R.	Thomas, Susan C.	Dec. 25, 1856
Thornton, James T.	Atkinson, Virginia	Dec. 7, 1856
Gibson, Matthew J.	Goodman, Mary	Dec. 4, 1856

Page 158

Wise, James W.	Lindsey, Fanny J.	Dec. 26, 1856
Thompson, John H.	Burford, Nancy J.	Dec. 28, 1856
Mayo, James H.	Thomas, Eunicia A.	Jan. 1, 1857
Clark, Thos. F.	Clark, Nancy F.	July 20, 1856
Mann, Joel	Hunter, Sarah J.	Jan. 17, 1857
Redman, Wm. T. C.	Maddux, Sarah Eliz.	Dec. 17, 1857

Page 159

Colwell, A. J.	Grice, Polly Ann	Aug. 10, 1856
McKibben, Samuel	Harkness, Mary Ann	Apr. 4, 1852

Thaxton, Yelverton	Campbell, Susan	Apr. 20, 1856
Faulkner, J. H.	Fears, S. C.	Jan. 15, 1857
Duke, Aristotle G.	Lewis, Mary Jane	Dec. 8, 1856

Page 160

Thompson, John R.	Hails, Susan J.	Jan. 31, 1856
Collins, Irbin	Kindrick, Mary	Dec. 18, 1856
Mayo, Joseph A. G.	Hardin, Margaret R.	Feb. 7, 1856
Gilleland, Thos.	Nosworthy, Samantha	Jan. 13, 1856
Elder, W. James	Yarbrough, Mary S.	Nov. 23, 1856
Grier, Algerson S.	Cook, Drucilla	July 10, 1856
Vardeman, Simeon	Hoard, Eliz	Jan. 12, 1857

Page 161

Strickland, Solomon	Carter, Julia	Mar. 20, 1857
Garr, Joseph H.	Still, Sarah Eliz.	Jan. 14, 1857
Nelems, Thos. A.	Garr, Sugar E.	Jan. 15, 1857
Evans, Wm. H.	Underwood, Eliz.	Jan. 11, 1857
Amos, Joel B.	Brownlee, Catherine	Jan. 29, 1857
Giles, Frederick	Wise, Elizabeth A.	Jan. 15, 1857
Coleman, R. W.	Head, Mary Jane	Jan. 25, 1857

Page 162

Mills, Morgan M.	Blisset, Mary A.	Feb. 16, 1857
Giles, Thos. E.	Maddux, Penica	Mar. 10, 1857
Moore, Andrew J.	Pye, Sarah J.	Mar. 8, 1857
Willis, W. L.	Roberts, E. A.	Oct. 22, 1857
Morris, Samuel H.	Barlow, Mahaly A.	Aug. 6, 1854
Harkness, Thos. M.	Daniel, Amelia O.	Dec. 13, 1855

Page 163

Dodson, Charles	Giles, Susan	June 2, 1857
Kelly, Jefferson	Witcher, Jane	Mar. 15, 1857
Dawkins, Thos. J.	Tucker, Nancy A.	Aug. 30, 1857
Herndon, Chas J.	Beasley, Frances	Aug. 16, 1857
Roberts, Seth V.	Cash, E.	July 11, 1857
Heninton, Pompey	Wilson, Caroline	Aug. 23, 1857
Kelly, John	Grant, Mary	Sept. 17, 1857
McMichael, W. G.	Sims, Julia A.	Oct. 13, 1857

Page 164

Jinks, Gale	McDowell, Elizabeth A.	Dec. 23, 1857
Nelms, William	Powell, Corrinda	Dec. 29, 1857
Herring, Jesse	Crane, Sarah Jane	Jan. 3, 1858
Braziel, Lawson Marion	Powell, Sarah	Nov. 10, 1857
Hamil. J. L.	Hightower, E. R.	Nov. 5, 1857
Kimble, James G.	Sims, Frances A.	Nov. 24, 1858
Wilson, Wm. H.	Foster, Rebecca E.	Feb. 6, 1858

Page 165

Williams, Thos. B.	Duffey, Rebecca Jane	Jan. 12, 1858
Head, Thos. J.	Johnson, Mary A.	Jan. 28, 1858
Duncan, Jas. N.	Fish, Mary Ann	Jan. 10, 1858
Carmichael, Robert C.	Harkness, Rosannah	Jan. 24, 1858
Spencer, Thos. A.	Ball, Sarah E.	Dec. 6, 1857
Tollison, Burrell	Ellis, Mary Ann	Feb. 15, 1858
Stewart, John O.	Dillon, Catherine R.	May 27, 1858

Page 166

Wilson, Leander G.	Slaten, Mandane C.	June 6, 1858
Crawel, Wm. E.	Tante, Henryeter	Aug. 8, 1858
Holifield, Thos. J.	Barnes, Mary Frances	Sept. 21, 1858
Shaw, John	Dogget, Mary	Sept. 23, 1858
Wise, Francis M.	Giles, Mary E.	Oct. 28, 1858
Bankston, Andrew J.	Dogget, Levicia	Oct. 5, 1858
Folds, Wm. T.	Folds, Chloe Ann F.	Oct. 7, 1858

Page 167

| Pace, Wm. A. | Bond, Juda A. | Dec. 30, 1858 |

Jinks, Burel J.	Ingraham, Martha Susan	Dec. 14, 1858
Gray, James R.	Lewis, Mary Ann	Dec. 16, 1858
Evans, Willis J.	Carr, Sarah	Dec. 16, 1858
Carter, Jesse L.	Hamil, Mary	Dec. 20, 1858
Hammond, Charles C.	Stodghill, Mary Ann	Jan. 20, 1859
Hall, John	Stewart, Miley M.	Jan. 13, 1859

Page 168

Evans, John B.	Andrews, Mary Ann	Feb. 10, 1859
McDaniel, Simeon	Johnson, Frances M.	Apr. 21, 1859
Sharpe, George W.	Hinton, Mary	Apr. 3, 1859
Puckett, Jesse H.	Thurston, Mary A.	May 5, 1859
Duffey, Florence P.	Webb, Martha F.	June 19, 1859
Nolen, Thomas	Tollison, Mary E.	June 23, 1859
Gilbert, Wm. S.	Ferrell, Nancy E. F.	June 26, 1859

Page 169

Gray, Aaron W.	Lewis, Caroline	July 17, 1859
Pitts, George	McDaniel, Mary	July 7, 1859
Thomas, James M.	Murrey, Mary	Aug. 29, 1859
Wilson, Simon	Roe, Rosa	Aug. 8, 1858
Crenshaw, S. R.	Slaten, Martha A.	Aug. 28, 1859
Curry, Wm. D.	Barnes, Olive	Dec. 5, 1859
Hughey, Henry H.	McCord, Sarah J.	Oct. 2, 1859

Page 170

Bullard, John D.	Kindrick, Adeline J.	Sept. 22, 1859
Mangham, Willis	Thaxton, Nancy G.	Nov. 2, 1859
Evans, James	Thaxton, Mary Ann	Nov. 6, 1859
Bond, John M. D.	Goddard, Charity	Dec. 25, 1859
Bankston, Leonard A.	Beauchamp, Nannie	Dec. 25, 1859
Willard, Green	Edson, Martha	Sept. 11, 1859

Page 171

Lindsey, Robert	Wilkerson, Mary Jane	Jan. 1, 1860
Rodgers, Thos.	Edson, Nancy A.	Oct. 22, 1854
Byars, Richard	Jones, Mary Ann	Dec. 22, 1859
Brownlee, George	Coody, Nancy Caroline	Dec. 18, 1859
Nutt, Samuel D.	Woodward, Chloe Ann	Oct. 11, 1859
Turner, Geo. W. T.	Ellis, Catherine	Dec. 16, 1858

Page 172

Goodson, Wm.	Grant, Georgian	July 29, 1858
Moore, James	Thurmon, Elizabeth	July 17, 1859
Leonard, John	Witcher, Martha	Dec. 21, 1859
Langford, Jefferson	Willis, Bertha	Dec. 11, 1859
Nelson, Parham L.	Wilson, Lavonia E.	Jan. 9, 1859
Aiken, Robt. W.	Thaxton, Amanda E.	Dec. 18, 1859

Page 173

Dickerson, Wiley R.	Gilleland, Ellen	Jan. 20, 1860

Page 174

Towles, Adam L.	Williams, Sarah W.	Jan. 15, 1860

Skips from page 174 to page 181

Page 181

Bankston, Alfred L.	Crumbley, Martha	Oct. 30, 1859
McElheney, J. V.	Wise, Frances	Jan. 1, 1860
Moore, Daniel A.	Harkness, Nancy M.	Aug. 1, 1858

Page 182

Kimbrough, C. M.	Jones, Eliza	Apr. 12, 1860
Goddard, Lucius	Autry, Mary A.	May 17, 1860
Gilmore, Henry J.	Crowels, Frances E.	Feb. 19, 1860

Page 183

Dickerson, William T.	Edwards, Frances	July 18, 1860

| Pritchett, Thos J. | Williamson, Florida | July 31, 1860 |
| Tinsley, Elias C. | Darden, Sarah Eliz | Aug. 2, 1860 |

Page 184
Lummus, Wm. D.	Stodghill, Susan A.	July 31, 1860
Smith, William	Crickett (Crockett), Eliz	Feb. 21, 1861
Moore, Isaac C.	Mayo, May C.	Sept. 6, 1860

Page 185
King, Henry H.	Gray, Mary A.	May 12, 1861
Maddux, James C.	Wise, Sarah F.	Dec. 20, 1860
Rosser, Geo. S.	Collins, Nancy Ann	Dec. 8, 1860

Page 186
Edwards, Rubin R.	Hay, Mary Ann	Sept. 5, 1861
Key, Wm. H.	Barnes, Mollie M.	Aug. 25, 1860
Whitington, John W.	Jones, Susan E.	July 3, 1860

Page 187
Shaw, Nathaniel M.	Gilliland, Sarah	May 30, 1855
Campbell, Joseph	Tollison, Mrs. Volinda	Oct. 8, 1860
Pittman, C. C.	White, M. P.	Nov. 12, 1857

Skips from page 187 to page 190

Page 190
Higgins, Early	Smith, Nancy	Nov. 18, 1860
McBride, John W.	Elderman, Susan E.	Apr. 18, 1861
McGough, Joseph H.	Finnie, Sallie C.	Aug. 19, 1860

Page 191
Dupree, Lewis J.	Head, Susannah E.	May 12, 1861
Jones, R. Augustus	Byars, Lucy	Dec. 29, 1860
Barnes, Thos. J.	Bailey, Jimmie A.	Aug. 27, 1861

Page 192
Fears, Riley S.	Cook, Elizabeth Ann	July 26, 1860
Hoard, Arthur D.	Atwood, Mrs. A. M.	Dec. 22, 1861
Weaver, James J.	Pace, Julia A.	Aug. 7, 1860

Page 193
| Thompson, E. J. | James, A. H. J. | Nov. 8, 1862 |
| Thaxton, Wiley W. | Carr, Margaret E. | Dec. 23, 1860 |

Page 194
Swan, James W.	Lummus, Margaret	Oct. 8, 1895
Sigler, Leory	Hinton, May E.	Sept. 28, 1860
Proctor, Wm. W.	King, Elizabeth F.	Oct. 25, 1860

Page 195
| Howell, Joseph I. | Boughan, M. A. | Apr. 23, 1860 |
| Brooking, S. L. | Fold, Penelope N. | Dec. 15, 1860 |

Page 196
Thurston, James R.	Rich, Sarah	Aug. 30, 1860
Brownlee, James M.	Hoard, Elisabeth	Dec. 28, 1860
Baileu, S. B.	Lindsey, A. B.	June 6, 1862

Page 197
Moore, Riley R.	Heard, Jane N.	Oct. 10, 1860
Martin, Henry F.	Jinks, Mary Frances	July 4, 1860
Thompson, E. J.	Byars, Mrs. E. J.	Jan. 24, 1861

Page 198
White, Wm. R.	Mayo, M. S.	Jan. 17, 1861
O'Neal, Lemuel N.	Shields, Martha A.	Jan. 20, 1861
Sellars, Francis	Campbell, Elvie	Dec. 28, 1860

Page 199
| Blanks, Simon F. | Deason, Mary A. | Feb. 1, 1861 |

Powell, John G.	Cole, Mary E.	Feb. 12, 1862
Edge, Rubin D.	Gossett, Louisa C.	July 22, 1861

Page 200

Knowles, James B.	Williamson, Lavonia C.	Nov. 3, 1861
Willis, James R.	Curtis, Maria F. H.	July 1, 1861
Brady, John W.	Moore, Emily	Dec. 13, 1860

Page 201

Evans, David Frankley	Johnson, Nancy A.	Feb. 14, 1861
Goin, Robt W.	Webb, Mary E.	June 5, 1861
Jinks, Wm. M.	Smith, Nancy J.	Jan. 13, 1861

Page 202

Bearden, Thos M.	Saunders, Louisa E.	Aug. 19, 1861
Slaten, C. W.	Lyons, Margaret L.	Oct. 6, 1863
Crane, Josiah	Smith, Maria	June 11, 1863

Page 203

Hudgens, Wm. S.	Leonard, Martha A.	Sept. 6, 1863
Ridgeway, Samuel	Morris, Mrs. Mahala D.	May 31, 1863
Lewis, Benjamine	Hoard, Martha C.	Jan. 25, 1863

Page 204

Butler, Thos H.	Carter, Sarah	June 24, 1863
Rhodes, John D.	Nelson, Lavonia	Dec. 28, 1863
Kelly, Lemuel	Welborn, Sarah E.	July 30, 1863

Page 205

Thurston, George W.	Collins, Malvina	Sept. 24, 1863
Wynn, N. B.	Blankston, Amanda J.	Sept. 24, 1863
Brooks, Hillary	Standard, Fannie	Jan. 1, 1864

Page 206

Jolly, Jesse	Hine (Hail), Delanney	Jan. 31, 1864
Thompson, David	King, Rebecca C.	Jan. 14, 1864
Towles, Thos J.	Nolan, Nancy A.	Feb. 14, 1864

Page 207

Herron, John H.	Barnett, Marie J.	Dec. 13, 1863
Hodges, Geo. W.	Deason, Martha J.	Jan. 5, 1864

Page 208

Hall, John I.	McMichael, Eliz A.	Mar. 7, 1864
Willis, James R.	Keith, Susan F.	Mar. 6, 1864
Thomas, John B.	Lummus, Sarah Ann	Jan. 10, 1864

Page 209

Reynolds, Benjamin	Hartsfield, Susan	Oct. 24, 1867
McKibben, Thomas	Foster, Penelope B.	Oct. 3, 1867
Harkness, Zarhariah T.	Moore, Parham M.	Nov. 28, 1867

Page 210

Yancey, Thos J.	Herring, Martha J.	Aug. 20, 1867
Herring, Joel	Carter, Sarah M.	Aug. 18, 1867
Morgan, J. W.	Smith, Ophelia J.	Sept. 12, 1867

Page 211

Manley, Richard C.	McCord, Mary E.	Mar. 28, 1864
Turner, Berry S.	Britton, Martha Jane	Jan. 12, 1864
McElroy, Jesse	Johnston, Lucy A.	Mar. 15, 1864

Page 212

Parker, John C.	Holifield, Emily	June 8, 1864
Gregory, John	Jones, Susan	Aug. 7, 1864
Moore, Jason G.	Edwards, Martha A.	Oct. 8, 1864

Page 213

Hardy, Robt. M.	McClure, Amandy J.	Aug. 25, 1864

Gentry, Jesse	Moore, Martha E.	Dec. 28, 1864
Sparks, James A.	Stodgill, Elizabeth J.	Oct. 15, 1865

Page 214
Carr, James M.	Coody, Narcissa	Jan. 11, 1866
Weaver, Jarrette C.	McNair, Susan A.	Mar. 25, 1866
Washington, J. I. W.	Coody, M. J.	Apr. 18, 1866

Page 215
Dodson, Chas.	Herren, Mrs. Sarah	Apr. 17, 1866
Cook, Elam	Wilson, Rose	Apr. 5, 1866
Grant, Benjamin F.	Martin, Louisa E.	Apr. 22, 1866

Page 216
Ingram, James M.	Burford, Susan T.	Dec. 20, 1865
Tyson, Henry F.	Hay, Sarah A.	May 31, 1866

Page 217
Kitchens, Thos	Grant, Martha F.	Apr. 8, 1866
Fincher, S. C.	Mounes, F. M.	July 1, 1866
Mason, J. N.	L. E. Guin (LeGuin), Sarah	July 3, 1866
Hall, S. L.	Grier, Drucilla	Oct. 13, 1864

Page 218
Fincher, John F.	Dearing, Sara	May 15, 1864
Herriot, B. M.	Sherwood, Laura V.	Jan. 22, 1865
Neal, James P.	Bankston, Willa	July 18, 1865

Page 219
McCord, John Wm.	Crawford, Mary J.	Oct. 12, 1865
Byars, Harrel N.	Nutt, Mary J.	Nov. 25, 1865
Roberts, J. M.	Castleberry, Martha E.	Dec. 4, 1865

Page 220
Barnes, George A.	Powell, Mrs. A. E.	Dec. 16, 1865
Wise, T. M.	Moore, Mrs. Jane H.	Jan. 8, 1866
Gunn, J. A.	Hall, Jane H.	Jan. 28, 1866

Page 221
Preston, John R.	Strickland, Elizabeth	June 11, 1866
Higgins, Oliver S.	Higgins, Nancy E.	Jan. 28, 1866
Thompson, David	Watkins, Sarah A.	Feb. 4, 1866

Page 222
Sparks, Z. T.	Stodghill, Lucy J. A.	July 18, 1866
White, Wm.	Patrick, Susan	July 8, 1866
Gaston, Charles R.	Mackey, Mary	July 15, 1866

Page 223
Hendricks, Franklin	Cloud, Sally	July 19, 1866
Lewis, John H.	Gray, Eliz A.	Jan. 28, 1866
Sellers, W. L.	Lummus, Mrs. S. A.	Aug. 26, 1866

Page 224
Holifield, Henry	Weaver, Mrs. Catherine	Aug. 19, 1866
Head, Wm.	Jenkins, Eliz.	Sept. 19, 1866
Hale, Walter R.	Gilmore, Frances E.	Sept. 4, 1866

Page 225
Johnson, G. W.	Maddox, Frances E.	Oct. 14, 1866
Carter, Washington	Gunn, Louise	Oct. 14, 1866
Gunn, Jesse T.	Kitchens, Frances	Oct. 8, 1866

Page 226
McMichael, James M.	Bailey, Nannie	Oct. 26, 1866
Nelums, Epps	Kitchens, Adline M.	Nov. 18, 1866
Underwood, W. M.	Harris, M. J.	Nov. 8, 1866

Page 227
Hendrick, Obidiah   Barnes, E. C.   Nov. 15, 1866
Watson, L. D.   Buttrill, Mary E.   Nov. 15, 1866
Cawthon, E. C.   Thompson, E. J.   Nov. 1, 1866

Page 228
Barnes, H. T.   Lindsey, L. M.   Nov. 15, 1866
Moore, G. W.   Evans, Mary A.   Dec. 6, 1866
Jolly, Joseph   Dickson, Emma W.   Dec. 5, 1866

Page 229
Higgins, Benjamin F.   Smith, Josephine   Dec. 6, 1866
Norris, W. D.   Strange, Mary A.   Dec. 4, 1866
Rich, Wm. F.   Lynch, Emeline C.   Dec. 12, 1866

Page 230
Higgins, H. H.   Plymale, Georgia A.   Dec. 6, 1866
Still, Louis H.   Brownlee, Eliz P.   Dec. 20, 1866
McGough, James R.   Bankston, E. J.   Dec. 18, 1866

Page 231
McClure, Thos J.   Campbell, Sarah P.   Mar. 20, 1866
Beardin, J. G.   Saunders, E. R.   Dec. 13, 1866
Lemon, Wm.   Giles, Eliz K.   Dec. 8, 1866

Page 232
Thaxton, Wm. W.   Hamil, M. M.   Dec. 9, 1866
Horton, Wm. A.   Benson, Rutha A. L.   Dec. 23, 1866
Maddox, James   Thaxton, Harriett   Jan. 1, 1867

Page 233
Doby, Silas   Blank, Mrs. Mary Ann   Jan. 13, 1867
Gilmore, Robert P.   Harris, Elvay   Jan. 8, 1867
Weaver, Willis C.   Witcher, Lou   Jan. 11, 1867

Page 234
Goddard, James F.   Heath, M. E.   Jan. 31, 1867
Parker, W. R.   Jolly, Eugene   Jan. 23, 1867
Walthal, Felix L.   Moore, Lizza   Jan. 31, 1867

Page 235
Bell, David A.   Thaxton, Fannie G.   Feb. 12, 1867
Thompson, James M.   Bond, Mrs. C. S.   Feb. 7, 1867
White, W. G.   Amos, A. S.   Feb. 5, 1867

Page 236
Mayo, John M.   Dodson, Mary J.   Feb. 10, 1867
O'Neal, E. W.   Weaver, Julia A.   Feb. 21, 1867
Crain, John T.   Dodson, Martha   Mar. 4, 1867

Page 237
McElhay, W. F.   Wise, E. H.   Mar. 3, 1867
Jones, J. F.   Myars, Georgia   Mar. 8, 1867
Coker, M. J.   McGibbon, Martha A.   Apr. 16, 1867

Page 238
Fogg, Miscah   Goins, Margaret   May 18, 1867
Wells, P. B. M.   Stillwell, Martha F.   June 27, 1867
Barnes, W. J.   Preston, Martha A.   July 30, 1867

Page 239
Nutt, John H.   Hodges, Samantha   Nov. 21, 1867
Britt, Thos.   Barnett, G. A.   Nov. 17, 1867
Bearden, John I.   Benton, Mary Emma   Nov. 29, 1867

Page 240
Brown, R. L.   Goodrum, J. A.   Dec. 5, 1867
Harris, J. N.   Beaver, Nancy J.   Dec. 5, 1867
Roberts, A. J.   Willis, Phronay E.   Dec. 5, 1867

Page 241
Shields, Wm.   McMichael, Martha J.   Dec. 15, 1867
McCord, James A.   Tomlinson, Eliz   Dec. 17, 1867
Preston, Archable G.   Mayo, Martha E.   Dec. 19, 1867

Page 242
Crumbley, John J.   Spears, Eliz H.   Dec. 19, 1867
Cole, Thos J.   Leftwich, Sarah   Dec. 12, 1867
Duke, Green R.   Singley, Mrs. Mary   Dec. 3, 1867

Page 243
Elder, John G.   Dumble, Mary E.   Dec. 4, 1867
Smith, John Wm. F.   Preston, Mary T.   Dec. 24, 1867
McKey, Thurmond   Nelson, Annie   Dec. 24, 1867

Page 244
Reeves, Thos. J.   Crain, Rachel A.   Dec. 26, 1867
Henderson, Thos J.   Mangum, Mrs. Mary   Dec. 31, 1867

Page 245
Pye, John   Fears, Charlotte   Jan. 9, 1868
McGarity, Eual   Heath, Mary A.   Feb. 20, 1868
Henderson, McD   Barber, Lue   Feb. 13, 1868

Page 246
Lindsey, James   Moore, Caroline   Mar. 8, 1868
Mayo, Thos J.   Gunnells, Eliz D.   Mar. 1, 1868
Johnson, Wm. M.   Mayfield, Mary A. E.   Apr. 13, 1868

Page 247
Bledsoe, John   Bailey, Susan B.   Apr. 16, 1868
Singley, John H.   Preston, Emily T.   May 3, 1868
Thaxton, M. D. F.   Tucker, Martha E.   May 19, 1868

Page 248
Heard, Hugh H.   Preston, Jane M.   July 11, 1868
Willis, John J.   Duke, Sally R.   Aug. 6, 1868
Pain, Wm. H.   Moore, Martha J.   Sept. 13, 1868

Page 249
Moore, Henry F.   Brooks, Martha E.   Oct. 26, 1868
Barnett, G. M. D.   King, F. R.   Oct. 22, 1868
Roberts, Wm. M.   Maddux, Caroline   Oct. 14, 1868

Page 250
Goodman, Wiley   Tennant, Frances V.   Nov. 11, 1868
Thaxton, Wm. R.   Goodman, Lucy V.   Nov. 12, 1868
Fletcher, Wm.   Harkness, Sarah E.   Nov. 26, 1868

Page 251
Waldrop, Wm.   Nelson, Ellen   Dec. 3, 1868
Standard, Thos.   Preston, Mary F.   Dec. 24, 1868
Mayo, Elisha F.   Godsey, Louisa   Dec. 27, 1868

Page 252
Mayo, J. T.   Smith, Eliz. R.   Dec. 24, 1868
Thurston, Thos. J.   Rich. Sarah F.   Dec. 17, 1868
Lavender, Robt. G.   Wise, Eliz.   Dec. 24, 1868

Page 253
Wise, John M.   Patrick, Sarah F.   Jan. 12, 1869
Gunn, Augustus   Kitchens, Eliz.   Jan. 17, 1869
Gilmore, Humphry J. W.   Coleman, Margaret   Jan. 17, 1869

Page 254
Thaxton, Henry J. C.   Carson, Josephine L.   Mar. 10, 1869
Elder, Wm. A.   Saunders, Virginia   Apr. 27, 1869
Wilson, R. J.   Lathran, Mrs. M. J.   Jan. 20, 1869

132

133

Page 269

Dumble, John B.	Goddard, Martha S.	Nov. 21, 1869
Dardin, Wm.	Johnson, Martha	Nov. 13, 1869
King, James	Pye, Fanny	Dec. 30, 1869

Page 270

Shephard, Thos. H.	Autry, F. R.	Dec. 13, 1869
Wise, Riley	Watts, Emily	Dec. 9, 1869
McMichael, George	Shields, Laura A.	Dec. 23, 1869

Page 271

Pittman, John R.	Moreland, Martha	Dec. 29, 1869
Andrews, Jim	Henley, Betsy	Jan. 1, 1869
Gray, Monroe	Maddox, Sarah F.	Dec. 23, 1869

Page 272

Pope, Daniel	Ward, Rosannah	Dec. 26, 1869
Phillips, Minor	Fish, Sally	Dec. 3, 1869
Bell, Chas. C.	Reeves, Mary	Dec. 2, 1869

Page 273

Harper, Richard M.	Maddux, M. L.	Dec. 13, 1869
Kitchens, John	Bryant, Martha	Dec. 5, 1869
Dennis, William	Benton, Mary	Jan. 2, 1870

Page 274

Lindsey, Daniel	Tanner, Elizabeth	Dec. 28, 1869
Hardy, W. G.	Stodghill, Isabelle	Dec. 25, 1869
Lofton, Andrew	Mann, Stephena L.	Dec. 9, 1869

Page 275

Stillwell, Abraham	Andrews, Mary	Dec. 26, 1869
Collins, Green	Duke, Ella	Dec. 9, 1869
Gourren, Edmund	Thurman, Laura	Jan. 26, 1870

Page 276

Fitzpatrick, James	Watson, Jinnie	Jan. 22, 1870
Head, Gillan	Gilmore, Jane	Jan. 8, 1870
Redman, Wiley	Varson, Easter	Jan. 27, 1870

Page 277

Scarborough, Warren A.	Castleberry, Susan F.	Jan. 18, 1870
Hiney, T. J.	Gunn, Georgia A.	Mar. 19, 1870

Page 278

Price, Wesley	McMichael, Angelina	Apr. 14, 1870
Moore, Oliver W.	Pittman, Susan T.	Feb. 23, 1870
Waldrop, J. A.	Moore, Mollie	Feb. 24, 1870

Page 279

McMichael, John M.	Bailey, Sallie J.	Apr. 14, 1870
Carson, Moses	Stewart, Jane	May 15, 1870
Dennis, J. F.	Nutt, Maggie	May 26, 1870

Page 280

McMames, Charles	Greer, Rosin	May 17, 1870
Sims, Robert	Austin, Kesiah	Sept. 12, 1870
Clark, Andrew	Walthall, Abby	June 18, 1870

Page 281

Barber, Dallis	Nutt, Mariah	June 5, 1870
Bradley, John	Dickerson, Sarah	July 28, 1870
Willingham, Eliga	McMichael, Carrie L.	July 3, 1870

Page 282

Lummus, Wm.	Thomas, Nancy A.	July 26, 1870
Neal, Daniel Odum	Smith, Jennie S.	July 12, 1870
Cargile, John M.	Holifield, Caroline	July 5, 1870

Page 299
Heath, J. S.   Lynch, Sallie F.   Aug. 20, 1871
Weiderman, G. T.   Newell, K. M.   Aug. 3, 1871
Crawford, Caleb   Wise, Fannie   Sept. 7, 1871

Page 300
McKibben, Gifford   Stillwell, Cinda   Oct. 31, 1871
Williams, Henry   Greer, Josephin   Oct. 8, 1871
Jester, Ransom   Thaxton, Angeline M.   Oct. 3, 1871

Page 301
McMichael, J. A.   Slaughter, Sallie J.   Nov. 3, 1871
Morrell, Adolphus   Maddox, Martha   Nov. 16, 1871
Smith, Wilson   Watkins, Mary A.   Nov. 16, 1871

Page 302
Castleberry, Jeptha T.   Willis, Maggie L.   Nov. 25, 1871
Thornton, R. A.   Moore, Sarah V.   Nov. 15, 1871
Carter, George   Still, Amanda   Nov. 19, 1871

Page 303
Bledsoe, George   McCune, Louise   Nov. 18, 1871
Aikin, George   Bledsoe, Caroline   Dec. 18, 1871
McGarity, M. G.   Heath, Martha B.   Nov. 16, 1871

Page 304
Gilmore, A. S.   Hoard, M.   Dec. 24, 1871
Head, Major   Rose, Allie   Dec. 30, 1871
Bennett, J. M.   Waldrop, M. P.   Dec. 28, 1871

Page 305
Beasley, Read   Fears, Mary   Dec. 29, 1871
McKibben, Dave   Duke, Mollie   Dec. 27, 1871
King, James A.   O'Neal, Mary F.   Dec. 7, 1871

Page 306
Sims, Henry   Jinks, Elizabeth   Dec. 31, 1871
Hendrick, Noah   Britten, Sarah J.   Dec. 28, 1871
Vason, Shadrick   Kelly, Salley   Dec. 27, 1871

Page 307
Wise, Isaac   Lyons, Jane   Jan. 1, 1872
Goodman, Ausburn   Berry, Dinah   Jan. 6, 1872
Bennett, S. J.   Waldrop, F. A.   Jan. 4, 1872

Page 308
Williams, John   Roberson, Fanny   Jan. 15, 1872
Benson, M. A.   Bishop, R. C.   Jan. 15, 1872
McKibben, Van   Fletcher, E. J.   Jan. 28, 1872

Page 309
Moss, Benjamin   Gray, Sarah Ann   Jan. 4, 1872
Stodghill, James   Fuller, Martha   Feb. 22, 1872
Laney, Abraham   Byars, Georgia Ann   Mar. 14, 1872

Page 310
Wilkerson, M. B.   Osborn, Ella   Apr. 16, 1872
Harvey, H. H.   Hodges, V. W.   Apr. 6, 1872
Goodrum, Aaron   Cardwell, Jane   May 12, 1872

Page 311
Lacy, Henry   McKibben, Rhoda   May 2, 1872
Carson, David P.   Webb, Mary J.   July 7, 1872
Moore, Joseph T.   Edwards, Sarah C.   July 13, 1872

Page 312
Leverett, T. J.   Lunsden, Emma W.   Sept. 17, 1872
Mangham, Chas. T.   Evans, Narsia J.   Sept. 4, 1872
Strawn, D. T.   Cook, S. E.   Sept. 15, 1872

Cook, Ben	Johnson, Hannah	Sept. 4, 1871
Watson, Clem	Winn, Mariah	Jan. 14, 1873
Harris, Wiley	Finney, Aldine	July 13, 1873

Page 328
Higgins, John	Slaughter, Matilda	Aug. 3, 1873
Crawford, Wm.	Martin, Hannah	Aug. 13, 1873

Page 329
Shivers, Joe	Pullin, Ann	Aug. 8, 1873
Rowan, Asa A.	Hendrick, Harriett	Aug. 25, 1873
Barnes, Henry	Steward, Eliza	Aug. 28, 1873

Page 330
Reese, Moses	Grady, Mary	Sept. 13, 1873
Burney, Thos J.	Riorden, M. M.	Oct. 3, 1873
Logan, Nelson	Mann, Fannie	Sept. 20, 1873

Page 331
Wimbush, Moses	Gunn, Ritta	Oct. 12, 1873
Phillips, Lewis	Heath, Donna Ann	Oct. 16, 1873
Phillips, Minor	Carr, Harriett	Oct. 28, 1873

Page 332
Lummus, Reuben	Gunn, Ollie	Oct. 30, 1873
Wright, George	Harkness, Jane	Oct. 30, 1873
Goodrum, James	Childs, Molly	Oct. 30, 1873

Page 333
Greer, O. H. P.	Cole, Alice	Nov. 26, 1873
Brown, Henry M.	Roper, Sarah A. E.	Nov. 25, 1873
Ham, Frederick	Cornell, Winnie	Nov. 23, 1873

Page 334
Lyons, Henry	Ponder, Catherine	Dec. 19, 1873
Minter, Squire	Crawford, Martha	Oct. 21, 1873
Thornton, Milton	Kelly, Minerva	Dec. 25, 1873

Page 335
Talmadge, Martin	Barkley, Sarah Ann	Dec. 20, 1873
Phillips, Mark	Heath, Louella	Nov. 20, 1873
Miller, Anderson	Carr, Jane	Dec. 18, 1873
McElroy, Tillman O.	Barnett, Lucy L.	Dec. 3, 1873
McMichael, Miles	Banks, Nellie	Jan. 1, 1874
Berry, George	Hall, Hannah	Jan. 1, 1874
Hodges, F. M.	White, Kate	Dec. 23, 1873
Collins, Lewis	Roberts, Kesiah	Jan. 25, 1874
Ingram, Wm. B.	Edison, Mary M.	Jan. 22, 1874

Page 338
Harmon, Wm.	Carr, Phereby	Jan. 29, 1874
Slaughter, Warren	Shivers, Betty	Jan. 25, 1874
Shivers, James	McMichael, Sarah	Jan. 24, 1874

Page 339
Hardy, Green	Hall, Sally	Jan. 31, 1874
Jester, Stephens	McKibben, Sarah	Dec. 25, 1873
Kelly, L. P.	Smith, Susan S.	Jan. 29, 1874

Page 340
Smith, John F.	Barnett, Julia C.	Jan. 15, 1874
Kelly, Lewis	Slaughter, Prudie	Jan. 4, 1874
Ross, Edinbrough	Butler, Josephine	Apr. 10, 1874

Page 341
Ringfield, Jim	McDune, Louisa	May 3, 1874
Barnes, Chas. B.	Weaver, Lizzie	May 18, 1874
Davis, Thos N.	Evans, Laura E.	June 28, 1874

Page 342
Bishop, Silas N.   McNair, Mattie   June 18, 1874
Yancey, John W.   Barnes, Ludie   July 30, 1874
Leverett, James H.   Barnett, Elmina S.   July 20, 1874

Page 343
Gordon, Seaborn   Pye, Fannie   Aug. 15, 1874
Ward, Andrew J.   Mitchell, Louise   Aug. 15, 1874
Barber, Ben   Price, Angeline   Aug. 25, 1874

Page 344
Carr, Andy   Mays, Frances   Sept. 2, 1874
Spark, W. W.   Stewart, Allie   Sept. 6, 1874
Vaughn, Henry M.   King, Nancy A.   Sept. 15, 1874

Page 345
Dawson, Simon   Sandifer, Rose   Sept. 2, 1874
Pittman, Moses   Douglas, Winnie   Sept. 26, 1874
Crow, John M.   Maddox, Marry E.   Sept. 28, 1874

Page 346
Collins, Stephen   Foster, Sally   Oct. 12, 1874
Berry, Rufus   Hall, Sally   Oct. 21, 1874
Goodman, Jim   Minter, Celia   Nov. 1, 1874

Page 347
Hammond, Henry   Buckner, Emily   Nov. 1, 1874
Kitchens, A. S.   Cook, Sarah E.   Nov. 8, 1874
McKibben, Valentine   Aplin, Martha Jane   Aug. 24, 1874

Page 348
Duke, Mollie L.   Fletcher, Emma S.   Nov. 22, 1874
Byars, George W.   Barnett, Honey   Dec. 11, 1874
Barnes, J. C.   Moore, Susan I.   Dec. 10, 1874

Page 349
Mason, F. B.   LeGuin, Rebecca   Dec. 13, 1874
Slaughter, Isaac   Saunders, Susie   Dec. 13, 1874
Allen, Alexander Jr. Roberts, Amanda   Nov. 1. 1874

Page 350
Rogers, John   Preston, Elvira   Dec. 15, 1874
Hardy, Zachariah   Giles, Laty   Dec. 22, 1874
Bivins, Lewis   Gunn, ___?   Dec. 12, 1874

Page 351
Garden, Pleasant   McCune, Clara   Dec. 23, 1874
Johnson, Jesse   McCune, Jinnie   Dec. 24, 1874
McCord, James H. Jr. Owen, Molly   Dec. 24, 1874

Page 352
Burns, Sebron   Yancey, Margaret   Dec. 27, 1874
Dearing, H. G.   Tucker, Molly   Dec. 6, 1874
Crabtree, Zelie   Hardy, Susan   Dec. 15, 1874

Page 353
Gray, James H.   Finley, Martha   Dec. 29, 1874
Ham, J. H.   McMichael, Nanie O.   Dec. 27, 1874

Page 354
Hardy, LeRoy   Fincher, Julia   Dec. 31, 1874
Etheridge, C. F.   Smith, Sarah A.   Jan. 19, 1875
Williams, Sam   Proctor, Nellie   Jan. 16, 1875
Robert, Hubbard   Roberts, Martha   Jan. 22, 1875

Page 355
Harkness, Charles   Benton, Allie   Jan. 14, 1875
Parnell, James   Leverett, Celia Ann   Dec. 22, 1875
Phillips, Abram   Barkley, Amanda   Dec. 30, 1875

Page 356		
Aikin, Calvin	Gunn, Minnie	Nov. 17, 1874
Moore, Henry	Bond, Airy	Dec. 8, 1874
Folds, Robert	Johnson, Sallie	Jan. 5, 1875
Page 357		
Head, Nathan	Roath, Lucinda	Jan. 20, 1875
Page 358		
Towles, Adam	Glover, Angeline	Feb. 21, 1875
Jackson, Wm.	Harkness, Hariette	Feb. 21, 1875
Hardy, Joseph	Giles, Martha	Mar. 8, 1875
Page 359		
Isdel, J. S.	Darnell, Mollie	Feb. 11, 1875
Greer, Chas.	Adams, Amanda	Jan. 7, 1875
Bailey, Wm.	Fish, Sarah	Mar. 8, 1875
Page 361		
Dick, Wm. M.	Blippett, Mary J.	Sept. 14, 1874
Page 362		
Carr, James M.	Bishop, Mary J.	Feb. 10, 1875
Maddox, J. H.	Stewart, Georgia J.	Feb. 10, 1875
Snow, James M.	Capps, Vina	Oct. 8, 1875
Roper, Wm. M.	Thompson, M. O.	Nov. 19, 1874
Page 363		
Roper, Daniel	Tolleson, Sarah F.	Jan. 5, 1874
Capps, James W.	Thurston, Eliza	Feb. 8, 1873
Page 364		
Thaxton, David	Carmichael, Margaret	Nov. 3, 1873
Fears, Thos. E.	Giles, Mollie E.	Mar. 21, 1875
Rainy, Bird	Gogin, Fannie	Apr. 16, 1875
Page 365		
White, G. W.	Weaver, Lucinette	Dec. 24, 1874
Hunt, C. W.	Griffin, Sophronia	May 9, 1875
Willis, Frank	Holland, Mina	June 20, 1875
Page 366		
Jackson, Wm.	Prichett, Joseph	June 20, 1875
Page 368		
Foster, Bailey	Jester, Anna	Jan. 18, 1876
Page 369		
Harris, B. F.	Byars, Mahalia	Jan. 8, 1876
Carpenter, Levi W.	Kimbell, Mrs. Margaret	Dec. 8, 1864
Page 370		
Evins, Pleasant	Thompson, Harriett H.	Feb. 21, 1864
Wise, John M.	Thomason, Nanny Jane	Dec. 21, 1865
Page 371		
Glover, J. W. C.	Bledsoe, Mary Susan	Dec. 20, 1864
Ray, Geo. W.	Atkinson, Emma D.	Dec. 26, 1864
Page 372		
Hopson, Wm. B.	Darden, Ora E. T.	Jan. 24, 1865
Strawn, Abraham	Cook, Mary E. P.	Mar. 18, 1865
Page 373		
Nelms, David	Hilley, M. J.	Feb. 12, 1865
Gaston, Matthew S.	McMichael, Laura A.	Apr. 8, 1865
Page 374		
Haley, Thos. H.	Elder, Laura M.	May 8, 1865
Jinks, Minton	Harris, Elizabeth	May 25, 1865

Page 375
Thurman, Jas. G.   Giles, Mary J.   June 1, 1865
Skinner, L. A.   LeGuin, T. A.   June 15, 1865

Page 376
Hail, Walter H.   Goddard, Margaret   June 13, 1865
Varner, John C.   Gordon, Aldine   June 25, 1865

Page 377
Baxley, Geo. W.   Lindsey, Amey   July 11, 1865
Roberts, L. T.   Willis, C. E.   Aug. 3, 1865

Page 378
Jenkins, Wm. H.   Crumbley, Nancy A.   Aug. 18, 1865
Carter, W. J.   Lindsey, Martha   Aug. 15, 1865

Page 379
Lindsey, C. P.   Dodd, Mrs. Julia   Aug. 31, 1865
Bishop, Chas.   Thurston, Martha   Aug. 18, 1865

Page 380
Crain, Marcus   Barnes, Martha C.   Sept. 14, 1865
Garrett, P. M.   Maddux, Ann   Oct. 1, 1865

Page 381
Lynch, Geo. S.   Rich, Mary E.   Sept. 10, 1865
Peek, A. J. W.   Thompson, Nancy E.   Sept. 10, 1865

Page 382
Henderson, Anderson B.   Saunders, Mamie B.   Nov. 16, 1865
Britton, Jas. P.   Knowland, Anna E.   Oct. 5, 1865

Page 383
Buffington, John J.   Williamson, Mary E.   Nov. 30, 1865
Moore, Jas. H.   Barlow, Margaret H.   Nov. 2, 1865

Page 384
Weaver, Joseph E.   Carr, Victoria   Nov. 7, 1865
Thomas, Wm. D.   Thaxton, Mary J.   Dec. 7, 1865

Page 385
Douglas, Wm. F.   Watkins, Maggie   Nov. 7, 1865
Curry, Willis W.   Crowell, Hargetta   Dec. 17, 1865

Page 386
Smith, John M.   Lummus, Mrs. Ernestine   May 27, 1865
Philips, John W.   Jones, Emily   Oct. 12, 1865

Page 387
Cooper, John N.   Douglas, Martha R.   Nov. 6, 1865
Hendrick, Mastin   Willis, Mrs. E. H.   Dec. 18, 1865

Page 388
Bearden, H. G.   Lassiter, M. J.   Dec. 19, 1865
Flint, Frank   Duke, Ellen E.   Dec. 24, 1865

Page 389
McCallum, J. H.   Carr, Mary   Dec. 14, 1865
Potts, Moses A.   Jones, Catherine R.   Dec. 26, 1865

Page 390
Heard, Chas. L.   Gilmore, Amanda A.   Jan. 2, 1866
White, P. L.   Macky, Ellen   Jan. 9, 1866

Page 391
Hail, Henderson   Brownlee, Eliz.   Feb. 1, 1866
Hoard, William   Lewis, Sarah   Feb. 8, 1866

Page 392
Dickerson, C. M.   Hartsfield, Lizzie   Feb. 16, 1866

141

Collins, Samuel   Bankston, Lavisa   Feb. 22, 1866

Page 393
Hilley, John M.   Carter, E. T.   Feb. 9, 1865
Strange, Wm. E.   McCord, Elvira E.   Apr. 16, 1865

Page 394
Frasier, D. W.   Foster, Sarah   Apr. 16, 1865
Given, Dave   Sims, Julia   Jan. 6, 1873

Page 395
Walker, Benson   Buttrill, Amanda   Apr. 2, 1872
Thompson, Ensign   Byars, Bobbie   Sept. 25, 1873

Page 396
Shaw, George   Buttrill, Martha   June 25, 1875
Jackson, Burwell   Cannon, Jane   June 27, 1875
McLeroy, Chas.   Allen, Frances   June 27, 1875
McMichael, Henry   Berry, Susan   July 24, 1875
Wynn, Owen   Laquin, Susan   May 30, 1875
Jackson, Augustus   Slaughter, Amanda   Aug. 21, 1875

Page 397
Douglas, Ephraim   Hendrick, Adaline   Sept. 6, 1875
Dutton, B. Z.   Edge, Jennie   July 28, 1875
Collins, J. F.   Shaw, Elia   Aug. 24, 1875
Mayfield, Robert   Plymale, Mary Jane   Sept. 24, 1875
Davis, A. C.   Tolleson, Mary A.   Sept. 19, 1875
Wood, J. A. P.   Elder, Georgia   Oct. 11, 1875

Page 398
Weaver, W. J.   Meredith, S. E.   Oct. 24, 1875
Smith, Clovis   Walthall, Luda   Aug. 22, 1875
Washington, W. W.   Griffin, D. A.   Nov. 14, 1875
Causey, S. A.   Clark, Mattie V.   May 25, 1875
Maddux, Lucian   Cole, Susan   Nov. 21, 1875
Ward, Wesley   Goodrum, Angeline   Dec. 5, 1875
Brown, Simon   Wilkerson, Lucy   Dec. 12, 1875

Page 399
Walker, Andrew   Gotier, Lydia   Dec. 12, 1875
Tucker, William   Mayo, Martha Jane   Dec. 2, 1875
Bledsoe, Roy   Bledsoe, Emma   Dec. 9, 1875
Simonton, David   McMichael, Angeline   Dec. 4, 1875
Thornton, Chas. H.   McKibben, Mattie   Dec. 21, 1875
Grubbs, George   Dickerson, Frances   Dec. 20, 1875
Cleveland, Jesse F.   Collier, Susie F.   Dec. 15, 1875
Head, Anderson   Redman, Milley   Dec. 25, 1875

Page 400
Norsworthy, Pharo   Mayo, Sarah   Sept. 11, 1875
Sims, Anderson   Smith, Amanda   Dec. 23, 1875
Brewster, Peter   Murray, Susan   Dec. 23, 1875
Matthews, Lewis   White, Polly   Sept. 15, 1875
Cornell, Geo. P.   Elder, Lucerne (Lucine)   Nov. 11, 1875
Hardy, John   Mote, Lizzie   Nov. 3, 1875

Page 401
Powell, John   Mason (Vason), Amanday   Dec. 20, 1875
Davis, E. O. N.   Nolen, Alice   Jan. 11, 1876
Douglas, Washington   Clark, Martha J.   Dec. 12, 1875
Rogers, Sydney   Spiers, Harriet J.   Dec. 2, 1875
Thurman, Sanford   Cardwell, Isabella   June 2, 1875
Jarrell, Newton   Appling, Clema   Dec. 30, 1876
Thurman, Alex.   Bledsoe, Sarah Ann   July 27, 1876

Page 402
Clark, Andrew   Watkins, Amanda   July 27, 1876
Tanner, John   Proctor, Jane   Sept. 1, 1876

Asbury, Daniel	Mayo, Araminta	Oct. 9, 1875
Barnes, George	Caloway, Mattie	Jan. 25, 1873
Redman, Reaben	Clark, Celia	Feb. 25, 1875
Barnes, Eliza	Cook, Laura	Dec. 30, 1872
Mayfield, E. M.	Duke, E. J.	May 6, 1872

Page 403

Smith, Simon R.	Sutton, Martha A.	Dec. 2, 1875
Plymale, Wm. A.	Kelly, Mary J.	Feb. 20, 1876
Maddux, C. W. F.	Baughan, N. J.	Mar. 12, 1876
McLeroy, Thos.	Deason, Margaret	Dec. 3, 1875
Pitman, Thos	Cook, Jinnie	Dec. 3, 1874
Hurd, Stephen M.	Barkley, Amelia	Dec. 23, 1875
Wilson, Chas. Patrick	Rice, Turtilla W.	Oct. 27, 1875
Tucker, Thos.	Willis, Mary	June 26, 1876

Page 404

Hendrick, Green	Wise, Lucina	July 15, 1876
Clements, Thos.	Watson, Sallie	Aug. 19, 1876
Roberts, Gilbert	McCune, Ida	Nov. 28, 1876
Hardy, Louis	Head, Fanny	Dec. 28, 1876
Tanner, Andrew	Bailey, Sylvia	Feb. 10, 1877
Davis, Arthua	Duke, Malissa	Feb. 11, 1877

Page 405

Brownlee, App	Price, Nancy	Mar. 8, 1877
Bailey, James	Chambliss, Rhena	Apr. 15, 1877
Buttrill, Moses	Hall, Margaretta	June 14, 1877
Vason, Shadrac	Aiken, Mollie	Dec. 8, 1877
Redman, Wash	Brown, Jennie	Jan. 24, 1879

Page 406

Brown, Noah	Buttrill, Martha	July 8, 1876
Butler, Wm.	Stark, Carrie	Apr. 5, 1876
Ingram, Newton	Clark, Phillips	Dec. 3, 1875
Harkness, Green	Roberts, Emaline	Sept. 21, 1876
Washington, Henry	Taylor, Frances	Aug. 19, 1876
Taylor, Jordan	Spencer, Flora	July 15, 1876
Maddux, Mark	Collins, Jennie	Dec. 27, 1876

Page 407

McMichael, Richard	Lawrence, Lucinda	Jan. 24, 1877
Roberts, Milton	Berry, Eady	Dec. 17, 1876
Berry, Henry	Whitehead, Jenny	Feb. 9, 1877
Burford, Columbus	Aiken, Mattie	Jan. 21, 1877
Whitehead, Isaac	Holt, Ella	Mar. 10, 1877
Vickers, Henry	James, Caroline	Mar. 25, 1877

Page 408

Tanner, Prince	Proctor, Lucreta	Mar. 10, 1877
Duncan, Wm.	Nobles, Lucy	Sept. 29, 1877

Page 409

Wright, Albert	Barlow, Easter	Oct. 11, 1877
Hodges, Jeff	Brown, Mariah	Nov. 15, 1877
Barlow, Tom	Byars, Sallie	Aug. 14, 1877
Hodges, Solomon	Jones, Lizzie	Aug. 8, 1877
Key, Emanuel	Ellerson, Cena	June 30, 1877
Flemister, Alex	Ross, Ann	Dec. 6, 1877
Jester, Stephen	Greer, Katie	Dec. 20, 1877
Carter, George	Garner, Amanda	Dec. 2, 1877
Berry, Simon	Brownlee, Amanda R.	July 10, 1877
Ham, Benton	Burford, Rhoda	Dec. 4, 1870

Page 410

Jolly, Oke	Mason, Georgia	Dec. 24, 1877
Banks, Joe	Harkness, Martha	Dec. 27, 1877
Maddox, Joe	Williams, Mary	Jan. 6, 1878
Bailey, Squire	Darden, Lucinda	Jan. 6, 1878

Page 411

Williamson, Chas.	McCune, Frances	Dec. 27, 1877
Render, Geo.	Sims, Antonett	Jan. 1, 1878
Price, David	Goolsby, Lucy Ann	Dec. 27, 1878
Ball, Joe	Dicken, Patsy	Jan. 3, 1878
Wilkerson, Joe	Barkley, Frances	Dec. 28, 1877

Page 412

McKibben, Gilbert Gay	Newton, Winnie	Dec. 15, 1878
Corley, Elbert	Phinazee, Lucy	Jan. 10, 1878
Brown, Bill	McMichael, Clarisy	Dec. 20, 1877
Byars, Frank	Campbell, Sallie	Dec. 27, 1877
Byars, Joe	Wynn, Amanda	Jan. 30, 1877
Barber, Burrell	Ingram, Susan	Dec. 27, 1877

Page 413

Ham, John	Greer, Jinnie	Dec. 31, 1878
McMichael, Robt.	Berry, Martha	Jan. 6, 1878
Mayfield, Greer	Byas, Margaret	Dec. 31, 1877
Watson, Henderson	Watson, Fanny	Dec. 27, 1877
Shepherd, Elie	Berry, Louise	Dec. 13, 1877
Shaws, Henry	Stewart, Laura	Oct. 5, 1878
Harkness, Simon	Barkley, Margaret	Nov. 21, 1878

Page 414

Minter, Madison	Roberts, Rosanah	Dec. 15, 1877
Roddy, John	Watson, Jane	Mar. 14, 1878
Head, Moses	Tiler, Sarah	Dec. 30, 1877
Saunders, Pleasant	Ross, Emma	Feb. 10, 1878
Thomas, Green	Cook, Polly	Jan. 30, 1878

Page 415

Brady, Tom	Smith, Georgia Ann	Sept. 30, 1877
Calhoun, Chas.	Fears, Josephine	Dec. 28, 1877
Walker, Samuel	Bankston, Ellen	Mar. 23, 1878
Talmage, Martin	Mackey, Florence	Apr. __, 1878
Burford, Frank	Ball, Sallie	Dec. 9, 1878
Goodrum, Jesse	Barber, Lucy	Jan. 25, 1877

Page 416

McKibben, Burney	Hall, Joanna	Aug. 29, 1878
Ursery, Moses	Gardner, Betsey	Sept. 9, 1878
Peoples, Harvey	Hendrick, Fanny	Nov. 28, 1878
Cash, John	Bledsoe, Angaline	Dec. 11, 1878

Page 417

Morgan, Sam	Thompson, Anna	Dec. 19, 1878
Berry, Oliver	Goodman, Laura	Jan. 22, 1879
Vaughn, Rawson	Sims, Martha	Jan. 24, 1879
Buttrill, Moses	Watson, Mariah	Jan. 4, 1879
Walker, James	Whitehead, Amanda	July 6, 1879
Byans (no name)	Roberson, Ellen	Dec. 26, 1878

Page 418

Woodward, Tony	Ridgeway, Georgia Ann	Jan. 16, 1879
Bowdoin, Ned	Hart, Ellzie	Mar. 6, 1879
Harkness, Charles	Thurman, Matilda	Mar. 20, 1879
Redding, Jim	Bradley, Polly	Dec. 29, 1878
King, Oliva	Barnes, Tabitha	Jan. 25, 1879
Ridgeway, Columbus	Hodges, Sophia	Dec. 26, 1878

Page 419

Hendrick, Thos.	Mays, Ollie	Dec. 12, 1878
McCune, Levi	Hodges, Isabella	Apr. 3, 1879
Sims, Wiley	Morris, Mary	May 4, 1879
Taylor, Peter	Campbell, Frances	Mar. 23, 1879
Thomaston, Henry	Sims, Terrissa	Aug. 24, 1879
King, John	Whitehead, Caroline	Sept. 1, 1879

Barkley, Frank	Carr, Celia	Sept. 28, 1879
Johnson, Webster	Byars, Allie	Dec. 9, 1879
Simons, Presley	Fears, Fannie	Jan. 9, 1877
Mathis, Lewis	Hendrick, Harriet	Mar. 2, 1879
Carson, Charlie	Woodward, Sallie	Nov. 2, 1879
Stewart, Albert	Hines, Bettie	Nov. 7, 1879
Johnson, Caroline	Turner, Josey	July 2, 1876

Page 421

Greer, Henry	Redding, Nancy	Jan. 29, 1879
Jones, John	Bailey, Irena	Dec. 24, 1878
Back, Henry	Woodward, Mollie	Nov. 2, 1879
Greer, Benjamin	Head, Sena	Oct. 25, 1879
Carr, Bill	Thompson, Sallie	Dec. 18, 1879
Burford, Ellick	Brownlee, Lou	Dec. 25, 1879
Jester, Peter	Hentry (Gentry?), Vina	Nov. 30, 1879

Page 422

Benton, Milton	Hall, Caroline	Dec. 27, 1879
Winn, Glover	Goodrum, Emiline	Dec. 24, 1879
Thomas, Ben	Johnson, Josephine	Jan. 22, 1880
Woodward, Monroe	Berry, Georgia	Jan. 15, 1880
Gotarire, Wiley	Head, Ella	Apr. 15, 1880
Bledsoe, Leroy	Barber, Mary	Apr. 8, 1880
Huddleston, Aaron	Mays, Polly Ann	May 14, 1880
Berry, John	Price, Marietta	July 1, 1880
Heard, John	Byars, Susan	June 20, 1880
Laney, Abe	Watts, Lettie	July 10, 1880
Fretwell, Green	Lester, Fannie	Aug. 29, 1880
Bailey, Joe	Moore, Susan	July 11, 1880
Worthy, Fleming	Willis, Winnie	Nov. 6, 1880
McElroy, Charles	Redding, Millie	Nov. 13, 1880
Clark, Mastus	Mann, Lulor	Oct. 25, 1880
Reeves, Dempse	Shepherd, Mollie	Dec. 5, 1880
Lynch, Monroe	Cook, Betsey	July 3, 1881
Brown, Milton	Trimble, Emma	Dec. 21, 1879
White, Daniel	Goodman, Martha	Dec. 12, 1879
Barnes, Willis	Shepherd, Amanda	Dec. 25, 1879
Vason, Alfred	Banks, Ella	July 4, 1881
Roach, Frank	Redman, Lumie	Apr. 20, 1880
Shepherd, Jack	Berry, Winny	Dec. 22, 1879
Fortner, W. M.	Johnson, Rebecca	July 18, 1880
McGee, Squire	Scott, Peggy	Oct. 17, 1880
McMichael, Tom	Goodman, Josie	Sept. 18, 1880
Goodrum, Mike	Heard, Georgia A.	Sept. 18, 1880
Rush, Alex	Howard, Matt	Sept. 18, 1880
Johnson, Irvin	Ponder, Amy	Jan. 30, 1881
Andrews, Riley	Woodward, Sallie	Feb. 6, 1881
Masten, Lawson	Beasley, Emma	Feb. 10, 1881

Page 436

Greer, Jack	Berry, Annetta	Feb. 19, 1881

Page 438

Taylor, Erminah	Lyons, Levena	Mar. 12, 1881
Monroe, Atlas	Clark, Emma	Mar. 17, 1881
Jester, Willis	Price, Julia	Mar. 27, 1881
Dixon, Abe	Foster, Eliga	Apr. 7, 1881

Page 429

Waits, Andrew	Gant, Sidney	Mar. 24, 1881
Start (Stark), Lucian	McMichael, Matilda	Mar. 28, 1881
Norris, Jack	Harkness, Queen	July 15, 1881
Knight, Wiley	Gualt, Lizzie	Apr. 21, 1881
Waits, Wm.	Ganet, Phillipa	Apr. 21, 1881
Peeples, Thos	McKibben, Charlotte	Apr. 30, 1881

Page 436

Lawson, Martin	McMichael, Agneline	June 19, 1881

Gunn, Chas.	Jolly, Sadie	Feb. 7, 1881
Henderson, G. Thos	Watson, Hester	June 23, 1881
Greer, Joe	Watson, Lottie	June 12, 1881
Wilson, Nelson	Byars, Celia	Sept. 14, 1881

Page 431
Mays, Thos	Fears, Adaline	Sept. 22, 1881
Henderson, John Henry	Nobels, Sarah	Oct. 4, 1881
Sullivan, Wm.	Doomis, Jennie	Oct. 16, 1881

Page 432
Benson, Harrison	Lyons, Mary	Aug. 16, 1881
McCord, Andrew	Ogletree, Eliza	Nov. 17, 1881
Kelly, Mack	Greer, Shady	Nov. 17, 1881

Page 433
Folds, Edmon	Mayfield, Madora	Dec. 29, 1881
Banks, Robert	Mayo, Julia A.	Sept. 17, 1881
Clowers, Joshua	Thomas, Queen Ann	Dec. 24, 1881
Carson, Charles	Moore, Hattie	Dec. 28, 1881

Page 434
McKibben, Dave	Stark, Sallie	Dec. 28, 1881
Gaston, Freeman	Lawson, Ann	Jan. 10, 1882
Berry, Lyman	Norris, Louise	Feb. 5, 1882
Berry, Russell	McMichael, Amy	Feb. 9, 1882

Page 436
| Fambrough, James | Beasley, Carrie | Jan. 22, 1882 |

Page 437
Shaw, Tell	Collins, Martha	Nov. 3, 1875
Riches, Wm. G.	Collins, Mary C.	Oct. 6, 1873
Collins, J. J.	Collins, Sallie	Dec. 17, 1874
Woodward, Newdigate H.	Stilwell, Lizzie	Sept. 1, 1874
Johnson, A. J. T.	Clark, Cora	Dec. 23, 1875
Rich, John B.	Collins, Sarah J.	Dec. 14, 1875
Crawford, W. D.	Collins, M. B.	Dec. 23, 1875

Page 438
Stewart, Samuel A.	Sharks, Mattie	Jan. 6, 1876
Dickerson, Abe	McDaniel, Liza	Jan. 6, 1877
Mouland, Albert	Barkley, Rhoda	Jan. 20, 1878
Hodge, Sebron	Watkins, Anna	Dec. 4, 1879
Aldridge, Ben	Moore, Mariah	Sept. 4, 1881

Foreward: Henry, an original Georgia County, was created May 15, 1821 from the Creek Indian Cession of Jan. 8, 1821. McDonough has always been the County seat.

All of the land in the original Henry County was surveyed by the State of Georgia into land lots of 202 1/2 acres each, with minor exceptions along river, and these were offered to Georgia citizens generally by means of the Land Lottery of 1821.

The original area which embraced Henry County began almost immediately to be cut off to form new counties, as follows: Newton County, Dec. 24, 1821, DeKalb County, Dec. 9, 1822, Butts County, Dec. 24, 1825.

On Dec. 20, 1853 the westernmost part of DeKalb County was cut off to form Fulton County to which Atlanta is the county seat, so much of the considerable land area of the original Henry County is today included in the densely populated area comprising metropolitan Atlanta.

Henry County's records have been well preserved from the earliest time. They may be found at the court house in McDonough or on microfilm at the Georgia Department of Archives and History in Atlanta.

DEED BOOK A

March 22, 1824: JAMES MONCRIEF of Lincoln Co., Ga. to JOSEPH HAND of Henry Co.; $320; Lot No. 246 of the 6th Dist. Henry County. Witnesses: Johathan AMMONS and JOHN DUNN, J.P. (Un-numbered page at beginning of the book.)

Feb. 18, 1822: Bill of sale made in Jackson Co., Ga. by AUSTIN FULCHER to PETER Z. WARD of Henry Co.; $250; a negro boy named Ephraim. Witnesses: Dillon FULCHER, J.P. and JOHN LOVEJOY. (Un-numbered page at beginning of the book.)

March 17, 1823: Power of attorney by ROBERT WOODS to JOHN FILLMORE empowering GILLMORE to sell Lot No. 65 of the 2nd Dist. Henry County. (Un-numbered page at beginning of the book.)

Page 1: May 7, 1822. JOHN PHILLIPS and wife MARY "formerly MARY WILKINSON of Mills District, Chatham County, Ga." to THOMAS ELKINS; $100; Lot No. 71 of the 16th Dist. Henry County. Deed was signed "JOHN F. PHILLIPS" and MARY (X) PHILLIPS." Witnesses: JOHN DILLON, J.P., JOHN ALLEN, JAMES WASHINGTON. MARY PHILLIPS relinquished her dower at Savannah, Ga. May 7, 1822 and "JOHN FRANK PHILLIPS" acknowledged the transaction at Savannah on May 8, 1822.

Page 3: Feb. 6, 1822. Deed made in Twiggs Co., Ga. by MACKSIE (X) BUTLER of Telfair Co., Ga. to JOHN B. ALEXANDER of Bryan Co., Ga.; $150: Lot 325 of the 18th Dist. Henry Co. Witnesses: THOMAS FULTON, LAIRD MCMURRAY, J.P.

Page 3: April 9, 1822. Deed made in Walton Co., Ga. by JOHN B. ALEXANDER of Bryan Co., Ga. to JOHN T. BLACKMAN of Walton Co. Lot No. 225 of the 18th Dist. Henry Co. on Nancy Creek, drawn by MACKSIE BUTLER in the Lottery of 1821. Witnesses: DAVID J. BRITT, EDWARD BRITT.

Page 4: Feb. 13, 1822. Deed made in Clarke Co., Ga. by CHRISTOPHER BROCK of Jackson Co., Ga. to STEPHEN THOMAS; $300; Lot No. 109 of the 11th Dist. Henry Co. Witnesses: WILLIAM MITCHELL, S. BROWN, J.P.

Page 4: Jan. 7, 1822. Deed made in Telfair Co., Ga. by THOMAS DENT to CHARLES J. SHELTON, both of Telfair Co. $200; Lot No. 5 of the

3rd Dist. Henry Co., drawn by said DENT in the lottery. Witnesses:
ARTHUR BREWS (BRUCE?), NATHANIEL ASHLEY, J.I.C.

Page 5: Jan. 7, 1822. Deed made in Telfair Co., Ga. by WILLIAM L.
CURRY to CHARLES J. SHELTON both of Telfair Co. $200; Lot No. 87 of
the 17th Dist. Henry Co. Witnesses: Lewis A___?, ___ LUMPKIN,
NATHANIEL ASHLEY, J.I.C.

Page 6: Jan. 9, 1822. Deed made in Guinnett Co., Ga. by WILLIAM
W. (X) ADAMS with ISAAC TOWERS, SENR. to HIRAM E. C. HARRIS. Lot No.
237 of the 14th Dist. Henry Co. Witnesses: JAMES WARDLAW, JAMES MCLIN.

Page 6: Feb. 23, 1822. Deed made in Baldwin Co., Ga. by HENRY (X)
COURSEY of Houston Co., Ga. to MOSES COX of Henry Co. $300; Lot No. 207
of the 1st Dist. Henry Co. Witnesses: SLIAS HARRIS, MARLOW L. PRYOR,
J.P.

Page 7: June 12, 1822. JAMES MCVAY to HUGH HAMMETT, both of Henry
Co.; $250 Lot No. 16 of the 1st Dist. Henry Co. Witness: MOSES COX,
J.P.

Page 8: June 18, 1822. JOHN F. WILLIAMS of Habersham Co., Ga. to
JOHN T. HUMPHRIES of Pendleton District, S. C. $100; Lot N. 288 of the
16th Dist. Henry Co. granted to JOHN F. WILLIAMS March 18, 1822.
Witnesses: EDMAND POWELL, ELIZA POWELL, DAVID HUMPHREY, SENR.

Page 9: July 29, 1822. Deed made in Putnam Co., Ga. by ALEXANDER
P. HOLLY to ROBERT RIGHT, both of Putnam Co. $100; Lot No. 21 of the 14th
Dist. Henry Co. Witnesses: NICHOLAS TOMPKINS, ISAAC THRASH.

Page 9: Feb. 2, 1822. SUSANNAH (X) COOPER of Elbert Co., Ga. to
JAMES HENRY of Jackson Co., Ga. $30; Lot No. 27 of the 11th Dist. Henry
Co. Witnesses: NATHANIEL H. WHITE, JOHN WATSON.

Page 10: July 9, 1822. Power of attorney made in Telfair Co., Ga.
by JOHN (X) MOSELEY "of the Province of East Florida" to REDDIN W.
PARRAMORE of Telfair Co. "for divers causes and considerations" to
empower the said REDDIN to sell Lot No. 109 of the 16th Dist. Henry
Co. Witnesses: THOMAS S. SWAYN, WILLIAMSON SMITH, JOHN COFFEE, J.I.C.
Next following is recorded a deed dated July 15, 1822, by REDDIN
W. PARRAMORE as attorney in fact for JOHN MOSELEY of the Province of
East Florida to JOHN PARRAMORE, both of Telfair Co., conveying for
$100 the lot described in the foregoing power of attorney. Witnesses:
SAMUEL WATSON, APPLETON ROSSETER, J.I.C.

Page 11: No date. Power of attorney made in Telfair Co., Ga. by
JOHN P. TURNER of Appling Co., Ga. to General JOHN COFFEE of Telfair
Co. to empower General COFFEE to sell Lot No. 156 of the 8th Dist. and
Lot No. 151 of the 11th Dist. Henry Co. Recited that the lots were
drawn in the Lottery of 1821 by PHERIBY CARVER and that JOHN P. TURNER
was authorized to sell the lots "since his marriage to the said PHERIBY
CARVER." Witnesses: J. H. REID, N. PARRAMORE, J.I.C. Next following
(on Page 12) is recorded a deed dated Feb. 15, 1822, by JOHN COFFEE
as attorney in fact for JOHN TURNER to JOHN PARRAMORE conveying for $500
the two lots described in the foregoing power of attorney. Witnesses:
REDDIN W. PARRAMORE, N. PARRAMORE, J.I.C.

Page 13: Aug. 16, 1822. DANIEL STAGNER of Jasper Co., Ga. to
ELIJAH RAY of Henry Co.; $100; Lot No. 80 of the 11th Dist. Henry Co.
Witnesses: JORDAN GAY, J.I.C., WILLIAM HARDEN, Clerk, Superior Court.

Page 13: Aug. 16, 1822. ELISHA (X) RAY of Henry Co. to MARLIN
MILLER of Jasper Co. $67; Lot No. 87 of 11th Dist. Henry Co. Witnesses:
JORDAN GAY, J.I.C., WILLIAM HARDEN, Clerk, Superior Court.

Page 14: Feb. 25, 1822. Power of attorney made in Laurens Co.,
Ga. by KINYARD STRICKLAND of Chatham Co., Ga. to GEORGE W. WELCH of
Laurens Co. to empower WELCH to sell to BENNETT S. GRIFFIN of Laurens
Co. the following lots; Lot No. 227 of the 7th Dist. Henry Co.; Lot No.

162 of the 12th Dist. Houston Co., Ga. Witnesses: DAVID J. GRIFFIN, ROBERT COLMAN, J.I.C. Next following (on Page 15) is recorded a deed dated Feb. 26, 1822 by GEORGE W. WELCH as attorney in fact for KINYARD STRICKLAND to BENNETT S. GRIFFIN conveying for $150 the lots described in the foregoing power of attorney, with the same witnesses.

Page 16: Aug. 3, 1822. Deed executed in Hancock Co., Ga. by WILLIAM ALFORD, Jun'r. to LEVIN ELLIS, both of Hancock Co.; $219; Lot No. 234 of the 6th Dist. Henry Co. Witnesses: JAMES H. JONES, JOHN BINION, J.I.C. Next following is recorded a deed, same date, by LEVIN (X) ELLIS of Hancock Co. to JAMES BUTTS of Jasper Co., Ga., conveying for $200 the lot described above, with the same witnesses.

Page 17: April 28, 1822. WILLIAM GILBERT of the City of Savannah, Ga. to MICHAEL O'CONNER of the same place; $50; Lot No. 248 of the 7th Dist. Henry Co. Witnesses: SAMUEL GRIGGS, ISAAC RUSSELL, J.P. ISABEL R. GILBERT relinquished her dower interest same date.

Page 19: April 25, 1822. CHRISTIAN TRISPERS, blacksmith of the city of Savannah, Ga., to MICHAEL O'CONNER, shopkeeper of the same place; $91; Not No. 225 of the 8th Dist. Henry Co. Witnesses: W. BROWNHOHN, ISAAC RUSSELL, J.P.

Page 21: Sept. 3, 1822. Sheriff's Deed by JAMES FLETCHER, Sheriff, to LAZARUS SUMMERLIN: $350; Lot No. 204 of the 1st Dist. Henry Co. Sold as the property of WILLIAM H. WORSHAM to satisfy indebtedness to JAMES LINDLEY of Walton Co., Ga.

Page 22: April 1, 1822. WILLIAM BETSILL to THOMAS GLENN, $700; Lot No. 6 of the 6th Dist. Henry Co., drawn by the said BETSILL in the lottery. Witnesses: BENJAMIN TARVER, W. BROWN, J.I.C.

Page 23: March 19, 1822. Deed made in Baldwin Co., Ga. by JOHN H. SMITH of Baldwin Co. to THOMAS MCKNIGHT of Walton Co., Ga. $612.50; Lot No. 150 of the 11th Dist. Henry Co. Witnesses: J. B. BECKHAM, D. JUSTICE, J.P. SELAH SMITH relinquished her dower interest the same day.

Page 26: Jan. 25, 1822. Power of attorney made in Twiggs Co., Ga. by C. W. MCMURRAY to C. LAIRD MCMURRAY both of Twiggs Co., empowering the latter to sell Lot No. 4 of the 11th Dist. Henry Co., drawn by C. W. MCMURRAY in the lottery. Next following is recorded a deed made in Twiggs Co. March 13, 1822 by LAIRD MCMURRAY of Twiggs Co. to ALLEN GAY of Jasper Co., Ga. conveying for $100 the lot described in the foregoing item. Witnesses: WILLIAM BROCK, WILLIAM MELTON, J.I.C.

Page 27: Aug. 29, 1822. BENNETT S. GRIFFIN of Laurens Co., Ga. to WILLIAM HARDEN of Henry Co. $100; Lot No. 227 of the 7th Dist. Henry Co. Witnesses: JOHN WALKER, HARDY SMITH.

Page 28: February 22, 1822. Deed made in Jackson Co., Ga. by AARON VICKERY to HARDY STRICKLAND. $500; Lot No. 100 of the 3rd Dist. Henry Co. Witnesses: CULLEN DAVIS, ASHLEY (X) CONESTON. Next following is recorded a deed dated July 22, 1822 by HARDY STRICKLAND of Jackson to H. J. WILLIAMS of Henry Co. conveying for $400 the lot described in the foregoing deed. Witnesses: DREWRY HARRINGTON, THOMAS RAMSEY, SOLOMON STRICKLAND.

Page 29: Oct. 1, 1822. Sheriff's Deed. By JAMES FLETCHER, Sheriff to JAMES P. HOLMES. $705; Lot No. 156 of the 18th Dist. Henry Co. Sold as the property of ANDREW MCBRIDE to satisfy indebtedness in Jasper Co., Ga. to WILLIAM CALDWELL.

Page 30: Oct. 1, 1822. Sheriff's Deed. By JAMES FLETCHER, Sheriff, to WILLIS BAKER of Wilkes Co., Ga. $26; Lot No. 199 of the 12th Dist. Henry Co. Sold as the property of WILLIAM STEPTOE of Wilkinson Co., Ga. to satisfy indebtedness to the said BAKER.

Page 31: Oct. 1, 1822. Sheriff's Deed. JAMES FLETCHER, Sheriff to AUGUSTUS HAYWARD. $260; Lot No. 89 of the 11th Dist. Henry Co. Sold as the property of the heirs of JAMES TRUETT to satisfy indebtedness to BENJAMIN W. PETERSON, for the benefit of JACOB PETERSON.

Page 32: Sept. 4, 1822. Deed made in Hancock Co., Ga. by JOHN J. BERRY of Hancock Co. to JEHU PUGH of Jasper Co., Ga. $208; Lot No. 152 of the 1st Dist. Henry Co. Witnesses: NICHOLAS LANIER, GEORGE RIVERS, J.P.

Page 32: Sept. 3, 1822. Sheriff's Deed. JAMES FLETCHER, Sheriff to WILLIAM WALLER SENR. of Washington Co., Ga. $78; Lot No. 243 of the 1st Dist. Henry Co. Sold as the property of JAMES WALLER to satisfy various items of indebtedness in Washington Co. to WILLIAM JOHNSON.

Page 33: Feb. 11, 1823. SAMUEL M. GARNETT to JOSEPH G. BLANCE. $400: Lot No. 16 of the 15th Dist. Henry Co. Witnesses: GEORGE GRAY, JOHN DILLON, J.P. ANN GARNETT relinquished her dower right on Feb. 15, 1823 in Chatham Co., Ga.

Page 35: March 1, 1822. Deed of trust by JOHN C. BLANCE to JOSEPH G. BLANCE. $100; Lot No. 191 of the 17th Dist. Henry Co. Witnesses: GEORGE RILEY, JOHN A. HORN, JOHN DILLON, J.P.

Page 37: Dec. 21, 1822. Deed made in Bryan Co., Ga. by HENRY (X) STONE and wife PRISCILLA (X) to GEORGE H. SHEWMAN, all of Bryan Co. $200; Lot No. 276 of the 18th Dist. Henry Co. Witnesses: WILLIAM ENGLISH, SHADRACH HARPER, ANDREW BIRD, J.I.C. PRISCILLA STONE relinquished her dower right same date.

Page 37: Nov. 27, 1822. Deed made in Jasper Co., Ga. by JAMES JUSTICE of Jasper Co. to JESSE SMITH of Newton Co., Ga. $100; Lot No. 148 of the 6th Dist. Henry Co. on Walnut Creek. Witnesses: RICHARD Q. (?) LANE, DANIEL ROBERTS, THOMAS B. GAY, J.P.

Page 39: Jan. 25, 1823. ARCHIBALD MILLER of Appling Co., Ga. to JOHN T. BENTLEY of Henry Co. $118; Lot No. 159 in the 3rd Dist. Henry Co. Witnesses: JOHN (X) MILLER SENR., CHRISTOPHER EDWARDS, J.P. Next following is recorded (on page 40) a deed dated March 21, 1823 by JOHN T. BENTLEY of Henry Co. to CHARLES HUDSON of Walton Co., Ga. conveying for $300 the lot described in the foregoing deed. Witnesses: JAMES KIMBROUGH, JAMES HENRY, J.P.

Page 41: Dec. 29, 1821. Deed made in Twiggs Co., Ga. by GEORGE PARMER of Twiggs Co. to CHARLES WILDER of Jasper Co., Ga. $150; Lot No. 208 of the 3rd Dist. Henry Co. on Towaligah River. Witnesses: JACOB COBB, H. PERRYMAN.

Page 41: Jan. 28, 1822. Deed made in Newton Co., Ga. by ARCHIBALD RICH to PETER TAYLOR both of Newton Co. $800; Lot No. 144 to the 2nd Dist. Henry Co. Witnesses: WILLIAM WOOD, JAMES SWINNEY.

Page 42: April 14, 1823. WILLIAM B. TATE of DeKalb Co., Ga. to SAMUEL HOUSTON of Henry Co. $300; Lot No. 54 to the 7th Dist. Henry Co. on Walnut Creek. Witnesses: WILLIAM MALONE, JAMES HENRY, J.I.C.

Page 43: April 4, 1822. Deed made in Baldwin Co., Ga. by DAVID HILLIARD of Jones Co., Ga. to JESSE GEORGE of Jasper Co. $150; Lot No. 24 of the 9th Dist. Henry Co. Witnesses: BENJAMIN C. SCOTT, MARLOW PRYOR, J.P.

Page 43: Feb. 11, 1823. Power of attorney made in Baldwin Co., Ga. by ALBERT C. HORTON to BENJAMIN J. THOMAS both of Jones Co., to empower the latter to sell the following property: Lot No. 270 of the 18th Dist., Henry Co.; Lot No. 42 of the 12th Dist. Henry Co.; Lot No. 180 of the 11th Dist. Henry Co.; Lot 106 of the 1st Dist. Houston Co., Ga. Witnesses: WILLIAM H. TORRENCE, JAMES ROUSSEAU, J.P.

Page 44: March 20, 1823. Deed made in Jones Co., Ga. by BENJAMIN

THOMAS, as attorney in fact for ALBERT HORTON to MICHAEL HAILEY. $100;
Lot No. 180 of the 11th Dist. Henry Co. Witnesses: ROGER MCCARTHY,
G. W. COOKE, D. T. MILLING, J.P.

Page 45: Dec. 22, 1821. WILLIAM A. ROBERTSON of Jones Co., Ga. to
MICHAEL HAILEY of the same place. $500; Lot No. 88 of the 2nd Dist.
Henry Co. Witnesses: ARCHIBALD P. BENTON, ROGER MCCARTHY.

Page 46: March 20, 1823. Deed made in Jones Co., Ga. by BENJAMIN
J. THOMAS as attorney in fact for ALBERT C. HORTON of Jones Co. to MICHAEL
M. HAILEY. $100; Lot No. 42 of the 12th Dist. Henry Co. Witnesses:
ROGER MCCARTHEY, K. W. COOKE, D. T. MILLING, J.P.

Page 47: March 9, 1822. WILLIAM H. RAMSAY of Jones Co., Ga. to
A. DORROUGH. $100; Lot No. 234 of the 2nd Dist. Henry Co. Witnesses:
W. DAILE, JOHN GAMUX, J.P.E.C. Signed and sealed at "Pensacola Province
of West Florida."

Page 47: Nov. 5, 1822. Deed made in Habersham Co., Ga. by
BENJAMIN CLEVELAND of Habersham Co. to JOHN COOK of Morgan Co., Ga. $600;
Lot No. 90 of the 11th Dist. Henry Co. Witnesses: W. WHATLEY, JAMES
STRAWN, J.I.C.

Page 48: March 1, 1823. Deed made in Jasper Co. Ga. by WILLIAM
F. GERALD of Henry Co. to JOHN W. BURNEY and ALEXANDER MCDONALD of Jasper
Co., Ga. $300; Lot No. 190 of the 7th Dist. Henry Co. Witnesses:
JAMES S. WEEKS, WM. PENN.

Page 49: May 14, 1822. SAMUEL MCCULLOUGH of Richmond Co., Ga. to
JAMES MCLAWS of the same place. $125; Lot No. 156 of the 3rd Dist.
Henry Co. Witnesses: JAMES M. GLYNN, DAVID SAVAGE.

Page 50: June 14, 1822. JAMES MCLAWS of Richmond Co., Ga. to
THOMAS CRAYTON. $300; Lot No. 156 of the 3rd Dist. Henry Co. Witnesses:
RALPH KETCHUM, J.I.C. Richmond Co., JOHN S. HOLT. ELIZA V. MCLAWS
relinquished her dower interest the same day in Richmond Co.

Page 51: Sept. 27, 1822. WILLIAM D. WHITE to THOMAS CRAYTON both
of Richmond Co., Ga. $100; Lot No. 123 of the 7th Dist. Henry Co.
Witnesses: WILLIAM J. MCMILLING, R. BUSH, J.P.

Page 52: March 10, 1823. JOHN LIGON of Richmond Co., Ga. to
THOMAS CRAYTON. $120; Lot No. 115 of the 3rd Dist. Henry Co. Witnesses:
THOMAS FARROW, COLLINS H. BELCHER.

Page 54: April 2, 1823. JOHN C. GRIFFIN to THOMAS CRAYTON both of
Richmond Co., Ga. $120; Lot No. 3 of the 3rd Dist. Henry Co., drawn by
JOHN C. GRIFFIN in the lottery and granted March 31, 1823. Witnesses:
JACOB FREDERICK, R. BUSH, J.P.

Page 55: March 10, 1823. THOMAS TALMADGE of Richmond Co., Ga. to
EDWARD TALMADGE OF Chatham Co., Ga. $150; Lot No. 208 of the 6th Dist.
Henry Co. Witnesses: JAMES RENS, R. BUSH, J.P.

Page 56: Jan.7, 1823. Sheriff's Deed. JAMES FLETCHER, Sheriff,
to DAVID JOHNSON. $33; Lot No. 50 of the 2nd Dist. Henry Co. Sold as
the property of JOSEPH M. PORTER to satisfy indebtedness to W. W. BLACK.

Page 57: March 18, 1823. JOHN SIMMONS of Elbert Co., Ga. to
WILLIAM MCCONNELL of Henry Co. $300; Lot No. 29 of the 12th Dist. Henry
Co. Deed signed: "JOHN SIMMONS by HOLMAN F. SIMMONS." Witnesses:
JOHN HEAD, J.P., MICHAEL DICKSON.

Page 57: April 23, 1823. Deed made in Twiggs Co., Ga. by JOHN B.
TEAL of Twiggs Co. to TURNER EVANS of Henry Co. $500; Lot No. 134 of the
7th Dist. Henry Co. Witnesses: JOHN WOOD, MARLOW PRYOR, J.P. ELIZABETH
(X) TEAL relinquished her dower interest Aug. 9, 1824.

Page 58: July 19, 1822. Deed made in Twiggs Co., Ga. by JEREMIAH (X) DIXON of Twiggs Co. to WILLIAM STROUD of Henry Co. $150; Lot No. 72 of the 9th Dist. Henry Co. Witnesses: D. D. COPP, DAVID GRAYHAM.

Page 59: Dec. 23, 1822. Deed made in Putnam Co., Ga. by WILLIAM H. KIMBROUGH of Putnam Co. to MILLENTON POWELL: $150; Lot No. 201 of the 1st Dist. Henry Co. Witnesses: ROBERT LITTLE, JESSE LITTLE, J.P.

Page 60: March 10, 1823. SAMUEL M. WILSON to JAMES HARKNESS of Henry Co. $381; Lot No. 106 of the 1st Dist. Henry Co., drawn by said WILSON in Warren Co., Ga. Witnesses: JOHN FOUNTAIN, CLARK BLANFORD.

Page 60: Jan. 14, 1823. CHARLES P. COLLIER of Jasper Co., Ga. to JAMES HARKNESS of Henry Co. $320; Lot No. 119 of the 1st Dist. Henry Co., drawn by the said COLLIER in the lottery. Witnesses: WILLIAM B. STOKES, JESSE LOYALL, J.P. SARAH (X) COLLIER relinquished her dower interest on April 8, 1824 in Jasper Co., Ga.

Page 62: Feb. 26, 1823. Deed made in Bibb Co., Ga. by BURWELL WISE of Bibb Co. to THOMAS YARBROUGH of Henry Co. $95; Lot No. 92 of the 11th Dist. Henry Co. Witnesses: ROBERT SHAW, JAMES MCDONALD, JOHN TREADWELL, J.P.

Page 63: May 14, 1822. Deed made in Baldwin Co., Ga. by LEONARD PERKINS to THOMAS B. BURFORD of Greene Co., Ga. $500; Lot No. 214 of the 1st Dist. Henry Co. Witnesses: SAMUEL P. B. BURFORD, JAMES ROUSSEAU, J.P.

Page 63: Aug. 26, 1822. Deed made in Wilkes Co., Ga. by HUGH RUNNELLS of Wilkes Co., Ga. to NOAH CALLAWAY of Jasper Co., Ga. $69; Lot No. 154 of the 12th Dist. Henry Co. granted to the said RUNNELLS Aug. 23, 1822. Witnesses: SIMEON PETEET, HENRY HOLTZCLAW.

Page 64: Feb. 4, 1823. Sheriff's Deed. JAMES FLETCHER, Sheriff, to THAD B. REES. $116; Lot No. 100 of the 2nd Dist. Henry Co. Sold as the property of MARTIN NALL to satisfy indebtedness in Putnam Co., Ga. in a suit by IRBY and JOHN HUDSON vs. MARTIN NALL. Witnesses: CHAS. COCHRAN, WILLIAM MCCONNELL, J.P.

Page 65: May 23, 1822. THOMAS BURKS SENR. of Hall Co., Ga. to SAMUEL ARMSTRONG of the same place. $300, Lot No. 136 of the 3rd Dist. Henry Co., granted to the said BURKS May 18, 1822. Witnesses: WILLIAM D. BYRD, ROBERT (X) YOUNG.

Page 66: Feb. 4, 1822. LEWIS (X) TAYLOR of Washington Co., Ga. to ELI COOPER of Monroe Co., Ga. $300; Lot No. 87 of the 2nd Dist. Henry Co. Witnesses: JAMES BOZEMAN, JAMES MAY. Deed was proved by JAMES MAY in Jasper Co., Ga. Feb. 1, 1823. Recorded May 10, 1823. Next following (on page 67) is recorded a deed made in Jasper Co., Ga. Nov. 27, 1822 by ELI COOPER to GEORGE MORRIS, conveying for $750 the lot described in the foregoing deed. Witnesses: JOHN COMPTON, P. COMPTON J.P. Recorded May 10, 1823.

Page 68: Dec. 25, 1822. JONATHAN W. DAVIS of Fayette Co., Ga. to JAMES B. CRAIN of Morgan Co., Ga. $219; Lot No. 14 of the 2nd Dist. Henry Co. Witnesses: AMOS H. HOLLEY, BENJAMIN CANNAFORD, J.P.

Page 68: Aug. 31, 1822. Deed made in Washington Co., Ga. by BANJAMIN FORGUSON to HENRY J. WILLIAMS, both of Washington Co. $119; Lot No. 218 of the 3rd Dist. Henry Co. Witnesses: THOMAS RAMSEY, WILLIAM MOYE.

Page 69: Nov. 1, 1822. CHURCHWELL T. HINES of Washington Co., Ga. to HENRY J. WILLIAMS of Henry Co. $200; Lot No. 48 of the 2nd Dist. Henry Co. Witnesses: WILLIAM P. HARDWICK, BENJAMIN BROOKINS, J.P.

Page 70: Dec. 4, 1822. Deed made in Morgan Co., Ga. by HENRY SMITH of Clarke Co., Ga. to HENRY J. WILLIAMS of Henry Co. $500; Lot No. 80 of the 2nd Dist. Henry Co. Witnesses: JOHN L. KIRBY, THOMAS NELSON, J.P.

Page 70: Feb. 11, 1823. Sheriff's Deed. JAMES FLETCHER, Sheriff, to HENRY J. WILLIAMS of Henry Co. $95; Lot No. 19 of the 2nd Dist. Henry Co. Sold as the property of MEREDITH JOYNER to satisfy indebtedness to HENRY BUNN in Twiggs Co., Ga.

Page 71: March 23, 1823. Deed made in Washington Co., Ga. by PATRICK SMITH of Washington Co. to SOLOMON STRICKLAND of Henry Co. $500; Lot No. 142 of the 2nd Dist. Henry Co. Witnesses: ALLEN SMITH, ENOCH B. SMITH, JOSIAH MOORE, J.P.

Page 72: March 10, 1823. JACKSON CONE of Baldwin Co., Ga. to SAMUEL MCCLENDON of Henry Co. $309; Lot No. 152 of the 11th Dist. Henry Co. Witnesses: Rebecca (X) PERDUE, JAMES A. PERDUE, J.P.

Page 73: March 5, 1823. WILLIAM KEOWN to DAVID MANLEY. $500; Lot No. 117 of the 2nd Dist. Henry Co. Witnesses: JAMES H. JOHNSON, JOHN T. MANLEY, DAVID JOHNSON, J.P.

Page 73: May 30, 1822. Deed made in Walton Co., Ga. by JAMES HIGGINS of Walton Co. to JAMES A. CROMBIA (ABERCROMBIE) $150; Lot No. 101 of the 6th Dist. Henry Co. Witnesses: JONATHAN GARRETT, JAMES CAMP, J.I.C.

Page 74: Nov. 19, 1822. JACOB DAVIS of Telfair Co., Ga. to JAMES HARKNESS of Henry Co. $320; Lot No. 31 of the 9th Dist. Henry Co. Witnesses: RICHARD HOLMES, C. MCCARTY, J.P.

Page 75: July 18, 1823. JOHN B. CARMICHAEL of Jasper Co. to KENNETH GILLIS of Henry Co. $100; Lot No. 203 of the 2nd Dist. Henry Co. Witnesses: CYRUS SHARP, JAMES HUMPHRIES, J.I.C.

Page 75: March 24, 1823. GREEN B. TURNER of Newton Co., Ga. to THOMAS ROWLAND of Warren Co., Ga. $100; Lot No. 110 of the 8th Dist. Henry Co. Witnesses: WILLIAM THOMASON, JOHN B. THOMASON.

Page 76: Jan. 13, 1823. PETER KERLIN to BURWELL JENKS, both of Henry Co. Lot No. 77 of the 1st Dist. Henry Co. (The consideration paid is not shown) Witnesses: ELISHA CREWS, RICHARD COTTEN.

Page 77: Nov. 11, 1822. Power of attorney made in Laurens Co., Ga. by NANCY (X) SMITH to JESSE CORBIT of Laurens Co. to empower the latter to sell Lot No. 88 of the 12th Dist. Henry Co., drawn by NANCY SMITH in the lottery. Witnesses: WILLIAM MOORE, J. P., KINDRED PARTAIN. Next following is recorded power of attorney dated Dec. 13, 1822 by JESSE CORBIT of Laurens Co. to JEPTHA V. SMITH, empowering the latter to sell the property described in preceding item, as attorney in fact for NANCY SMITH. Witness: ISHAM BAILEY. Next following (on page 78) is recorded a deed dated Jan. 25, 1823 by JESSE (X) CORBIT, as attorney in fact for NANCY SMITH to JEPTHA V. SMITH conveying for $200 the property described above. Witnesses: MITCHELL ROBERTS, JOHN B. SMITH, JULUS (X) ROBERTS, WILLIAM MCCONNELL, J.P. The deed signed by JESSE CORBIT and NANCY SMITH.

Page 79: Jan. 15, 1823. Deed made in Morgan Co., Ga. by JOHN (X) BARRETT of Putnam Co., Ga. to THOMAS EASON of Morgan Co. $200; 101 ½ acres of Lot No. 91 of the 11th Dist. Henry Co. on Cotton Indian River. Witnesses: SAMUEL H. (X) WATSON, CHARLES HARRINGTON, JOHN WELCH.

Page 80: Nov. 9, 1818. JAMES WYATT of Morgan Co., Ga. to JOHN WYATT of Jasper Co., Ga. $100; Lot No. 127 of the 14th Dist. of Wilkinson Co., Ga. on waters of Crooked Creek. Witnesses: DANIEL DUNCAN, JAMES HEARD, J.P. Recorded Oct. 21, 1823.

Page 80: Dec. 21. 1822. Deed made in Oglethorpe Co., Ga. by JOHN MCKEE to PHILIP WATKINS both of Oglethorpe Co. $2000; Lot No. 102 of the 3rd Dist. Henry Co. Witnesses: Kirk [sic] Goolsh [sic], PHILIP WATKINS JUNR., JOHN M. SIMS, J.P.

Page 81: May 24, 1823. GEORGE U. TIPPINS of Tatnall Co., Ga. to JAMES BRADY of Henry Co. $400; Lot No. 19 of the 1st Dist. Henry Co. Witnesses: STARLING CAMP, POLLY CAMP, NATHAN BREED, J.P.

Page 82: Dec. 27, 1822. Deed made in Hall Co., Ga. by JOSEPH GAILEY of Hall Co. to ELI COOPER of Henry Co. $400; Lot No. 93 of the 2nd Dist. Henry Co. Witnesses: WILLIAM ROBINS, J.P., D. BURNS.

Page 82: Feb. 6, 1823. WILLIAM (X) LEACROY to WILLIAM MESSER both of Henry Co. $75; Lot No. 254 of the 1st Dist. Henry Co. Witnesses: ELIZABETH MABRY, HENRY WAIGHTS, R.E. MABRY, J.I.C.

Page 83: Feb. 3, 1823. Deed made in Jefferson Co., Ga. by NOAH (X) ADAMS to WILKINS HARPER, both of Jefferson Co.; $200 Lot No. 35 of the 1st Dist. Henry Co. Witnesses: JAMES ADAMS, WILEY SUTTON, J.P.

Page 83: Deed made in Newton Co., Ga. Nov. 29, 1823 by DRAKEFORD T. TRAMMELL to FARR H. TRAMMELL; $400; Lot No. 101 of 12th Dist. Henry Co. Witnesses: JOSEPH BROOKS, JOSIAH PERRY, J.P.

Page 84: Jan. 18, 1822. Deed made in Oglethorpe Co., Ga. by AARON (X) BRIDGES to FREDERICK PATTERSON: $150; Lot No. 135 of 1st Dist. Henry Co., drawn by AARON BRIDGES of Flannigan's Dist., Jackson Co., Ga. in the Land Lottery of 1821. Witnesses: WM. M. STOKES, THOMAS S. COOK, JOHN BUZBY.

Page 85: July 3, 1823. Deed made in Jackson Co., Ga. by JOHN ANGER to THOMAS JOHNSON both of Jackson Co.; $200; Lot No. 174 of 3rd Dist. Henry Co. on Thompson's Creek. Witnesses: ISAAC BURSON, JOSEPH LANDRUM, J.P.

Page 85: Oct. 7, 1823. SAMUEL PATTON of Morgan Co., Ga. to TIMOTHY JONES of Henry Co.; $500; Lot No. 255 of 2nd Dist. Henry Co. Witnesses: JOHN WELCH, SAMUEL H. WATSON, LUKE WELCH, J.P.

Page 86: Aug. 1, 1823. Deed made in Morgan Co., Ga. by JESSE REID of Morgan Co. to JOHN A. ELLIA of Oglethorpe Co., Ga.; $139; Lot No. 190 of 2nd Dist. Henry Co. Deed was signed "JESSE REID" and "RUTH REID." Witnesses: JOHN HUBBARD, E. DUKE, J.P.

Page 87: March 22, 1823. JESSE LANDERS of Walton Co., Ga. to DAVID SMITH of Henry Co.; $325; Lot No. 255 of 3rd Dist. Henry Co. on Cabin Creek. Witnesses: JOSEPH JAMES, JAMES LINDLEY, J.P.

Page 88: Dec. 7, 1822. Deed made in Richmond Co., Ga. by SAMUEL SMITH of Richmond Co. to YERBY STROUD of Jasper Co., Ga.; $100; Lot No. 138 of 8th Dist. Henry Co. Witnesses: JOHN R. TARVER, E. TARVER, J.P.

Page 89: . . . 1822. Sheriff's Deed: JAMES FLETCHER, Sheriff to YERBY STROUD; $100; Lot No. 150 of 8th Dist. Henry Co. Sold as the property of JESSE SIMMONS to satisfy indebtedness of WILLIAM H. KIMBROUGH.

Page 90: Nov. 23, 1822. THOMAS BAKER to DAVID MANLY; $500; part of Lot No. 106 of 2nd Dist. Henry Co. on Towaligah Creek. Witnesses: BENJAMIN BROWN, JOHN T. MANLY, DAVID JOHNSON, J.I.C.

Page 90: Dec. 8, 1823. Deed made in Effingham Co., Ga. by ABRAHAM (X) BLITCH and THOMAS (X) BLITCH, jointly of Effingham Co. to SHEPPARD WILLIAMS of Bulloch Co., Ga.; $180; Lot No. 135 of 7th Dist. Henry Co., drawn by THOMAS BLITCH in the Land Lottery of 1821. Witnesses: JOHN S. ACORD, JOHN BLITCH.

Page 91: Nov. 15, 1823. Deed made in Franklin Co., Ga. by JAMES MCDONALD of Franklin Co. to EDWARD LOVEJOY of Jasper Co.; $200; Lot No. 6 of 2nd Dist. Henry Co. Witnesses: SAMUEL JOHNSON, JOHN JOHNSON, J.P.

Page 92: Oct. 1, 1822. Quiteclaim deed by THOMAS WATTS of Chatham Co., Ga. to THOMAS ELKINS of Effingham Co., Ga.; $45; Lot No. 202 of 12th Dist. Henry Co. Witnesses: JOHN SCOTT, B. DOBBINS, J.P.

Page 94: Oct. 1, 1822. Quitclaim deed by PETER STRONG of Chatham Co., Ga. to JAMES WASHINGTON of Savannah, Chatham County; $50; Lot No. 115 of 12th Dist. Henry Co. Witnesses: T. SMYTH, B. DOBBINS, J.P.

Page 96: Jan. 6, 1824. Sheriff's Deed: JAMES FLETCHER, Sheriff to JEFFRY BARDSDALE; $115; Lot No. 242 of 1st Dist. Henry Co. Sold as the property of DANIEL BARKSDALE to satisfy indebtedness to JOHN SMITH of Hancock Co., Ga.

Page 97: July 30, 1822. DANIEL DUNLEVEY of Chatham Co., Ga. to JAMES WASHINGTON; $40; Lot No. 112 of 12th Dist. Henry Co. Witnesses: EDMUND MAHER, B. DOBBINS, J.P.

Page 98: Feb. 10, 1824. SAMUEL HOUSTON to SAMUEL MATTOX; $200; 125 acres of Lot No. 54 of 7th Dist. Henry Co. Witnesses: WILSON (X) WHITE, CARTER HOUSTON.

Page 99: Aug. 9, 1823. Deed made in Morgan Co., Ga. by WILLIAM (X) GREEN to JOHN C. WILLIS both of Morgan Co. $400; Lot No. 50 of 1st Dist. Henry Co. Witnesses: THOMAS C. PINCKARD, JOHN STILLWELL, J.P.

Page 100: Oct. 15, 1823. Deed made in Putnam Co., Ga. by AZERIAH C. SAMPLES to EZEKIEL CLOUD, both of Putnam Co.; Lot No. 150 of 12th Dist. Henry Co., drawn by THOMAS R. SPAIN of Jasper Co., Ga. in the Land Lottery of 1821. Witnesses: IRBY HUDSON, J.I.C., ROBERT ASHWORTH, J.P.

Page 101: Mar. 11, 1824. Deed of trust executed in Henry Co. by ZACHARIAH ESTERS to DANIEL BROWN as Trustee, "in consideration of the love and affection I have for my sister's children, GEORGE W. PACE, MATILDA PACE, THOMAS J. PACE, LUCINDA PACE and ZACHARIAH PACE." Three featherbeds and furniture; 1 bedstead; 2 fine chests; 2 fine tables; 2 big wheels; 1 flax wheel; 1 set of common chairs; 1 set of Windsor chairs; 1 check real; 1 pot oven; 3 pairs of hooks; 1 cupboard; 1 dresser; 1 cow and calf; 1 heiffer; 1 sow; 5 pigs; 5 shoats; 2 empty barrels; 1 "pale"; 2 piggens [sic]; 1 cedar churn; 1 washing tub. The Trustee, DANIEL BROWN, was empowered to dispose of the aforesaid property for the benefit and use of the said children. Witnesses: OWEN H. KINARD, SAMUEL CLAY. The deed was signed "Z. ESTICE."

Page 101: June 20, 1822. CHARLES R. WALLER to HANDY WALLER both of Putnam Co., Ga.; $200, Lot No. 161 of 2nd Dist. Henry Co. Witnesses: H. W. ECTOR, WILLIAM REESE, MIRABEAU B. LAMAR, J.P.

Page 102: Mar. 19, 1822. Deed made in Montgomery Co., Ga. by ALEXANDER (X) MCINTOSH of Montgomery Co. to JAMES ALSTON; $100; Lot No. 231 of 12 th Dist. Henry Co. Witnesses: EDWARD FEATHERSTONE, DANIEL M. CRAINE, J.I.C.

Page 103: Nov. 12, 1823. Next following the foregoing recording, JAMES ALSTON of Montgomery Co., Ga. sells the above described lot to ADAM G. SAFFOLD of Morgan Co., Ga. for $300. Witnesses: THOMAS STOCKS, AUGUSTUS B. LONGSTREET, J.I.C.

Page 104: May 13, 1824. POINTON (X) ASHMORE to LEWIS HOPGOOD; $115; Lot No. 71 of 3rd Dist. Henry Co. Witnesses: JOHN C. HAND, HUGH LONGINO, J.P.

Page 104: Mar. 20, 1824. ROBERT COCHRAN to JOHN FLOYD; $300; Lot No. 26 of 9th Dist. Henry Co. Witnesses: THOMPSON FLOYD, WM. BARKLEY, J.P.

Page 105: April 28, 1823. JAMES TOMLINSON of Baldwin Co., Ga. to PETER MILNER of Jones Co., Ga.; $600; Lot No. 49 of 1st Dist. Henry Co., drawn by the said TOMLINSON in the Land Lottery of 1821. Witnesses: ELIZABETH SIMS, JOHN H. MILNER.

Page 106: June 7, 1823. HENRY JOYCE to SMITH BONNER; $150, Lot No. 154 of 11th Dist. Henry Co. Witnesses: DANIEL STONE, JAMES DYMOND, J.P., JOHN TERRY.

Page 106: June 2, 1824. WILLIAM HARDIN to EZEKIEL CLOUD; $100; Lot No. 59 of 7th Dist. Henry Co. Witnesses: Hardy Smith, Joseph Benton, J.P.

Page 107: Feb. 8, 1822. Deed made in Warren Co., Ga. by ELLENDER (X) STANFORD to REUBEN MCGEE both of Warren Co.; $100; Lot No. 9 of 12th Dist. Henry Co. Witnesses: JAMES MORRIS, ELIJAH STANFORD

Page 108: July 6, 1824. Sheriff's Deed: by JESSE JOHNSON, Sheriff, to LAIRD W. HARRIS and ROBERT YOUNG; $63; Lot No. 256 of 6th Dist. Henry Co. Sold as the property of JAMES D. WILSON to satisfy indebtedness of GABRIEL and LAIRD W. HARRIS in Putnam Co., Ga.

Page 109: July 6, 1824. Sheriff's Deed: JESSE JOHNSON, Sheriff, to STEPHEN W. MILLER; $5.00; Lot No. 164 of 7th Dist. Henry Co. Sold as the property of JOHN MILLER to satisfy indebtedness to PHILIP STROUD.

Page 110: May 14, 1824. Power of attorney executed by JAMES HOWARD to JOHN C. KENNEDY, both of Henry County to empower the latter to make titles to Lot No. 100 of 7th District Henry Co. Witness: JACOB SIKES.

Page 110: Feb. 6, 1824. DAVID MCMURRARY of Newton Co., Ga. to LAWSON S. HOLLAND of Jasper Co., Ga.; $250; part of Lot No. 16 of the 8th Dist. Henry Co. on the west side of Ocmulgee R. adjoining ROBERT LANG and PARKER NOLES. Deed was signed "DAVID (X) MCMURRAY" and "HANNAH (X) MCMURRAY." Witnesses: GUY W. SMITH, RODERICK HARPER, WILEY BEARDIN.

Page 111: Jan. 7, 1823. Sheriff' Deed: JAMES FLETCHER, Sheriff, to WILLIAM RUFF; $112.25; Lot No. 105 of the 7th Dist. Henry Co., sold as the property of JAMES and JOHN G. JONES to satisfy indebtedness to WILEY GLOVER, all of Henry Co.

Page 113: July 22, 1822. Deed made in Putnam Co., Ga. by THOMAS B. SWANN of Monroe Co., Ga. to EZEKIEL CLOUD of Putnam Co.; $224; Lot No. 261 of 7th Dist. Henry Co. Witnesses: JOHN L. WILLIAMS, JAMES LAWRENCE, J. B. SWANN.

Page 114: July 27, 1822. Deed made in Elbert Co., Ga. by JAMES (X) B. BRADY to WILLIAM KEOWN of Pendleton District, S. C.; $78; Lot No. 117 of 2nd Dist. Henry Co. Witnesses; JACOB BECK, JR., ALLEN ALEXANDER.

Page 114: Dec. 28, 1821. Deed made in Baldwin Co., Ga. by THOMAS HANNAH of Jefferson Co., Ga. to WILLIAM HENRY of Henry Co.; $360; Lot No. 27 of 18th Dist. Henry Co., drawn by the said Hannah in the Land Lottery of 1821. Witnesses: L. FLEMING, APPLETON ROSSETER, J.I.C.

Page 115: Mar. 14, 1822. Deed made in Wilkes Co., Ga. by WILLIAM M. S. HOUGHTON of Wilkes Co. to WILLIAM HENRY of Jackson Co., Ga.; $410; Lot No. 152 of the 12th Dist. Henry Co. Witnesses: C. BROOKS, THOMAS LASLEY, J.P.

Page 116: Oct. 17, 1822. SAMUEL SANDERS of Wilkinson Co., Ga. to WILLIAM BARNETT of Henry Co.; $260; Lot No. 249 of the 8th Dist., Henry Co. Witnesses: J. CAMAK, WILLIAM HARDIN, Clerk, Superior Court, Henry Co.

Page 117: July 8, 1822. "SAMUEL J. BRYAN & Brother" of Chatham Co., Ga. to "DANIEL NOLLEY & CO." $200; Lot No. 9 of the 1st Dist. Henry Co. Deed was signed "SAMUEL J. BRYAN & Brother." Witnesses: J. D. MANN, JAMES LOW, J.P.

Page 117: April 1, 1822. Deed made in Wilkinson Co., Ga. by JAMES VENTRESS to LEWIS BOND both of Wilkinson Co. $200; Lot No. 112 of the 13th Dist. Henry Co. Witnesses: LEONARD T. MARSHALL, LEWIS (X) A. BOND, JOHN (X) ODOM.

Page 118: Oct. 24, 1822. Deed made in Gwinnett Co., Ga. by
DEMPSEY MILLER of Gwinnett Co. to WILLIAM JENKS of Henry Co.; $50; Lot
No. 199 of the 3rd Dist. Henry Co. Witnesses: WESTON (X) JENKS, PETER
JOHNSON.

Page 119: Feb. 13, 1822. Deed made in Baldwin Co., Ga. by JOHN
CANNON of Wilkinson Co., Ga. to BENJAMIN SANSING of Jasper Co., Ga.;
$345; Lot No. 105 of the 2nd Dist. Henry Co. Witnesses: WM. PEAVY,
APPLETON ROSSETER, J.I.C.

Page 120: Jan. 25, 1822. JOHN LANE of Jefferson Co., Ga. to
WILEY HEFLIN of Henry Co.; $100; Lot No. 107 of the 2nd Dist. Henry Co.
Witnesses: GEORGE MORRIS, BENJAMIN BLESSET. Deed was proved in Jasper
Co., Ga. by BENJAMIN BLESSET on April 16, 1822.

Page 121: Feb. 16, 1822. WILLIAM (X) DAVIS of Henry Co. to BEN-
JAMIN SANSING of Jasper Co., Ga.; $300; Lot No. 104 of the 2nd Dist.
Henry Co., drawn by the said DAVIS in the Land Lottery of 1821. Wit-
nesses: BALAAM PETERS, JOHN DAVIS, DAVID JOHNSON, J.P.

Page 122: Jan. 25, 1822. CORNELIUS TAYLOR of Twiggs Co., Ga. to
WILEY HEFLIN of Henry Co.; $400; Lot No. 70 of the 2nd Dist. Henry Co.
Witnesses: GEORGE MORRIS, BENJAMIN BLESSET, A. YOUNG, J.P.

Page 123: July 4, 1822. Power of attorney executed in Hancock
Co., Ga. by THOMAS H. KINDALL to THOMAS L. LATTIMORE both of Hancock Co.,
empowering the latter to convey one-half of Lot No. 71 of the 2nd Dist.
Henry Co., granted to JESSE HICKMAN of Warren Co., Ga. in the Land
Lottery of 1821. Witnesses: THOMAS LANDRETH, L. SMITH, J.P. Next
following is recorded a deed dated July 8, 1822 by THOMAS H. KINDALL
and THOMAS L. LATTIMORE of Hancock Co., jointly conveying the above
described land to WILEY HEFLIN for $200. The deed was signed "THOMAS L.
LATTIMORE by Power of Attorney, for T. H. KINDALL." Witnesses: EDWARD
LATTIMORE, JOSEPH CHEELEY, LUKE (X) PATRICK.

Page 124: Jan. 15, 1822. JAMES W. HICKS of Gwinnett Co., Ga. to
THOMAS BROWN of Morgan Co., Ga.; $500; Lot No. 197 of the 5th Dist.
Henry Co. Witnesses: LEWIS M. GILBERT, RICHARD M. GILBERT, J.P.

Page 125: Nov. 16, 1822. Deed of gift executed by GEORGE UPTON
of Henry Co. for love and affection to "my three sons. . . JOHN UPTON,
PHILIP UPTON and NATHANIEL UPTON." Goods and chattels not described.
Witnesses: WILLIAM (X) KILPATRICK, HUGH (X) KILPATRICK, MARTIN LUKEN
(or LUKER?).

Page 125: Dec. 12, 1821. Deed made in Putnam Co., Ga. by JOHN
TURNER, SR. of BLEDSOE'S District, Putnam Co. to THADDEUS B. REES of
the same place. $50; Lot No. 2 of the 10th Dist. Henry Co. on Cotton
River. Witnesses: JAMES NICHOLSON, J.B. WILLIAMSON, JAMES M. DUNN, JP.

Page 126: Nov. 5, 1822. Sheriff's Deed: JAMES FLETCHER, sheriff
to HARRIS ALLEN; $100; Lot No. 101 of the 2nd Dist. of Henry Co. on
Indian Creek. Sold as the property of ISAAC T. CUSHING to satisfy
indebtedness to SANFORD & BETTS of Baldwin Co., Ga.

Page 127: Nov. 5, 1822. Sheriff's Deed: JAMES FLETCHER, Sheriff,
to THADDEUS B. REES; $100; Lot No. 17 of 2th Dist. Henry Co. on Cotton
Indian River. Sold as the property of JAMES GRIFFIN to satisfy indebtedness to SAMUEL JOHNSON of Jones Co., Ga.
***See Page 170 for Deed 128.

Page 129: Jan. 18, 1822. Deed made in Jackson Co., Ga. by ROBERT
HENDERSON of Jackson Co., Ga. to JOHN BOYLE; $250; Lot No. 178 of the
16th Dist. Henry Co. drawn by the said HENDERSON in the Land Lottery
of 1821. Witnesses: JONES HENDERSON, W. D. MARTIN, J.I.C.

Page 130: June 19, 1822. Deed made in Liberty Co., Ga. by
WILLIAM HUGHES of Liberty Co. to EDWARD KENT of Jackson Co., Ga.; $200;
Lot No. 122 of the 17th Dist. Henry Co. Witnesses: SAMUEL LEWIS,

THOMAS MALLARD, J.I.C., Liberty Co., Ga.

Page 130: Nov. 11, 1822. Deed made in Jasper Co., Ga. by ALEXANDER MCALLISTER to JOHN CALLOWAY: $100; Lot No. 237 of the 3rd Dist. Henry Co. Witnesses: JOHN A. MCPARMER(?), THOMAS WYATT, THOMAS B. GAY, J.P.

Page 131: Dec. 10, 1821. Deed made in Putnam Co., Ga. by JOHN TURNER, JR. and JOHN TURNER, SR., jointly to WILLIAM VARNER all of Putnam Co. $1000; Lot No. 2 of the 6th Dist. Henry Co., drawn by JOHN TURNER, JR. in the Land Lottery of 1821. Witnesses: AUG. HAYWARD, PLEASANT H. ROGERS.

Page 132: Nov. 11, 1822. ABNER SERMON of Emanuel Co., Ga. to MARTIN PALMER of Baldwin Co., Ga.; $79; Lot No. 84 of the 12th Dist. Henry Co. Witnesses: CHRISTOPHER PALMER, WILLIAM PARKER, J.P.

Page 133: Sept. 3, 1822. Sheriff's Deed: JAMES FLETCHER, Sheriff to WILLIAM MCKNIGHT, for $351, one-half of Lot No. 85 of the 11th Dist. Henry Co. on the southwest side of South River. Sold as the property of GEORGE W. TALBOT to satisfy indebtedness to FRANCIS WEST of Morgan Co., Ga.

Page 134: June 10, 1822. DICEY (X) PARKER of Greene Co., Ga. to MOOREFIELD OWEN of same place; $75; Lot No. 213 of the 7th Dist. Henry Co. Witnesses: JOHN MONTFORT, THOMAS HART.

Page 135: September 3, 1822. Next following is recorded a deed made in Greene Co. by MOOREFIELD OWEN of Greene Co., conveying the above described land to WEST & SANFORD, also of Greene Co., for $92. Witnesses: JOHN MONTFORT, JONATHAN BICKERS, W. MCGIBBONEY.

Page 135: September 2, 1822. Deed made in Houston Co., Ga. by HENRY LIGON of Houston Co. to DAVID TEDFORD of Henry Co.; $250; Lot No. 187 of the 15th Dist. Henry Co. Witnesses: R. RUFFIN, H. C. HUTCHISON, H. BLANKENSHIP. Deed was proved by H. BLANKENSHIP in Clarke Co., Ga., Sept. 9, 1822.

Page 136: Dec. 5, 1822. WILLIAM HARDIN of Henry Co. to EZEKIEL CLOUD of Putnam Co., Ga., $132; Lot No. 227 of the 7th Dist. Henry Co. Witnesses: JOHN C. HAND, J.P., JOSIAH HAND.

Page 137: Dec. 3, 1822. Sheriff's Deed: JAMES FLETCHER, Sheriff, to EZEKIEL CLOUD of Putnam Co., Ga., for $111, Lot No. 213 of the 6th Dist. Henry Co. Sold as the property of JOHN WATSON to satisfy indebtedness in Clarke Co., Ga. in favor of THOMAS STAMPS.

Page 138: Dec. 3, 1822. Sheriff's Deed: JAMES FLETCHER, Sheriff, to EZEKIEL CLOUD of Putnam Co., for $55, Lot No. 248 of the 2nd Dist. Henry Co. Sold as the property of THOMAS RUSSELL to satisfy indebtedness in Twiggs Co., Ga. in favor of JAMES SPURLOCK.

Page 139: Nov. 3, 1822: Sheriff's Deed: JAMES FLETCHER, Sheriff, to LEROY MCCOY of Morgan Co., Ga., for $32, Lot No. 192 of the 7th Dist. Henry Co. Sold as the property of WILLIAM DRENNON to satisfy indebtedness in Morgan Co. In favor of GREEN & COOK.

Page 140: Dec. 3, 1822: Sheriff's Deed: JAMES FLETCHER, Sheriff, to ROBERT MARTIN, for $56, Lot No. 212 of the 1st Dist. Henry Co. Sold as the property of JOHN R. WARNER to satisfy indebtedness in Chatham Co., Ga. in favor of VANWICK MIELESS & LESTER.

Page 141: Dec. 3, 1822. Sheriff's Deed: JAMES FLETCHER, Sheriff, to KINCHEN W. HARGROVES of Twiggs Co., Ga., for $115, Lot No. 15 of the 3rd Dist. Henry Co. Sold as the property of MOSES DICKSON to satisfy indebtedness in Twiggs Co. in favor of JAMES SPURLOCK.

Page 142: Dec. 3, 1822. Sheriff's Deed: JAMES FLETCHER, Sheriff, to BENJAMIN L. LESTER of Baldwin Co., Ga. for $56.50, Lot No. 62 of the 18th Dist. Henry Co. Sold as the property of GEORGE ROWLAND to satisfy indebtedness in Wilkinson Co., Ga. in favor of J. and L. TISON.

Page 143: Feb. 11, 1822. Power of attorney exeucted in Jones Co., Ga. by N. D. DICKENS of Jefferson Co., Ga. to JAMES JONES of Jones Co., empowering the latter to convey Lot No. 318 of the 9th Dist. Henry Co. Witnesses: ROBERT B. SHELLMAN, JOSEPH HALL, J.I.C. Next following is recorded a deed, dated Feb. 18, 1822 by JAMES JONES of Jones Co., as attorney in fact for N. D. DICKENS of Jefferson Co., to WILLIAM JONES of Jones Co., conveying the above described land for $500. Witnesses: SAMUEL LUTHER, JAMES SMITH, ROBERT CUNNINGHAM, J.I.C.

Page 144: Apr. 26, 1822. Deed made in Greene Co., Ga. by NANCY (X) BALLARD to ARCHIBALD H. SCOTT both of Greene Co.; $500; Lot No. 78 of the 15th Dist. Henry Co., Witnesses: Y. P. KING, ALEX. KING.

Page 145: Feb. 16, 1822. Power of attorney exeucted by ALLEN (X) FINCH of Bulloch Co., Ga. to JAMES JONES of Jones Co., empowering the latter to sell Lot No. 24 of the 6th Dist. Henry Co. to WILLIAM JONES also of Jones Co., for $150. Witnesses: DAVID YOUNG, W. B. BEESLEY, ISAAC BEESLEY. (On page 146 is recorded a deed, dated March 2, 1822, conveying the said land.)

Page 147: Dec. 20, 1821. HENRY SHOFNER of Wilkinson Co., Ga. to JOHN GRIFFIN of Oglethorpe Co., Ga.; $325; Lot No. 205 of the 3rd Dist. Henry Co., drawn by HENRY SHOFNER in the Land Lottery of 1821. Witnesses: ALBETON THAXTON, JAMES (X) HENDERSON, GREEN (X) MARTIN. Deed was proved by YALVERTON THAXTON in Jasper Co., Ga. Dec. 15, 1822.

Page 148: May 21, 1822. ALLEN (X) COOK to ABSOLOM WOFFORD. $500; Lot No. 198 of the 1st Dist. Henry Co. Witnesses: NATHAN LOWERY, JOHN WALLACE. Proved by WALLACE in Jackson Co., Ga., June 1, 1822.

Page 148: Jan. 18, 1822. EADY JONES of Baldwin Co., Ga. to JOHN GRIFFIN of Henry Co.; $400; Lot No. 206 of the 3rd Dist. Henry Co. Deed was signed "GIDEON JOHNSON for EADY JONES." Witnesses: JESSE JOHNSON, JAMES P. REDDING, JAMES P. DOZIER, J.P.

Page 149: Nov. 9, 1822. Deed made in Clarke Co., Ga. by ECHO (X) THACKER of Hall Co., Ga. to WILLIAM FAMBROUGH; $400; Lot No. 242 of the 3rd Dist. Henry Co. Witnesses REUBEN HARRISON, C. S. PRINGLE, WILLIAM FAMBROUGH, J.P.

Page 150: June 11, 1822. JAMES WASHINGTON, for $462.50, relinquished his right, title, interest and claim in Lot No. 71 of the 16th Dist. Henry Co. Witnesses: WILLIAM POWELL, LEVI PHILLIPS.

Page 150: Dec. 14, 1822. EZEKIEL CLOUD of Putnam Co., Ga. to WILLIAM HARDIN of Henry Co.; $130; Lot No. 241 of the 7th Dist. Henry Co. Witnesses: THOMAS YARBROUGH, MARTHA (X) YARBROUGH.

Page 151: Sept. 28, 1822. SHADRACH EASTERLING of Twiggs Co., Ga. to DAVID FRANKLIN of Morgan Co., Ga.; $450; Lot No. 160 of the 15th Dist. Henry Co. Witnesses: LEVI BETTERTON, JOHN BOZEMAN, J.P.

Page 151: October 26, 1822. Next following is recorded a deed by DAVID (X) FRANKLIN of Morgan Co. conveying the above described land to LEVI BETTERTON of Henry Co. for $225. Witnesses: ROBINSON HENDON and JAMES DENMARK, J.P.

Page 152: Jan. 17, 1822. Deed made in Morgan Co., Ga. by LEMUEL B. SCAGGS to SAMUEL MCCLENDON: $750; Lot No. 170 of the 11th Dist. Henry Co. Witnesses: NICHOLAS MORGAN, WILLIAM (X) ALLEN.

Page 153: Dec. 10, 1821. Deed made in Baldwin Co., Ga. by FRANCIS MILLER of Washington Co., Ga. to DRAKEFORD L. TRAMMELL of Clarke

Co., Ga.; $300; Lot No. 101 of the 12th Dist. Henry Co. Witnesses:
JOSIAH BLACKWELL, APPLETON ROSSETER, J.P.
**Note: See Page 170 for 2nd Deed on Page 153.

Page 154: Oct. 1. 1822. Sheriff's Deed: JAMES FLETCHER, Sheriff,
to WILLIAM H. KIMBROUGH of Putnam Co., Ga., for $211, Lot No. 201 of
the 1st Dist. Henry Co. Sold as the property of MANNING D. HILL to
satisfy indebtedness in Putnam Co. in favor of the estate of BENJAMIN
LANE, deceased.

Page 155: Oct. 3, 1822. URIAH BROWN of Baldwin Co., Ga. to DAVID
R. SULLIVAN of Henry Co.; $150; Lot No. 82 of the 15th Dist. Henry Co.
Witnesses: A. B. BECKHAM, JOHN BOZEMAN, J.P.

Page 156: Feb. 8, 1822. Deed made in Elbert Co., Ga. by WILLIAM
BURNS of Elbert Co. to WILLIAM HOWELL of Newton Co., Ga.; $300; Lot No.
110 of the 6th Dist. Henry Co., drawn by the said BURNS in the Land
Lottery of 1821. Witnesses: E. RAGLAND, WILLIAM WOODS, J.I.C.

Page 157: Dec. 3, 1822. Sheriff's Deed: JAMES FLETCHER, Sheriff,
to JAMES H. WILLIAMS of Jasper Co., Ga.; $5.00; Lot No. 150 of the 8th
Dist. Henry Co. Sold as the property of JESSE SIMMONS to satisfy indebtedness in Putnam Co., Ga. in favor of ZACHARIAH COX.

Page 158: Dec. 3, 1822. Sheriff's Deed: JAMES FLETCHER, Sheriff,
to DABNEY A. MARTIN of Wilkes Co., Ga., for $110, Lot No. 98 of the 16th
Dist. Henry Co. Sold as the property of ASA LANHAM to satisfy indebtedness in Wilkes Co. in favor of DABNEY A. MARTIN.

Page 159: Oct. 19, 1822. Power of attorney executed in Pulaski
Co., Ga. by ALEXANDER (X) BANNISTER to NATHAN PARRIS, both of Pulaski
Co. empowering the latter to sell Lot No. 105 of the 11th Dist. Henry
Co. Witness: LEWIS YARBROUGH, J.I.C. Next following is recorded a
deed made in Baldwin Co., Ga. Nov. 24, 1822 by NATHAN PARRIS as attorney
in fact for ALEXANDER BANNISTER conveying the above described land to
JAMES DICKEN for $200. Witnesses: GANAWAY MALCOLM, JAMES FLEMING, J.P.

Page 160: July 5, 1822. Deed made in Elbert Co., Ga. by ROBERT
(X) BEARD to SAMUEL F. BEARD both of Elbert Co.; $500; Lot No. 99 of
the 12th Dist. Henry Co. on Middle Creek. Witnesses: A. MEANS, REUBEN
CHRISTIAN, J.P.

Page 161: Sept. 14, 1822. RICHARD MITCHELL of Newton Co., Ga.
to THOMAS CREEL of the same place; $500; Lot No. 39 of the 11th Dist.
Henry Co. Witnesses: WILLIAM HOLLIS, E. DODSON, J.P.

Page 162: Nov. 16, 1822. MARTIN PALMER of Baldwin Co., Ga. to
RICHARD CURD: $150; Lot No. 84 of the 12th Dist. Henry Co. Witnesses:
PETER MCKINZIE, F. MERCER, J.P.

Page 162: Jan. 6, 1822. SAMUEL GARNETT of Chatham Co., Ga. to
JOHN WOMMACK: $20; Lot No. 15 of the 16th Dist. Henry Co., drawn by
said Garnett in Land Lottery of 1821. Witnesses: J. A. KUCHHILL,
WILLIAM C. BARTON, J.P.

Page 164: Dec. 20, 1822. JAMES DICKEN of Morgan Co., Ga. to ROBERT
SHAW of Henry Co.; $250; Lot No. 105 of the 11th Dist. Henry Co.
Witnesses: SIMEON WILDER, ELI (X) NARON. Deed was proved by the
witnesses in Newton Co., Ga., Dec. 27, 1822.

Page 165: Mar. 8, 1822. Deed made in Warren Co., Ga. by JOSEPH
GRAY of Wilkes Co., Ga. to JESSE BENTON of Henry Co.; $150; Lot No.
195 of the 8th Dist. Henry Co. Witnesses: THOMAS GRIER, AARON W.
GRIER, J.P.

Page 166: Dec. 26, 1822. Deed made in Warren Co., Ga. by CAIN
KENT to JOHN HARRY; $350; Lot No. 91 of the 6th Dist. Henry Co.
Witnesses: ELISHA HURST, ADAM JONES, J.P.

Page 167: Jan. 7, 1823. Sheriff's Deed: JAMES FLETCHER, Sheriff, to ROBERT RAKESTRAW of Oglethorpe Co., Ga.; $230; Lot No. 166 of the 1st Dist. Henry Co. Sold as the property of ANDREW HARTSFIELD to satisfy indebtedness of Oglethorpe Co. in favor of RAKESTRAW & RUPORT.

Page 168: Nov. 5, 1822. Sheriff's Deed: JAMES FLETCHER, Sheriff, to LEROY NAPPIER & Co.; for $62, Lot No. 280 of the 18th Dist. Henry Co.; sold as the property of JACOB COBB to satisfy indebtedness in Putnam Co., Ga. to the aforesaid company.

Page 169: Oct. 12, 1822. SAMUEL LADSOE SPIESSEGGAR of Chatham Co., Ga. to ADAM TALMADGE (referred to variously as AARON TALMADGE); $100; Lot No. 3 of the 13th Dist. Henry Co., granted to the said SPIESEGGAR Oct. 5, 1822. Witnesses: BERNARD ROCHELAN (or ROCHELAR), JOHN DILLON, J.P. MARTHA B. SPIESSEGGAR relinquished dower interest same date. Witnesses: ELIZABETH GROVES and J. DILLON, J.P.

Page 171: Sept. 10, 1822. CHRISTIANA WRIGHT of Washington Co., Ga., Wimberly District, to THOMAS TALMADGE of Richmond Co., Ga.; $200; Lot No. 218 of the 18th Dist. Henry Co. on the waters of Mountain and Camp Creek, drawn by CHRISTIANA WRIGHT in the Land Lottery of 1821. Witnesses: R. F. BUSH, R. BUSH, J.P. Deed was signed "CHRISTINA (X) WRIGHT."

Page 172: Dec. 16, 1822. JOSEPH CRAIN of Luthers District, Richmond Co., Ga. to THOMAS TALMADGE of Richmond Co.; $100; Lot No. 208 of the 6th Dist. Henry Co. Witnesses: ELLIOTT HONEYWELL, R. BUSH, J.P.

Page 173: Jan. 5, 1823. RICHARD (X) MITCHELL of Henry Co. to WILLIAM MITCHELL of Clarke Co., Ga.; $250; one-half of Lot No. 39 of the 11th Dist. Henry Co. Witnesses: JOHN KIMBROUGH, JORDAN GAY, J.I.C.

Page 174: April 2, 1822. Deed made in McIntosh Co., Ga. by JOHN FLORY to ALLEN B. POWELL, both of McIntosh Co.; $110; Lot No. 83 of the 1st Dist. Henry Co., drawn by the said FLORY in the Land Lottery of 1821 and granted March 2, 1822. Witnesses: GEORGE ATKINSON, WILLIAM A. DUNHAM, J.I.C. SUSANNAH (X) FLORY relinquished her dower interest the same date in McIntosh Co.

Page 176: June 8, 1822. Deed made in McIntosh Co., Ga. by THOMAS HAROLD to ALLEN B. POWELL, both of McIntosh Co.; $60; Lot No. 85 of the 8th Dist. Henry Co., drawn by the said HAROLD in the Land Lottery of 1821 and granted May 13, 1822. Witnesses: P. HARG, MO [sic] HUNTER, J.I.C.

Page 177: Jan. 7, 1823. Sheriff's Deed: JAMES FLETCHER, Sheriff, to ROBERT MARTIN of Clarke Co., Ga., for $233, Lot No. 75 of the 8th Dist. Henry Co. Sold as the property of WILLIS JENKS to satisfy indebtedness in Gwinnett Co., Ga. in favor of ANDREW BOYD.

Page 178: Aug. 6, 1822. Sheriff's Deed: JAMES FLETCHER, Sheriff, to JENNINGS HULSIE, for $100, Lot No. 158 of the 11th Dist. Henry Co. Sold as the property of JAMES ARNOLD to satisfy indebtedness in favor of JOHN STOVALL of Wilkes Co., Ga.

Page 179: Oct. 21, 1822. NATHANIEL GUESS of Franklin Co., Ga. to WILLIAMRUFF of Henry Co. $50, Lot N. 93 of the 7th District Henry Co. on Walnut Creek. Witnesses: FRANCIS ABNEY MORRIS, JOHN H. CARTER, J.P.

Page 179: . . . 182_. Deed made in Effingham Co., Ga. by MOSES (X) CARTER of Scott's District, Chatham Co., Ga. to CLEM POWERS of the same place and GEORGE H. SURMAN [sic] deceased: $75; Lot No. 52 of the 2nd Dist. Henry Co. on Cabin Creek, granted Aug. 29, 1822. Witnesses: JOHN G. BUTLER, J.P., MARY FOX, SARAH (X) CARTER relinquished her dower interest Oct. 29, 1822 in Chatham Co. before the same witnesses.

Page 181: Feb. 9, 1822. JOHN DOROUGH of Jones Co., Ga. to THOMAS MCCLENDON; $205; Lot No. 106 of the 2nd Dist. Henry Co. on Towaligah

River. Witnesses: JAMES MCBRIDE, H. WATT, J. P. Deed was signed "JOHN DUROUGH."

Page 181: Feb. 17, 1823. Deed made in Jefferson Co., Ga. by JESSE HERRING of Jefferson Co. to CHARLES MILLER of Henry Co.; $250; Lot No. 90 of the 8th Dist. Henry Co. Witnesses: WILLIAM PARRADICE, WILLIAM LIVINGSTON, J.P.

Page 182: Oct. 10, 1822. Deed made in Jasper County, Ga. by CANNON JONES of Covington County, Ala. to JAMES BETTS of Jasper Co., for $100., Lot No. 96 of the 1st Dist., Henry County. Witnesses: JOHN FAULKNER, JOHN (X) MANRY. Proved in Jasper County by JOHN MANRY on Jan. 18, 1823.

Page 183: Jan. 21, 1822. JAMES CONNER of Tatnall Co., Ga. to ZACHARIAH FAULKNER of Jasper Co., Ga., for $250, Lot No. 51 of the 11th Dist., Henry Co. Witnesses: JAMES CASWELL, HENRY STRICKLAND, J.P.

Page 183: Jan. 25, 1823. Deed made in Warren Co., Ga. by ISHAM R. BUCKHALTER of Warren Co. to ROBERT SHAW for $150., Lot No. 41 of the 11th Dist. Henry Co. Witnesses: JER. BUCKHALTER, JOHN NEAL, J.P.

Page 184: Nov. 1, 1822. Deed made in Jasper Co., Ga. by JAMES BETTS of Jasper Co. to GEORGE J. SPEAK, for $170., Lot No. 96 of the . . . Dist., Henry Co. Witnesses: WILLIAM W. SMITH, JESSE LOYALL, J.P.

Page 185: Feb. 4, 1823. Sheriff's deed. JAMES FLETCHER, Sheriff to THADEUS B. REES for $203.50 at public sale, Lot No. 132 of the 1st Dist., Henry Co., sold as the property of DAVID HOLT on fi fa from Putnam County, Ga. Inferior Court in a suit for debt. ELI BRUNAH vs DAVID HOLT. Recorded Feb. 8, 1825.

Page 186: Dec. 14, 1821. Power of attorney, Appling Co., Ga. by SAMUEL (X) LUNSFORD of Appling Co. to THOMAS HUGHS SEN'R. of Montgomery Co., Ga. empowering the latter to obtain in the said Lunsford's name a grant from the State of Georgia, it being Lot No. 110 of the 3rd Dist., Henry Co. Witnesses: JESSE VAUGHN, JAMES CHAINEY, J.P.

Page 187: Dec. 31, 1821. SAMUEL LUNSFORD of Appling Co., Ga. by his attorney in fact, THOMAS HUGHS to WILLIAM B. WALE (or WALL) for $30, the lot described in preceding item. Witnesses: L. S. WARNER, DEMPSEY (X) ALGOOD JUN'R. Proved in Montgomery Co., Ga. Jan. 22, 1823.

Page 188: Jan. 18, 1823. JOHN ARRINGTON of Jefferson Co., Ga. to JOHN GRIFFIN of Henry Co. for $359, Lot No. 179 of the 3rd Dist. of Henry Co. Witnesses: GEAN EVANS, SILAS (X) ARRINGTON, DAVID EVANS. Proved in Jefferson Co. Jan. 9, 1823

Page 189: Feb. 8, 1822. Deed made in Columbia Co., Ga. by THOMAS SOMMERS of Columbia Co. to JOHN WATSON and ELISHA H. BARRETT of the same place, for $100., Lot No. 20 of the 11th Dist., Henry Co. Witnesses: THOMAS DOLLEY, AUGUSTUS WOOD. Proved in Columbia Co. Feb. 24, 1823.

Page 190: Feb. 7, 1823. Deed made in Jasper Co., Ga. by WILLIAM ALLEN of Jasper Co. to WILLIAM RUFF of Henry Co., for $200, Lot No. 68 of the 11th Dist, Henry Co. Witnesses: GEORGE W. RICHARDS, BENJAMIN BARNES, J.P.

Page 190: April 9, 1822. JOHN LEAK of Haggard's Dist., Jackson Co., Ga. to SAMUEL HENSON of Ralton Co., Ga. for $400, Lot No. 128 of the 12th Dist, Henry Co., granted to said JOHN LEAK March 7, 1822. Deed signed: "JOHN B. LEAK." Witnesses: WESTLEY MARTIN, DAVID ROGERS. Proved in Newton Co., Ga. Oct. 25, 1822.

Page 192: Feb. 27, 1822. Deed made in Columbia Co., Ga. by HENRY (X) HAND of Warren Co., Ga. to JOHN WATSON & ELIJAH BARRETT both of Columbia Co. for $1000, Lot No. 60 of the 12th Dist., Henry Co. granted to HENRY HAND Feb. 4, 1822. Witnesses: WILLIAM (X) HAND, THOMAS WATSON JUN'R. Proved in Columbia Co. Feb. 24, 1823.

Page 193: April 18, 1822. RICHARD DAVIS of Hall Co., Ga. to WILLIAM J. DAVIS of Morgan Co., Ga. for $250, Lot No. 62, of the 2nd Dist., Henry Co. Witnesses: WILLIAM E. DAVIS, JOHN EBERHARDT.

Page 193: Mar. 16, 1822. Deed made in Wayne Co., Ga. by WILLIAM MUNDEN of Wayne Co. to ALLEN B. POWELL of McIntosh Co., Ga. for $100, Lot No. 124 of the 7th Dist., Henry Co. The tract was drawn by WILLIAM MUNDEN of O'Neal Dist., Wayne Co. in the Land Lottery of 1821 and granted Mar. 11, 1822. Also the adjoining Lots Nos. 101, 138, 123, and 125 of the same land district. Deed signed: "WILLIAM MUNDEN, SARAH MUNDEN." Witnesses: STEPHEN PILCHER, WILLIAM STAFFORD, J.P., SARAH MUNDEN, wife of WILLIAM MUNDEN, relinquished her dower interest (by mark) in Wayne Co. the same date.

Page 195: Feb. 12, 1822. Deed made in Putnam Co., Ga. by JOHN FARMER of Elbert Co., Ga. to THOMAS HALL of Putnam Co., for $205, Lot No. 222 of the 8th Dist., Henry Co. Witnesses: HENRY A. HARPER, THOMAS MCMULLEN, WILLIAM DOOLEY, J.P.

Page 195: Feb. 27, 1823. Morgan Co., Ga. relinquishment of claim by LEWIS (X) WHEELUS of Morgan Co., in which he recited that in the Land Lottery of 1821 he gave in his name as a resident of CAPT. WRIGHT'S Militia District of Morgan County, as a consequence of which he drew Lot No. 196 of the 5th Dist., Early County. Unaware that he had drawn this lot he again gave in his name in the lottery, as a consequence of which he drew Lot No. 251 of the 6th Dist., Dooly County, and also Lot No. 242 of the 7th Dist., Henry County. By ther terms of this document he wished to relinquish his right, title and interest in the last two tracts. Witnesses: M. C. WILLIAMSON, WILLIAM MULLIN, J.P.

Page 196: Mar. 3, 1823. Newton Co., Ga. Relinquishment of claim by WILLIAM MITCHUM of Newton Co., reciting that in the Land Lottery of 1821 he gave in his name in CAPT. SHROPSHIRE'S District, Jones County, as a consequence of which he drew Lot No. 238 of the 5th Dist., Gwinnett Co., not knowing at the time that he had drawn it, wherefore, he again gave in his name in CAPT. KOLB'S Dist., Walton Co., for two draws, as a consequence of which he drew Lot No. 396 of the 16th Dist., Henry Co. By the terms of this document he relinquished his right, title and interest in the Henry Co. tract. Witnesses: M. C. WILLIAMSON, JOHN TRAYLOR, J.P.

Page 196: Feb. 1822. Deed made in Jones Co., Ga. by JOHN ANDREWS of Houston Co., Ga. to ZACHARIAS O'NEAL of Jasper Co., Ga. for $250. Lot No. 249 of the 1st Dist. Henry Co., drawn by JAMES MORAN of Capt. PARMENTER'S Dist., Jones Co. in the Lottery, and granted to him Feb. 13, 1822. Witnesses: LOUISA C. CANDLER, JOHN JENKINS, J.P.

Page 197: Feb. 27, 1822. Deed made in Columbia Co., Ga. by ICHABOD FINCH of Warren no., Ga. to JOHN WATSON and ELIJAH BARRETT of Columbia Co. for $1000., Lot No. 140 of the 12th Dist., Henry Co. Witnesses: JOSEPH BERSON, THOMAS WATSON JUN'R., WILLIAM (X) HAND. Proven in Columbia Co. Feb. 24, 1823.

Page 198: Feb. 7, 1822. Deed made in Columbia Co., Ga. by HANNAH (X) NEWBERRY of Warren Co., Ga. to JOHN WATSON and ELIJAH BARRETT of Columbia Co., for $1,000., Lot No. 185 of the 5th Dist., Henry Co., granted to HANNAH NEWBERRY Feb. 4, 1822. Witnesses: WILLIAM (X) HAND, THOMAS WATSON JUN'R. Proved in Columbia Co. Feb. 24, 1823.

Page 199: Feb. 17, 1822. Deed made in Baldwin Co., Ga. by "RICHARD SALTER as Agent for OWEN DUFFY" of Baldwin Co., Ga. to JESSE JOHNSON of Henry Co., for $250., Lot No. 207 of the 3rd Dist., Henry Co. Deed signed: "RICHARD SALTER as Agent for OWEN DUFFY." Witnesses: JOHN BOON, JOHN GRIFFIN, APPLETON ROSSETER.

Page 200: Jan. 17, 1823. HUMPHREY DAVIS of Elbert Co., Ga. to JESSE JOHNSON of Henry Co. for $200, Lot No. 150 of the 3rd Dist., Henry Co. Witnesses: HARRIS HOWELL, SAMUEL JOHNSON, JOHN PENTON.

Page 201: June 28, 1821. Power of attorney, Baldwin Co., Ga. by OWEN DUFFY to RICHARD SALTER of Baldwin Co., to empower the latter to receive title to any land drawn by the said DUFFY in the Land Lottery of 1821 and to dispose of it in his (DUFFY'S) name. Witness: JAMES MCKNIGHT.

Page 202: Mar. 2, 1822. Deed made in Pulaski Co., Ga. by MARY (X) BRYANT to JESSE SUTTON both of Pulaski Co. for $200, Lot No. 170 of the 3rd Dist., Henry Co. Witnesses: JAMES ALLEN, J.P., WILLIAM (X) CUSSIN (for "COUSINS"?)

Page 202: Feb. 12, 1823. JESSE SUTTON of Pulaski Co., Ga. to JESSE JOHNSON of Henry Co., for $50, Lot No. 170 of the 3rd Dist., Henry Co. Witnesses: SAMUEL JOHNSON, ISAIAH HAND, JOHN C. HAND, J.P.

Page 203: Dec. 27, 1822. JEREMIAH GILCREASE of Montgomery Co., Ala. to JESSE JOHNSON of Henry Co., for $130, Lot No. 140 of the 2nd Dist., Henry Co. Witnesses: JOHN GRIFFIN, SAMUEL JOHNSON, JOHN C. HAND, J.P.

Page 203: Feb. 11, 1823. JETHRO HARRELL of Henry Co. to JAMES FLETCHER of the same place, for $1000, Lot No. 57 of the 5th Dist., Henry Co. Witnesses: JAMES CALDWELL, ELI W. HARRISON, WILLIAM P. NEWELL, J.P.

Page 204: Aug. 27, 1822. Deed made in Wilkes Co., Ga. by ROBERT MOSS of Wilkes Co. to JOHN SELLERS of Oglethorpe Co., Ga. for $200, Lot No. 148 of the 3rd Dist., Henry Co. Witnesses: WILLIAM B. SMITH, JOHN W. POYNER, J.P.

Page 205: Feb. 22, 1823. Deed made in Burke Co., Ga. by RICHARD PONDER of Burke Co. to SOLOMON STRICKLAND of Henry Co., for $300, Lot No. 116 of the 2nd Dist., Henry Co. Witnesses: THOMAS RAMSEY, EPHRAIM PONDER.

Page 206: Jan. 12, 1822. Deed made in Wilkes Co., Ga. by WILLIAM (X) MATTHEWS of Lincoln Co., Ga. to ABNER WELLBORN for $100, Lot No. 10 of the 1st Dist., Henry Co. Witnesses: WINSTON MILLER, EDWARD SUMVALL (SUMMERVILLE?), JOHN QUINN, J.P.

Page 207: Jan. 10, 1822. Deed made in Wilkes Co., Ga. by POLLY (X) BESS, widow of Wilkes Co. to ABNER WELLBORN of the same place for $100, Lot No. 2 of the 9th Dist., Henry Co., granted to the said POLLY BESS, widow on Jan. 7, 1822 in the Land Lottery of 1821. Witnesses: SANFORD (X) PARISH, C. WELLBORN. In proving the deed in Wilkes Co., Jan. 10, 1823, the witness C. WELLBORN is shown as "CARLTON WELLBORN."

Page 208: Mar. 10, 1823. Jones Co., Ga. Relinquishment of claim by MARK WOMACK and GREEN WOMACK as orphans of WILLIAM WOMACK, reciting that they drew Lot No. 282 of the 12th Dist., Early Co., in the Land Lottery of 1821. Being then unaware that they had drawn the said lot, MARK WOMACK gave in his name as a registrant in Buckhalter's Dist., Jones Co., as a consequence of which he drew Lot No. 30 of the 7th Dist., Henry Co. By the terms of this document, MARK WOMACK relinquished his individual right, claim and title in the tract in Henry County. Witnesses: MICAJAH C. WILLIAMSON, STEPHEN RENTFROW, J.P.

Page 208: Mar. 20, 1823, Jones Co., Ga. Relinquishment of Claim by WRIGHT GROOMS, wherein he recited that in the Land Lottery of 1821 he gave in his name in CAPT. SAMUEL'S Dist., Jones Co., as a consequence of which he drew Lot No. 239 of the 3rd Dist., Irwin Co. Being then unaware that he had drawn the said lot, he gave in his name in Houston's Dist., Baldwin Co., as a consequence of which he drew Lot No. 244 of the 7th Dist., Henry Co. By the terms of this document he relinquished his right, claim and title to the tract in Henry Co. Witnesses: D. T. MILINER, J.P., MICAJAH C. WILLIAMSON, J.P.

Page 209: Dec. 13, 1822. Deed made in Jasper Co., Ga. by JAMES H. WILLIAMS to THOMAS DAVIDSON both of Jasper Co., for $100, Lot No. 150 of the 8th Dist., Henry Co. Witnesses: EBEDNEGO TURNER and B. J. WEEMS.

Page 209: Oct. 19, 1822. Deed made in Wilkinson Co., Ga. by ISAAC

JACKSON to LEWIS BOND both of Wilkinson Co. for $100, Lot No. 174 of the 18th Dist., Henry Co. Witnesses: ROBERT ETHEREDGE, JOHN HANCOCK.

Page 210: Oct. 30, 1822. Deed made in Wilkinson Co., Ga. by ANSON MIMS of Lee's Dist., Wilkinson Co., to LEWIS BOND, for $230, Lot No. 208 of the 7th Dist., Henry Co. Witnesses: RIGHT MIMS, SAMUEL CLARK, PETER MCARTHUR, J.I.C.

Page 211: July 10, 1822. Deed made in Wilkes Co., Ga. by JAMES (X) GRISSIP and wife NANCY to ALEXANDER POPE and HOPKINS W. BREWER all of Wilkes Co. for $300, Lot No. 53 of the 15th Dist., Henry Co. Witnesses: THOMAS D. BORSIER, JOHN M. COOPER, J.P. NANCY GRISSIP, wife of JAMES GRISSIP, relinquished her dower (by mark) in Wilkes Co. the same date.

Page 213: Power of attorney, Telfair Co., Ga. by WILLIAM (X) PETERSON to BENJAMIN CRUM both of Telfair Co., to empower the latter to execute a deed in fee simple, to Lot No. 245 of the 8th Dist., Henry Co., to CHARLES J. SHELTON of Telfair Co. The tract was drawn by the said Peterson in the Land Lottery of 1821. Witness: N. PARAMORE, J.I.C.

Page 213: Jan. 7, 1823. Deed made in Telfair Co., Ga. by BENJAMIN CRUM as attorney in fact for WILLIAM PETERSON to CHARLES J. SHELTON both of Telfair Co., for $500, the tract described in the foregoing item. Witnesses: H. H. BRICKELL, NATHANIEL ASHLEY, J.I.C.

Page 214: May 17, 1823. WILLIAM MCKNIGHT to JOHN TREADWELL JUN'R. both of Henry Co., for $451, Lot No. 85 of the 11th Dist., Henry Co., drawn in the Land Lottery of 1821 by WASHINGTON G. TALBOT of Shaw's Dist., Morgan Co., Ga. The tract situated on the south side of South River. Witnesses: JOHN T. BENTLEY, WILLIAM MCCONNELL, J.P.

Page 215: May 8, 1822. Deed made in Tatnall Co., Ga. by JOSEPH DURRANCE, as attorney in fact for JOSIAH PORCHIN to JAMES A. TIPPENS, all of Tatnall Co. for $1250, Lot No. 143 of the 5th Dist., Henry Co. Witnesses WILLIAM R. HOOKER, GEORGE W. TIPPENS, J.P.

Page 216: Apr. 18, 1822. Power of attorney, Tatnall Co., Ga. by JOSIAH PORCHIN to JOSEPH DURRANCE to empower the latter to sell the tract of land in Henry Co., described in for foregoing item. Witnesses: AARON DANIEL, D. J. BLACKBURN.

Page 216: Oct. 10, 1822. JOHN (X) SMITH SEN'R. to HENRY COLLINS both of Jackson Co., Ga. for $400. Lot No. 82 of the 8th Dist., Henry Co., granted to JOHN SMITH in the Lottery of 1821. Witnesses: SAMUEL TREET, STEPHEN BORDER, J.P.

Page 217: June 3, 1823. Sheriff's deed. JAMES FLETCHER, Sheriff to ELISHA BURNSON for $81, Lot No. 24 of the 11th Dist., Henry Co., sold as the property of WILEY SPIVEY to satisfy indebtedness to HENRY WILLIAMS in Columbia Co., Ga.

Page 218: Aug. 6, 1822. Deed made in McIntosh Co., Ga. by THOMAS P. BUNKLEY of Camden Co., Ga. to ANSON KIMBERLY of McIntosh Co., for $60, Lot No. 69 of the 12th Dist., Henry Co. Witnesses: JOHN BLAIR, WILLIAM NIBLACK, J.P., REBECCA BUNKLEY, the wife of THOMAS P. BUNKLEY relinquished her dower interest in Canden Co., Ga. the same date.

Page 219: Aug. 1822. Deed made in McIntosh Co., Ga. by JAMES A. CLUBB of Camden Co., Ga. to ANSON KIMBERLY of McIntosh Co., for $60., Lot No. 76 of the 2nd Dist., Henry Co. Witnesses: JOHN BLAIR, WILLIAM NIBLACK, J.P. REBECCA CLUBB, wife of JAMES A. CLUBB, relinquished her dower interest the same date.

Page 200: Apr. 18, 1822. Deed made in McIntosh Co., Ga. by JAMES HUDSON to ANSON KIMBERLEY both of McIntosh Co., for $40., Lot No. 53 of the 6th Dist., Henry Co. Witnesses: ANN (X) THOMAS, JOHN ORME, J.P., MARY HUDSON the wife of JAMES HUDSON relinquished her dower interest (by mark) the same date in McIntosh Co.

Page 221: July 3, 1821. Power of attorney, Chatham Co., Ga. by THOMAS H. CANDY (?) to ELIAS BLISS to empower the latter to convey any land that might be drawn by the said CANDY in the Lottery of 1821. Witnesses: EDWIN BARTLETT, N. HOLMSTED.

Page 222: Power of attorney, Laurens Co., Ga., by JOHN CARY to ALEXANDER TURNER, both of Laurens Co., to empower the latter to sell Lot No. 165 of the 8th Dist., Henry Co., drawn by the said CARY in the Lottery of 1821. Witnesses: HENRY BAILEY, THOMAS MOORE.

Page 223: Nov. 10, 1822. Deed made in Newton Co., Ga. by ALEXANDER TURNER of Laurens Co., Ga. to JOHN MCBRIDE of Newton Co., for $100, the lot described in the foregoing item. Witnesses: CHARLES (X) STEWART, JOSHUA (X) CREECH. Proved in Henry Co., June 2, 1823.

Page 224: Feb. 12, 1822. SAMSON (X) WEST of Twiggs Co., Ga. to JOHN MCBRIDE of Henry Co., for $250, Lot No. 157 of the 8th Dist., Henry Co. Witnesses: CHARLES SCAGGS, APPLETON ROSSETER, J.I.C.

Page 225: July 20, 1822. HENRY WALKER of Jefferson Co., Ga. to JOHN MCBRIDE of Newton Co., Ga. for $200, Lot No. 133 of the 8th Dist., Henry Co. Witnesses: JULIUS JOHNSON, STEPHEN NOLLEN.

Page 226: Mar. 18, 1823. ROBERT RAKESTRAW of Oglethorpe Co., Ga. to ELIZABETH COHRON (?) of Walton Co., Ga. for $350, Lot No. 166 of the 1st Dist., Henry Co. Witnesses: JOHN LOYD, WILLIAM COHRON(?).

Page 227: Aug. 17, 1822. Deed made in Jasper Co., Ga. by JAMES SMITH to PEYTON PINCKARD both of Jasper Co., for $500, Lot No. 61 of the 2nd Dist., Henry Co. Witnesses: NORBON B. POWELL, JESSE LOYALL, J.P.

Page 227: Apr. 12, 1822, THOMAS MCCLENDON to THOMAS BAKER, both of Henry Co., "all his rights only to the part of the lot of land lying on the east side of Towaliga River." Witnesses: THOMAS (X) MCCLENDON SEN'R., ENOCH MCCLENDON, DAVID JOHNSON, J.I.C. Recorded July 5, 1825. (Note: The lot and district neumbers of the tract conveyed are not specified in the recording, and no consideration is shown.)

Page 228: Feb. 28, 1822. JOHN KING SEN'R. to HUGH MORRIS both of Henry Co., for $199, Lot No.112 of the 1st Dist. Henry Co., on the waters of Yellow River. Witnesses: WILLIAM SAMPLE, JONATHAN LONG. Proved in Putnam Co., Ga. Mar. 8, 1822 by JONATHAN LONG before GEORGE OSBORN, J.I.C.

Page 229: Nov. 6, 1822. Deed made in Baldwin Co., Ga. by SOLOMON ROBERTSON of Hancock Co., Ga. to ROBERT BARNWELL of Henry Co., for $250 Lot No. 28 of the 12th Dist., Henry Co. Witnesses: BRADWELL W. STUBBS, JAMES FLEMING, J.I.C.

Page 230: July 1, 1823, Sheriff's deed. JAMES FLETCHER, Sheriff to JAMES HARKNESS, for $10.50, Lot No. 106 of the 1st Dist., Henry Co., sold as the property of SAMUEL M. WILLSON to satisfy indebtedness in Warren Co., Ga. in a suit: Foutaine & Hargroves vs SAMUEL M. WILLSON.

Page 231: Oct. 9, 1822. Deed made in Jefferson Co., Ga. by THEOPHILUS DILLARD of Jefferson Co. to BENJAMIN BLESSET of Jasper Co., Ga. for $150, Lot No. 110 of the 1st Dist., Henry Co. Witnesses: MUND GROSS, STEPHEN BLESSET. Proved in Jasper Co. Oct. 18, 1822 by STEPHEN BLESSET.

Page 232: Feb. 29, 1822. Deed made in Chatham Co., Ga. by BARTHO-LOMEW ROBERTS of Chatham Co. to GEORGE W. TIPPINS of Tatnall Co., Ga. for $200, Lot No. 19 of the 1st Dist., Henry Co. Witnesses: LEVI STEAVENS, JAMES EPPINGER, J.P.

Page 232: Feb. 27, 1823. CHARLES JORDAN of JESSE JOHNSON both of Henry Co., for $150, 101¼ acres or half of Lot No. 98 of the 9th Dist., Henry Co., being the east half of the said lot. Witnesses: ASA HEARN, THOMAS CARPENTER, HUGH LONGINO, J.P.

Page 233: Mar. 1, 1823. Deed made in Baldwin Co., Ga. by THOMAS WHIGHAM of Jefferson Co., Ga. to ELISHA BLESSIT of Henry Co., for $350 Lot No. 64 of the 2nd Dist., Henry Co. Witnesses: ROBERT B. WASHINGTON, JAMES FLEMING, J.P. Recorded July 11, 1825.

Page 234: July 1, 1823. Sheriff's deed. JAMES FLETCHER, Sheriff to JOSHUA EVANS of Henry Co. for $70, Lot No. 40 of the 2nd Dist., Henry Co. sold as the property of WILLIAM STONE for indebtedness to MORGAN BROWN of Washington Co., Ga.

Page 235: Apr. 30, 1823. FRANCIS (X) GRESHAM of Jones Co., Ga. to GEORGE T. LONG of Newton Co., Ga. for $200, Lot No. 59 of the 6th Dist., Henry Co. Witnesses: JESSE PARTRIDGE, EDWARD GRESHAM, J.P.

Page 236: July 24, 1822. Deed made in Walton Co., Ga. by ABEL (X) SPARKES to HINCHE MITCHELL both of Walton Co., for $275, Lot No. 153 of the 12th Dist., Henry Co. on Paris Creek. Witnesses: ELIJAH SHAW, JOHN CAMPBELL.

Page 237: Nov. 2, 1822. Deed made in Columbia Co., Ga. by RHODY (X) REYNOLDS of Columbia Co. to SAMUEL JOHNSTON of Oglethorpe Co., Ga. for $100, Lot No. 141 of the 3rd Dist., Henry Co., on Little Sandy Creek. Witnesses: ZEPHANIAH BLACKSTONE, MILTON MCDONALD. Proved by ZEPHANIAH BLACKSTONE in Columbia Co. June 18, 1823.

Page 238: Apr. 4, 1823. Deed made in Wilkinson Co., Ga. by ANN (X) SMITH of Wilkinson Co. to ELI NAIRN of Newton Co., Ga. for $300, Lot No. 46 of the 11th Dist. Henry Co. Witnesses: JAMES ROSS, ISAAC HALL, J.P.

Page 239: Mar. 4, 1823. Sheriff's deed. JAMES FLETCHER, Sheriff, to BARNA. DUNN for $151., Lot No. 15 of the 7th Dist., Henry Co., sold as the property of RICHARD DAVIS to satisfy indebtedness to SAMUEL TAIT in Franklin Co., Ga.

Page 240: May 4, 1823. MARTIN (X) MILLEN(?) of Fayette Co., Ga. to ELISHA KAY of Jasper Co., Ga. for $100, 50 3/4 acres of Lot No. 87 of the 11th Dist., Henry Co. Witnesses: JAMES N. WRIGHT, DOTSON HARRELL.

Page 241: Apr. 29, 1823. ELI (X) NAIRN of Newton Co., Ga. to JESSEE RUSSELL of Henry Co., for $500, Lot No. 46 of the 11th Dist., Henry Co. Witnesses: THOMAS NAIRN, JOHN TREADWELL, J.P.

Page 242: May 21, 1823. Deed made in Richmond Co., Ga. by AUGUSTUS HEYWARD to WILLIAM ALLEN both of Richmond Co., for $229, Lot No. 89 of the 11th Dist., Henry Co. Witness: P. H. MANLEY, J.P.

Page 243: Nov. 12, 1823. WILLIAM HARDIN of Henry Co. to WILLIAM WARREN of Jackson Co., Ga. for $500, Lot No. 241 of the 7th Dist., Henry Co. Witnesses: ANDREW M. BROWN, JOHN (X) NAILS.

Page 244: Dec. 12, 1822. Deed made in Baldwin Co., Ga. by JAMES M. FRANKLIN of Washington Co., Ga. to WILLIAM CURRIE of Morgan Co.,Ga. for $266, Lot No. 66 of the 9th Dist., Henry Co. Witnesses: EBENEZER SKINNER, JAMES FLEMMING, J.P.

Pages 245: Jan. 28, 1823. EDWARD BASS of Jones Co., Ga. to HIRAM GLAZIER of Jasper Co., Ga. for $600., Lot No. 61 of the 1st Dist., Henry Co. Witnesses: WILLIAM PAULK, BENJMAIN F___?, J.P. (surname indistinguishable)

Page 246: Jan. 1, 1822. JOSEPH DAVID of Columbia Co., Ga. to EDWARD BASS of Jones Co., for $500, Lot No. 61 of the 1st Dist., Henry Co., drawn by the said DAVIS in the Land Lottery of 1821. Witnesses: JOHN S. BORDEN, JAS. BOZEMAN.

Page 247: Aug. 5, 1823. Sheriff's deed. JAMES FLETCHER, Sheriff, to EZEKIEL CLOUD for $53.75, Lot No. 197 of the 2nd Dist., Henry Co., sold as the property of JOHN SLAUGHTER to satisfy indebtedness in Baldwin Co., Ga. to JAMES SANDIFORD.

Page 248: Aug. 4, 1823. Sheriff's deed. JAMES FLETCHER, Sheriff to EZEKIEL CLOUD for $51.50, Lot No. 244 of the 3rd Dist., Henry Co. sold as the property of TURNER SCARBROUGH for indebtedness to JAMES HUNT in Jefferson Co., Ga.

Page 249: Sept. 11, 1822. Deed made in Putnam Co., Ga. by SION L. HILL to EDMUND ALLUMS for $500, Lot No. 25 of the 6th Dist., Henry Co. Witnesses: JAMES DISMUKES, RICHARD WRIGHT. Proved in Putnam Co. Sept. 21, 1823 by RICHARD WRIGHT.

Page 250: Mar. 28, 1822. HARDY (X) ANDERSON of Chosen's Dist., Emanuel Co., Ga. to EDMUND ALLUMS of Putnam Co., for $200, Lot No. 74 of the 6th Dist., Henry Co. Witnesses: EDWARD ALLUM, FREELAND BUCKNER. Proved in Putnam Co., Sept. 21, 1823.

Page 251: Feb. 23, 1822. Deed made in Jasper Co., Ga. by JOHN (X) MATOX of Jasper Co. to AARON PARKER of Clarke Co., Ga. for $400, Lot No. 229 of the11th Dist., Henry Co. Witnesses: ELIJAH CORNWELL, KITTY (X) CORNWELL, KATY (X) TAYLOR, ANDREW NUTT, J.P.

Page 252: Nov. 27, 1823. TURNER EVANS to JOHN WOOD, both of Henry Co., for $40, one acre "near the Court House in said County (Henry) lying east of the Road leading from the southeast corner of the public square to the Court House in Monroe County." Witnesses: JOHN GUYDEN, JAMES KIMBROUGH, J.P.

Page 253: Feb. 16, 1822. Deed made in Putnam Co., Ga. by HENRY COATS to WILLIAM C. ANDERSON both of Henry Co., for $150, Lot No. 104 of the 12th Dist., Henry Co. Witnesses: MERRIDA HENDERSON, EDMUND ALLUMS, J.P.

Page 254: Dec. 24, 1822. MATTHIAS E. GARY to JORDAN COMPTON both of Jasper Co., Ga. for $200, Lot No. 52 of the 9th Dist., Henry Co. Witnesses: WILEY TRAYLOR, WILLIAM HEAD.

Page 255: Jan. 4, 1822. Deed made in Putnam Co., Ga. by LARKIN SIMS to JOHN MORELAND both of Putnam Co., for $300., Lot No. 250 of the 1st Dist., Henry Co. Witnesses: COLSON MORELAND, JOHN MORELAND.

Page 256: Nov. 25, 1823. SARAH (X) SMITH of Morgan Co., Ga. to PARNELL HENDERSON of Henry Co., for $200, Lot No. 72 of the 6th Dist., Henry Co. Witnesses: S. SHIELDS, GEORGE CHATFIELD, J.P.

Page 256: Nov. 14, 1823. JESSEE JOHNSON, as attorney in fact for ALLEN WEBB and LEWIS MOORE to WILLIAM PATE for $150, Lot No. 20 of the 6th District, Henry Co. Witnesses: JACOB HINTON, J.I.C., WILLIAM HARDIN.

Page 258: Aug. 1, 1822. Power of attorney by LEWIS MOORE of Emanuel Co., Ga. to JESSEE JOHNSON of Henry Co., to empower the latter to receive grnat to Lot No. 20 of the 6th Dist., Henry Co. Witnesses: JOHN GRIFFIN, JOHN C. HAND, J.P.

Page 259: Aug. 28, 1823. EDWARD ALLUMS to BRITAIN ALLUMS both of Henry Co., for $250(?) 100 acres of Lot No. 25 of the 6th Dist., Henry County. Witnesses: HENRY KING, BRIGGS ALLUMS. (Comment: The deed is signed, in the recording, as "Edmund Allums" but is shown as "Edward Allums" when it was proved in Henry County Dec. 21, 1823.)

Page 260: Jan. 6, 1823. Sheriff's deed. JAMES FLETCHER, Sheriff to DAVID RALSTON for $120, Lot No. 60 of the 9th Dist., Henry Co., sold as the property of WILLIAM GRIMES to satisfy indebtedness to MCKINNEY & B___? in Twiggs Co., Ga.

Page 261: Dec. 2, 1823. TURNER EVANS to EZEKIEL CLOUD of Putnam Co., Ga. for $850, 70½ acres of Lot No. 155 of the 7th Dist., Henry Co. Witnesses: JOHN WOOD, ANDREW M. BROWN. On page 263 is recorded the relinquishment of dower interest by RIDLEY EVANS, the wife of TURNER EVANS on March 14, 1823.

Page 262: Nov. 9, 1822. Deed made in Putnam Co., Ga. by THAD B. REES of Putnam Co. to AWSLEY BEVERS of Morgan Co., Ga., for $150, Lot No. 17 of the 12th Dist., Henry Co. Witnesses: JOHN C. MASON, LUKE J. MORGAN, THOMAS R. SMITH, J.P.

Page 263: Oct. 17, 1822. Deed made in Jones Co., Ga. by TRUMAN GRIDLEY of Tatnall Co., Ga. to HARDY HARRELL of Jones Co., Ga. for $200, Lot No. 107 of the 1st Dist., Henry Co. Witnesses: JAMES HOLDERNESS, WILLIAM HARRELL. Proved in Bibb Co., Ga. Jan. 31, 1824 by JAMES HOLDERNESS before E. B. GRACE, J.P.

Page 264: July 25, 1821. Power of attorney, Jackson Co., Ga.by JOHN F. HOWARD of Jackson Co. to JAMES PRICE of Hall Co., Ga. to empower the latter to receive in his (Howard's) name any land drawn by the said Howard in the Land Lottery of 1821, and to convey the same in his name to JOHN YOUNG of Jackson Co. Witnesses: ISAAC WHORTON, ALEXANDER SPENCE, J.P.

Page 264: Jan. 2, 1824. JAMES (X) PRICE as attorney in fact for JOHN F. HOWARD of Jackson Co., Ga. to JOHN YOUNG of the same place for $60, Lot No. 86 of the 3rd Dist., Henry County. Witnesses: JOHN (X) SUTHARD, JOHN (X) ALBRITON. Proved by JOHN SUTHARD in Jackson Co.

Page 265: Aug. 14, 1823. DEMSY JOHNSON of Henry Co. to JOSEPH KITCHEN of Greene Co., Ga. for $450, Lot No. 41 of the 11th Dist., Henry Co. Witnesses: JOHN TOWNSEND, JOHN T. BENTLEY, J.P.

Page 266: Apr. 2, 1822. CALEB BAILEY of Newton Co., Ga. to AZARIAH BAILEY of Morgan Co., Ga. for $600, Lot No. 122 of the 6th Dist., Henry Co. on Walnut Creek drawn by CALEB BAILEY of Koble's Dist., Walton Co., Ga. in the Land Lottery of 1821 and granted Mar. 28, 1822. Witnesses: EPHRAIM HEARD, BENJAMIN H. BAILEY, JONATHAN (X) MOORE. Proved in Morgan Co. by EPHRAIM HEARD before BENJAMIN TILMAN, J.P. Recorded Mar. 22, 1824.

Page 267: Mar. 2, 1824. EZEKIEL CLOUD to JOHN BARTON both of Henry Co., for $125, Lot No. 241 of the 7th Dist., Henry Co. Witnesses: WILLIAM HARDIN, JAMES KIMBROUGH, J.P.

Page 268: Dec. 9, 1822. Power of attorney, Habersham Co., Ga. by ELEAZER QUARLES of Habersham Co. to WILLIAM R. HARVEY(?) of the same place, to empower the latter to convey Lot No. 133 of the 7th Dist., Henry Co. Witnesses: ABR. THOMPSON, JOHNAS(?) BROCK, J.P.

Page 268: Feb. 5, 1824. Deed made in Newton Co., Ga.by WILLIAM R. HERVY(?) as attorney in fact for ELEAZER QUARLES of Habersham Co., Ga. to ALEXANDER THOMPSON of Greene Co., Ala., for $200, Lot No. 133 of the 7th Dist., Henry Co. Witnesses: EPHRAIM HEARD, BENJAMIN H. BAILEY, JONATHAN (X) MOORE. Proved by EPHRAIM HEARD in Morgan Co., Ga. before BENJAMIN TILMAN, J.P.

Page 269: Mar. 2, 1824. Sheriff's deed. JESSEE JOHNSON, Sheriff to JOHN SIMMS for $150, at public sale, Lot No. 141 of the 1st Dist., Henry Co., sold as the property of THOMAS BABBITT for indebtedness in Jones County, Ga.

Page 270: Mar. 2, 1824. Sheriff's deed. JESE JOHNSON, Sheriff, to LEONARD ROWE of Henry Co., for $96, Lot No. 37 of the 1st Dist., Henry Co., sold as the property of EZEKIEL STEPHENS to satisfy indebtedness to JEREMIAH CASTLEBERRY in Madison Co., Ga.

Page 271: Deed dated 2 Oct. 1823 in Oglethorpe County, Ga. between JESSE STANSELL... conveys Lot. No. F in 7th Dist., Henry Co. Signed: GEORGE T. LYON. Wit: S. H. CAM(BE?), JOHN TAY(NUR?). Rec. March 2, 1824.

Page 272: Deed dated 25 Dec. 1822 bet. ELIZABETH RAMSEY and CLABON O. DOSS both of Henry Co...sd. ELIZABETH RAMSEY for consid. of $224...conveyed tract known by half of that Lot No. 254 in 8th Dist.

of afsd County, being on No. half of afsd. Lot and bounded by E. MAYBERRY and Lot No. 227. Signed: ELIZABETH (X) RAMSEY. Wit: ROBERT COCKRAN, JOSEPH BENTON, J.P. Rec. March 6, 1824.

Page 273: Deed dated April 20, 1823 bet. JESSEE JOHNSON of Henry Co. and THOMAS COCKRAN of same...sd. JESSEE JOHNSON for consid. of $200... conveys a Lot in 3rd Dist. of sd. Co. being No. 207 cont. 20 acres. Signed: JESSEE JOHNSON. Wit: WILLIAM TUGGLE, JOHN (X) PENTON, JOHN C. HAND, J.P. Rec. March 6, 1824.

Page 273: Power of Attorney made in Early Co., Ga. by THOMAS FOLLOWER of Henry Co. to OBEDIAH DECK to dispose of tract of land in Henry Co. in 11th Dist. which he drew by Lot in last Land Lottery as an orphan at the time and living in Twiggs Co...and he appoints WILLIAM MATTHEWS and JOSEPH GUYTON to act for sd. DICK if required. Signed: THOMAS (X) FOWLER. Wit: BENJAMIN HODGES, J.I.C. Dated 11 Aug. 1823. Rec. 6 March 1824.

Page 274: Sheriff's Deed JESSE JOHNSON, Sheriff on order for Superior Ct. of Screven Co. sold to JOHN LONG at public outcry on 3 Feb. 1824 property of THOMAS COLDING for indebtness to SAMUEL and JACOB BRYAN for sum of $108, Lot in 11th Dist. being No. 86 cont. 202 ½ acres. Signed: JESSE JOHNSON. Wit: WM. TUGGLE, JAMES KIMBROUGH, J.P. Rec. March 13, 1824.

Page 275: Sheriff's Deed. JESSE JOHNSON, Sheriff on order from Justices Court of Columbia County, sold property of DANIEL YOUNG for indebtedness to JONATHAN SAFFOLD on 3 Feb. 1824...to WILLIAM BARNWELL for $81, being in 20th Dist. and Lot No. 39 cont. 202 1/2 acres. Signed: JESSE JOHNSON. Wit: WILLIAM TUGGLE, JAMES KIMBROUGH, J.P. Rec. 13 March 1824.

Page 276: Deed dated 22 Nov. 1824 bet. ARTHUR ALEXANDER of Habersham County and JAMES KING of Jasper County...sd. ALEXANDER for consid. of $330...conveys tract in Henry Co. in 1st Dist. Lot No. 60, cont. 202 1/2 acres. Signed: ARTHUR ALEXANDER. Wit: WILLIAM B. STAKS, JESSE (PAYALL?) J.P. Rec. 13 March 1824.

Page 278: Deed made in Baldwin Co. and dated 8 March 1822, bet. ROBERT COACHRAN of Henry Co. and JAMES MCHAMILTON of Gwinett...sd. MCHAMILTON for consid. of $200 conveys tract cont. 202 1/2 acres in Henry Co., Lot No. 26 in 9th Dist. Signed: JAMES (X) HAMILTON. Wit: J. N. BLACKWELL, APPLETON ROSSETER, J.I.C. Rec. 15 March 1824.

Page 279: Deed made in Richmond Co. dated 25 Dec. 1823, bet. HILLARY FRAZIER of Richmond Co. and JOHN MCMICHAEL of Henry Co...sd. FRAZIER for consid. of $500...conveys tract in Henry Co., Lot No. 120 in 1st Dist. Signed: HILLERY B. FRAZIER. Wit: JOHN R. CARGILE, R. BUSH, J.P. Rec. 13 March 1824. LEVINAH FRAZIER wife of HILLERY FRAZIER Rel. Dower on 13 Dec. 1823.

Page 280: Deed dated 29 Jan. 1824 bet NANCY BUCK of Richmond Co. and JESSE JOHNSON of Henry Co...sd. NANCY BUCK for consid. $600, conveys tract in Henry Co...sd. NANCY BUCK for consid. $600, conveys tract in Henry Co. Lot No. 180, Dist. (?) cont. 202 1/2 acres. Signed: NANCY (") BUCK. Wit: WILLIAM (+) WALKER, T. PALMUR, J.P. Rec. March 26, 1824. HANNAH BUCK certifies that her daughter NANCY BUCK is 21 dated 29 Jan. 1824.

Page 281: Deed made in Putnam Co., Dated 1 March 1824 bet. AQUILLA BEARDEN of one part and ANSALOM EVANS of other, both of the Co. and state afsd...sd. AQUILLA BEARDEN for consid. of $150...conveys tract in Henry Co. on Tussahaw Creek cont. 202 1/2 acres, being Lot No. 231 in 1st Dist. Signed: AQUILLA BEARDEN. Wit: TURNER H. TRIPPUR, JNO. J. SMITH, J.I.C. Rec. 26 March 1824.

Page 282: Deed dated 10 March 1824 bet. JESSE JOHNSON of Henry Co. and WILLIAM GRIFFIN of same...consid of $600, conveys to sd. GRIFFIN tract in 3rd Dist. of Henry Co. Lot No. 180 cont. 202 1/2 acres. Signed: JESSE JOHNSON. Wit: RICHARD A. RISON, JOHN GRIFFIN. Rec. March 26, 1824.

Page 283: Power of Attorney made in Henry Co. on 8 August 1822, from HUMPRIES DAVIS of Henry Co. to JESSE JOHNSON of same...to apply for plat & grant of Land in 3rd Dist. Lot No. 150 drawn by sd. DAVIS. Signed: HUMPHRY DAVIS. Wit: JOHN HAND, J.P. Rec. 30 March 1824.

Page 283: Deed made in Liberty Co., dated 28 Feb. 1824 bet JOHN O. BAKER of Co. afsd. and JAMES RANSOM of Henry Co...sd. BAKER for consid. of $112...conveys tract in Henry Co., being Lot No. 140 in 3rd Dist. Signed: J. O. BAKER. Wit: JAMES SMYLO, J.I.C., JAMES I. SHEPHERD. Rec. March 29, 1824.

Page 284: Deed dated 13 Jan. 1823 bet JESSE JOHNSON agent for HUMPHRIS DAVIS of State and Co. afsd. and JAMES RANSOM of other part...sd. JESSE JOHNSON as Agent for consid. of $400, conveys Lot No. 150 in 3rd Dist. Henry Co. cont. 202 1/2 acres. Signed: JESSE JOHNSON, Agent for HUMPHRY DAVIS. Wit: LITTLETON (X) CULLHOUND, JAMES (X) RANSOM, JOHN GRIFFIN. Rec. 31 March 1824.

Page 285: Deed dated 29 March 1824 bet. JESSE JOHNSON of Henry Co. and JAMES RANSOM of same...for consid. of $400, conveys Tract in Henry Co. Lot No. 150 in 3rd Dist. cont. 202 1/2 acres. Signed: JESSE JOHNSON. Wit: JAMES KIMBROUGH, J.P., JOHN GRIFFIN. Rec. 31 March 1824.

Page 285: Deed of Gift from EDMOND ALLUMS dated 10 March 1824 to his son HOPSON ALLEN of a tract in 6th Dist. Henry Co. cont. 102 1/2 acres...Lot No. 25 with an exception "of my self, my wife and her son JOHN ALLUMS living on it during our natural lives"...Signed: EDMOND ALLUMS. Wit: E. W. HARRISON, WILLIAM SMITH, MARY KING. Rec. April 3, 1824.

Page 286: Deed dated 8 March 1824 bet. BRITIAN ALLUM of Henry Co. and BRIGGS ALLUM of same, for consid. of $300...conveys unto sd. BRIGGS ALLUM tract in 6th Dist. Henry Co. on waters of Cotton River, Lot No. 25, cont. 100 acres more or less. Signed: BRITTON ALLUM. Wit: WILLIAM ALLUM, JOHN ROOKS. Rec. 3 April 1824.

Page 287: Deed of Gift headed Columbia Co., Dated 8 March 1822 from THOMAS O. MARTIN of Columbia Co. for "affection towards my wife REBECCA" and my daughter ELLENOR MARTIN, SARAH MARTIN and ELIZA MARTIN do convey tract of land cont. 200 acres in 8th Dist. of Henry Co., Lot No. 136 and other part of land in 11th Dist. of Early Co. being No. 1 6 cont. 250 acres. Signed: THOMAS O. MARTIN. Wit: GILLIAM WATKINS, WM. SATTER WHITE, JAMES WOOD, LEOD. THOMPSON, J.P. Rec. 6 April 1824.

Page 288: Deed headed Jasper County, dated 5 Jan. 1824, bet. ABEL BROWN of Morgan Co. and DAVID CARRELL of Jasper Co...consid. of $450... conveys tract in 11th Dist. Henry Co., Lot No. 104, cont. 202 1/2 acres. Signed: ABEL BROWN. Wit: EDWARD PRICE, ARON SMITH, J.P. Rec. 6 April 1824.

Page 289: Sheriff's deed, dated 20 Dec. 1823 JAMES FLETCHER, Sheriff on Order from Superior Court of Elbert Co. sells land of SOLOMON GUISE at public auction on 7 Oct. 1823 to WILLIAM GRAY for sum of $100 in 8th Dist. Henry Co., Lot No. 182 cont. 202 1/2 acres. Signed: JAMES FLETCHER. Wit: TANDY W. KEY, JAMES KIMBROUGH, J.P. Rec. 7 April 1824.

Page 290: Deed dated 6 April 1824 bet. WM. GRAY of Henry Co. and WILLIAM DUNLAP of Elbert Co...consid. of $300...sd. GRAY conveys lot in 8th Dist. Henry Co., Lot No. 182, cont. 202 1/2 acres. Signed: WM. GRAY. Wit: THOS. D. JOHNSON, JAMES KIMBROUGH, J.P. Rec. 7 April 1824.

Page 292: Deed dated 3 Feb. 1824 bet ALEXANDER THOMPSON of State of Alabama and SILAS MOSELY of Henry Co., Ga...consid. of $700...conveys tract in Henry Co. 7th Dist. Lot No. 133 cont. 202 1/2 acres...Signed: ALEXANDER THOMPSON. Wit: JAMES SCARBROUGH. Rec. April 7, 1824.

Page 293: Deed dated 14 Feb. 1824 bet. SILAS MOSELY of Henry Co. and THOMAS KEY of other part...consid. of $560...conveys to THOMAS KEY tract of land known as Lot No. 133 in 7th Dist. of Henry Co. Signed:

SILAS MOSELY. Wit: WM. L. CRAYTON, JAMES KIMBROUGH, J.P. Rec. 7 April, 1824.

Page 294: Deed dated 20 March 1824, bet WILLIAM MCKNIGHTof Henry Co. and WILLIAM GURLEY of same...consid. $85...conveys to WILLIAM GURLEY tract in Henry County, being Lot No. 123 in Dist. 11th, cont. 100 and 1/4 acres, being equal half of sd. Lot of land. Signed: WM. MCKNIGHT. Wit: JOHN SMITH, JOHN T. BENTLY, J.P. Rec. 6 April 1824.

Page 295: Deed dated 11 Oct. 1823 bet. WILLIAM JOHNS of Henry Co. and JOHN LANG of same, for consid. of $150, conveys tract in 11th Dist. Monroe County, Lot No. 57. Signed: WILLIAM (X) JOHNS. Wit: GUY W. SMITH, THOMAS INGRAM. Rec. April 8, 1824. (Note: this name could be LONG instead of LANG...diff. to tell, Ed.)

Page 296: Deed dated 13 Dec. 1823, bet. DEMPSEY JOHNSON of Henry Co. and WILLIAM CRAWFORD of Greene Co., Ga...conveys tract of 202 1/2 acres for consid. of $350 in 11th Dist. of Henry Co. known by Lot No. (2?), gtd. to WM. BROWN, Gilders Dist. Irwin Co., Signed: DO. JOHNSON. Wit: ALEXANDER MOORE, JAMES HENRY, J.I.C. Rec. 9 April 1824.

Page 296: Deed dated 13 Dec. 1823 bet DEMPSEY JOHNSON of Henry Co. and WILLIAM CRAWFORD of Greene Co., Ga...tract of 202 1/2 acres for consid. of $350 in __ Dist. Henry Co., Lot No. one, gtd. to GEORGE LITTLE of Halls Dist. Twiggs Co. Signed: D. JOHNSON. Wit: ALLEXANDER MOORE, JAMES HENRY, J.I.C. Rec. April 9, 1824.

Page 297: Deed made in Bibb County, Dated 7 Jan. 1824 bet. HARDY HARROLD of Bibb Co. and JAMES HARKNESS of Henry...consid. of $300 conveys tract in Henry Co., Lot No. 107 and 1st. Dist., cont. 202 1/2 acres drawn by and gtd. TRUMAN GRIDLEY of the 271st. Dist. McIntosh Co. Signed: HARDY HARRELL. Wit: HENRY G. ROSS, ELINZAR MCCALL, J.P. Rec. 9 April 1824.

Page 299: Sheriff's Deed dated 6 April 1824 JESSE JOHNSON, Sheriff of Henry County on order from Sup. Ct. of McIntosh Co., at suit of JOSEPH LAURENCE agst. HENRY CANNON, sold land of HENRY CANNON at public auction on 6 April 1824 to BENJAMIN MOSELY and SILAS MOSELY of Henry Co. for consid. of $79, being Lot No. 126 in 11th. Dist. of Henry Co. Signed: JESSE JOHNSON. Wit: (ROWAN?) McKEE, WM. HARDIN, Clk. Sup. Ct. Rec. 9 April 1824.

Page 300: Receipt made in Putnam Co., dated 3 Jan. 1824 Rec'd of LEVY CLOUD $100 in full payment for Lot in 20th Dist. Henry County, drawn by THOMAS R. SPAIN and being Lot No. 150 cont. 202 1/2 acres by EZEKIEL CLOUD. Wit: JESSE DUP__?, JESSE LITTLE, J.P. (Note: Bottom of deed is illeg. on microfilm where signed.)

Page 301: Receipt dated 25 Sept. 1822 of RHODERIK HARPER $140 in full compensation for right and title to Lot No. 46 in 7th Dist. Henry Co. cont. 202 1/2 acres. Signed: ISAAC CLEATE.

Page 301: Deed dated 25 Setp. 1822 by ISAAC CLIATT of Columbia Co. from RHODERICK HARPER of Jasper Co. for Lot No. 46 in 7th Dist. Henry Co., Receipt above signed and given, drawn by me in Land Lottery. ISAAC CLIATT appt's trusty friend THOMAS HARPER of Morgan Co. his lawful attorney to execute title to sd. land. Signed: ISAAC CLIATT. Wit: ASA (X) GOODEN, JAMES SELLORS, J.P. Rec. April 9, 1824.

Page 302: Deed dated 25 Dec. 1823, bet. ISAAC CLIATT of Columbia Co. and RHODERICK HARPER of Henry Co...consid. of $140...conveys tract in Henry Co. drawn by ISAAC CLIATT, cont. 202 1/2 acres, lot No. 46 in 7th Dist. Henry Co. Signed: ISAAC CLIATT. Wit: JAMES SELLORS, J.P., WARD H. TURNER, J.I.C. Rec. 9 April 1824.

Page 303: Deed headed Morgan Co. Dated 2 Jan. 1824 bet WILLIAM CURRY of Morgan Co. and ROBERT CURRY, JUR. of Morgan Co., for consid. of $280...conveys tract to ROBERT CURRY, JUNR. cont. 202 1/2 acres in 9th Dist. Henry Co., Lot No. 66. Signed: WM. CURRY. Wit: THOS. S. BANNER, WM. PATTRICK. Rec. 12 April 1824.

Page 304: Receipt dated Jan. 26, 1818 in Henry Co. from THOS. C. RUSSELL $300 in payment for a negro boy Armsted to CAPT. RICHD. AYCOCK. Signed: RICHARD AYCOCK. Wit: ROBT. BURTON. On 23 July 1823 in Wilks Co., Ga. ROBT. BURTON swore that he was a subscribing. Wit: to the receipt of RICHARD AYCOCK to THOS. C. RUSSELL bef. ROWLAND BEASLY, J.P. Rec. 3 May 1823.

Page 304: Deed dated 16 April 1824 bet. JESSE STANSILL and JOEL STANSILL...for consid. of $100...conveys tract cont. 140 acres, part of Lot No. 5 in 7th Dist. of Henry Co. Signed: JESSE STANSILL. Wit: WILLIAM MCKNIGHT, JOHN T. BENTLY, J.P. Rec. May 4, 1824.

Page 305: Deed headed Greene Co., Ga. dated 12 Jan. 1824 bet. ROBERT DUNCAN of Greene Co. and PARKER EASON of Henry Co...consid. of $425...conveys tract in Henry Co. on waters of Towaliga, cont. 202 1/2 acres, being Lot No. 181 in 3rd Dist. of Henry Co. Signed: ROBT. DUNCAN. Wit: JAMES RAMSOM, PETER JOHNSON. Rec. 4 May 1824.

Page 306: Deed dated 3 Dec. 1822, bet ISAAC BRYANT of Putnam Co. and JAMES BRYANT of afsd. Co...consid. of $100...conveys to JAMES BRYANT tract being Lot No. 75 in 7th Dist. of Henry Co. adj. Lots No. 76 and 74 and 72 cont. 152 acres. Signed: ISAAC (X) BRYAN. Wit: JOHN BRYANT, SAML. WRIGHT, J.P. Rec. 14 May 1824.

Page 307: Deed headed Gwinnett Co. and dated 24 April 1824 bet HENRY C. BUTLER of Co. afsd. and HENRY HAYNES of Henry Co., for consid. of $725...conveys Lot No. 48 in 7th Dist. of Henry Co. adj. Lot No. 49 cont. 100 1/4 acres. Signed: HENRY C. BUTLER. Wit: WM. BEACHAMP, WILLIS ROWLAND, J.P. Rec. 17 May 1824.

Page 307: Deed dated 13 Feb. 1824 bet. JONATHAN WOOD of Columbia Co. and MICAJAH FERRILL of Henry Co...consid. of $850...conveys tract in Henry Co. being Lto No. 228 in 1st Dist. cont. 202 1/2 acres. Signed: JOHNATHAN WOOD. Wit: JOHN PULLEN, THOMAS BAYLESS, J.P. Rec. May 17, 1824.

Page 308: Sheriff's Deed dated 2 Dec. 1823 JAMES FLETCHER, Sheriff on order from Justice Court of Jackson Co., at the suit of JAMES KIRK PATTRICK agst DAVID BURGANS,...sold property of DAVID BURGAN at public outcry on 2 Dec. 1823, with ENOCH HILL being highest bidder, for sum of $101.62 1/2 cents, tract being Lot No. 87 in 3rd Dist. Henry Co. Signed: JAMES FLETCHER. Wit: LEWIS HAYGOOD, DAVID JOHNSON, J.I.C. Rec. May 17, 1824.

Page 309: Sheriff's deed, dated 6 Jan. 1824 JAMES FLETCHER, Sheriff on order from Inferior Court of Jones Co., in suit of ANDREW MCBRYAN agst. JOHN FARRALL, sold land on 6 Jan. 1824 at public outcry and bought by ENOCH HILL for $117.50 in 2nd Dist. Lot No. 250, cont. 202 1/2 acres. Signed: JAMES FLETCHER. Wit: THOS. BOU_ING, DAVID JOHNSON, J.I.C. Rec. May 18, 1824.

Page 311: Blank.

Page 312: Deed headed McIntosh Co., dated 22 April 1823, bet. ALLEN B. POWELL of McIntosh Co. and WILLAIM HARDIN of Henry Co. consid. $250 conveys to WILLIAM HARDIN tract in 7th Dist., Lot No. 124 cont. 202 1/2 acres, drawn by WILLIAM MUNDEN of Wayne Co. and gtd. 11 March 1822. Signed: ALLEN B. POWELL. Wit: SCOTT GRAY, JNO. SAWYER, J.P. Rec. June 16, 1823.

Page 312: Deed headed Jasper Co., dated 27 Jan. 1823 bet. WILLIAM JOHNSON of Jasper Co. and MOSES BROOKS of Henry Co...consid. of $400 conveys tract in 3rd Dist., Henry Co., Lot No. 247 cont. 202 1/2 acres. Signed: Wit: E. ELI STRICKLAND, JOSEPH WILLIAMS. Rec. June 27, 1823. Signed: WM. JOHNSON.

Page 313: Deed headed Wilkes Co., dated 4 Jan. 1823 bet. ROBERT M. JOHNSON of state and Co. afsd. and WILLIAM W. CALLAWAY of Jasper Co... consid. of $50...conveys tract cont. 202 1/2 acres in 2nd Dist. Henry

Co., Lot No. (not given). Signed: R. M. JOHNSON. Wit: C. ORR, JOHN
S. ROLLIN. Rec. July 1, 1823.

Page 314: Deed dated 12 Oct. 1822, bet. JESSE BRYAN of Newton Co.,
Ga. and WILLIAM WAKEFIELD of Henry Co...consid. of $70...conveys tract
of 50 1/2 or the 4th of Lot No. 45 in So. corner of land Lot on waters
of Cotton River in 11th Dist. of Henry Co., Signed: JESSE BRYAN. Wit:
DAVID W. HAM, JESSE BRYAN, JUNR. Rec. July 2, 1823.

Page 315: Deed headed Jones Co., Dated 15 Feb. 1823 bet. SARAH
TALLY of state & Co. afsd. and JOHN ROSE of other...consid. of $150...
conveys tract to JOHN ROSE in Henry Co., Lot No. 39 in 2nd Dist. cont.
202 1/2 acres, orig. gtd. to SARAH TALLY and grant dated 15 Feb. 1822.
Signed: SARAH (X) TALLY. Wit: WILLIAM BALLARD, SARAH GARRETT, JOHN T.
POPE, J.P. Rec. 5 July 1823.

Page 316: Deed dated 8 March 1823 bet JOHN RESE of Jones Co. and
PEYTON PINKARD of Henry Co., consid. of $200...conveys tract in Henry
Co., Lot No. 39 in 2nd Dist. of Henry Co., cont. 202 1/2 acres, gtd. to
SARAH TALLY on 15 Feb. 1822. Signed: JOHN BRYAN. Wit: MARY H. (+)
KNIGHT, WOODY R. KNIGHT. Rec. 5 July 1823.

Page 317: Power of attorney headed Screven Co., dated (not dated)
from JAMES CONNER to JAMES CONNER to sell Lot No. 69 in 2nd Dist. Henry
Co. Signed: JAMES CONNER. Wit: WILLY YOUNG, M. N. MCCALL, J.P. Rec.
July 5, 1823.

Page 317: Deed headed Baldwin Co., dated 19 Dec. 1822 bet JAMES
CONNER, JR., Attorney for JAMES CONNER, SR. of Screven Co. of the one
part and PEYTON PINKARD of Henry Co...consid of $500...conveys tract of
202 1/2 acres in 2nd Dist. Henry Co., Lot No. 69. Signed: JAMES CONNER,
JR. for JAMES CONNER, SR. Wit: ELY COACHRAN, EBINZAR S. RINNER, JAS.
FLUNG, J.P. Rec. July 7, 1823.

Page 318: Deed dated 29 Jan. 1822 bet. WALTER AUSTIN of Greene Co.
and JOHN GARNER consid. of $300...conveys tract cont. 202 1/2 acres in
8th Dist. Henry Co., Lot No. 59 on South prong of the Ockmulgee River.
Signed: WALTER AUSTIN. Wit: HENRY DAVIS, H. H. MABRY, J.P. Rec. July
7, 1823.

Page 319: Deed dated Jan. 20, 1823 bet THOMAS P. HAMILTON of Jasper
Co. and WILLIAM S. GARNER of Greene Co...consid. of $325...conveys tract
in 8th Dist. Henry Co. Lot No. 71, drawn by sd. THOMAS P. HAMILTON, cont.
202 1/2 acres. Signed: THOMAS P. HAMILTON. Wit: JOHN WILLSON, THOS.
GALLOW, J.P. Rec. July 7, 1823.

Page 319: Deed dated 24 August 1822 bet. ALLEN B. POWELL of McIntosh
Co. and ELISHA BLESSETE of Henry Co., for consid. of $300 conveys tract
in 1st Dist. Henry Co., Lot No. 80, cont. 202 1/2 acres drawn by JOSEPH
J. WINN of McIntosh Co. and gtd. 1 March 1822. Signed: A. B. POWELL.
Wit: JOSEPH W. TODD, JOHN W. DONALSON, SAML. BREEDLOVE. (The name looks
as if it is BLESSETT). Rec. July 7, 1823.

Page 320: Sheriff's deed, JAMES FLETCHER, Sheriff of Henry Co.
on order from Justice Court of Jasper Co. in suit of THOMAS WILLIAMS
agst. WHITMELL EASON, JAMES FLETCHER did sell land of WHITMELL EASON on
4 Feb. 1823 to ZACHARIAH WHITE for $100 and made deed dated 1 May 1823
to tract in Henry Co. in 18th Dist. Lot No. 332. Signed: JAMES FLETCHER.
Wit: ALLEN GAY, JAMES SALLONS, J.P. Rec. 16 July 1823.

Page 322: Deed headed Putnam Co., dated 5 Jan. 1822 bet. HENRY G.
EZELL of Jasper Co. and DANIEL C. MAUND of Putnam Co., for consid. of
$1,000 conveys tract in Henry Co. on waters of Cotton River in 20th
Dist. Henry Co. surveyed by B. B. FOUNTAIN, district surveyor on 20
Aug. 1821. Signed: HENRY G. EZELL. Wit: ___ HARWELL?, NEHEMIAH DAVIS,
JOHN SPARKS, J.P. Rec. July 16, 1823. (Note: The first part of this
deed had names of grantor and Grantee written in between the lines in
very small script and diff. to read, and the county of residence may have
been reversed from way stated above, as was diff. to tell, Ed.)

Page 322: Deed dated 14 July 1823, bet. TURNER EVANS of Co. of __ and the Honorable Justices of Inf. Ct. of Henry Co., to wit: JACOB HINTON, JAMES HENRY, DAVID JOHNSON, WILLIAM PATE, REASON E. MARBERRY... for consid. of $400, conveys to sd. Justices tract of land cont. 100 acres at N. E. corner of Lot No. 134 in 7th Dist. of Henry Co. Signed: TURNER EVANS. Wit: WM. HARDEN, WM. MULON the dower page 17. Rec. July 18, 1823.

Page 323: Deed dated 11 Oct. 1822 bet. HENRY T. BILBRO of Henry Co. and GEORGE HEARD of Greene Co., for consid. of $300, conveys tract in 6th Dist. of Henry Co., Lot No. 65. Signed: HENRY T. BILBRO. Wit: HENRY GIBSON, R. BUSH, J.P. Rec. July 19, 1823.

Page 324: Deed dated 8 Jan. 1823 bet WILLIAM H. WHITNEY of City of Savannah and WILLIAM WILLIAMS of City and state afsd...for consid. of $50, conveys tract in Henry Co., lot No. 241 in 2nd Dist., drawn in Land Lottery by orphans of HENRY (CRGG?) (Possibly GRAGG?) dec'd, sd. orphan was married to sd. WILLIAM H. WHITLEY. Signed: WILLIAM H. WHITNEY. Wit: WILLIAM STOW, JOHN ASHTON, J.P. Rec. 21 July 1823.

Page 325: Relinquishment of Dower of RIDLY EVANS wife of Turner Evans to land mentioned in Deed on Page 322, just mentioned above, bef. WILLIAM HARDIN Clk. S. C., JOHN C. HAND, J.P. Rec. July 22, 1823. (Note at top says see dower page 14.)

Page 325: Deed dated 12 March 1822 bet. WM. D. COTTINGHAM of Appling Co. and DURANT GREEN of Twiggs Co...consid. of $25...conveys Lot of land cont. 202 1/2 acres in 7th Dist. Henry Co., Lot No. 70. Signed: WM. D. COTTINGHAM. Wit: DANIEL GEORGE, GEORGE HEARDON, JOHN LAWTHER. Rec. July 22, 1823. DANIEL GEORGE swore to signature on 12 March 1822 bef. ROBT COLEMAN, J.P. of Lawrence Co.

Page 326: Deed dated 25 May 1822, bet. SIMON SAMSUMONS of Chatham Co. and ELIAS BLESS of Chatham Co., City of Savannah, for consid. of $500 conveys Lot No. 54 in 8th Dist. Henry Co., land drawn by SIMON SAMSUMONS 15 May 1822. Signed: S(GAMSIMONS?). Wit: OLIVER LILLEBRIDGE, JAMES EPPINGER, J.P. Rec. July 24, 1823. Signature on Receipt looks like S. SAMSIMONS, Ed.

Page 329: Deed headed Richmond Co., dated 15 May 1822 bet. JOHN W. PRICHARD and JOHN D. ANDERSON...for consid. of $100, conveys tract of 202 1/2 acres in 6th Dist. Henry Co., Lot No. 168. Signed: JOHN W. PRICHARD. Wit: BENJAMIN F. HENRICK, R. BUSH. Rec. July 26, 1823. Mrs. PRICHARDS Dower, see Page 492.

Page 330: Deed dated 7 April 1823 bet. JOHN GILMORE of Henry Co. and ELISHA BLESSETT of Co. afsd...consid. of $300, conveys tract in Henry Co., Lot No. 65 in 2nd Dist. cont. 101 1/4 acres. Signed: JOHN GILMORE. Wit: WILEY HEFLIN, ELIZABETH (+) PATTRICK.

Page 331: Deed headed Baldwin Co., dated 4 Dec. 1822, bet. JAMES SMITH of Pulaski Co. and JOHN LOVEJOY of Jackson Co., consid. of $300, conveys tract in Henry Co. in 12th Dist, Lot No. 102, gtd. to JAMES SMITH Dec. 1822. Signed: JAMES SMITH. Wit: W. WATLEY, JAMES STRAWN, J.I.C. Rec. 4 Aug. 1823.

Page 331: Deed dated 25 Dec. 1822 bet. FARLDING PEARCE of Putnam Co. and JOEL JOBEZ of Henry Co., consid. of $400, conveys tract in Henry Co., cont. 202 1/2 acres, Lot No. 50 in 11th Dist...Signed: FARLDING PEARCE. Wit: WM. MADDOX, IRBY HUDSON, J.I.C. Rec. Aug. 6, 1823.

Page 332: Sheriff's Deed, JAMES FLETCHER, Sheriff on order from Sup. Ct. of Jones Co. in suit of FRANCIS F. JOHN IRWIN agst. ALLEN ROBINETTE did sell property of sd. ALLEN ROBINETTE on 5 Aug. 1823 for $40.50 to FRANCIS ERWIN. Deed made 5 Aug. 1823 to Lot No. 88 in 1st Dist. Henry Co. cont. 202 1/2 acres. Signed: JAMES FLETCHER. Wit: JAMES RANSOM, JR., JAMES MORSE, J.P. Rec. 1823.

Page 333: Deed of Sale headed Jackson Co., dated 18 Feb. 1822 by AUSTIN FULCHER of Co. afsd. for sum of $300, sells to PETER Z. WARD

177

of sd. Co. and State, a negro boy named Ephriam about 9 or 10 years of age. Signed: AUSTIN FULCHER. Wit: DILLIN FULCHER, JOHN LOVEJOY. Rec. July 26, 1823.

Page 334: Sheriff's Deed, JAMES FLETCHER, Sheriff on order of Justice Ct. of Jasper Co. in suit of U. & J. SAMPLE agst. THOMAS SPAIN, sells on 5 Aug. 1823 to URIAH C. SAMPLE for $58, Deed dated 5 Aug. 1823 Lot No. 150 in 12th Dist. Henry Co. cont. 2 1/2 acres. Signed: JAMES FLETCHER. Wit: JAMES RANSOM, JAMES SELLORS, J.P.

Page 335: Deed headed Jefferson Co., dated 24 Jan. 1823 bet. ROBERT LANSBY of Warren Co. and RISIN COLLY of Jefferson Co., for consid. of $400, conveys tract cont. 202 1/2 acres in 3rd Dist. Henry Co., Lot No. 185 drawn by RISIN COLLY and gtd. 10 Jan. 1820. Signed: REASON (X) COLLY (could be COLBY, Ed.) Wit: JOHN RENT, ELISHA JOHNSON, ELY (X) LASSIN. Rec. Aug. 23, 1823. Singature sworn to in Jefferson Co. bef. DANIEL CONNELL, J.P. by ELIJAH JOHNSON on 5 Jan. 1823.

Page 335: Deed headed Oglethorpe Co., dated 5 Oct. 182_, bet. WILLIAM A. BENTLY of Co. afsd. and CLABON DOSS of Henry Co., consid. of $200, conveys to sd. CHARLES DOSS tract of land in 8th Dist. Henry Co., cont. 202 1/2 acres, Lot No. 256 gtd. to sd. WILLIAM BENTLY 3 Jan. 1822. Signed: WILLIAM A. BENTLY. Wit: HAMPTON THOMPSON,BENJAMIN AVENTZ, JOHN THORNTON, J.P. Rec. 25 Aug. 1823.

Page 335: Deed headed Jones Co., dated 2 Jan. 1823, bet. RICHARD SEABORN of Jones Co. and BENJAMIN WEBSTER of Henry Co., consid. of $200 conveys tract of 202 1/2 acres in 11th Dist. Henry Co., Lot No. 184. Signed: RICHARD (X) SEABORN. Wit: JOHN BATEMAN, JOSHUA ECKLES, J.P. Rec. 26 Aug. 1823.

Page 337: Deed dated 10 Aug. 1822 bet. JESSE GATES, Cratz Dist. LawrenceCo. by his attorney in fact DANIEL MARTIN of one part and WILLIAM TERRILL of Habersham Co. by Power of Attorney to DANIEL MARTIN by JESSE GATES dated 8 Aug. 1822...consid. of $200... conveys tract cont. 202 1/2 acres in 7th Dist. Henry Co., Lot No. 8. Signed: JESSE GATES by his Attorney DANIEL MARTIN. Wit: ALEY ANN JOHNSON, LOCKTIN JOHNSTON, J.P. Rec. Aug. 26, 1823. (This name may have been YATES instead of GATES, as was diff. to distinguish a cpaital G from Y, Ed.) Power of Attorney follows the deed and states DANIEL MARTIN of Franklin Co., Ga. and was Wit: by J. (C or U) JAMES, ROBERT COATZ and Recorded 26 Aug. 1823 in Laurens Co., Ga.

Page 339: Sheriff's Deed, JAMES FLETCHER, Sheriff on order from Superior Ct. of Twiggs Co. in suit of POLY ROSE, Admnr. against GEORGE LITTLE...sold on 4 Feb. 1823 to JOEL STANSEL_ for $129...Deed dated 4 Feb. 1823 for tract in 11th Dist. Henry Co., cont. 202 1/2 acres, Lot No. 1. Signed: JAMES FLETCHER. Wit: CH. COCHRAN, WM. MCCONNELL, J.P. Rec. Sept. 1, 1823.

Page 340: Deed headed Jones County, Dated 4 Jan. 1823, bet JOHN SIMMONS of Jones Co. and JOHN DOROUGH of same Co. and state afsd...consid of $400, conveys tract in Henry Co. on Towale River in 2nd Dist., Lot No. 106 cont. 202 1/2 acres. Signed: JOHN (X) SIMMONS. Wit: JAMES (SENTOR?) CHAS. PHILIPS, J.P. Rec. Sept. 1, 1823.

Page 340: Deed dated 24 July 1823 bet. JOHN DOROUGH of Jones County and THOMAS MCLENDON of Henry Co...consid. of $400...conveys tract in Henry County on Towale River in 2nd Dist., Lot No. 106 cont. 202 1/2 acres, gtd. to JOHN SIMMONS on 24 Jan. 1822. Signed: JOHN DOROUGH. Wit: GEORGE MORGAN, THOMAS MCLENDON, SR. Rec. 1 Sept. 1823.

Page 341: Sheriff's Deed, JESSE JOHNSON, Sheriff of Henry Co. on order from Justices Court of Wilkinson Co. in suit of MORGAN BROWN agst. JOHN CANNON...did sell property of JOHN CANNON on 2 Sept. 1823 for $10 to BENJAMIN SANSING Deed dated 2 Sept. 1823 for tract of land in 2nd Dist. Henry Co. Lot No. 105. Signed: JESSE JOHNSON. Wit: W. L. CRAYTON, JOHN GRIFFIN, SAMUEL JOHNSON, J.P. Rec. 2 Sept. 1823.

Page 342: Receipt dated 15 Nov. 1822 by JOHN EXLY of Savannah $180 from JOHN C. HELVANSTON for 2 tracts of land, viz: 114 in 8th Dist. of Henry County and No. 228 in 2nd Dist. Houston Co. Signed: JOHN EXLY. Wit: K. TYNER, WM. C. MILLS, J.P. Rec. Sept. 19, 1823.

Page 343: Deed dated 4 Sept. 1823 bet. WM. REFF of Henry Co. and WILLIAM HARDIN of same...consid. of $100...conveys tract in 7th Dist... Henry Co., Lot No. 93 being half of sd. Lot, cont. 101 1/4 acres. Signed: WM. (+) REFF. Wit: MARTIN LUKER, WM. MCCONNELL, J.P. Rec. Sept. 25, 1823.

Page 344: Deed headed Oglethorpe Co., dated 12 April 1823 bet. JOHN BOWLING of Co. and State afsd. and COLEMAN S. PRINGLE of Clark Co... consid. of $60...conveys tract in Henry Co., Lot No. 245 in 1st Dist. Signed: JOHN BOWLING. Wit: CHRIST. BROWN, J.I.C. JOHN TARPLEY, J.P. Rec. Sept. 9, 1823.

Page 344: Deed headed Morgan Co., dated 14 Nov. 1822, bet. WILLIAM PACE of state and Co. afsd. and THOS. DAVIS of same...consid. of $500 conveys tract in 1st. Dist. Henry Co., grant to sd. WM. PACE dated Nov. 12, 1822. Signed: WILLIAM PACE. Wit: __? KEY BEAVERS, THOS. WILSON, J.P. Rec. Sept. 9, 1823.

Page 345: Sheriff's Deed, JAMES FLETCHER, Sheriff of Henry Co. on order from Inf. Ct. of Jones Co. in suit of REID WOODROFF agst. LEWIS SHEPHERD...did sell property of sd. LEWIS SHEPHERD on 5 Aug. 1823 for sum of $51. to JULIAS TURNER...Deed dated 5 Aug. 1823, conveys tract in 12th Dist. Henry Co. Lot No. 106 cont. 202 1/2 acres. Signed: JAMES FLETCHER. Wit: FRANCIS (+) PEARSON, JAMES STANZ, J.P. Rec. Sept. 20, 1823.

Page 346: Deed headed Morgan Co., dated 17 Dec. 1822 bet. THOS. DAVIS of State and Co. afsd. and THOS. COOK of Henry Co...consid. of $500 conveys tract in 1st. Dist. Henry Co., Lot No. 226, gtd. to WELBRON PACE. Signed: THOMAS DAVIS. Wit: JOHN S. RANDLE, THOMAS WILLSON, J.P. Rec. Sept. 14, 1823. (Note: Deed on page 344 shows him signing as WILLIAM PACE).

Page 347: Deed headed Clark Co., dated 20 May 1822 bet. ROBERT STRINGFELLOW of Greene Co. and EDWARD HILLARY of the other part...consid. of $150...conveys tract in Henry Co., 1st Dist., Lot No. 231, bearing date 24 April 1822. Signed: ROBERT STRINGFELLOW. Wit: JOHN JACKS, JOHN OSBORN, JOHN MARTINDALE, J.P. Rec. Sept. 11, 1823.

Page 347: Deed headed Clark Co., dated 24 Feb. 1823 bet EDWARD H. MAXEY and HIRAM MAGBEE both of Co. and state afsd...consid of $150 conveys tract in Henry Co., Lot No. 230 in 1st Dist. Signed: EDWARD H. MAXEY. Wit: WM. TURNER, W. W. BROWN, JOHN PARK, J.P. Rec. Sept. 12, 1823.

Page 348: Power of Attorney headed Morgan County, dated 10 Jan. 1823 from WILLIAM TOMER of Decalb (i.e. DeKalb), Appoints WILLIAM JONES his lawful att. to conve- unto WILLIAM BAKER of Morgan Co., Lot No. 251, 1st Dist. Henry Co. Signed: WILLIAM TOMER, Wit: JOHN CHATFIELD, GEORGE CHATFIELD, J.P. Rec. Sept. 12, 1823.

Page 348: Deed headed Morgan Co., dated 20 Jan. 1823 bet. WILLIAM TOWERS of DeKalb Co. and WILLIAM BAKER of Morgan Co., for consid. of $250 conveys tract in Henry Co. 1st Dist. Lot No. 251 on waters of Tusshaws. Signed: WILLIAM TOWERS, WILLIAM JONES, Agent. Wit: THOMAS JONES, THOMAS COLEMAN, D. LEANNEAR, J.P. Rec. Sept. 12, 1823.

Page 349: Power of Attorney headed Habersham County, Dated 1 Nov. 1822 from ELISHA UTLY of State and Co. afsd. to WILLIAM MCKNIGHT of Henry Co. to take out grant and plat for tract in 11th Dist. of Henry Co. Lot No. 138, and also empowers him to sell same. Signed: ELISHA UTTLEY. Wit: JOHN T. BENTLY, JOHN O'BANNER. Rec. Sept. 12, 1826.

Page 350: Deed headed Wilks Co., Dated 20 Sept. 1820 bet. HENRY B.
GIBSON of Co. and State afsd. and LABON MAGBEE of Clark Co...consid. of
$500...conveys tract cont. 202 1/2 acres, Lot No. 252. Signed: HENRY B.
GIBSON. Wit: R. L. DICKERSON, JAMES CH___, J.P. Rec. Sept. 12, 1823.

Page 351: Deed dated 16 Sept. 1822 bet. ELISHA BRITTINGHAM of
Jasper Co. and Jennings Hulsir of Henry Co...consid. of $350...conveys
tract in Henry Co., Lot No. 96 in 11th Dist., cont. 202 1/2 acres.
Signed: ELISHA (X) BRITINGHAM. Wit: JAMES SESSIOM, AARON PARKER, Rec.
Sept. 16, 1823.

Page 352: Deed headed Jasper Co., dated 16 Nov. 1820 bet JOSEPH
BAKER of Co. and state afsd. and DAVID GEORGE of Henry Co. consid of
$103...conveys tract cont. 202½ acres, Lot No. 128 in 118th Dist. of
Henry Co. Signed: JOSEPH (X) BAKER. Wit: JESSE (+) GEORGE, ___
BROWN, J.P. Rec. Sept. 17, 1823.

Page 352: Deed headed Walton County, dated 12 May 1823, bet.
JOHN LIGGERS of Co. and state afsd. and ALLEN CLARK of Henry Co...consid.
of $200...conveys tract cont. 202 1/2 acres in 12th dist. Henry Co., Lot
No. 168. Signed: JOHN (X) LIGGERS. Wit: ROBT. MOORE, J.P., ZACHARIAH
MOORE, Rec. Sept. 17, 1823.

Page 353: Power of Attorney headed Newton County, dated 7 Nov.
1822 from WILLIAM OGLETREE of Alabama State and Marengo County...Appt's.
WILLEY BRIDGES of Newton County his attorney to take out grant of tract
of land in the 6th. dist., Lot No. 19 of Henry Co. and for him to sell
or dispose of it...Signed: WM. OGLETREE. Wit: THOMAS B. GAY, J.P.
(O. D. LAW?)

Page 353: Receipt dated 28 July 1823, bet. WILLY BRIDGES of Newton
Co., Ga. attorney in fact for WILLIAM OGLETREE of Morgan County and
State of Alabama (former states Morengo Co., which your editor believes
is more approp. There is a Morgan Co., Ala. but date of its formation
if not know by editor) and THOMAS B. GAY of Newton Co., Ga. for tract
of land in 6th Dist. Henry Co., Lot No. 19, drawn by and gtd. to sd.
WILLIAM OGLETREE. Signed: WILLY BRIDGES, Atto. in fact. Wit: GEO.
W. BENNY, JAMES BLOOD. Rec. Sept. 20, 1823.

Page 354: Deed headed Jasper County, dated 20 Jan. 1823 bet.
ZACHARIAH MCLAIN and GEORGE A. (KAY?) of Morgan and state afsd.
of the one part and JOSIAH SANDERS of Henry Co...convey tract in 7th
Dist. Henry Co., Lot No. 66 cont. 202 1/2 acres for sum of $200. Signed:
ZACHARIAH D. MCLAIN (in places this looks somewhat like DILLLAIN but
am almost sure it is D. MCLAIN, Ed.) GEO. A (X) KAY Ior RAY, as R & K
are diff. to distinguish). Wit: JOHN (X) SANDERS, ELISHA (X) JOHNSON.
Rec. Sept. 27, 1823.

Page 355: Deed dated 20 Jan. 1823 bet. PETER CEARLIN of Henry Co.
and HUGH HAMEL of same Co...consid. of $100...conveys tract in 1st
Dist. Henry Co., Lot No. 77, cont. 202 1/2 acres. Signed: PETER CERTIN.
Wit: CLARK HAMEL, BRYANT HAMEL. Rec. 27 Sept. 1823. Sworn to bef.
MOSES COX, J.P. 23 Sept. 1823.

Page 356: Deed headed Morgan Co., dated 2 Dec. 1822 bet. GEORGE
HENDRY of Co. afsd. and RICHARD H. J. HOLLY of Walton Co..consid. of
$260...conveys tract in 1st Dist. Henry Co., Lot No. 138 cont. 202 1/2
acres, gtd. to ENOCH JOHNSON 18 Nov. 1822. Signed: GEORGE HOLLY.
Wit: HOWELL HOLLY, ROBERT HENDRY, GREEN(BRO?) HOLLY. Rec. Sept. 27,
1823. Sworn to bef. OLIVER HIGGANBOTHAM, J.P. 18 Dec. 1822 and signed
by LANKIN HOLY. (This must be EARICK JOHNSON instead of ENOCH as seen in
next deed. Ed.)

Page 357: Deed headed Liberty Co., dated 25 Nov. 1822 bet EARICK
JOHNSON of Co. afsd. and GEORGE HENDRY of Morgan Co...consid of $150
conveys tract in 1st. dist. Henry Co., Lot No. 138, cont. 202 1/2 acres,
gtd. sd. EARICK JOHNSON 18 Nov. 1822. Signed: EARICK JOHNSON. Wit:
NANCY HENDRY, ROBERT HENDRY, JR., J.P. Rec. Sept. 27, 1823.

Page 358: Deed headed Jackson Co., dated (no date shown) bet. ISAAC BETZ of afsd. Co. and JAMES YARBOROUGH of Henry Co...for consid. of $100...conveys tract, Lot No. 92 in Henry Co., 11th dist. cont. 202 1/2 acres. Signed: ISAAC (+) BETTS. Wit: GEORGE PENTACOST. THOMAS (+) YARBROUGH. Rec. Oct. 11, 1823.

Page 359: Deed headed Baldwin Co., dated 5 Jan. 1822, bet. BASEL LAW of Jefferson Co. and STARLING KAMP of Jasper Co...consid. of $325 conveys to STIRLING CAMP in 2nd Dist. Henry Co., No. 68 and comes on the waters of Towadega. Signed: BASEL LAW. Wit: JOSIAH BLACKWELL, APPLETON ROSSETER, J.I.C. Rec. 16 Oct. 1823.

Page 360: Deed headed Franklin Co., dated 11 March 1822 bet. JOHN MCCLURE of Co. afsd. and A. P. KNOX of sd. state and Co. afsd...consid of $__?...conveys tract cont. 202 1/2 acres in Henry Co., 4th Dist... Signed: JOHN (X) MCCLURE. Wit: H. GRAY, RICHD. GRAY, J.P. Rec. Oct. 23, 1823.

Page 360: Deed headed Jones Co., dated 25 June 1823 bet. PETER SMITH of state and Co. afsd. and JOHN A. ELLIS of Oglethorpe Co...consid. of $500, conveys tract in Henry Co., Lot No. 191 in 3rd. Dist. Signed: PETER SMITH. Wit: HARDAMAN OWEN, JEREMIAH SMITH, J.P. Rec. Oct. 24, 1823.

Page 361: Deed headed Jackson Co., dated 18 Oct. 1823, bet. ELIAS GREEN of State and Co. afsd. and FRANCIS PEARSON of Henry Co...consid. of $350...conveys tract in Henry Co., Lot No. 80 in 7th Dist., cont. 202 1/2 acres. Signed: ELIAS GREEN. Wit: PETTER E. MCMILLEN, J.P., JAMES SELLORS. Rec. Oct. 27, 1823.

Page 362: Promissory Note headed Jasper Co., dated 24 May 1823 bet. GEORGE LEWIS of Co. afsd. and JOHN A. ELLIS of Oglethorpe Co...has conveyed his promissory note for $123.25 payable on or before 25 Dec. next and securing the sd. promissory note GEORGE LEWIS has conveyed tract in Henry Co., Lot No. 91, 2nd Dist., cont. 202 1/2 acres. Signed: GEORGE (X) LEWIS. Wit: W. B. BUCKHANNON, E. DODSON, J.P. Reco. Oct. 29, 1823.

Page 363: Deed headed Jones Co., dated 13 Dec. 1821 bet HENRY HARRALLD of Co. afsd. and JOHN QUINN of same...consid. of $500...conveys tract in 1st. Dist. Henry Co., Lot No. 220, orig. gtd. to HENRY HARROLD on 11 Dec. 1821, cont. 202 1/2 acres. Signed: HENRY (X) HARROLD. Wit: GIDEON POPE, GEORGE KENEDY. Rec. Nov. 1, 1823.

Page 364: Deed headed Henry Co., dated 14 Feb. 1823 bet JAMES FLETCHER, Sheriff of Henry Co. and JOHN A. ELLIS of Oglethorpe Co...consid of $356 conveys tract in Henry Co., 2nd Dist., Lot No. 91, cont. 202 1/2 acres __ on by FRANCIS PEARSON constable of sd. Co. and returned to Mr. __ as the property of JAMES DYAR to satisfy sundry __ issues out of a Justices Ct. of Hancock Co. in favor of JACOB P. TURNER and others and sold at public outcry on 1st. Tues. in Feb. 1823. Signed: JAMES FLETCHER. Wit: THAD. B. RUZ, WM. HARDIN, Clk. S. C. Rec. Nov. 1, 1823.

Page 365: Promissory Note headed Jasper Co., dated 7 Aug. 1823 bet. ROBERT MEEK of State of N. C. and County of Mecklenburg and JOHN A. ELLIS of Oglethrope Co., Ga... sd. ROBT. MEEK conveys his promissory note payable on or before 25 Dec. 1824 for $360...and secures the sd. note by a tract of land in Henry Co., Lot No. 190 in 2nd Dist. Signed: ROBERT MEEK. Wit: ELI CONGER, JAMES L. BURKES, J.P. Rec. Nov. 4, 1823.

Page 367: Deed headed Jasper Co., dated 9 Aug. 1822 bet. WADE H. TURNER of State and Co. afsd. and SCILAS MOSELY of Putnam Co...sd. SCILAS MOSELY for consid. of $700... conveys tract in 7th Dist. Henry Co. Lot No. 191...cont. 202 1/2 acres... Signed: SCILAS MOSELEY. Wit: T. J. H. SHARPE, M. C. HARPER, J. WILKINSON, J.P. Rec. Nov. 14, 1823.

Page 367: Receipt headed Warren Co., dated 15 Sept. 1823, bet ROWEL ADAMS for consid. of $50 received from JAMES FLETCHER...conveys tract in Henry Co., Lot No. 33 in 11th Dist. Signed: ROWEL ADAMS, Wit: WIKE IVEY, ELIAS WILLSON, J.P. Rec. Nov. 14, 1823.

Page 368: Deed headed Jasper Co., dated 2 Oct. 1823 bet. ARCHIBALD BACHELLOR of Jones Co. and JOHN A. ELLIS of Oglethorpe Co...consid. of $500...conveys tract in Henry Co., Lot No. 206, 2nd Dist. Signed: ARCHIBALD BATCHELLOR. Wit: AARON SMITH, J.P., HARDAMAN OWEN. Rec. Nov. 19, 1823.

Page 368: Deed dated 18 Feb. 1823 bet. GEORGE N. BURROUGHS of Franklin Co., Ga. and THOMAS HORTON of Elbert Co...consid of $175... conveys tract cont. 202 1/2 acres in 3rd Dist. Henry Co., Lot No. 231. Signed: GEORGE N. BURROUGHS. Wit: FREDERICK (DE) DEEN, ROYAL BRYAN, J.P. Rec. Nov. 19, 1823.

Page 369: Receipt dated 4 Feb. 1822 headed Franklin Co., bet. WILLIAM BROWN for consid. of $80 paid by BENJAMIN STRINGFELLOW conveys tract in 2nd. Dist. Henry Co., Lot No. 107. Signed: WILLIAM BROWN. Wit: ABM. NICHOLS, MARSHALL WILBANKS. Rec. Nov. 20, 1823. Sworn to in Franklin Co. bef. MARSHALL WILBANKS and wit by ELIJAH STEPHENS, J.P. on 19 March 1822.

Page 369: Deed headed Henry Co., dated 15 Nov. 1823 bet. ELIJAH RAY and DOTTSON HARVELL both of same state and Co. first above...consid. of $120, conveys tract in Henry Co., Lot No. 87, being part of sd. lot, say one fourth in 11th Dist. cont. 50 1/4 acres, gtd. to DANIEL STAGNER. Signed: ELIJAH (X) RAY. Wit: JOHN T. BENTLY, J.P., ROBERT SHAW. Rec. Nov. 21, 1823.

Page 370: Deed headed Henry Co., dated 30 Jan. 1823 bet. URIAH TAYLOR of Jasper Co. and DAVID COX of Henry Co...consid of $500...conveys tract in 1st Dist. Henry Co., Lot No. 178 cont. 202 1/2 acres. Signed: URIAH (T) TAYLOR, NANCY (T) TAYLOR. Wit: EPHRIAM COX, MOSES COX, J.P. Rec. Dec. 8, 1823.

Page 371: Deed of Conveyance, headed Camden Co., dated 19 March 1823, bet. WILLIAM CLUBB of Co. and State afsd. and ANSON KIMBERLY of McIntosh Co...consid. of $30...conveys tract in Henry Co., Lot No. 198 in 6th Dist. cont. 202 1/2 acres. Signed: WILLIAM CLUBB. Wit: JOHN J. MORGAN, B. R. BUNKLEY, J.P. Rec. Dec. 8, 1823. SARAH CLUBB wife of WILLIAM CLUBB rel. dower in Camden Co. on 19 March 1823, bef. B. R. BUNKLEY, J.P.

Page 372: Deed headed McIntosh Co., dated 7 Dec. 1822, bet. JOHN J. DEETS of McIntosh Co. and AMSON KIMBERLEY of same...consid. of $50... conveys tract in 7th Dist. Henry Co., Lot No. 91. Signed: JOHN J. DEETS. Wit: WM. D. WILLIAMS, JOHN HUNTER, J.I.C. Rec. Dec. 8, 1823.

Page 372: Morgan Co., Ga. David McMahan swore that he saw JESSE BRYAN(T) signed his name on 11th Oct. 1823 before E. DUKES, J.P. Rec. Dec. 12, 1823.

Page 373: Deed of Gift, dated 20 Dec. 1823, headed Henry Co., from HENRY KING for love and affection he has for his son ABNER H. KING, gives him a certain negro girl called Mariah about 13 years of age and also one feather bed and furn. when he comes to 21 yrs. of age, extra of an equal division with the rest of his heirs at his decease. Signed: HENRY KING. Wit: EDWARD ALLAMS, WM. MCCONNELL, J.P. Rec. Dec. 22, 1823.

Page 373: Deed dated 1 March 1823 bet. SAMUEL J. BRYAN of Chatham Co., Ga. and ROBERT GRIMMETof Henry Co...consid. of $500...conveys tract in Henry Co., Lot No. 247 in 1st Dist. cont. 202 1/2 acres, drawn by JAMES KEY and Transferred by him to SAMUEL J. BRYAN on 13 Feb. 1823. Signed: SAMUEL J. BRYAN. Wit: JOHN KELLEN, JAMES EPPINGER, J.P. Rec. Dec. 22, 1823.

Page 375: Deed headed Walton Co., dated 17 Dec. 1823 bet CHARLES GARRETT of sd. Co. and State and JOHN BROOKS of Henry Co...consid. of $500...conveys tract in Henry Co., 11th Dist. Lot No. 38, cont. 202 1/2 acres. Signed: CHARLES GARRETT. Wit: WILLIAM HENDERSON, JAMES PHILIPS, J.P. Rec. Dec. 23, 1823.

Page 375: Deed headed Jackson Co., dated 24 June 1822, bet. JOHN

BURTON of Jackson Co. and ABRAHAM ROWAN of Clark Co., Ga...consid. of $500...conveys tract drawn by sd. JOHN BURTON of Capt. HANSON'S Dist. of Jackson Co. sit. in 6th Dist. Henry Co., Lot No. 115 cont. 202 1/2 acres. Signed: JOHN (X) BURTON. Wit: DAVID AULUN, MOSES CALLAHAN, ASA NA_NM, J.P.

Page 376: Deed headed Jasper Co., dated 17 Dec. 1822 bet. SAMUEL ETHERIDGE of Wilkinson Co. and WILLIAM TAYLOR of Henry Co...consid of $100...conveys tract in Henry Co. Lot No..237 in 1st Dist. drawn by sd. SAMUEL and gtd. 16 Dec. inst. cont. 202 1/2 acres. Signed: SAMUEL ETHERIDGE. Wit: JAMES WILLIAMS, TANDY W. KEY, J.P. Rec. Dec. 29, 1823.

Page 377: Deed dated 4 Jan. 1823 bet BENJAMIN KEMP of Wilkinson Co. and SIMEON KEMP of Baldwin Co...consid of $300...conveys tract in Henry Co., Lot No. 156 in 1st. Dist. drawn by sd. BENJAMIN KEMP. Signed: BENJA. KEMP. Wit: DANIEL NOLLEY, JAMES LOW, J.P. Rec. Dec. 30, 1823.

Page 378: Deed headed Baldwin Co., dated 6 Jan. 1823 bet. SIMEON KEMP of Baldwin Co. and JESSE GOODWYN of Baldwin Co...consid of $300... conveys tract in Henry Co., Lot No. 156 in 1st Dist. Signed: SIMEON KEMP. Wit: J. G. WORSHAM, C. MCARTY, J.P. Rec. 30 Dec. 1823.

Page 379: Deed dated 1 Jan. 1823 bet. AARON HAM of Burk Co. and ABRAHAM BETTS of Jasper Co...consid. of $100...conveys tract in 8th Dist., Henry Co., cont. 202 1/2 acres, Lot No. 219, drawn by sd. AARON HAM. Signed: AARON (X) HAM. Wit: WILLIAM MANNER, LEONARD ROAN, JOHN VANCE, J.P. Rec. Jan. 1, 1824.

Page 379: Deed headed Jackson Co., dated 9 March 1823 bet. MICHAEL MCDONELL of Jackson Co. and ALLEN C. MCDONELL of Jackson Co...consid. of $300...conveys tract in 11th Dist. Henry Co., Lot No. 65, cont. 202 1/2 acres, gtd. to JESSE ROBINETT on 10 July 1822. Signed: M. MCDONELL. Wit: FRANCIS MERIWETHER, M. D. MARTIN, J.P. Rec. June 1, 1824.

Page 380: Deed headed Jackson Co., dated 4 June 1823 bet. SEABORN J. SCROGGINS and JOHN BOYLE both of State and Co. afsd...consid. of $250 conveys tract in 11th Dist. Henry Co., Lot No. 129, cont. 202 1/2 acres. Signed: SEABORN J. SCROGGINS. Wit: JOSHUA ROBERTS, Wit: JOSHUA ROBERTS, GEORGE SHAW, J.P. Rec. Jan. 1, 1824.

Page 381: Deed headed Enauel County, Ga. dated 14 Nov. 1823 bet. THOMAS T. JOHNSON of sd. Co. and GEORGE NOWLAN of Henry Co... consid of $150...conveys tract in 8th dist. Henry Co., Lot No. 49, cont. 202 1/2 acres. Signed: THOMAS T. JOHNSON. Wit: ANDREW YOUNG, ELDRED SWAIN, J.P. Rec. Jan. 1, 1824.

Page 381: Deed dated 14 Nov. 1823 bet. ELISHA MOSELEY of Henry Co. and JONATHAN BEAN of same...consid of $300...conveys tract in 8th Dist. of Henry Co., Lot No. 107. Signed: ELISHA MOSELEY. Wit: TANDY W. KEY, WILLIAM TUGGLE. Rec. Jan. 1, 1824.

Page 382: Deed dated 2 Feb. 1822 bet. BETHEAL MORGAN of Madison Co., Ga. and SOLOMON FOWLER of Franklin Co., Ga...consid. of $100...conveys tract in 7th Dist. Monroe Co., cont. 202 1/2 acres, Lot No. 100. Signed: BETHEL MORGAN. Wit: EDWARD L. CRISTAIN, ISAAC GILBERT, JOEL FREEMAN, J.P. Rec. Jan. 7, 1824.

Page 383: Deed dated 18 Jan. 1823 bet H. J. WILLIAMS of Henry Co. and SOLOMON FOWLER of state and Co. afsd...consid. of $140...conveys tract in 3rd Dist. of sd. Co., Lot No. 218. Signed: H. J. WILLIAMS. Wit: THOMAS RAMSEY, DAVID JOHNSON, J.P. Rec. Jan. 7, 1824.

Page 384: Power of Attorney, headed Burk Co., Ga. dated 8 Feb. 1823 from THOMAS SMITH of Co. and State afsd. to JAMES HOWARD of Co. and State afsd., his lawful attorney to dispose of tract in Henry Co. and 7th Dist. Signed: THOS (X) SMITH. Wit: JOHN NATWORTHY, JOHN LODGE, J.P. Rec. 7, 1824.

Page 385: Deed headed Morgan Co., dated 7 May 1823 bet. WILLIAM HOLLIS and THOMAS WYATT both of sd. Co...consid. of $700...conveys tract in Henry Co. on waters of Shoal Creek, Lot No. 134 in 8th Dist. cont. 202 1/2 acres. Signed: WM. HOLLIS. Wit: THOMAS FEILDER, BENJA. SELLOR, J.P. Rec. Jan. 7, 1824.

Page 385: Power to Attorney, headed Hall Co., dated 6 Jan. 1823 from MOSES ELLISON of State and Co. afsd. to JOSEPH HAMBRICK of Newton Co...his lawful att. to sell tract of land in Henry Co., Lot No. 53 in 2nd Dist. Signed: MOSES (X) ELLISON. Wit: THOMAS PHARR, NATHAN CENTER. Rec. Jan. 8, 1824.

Page 386: Deed headed Henry Co., dated 13 Oct. 1823 bet. JAMES A. CROMBIE of Co. afsd. and JOSEPH YARBROUGH of same...consid of $500... conveys tract in 6th Dist. Henry Co., Lot No. 101, cont. 202 1/2 acres. Signed: JAMES A. CROMBIE. Wit: JAMES FLETCHER, MATHEW (X) WALLDROOP, SAMUEL HENDERSON. Rec. Jan. 8, 1824.

Page 387: Power of Attorney headed Tatnall County, dated 30 June 1822 from WILLIAM DURRANE (DURRENCE?) of Co. afsd. to LEMUEL TIPPINS of same...his lawful attorney to take out and sell Lot No. 234 in 1st. Dist. Henry Co. Signed: WILLIAM DURRANE. Wit: JOHN BROWN, JOSEPH DURRENE. Rec. Jan. 8, 1824.

Page 388: Deed headed Henry Co., dated 15 Aug. 1822 bet. WILLIAM DURRENE, SENR. of Co. of Tatnall and State of Ga. by his Attorney LEMUEL TIPPINS and JAMES A. MCCANE of state and co. afsd...consid of $400... conveys tract of 202 1/2 acres on Tupehaw Creek in 1st. Dist. Henry Co. Lot No. 234. Signed: LEMUEL TIPPINS, Attorney for WILLIAM DURRENE. Wit: JOHN TERRILL, ALLEN JONES. Rec. Jan. 9, 1824.

Page 388: Deed of Conveyance headed Jasper Co., dated 5 April 1823 bet. HEZEKIAH ALLEN of Jasper Co. and BENAGER SEXTON of Henry Co., consid. of $140 conveys tract in 3rd Dist. Henry Co., Lot No. 112, cont. 202 1/2 acres. Signed: HEZEKIAH ALLEN. Wit: JOHN WEST, RUFUS WEST. Rec. Jan. 9, 1824.

Page 389: Deed dated 23 April 1823 bet. JOHN B. BUSH of Pulaski Co., and WILLIAM HOLLIS of Morgan Co., Ga...consid. of $150, conveys tract in 8th dist. Henry Co., Lot No. 134, cont. 202 1/2 acres. Signed: JOHN B. BUSH. Wit: SANDERS BUSH, JAMES M. ADAMS. Rec. Jan. 9, 1824.

Page 390: Deed headed Henry Co., dated 23 Dec. 1823 bet. CHARLES WILDER and CHARLES JURDIN both of Co. and State afsd...consid of $800, conveys to CHARLES JORDAN tract in Henry Co. on waters of Toweliga River, cont. 202 1/2 acres, Lot No. 208 in 3rd Dist. gtd. to GEORGE PARMER on 27 Dec. 1821. Signed: CHARLES WILDER. Wit: STEPHEN SMITH, JAMES D. (X) JORDAN, JOHN C. HAND, J.P. Rec. Jan. 9, 1821.

Page 390: Deed headed Henry Co., dated 8 Aug. 1823 bet. THOMAS MCCLENDON of Co. afsd. and WILLEY HEFFLIN of same Co...consid of $600, conveys tract on Toweliga River in 2nd Dist. Henry Co., Lot No. 106, except what lies on east side of Toweliga River. Signed: THOMAS MCCLENDON. Wit: JAMES H. JOHNSON, H. J. WILLIAMS, J.P. Rec. Jan. 10, 1824.

Page 391: Power of Attorney headed Pulaski Co., dated 19 Dec. 1823, from JEFFREY MUNFORD of Co. afsd. to "trusty friend" JAMES GARNETT of Madison Co. his lawful att. to dispose of tract of land in Henry Co., Lot No. 188 in 7th Dist. drawn by "myself" Signed: JEFFREY (X) MUNFORD. Wit: ORRIN D. WATSON, GEORGE COOPER, J.P. Rec. Jan. 4, 1824.

Page 392: Deed headed Jefferson Co., dated 16 March 1822, bet. JOHN DEBINGPORT of Jefferson Co. and PATRICK B. CONNELLY of Jefferson Co., consid. of $300, conveys tract in 8th Dist. Henry Co., Lot No. 135 cont. 202 1/2 acres. Signed: JOHN (X) DEBINGPORT. Wit: RANDOL MCDONALD, SHEPHERD GREEN, J.P. Rec. Jan. 10, 1824.

Page 393: Deed headed Ogelthorpe Co., dated 15 March 1823, bet.
JOHN A. ELLIS of Co. afsd. and LAZARUS SUMMERLIN of Clarke Co...consid.
of $800...conveys tract in Henry Co., 8th Dist., Lot No. 223 on south
fork of Oakmulga River cont. 202 1/2 acres, gtd. to JOHN A. ELLIS 4
Feb. 1823. Signed: JOHN A. ELLIS. Wit: JOHN HALE, SANKY T. JOHNSON,
J.P. Rec. Jan. 12, 1824.

Page 394: Deed headed Richmond Co. dated 13 Sept. 1823 bet.
ZEPHENIAH BLACKSTON and JOHN C. WINSLETT...consid. of $500...conveys
tract in 6th Dist. Henry Co. cont. 202 1/2 acres, Lot No. 130, surveyed
on 10 Aug. 1821 by JAMES WATSON Surveyor, drawn by ZEPHENIAH BLACKSTON of
PALMERS Dist., Richmond Co...Signed: ZEPHENIAH BLACKSTON. Wit: W. J.
CULLENERTS, ABNER FULLER, J.P. Rec. Jan. 13, 1824.

Page 395: Sheriff's Deed headed Henry Co., on writ from Superior
Ct. Oglethorpe Co. in suit of FLEMING & LEWIS J. JORDAN agst. WADE
GOOLSBY, JAMES FLETCHER, Sheriff of Henry Co., seized property of sd.
WADE GOOLSBY and on 6 Jan. 1824 sold same to FLEMING JORDAN for sum of
$170...Deed dated 6 Jan. 1824, for consid of $170...tract in Henry Co.
Lot No. 239. Signed: JAMES FLETCHER, Sheriff. Wit: THO. C. BENNING,
DAVID JOHNSON, J.P. Rec. Jan. 15, 1821.

Page 396: Sheriff's Deed from JAMES FLETCHER, Sheriff Henry Co. on
writ from Justice Court of Elbert Co., in suit of F. & R. JORDAN agst.
JOEL BRAWNER, seized land on 6th Jan. 1824 sold same to FLEMING JORDAN
for sum of $50. Deed dated 6 Jan. 1824 for tract in Henry Co., Lot No.
218 in 12th Dist. Signed: JAMES FLETCHER, Sheriff. Wit: THOS. C.
BENNING, DAVID JOHNSON, J.P. Rec. 15 Jan. 1824.

Page 397: Sheriff's Deed headed Henry Co. from JAMES FLETCHER,
Sheriff on writ from Justice Court of Pulaski Co. in Suit of JORDEN
DYKES agst. HAYS HOLLY, seized lot and sold same on 6 Jan. 1824 to SMITH
BONNER for sum of $171. Deed dated 6 Jan. 1824 for Tract in Henry Co.,
Lot No. 102 in 6th Dist. Signed: JAMES FLETCHER, Sheriff. Wit:
THOS. C. BENNING, WILLIAM TUGGLE, JAMES SELLERS, J.P. Rec. Jan. 15, 1824
(Note: In body of Deed HAYES is also found spelled HAYNES HOLLEY.)

Page 398: Deed headed Jefferson Co., dated 20 March 1823, bet.
PATRICK B. CONNELLY of Jefferson Co. and WILLIAM HOWARD of Burk Co.
consid. of $245 conveys tract in Henry Co. in 8th Dist., Lot No. 135
drawn by JOHN DEBINGPORT. Signed: PATRICK B. CONNELLY. Wit: BALDWIN
RAIFORD, JAMES (X) HILLIARD. Rec. Jan. 17, 1824.

Page 399: Deed headed Elbert Co., dated 31 March 1823 bet. JACOB
W. KING and MARY his wife and ANDREW WEST all of Co. afsd...consid. of
$300...conveys tract which sd. JACOB W. KING and MARY his wife have
interest or claim in gtd. to JOHN G. WINGFIELD in Henry Co., Lot No. 207
in 8th Dist. cont. 202 1/2 acres. Signed: JACOB W. KING,MARY A. KING.
Wit: SAMUEL G. RAND, DAVID R. JAMES. Rec. Jan. 17, 1824.

Page 400: Deed headed Baldwin Co., dated 26 Sept. 1823, bet.
VINCENT E. VICKERS of Baldwin Co. and JOHN BATEMAN of Co. afsd...consid.
of $300 conveys tract in 3rd Dist. Henry Co., cont. 202 1/2 acres, Lot
No. 56. Signed: VINCENT E. VICKERS. Wit: E. UNDERWOOD, H. ALLEN,
J.I.C. Rec. Jan. 20, 1824.

Page 400: Sheriff's Deed headed Henry Co., from JAMES FLETCHER,
Sheriff on writ from Superior Ct. of Wilkinson Co. in suit of JAMES
HATCHER and ROBERT CLAY agst. JAMES SHIRER, JOHN HATCHER and JOHN S.
SHIRER...sd. JAMES FLETCHER seized land of sd. JAMES SHIRER and on 6
Jan. 1824 sold same to SAMUEL WILLIAMS for $127. Deed dated 6 Jan.
1824 for Tract in Henry Co., 6th Dist. Lot No. 192, cont. 202 1/2 acres.
Signed: JAMES FLETCHER. Wit: THOS. C. BENNING, WAID H. TURNER, J.I.C.
Rec. Jan. 20, 1824.

Page 401: Deed headed Henry Co. dated 5 Dec. 1824 bet. WILLIAM
HOWARD of Co. afsd. and JAMES HOWARD of same place...consid. of $300
conveys tract in 8th Dsit. Henry Co., Lot No. 135. Signed: WILLIAM
HOWARD. Wit: WILLIAM TUGGLE, JAMES SELLERS, J.P. Rec. Jan. 21, 1824.

Page 402: Sheriff's Deed headed Henry Co., from JAMES FLETCHER, Sheriff on writ of Justice Court of Washington Co., in suit of GREEN and HARDING agst. JOHN LORD, sd. FLETCHER seized land of sd. JOHN LORD and on 3 March 1824, sold same to THOMAS CARPENTER for $301. Deed dated 19 Nov. 1823 for tract in 3rd Dist. Henry Co., Lot No. 143 cont. 202 1/2 acres. Signed: JAMES FLETCHER. Wit: WM. SMITH, WM. BRYANT, ALEXANDER SMITH, JAMES SELLERS, J.P. Rec. Jan. 21, 1824.

Page 403: Deed headed Jasper Co., dated 7 Nov. 1822, bet. WILLIAM BENNET of Irwin Co. and THOMAS ROBINSON of Jasper Co...consid. of $125 conveys tract cont. 202 1/2 acres, Lot No. 136 in 1st Dist. Signed: WILLIAM BENNET. Wit: ABEL L. ROBINSON, VALINTEN NASH. Rec. 3 Feb. 1824.

Page 404: Deed headed Baldwin Co., dated 19 Jan. 1822, bet. JOHN GILASPY of Hancock Co. and WILLIAM BARKLEY of Morgan Co...consid. of $200...conveys tract in 9th Dist. Henry Co., Lot No. 35, drawn by sd. JOHN GILASPY of Capt. LOYD'S Dist. Hancock Co. Signed JOHN GILASPY. Wit: JOHN B. HINES, JAMES RUSELLE, J.P. Rec. Feb. 3, 1824.

Page 405: Deed headed Jasper Co., dated 19 Aug. 1822 bet. DANIEL STAGNER of Jasper Co. and SANDERS DUKE of Jasper Co...consid. of $150... conveys tract in 11th Dist. Henry Co., Lot No. 87, cont. 101¼ acres, being drawn by sd. DANIEL STAGNER, it being the north half of sd. Lot 87 adj. 106 and lying in Camp Creek. Signed: DANIEL (X) STAGNER, Wit: GIDEON H. BROKTON, JOHN C. GIBSON, J.P. Rec. 4 Feb. 1824.

Page 406: Deed headed Jasper Co. dated 23 Oct. 1822, bet. JOHN CAMPTON and ADAM LANSON of other of Co. afsd...consid. of $200...conveys tract in 9th Dist. Henry Co., Lot No. 54 cont. 202 1/2 acres. Signed: JOHN CAMPTON. Wit: JOHN R. CARGIL, JAMES DICK, JOHN M. MARKS. Rec. Feb. 5, 1824.

Page 406-411: Deed headed Georgia, City of Savannah, dated 18 May 1822 bet. GEORGE MILLER of City of Savannah and his wife and JOHN ADAMS of City of Savannah of 2nd part. consid. of $5,130.00...conveys following parts of land to wit: Lot No. 241 in 8th Dist. Henry Co., drawn by JOHN A. STEPHENS, SEN., Lot No. 77 in 15th Dist. Houston Co., drawn by JOHN A. STEPHENS SEN., Lot No. 117 in 17th Dist., Henry Co. drawn by RANICE CLEVICE PITIT... Lot No.199 in 12th Dist. Henry Co., drawn by JOSEPH BRANTLEY, Lot No. 66 in 14th Dist. Henry Co., drawn by DEMPRY GRIFFIN. Lot No. 153 in 13th Dist. Monroe Co. drawn by JOHN DIMICK, Lot No. 187 in 18th Dist. Monroe Co. drawn by WILLIAM MONLY, Lot No. 188 in 7th Dist. Monroe Co. and Lot No. 207 in 9th Dist. Houston Co. drawn by FRANCIS EIPEELLETT, Lot No. 161 in 6th. Dist. Henry Co., drawn by JOHN BATTERSTONE, Lot No. 154 in 15th Dist. Houston Co. drawn by JOHN CARTIN, Lot No . 253 in Dooly Co. drawn by JOHN MITCHELL. Lot No. 78 in __ Dist. Henry Co. drawn by LITTLE WHITE: Lot No. 57 in 2nd Dist. Monroe Co. drawn by PETER WHITE; Lot No. 128 in 4th Dist. Dooly Co. drawn by HENRY MATTHEWS...Lot No. 158 in 13th Dist. Henry Co. drawn by SOLOMON DURNHAM; Lot No. 238 in 10th Dist. Houston Co. drawn by SOLOMON DURNHAM; Lot No. 132 in 19th Dist. of Early Co. drawn by EZRA KINK, Lot No. 227 in 7th Dist. Henry drawn by KINAND STRICKLAND, Lot No. 162 in 12th Dist. Houston drawn by KINAND STRICKLAND, Lot No. 100 in 8th Dist. Monroe Co. drawn by RODRICK W. MCH_NEOR, Lot 47 in 5th Dist. Henry Co. drawn by LOT HAMILTON, Lot No. 60 in 7th Dist. Monroe Co. drawn by GIDEON HAMILTON; Lot No. 8 in 15th Dist. Houston drawn by GIDEON HAMILTON; Lot No. 164 in 9th Dist. Houston drawn by HAMIT JOHNSON; Lot No. 164 in 4th Dist. Houston drawn by JOSEPH BALDWIN; Lot 56 in 4th Dist. Dooly drawn by WILLIAM BUTLER; Lot No. 76 in 4th Henry Co. drawn by LEWIS MILLS; Lot No. 76 in 8th Dist. Early Co. drawn by WILLIAM C. MILLS; Lot No. 99 in 14th Dist. Monroe drawn by JOSEPH HERRANE; Lot No. 372 in 1st Dist. Appling drawn by JOHN BEAN; Lot No. 248 in 11th Dist. Dooly drawn by BRIAN DOTTINS; Lot No. 7 in 14th Dist. Fayette Co. drawn by JOHN W. ASHTON; Lot No. 104 in 4th Dist. Henry Co. drawn by JOHN KEANE; Lot No. 115 in 8th Dist. Dooly drawn by ELIZAB ETH KEAN; Lot No. 10 in 18th Dist. Henry Co. drawn by ELIZA MULLIN. Signed: GEO. MILLER, ELISA JANE W. MILLER, JOHN ADAMS. Wit: IVERY MACKPAL. WM. C. BARTON, J.P. Chatham Co. ELIZA JANE W. MILLER wife of GEORGE MILLER renounces dower on May 20, 1822 bef. AM. C. BARTON, J.P. Rec. 9 Feb. 1824.

Page 411: Deed headed Chatham Co., dated 21 Jan. 1822, bet. JOHN BEVITISTE of Chatham Co. and GEORGE MILLER of Chatham Co...consid. of $25...conveys tract in 6th Dist. Henry Co., Lot No. 161 cont. 202 1/2 acres, drawn by sd. JOHN BEVITISTE in 1821. Signed: JOHN BEVITISTE. Wit: W. (CAP?) B. ROBINS, J.P. Rec. 9 Feb. 1824.

Page 412: Deed headed Chatham Co., dated 11 Feb. 1822, bet. KYNEARD STRICKLAND of Chatham Co. and GEORGE MILLER of City of Savannah...consid. of $50...conveys tract in 7th Dist. Henry Co. cont. 202 1/2 acres Lot No. 227. Signed: KYNEARD STRICKLAND. Wit: S. SIMMONS, B. DOBBINS, J.P. Rec. 9 Feb. 1824.

Page 414: Deed headed Telfair Co., dated 20 March 1823, bet. JOSEPH WILSON of Telfair Co. and NATHANIEL ASHLEY of Telfair Co...consid. of $159...conveys tract in 12th Dist. Henry Co., Lot No. 138 cont. 202 1/2 acres, gtd. to sd. JOSEPH WILSON. Signed: JOSEPH WILSON. Wit: JASON BRINSON, CORNELIUS R. ASHLEY. Rec. 11 Feb. 1824.

Page 415: Sheriff's Deed headed Henry Co. from JAMES FLETCHER, Sheriff on writ from Superior Ct. of Elbert Co. in suit of WILLIAM B. HARDY agst. JOHN JOHNSON...sd. Fletcher sezied land and sold on 5 Nov. 1822 to WILLIAM NELSON for $25...Deed dated 5 Nov. 1822 to WILLIAM NELSON of Morgan Co. for tract in 7th Dist. Henry Co., Lot No. 156. Signed: JAMES FLETCHER. Wit: WM. MCCONNELL, RICHARD GROGAN, J.P. Rec. Feb. 12, 1824.

Page 416: Deed headed Morgan Co., dated 12 Aug. 1823 bet. JANE L. FRETWELL and HENRY C. MERRITT of Co. afsd...consid. of $900...conveys tract cont. 202 1/2 acres in 11th Dist. Henry Co., Lot No. 67 gtd. to sd. JANE FRETWELL, Widow of Fitzpatrick's Dist. Morgan Co. Signed: JANE L. FRETWELL. Wit: EDWARD PATE, RICHARD M. GILBERT, J.P. Rec. 13 Feb. 1824.

Page 417: Deed headed Henry Co., dated 1 Jan. 1824 bet. WILLEY HEFFLIN of Co. afsd. and JOSHUA STEPHENS of Clarke Co...consid. of $1100.. conveys tract on Toweliga River in 2nd Dist. Henry Co., Lot No. 106. Signed: WILLEY HEFFLIN. Wit: ENOCH MCCLENDON, GEORGE (X) MORRIS, NATHAN BREED, J.P. Rec. Feb. 13, 1824.

Page 417: Deed headed Henry Co., dated 25 Dec. 1823 bet. EDMUND ALLUMS of Co. afsd. and SAMUEL HENDERSON of same...consid. of $125... conveys tract in 6th Dist. Henry Co. Lot No. 74, cont. 202 1/2 acres. Signed: EDMUND ALLUMS. Wit: JAMES FLETCHER, MATTHEW (X) WALDROPE, JOHN (X) JOHNSON. Rec. Feb. 15, 1824.

Page 418: Deed headed Henry Co., dated 13 Jan. 1824 bet. JETHREW HARRELL of Co. afsd. and JESSE JOHNSON of same...consid. of $300...conveys tract in 3rd Dist. Henry Co., Lot No. 213...cont. 202 1/2 acres. Signed: JETHRO HARRELL. Wit: WILLIAM HARRY, JOSEPH HARRELL, JAMES FLETCHER. Rec. Feb. 16, 1824.

Page 419: Deed headed Henry Co., dated 28 Jan. 1824 bet. WILLIAM YARBOROUGH of Co. afsd. and THOMAS YARBOROUGH of same...consid of $100 conveys tract in 11th Dist. Henry Co., part of Lot No. 69, cont. 50 acres on north side of above tract, gtd. WILLIAM YARBOROUGH 10 Oct. 1822. Signed: WILLIAM YARBROUGH. Wit: ROBERT SHAW, JOHN T. BENTLY, J.P. Rec. Feb. 17, 1824.

Page 420: Deed headed Newton County, dated 25 Feb. 1823, bet. WILLIAM JONES and of one part SILAS GORDEN of Morgan Co...consid. of $1,000...conveys tract in 11th Dist. Henry Co., Lot No. 131, gtd. to JOHN (DORLTON?). 12 Dec. 1821. Signed: WILLIAM (X) JONES. Wit: SAMUEL MCCLENDON, JOEL JONES. Rec. Feb. 17, 1824.

Page 421: Deed headed State of Georgia, DeKalb Co., dated 23 Jan. 1824 bet. SAMUEL REID of afsd. Co. and JESSE JOHNSON of Henry Co...consid. of $150...conve-s tract in 3rd Dist. Henry Co., cont. 202 1/2 acres. Signed: SAMUEL REED. Wit: JOSEPH MCCONNELL, JAS. FLETCHER, ABSALEM STEWART, J.I.C. Rec. Feb. 17, 1824.

Page 421: Deed dated 15 Jan. 1825 bet. WILLIAM HARDIN and JACOB SIKES both of Henry Co...consid of $100...conveys tract in 7th Dist. Henry Co. Lot No. 93...(description of land mentions running to Walnut Creek and down Creek to where present Spring Branch empties in sd. Creek reserving sd. land near sd. Creek that every may be covered by waters raised at WILLIAM RUFFS Mill Dam). Signed: WILLIAM HARDIN. Wit: ANDRED M. BROWN, JAMES KIMBROUGH, J.P. Rec. Feb. 17, 1824.

Page 422: Power of Attorney headed Camden Co., dated 13 July 1820 from JAMES D. WILSON of same County...appt's. BOLTON A. CAPP his lawful att. to dispose of tract in 6th Dist., Lot No. 256. Signed: JAMES D. WILSON. Wit: LEMUEL CHURCH, M. H. HIBBARD, J.P. Rec. 18 Feb. 1824.

Page 423: Camden Co. Sale of "Chance in the land Lottery shortly to take place" by BOLTON A. CAPP for sum of $7.50 by JAMES D. WILSON who also gives BOLTON A. CAPP Power of Att. to dispose of sd. tract. Signed: JAMES D. WILSON. Wit: LEMUEL CHURCH, MICHAEL JOHNSTON, M. H. HILBARD, J.P. Rec. Feb. 18, 1824.

Page 424: Deed headed Putnam Co., dated 19 Feb. 1822 bet GEORGE W. PHILIPS and WILLIAM MANGHAM and JOHN BOWLING of other part, sd. PHILIPS of Greene Co. and MANGHAM and BOWLING of Putnam Co...consid. of $150... conveys tract in 7th Dist. Henry Co., Lot No. 34. Signed: GEORGE W. PHILIPS. Wit: BRYANT S. MANGHAM, STITH DANIELL, J.P. Rec. Feb. 15, 1824.

Page 425: Sheriff's Deed headed Henry Co., on writ from Justices Court of Putnam Co. in suit of GOODRIDGE and CARSTARPHEN agst. LEWIS TAYLOR, JESSE JOHNSON, Sheriff of Henry Co. seizes tract of LEWIS TAYLOR and sells on 3 Feb. 1824 to ELY COOPER for $10...Deed dated 3 Feb. 1824 for tract in 2nd. Dist. Henry Co., Lot No. 87. Signed: JESSE JOHNSON, Sheriff. Wit: BENJAMIN SANSING, JAMES SELLERS, J.P. Rec. Feb. 20, 1824.

Page 426: Sheriff's Deed headed State of Georgia on writ from Justices Court of Putnam Co. in suit of OBADIAH EDGE agst. CORNELIUS FOGARITY, JAMES FLETCHER, Sheriff, sells land of sd. FORGARITY to OBADIAH EDGE for $55...Deed dated April 1, 1823 for tract in 6th Dist. Henry Co. Lot No. 202, cont. 202 1/2 acres. Signed: JAMES FLETCHER, Sheriff. Wit: TURNER EVAN, MARLIN EDGE. Rec. Feb. 26, 1824.

Page 427: Deed headed Georgia, dated 29 April 1823, bet. JOHN ROE of Early Co. and EZEKIEL REGISTER of State of Alabama...consid. of $218... conveys tract cont. 202 1/2 acres in 2nd Dist. Henry Co., Lot No. 9. Signed: JOHN ROE. Wit: JOHN SICKES, TOM PETER CHAIRRES, THOMAS GIBSON. Rec. March 5, 1824. (Note: There is an * by the name TOM which looks as if it were written in a diff. hand from PETER CHAIRRES, Ed.) The signing is sworn to on page 428 bef. JOHN E. PARRAMORE a Justice for Early Co. in which he mentions JONES PETER CHAIRRES as being a wit. Dated 30 April 1823. Underneath this is a note saying "see TOM PETER CHAIRRES affidavit P. 493, also WM. MCCARTY acting Gov. of Fla. on same page.)

Page 428: Deed headed Monroe Co., dated 5 Feb. 1824 bet. EZEKIEL REGISTER of State of Alabama and County of Henry and EDMUND STEPHENS of Monroe Co...consid. of $228...conveys tract in 2nd Dist. Henry Co., Lot No. 9. Signed: EZEKIEL REGISTER. Wit: JOHN C. WILLIS, JOHN C. GOSS, STEPHEN BARKWELL. Sworn to in Pike Co., Ga. bef. LEVI MARTIN, J.P. and Reg. March 5, 1824.

Page 429: Deed headed Georgia, dated 9 Oct. 1823 bet. POINTON ASH-MORE of Henry Co. and LEWIS HOPGOOD of Henry Co...consid of $150...conveys tract in 3rd Dist. Henry Co., Lot No. 71, drawn by sd. POINTON ASHMORE, cont. 101 1/4 acres. Signed: POINTON (X) ASHMORE. Wit: ROBERT CROSS, DREW HERRINGTON. Rec. March 11, 1824.

Page 430: Deed headed Putnam Co., dated 8 March 1824 bet. WILLIAM VARNER and THAD B. REES of Co. and State afsd...of one part and SAMUEL

PILES of other...consid. of $450 conveys tract in 6th Dist. Henry Co., Lot No. 2 on waters of Cotton River, cont. 202 1/2 acres. Signed: WILLIAM VARNER, THAD. B. REES. Wit: JAS. W. WRGITH, IRBY HUDSON, J.I.C. Rec. March 12, 1824.

Page 431: Deed headed Bibb Co., dated 17 Sept. 1823 bet MOSES STRIPLING of Bibb Co. and PARKES W. SMITH of same state and Co. of Oglethorpe...consid. of $1150...conveys tract in 2nd Dist. Henry Co. on waters of Indian Creek cont. 202 1/2 acres. Signed: MOSES (X) STRIPLING. Wit: THOMAS (X) TYE, JOHN B. SMITH, WM. M. STOKES, J.P. Rec. March 13, 1824.

Page 431: Deed headed Georgia, dated 25 Oct. 1823 bet. THOMAS NICHOLS of Oglethorpe Co. and JOHN MCMICHAEL of Jasper Co...consid of $500... conveys tract in 1st. Dist. Henry Co., Lot No. 121. Signed: THOS. NICHOLS. Wit: JAMES HARKNESS, THOMAS LOVE, ISAAC WELDEN. Rec. March 13, 1824.

Page 432: Deed headed Jasper Co., dated 6 Feb. 1824 bet. JURDEN THORNTON of Newton Co. and STEPHEN KNIGHT of Henry Co...consid of $300... conveys tract in 9th Dist. Henry Co., Lot No. 39. Signed: JURDEN THORNTON. Wit: JOHN R. CARGIL, EZEKIEL FEARS. Rec. 13 March 1824.

Page 433: Deed headed Scriven Co., dated 11 March 1822, bet. JOHN ADKINS of one part and SAMUEL B. COULDING of other, both of Co. afsd... consid. of $200...conveys tract cont. 202 1/2 acres in 3rd Dist. Henry Co., Lot No. 213. Signed: JOHN ADKINS. Wit: JAMES W. (RITTLES?), HOPE BRANNE, J.P. Rec. March 13, 1824.

Page 434: Deed headed Henry Co., dated 26 Dec. 1823 bet JOHN SIMMONS of Henry Co. and JOHN MCMICHAEL of sd. Co...consid. of $180... conveys tract in 1st. Dist. Henry Co. cont. 202 1/2 acres drawn by JARRUSHED KNIGHT, widow of Bullock Co. and gtd. to her 8 Nov. Signed: JOHN SIMMONS. Wit: D. ANDREWS, SILAS ELLIOTT. Rec. March 15, 1824.

Page 435: Deed headed Jones Co., dated 9 June 1823 bet JOHN SIMMS of Ogelthorpe Co. and PITT MILNER of Jones Co...consid of $700...conveys tract drawn by JAMES TOMLINSON, Lot No. 49 in 1st Dist. Henry Co. on waters of Sandy Creek. Signed: PITT MILNER. Wit: PARKER EASON, STEPHEN VINTREP, J. L. BLACKBURN, J.P. Rec. March 15, 1824.

Page 436: Deed headed Henry Co., on order from Justices Ct. of Hancock Co. in suit of JEFFREY BARKSDALE agst. HENRY H. LANGFORD...JESSE JOHNSON Sheriff of Henry Co., sold land of LANKFORD on 2 March 1825 to JEFFREY BARKSDALE for $57...Deed dated 2 March 1824. for tract in 12th Dist. Henry Co. Lot No. 173 cont. 202 1/2 acres. Signed: JESSE JOHNSON, Sheriff. Wit: THO. C. BENNING, JOHN FERRELL, J.P. Rec. 17 March 1824.

Page 437: Deed headed Georgia, dated 18 Oct. 1823 bet. ISIAH and BENTLY ROWLIN of one part and PAYTON PINKARD of other, both of Henry Co., consid. of $225, conveys tract in 2nd Dist., Henry Co., Lot No. 60 cont. 101 1/4 acres. Signed: ISAIAH (+) ROWLIN, BENTLY A. ROWLIN. Wit: THOS. MCCLENDON, NATHAN BREED, J.P. Rec. March 31, 1824.

Page 437: Deed headed Georgia, dated 24 April 1823, bet. JAMES BOYKIN of Baldwin Co. and JOHN SIMMS of Oglethorpe Co...consid. of $500... conveys tract in 1st. Dist. Henry Co., Lot No. 47, cont. 202 1/2 acres. Signed: JAMES BOYKIN. Wit: BENJ. MILNER, JAMES FLEMING, J.P. Rec. March 31, 1824.

Page 438: Deed headed State of Georgia, DeKalb Co., dated 9 Feb. 1823 bet. CHARLES REYNOLDS of Co. of Elbert and BENTON SMITH of Co. afsd... consid. of $250...conveys tract in 1st Dist. Henry Co., Lot No. 177, cont. 202 1/2 acres. Signed: CHARLES REYNOLDS. Wit: WILLIAM TERRY, ABSALOM STEWARD, J.I.C. Rec. 19 March 1824.

Page 439: Deed headed Baldwin Co., dated 7 June 1823 bet. THOMAS JORDAN of Jefferson Co. and JOHN SIMMS of Oglethrope Co...consid. of $250...conveys tract in 2nd Dist. Henry Co., Lot No. 33 cont. 202 1/2 acres. Signed: THOMAS JORDAN. Wit: B. P. STUBBS, JAS. FLEMING, J.P. Rec. March 26, 1824.

Page 440: Deed headed Putnam Co., dated 13 March 1824 bet. DIXON HALL of one part and JOHN ROOKS of other both of Co. afsd...consid. of $300...conveys tract in 9th Dist. Henry Co., Lot No. 27 cont. 202 1/2 acres. Signed: DIXON HALL. Wit: JOSEPH STANFORD, LARD H. HARRIS, J.P. Rec. March 26, 1824.

Page 441: Deed headed Oglethrope Co., dated 31 May 1823 bet. THOMAS COOKSEY of Wilkes Co. and JAMES ANDREWS of Co. afsd. and WILLIAM FARMER of Oglethrope...consid. of $600...conveys tract cont. 202 1/2 acres in 2nd Dist. Henry Co., Lot No. 2 on waters of Towaliga drawn by sd. THOMAS COOKSEY of Moore's Dist. Wilkes Co. Signed: THOMAS COOKSEY. Wit: HENRY COMMONS, JR., HAMILTON GOSS, JOHN SIMS. Rec. March 31, 1824.

Page 442: Deed headed Georgia, dated 11 May 1822 bet. WILLIAM MOORE of one part and JOSIAH HRON both of Laurens Co...consid. of $200...conveys tract in 1st. Dist. Henry Co., Lot No. 223, cont. 202 1/2 acres, orig. gtd. to sd. WILLIAM MOORE. Signed: WILLIAM MOORE. Wit: THOMAS W. HART, LEWIS HOLLAND, J.P. Rec. March 31, 1824.

Page 443: Deed headed Georgia, dated 11 March 1823 bet. JOSIAH HORN of Laurens Co. and BENJAMIN MAY of Jones Co...consid. of $300...conveys tract in 1st Dist. Henry Co. Lot No. 223, cont. 202 1/2 acres, gtd. to WILLIAM MOORE. Signed: JOSIAH HORN.

Page 444: Deed headed Oglethrope Co., dated 21 Dec. 1823 bet. JAMES ANDREWS of Co. afsd. and HENRY FARMER of same...consid of $375...conveys tract cont. 202 1/2 acres in 2nd Dist. Henry Co., Lot No. 2 on Waters of Towaliga, drawn by THOMAS COOKSEY of Wilkes Co., Signed: JAMES ANDREWS. Wit: ROBERT G. CARTER, CHARLES CARTER, EDWARD CARTER, SR. Rec. March 31, 1824.

Page 445: Deed headed Oglethrope Co., dated 8 March 1824 bet. HENRY FARMER and WILLIAM FARMER of Oglethrope Co. and JOHN SIMS of same...consid. of $700...conveys tract cont. 202 1/2 acres in 2nd Dist. Henry Co., Lot No. 2 on waters of Towaliga, drawn by THOMAS COOKSEY of Wilkes Co. Signed: HENRY FARMER, WILLIAM FARMER. Wit: GEORGE LESTER, THOMAS CARTER, WM. M. STOKES, J.P. Rec. April 3, 1824.

Page 446: Deed headed Morgan Co., dated 26 Feb. 1824 bet. ELIZABETH HEMPHILL of Co., afsd. and WADE HEMPHILL of sd. Co. of other part...consid. of $400...conveys tract in 11th Dist. Henry Co., Lot No. 29, cont. 202 1/2 acres. Signed: ELIZABETH HEMPHILL. Wit: JESSE ROBERTS, JOHN ROBERTS, J.P. Rec. April 6, 1824.

Page 447: Deed headed Georgia, dated 24 Feb. 1824 bet. HENRY EDWARDS of Greene Co. and ELIZABETH HEMPHILL of Morgan Co...consid. of $420...conveys tract in 11th. Dist. Henry Co., Lot No. 29, cont. 202 1/2 acres. Signed: HENRY EDWARDS. Wit: WILLIAM C. DAWSON, THOS. J. MCCASKY, J.P. Rec. 6 April 1824.

Page 447: Deed headed Jasper Co., dated 6 April 1823 bet. ANDREW NUTT of Jasper Co. and ELISHA BROOKS of same...consid. of $1000...conveys tract in 7th Dist. Henry Co., Lot No. 73, drawn by WILLIAM MORRIS 5th April last. Signed: ANDREW NUTT. Wit: JOSEPH (X) TURNER, TANDY W. KEY, J.P. Rec. April 6, 1824.

Page 448: Deed headed Henry Co., dated 4 March 1823, bet. JAMES FLETCHER, Sheriff of Henry Co...consid of $16...conveys tract in 11th. Dist. Henry Co. Lot No. 20, cont. 202 1/2 acres, levied on as property of THOMAS SIMMONS on order of Justices Court of Columbia Co. in favor of TILMAN ANLY and sold on 1st. Tues. in March 1823, when ROBERT SHAW was highest bidder. Signed: JAMES FLETCHER. Wit: HENRY N. POPE, JAMES HENRY, J.I.C. Rec. 10 April 1824.

Page 449: Deed headed Wilkinson Co., dated 31 Jan. 1824 bet. JAMES JOHNSON of Co. afsd. and JAMES MANN of Henry Co...consid of $212...conveys tract in 2nd Dist. Henry Co. cont. 202 1/2 acres, Lot No. 182. Signed: JAMES JOHNSON. Wit: JEREMIAH D. MANN, DAVID JOHNSON, WM. M. BROWN.

Page 450: Deed headed Georgia, dated 20 Jan. 1823 bet. WILLIAM

BLAKE of Gwinnett Co. and REPS OSBORN of Jackson Co...consid of $200..
conveys tract to REPS OSBORNE SENR. in 6th Dist. Henry Co., Lot No. 115,
which land was gtd. to CHARLES YANCY of Jackson Co. (could be YANAY,
instead of YANCY, Ed.) Signed: WILLIAM BLAKE. Wit: CHARLES PRICE, NANCY
PRICE. Rec. April 19, 1824.

Page 451: Deed headed Elbert Co. from DAVID BARRON of Co. afsd. who
conveys to JAMES MORRISON of Co. afsd. for consid. of $400...conveys tract
in 3rd. Dist. Henry Co., Lot No. 220. Dated 20 Nov. 1823. Signed:
DAVID BARRON. Wit: T. MORRISON, WM. DAVIS. Rec. 18 April 1824.

Page 452: Deed headed Henry Co., dated 26 Sept. 1822, bet. IRA LEWIS
of Co. afsd. and THOMAS HARPER of Morgan no...consid of $100...conveys
tract cont. 100 acres, in Henry Co. on waters of Big Walnut Creek,known
as part of Lot No. 51 in 7th Dist. Signed: IRA LEWIS. Wit: RHODRICK
HARPER, JAMES SELLERS, J.P. Rec. 22 April 1824.

Page 453: Deed dated 7 Nov. 1823 bet. MILES C. NESBIT of Morgan Co.
and JAMES H. ROBERTS of State and Co. afsd. (Not stated) consid. of $509..
conveys tract in 1st. Dist. Henry Co. on waters of Tuzshaw Creek, cont.
202 1/2 acres. Signed: MILES C. NESBIT. Wit: ROBERT WATSON, JOHN
ROBERTS, J.P. Rec. 23 April 1824.

Page 454: Dower headed Morgan Co., MARTHA S. NESBIT wife of within
named MILES C. NESBIT relinquished Dower on 11 Nov. 1823. Wit: ROBERT
WATSON, JOHN ROBERTS, J.P. Rec. 23 April 1824.

Page 454: Deed headed Green Co., dated 25 Feb. 1823 bet. LITTLEBERRY
BOSTICK of Co. afsd. and ARCHIBALD GRAY of same...consid. of $200...con-
veys tract known as Lot No. 14 in 11th Dist. Henry Co., cont. 202 1/2
acres. Signed: LITTLEBERRY BOSTICK. Wit: EVERETH WOODHAM, HENRY
DAVIS. Rec. 26 April 1824.

Page 455: Deed dated 31 Dec. 1823 bet. WALTER AUSTIN of Gwinnett
Co. and HENRY DAVIS of Green Co...consid of $100...conveys tract in Henry
Co. 2nd Dist. Lot No. 22. Signed: WALTER AUSTIN. Wit: JACOB RILEY,
J.P. D. MOBLEY, J.P. Rec. 26 April 1824.

Page 456: Deed headed Henry Co., dated 19 Dec. 1822, bet. ELIZABETH
RAMSEY and R. C. MAYBERY both of Co. afsd...consid of $350...conveys 1/2
of lot of land in Henry Co., known as Lot No. 254 in 8th Dist. Signed:
ELIZABETH (X) RAMSEY. Wit: ROBERT COCHRAN, JOSEPH BENTON, J.P. Rec.
26 April 1824.

Page 456: Power of Attorney headed Burk Co., from WILLIAM DREW of
sd. Co. to PARKER KNOWLES of Jasper Co. to demand and dispose of tract of
land Lot No. 16 in 7th Dist. Henry Co. drawn by me. Signed: WILLIAM
DREW. Wit: WILLIAM HOWARD, JOHN LODGE, J.P. Rec. 26 April 1824.

Page 457: Deed dated 20 March 1822, bet. WILLIAM DREW of Burk Co. and
PARKER KNOWLES of Jasper Co...consid. of $155...conveys tract Lot No. 16
in 7th Dist. Henry Co. Signed: WILLIAM DREW by his Attorney PARKER (X)
KNOWLES. Wit: RODRICK HARPER, JAMES KIMBROUGH, J.P. Rec. April 27,
1824.

Page 458: Deed headed Morgan Co., dated 22 Jan. 1824 bet. GEORGE L.
BIRD of Co. afsd. and VASHTI BOYKIN of Henry Co., consid. of $400, conveys
tract in 8th Dist. Henry Co., Lot No. 201 cont. 202 1/2 acres. Signed:
GEORGE L. BIRD. Wit: JOEL S. BIRD, JAMES REPLEY, J.P. Rec. April 28,
1824.

Page 458: Deed headed Walton Co., dated 1 May 1824 bet. HAWKINS
HOWARD of one part and DAVID WRIGHT of Co. afsd...consid. of $100..
conveys tract in Henry Co. cont. 202 1/2 acres, Lot No. 90 in 7th Dist.
Signed: HAWKINS HOWARD. Wit: JOHN M. GILES, ANDREW BROWN, J.P. Rec.
5 May 1824.

Page 459: Deed headed State of Georgia, dated 3 May 1824 bet. DAVID
WRIGHT and JEREMIAH DOSS of one part and WILLIAM L. CRAYTON of other...
consid. of $200...conveys tract, Lot No. 90 in 7th Dist. Henry Co., cont.

202 1/2 acres, surveyed by WILLIAM LITTLE and drawn by HAWKINS HOWARD
on 19 April 1824. Signed: DAVID WRIGHT, JEREMIAH DOSS. Wit: WILLIAM
TUGGLE, JAMES KIMBROUGH, J.P. Rec. 5 May 1824.

Page 460: Deed headed Baldwin Co., dated 25 Nov. 1823, bet. SHERARD
SHEFFIELD Attorney for BRIANT SHEFFIELD of Wayne Co. and DAVID WRIGHT of
Walton Co...consid. of $200...conveys tract in 1st. Dist. Henry Co., Lot
No. 244...cont. 202 1/2 acres. Signed: SHERARD HSEFFIELD for BRIANT
SHEFFIELD. Wit: ISHAM SHEFFIELD, HUGH BROWN, J.I.C. Rec. May 7, 1824.

Page 461: Deed dated 8 Jan. 1823 bet. THOMAS HUDSON of Newton Co.
and JESSE KELLY and of Henry Co...consid of $400...conveys tract in 2nd
Dist. Henry Co., Lot No. 30 on waters of Towaliga, cont. 202 1/2 acres.
Signed: THOMAS HUDSON. Wit: GEORGE THOMPSON, J.P., MATTHEW OLEMPA,
WILLIAM SIMMONS, CHARLES OLIVER. Rec. May 8, 1824.

Page 461: Deed headed Chatham Co., dated 23 March 1824 bet. WILLIAM
WILLIAMS of afsd. Co. and JOHN ADAMS of same place...consid. of $130...
conveys tract in Henry Co. cont. 202 1/2 acres. Lot No. 241 in 2nd Dist.
Signed: WILLIAM WILLIAMS. Wit: WM. MORRELL, Clk. S.C.C.C., JACOB
CHATBOURN, J.P. Rec. May 10, 1824.

Page 462: Deed headed Monroe Co., dated 7 April 1824 bet. WILLIS P.
BAKER of Wilkinson Co. and JOHN ADAMS of City of Savannah...consid. of
$200...conveys tract in 12th Dist. Henry Co., Lot No. 199. Signed:
WILLIS P. BAKER. Wit: A. N. CLOPTON, ANDERSON BALDWIN, J.P. Rec. May
10, 1824.

Page 463: Deed headed Burk Co., dated 8 April 1824 bet. SEABORN
THOMPSON of Co. afsd. and JOHN ADAMS of City of Savannah...consid. of $200
conveys tract in 1st. Dist. Henry Co., cont. 202 1/2 acres, hot No. 67.
Signed: SEABORN (X) THOMPSON. Wit: JOHN BRIGHAM, JOEL RACKLY, JOHN S.
ROYAL, J.P. Rec. May 10, 1824.

Page 464: Deed headed Appling Co., dated 25 Dec. 1821 bet. SAMUEL
LUNSFORD of Co. afsd. and HENRY HOGAN of same place...consid of $100...
conveys tract in 3rd Dist. Henry Co., Lot No. 110 cont. 202 1/2 acres.
Signed: SAMUEL (X) LUNSFORD. Wit: ZACHARIAH DAVIS, BALDY BRITT. Rec.
May 12, 1824.

Page 465: Deed headed Henry Co., dated 28 April 1824 bet. JENNINGS
HULSIE of one part and JOHN HAMBRICK both of state above written...consid.
of $140...conveys tract in 11th Dist. Henry Co., Lot No. 158, cont. 202 1/2
acres. Signed: JENNINGS (X) HULSIE. Wit: JOHN T. BENTLY, JOHN TREAD-
WELL, J.P. Rec. May 12, 1824.

Page 465: Sheriff's Deed headed Henry Co., on writ from Justices
Court of Henry Co. in suit of THOMAS HUDSON and JOHN NESBITT agst. ELIJAH
WILSON, WILLIAM HOWARD, JESSE JOHNSON, Sheriff sold land of sd. WILLIAM
HOWARD on May 4, 1824...Deed dated May 4, 1824 for consid. of $75...tract
sold at highest bidder to JOHN SELLERS in 8th Dist. Henry Co., Lot No.
135 cont. 202 1/2 acres. Signed: JESSE JOHNSON. Wit: WILLIAM TUGGLE,
JAMES SELLERS, J.P. Rec. 13 May 1824.

Page 467: Deed headed Henry Co., dated 13 May 1824 bet. WILLIAM
TERRY of Gwinnett Co. and SMITH BONNER of Henry Co...consid. of $800...
conveys tract in 11th Dist. Henry Co., Lot No. 18. Signed: WM. TERRY.
Wit: WILLIAM GRAY, WILLIAM MCCONNELL, J.P. Rec. May 13, 1824.

Page 467: Deed headed Bibb Co., dated 9 March 1824 bet. LEWIS
WIMBERLY, JUNR. of Bibb Co. and ADAM SAFFOLD of Morgan Co...consid of
$200...conveys tract in 1st. Dist. Henry Co., Lot No. 43 cont. 202 1/2
acres. Signed: LEWIS WIMBERLY, JUNR. Wit: SAMUEL LAUTHEN, ELI S.
SHORTER, J.I.C. Rec. May 14, 1824.

Page 468: Sheriff's Deed headed Henry Co., on order from Superior
Ct. of Baldwin Co. in suit of JOSIAH NEWTON agst. PETER B. STOUGHTEN-
BOROUGH, JESSE JOHNSON, Sheriff sold land of sd. STOUTENBOURGH on 4 May
1824 to SEABORN JONES for $130...Deed dated 15 May 1824 for tract in 1st.
Dist. Henry Co., Lot No. 216. Signed: JESSE JOHNSON. Wit: THO. C.

BENNING, SAML. JOHNSON, J.P. Rec. 18 May 1824.

Page 469: Deed headed Georgia, dated 31 Dec. 1823, bet. JAMES HARK-
NESS of Henry Co. and WILLIAM BUTRILL of Jasper Co...consid. of $1200...
conveys tract in 1st. Dist. Henry Co. Lot No. 106 cont. 202 1/2 acres.
Signed: JAMES HARKNESS. Wit: WM. BAKER, JESSE LOYALL, J.P. Rec. 18
May 1824.

Page 470: Dower headed Henry Co., dated 27 Feb. 1824 by ROSANNAH
HARKNESS wife of within named JAMES HARKNESS before WOODY DOZIER, J.I.C.
and Rec. 18 May 1824.

Page 471: Deed headed Georgia, dated 31 Dec. 1823 bet. JAMES HARKNESS
of Henry Co. and WILLIAM BUTTEWILL of Jasper Co...consid. of $1200...
conveys tract in 1st. Dist. Henry Co. Lot No. 119, drawn by CHARLES P.
COLLIER of Capt. NEWTON'S Dist. Jasper Co. cont. 202 1/2 acres. Signed:
JAMES HARKNESS. Wit: WM. BAKER, JESSE LOYALL, J.P. Rec. May 19, 1824.
ROSANNAH HARKNESS wife of JAMES rel. dower on 27 Feb. 1824 bef. WOODY
DOZIER, J.I.C. and Rec. May 19, 1824.

Page 472: Deed headed Georgia, dated 6 Jan. 1824 bet. JOHN T. BOYKIN
admnr. of WM. P. BOYKIN, dec'd. of Jasper Co. and DREWRY ROGERS of Henry
Co...consid. of $500... conveys tract in 2nd Dist. Henry Co., Lot No. 15
cont. 202 1/2 acres, drawn by WM. P. BOYKIN of Capt. THOMAS'S Dist. Jasper
Co. Signed: JOHN T. BOYKIN. Wit: JNO MARTIN, JOHN HILL, J.P. Rec. May
19, 1824.

Page 473: Deed headed Henry Co., dated 15 Aug. 1823 bet. CHARLES
HULSIE of Henry Co. and ALANCEN MOSELY of Co. afsd. .consid of $75...con-
veys tract cont. 20 acres in 8th Dist. Henry Co., part of Lot No. 221.
Signed: CHARLES HULSEY. Wit: THOMAS BENTON Rec. 20 May 1824.

Page 473: Sheriff's deed headed Henry Co., on order from Justices
Court of Newton Co. in suit of JAMES BYARS agst. JOHN F. HOWARD, JESSE
JOHNSON, Sheriff sold property of JOHN F. HOWARD on 4 May 1824 to JOHN
YOUNG of Jackson Co. for #3.00. Deed dated 13 May 1824 for tract in Henry
Co., Lot No. 86 in 3rd Dist. Signed: JESSE JOHNSON. Wit: D. YOUNG,
ABSALOM STEWARD, J.I.C. Rec. 20 May 1824.

Page 475: Deed headed Henry Co., dated 11 Feb. 1824 bet. ELIJAH
M. CHAPMAN of Monroe Co. and MICAJAH BROOKS of other part...consid. of
$500...conveys tract in 3rd Dist. Henry Co., Lot No. 122. cont. 202 1/2
acres, drawn by CASEN MOORE and gtd. on 2 Feb. 1824. Signed: ELIJAH M.
CHAPMAN. Wit: ROBERT CROSS, LEVI MARTIN. Rec. 20 May 1824.

Page 476: Deed headed Henry Co., dated 7 Feb. 1823 bet. BENJAMIN
GEORGE of Henry Co. and ALANSON MOSELY (MOSSLY?)...consid. of $275...
conveys tract cont. 80 acres (along HULSIE'S Line) in 8th Dist. Henry Co.,
Lot No. 221. Signed: BENJAMIN (X) GEORGE. Wit: THOMAS BENTON, JOSEPH
BENTON, J.P. Rec. 20 May 1824.

Page 477: Deed headed Putnam Co., dated 18 Feb. 1824 bet. JOHN
MORELAND of Co. afsd and JAMES WEBB of State of S. C. of other...consid.
of $350...conveys tract in 1st Dist. Henry Co., Lot No. 240, cont. 202½
acres. Signed: JOHN MORELAND. Wit: ISHAM SHIRLING, WM. A. SLAUGHTER,
J.P. Rec. May 20, 1824.

Page 477: Deed headed Henry Co., dated 18 June 1823 bet. JOHN E.
GLOVER of one part and JAMES PHILIPS of other...consid. of $200...conveys
tract cont. 202½ acres. Lot No. 119 in 12th Dist. Henry Co. lying on
waters of Cotton Indian. Signed: JOHN E. GLOVER. Wit: WILLIAM PARKS,
S. MALONE, J.P. Rec. 22 May 1824.

Page 478: Deed headed Henry Co., dated 14 Feb. 1824 bet. HENRY
WILLIAMS of Henry Co. and JOHN ROGERS of Henry Co...consid of $400...
conveys tract in 2nd Dist. Henry Co. Lot No. 16 (...to corner of ISRAEL
PARKERS land...head of WILLIAM SALLY'S spring branch. Signed: HENRY J.

WILLIAMS. Wit: WILLIAM SALLEY, DRURY (X) ROGERS, HENRY J. WILLIAMS, J.P. Rec. May 25, 1824.

Page 479: Deed headed Henry Co., dated 17 May 1824 bet. WILLIAM HARDIN of Henry Co. and THOMAS C. RUSSELL of Co. afsd. consid. of $725... conveys tract in 7th Dist. Henry Co., Lot No. 124 cont. 165 acres, gtd. to WILLIAM MUNDER of O'NEAL'S Dist., Wayne Co. Signed: WILLIAM HARDIN. Wit: JACOB MADDUX, JAMES KIMBROUGH, J.P. Rec. May 25, 1824. NANCY HARDIN wife of within named WILLIAM HARDIN rel. dower on 17 May 1824 bef. JAMES KIMBROUGH, J.P. and Rec. 25 May 1824.

Page 480: Deed headed Jones Co., dated 7 Feb. 1824 bet. CASON MOORE of Washington Co. and ELIJAH M. CHAPMAN of Monroe Co...consid. of $300... conveys tract in Henry Co., Lot No. 122 in 3rd Dist. cont. 202 1/2 acres. Signed: CASON (X) MOORE. Wit: JOHN SIMMONS, STEPHEN RENFROE, J.P. Recq 26 May 1824.

Page 481: Bill of Sale August 5, 1818, Bargained sold and delivered to JOSEPH MCCONNELL one negro woman named Peggy and her two children Easter and Sam which negroes I warrant and defend from all persons for sum of $1300. Signed: THOMAS RAMSEY. Wit: ROBERT W. RUSSELL. Rec. May 26, 1824.

Page 482: Deed headed Henry Co, dated 30 April 1823 bet. SOLOMON WALDROUP of Jasper Co. and JOSEPH MCCONNELL of Henry Co...consid. of $700 conveys tract in 12th Dist. Henry Co., Lot No. 31, drawn by sd. WALDROUP. Signed: SOLOMON WALDROUP. Wit: WILLIAM (X) COUCH. THOS. HURSTON, J.P. Rec. May 26, 1824.

Page 482: Sheriff's Deed headed Henry Co., on writ from Justices Court of Pulaski Co. in suit of JOHN N. DAVIS agst. JOHN PRESTCOAT, JESSE JOHNSON, Sheriff sold property of sd. PRESTCOAT on 3 Feb. 1824 to ABEL L. ROBERTSON for $50...Deed dated 20 May 1824 for tract in 2nd Dist. Henry Co. Lot No. 236. Signed: JESSE JOHNSON. Wit: WM. GRAY, JAMES KIMBROUGH, J.P. Rec. May 26, 1824.

Page 483: Power of Attorney headed Georgia from WILLIAM B. MORGAN of Appling Co. to JOHN M. GLOVER of Wayne Co. to sell tract in Henry Co., Lot No. 101, drawn to WILLIAM B. MORGAN. Signed: WILLIAM B. MORGAN. Wit: BRYANT LANE, JOHN WIGGINS. Rec. May 27, 1824.

Page 484: Deed headed Henry Co., dated 8 March 1824 bet. WILLIAM B. MORGAN of Appling Co. and THOMAS B. BURFORD of Co. afsd...consid of $100...conveys tract in 1st. Dist. Henry Co. cont. 202½ acres, Lot No. 101 surveyed by GABRIEL JONES on 20 Sept. 1821. Signed: WILLIAM B. MORGAN Wit: BENJAMIN F. TUCKER, GIDEON MATHES, MOSES COX, J.P. Rec. 28 May 1824.

Page 485: Deed headed Putnam Co., dated 23 Sept. 1822 bet. SALAWAY MCCALL of Irwin Co. and ISAAC BRIANT of Putnam Co...consid of $200... conveys tract in 9th. Dist. Henry Co., Lot No. 75, cont. 202½ acres. Signed: SALAWAY MCCALL. Wit: S. B. PECKE, J.P. Rec. 28, May 1824.

Page 485: Deed headed Clark Co., dated 1 Sept. 1823 bet. DANIEL CRAFT Junior of sd. Co. and HENRY N. POPE of Henry Co...consid. of $500...conveys tract in 11th Dist. Henry Co, Lot No. 34, whereon sd. POPE now lives cont. 202½ acres. Signed: DANIEL CRAFT. Wit: ALLEN STOKES, JOHN HAMILTON, J.P. Rec. 1 June 1824.

Page 486: Deed headed Henry Co., Dated 3 Sept. 1823 bet. JOSEPH BAYS of Co. afsd. and NATHANIEL BAYS of Henry Co...consid. of $300... conveys tract known by Lot No. 1 in 7th Dist. Henry Co. on waters of Cotton Indian cont. 202½ acres. Signed: JOSEPH (X) BAYS. Wit: AMBROSIS EDWARDS, HERRATIO A. B. NUNNELLY, J.P. Rec. June 1, 1824.

Page 487: Deed headed Henry Co., dated 31 Oct. 1823 bet. NATHANIEL BAYS of Henry Co. and ROWAN MCKEE of sd. Co...consid. of $425...conveys tract in Henry Co. cont. 202½ acres in 7th Dist. Lot No. 1. Signed: NATHANIEL (X) BAYS. Wit: LOVET HINTON, J.I.C. Rec. June 1, 1824. JACOB HINTON, J.I.C.

Page 487: Deed headed Henry Co., dated 25 Feb. 1824 bet. SAMUEL NUTT SENR. to SAMUEL R. NUTT for consid. of $200...conveys half of Lot No. 136 in 1st Dist. Henry Co., adj. JOHN MCMICHAEL. Signed: SAMUEL NUTT. Wit: WM. MCCORKLE, WM. B. NUTT. Rec. June 14, 1824.

Page 488: Deed dated 30 Aug. 1823 bet. JOEL STANSILL of Henry Co. and DEMPSEY JOHNSON of same...consid. of $455...conveys tract in 11th Dist. Lot No. 1 Henry Co. on waters of Cotton River, cont. 202½ acres, orig. gtd. to GEORGE LITTLE of Twiggs Co. Signed: JOEL STANSILL. Wit: ALLEN GAY, JAMES HENRY, J.P. Rec. 14 June 1824.

Page 489: Deed dated 3 Jan. 1825 bet. CULLIN HARP of Henry Co. and JAMES LILE of Morgan Co...consid of $700...conveys tract in 1st Dist. Henry Co., Lot No. 179 on waters of Malcoms Creek joining DAVID COX and JESSE CLAY. Signed: CULLIN (X) HARP. Wit: SAMUEL (X) PRICE, NANCY PRICE, JOHN HARDMAN. Rec. Nov. 10, 1825.

Page 490: Deed headed Henry Co., dated 9 March 1825 bet. JAMES MORRIS of Monroe Co. and ANDREW M. BROWN of Co. afsd...consid. of $112... conveys tract in 7th Dist. Henry Co., Lot No. 60. Signed: JAMES (D) MORRIS. Wit: NATHAN (X) JARVIS, E. G. BROWN, J.P. Rec. 7 March 1826... OLIVE MORRIS wife of within named JAMES MORRIS rel. dower March 9, 1825 bef. E. G. BROWN, J.P. and Rec. 7 March 1826.

Page 491: Deed headed Henry Co., dated 26 April 1824 bet. JOHN WOOD of Co. afsd. and ANDREW M. BROWN of same...consid. of $100...conveys one lot in 7th Dist. Henry Co. and part of Lot No. 134 on east side of street leading from town of McDonough to Pike Court House...to the beginning corner being the 1to where on JOHN HUTCHISON now lives. Signed: JOHN WOOD. Wit: TANDY W. KEY, JAMES KIMBROUGH, J.P. Rec. March 7, 1826.

Page 492: Relinquishment of Dower, headed Richmond Co. dated May 19, 1822, ANN PRICHARD wife of within named JOHN W. PRICHARD rel. dower in land to JOHN L. ANDERSON before R. BUSH, J.P. Rec. July 26, 1823.

Page 493: Power of Attorney, headed Newton Co. from ROBERT WOODS of Co. afsd. to JOHN GILMORE as lawful att. to make title to one half cert. tract in 2nd Dist. Henry Co., Lot No. 65. Signed: ROBERT WOODS. Dated 17 March 1823. Wit: JAS. MOORE, J.P. Rec. July 26, 1823.

Page 493: Territory of Florida, Leon County, Affidavit to Prove Deed Recorded Page 427 issued bet. JOHN ROE and EZEKIEL REGISTER, Personally appeared bef. me TOM PETER CHAIRES who being duly sworn deposeth and sayeth that he saw JOHN ROE sign, seal and delivery to written deed for purposes therein mentioned and he subscribed to same as a Wit. Dated Feb. 18, 1828 bef. JAMES WILLIAMS, J.P. Signed: TOM PETER CHAIRES. Rec. March 8, 1828.

Page 494: Power of Attorney, headed Tatnall County, from ALAN JOHNSON as Guardian of MARY S. E. LAMBERSOZ...appt's JAMES SELLERS of the Co. afsd. my true and lawful att. and demand and receive from JOHN T. BENTLY of Henry Co., such sums of money is due me a Gdn...in relation to a cert. tract of land Lot No. 149 in 11th Dist. Henry Co. at time of survey, now in Newton Co. Signed: A. JOHNSON. Wit: P. F. SAPP, WM. M. TIPPINS, J.P. JAMES PERRY Clerk of Sup. Co. swears that WILLIAM TIPPINS is an acting J.P. and dated 13 Feb. 1827. Rec. March 17, 1828.

Page 495: Deed headed Henry Co., Ga., dated 4 June 1827, bet. GARRY GRICE, JAMES (IDLEY?), WAID H. TURNER, THOS. C. RUSSELL and JOSEPH P. GREEN, Esq's Justices of Inf. Ct. for Co. afsd. and AMASA SPENCER of town of McDonough...consid. of $150...conveys town Lot No. 1 in Square B. cont. 125 feet of space, also half of lot known in plan of town as Lot No. 3 of the acre lots cont. 2 roads and 9 poles. Signed: GARRY GRICE, THOS. C. RUSSELL, JAMES SELLERS, WAIDE H. TURNER, JOSEPH P. GREEN. Wit: WILLIAM HARDIN, JOHN WOOD, J.P. Rec. March 20, 1828.

Page 496: Deed headed Henry Co. dated 2 Oct. 1826, bet. (above named persons in Page 495 to AMASA SPENCER) for $100...for a town lot on North

Fayette St. and known as Lot No. 14 of the acre lots cont. one acre more or less. wigned as in Deed Page 495. Wit: SANDFORD D. JOHNSON, J. G. BARNET, J.P. Rec. March 20, 1828.

Page 496: Deed headed Henry Co., dated 11 Feb. 1828, bet. (above named Justices of pages 495 and 496) and AMASA SPENCER...for town lot in city of MacDonough...consid. of $60...one town lot No. 13 of the acre lots bounded on west by THOMAS CHAPILLS land and by RUSSELLS town lot and by West Street and North Street. Signed as bef. Wit: SANFORD D. JOHNSON, J. G. BARNET, J.P. Rec. March 20, 1828.

Page 497: Deed headed Hancock Co., dated 20 Dec. 1827, bet. WM. J. TURNER of Henry Co. and SUSANNAH ANDERS of Co. afsd...consid. of two promissory notes and promises to pay $108 on or before 25 Dec. 1828 and also $116 on or bef. 25 Dec. 1829...conveys to SUSANNAH ANDERS tract in 8th Dist. Henry Co. cont. 202 1/2 acres, Lot No. 111. Signed: WILLIAM T. TURNER. Wit: DAVID KENDALL, BUTT L. CATO, J.P. Rec. March 21, 1828.

Page 498: Deed dated 16 April 1828, bet. ANDREW M. BROWN of Henry Co. and AMASA SPENCER of same...consid. of $40...conveys tract in Henry Co... Lot No. 156 in 7th Dist. lying on east side of sd. lot, bounded by: TURNER HUNTS land, THOS. C. BENNINGS land, SOLOMON WARLICKS land and ANDREW MCBRIDES land cont. 11 acres. Signed: ANDREW M. BROWN. Wit: JONATHAN M. PECK, THOS. D. JOHNSON, J.P. Rec. April 16, 1828.

Page 499: Deed headed Henry Co., dated 18 March 1828, bet. JOHN DAILEY of sd. Co. and SILAS BARREN...consid. of $140...sd. BARREN conveys to JOHN DAILEY tract in Henry Co. 3rd Dist., Lot No. 176 cont. 101½ acres. Signed: SILLAS BARRAN. Wit: DAVID DAILEY, THOS. D. JOHNSON, J.P. Rec. 21 April 1828.

Page 500: Mortgage headed Henry Co., dated 25 Feb. 1828, bet. JAMES FIELDS of Co. afsd. and JOHN DAILEY of same...consid. of $99...conveys tract in 6th Dist. Henry Co., Lot No 172 cont. 50 acres...following condition that JOHN DAILEY holds notes of sd. fields to amount of $99 in four notes the afsd. sum of money will be due 25 Dec. 1828 to secure payment for which this deed is intended to operate as a Mortgage. Signed: JAMES FIELDS, Wit: DAVID DAILEY, G. GRICE, J.I.C. Rec. 21 April 1828.

Page 500: Deed headed Henry Co., dated 5 Feb. 1828, bet. WILLIAM H. RAIFORD of Co. afsd. and JOHN DAILEY of afsd. Co...consid. of $71...conveys tract in 2nd Dist. Henry Co., Lot No. 204...said sum due 25 Dec. 1828. Signed: WILLIAM H. RAIFORD. Wit: A. BROOKS, G. GRICE, J.I.C. Rec. 21 April 1828.

Page 501: Deed headed Henry Co., dated 19 April 1828 bet. ALEXANDER BRYAN of Henry Co. and SAMUEL C. ROBINSON of Henry Co...consid of $500... conveys tract in 12th Dist. Henry Co., Lot No.147 cont. 202½ acres. Signed: ALEXANDER BRYAN. Wit: SAMPSON GRAY, THOS. D. JOHNSON, J.P. Rec. 21 April 1828.

Page 502: Deed dated 19 March 1828 bet. DANIEL NELSON and wife CATHERINE of City of Savannah and ALEXANDER BRYAN of Henry Co...consid. of $37...conveys tract in 12th Dist. Henry Co. Lot No. 147 drawn by DANIEL NELSON in 1821. Signed: DAVID NELSON, CATHERINE (X) NELSON. Wit: THOS. P__, JACOB C. HADBOUREN, Not. Pub. CATHERINE NELSON Rel. dower bef. JACOB CHADBOURN, N.P. Chatham Co. on 19 March 1828. Rec. 21 April 1828.

Page 504: Deed headed Henry Co., dated Feb. 1, 1828 bet. JEFFERSON MCCOY of Co. afsd. and JAMES M. BRYAN of same...consid. of $144. 87 on or bef. 25 Dec. next...conveys a negro girl Edneah about two years old. Signed: JEFFERSON MCCOY. Wit: THOS. S. WESTBROOK, ISAIAH HAND, JOHN C. HAND, J.P. Rec. 22 April 1828.

Page 505: Deed headed Henry Co., dated 11 Nov. 1826 bet. TANDY W. KEY of Henry Co. and JAMES BROWN of Jasper Co...consid. of $100...conveys tract in 2nd Dist. Henry Co., Lot No. 231, cont. 202 1/2 acres. Signed: TANDY W. KEY. Wit: JAMES KIMBROUGH, THOMAS D. JOHNSON, J.P.

Page 505-506: Sheriff's Deed headed Henry Co., on writ from 41st
Dist. Ct. of Tatnall Co. in suit of JOSEPH UNDERHILL agst. JAMES LARYMORE
and LEWIS GREEN, AARON BROOKS Sheriff of Henry Co. sold property No. 204
in 2nd Dist. Henry Co. cont. 202 1/2 acres of sd. LARYMORE...on 3rd July
1827 to THOMAS C. BENNING for $67...Deed dated 1 Jan. 1828 for tract.
Signed: A. BROOKS. Wit: THOS. PAT__, JAMES KIMBROUGH, J.P. Rec. 25
April 1828.

Page 506: Deed headed Henry Co., dated 2 Feb. 1828 bet. JAMES BROWN
of Co. afsd. and AARON CLOUD of same...consid. of $150...conveys tract in
2nd Dist. Henry Co., Lot No. 231. cont. 202½ acres. Signed: JAMES BROWN.
Wit: JAMES A. EDWARDS, THOMAS D. JOHNSON, J.P. Rec. 25 April 1828.

Page 507: Deed headed Henry Co., dated 18 April 1828 bet. WILLIAM
JUSTER and SARAH JUSTER his wife of BURGESS JUSTER and MARY JUSTER his
wife...the sd. SARAH JESTRO and MARY JESTER the orphans of JOHN HAY, dec'd.
of the one part and WILLIAM GRAHAM of the other part all of Henry Co...sd.
WILLIAM JESTER and SARAH JESTER his wife and BURGESS JESTER and MARY JESTER
his wife for consid. of $800...conveys tract in 7th Dist. Henry Co. on
waters of Walnut Cr-ek (land of HENRY HAYNES, WILLIAM JESTER ment.) cont.
150 acres, it being part of Lot No. 49 in 7th Dist. Henry Co. and was
drawn by afsd. SARAH JESTER and MARY JESTER orphans of JOHN HAY dec'd. and
gtd. 6 Nov. 1826. Signed: WILLIAM JESTER, SARAH (X) JESTER, BURGESS (X)
JESTER, MARY (X) JESTER. Wit: W. A. COPELAND, JAMES SELLERS, JIC,
SARAH and MARY Rel. Dower on 19 April 1828 bef. JAMES SELLERS, J.I.C.
Rec. 26 April 1828.

Page 508: Deed headed DeKalb Co., dated 14 Feb. 1828, bet. JOHN
KIRKPATRICK of Henry Co. and JAMES KIRKPATRICK of Decalb Co...consid. of
$5.00...for better securing payment of 3 promissory notes given by sd.
JOHN to sd. JAMES KIRKPATRICK...one note being for $400 bearing date 28
July 1824 and due 25 Dec. 1825...etc. conveys to sd. JAMES KIRKPATRICK
160 sides of leather in various stages of turning, 35 rawhides, currying
utencils...two cows and calves, one cow and yearling, 2 heifers and calf,
steer etc. 2 beds and furn. 2 tables chests, trunk, chairs,...rent due me
from CHARLES JORDAN for a field on JAMES KITCHENS lot of land, hogs, a
75 gallon still...etc...etc... Signed: JOHN KIRKPATRICK. Wit: G. B.
BUTLER, WILLIAM EZZARD. Rec. 29 April 1828.

Page 510: Deed headed Henry Co., dated 12 Oct. 1827. bet. CULLEN
HARPE of one part and ROBERT M. SIMMS of other...consid. of $150...conveys
tract cont. 101½ acres, being half of Lot No. 164 in 6th Dist. Henry Co.
Signed: CULLEN (H) HARP. Wit: JOHN ROLLANS, JOEL C. TOMME, ROWLAND
BROWN. Rec. 3 May 1828.

Page 511: Deed headed Bibb Co., dated 19 Nov. 1827 bet. RICHARD
SIMMONS of Co. afsd. and ROBERT W. HUNTER of Butts Co...consid. of $200...
conveys tract in 2nd Dist. Henry Co. Lot No. 237, cont. 202½ acres.
Signed: RICHD. SIMMONS. Wit: ABNER HAMMOND, DANIEL MATHISON, J.P.
Rec. 5 May 1828.

Page 511: Deed headed Jones Co., dated 18 Dec. 1822 bet. JAMES
SIMMONS of Co. afsd. and RICHARD SIMMONS of same...consid. of $450...
conveys tract Lot No. 237 in 2nd Dist. Henry Co., cont. 202½ acres.
Signed: JAMES (+) SIMMONS. Wit: ORRAY TECKNOR, ISAAC TECKNOR. Rec.
May 5, 1828.

Page 512: Deed headed Georgia, dated 24 July 1827, bet. DANIEL
HATCHERof Chatham Co. and JOHN HATCHER of same...consid. of $150...conveys
tract in 3rd Dist. Henry Co. Lot No. 177, cont. 202½ acres, drawn by
sd. DANIEL HATCHER. Signed: DANIEL HATCHER. Wit: LEVI S. D. LYON,
J. DESMATTA, JUNR.

Page 514: Sheriff's Deed headed Henry Co., on order from Justices
Ct. of Wilkinson Co. in suit of SAMUEL ROBINSON agst. DAVID ROBERTS, JESSE
JOHNSON, Sheriff of Henry Co. seized lot of land No. 161 in 7th Dist.
Henry Co. cont. 202½ acres and sold same on 4 March 1828 to ALEXANDER

BRYAN for $50...Deed dated 4 March 1828. Signed: JESSE JOHNSON. Wit: JOHN R. BAYS, THOMAS D. JOHNSON, J.P. Rec. May 7, 1828.

Page 515: Deed headed State of Ga., dated 4 July 1827 bet. JOHN HATCHER of Chatham Co. and ALEXANDER BRYAN of Henry Co...consid. of $150 conveys tract in 3rd Dist. Henry Co. Lot No. 177, cont. 202½ acres, drawn by DANIEL HATCHER. Signed: JOHN HATCHER. Wit: J. D. LAMATTA, JUNR., LEVI S. D. LYON. Rec. 7 May 1828.

Page 516: Deed headed Henry Co., dated 21 Feb. 1828 bet. MOSES BROOKS of Co. afsd. and AARON BROOKS of same...consid. of $800...conveys tract in 3rd Dist. Henry Co. Lot No. 247.. Signed: MOSES BROOKS. Wit: E. B. STRICKLAND, G. GRICE, J.I.C. Rec. 13 May 1828.

Page 517: Deed headed Burk Co., dated 28 December 1821, bet. VINSON BARFIELD of Co. and state afsd. and NATHAN VICKERS of same...consid $100.00 conveys tract sit. in Henry Co. and 3rd Dist., cont. 202 1/2 acres, Lot No. 168 North by Lot No. 186 East by Lot No. 166, South by Lot No. 154. Signed: VINSON BARFIELD. Wit: JOAB ROWELL, J. L. SCARBROUGH. Sworn to in Burke County, Ga. 20 July 1822, HENRY B. JAMES J.P. Rec. 13 May 1828.

Page 518: Deed headed Pulaski Co., dated 27 June 1827, bet. NATHAN VICKERS of Co. afsd. for sum of $200 paid, does convey to JAMES M. VICKERS, tract in 3rd Dist. Henry Co., Lot No. 167 cont. 202½ acres. Signed: NATHAN VICKERS. Wit: WILLIAM B. DARLING, W. B. (MSCHER.) J.P. Rec. 13 May 1828.

Page 519: Deed headed Henry Co., dated 16 Jan. 1827, bet. HENRY WAITE of Co. afsd. and AARON BROOKS of other...consid. of $200 paid...conveys tract in 2nd Dist. Henry Co., Lot No. 180 on Waters of Indian Creek, cont. 50 acres...being southest corner of said Lot. Signed: HENRY WAITS. Wit: MOSES ROSSER, HENRY COKER, JOSHUA (X) HORN. Rec. 14 May 1828.

Page 519: Deed headed Henry Co., dated 7 April 1828 bet. THOMAS BROOKS of Henry Co. and AARON BROOKS of same...consid. of $200 paid... conveys tract lying northeast of the Towelagga, known by No. 248 in 3rd Dist. Henry Co., adj. to Lot No. 247. Signed: THOMAS BROOKS. Wit: JOSEPH SMITH, DANIEL SMITH (J.P.?) Rec. 14 May 1828.

Page 520: Promissory Note headed Henry Co., dated 9 April 1828 bet. WILLIAM J. TARVIN of Marion Co. and State of Tennessee of one part and GEORGE BROWN of Cheshew and State of New Hampshire...sd. WILLIAM J. TARVIN hath made a del. to GEORGE BROWN a Promissory Note...and promises to pay $314.00 and 75 cents by the 1st. of March next ensuing...said WILLIAM J. TARVIN hath sold to GEORGE BROWN a lot of land in Henry Co., 1st. Dist. Lot No. 225 cont. 200 acres. Signed: WILLIAM J. TARVIN. Wit: HENRY LAWLESS, WILLIAM BOYNTON, WILLIAM BOYNTON of Twiggs Co., Ga. made oath that he saw HENRY LOYLESS assign the same as subscribing witness, 12 April 1828. Rec. 14 May 1828.

Page 521: Deed headed DeKalb Co., dated 29 Sept. 1827 bet. JOSIAH MELTON of Co. and State afsd. and ELBERT AWTRY of other...consid. of $300 paid conveys tract in Henry Co. in 12th Dist. No. 187. Signed: JOSIAH T. MELTON. Wit: ISAAC AWTRY, ELDRIDGE AWTRY. Rec. 16 May 1828.

Page 522: Deed headed Putnam Co., dated 5 March 1828 bet. WILLIAM H. KIMBROUGH and WILLIAM C. THOMAS of same...consid. $750...conveys tract in 12th Dist. Henry Co., Lot No. 16, cont. 202 1/2 acres...also one other tract in 5th Dist. Troup Co. known by No. 7...also one other tract in 6th Dist. Henry Co. cont. 202 1/2 acres, Lot No. 179. Signed: WILLIAM H. KIMBROUGH. Wit: W. WILSON, ALFORD CLOPTON, J.I.C. Rec. 16 May 1828.

Page 523: Deed headed Henry Co., dated 15 March 1828 bet. JOHN LOVE-JOY SENR. and BARNWELL MOBLEY of other part...consid of $450...conveys tract cont. 101 1/4 acres, it being the 1/2 of Lot No. 102 and the East of said lot adj. 101 in 12th Dist. Henry Co. Signed: JOHN LOVEJOY. Wit: WILLIAM WOODARD, WILLIAM MCCONNELL, J.P. Rec. 16 May 1828.

Page 524: Deed headed Jasper Co., dated 21 Jan. 1827 bet. SUSANNAH COLBERT of Co. afsd. and AARON BROOKS of Henry Co...consid. $400...conveys tract, Lot No. 146 in 2nd Dist. Henry Co. drawn by SUSANNAH COLBERT cont. 202 1/2 acres. Signed: SUSANNAH (X) COLBERT. Wit: S. J. LAWRENCE, JACOB MCCLENDON, J.P. Rec. 16 May 1828.

Page 524: Deed headed Henry Co., dated 29 April 1828 bet. AARON BROOKS of Co. afsd. and JOSHUA STEPHENS of same...consid. of $600...conveys tract in 2nd Dist. Henry Co., No. 146. Signed: A. BROOKS. Wit: JESSE GRICE, G. GRICE, J.I.C. Rec. 16 May 1828.

Page 525: Deed headed DeKalb Co., dated 11 Feb. 1828, bet. JOHN ADAMS of DeKalb Co. and WILLIAM HARDIN of Henry Co...consid. of $200...conveys tract in Henry Co., No. 161 in the 6th Dist. cont. 202 1/2 acres. Signed: JOHN ADAMS. Wit: J. H. KIRKPATRICK, A. CORDY, J.P. Rec. 17 May 1828.

Page 526: Deed headed Charleston, S. C. dated 4 June 1827 bet. WILLIAM KING formerly of City of Savannah, now of State of S. C. and JOHN BRIGHAM of Co. of Bu(rk?) and State of Ga...consid. of $700...conveys all these tracts, viz: all the tract in formerly Henry now DeKalb Co. cont. 202 1/2 acres, Lot No. 231 and this in the 15th Dist. Henry Co...also tract in Henry Co. Lot No. 93 in 11th Dist. Henry Co. cont. 202 1/2 acres. Signed: WILLIAM KING. Wit: CHARLES HOLMES, J.P., B. A. W. MAYHEW. Witnessed in Charleston Dist., S. C. before CHARLES HOLMES on 4 June 1827 and dated 11 Dec. 1827. Rec. 23, May 1827.

Page 527: Deed headed Pike Co., Ga. dated 22 Oct. 1827 bet. JOHN MILLER of Co. afsd. and JESSE STANLEY of Henry Co...consid. of $200... conveys tract in 6th Dist. Henry Co. Lot 145 cont. 202 1/2 acres. Signed: JOHN MILLER. Wit: R. M. SIMS, THOS. C. RUSSELL, J.I.C. Rec. 26 May 1828.

Page 527: Deed headed Henry Co., dated 28 May 1828 bet. JESSE STANLEY and WILLIAM H. COOPER...consid. of $200...conveys tract, Lot No. 145 in Henry Co. and 6th Dist. cont. 202 1/2 acres. Signed: JESSE STANLEY. Wit: JOHN DAILEY, JUNR., THOS. D. JOHNSON, J.P. Rec. 28 May 1828.

Page 528: Deed headed Henry Co., dated 19 April 1828 bet. JESSE STANLEY and PER(LY?) FORD both of Co. afsd...consid. of $150...conveys tract in 6th Dist. Henry Co., Lot No. 87 cont. 112 3/4 acres (land is further described by chains in various distances, Ed.) Signed: JESSE STANLEY. Wit: JOHN DAILEY, JUNR., THOS. D. JOHNSON, J.P. Rec. 28 May 1828.

Page 529: Deed headed Henry Co., dated 3 Nov. 1827 bet. STEPHEN TREADWELL of sd. Co. and JOHN TREADWELL, JUNR. of same...consid. of $175... conveys tract cont. 202 1/2 acres in 11th Dist. Henry Co. Lot No. 55. Signed: STEPHEN (X) TREADWELL. Wit: STEPHEN TREADWELL, JOHN R. RICHARDS, HENRY N. POPE, J.P. Rec. 29 May 1828.

Page 529: Sheriff's deed from Justices Court of Wilkes To. on suit bet. DAVID ALISON agst. WILLIAM RUTH and HOPKINS RUTH, JESSE JOHNSON, Sheriff did seize lot of land of WILLIAM & HOPKINS RUTH and HENRY J. WILLIAMS was highest bidder. Deed dated 24 May 1828 bet. JESSE JOHNSON Sheriff and HENRY J. WILLIAMS for sum of $50 conveyed tract in 2nd Dist. Henry Co., Lot No. 184 cont. 202 1/2 acres. Signed: JESSE JOHNSON, Sheriff. Wit: J. G. BURWILL, J.P., B. R. CROSBY. Rec. 29 May 1828.

Page 530: Deed headed Jasper Co., dated 2 Jan. 1828 bet. DAVID THOMPSON of Walton Co. and WILLIAM T. HUDMAN of Henry Co...consid. of $300...conveys tract in 6th Dist. Henry Co., No. 88 cont. 202 1/2 acres. Signed: DAVID THOMPSON. Wit: E. A. BRODDUS, JESSEE LOYALL, J.P. Rec. 29 May 1828.

Page 531: Deed headed DeKalb Co., dated 10 Oct. 1827 bet. GILBERT D. GREEN and STEPHEN TREADWELL of Henry Co...consid. of $250...conveys tract cont. 202 1/2 acres in 11th Dist. Henry Co., Lot No. 55. Signed: GILBERT D. GREEN. Wit: ELIAS CAMPBELL, JAMES CAMPBELL, J.P. Rec. 27 May 1828.

Page 532: Deed headed Jones Co., dated 23 July 1827 bet HARDY HERBERT of afsd. Co. and WILLIAM T. HUDMAN...consid. of $250...conveys tract of 202 1/2 acres, No. 87 in 6th Dist. Henry Co. Signed: HARDY HERBERT. Wit: SIMEON L. STEPHENS, THOMAS BROWN. Rec. 29 May 1828.

Page 533: Deed headed Crawford Co., dated 19 Sept. 1823 bet. WILLIAM GRAY of Co. afsd. and WILLIAM HUDMAN of Henry Co...consid. $300...conveys tract in Henry Co. on Walnut Creek cont. 202 1/2 acres, Lot No. 109 in 6th Dist. Henry Co. Signed: WILLIAM GRAY. Wit: JOHN MCALLISTER, JEREMIAH SMITH, J.P. Rec. 30 May 1828.

Page 533: Deed headed Henry Co., dated 3 June 1828, bet. JAMES R. GRAY of Pike Co. and JOHN DAILEY, SENR. of Henry Co...consid. of $500... conveys tract in Henry Co. Lot No. 7 in 11th Dist., cont. 202 1/2 acres. Signed: JAMES R. GRAY. Wit: SAML. JOHNSON, THOS. C. RUSSELL, J.I.C. Rec. 9 June 1828.

Page 534: Sheriff's Deed on Superior Court of Jones Co. in suit of CONSTANCE S. MCKINNEY Admnr. agst. GEORGE KENNEDY, JESSEE JOHNSON, Sheriff seized land described as property of GEORGE KENNEDY and put to public sale and WILLIAM T. HANSELL was highest bidder at $71.00. Deed dated 28 Feb. 1828 for land in 7th Dist. Henry Co., Lot No. 382. Signed: JESSE JOHNSON. Wit: THOMAS C. BINNING, WILLIAM HARDIN, Clk. S. C., H. C. Ga. Rec. 9 June 1828.

Page 535: Deed headed Henry Co., dated 8 May 1828 bet. JOHN SMITH of afsd. Co. and JESSEE JOHNSON of other...consid. of $100...conveys tract in Henry Co. cont. 202 1/2 acres, Lot No. 243 in 6th Dist. Signed: JOHN SMITH. Wit: B. RENOE CROSBY, THOMAS JARROTT, J. G. BARNETT, J.P. Rec. 7 June 1828.

Page 536: Deed headed Henry Co., dated 6 May 1828, bet. ALEXANDER BRYAN of afsd. Co. and JESSEE JOHNSON of same...consid. of $300...conveys tract cont. 202 1/2 acres, Lot No. 177 in 3rd Dist. Henry Co. Signed: ALEXANDER BRYAN. Wit: SAML. JOHNSON, THOS. C. RUSSELL, J.I.C. Rec. 9 June 1828.

Page 537: Promissory Note headed Henry Co. dated 1 April 1828 bet. ALEXANDER MURRAY of afsd. Co. and JOHN CAMPBELL of City of Augusta said ALEXANDER MURRAY has promised to pay JOHN CAMPBELL $751.27 on or before 1st May next and in consid. of $10.00 by sd. JOHN CAMPBELL, Sd. ALEXANDER MURRAY conveys to JOHN CAMPBELL tract in Henry Co. cont. 202 1/2 acres, Lot N. 239. Signed: ALEXANDER MURRAY. Wit: ANDREW R. MORE, THOS. D. JOHNSON, J.P. Rec. 9 June 1828.

Page 538: Sheriff's deed headed Henry Co., on writ of Inf. Court of Washington Co. at suit of HARRIET E. RIVERS and others agst. A. M. RUTHER-FORD and D. MCDOUGAL, JESSEE JOHNSON, Sheriff seizes tract of land as property of A. M. RUTHERFORD and sells at public outcry to JOHN DAILEY Senr., the highest Bidder for $450...Deed dated 3 June 1828 for tract in Henry Co. in 11th Dist. Lot No. 6, cont. 202 1/2 acres. Signed: JESSEE JOHNSON. Wit: WILLIAM Y. HANSELL, THOS. C. RUSSELL, J.I.C. Rec. 9 June 1828.

Page 539: Deed headed District of Georgia, dated May 1, 1826 bet. GEORGE T. MARSHALL deputy marshall of the sd. Dist. and WILLIAM Y. HANSELL of other part. whereas JOHN FAY did lately in Fed. Ct. obtain a judgment agst MARY BOYD, Admr. of SAMUEL BOYD, dec'd. for sum of $1910.53 1/2 with interest and also $18.00 for costs...writ to seize cert. parcel of land of SAMUEL BOYD, dec'd. in Henry Co., Lot No. 226 in 6th Dist. cont. 202 1/2 acres...and sold at public outcry...sd. Indenture GEORGE MARSHALL for sum of $6.50 pd. by sd. WILLIAM T. HANSELL. Signed: GEORGE T. MARSHALL, Deputy Marshall. Wit: H. G. HARPESS, J. T. CUHING, J. (?) Rec. 9 June, 1828.

Page 540: Deed headed Henry Co., dated 1 Nov. 1827 bet. MARTIN CRIDER of Co. afsd. and JACOB MILLER of same...consid. of $400...conveys tract of 77 1/2 acres, part of Lot No. 58 in 3rd Dist. Henry Co. (near

Wild Cat Creek). Signed: MARTIN (X) CRIDER. Wit: WM. MCKINNIE, JOHN W. POYNER, J.P. Rec. 12 June 1828.

Page 541: Deed headed Henry Co., dated 11 June 1828 bet. THOMAS C. RUSSELL of one part and LUCINDA HOLTSCLAW of other...consid. of the esteem regard and respect the sd. THOMAS C. RUSSELL hath and doth entertain for the sd. LUCINDA, conveys in fee simple all that tract on West Side of the DeKalb Street known and dist. in plan of town of McDonough, being the Eastern part of Lot No. 11, cont. one acre, fronting DeKalb street by 319 feet and extending 140 feet back...Signed: THOMAS C. RUSSELL, Wit: RICHARD B. WOOTEN, THOS. D. JOHNSON, J.P. Rec. 13 June 1828.

Page 541: Deed headed Charleston, S. C., dated 15 July 1827 bet. DANIEL DUNLEVY, formally of city of Savannah and State of Ga., now of Charleston of one part and JOHN BRIGHA, of Burke Co., Ga...consid. of $500 conveys tract in 12th Dist. Henry Co., cont. 202 1/2 acres, Lot No. 113 drawn by DANIEL DUNLEVY. Signed: DANIEL DUNLEVY. Wit: J. F. LAPEWINE, THOMAS ELSE, J.P. Rec. 13 June 1828.

Page 542: Deed headed Henry Co., dated 14 June 1828, bet. THOMAS C. BENNING of Co. afsd. and THOMAS C. RUSSELL, JAMES SELLERS, WARD H. TURNER, HUNDLEY BRIMER and JOSHUA HAMES, Justices of the Sup. Ct.---for consid of a lot of land cont. 4 acres in town of McDonough, whereon the old grave-yard stands a deed to which sd. land is hereby ack. to have been rec'd... sells and exchanges all that lot of land in 7th Dist. sd. Co. being part of the west half of Lot No. 155, cont. 4 acres. Signed: THOS. C. BENNING. Wit: SAML. JOHNSON, THOS. D. JOHNSON, J.P. (The Plat shows graveyard land adj. Dr. MANSONS land and BENNINGS land and just off the Monroe Street or Road.)

Page 543: Deed headed Henry Co., dated 21 June 1828 bet. WILLIAM MCCONNELL of Co. afsd. and THOMAS CARTER (CARTEN?) of same...consid. of $900...conveys 202 1/2 acres in 12th Dist. Henry Co. Lot No. 29 which was gtd. 8 Feb. 1823 to JOHN SIMMONS of Richards Dist., Elbert Co. Signed: WILLIAM MCCONNELL. Wit: FREDERICK RA(?), HENRY N. POPE. Rec. 24 June 1828.

Page 544: Deed headed Baldwin Co., dated 21 June 1827 bet C. MCCARTY of Henry Co. and WYATT FORD of Baldwin Co...consid. of $1050.00 conveys tract cont. 202 1/2 acres in 3rd Dist. Henry Co., Lot No. 164. Signed: C. MCCARTY. Wit: SIMEON L. STEVENS, RHODOM A. GREEN swore to deed in Baldwin Co. 29 May 1828. Rec. 25 June 1828.

Page 545: Deed headed Putnam Co., dated 27 Feb. 1827 bet. WILLIAM H. KIMBROUGH of Co. afsd. and ELI E. GAITHER of same whereas on 2 Aug. 1826 sd. WILLIAM H. KIMBROUGH together with WILLIS BRYANT made his joint and several promissiory note payable to ELI E. GAITHER or bearer...now for consid. of $5.00 paid by sd. WILLIAM H. KIMBROUGH to ELI. E. GAITHER... conveys tract in 7th Dist. Henry Co., Lot No. 169 cont. 202 1/2 acres... Signed: WM. H. KIMBROUGH. Wit: TURNER H. TRIPPE, GREENBURY GAITHER. Rec. 27 June 1828.

Page 546: Deed headed Henry Co., dated 25 Dec. 1827 bet. ELISHA MOSEBY of Henry Co. and HIRAM WARTICK of same...consid $150...conveys tract cont. 25 acres in 7th Dist. Henry Co. part of Lot No. 156 cont. 25 acres...bounded by East by ANDREW MCBRIDE, North by PETER JOHNSON, North by TANDY W. KEYS and West by THOMAS C. BENNING. Signed: ELISHA MOSEBY. Wit: ROBERT BRADBERRY, JAMES KIMBROUGH, J.P. Rec. 27 June 1828.

Page 547: Deed headed Henry Co., dated 8 Jan. 1828 bet. HIRAM WAR-TICK of Co. afsd. and SOLOMON WARTICK of same...consid of $140...conveys tract cont. 25 acres in 7th Dist. Henry Co., part of Lot No. 156. Signed: HIRAM WARTICK. Wit: WM. C. LOVE, JAMES KIMBROUGH. Rec. 27 June 1828.

Page 548: Deed headed Baldwin Co., dated 16 June 1828 bet. ALEXIS TARDY SENR. by his agent and Att. of County of Tuscaloosa in Alabama and WILLIAM H. GREEN of Henry Co...consid. of $150 conveys tract in 11th

Dist. Henry Co., cont. 202 1/2 acres, drawn by sd. ALEXIS TARDY, SENIOR, then of Richmond Co., Ga... Signed: ALEXIS TARDY by his Attorney and Agent WILLIAM Y. HANSELL. Wit: ___M. ORME, S. ROCKWELL, Not Pun. Rec. 28 June 1828.

Page 549: Tuskaloosa Co., Ala. know all men that I ALEXIS TARDY of Co. and State afsd. appt. WILLIAM Y.HANSELL of Ga. my agent and attorney to sell tract in 11th Dist. Henry Co. in my name. Signed: ALEXIS TARDY. Wit: A. M. ROBINSON, LEVIN POWELL, J.P. State of Alabama, Tuskaloosa Co. JOHN A. HODGES Clerk of Co. Court of afsd. do certify that LEVIN POWELL Esq. who ack. power of Att., was acknowledged at the taking and is an acting J. P. for sd. Co. Dated 22 Sept. 1827.

Page 550: Deed headed State of Georgia, dated 19 July 1827 bet. JOHN S. HOLT of City of Augusta and ISAAC R. ST. JOHN of City and State afsd... consid. of $700...conveys tract cont. 500 acres in Franklin Co., Ga. on waters of North fork of Broad River, which was gtd. to DAVID TORONDITS dated 27 June 1786...and bounded northeasterly by JOHN HERRINGTON and JULIUS HOWARD, Southasterly by an old line and all other sides, vacant...also one other lot of land cont. 250 acres in 6th Dist. Gwinnett Co., Ga. Lot 251, gtd. to (?ISOM) J(S-M?) WATKINS dated 19 Feb. 1828...also one other part of land in 12th Dist. Henry Co. Lot No. 190 cont. 202 1/2 acres gtd. to NIMROD RAGES 1 Aug. 1822 and by him conveyed to sd. HOLT by indenture 24 June 1828. Signed: JOHN S. HOLT. Wit: SAML. H. PECK, WILLIAM B. THOMAS, J.P. Rec. 1 July 1828.

Page 551: Deed headed Walton County, dated March 19, 1828 bet. DARIUS ECHOLS, Att. in fact for STEPHEN CAUDELL (CANDELL?) of afsd. state and ABNER CAMP of State and Co. afsd. for the heirs of EDMUND CAMP dec'd... for consid. of $500 have conveyed unto ABNER CAMP, Admnr. of EDMUND CAMP, lot of land in Henry Co., Lot No. 20 in 2nd Dist., drawn by STEPHEN CAUDELL (CANDELL?) on 6 Dec. 1827. Signed: DARCY ECHOLS, Att. in Fact for STEPHEN CAUDELL. Wit: HIRAM CAMP. JONATHAN BETTS, J.P. Rec. 1. July 1828.

Page 552: Power of Attorney headed Franklin County, Ga. dated 12 March 1822, from STEPHEN CAUDELL of Co. afsd. to DARIUS ECHOLS of Habersham County as his Attorney in particular for sale of Cert. tract of land in Henry Co., Lot 20 in 2nd Dist. drawn by me in late land lottery. Signed: STEPHEN CAUDELL. Wit: JOHN MCCORNACK, SABEL ECHOLS. Rec. 1 June 1828.

Page 552: Deed of Gift from SAMUEL JOHNSON of Henry County, Ga. in year 1828 in consid. of affection which I bear for my friend CANDES TIPPAR daughter of WILEY TEPPER...grant to CANDAS TIPPUR a cow and calf. Signed: SAMUEL JOHNSON. Wit: THOS. C. RUSSELL, J.I.C., JOHN WOOD. Rec. 1 July 1828.

Page 553: Deed headed Henry County, dated 17 Jan. 1828 bet. SHERWOOD B. JOHNSON of Co. afsd. and ISAIAH HAND of same...consid. of $1,000.00 convey tract cont. 101 1/4 acres in 6th Dist. Lot No. 248 being the east half of lot of land. Signed: SHERWOOD B. JOHNSON. Wit: JOHN WILLIAMS, JOHN C. HAND, J.P. Rec. 2 July 1828.

Page 554: Sheriff's deed headed Henry Co. from Justices Court of Henry Co. at instance of STEPHEN MERCER against SELBY VINSENT...JESSE JOHNSON, Sheriff seizes land No. 145 in 7th Dist. of HENRY Co. cont. 80 1/4 acres as property of SELBY VINSENT and sold at public outcry 1 July 1828 to WAID H. TURNER for $47.00. Deed dated 1 July 1828. Signed: JESSE JOHNSON, Sheriff. Wit: SAMUEL JOHNSON, DAVID CRIM, J.P. Rec. 2 July 1828.

Page 555: Deed headed Henry Co., dated 18 July 1827 bet. THOMAS VESSELS of afsd. and FRANCIS MILLER of Butts Co...consid. of $1,000... conveys tract, hot No. 181 in 8th Dist. Henry Co., gtd. to DREWRY NAPPIER on 17 Dec. 1825, cont. 202 1/2 acres. Signed: THOMAS VESSALLS. Wit: ELI STRICKLAND, WILEY STRICKLAND, J.P. Rec. 5 July 1828.

Page 555: Bill of Sale headed Henry Co. dated 18 Feb. 1828 from
J. H. L. WILLIAMS unto JONATHAN MCKEY, 5 negroes for sum of $300...the
condition of the sale is that the above sum shall be paid to above
MCKEY in 4 months from this date with lawful interest in negotiable
bank bills then the above bill of sale to be null and void, otherwise
to remain in full force. Signed: H. J. WILLIAMS. Wit: JASON H.
MACKEY, JONATHAN C. MACKEY. Rec. 5 July 1828.

Page 556: Deed headed ELBERT COUNTY, Dated 9 Jan. 1827, bet. THOMAS
HAYNES of State and Co. afsd. and WYATT BROWN of Henry Co...consid. of
$700...conveys tract in Henry Co. cont. 202 1/2 acres, Lot No. 33 in 6th
Dist. Signed: WYATT BROWN. Wit: WILLIAM D. HAYNES, JAMES W. HAYNES.
Rec. 7 July 1828.

Page 557: Deed headed Henry Co., dated 21 May 1826 bet. JOHN KINARD
of Henry Co. and BARNED KINARD...consid. of $200...conveys tract cont.
100 1/4 acres in 1st Dist. Henry Co. Lot No. 211, adj. No. 206. Signed:
JOHN (K) KINARD. Wit: THOMAS W. HARRIS, MOSES COX, J.P. Rec. 7 July
1828.

Page 558: Deed headed Henry Co., dated 17 July 1828, bet. THOS. C.
RUSSELL, JAMES SELLERS, WAID H. TURNER, HENRY VARNER and JOSHUA (HARRIS
or HAMES?), Justices of Inf. Ct. of Henry Co. and WILLIAM L. CRAYTON...
consid. of $120...conveys all that lot in town of McDonough, known in
plan of town as No. 8 in Square 73, being 100 by 120 feet and bounded on
East by ANDREW MCBRIDES lot, south by a 30 ft. street, West by Pike St.,
and North by lots owned by W. L. CRAYTON and EZEKIEL CLOUD. Signed:
HENLEY VARNER, J.I.C., THOS. C. RUSSELL, J.I.C., WAID H. TURNER, J.I.C.
JAMES SELLERS, J.I.C., JOSHUA HAMES, J.I.C. Wit: AMASA SPENCER, THOS. D.
JOHNSON, J.P. Rec. 8 July 1828.

Page 559: Deed headed Henry Co. on 7 July 1828 by Justices of Inf.
Ct. (same as in Deed of Page 558 just preceding are named) to WILLIAM L.
CRAYTON...consid. of $152.00...convey the following lots in town of
McDonough, viz. Lot 27 being 450' by 480', 6"; Lot No. 20, being 450' by
272'6"; Lot No. 31 being 450' by 296'8" and Lot No. 32 being 450' by 300',
in 7th Dist. Henry Co. Signed: as signed in Deed Page 558. Wit: AMASA
SPENCER, THOMAS D. JOHNSON, J.P. Rec. 8 July 1828.

Page 560: Deed headed Henry Co., dated 1 Dec. 1826, bet. LEASTON
SNEED of (Bu--Butts?) Co. and WADE H. TURNER of Henry Co...consid. of
$325...conveys tract in Henry Co. in 7th Dist., No. 85 cont. 202 1/2
acres, drawn by THOMAS PHILLSON of McIntosh Co., transferred from sd. T.
PHILLSON to EDWARD W. RUSSELL of Liberty Co., Ga. Signed: LEASTON SNEED.
Wit: E. TURNER, T. JACKSON, EDWARD TURNER wit. that he saw T. S. JACKSON
do likewise on 28 July 1827. Rec. 8 July 1828.

Page 561: Deed headed Henry Co., dated 16 Nov. 1827, bet. JOHN
BROOKS of Henry Co. and CHARLES WEST of Washington County...sd. JOHN
BROOKS for consid. of $1650.00 conveys tract in 11th Dist. Henry Co., Lot
No. 37, also a part of No. 38 on South and West part of sd. lot and on
South side of North prong of Cotton River community and running down the
river till the old ford, thence up the old Road a Southwest course till
the line and thence to S. W. Corner...Signed: JOHN (X) BROOKS. Wit,
JAMES HENRY, GEORGE WEST. Rec. 7 July 1828.

Page 562: Deed headed Jefferson County, MARY HADDEN, Gdn. of person
and property of WILLIAM HADDEN, minor heir of WILLIAM HADDEN, dec'd. did
in late lottery of 1821 draw Lot No. 47 in 7th Dist. Henry Co. and said
orphans consisted of MARGARET HADDEN who has since intermarried with
BINNIAH S. CASWELL, GORDON HADDEN who are now both at legal discretion...
and WILLIAM HADDEN who is still a minor...Shere as MARY HADDEN did apply
at Ct. or Ord. of Jefferson Co. for leave to sell part of sd. tract that
belonged to minor heirs and with approbation of BEMNIAH S. CARSWELL and
sd. GORDON HADDEN. sd. land sold at public sale on 1st Tues. of June
instant...when same was knocked off to JOHN SELLERS of sd. County for sum
of $200. Signed: MARY HADDEN, BEMNIAH S. CARSWELL, GORDON HADDEN. Wit:
ROGER L. GAMBLE, ASA JOLT, J.P. Rec. 14 July 1828.

Page 563: Bill of Sale headed Henry Co. dated 28 Jan. 1828 bet.
WILLIAM W. BOYETTE and GEORGE MORRIS both of Co. afsd...sd. WILLIAM W.
BOYETTE has made 5 promissory notes for $30 each and 2 other notes one for
$22.09 and the other for $18.12 1/2 payable to ANTHONY DYRE or bearer and
payable on 25 Dec. next...sd. notes have been endorsed by sd. GEORGE
MORRIS lyable in the 2nd instance to MOSES ROPER (or ROSSER?)...now and for
consid. of sum of $5.00 by sd. GEORGE MORRIS to sd. WILLIAM W. BOYETTE
in hand paid...sells the following negroes to GEORGE MORRIS to wit:
JENNEY about 21, MARY about 8 months. Signed: E. W. BOYETT. Wit: JAMES
C. STELLE, WILLEY J. HEFFLIN. Rec. 14 July 1828. Witness to the signing
said his grantor was WILLIAM W. BOYETT and was dated 14 July 1828 bef.
THOS. FINCHER, J.P. Rec. 14 July 1828.

Page 565: Deed headed Jefferson County, dated 28 June 1827 from
ZACHARIAH BAILEY to BELTON ALESS for consid. of $225...conveys tract in
Henry Co. cont. 202 1/2 acres, known as Lot N. 77 in 7th Dist. Henry Co.
Signed: ZACHARIAH BAILEY. Wit: WILLIAM PROCTOR, WILLIAM BAILEY. Camden
Co., Ga. WILLIAM PROCTOR was sworn that he wit. signature of ZACHARIAH
and delivery of deed to BELTON ALESS, 15 Oct. 1828 this wit took place.
Rec. 15 July 1828.

Page 565: Deed headed Henry Co., dated 25 Nov. 1827, BELTON ALESS of
Camden Co. for consid of $350 paid by SAMUEL WYATT of Henry Co...conveys
tract of land, Lot No. 77 in 7th Dist. drawn by Z. BAILEY of Camden Co.,
cont. 202 1/2 acres. Signed: BELTON ALESS. Wit: WM. M. S. HAUGHTON,
JOHN WILLIAMS, J.I.C. Rec. 15 July 1828.

Page 566: Deed headed Henry Co., dated 18 Feb. 1828 bet. ROOSS
MOORE and JOHN MOORE of Co. afsd. and ROBERT L. HENDERSON of same...consid.
of $150...conveys tract in 6th Dist. of Henry Co., No. 199, cont. 202 1/2
acres, bounded by Lots 200, 20 , 198 and 186...Signed: ROSS MOORE, JOHN
MOORE. Wit: WILLIAM HAND, JOHN C. HAND, J.P. Rec. 18 July 1828.

Page 567: Deed headed Henry Co., dated 19 July 1828 bet. ELIAS
LANDRUM of Putnam Co. and JOHN GALLMAN of Henry Co...consid. of $300...
conveys tract in Henry Co. cont. 202 1/2 acres, Lot No. 86 in 6th Dist.
Signed: ELIAS LANDRUM. Wit: DAVID CRIM, THOMAS D. JOHNSON, J.P. Rec.
21 July 1828.

Page 567: Deed headed Henry Co., dated 23 Aug. 1827 bet HENRY HAGIN
of Apling Co., Ga. and NATHAN BREED of Henry Co...consid. $100...conveys
tract in 2nd Dist. Henry Co., Lot No. 54, cont. 202 1/2 acres...Signed:
HENRY HAGIN. Wit: WILLIAM FINCHER, JOHN (X) JAMES, WILLIAM C. FINCHER
swore to signing on May 3, 1828 bef. JOSHUA J. EVANS, J.P. Rec. 22 July
1828.

Page 568: Deed headed Warren Co., dated 2 Feb. 1822 bet. DANIEL
THOMAS and WILLIAM BREED both of afsd. Co...consid. of $200...conveys
tract in 2nd Dist. Henry Co., Lot No. 45 drawn by sd. DANIEL THOMAS on
28 Jan. last cont. 202 1/2 acres. Signed: DANIEL (X) THOMAS. Wit: BENJN.
RICKETON, D. DENNIS, J.P. Rec. 22 July 1828.

Page 569: Deed headed Henry Co., dated 8 Jan. 1828 bet. CORNELIUS
BLUNT of County of Gadsden, Fla. and WILLIAM BECK of other part...consid.
of $420...conveys tract in 3rd Dist. Henry Co. known by Lot No. 219 on
Waters of Wolf Creek, cont. 202 1/2 acres. Signed: CORNELIUS BLUNT.
Wit: BARNABAS STRICKLAND, JAMES H. RAMSEY, J.P. Rec. 22 July 1828.

Page 570: Sheriff's Deed, headed Henry Co., on writ from Court of
Pulaski Co. at instance of J. ROBINSON, H. GANTT, A. JONES, JESSE JOHNSON,
Sheriff of Henry Co. seized lot No. 180 in 12th Dist. Henry Co. cont.
202 1/2 acres as property of A. JONES and being advertised was sold at
public outcry to ALEXANDER BRYAN for sum of $21.00. Deed dated 1 July
1828 from JESSE JOHNSON, Sheriff to ALEXANDER BRYAN. Signed: JESSE
JOHNSON, Sheriff. Wit: ISAIAH HAM, CHARLES HULSEY, J.P. Rec. 30 July
1828.

Page 571: Deed headed Georgia, dated 12 June 1828 bet. MOSES SINQUE-
FIELD of Washington Co., Ga. and JOHN J. CHEATHAM of Co. of Jackson, Ga...

consid. $200...conveys tract cont. 202 1/2 acres in 7th Dist. Henry Co., drawn and gtd. to JOHN BURNS of Riddles Dist. Washington Co., bounding Lots 229, 251, 2, 253. Signed: MOSES SINQUEFIELD. Wit: W. P. HARDWICK, JOHN (X) STOWERS, SAML. BROWN, J.P. of Clark Co. Witnessed JOHN STOWERS signature. Dated 19 June 1828. Rec. 4 Aug. 1828.

Page 572: Deed headed Henry Co., dated 22 July 1828 bet. SAMUEL J. BRYAN and THOMAS C. BENNING of the 1st part and TURNER HUNT, SENR. of the 2nd part. consid. $300...convey tract in 7th Dist. Henry Co., Lot No. 167 cont. 202 1/2 acres. Signed: SAML. J. BRYAN, THOMAS C. BENNING. Wit: F. E. MANSON, JOSHUA HAMES, J.I.C. Rec. 4 Aug. 1828.

Page 573: Deed headed Henry Co., dated 28 Oct. 1826, bet. JOHN ADAMS of Co. afsd. and JOSEPH ATKINS of same...consid $500...conveys his interest in part of a tract in 3rd Dist. Henry Co., Lot No. 230 cont. 202 1/2 acres. Signed: JOHN ADAMS. Wit: D. M. (HEAY?)...G. GRICE, J.I.C. Rec. 5 Aug. 1828.

Page 574: Deed headed Jasper Co. dated 3 August 1827 bet. ROBERT FEARS of Co. afsd. and LEWELLEN MORGAN of Henry Co...consid. of $500, conveys tract in Henry Co., Lot No. 249 in 6th Dist. of Henry Cont. 202 1/2 acres, drawn by the sd. ROBERT FEARS and gtd. by the state. Signed: ROBERT FEARS. Wit: SANDERS WALKER, CHARLES MORGAN, J.P. Rec. 6 Aug. 1828.

Page 575: Deed headed Georgia, dated 4 March 1822, bet. ELIZABETH STONE of Clark Co. and GABRIEL A. MOFFETT of Co. of Clark of other... consid. of $500...conveys tract in 12th Dist. Henry Co., Lot No. 68 drawn by said ELIZABETH STONE in a late Lottery. Signed: ELIZABETH (X) STONE. Wit: DANIEL RAMSY (or RAMEY?), EDWARD JONES, J.P. Rec. 6 Aug. 1828.

Page 576: Deed headed Georgia, dated 6 Feb. 1828 bet. BRYANT ED-MUNDSON of Henry Co. and JONATHAN MACKEY of the other...consid. $1100... conveys tract cont. 202 1/2 acres in Henry Co., known as Lot No. 90 in 2nd Dist. Signed: B. EDMUNDSON. Wit: WILLIAM FINCHER, JONATHAN A. MACKEY. Sworn to by JONATHAN MACKEY and ELIJAH ALLEN on 23 July 1828. Rec. 6 Aug. 1828.

Page 557: Deed dated 18 Dec. 1826 bet. MATTHEW STOKER of Henry Co. and JEDIDIAH RICHARDS of Green Co...consid. of $400..conveys tract in Henry Co. cont. 202 1/2 acres, Lot No. 188 in 11th Dist., surveyed on 1 Aug. 1821 and gtd. to JOB JACKSON on 4 Nov. 1824. Signed: MATTHEW STOKER. Wit: EPHRIAM BO(MAR?), EDWD. D. ALFRIEND. Sworn to 18 Sept. 1827 by EPHRAIM BO(MAR?) that he with EDWARD D. ALFRIEND and JOHN HINES were subscribing witnesses.

Page 578: Deed headed Greene Co. dated 10 Feb. 1826 bet. JAMES CARTWRIGHT of Co. afsd. and THOMAS JOHNSON of Newton Co...consid. of $200.. conveys tract in Henry Co. in 7th Dist., Lot No. 119 cont. 202 1/2 acres. Signed: JAMES CARTWRIGHT. Wit: PETER C. JOHNSON, ABNER PERKINS, J.P. Rec. 11 Aug. 1828.

Page 579: Deed headed Burke Co., dated 13 June 1828 bet. GEORGE MCKAY of afsd. Co. and LEON DUGAS of sd. state and Co. of other...consid. of $200...conveys tract drawn by sd. GEORGE MCKAY known as Lot No. 99 in 6th Dist. Henry Co. cont. 202 1/2 acres...and sd. LEON P. DUGAS to hold same forever. Signed: GEORGE MCKAY. Wit: HEZEKIAH (X) GIBSON, MARTIN WILLEOR. Sworn to in Richmond Co. by MARTIN WILLEOR of Co. afsd. that he saw GEORGE MCKAY sign above and HEZEKIAH GIBSON made his mark and dated 20 June 1828. Rec. 15 Aug. 1828.

Page 580: Deed headed Georgia, dated 28 June 1828, bet. LEON P. DUGAS of Co. of Burke and E. L. Newton of Clark Co., Ga...consid. of $250...conveys tract drawn by GEORGE MCKAY of Burke Co., Lot No. 99 in 6th Dist. Henry Co. cont. 202 1/2 acres. Signed: LEON P. DUGAS. Wit: MARTIN WILLEOR, A. G. RAIFORD, J.P. Rec. 15 Aug. 1828.

Page 580: (Actually should be 581 as book shows 2 pages numbered 580)...Deed dated 21 March 1828 bet. WILLIAM T. HUDMON of Henry Co. and SAMUEL HENDERSON of same...consid of $150...conveys West half of tract or lot in Henry Co. in 6th Dist. Lot No. 88, cont. 101 1/4 acres... Signed: WILLIAM T. HUDMAN. Wit: E. D. VAUGHAN, J.P. WM. RUSSELL. Rec. 16 Aug. 1828.

Page 580: Deed headed Clark Co. (this begins midway of page 580 (581)...dated 6 March 1827 bet. MERRITT N. SERKINS of Co. afsd. and JOSHUA CALLAHAN of other part...consid. of $500...conveys tract in Henry Co. 7th Dist. Lot No. 7 cont. 202 1/2 acres, drawn in late lottery by HENRY GLAYSON. Signed: MERRITT N. SERKINS. Wit: GABRIEL R. THOMAS, (IRBY or JOBY?) HUDSON. Rec. 16 Aug. 1828. (Note, a letter deed shows PERKINS).

Page 581: Deed headed Henry Co., dated 25 July 1828 bet. WOODSON HUBBARD and WILLIAM MILES...consid. of $200...conveys tract, being one half of Lot No. 153 in 3rd Dist. of this Co., it being the East half of sd. lot...Signed: WOODSON HUBBARD. Wit: SAMUEL ARMSTRONG, JOHN W. PYNER, J.P. Rec. 16 Aug. 1828.

Page 581: Deed headed Henry Co., dated 12 Aug. 1828, bet. SOLOMAN BRYAN of Screven Co. and GEORGE T. LONG of Henry Co...consid of $500... conveys tract of land in Henry Co., Lot No. 68 in 6th Dist. cont. 202 1/2 acres. Signed: SOLOMON BRYAN. Wit: ALEXANDER BRYAN, JOHN ADAMS, J.P. Rec. 16 Aug. 1828.

Page 582: Deed headed Henry Co., dated 8 Jan. 1828 bet. PLEASANT S. BARNETT of Cowetaw Co. and State of Ga. and JOSEPH LET(ES?) of Henry Co.. consid. of $1000...conveys tract in 3rd Dist. Henry Co., Lot No. 214 cont. 202 1/2 acres. Signed: PLEASANT S. BARNETT. Wit: WM. GRIFFIN, ANDREW DINCK. Sworn to in Henry Co. 21 Mar. 1828. Rec. 16 Aug. 1828.

Page 583: Deed headed Clarke Co., dated 21 Feb. 1827 bet. HENRY GLASSON of Co. afsd. and MERETT N. PERKINS...consid. of $500...conveys tract in Henry Co. in 7th Dist., Lot No. 7 cont. 202 1/2 acres, drawn in late land lottery by sd. HENRY GLASSON. Signed: HENRY GLASSON. Wit: ABRAM DOOLITTLE, WILLIAM HOPKINS. Sworn to bef. WILLIAM CLARK, J.I.C. on 5 March 1827. Rec. 16 Aug. 1828.

Page 584: Deed headed Georgia, dated 23 July 1828, bet. WILLIAM SMITH of State of S. C. and Beaufort Dist. for himself and in right of his wife ANNATH SMITH formerly ANNATH KNIGHT and as Gdn. of the orphans and minor heirs of STEPHEN KNIGHT dec'd. late of sd. State first afsd. and SCREVEN CO. of the first part and SOLOMON BRYAN of Screven Co., Ga. of other sd. WILLIAM SMITH on 5 June 1826 appt'd by Honorable the Inf. Ct. of Screven Co. sitting for Ordinary purposes aypt'd Gdn. afsd. of the person, property of the orphans and minor heirs...on 7 May 1827 at public outcr- at the Cthse. in Henry Co. and publically advertised agreeable to the Ct. on the 1st. Tues. being the 6 May 1828 the following described tract of land drawn by heirs of sd. STEPHEN KNIGHT dec'd. in one of the land lotteries...when sd. SOLOMON BRYAN being highest bidder of same...consid. of $300.50...convey tract cont. 202 1/2 acres adj. Lot No. 67, 61, 69 and 93 as represented by the orig. plat in 6th. Dist. Henry Co. and known as Lot No. 68. Signed: WILLIAM SMITH, Guardian. Wit: SEABORN GOODALL, ALEXANDER KEMP, J.I.C. Rec. 18 Aug. 1828.

Page 585:(6): This Indenture made and confirmed this ___ Jan. 1826 bet. JAMES WHITE of DeKalb Co. and MARK MCCUTCHEN of Henry Co...sd. JAMES WHITE for and in consid. of $200...conveyed tract in 3rd Dist. Henry Co. Lot No. 223-cont. 202 1/2 acresin fee simple... Signed: WM. HARDIN, C.C.O. Wit: JAMES N. GEORGE, WESLY CAMP, J.P. Rec. 10 Aug. 1828.

Page 585: Deed made and confirmed 28 July 1828 bet. MARK MCCUTCHEN of Troup Co. and ANNA MCCUTCHEN, Extrx. of WILLIAM MCCUTCHEN dec'd. of Henry Co...sd. MARK MCCUTCHEN for consid. of $350...conveyed unto ANNA MCCUTCHEN Extrx. of WILLIAM MCCUTCHEN dec'd. tract in Henry Co. in 3rd Dist., Lot No. 223, cont. 202 1/2 acres. Signed: MARK MCCUTCHEN, WM. HARDIN, Clk. Wit: WILLIAM (C)AMISON, B. R. MCCUTCHEN, J.P. Rec. 18 Aug. 1828.

Page 586: Deed headed Gwinnett Co., dated 12 June 1828, bet. JAMES W. GRIMES, JR. of Co. afsd. and SAMUEL J. BRYAN of other part...consid. of $300...conveys tract in Henry Co. cont. 202 1/2 acres in 7th Dist. Lot No. 97 and drawn by sd. J. W. GRIMES... Signed: JAMES W. GRIMES, JUNR. Wit: SILAS LAWRENCE, ASAKEL R. SMITH, J.I.C. Rec. 18 Aug. 1828.

Page 587: Deed headed Henry Co., dated 15 Dec. 1827 bet. ALLEN KILLGORE of Perry Co., Alabama and ANNA MCCUTCHEN of Co. afsd...consid. of $100 to him paid...conveys tract in 3rd Dist. Henry Co., cont. 202 1/2 acres, Lot No. 194 drawn by EVE BEARD, Widow of Thorton's Dist. Ogel- thorpe Co. in late lottery and gtd. to sd. EVE BEARD on 11 Sept. 1824... Signed: ALLEN KILLGORE. Wit: WILLIAM CHRISTIAN, ELISABETH M. K. MC- CUTCHENS. Sworn to __ 1828. Rec. 18 Aug. 1828.

Page 588: Deed headed Oglethorpe Co., dated and concluded 29 Nov. 1827 bet. EVE BEARD of same and ALLEN KILLGORE of State and of Ala. and Co. of Perry. consid. of $300...conveys tract in 3rd Dist. Henry Co. cont. 202 1/2 acres, Lot No. 194 drawn by EVE BEARD, Widow of Thornton's Dist. in late lottery and gtd. to EVE BEARD 11 Sept. 1824. Signed: EVE (X) BEARD. Wit: BALOIX B. FAUST, JOHN FAUST, THOMAS DUKE, J.P. Rec. 18 Aug. 1828.

Page 588: Deed headed DeKalb Co., dated 10 ___ 1823 bet. LORANER TERRY of DeKalb Co. and CHARLES J. SHELTON of Telfair Co...consid of $200.. conveys tract in 3rd Dist. Henry Co. Lot No. 223 being the same land drawn by and in name of her the said. LORANER TERRY, Widow of Morgan Co... cont. 202 1/2 acres. Signed: LORANER (X) TERRY. Wit: JOHN TERRY, WILL- IAM TERRY. Sworn to bef. GEORGE CLIFTON J.I.C. of DeKalb Co. on 11 Sept. 1823. Rec. 18 Aug. 1828.

Page 590: Deed headed DeKalb Co., Ga. dated 11 Sept. 1823 bet. JAMES WHITE Territory of the County of DeKalb and CHARLES J. SHELTON of Telfair.. consid. of $200...conveys tract in 3rd Dist. Henry Co. Lot No. 223 being lot drawn by LORANER TERRY (Widow) of Morgan Co... Signed: CHARLES J. SHELTON. Wit: JAMES ADAMS, GEORGE CLIFTON, J.I.C. Rec. 18 Aug. 1828.

Page 591: Deed headed Bibb Co., dated 13 Jan. 1828, bet. JOHN FINCH of Co. afsd. and BIDWELL and CASEY of Richmond Co. Augusta...consid. of $200...conveys tract, eot No. 79 in 12th Dist. Henry Co. cont. 202 1/2 acres. Signed: JOHN (X) FINCHER. Wit: JEPHTHAN V. GEORGE, ROBT. M. REID. Sworn to 16 Aug. 1828. Rec. 18 Aug. 1828.

Page 592: Deed headed Henry Co., dated 2 Aug. 1828 bet. THOMAS YARBROUGH of one part and SAMUEL PHIFER of other...consid. of $200... conveys tract in 11th Dist. Henry Co., Lot No. 92 cont. 61 acres. Signed: THOMAS YARBROUGH. Wit: JOHN T. BENTLY, JNO. TREADWELL. Rec. 23 Aug. 1828.

Page 593: Deed headed Newton Co., dated 20 Jan. 1827 bet. JOHN CARLILE of Newton Co. and JOHN GAYDEN of Henry Co...consid. of $900...con- veys tract in 7th Dist. Henry Co., Lot No. 187, cont. 202 1/2 acres. Signed: JOHN CARLILE. Wit: JNO. MCCURDY, SAMUEL FEARS, J.P. Rec. 26 Aug. 1828.

Page 593: Deed headed Henry Co., dated 14 April 1828, bet. TURNER HUNT of Henry Co. and WILLIAM H. WHITE of Henry Co...consid of $600... conveys tract in Co. of Henry and town of McDonough known by Lot No. 18 one in the acre lots on Lot No. 134 in the 7th Dist...bounded No. by South Fayette St. West line of No. 133. Also one acre lying immediately west of sd. lot bounded No. by So. Fayette St. or Road and west by remain- ing part of as. lot, south by same lot, it being part of lot No. 133, whereon Dr. F. E. MANSAN now resides including his house. Signed: TURNER HUNT. Wit: WM. HARDIN, THOS. D. JOHNSON, J.P. Rec. 27 Aug. 1828.

Page 595: Deed headed Henry Co., dated March 10, 1827 bet. LEVI BEAUCHAMP of one part and JAMES WASHINGTON of other...consid. of $200 paid to sd. WASHINGTON...conveys Lot No. 115 in 12th Dist. Henry Co. joining Lot No. 114 and 110. Signed: JAMES WASHINGTON. Wit: CHARLES DAVIS, A. B. NICHOLS. Sworn to 2 July 1828 bef. WILLIAM MALONE, J.P. Rec. 9 Sept. 1828.

Page 596: Deed headed Oglethorpe Co., dated 10 Dec. 1827 bet. WILLIAM WILKS of one part and JOHN FREEMAN of other both afsd. Co...consid. of $250...conveys tract cont. 202 1/2 acres in 12th Dist. Henry Co., Lot No. 255. Signed: WILLIAM WILKS. Wit: ROBERT ALLISON, HENRY BRITAIN, JAMES B. LANDRUM. Rec. 12 Sept. 1828.

Page 596: Deed headed Henry Co., dated Oct. 13, 1827 bet. HENRY WAITZ of one part and WILLIAM COKER of other, both of afsd. Co...consid. of $200...conveys tract Lot No. 192 in 2nd Dist. Henry Co. cont. 101 1/4 acres. Signed: HENRY (X) WAITZ. Wit: JOHN A. ELLIS, MOSES COX, J.P. Rec. 15 Sept. 1828.

Page 596: Deed headed Henry Co., dated 9 Jan. 1826 bet. ELAXANDER NORTHCUT of one part and HENRY WATER of other...consid of 100...conveys tract in 1st Dist. Henry Co., Lot No. 192 cont. 202 1/2 acres of the west side of the lots of land. Signed: ELAXANDER (X) NORTHCUT. Wit: ELIAS F. WILSON. Sworn to 11 Sept. 1828 by ELIAS F. WILSON who saw ALEXANDER NORTHCUT sign his name and JAMES M. RICHARDSON also witness. Rec. 15 Sept. 1828.

Page 597: Deed headed Henry Co., dated 14 Aug. 1828, bet. BAZIEL PACE of Co. afsd. and JESSEE JOHNSON of same place...consid. of$150... conveys tract in 3rd Dist. Henry Co., being north west half of Lot No. 228 cont. 100 acres. Signed: BAZIEL PACE. Wit: D. MCCOY, J. G. BARNETT. Rec. 23 Sept. 1828.

Page 598: Deed headed Henry Co., dated 26 Nov. 1827 bet. JOHN TREADWELL, JUNR. of one part and JOSEPH P. GREEN of other, both of Co. afsd. consid of $600...conveys tract, Lot No. 55 in 12th Dist. Henry Co. Signed: JOHN (X) TREADWELL, JUNR. Wit: JESSE (X) __?, JNO TREADWELL, J.P. Rec. 25 Sept. 1828.

Page 599: Deed headed Henry Co., dated 13 July 1827, bet. JAMES M. VICKERS of Pulaska Co., Ga. and WILLIAM JINKS of Co. afsd...consid. of $350...conveys tract in 3rd Dist. Henry Co. Lot 167 cont. 202 1/2 acres. Signed: JAMES M. VICKERS. Wit: THOMAS HAYNOOD, WILLIAM JINKS, JUNR., THOMAS J. LIVINGSTON. Sworn to bef. WOODSON HUBBARD, J.P. on 12 Sept. 1828. Rec. 25 Sept. 1828.

Page 600: Deed headed Henry Co., dated 25 Oct. 1827 bet. RICHARD HOUSE of one part and ROBERT M. STEGAR of other both of Co. afsd... consid. of $800...conveys tract in Henry Co. on Waters of Cotton Indian Creek cont. 202 1/2 acres, Lot No. 97. Signed: RICHARD (X) HOUSE. Wit: JOHN MURRAY, ROLLEY (X) HIGHTOWER.

Page 600: Deed dated 29 Sept. 1827, bet. ABSALOM STEPHENS of Habersham Co., Ga. and VALENTINE BURNET of same and Co. of Henry...consid. of $150...conveys tract in Henry Co. Lot No. 171 in 12th Dist. Signed: ABSALOM STEPHENS. Wit: WM. STEPHENS, JAMES ALLEN, J.P. Rec. 25 Sept. 1828.

Page 601: Deed headed Henry Co., dated 15 Dec. 1827...bet. SOLOMON PATRICK of Henry Co. and ISAIAH HOLLENSWORTH of Co. afsd...consid. of $150.. conveys tract in 12th Dist. Henry Co., Lot No. 254...cont. 50 acres. Signed: SOLOMON PATRICK. Wit: HUBBARD HOLLOWAY, AARON PARKER, J.P. Rec. 26 Sept. 1828.

Page 602: Deed headed Henry Co., dated 11 Sept. 1828 bet. RANSON TAGGLE of Henry Co. and EDMUND LOW of Henry Co...consid. of $250...conveys tract to EDMUND LAW in town of McDonough, Lot No. 6 in the acrea and 5 acre plan cont. one or more or less bounded south by ABNER DAVISES land, West by 30 foot street north by JASPER Street, East by David Street... Signed: RANSOM TUGGLE. Wit: ABNER DAVIS, THOS. D. JOHNSON. Rec. 26 Sept. 1828.

Page 602: Deed headed Henry Co., dated 1 Sept. 1827 bet. HEZEKIAH MASK of Henry Co. and HOLBRY BROOKS of Oglethorpe Co...consid of $475... conveys tract in 3rd Dist. Henry Co., Lot No. 162 (adjoins MASK and MAT HENDERSON). To HELLERY BROOKS. Signed: HEZEKIAH MASK. Wit: MATTHEW ANDERSON, BRADFORD (X) ANDERSON, JOHN W. PYNER, J.P. Rec. 26 Sept. 1828.

Page 603: Deed headed Jasper Co., dated 4 Jan. 1828 bet. HARTWELL EZELL of afsd. Co. and DAVID RICHERSON of Henry Co...consid. of $100...

conveys tract cont. 202 1/2 acres in Henry Co. Lot No- 234 in 12 Dist.
Signed: HARTWELL (X) EZELL. Wit: EDWARD PRICE, J.P., ANN T. PRICE.
Rec. 26 Sept. 1826.

Page 604: Deed headed Henry Co., dated 1 Aug. 1828, bet. THOMAS C.
RUSSELL of afsd. and EDMUND LOW a regularly ordained Deacon and appt'd.
a proper representative of the Regular Baptist Church called Ramah in the
vicinity of McDonough...consid. of $75...conveys tract, part of Lot No.
133 in 7th Dist. of Henry Co. cont. 2 acres (adj. WYNN & RUSSELL, RUSSELL,
HANNAH.) Signed: THOMAS C. RUSSELL. Wit: JONATHAN M. PECK, DAVID C.
___?, J.P. Rec. 26 Sept. 1828.

Page 605: Deed headed Henry Co., dated (hard to read) 1825 bet.
WILLIAM GRAY of afsd. Co. and DICKSON BOWIN of same...consid. of $75...
conveys tract of 50 acres, Lot No. 58 in 11th Dist. Henry Co. Signed:
WILLIAM GRAY. Wit: WILLIAM CAMP. SILAS MOSEBY. Rec. 26 Sept. 1828.

Page 605: Deed headed Henry Co., dated 26 March 1828, bet. WILLIAM
JINKS, SENR. of one part and his son WILLIAM JINKS, JUNR. of other...
consid. of sum of $1000 conveys tract in 3rd Dist. Henry Co. Lot No. 186
cont. 202 1/2 acres. Signed: WILLIAM (X) JINKS. Wit: TILMAN BROWN,
WOODSON HUBBARD, J.P. Rec. 26 Sept. 1828.

Page 606: Deed headed Henry Co., dated 21 Feb. 1828 bet. SAMUEL
HOUSTON of Henry Co. and ROBERT KELTON of Monroe...consid. of $250...
conveys tract whereon SAMUEL HOUSTON now lives on in Henry Co...being part
of Lot No. 54 in 7th Dist. Henry Co. which lies on Southside of Big Walnut
Creek, orig. gtd. to WILLIAM B. TATE. Signed: SAMUEL HOUSTON. Wit:
CARTER HOUSTON, SAML. WELLES. Sworn to by CARTER HOUSTON bef. WILLIS
BARRINGTON on Sept. 16, 1828. Rec. 27 Sept. 1828.

Page 607: Deed headed Henry Co., dated 29 Aug. 1828, bet. JOSHUA
BRAUGHTON of Henry Co. and JESSEE BOWDEN of same...consid of $900...con-
veys tract, Lot No. 135 in 12th Dist. Henry Co. on Cotton Indian Creek
joining Lot No. 132 and Lot No. 134, and Lot 154 drawn by WM. HASBURRY
of Putnam Co. cont. 202 1/2 acres. Signed: JOSHUA BRAUGHTON. Wit:
ISAIAH SANDERS, HENRY N. POPE, J.P. Rec. 29 Sept. 1828.

Page 608: Deed headed Henry Co., dated 13 Sept. 1828, bet. IRWIN
YATES of Fayette Co. and THOMAS JARROTT of Henry Co...consid. of $500...
conveys tract in 6th Dist. Henry Co., Lot No. 210 cont. 202 1/2 acres.
Signed: IRWIN (X) YATES. Wit: JAMES C. STEEL, THOS. D. JOHNSON, J.P.
Rec. 1 Oct. 1828.

Page 609: Deed headed Putnam Co., dated 8 July 1828, bet. JOEL
___DON of Henry Co. and IRBY STROUD of other part...consid of $300...
conveys tract lying in __rest of deed is incomplete...and another deed
below follows.

Page 609: Deed headed Henry Co., dated Oct. (no day) 1828 bet.
WILLIAM YARBROUGH of afsd. and THOMAS YARBROUGH of other...consid. of
$300...conveys tract in 11th Dist. Henry Co., part of Lot No. 69 cont.
101 1/2 acres, orig. gtd. to WILLIAM YARBROUGH sd. grant bearing date 10
Oct. 1822... Signed: WILLIAM YARBROUGH. Wit: JOSEPH GRESHAM, JNO.
TREADWELL, J.P. Rec. 8 Oct. 1828.

Page 610: Deed headed Henry Co., dated 15 Sept. 1827 bet. BENJAMIN
ANGEL(Y?) of Twiggs Co. and WILEY HEFLIN of Henry Co...consid of $150...
conveys tract in Henry Co. cont. 202 1/2 acres, Lot N. 59 in 2nd Dist.
Signed: BENJAMIN (X) (ANGELY?). Wit: JOHN PAR(HARM?), WILLIAM (X)
DAVIS, JOSHO(ME?) J. EVANS, J.P. Rec. 8 Oct. 1828.

Page 610: Deed headed Henry Co., dated 14 Aug. 1823 bet. JAMES
BULLOCK of one part and ALPHOUS BEALL of other parts... consid. of $200...
conveys tract in Henry Co. Lot No. 68 in 3rd Dist. cont. 202 1/2 acres.
Signed: JAMES (X) BULLOCK. Wit: SAML. BEALL, JAMES LOW, J.P., ELIZABETH
BULLOCK wife of within JAMES BULLOCK did on 14 .ug. 1823 renounce her dower.
Signed: ELIZABETH (X) BULLOCK. Rec. 8 Oct. 1828.

Page 611: Deed headed Henry Co., dated 15 Jan. 1828, bet. ELI W. HARRISON of Co. afsd. and CHRISTIAN WARMER of same place...consid. of $150...conveys tract one half of Lot No. 40 in 6th Dist. Henry Co. cont. 202 1/2 acres. Signed: ELI W. HARRISON. Wit: HENRY KING, JOHN (X) JOHNSON. Sworn to 3 Oct. 1828. Rec. 8 Oct. 1828.

Page 612: Deed headed Burke Co., dated 20 Dec. 1826 bet DANIEL DUKES of Co. afsd. and AZARIAH DUKES of same...consid. of $100...conveys tract in Henry Co. cont. 202 1/2 acres, Lot No. 44 in 11th Dist. Signed: DANIEL DUKES. Wit: ELIJAH JOHNSON, JOHN DUKES, Ack. Dec. 10, 1829 bef. JNO. LEWIS, J.P. Rec. 10 Oct. 1828.

NEWTON COUNTY WILL BOOK 1
1823 - 1851

Pages 1-2: Georgia, Newton Co.: L. W. & T. of THOMAS HAIL... to wife MARGARET, two negroes Hannah and Mary... at her decease to son WILLIAM and negro Abram... also to WILLIAM a lot of land No. 270... to son ANDREW, 1/2 lot adj. to EDWARD NIX, No. 269 and negro Sam... to son JOHN, lot adj. JAMES EPPS, No. 267... to my daughter NANCY TRAILOR, three negroes... to my daughter ELIZABETH BERRY, three negroes... to son JOSEPH, negro Mark,... my four children ANDREW, JOHN, NANCY TRAILOR and ELIZABETH BERRY... to son THOMAS, negro Tom... to my daughter POLLY GIBSON, negro... to son WILLIAM.. 31 Mar. 1823... THOMAS HAIL (X). Wit: EDWARD NIX, JOHN E. B. LYONS, WILSON CONNER. Proven November Term. 1823 by JOHN E. B. LYONS and WILSON CONNER. Rec. Nov. 3(?), 1823.

Pages 3-4: L. W. & T. of JOHN WELSHER... being somewhat inferior in body... land on which I now live to be sold... horses, cattle, one yoke of oxen and cart, plantation tools, etc. to be sold and money to be distributed among my children Viz. DUKE WILLIAM WELSHER, CHARLES WELSHER, and NANCY BROWN and my present wife ELIZABETH WELSHER to have so much as she is of right... HARRISON JONES and WILLIAM COOPER, my executors... my daughter MARY RODINBURY should she apply shall be entitled to one dollar.. 21 Octr. 1823... JOHN WELSHER ( ). Wit: HARRISON JONES, WILLIAM COOPER. Codicil: My crop now shall be given to my wife ELIZABETH for her years support... 2 March 1824. Wit: ANDREW PATRICK, LEVICY HAMMOCK. Proven Newton County Court of Ordinary, May Term 1824 by LEVICY HAMMOCK, HARRISON JONES & WILLIAM COOPER, 3 May 1824 before STEPHEN HODGE, C.C.O. Rec. 5 May 1824.

Pages 5-7: L. W. & T. of WILIE BURGE transferred from Morgan County to Newton County at Sept. Term 1824... WILIE BURGE of Morgan County... unto my beloved wife VANDY, all estate real and personal during her life or widowhood... to sons THOMAS BURGE & WILEY BURGE & JAMES BURGE, $1000 when they arrive at age 21... to daughters ELIZA BURGE and NANCY BURGE when they arrive at 21, $1000... daughter PATSEY LAM and son HAMILTON BURGE, neighter shall have any part as I have given them $1000... RICHARD LAM, HAMILTON BURGE, JAMES HODGE, Exrs.. 5 June 1821... WILIE BURGE (SEAL), Wit: JACKSON HARWELL, ANDREW T. HODGE, RICHARD HARWELL. Proven by all three wit. in Morgan County 4 Nov. 1822, JOHN NESBET, Clk... Rec. 18 Sept. 1824.

Pages 7-8: Newton Co.: L. W. & T. of ELIZABETH BUCKHANON... being in low health... unto SOLOMON GRAVES, SENR. all my property real and personal, to take care and support my father JOHN BUCKEHANON during his natural life... after his death to his nearest relations living in the United States of American... SOLOMON GRAVES SNR., & JOSEPH LANE, Exrs... 9 Oct. 1824... E. G. BUCKANON. Wit: WELETON (?) JONES, REUBEN WINFREY, MARY WINFREY (X). Proven by WELDON JONES & REUBIN WINFREY... 1 Nov. 1824 before STEPHEN HODGE, O.C.O. Rec. 1 Dec. 1824.

Pages 8-9: L. W. & T. of ISHAM BERRY of Newton Co.... being weak in body... to my wife SALLY BERRY and my daughter ELIZABETH BERRY negro man Essex and negro woman Dicy... my lot of land #62, 10th Dist., of Henry Co.... my children MARY HART, CHARLES M. BERRY, JAMES BERRY, THOMAS BERRY, RHODY BERRY, GEORGE W. BERRY, CINTHIA BERRY & WILLIAM P.? BERRY. To son JESSE BERRY, $5, to daughter JUDY WINFREY, $5... to daughter RHODY BERRY, one bed and furniture... son WILLIAM P. BERRY, negro George and one bed and furniture... CHARLES M. BERRY and JAMES BERRY Exrs... 12 Oct. 1825... ISHAM BERRY (C). Wit: WM. MCMURRAY, THOMAS P. JONES, THOMAS WRIGHT. Proven by all three wit. 7 Nov. 1825, before STEPHEN HODGE, C.C.O. Rec. 9 Feb. 1826.

Pages 9-10: L. W. & T. of WILLIAM BURKE of Newton Co.... to wife ELIZABETH BURK, 50 A, plantation whereon I now live, lot #153 and one horse and saddle... to sister MELIA BURKE, 50A ... sister NANCY BURKE,

50 A... to my beloved ROBERT BURKE (no relation stated) one dollar,... to sister FRANCIS BURKE, $1... to sister ELIZABETH, one dollar... GREEN B. TURNER, Exr... WILLIAM BURKE (X) (SEAL). Wit: DAVID CRAWFORD, WM. J. KING, WILLIAM GRADY. Proven __ Aug. 1826. Rec. 29 Aug. 1826.

Pages 11-12: Newton County: L. W. & T. of JAMES WEBB... to wife CATHARINE WEBB, all my property both real and personal until my youngest child comes of age... an equal part of daughter MARTHA WEBB, son LEVI WEBB... brother in law LEVI WELDER, Exr... 6 Feb. 1826... JAMES WEBB (SEAL). Wit: FURMAN WATSHALL, JOHN WELCHER (?), EDMUND S(?) WEBB. Proven 4 Sept. 1826 before STEPHEN HODGE, C.C.O. by all three wit. Rec. 7 Sept. 1826.

Pages 12-14: L. W. & T. of WILLIAM GOBER... weak in body... to wife LUCY GOBER, all my estate real and personal... to my daughter DOROTHY HODGE a negro boy Platoe... to my daughter NANCY CLACKSOME negro boy Samuel... to my daughter SARAH GOBER negro boy Gilbert (?)... to my daughter LUCY GOBER, bed and furniture... to my daughter RODY BLACKWELL, negro girl Catharine... to son ROLEY GOBER, two negro girls Elizabeth and Aggy and the land on which I now live... to my son WILLIAM GOBER, $5.. to my son JOHN GOBER, $5... to son GEORGE GOBER, $5... to my daughter CLARY TAYLOR, $2... to my daughter ALCY PITCHFORD, $5... to son JAMES GOBER, $5... to my daughter ELIZABETH HARRIS, $1... to son DANIEL GOBER, $5... to my son RICHARD GOBER, $5... to my son LEWIS GOBER, $5... lot in Franklin County to be sold... wf LUCY and son ROLEY Exrs... 18 Oct. 1825... WILLIAM GOBER SENR. (X) (SEAL). Wit: WILLIAM HODGE, L. JOHNSON. Proven by WILLIAM HODGE and LUKE JOHNSON 24 Apr. 1826, before BARNABAS PACE & JOHN LOYALL, Esqr. Z. B. HARGROVE, D.C.C. Rec. 1 Sept. 1826.

Pages 15-16: Newton Co.: L. W. & T. of JOHN MOSS being weak in body... to wife ALENDER and four sons BURWELL MOSS, JOHN MOSS, THOMAS MOSS & WHITNER MOSS two lots where I now live and four negroes (named)... to my son as guardian and father JAMES MOSS, two negroes and bed and furniture... to my son as guardian and father, ANDY MOSS, two negroes and bed and furniture... remainder to be given to WILLIAM MOSS, JAMES MOSS, ANDY MOSS equally as to son WILLIS and daughter FANNY BROWN (??), I have given an equal portion heretofore, but will leave them one dollar each... 6th October 1825... JOHN MOSS (LS). Wit: JOHN STOCKS, BARNET MITCHAM, DAVID HARRIS (X). Proven by all three wit. 6th March 1827, before LAMBETH HOPKINS, Clk. C.O. Rec. 7th Mar. 1827.

Pages 16-19: 30 Mar. 1827, Will of JOHN HAMILTON of Newton Co... to my son CADER HAMILTON, two negroes (named), lot #207, 16th Dist., Henry, now Newton Co... to my son GEORGE K. HAMILTON, negro named Washington... my wife REBECCA HAMILTON... lot #108, 16th Dist., Henry, now Newton Co... daughter ELIZABETH SLANNERY (?)... daughter NANCY WARREN... daughter MORIAH WARREN... daughter JANE NORTON ... (date of will illegible) JOHN HAMILTON (X) (SEAL). Wit: Illegible. Rec. 8 Mar. 1827.

Pages 19-20: L. W. & T. of ELIJAH JONES (will very dim)... wife LUCY... (date illegible)... ELIJAH JONES (SEAL). Wit: JOSEPH MORRIS, JOHN W. MORRIS (X), JOSIAH STALLINGS. Proven 2 Apr. 1827.

Pages 20-23: Newton County: L. W. & T. of DAVID WELBORN... to my wife MARY WELBORN, Negro... three daughters MALINDA, ELIZABETH & ___ (remainder of will too dim to read, names several sons)... 25 Jan. 1827. DAVID WELLBORN (SEAL). Wit: GEORGE L. SMITH, MOSES TRIMBLE (?)... Proven 7 May 1827.

Pages 23-24: Newton County: L. W. & T. of THOMAS ? CURETON... to wife MARY A. CURETON during her life or widowhood, all estate real and personal... for the benefit of my children (not named)... wife Extx... T. J. CURETON (SEAL). Wit: JAMES BERRY, JOHN B. BAGLY, JACOB HARMAN. Prov. 2 July 1827. Will dated 9 May 1827.

Pages 24-26: Georgia, Hancock County: L. W. & T. of HARTWELL GAIRY (sic)... to son NATHANIEL GAIRY, $800, one bed bedstead and

furniture... to daughter JULIA MARTHEWS, one bed and furniture and $800...
to son NICHOLAS GAIRY, if he should marry a woman against my wish... to
my friend WILLIAM STANTON, tract which he is now possessed of deed to me
by the Sheriff of sd. county...to wife REBECCA GAIRY, to educate the
children... friends JOHN TURNER, FRANCIS JETER, and DAVID (?) HAMILTON
Esqr. my Exts... 10 May 1825... HARTWELL GARY (SEAL). Wit: GEORGE
HAMILTON, ELIZABETH HAMILTON, PETER SCOTT, DUKE HAMILTON... Proven in
Newton County by DUKE HAMILTON & PETER SCOTT 2 July 1827. Rec. 13 July
1827.

Pages 26-27: Georgia, Newton County: L. W. & T. of JOSEPH VANE
being infirm in body... to wife ELIZABETH JANE and the three youngest
children, ALBERT, JOSEPH & ISAAC... three eldest children NANCY,
LAURENCE (?) & EUDICIA (?)... 24 Jan. 1827... JOSEPH VANE (LS). Wit:
GEORGE L. SMITH, URIAH SPARKS, GEORGE __ WHIPPLE. Proven by URIAH SPARKS
14 Jan. 1828. L. C. HOPKINS, Clk.

Pages 28-29: Georgia, Newton County: L. W. & T. of MOSES CRIMBLE..
to my beloved children JAMES, JOHN, PHILIP and SARAH, $20 each within 12
months of my decease... to daughter ESTHER whatever my executor shall
think right... to sons MOSES & ELISHA, each 1/3 of the residue of my
estate... beloved wife CATHARINE... JOHN TRUMBLE, Exr... Feb. 1828...
MOSES TRIMBLE (LS). Wit: L. HOPKINS, JAMES TRIMBLE, C. COURSEY. Proven
by JAMES TRIMBLE and LAMBETH HOPKINS on 1 Sept. 1828. Registered 3
Sept. 1828.

Pages 29-31: L. W. & T. of DAVID HARRIS, being weak in body... to
wife HANNAH, an equal third of my estate... when my daughters marry, one
bed and furniture... if my wife marries, children to have an equal portion... when sons come of age, to have a horse and saddle... wife HANNAH
& sons TYRE (?) and LANFORD HARRIS, Exrs... 18 Feb. 1829... DAVID HARRIS
(X). Wit: JAMES E. TODD, THOMAS DACUS. Proven by THOMAS DACUS 4 May
1829. Proven by JAMES E. TODD 6 June 1829. Reg. 23 July 1829.

Pages 32-33: Newton County: L. W. & T. of THOMAS COCKRELL SENR...
to son SANFORD COCKREL, $2... to son JOHN COCKREL, 150 A whereon I now
dwell... wife MARY... to son THOMAS COCKREL, $2... to son GREGORY, $2...
to son JOHN, $2... to daughter JANE SAVAGE, $2... to daughter MARGARET
DOLSON (?), $2... to daughter LETTUCE ALEWINE, a negro girl... to daughter
MARY, $2... wife MARY, Extx... 5 Aug. 1829... THOMAS COCKRELL SENR. (X)
(SEAL). Wit: WM. W. JARROLL, WM. PARICH (+), GERARD CAMP. Proven by
all 3 wit. 5 Jan. 1830. Rec. 6 Jan. 1830.

Page 34: L. W. & T. of MICAJAH SAUSON of Newton County... being
of advanced age... to grand daughter ARTISSIMA MALONE, 1/3 part of land
I now live upon and all household furniture... MICAJAH SAUSON (X) (SEAL).
Wit: WILLIAM WALLACE, JOHN HENDRICK (X), WM. B. GRAVES. Proven 5 July
1830 by all 3 wit. Rec. 9 July 1830.

Pages 35-39: Georgia, Clark County: L. W. & T. of SOLOMON GRAVES
of Newton County... to wife JOANNA GRAVES, four negroes (named), all the
claim that she may have... to son JOHN, all the tract in Newton County
where he now lives, 312 1/2 A... to son SOLOMON GRAVES tract in Newton
Co., where he now lives, purchased of BOMAS (?), 250 A & 50 or 60 A
attached to it... to son BARZILLA GRAVES in trust for my son SIDNEY
GRAVES, 750 A... son JOURDAN (??)... daughter FRANCES GRAHAM... plantation on west side of Alcofanhatcher (?) River... son WILLIAM GRAVES...
son IVERSON (?)... 18 Sept. 1830... SO. GRAVES (LS). Wit: JOEL
WILLIAMS, JNO W. GRAVES, THOMAS F. FOSTER. Proven in Newton Co. 1
Nov. 1830, L. HOPKINS, Clk.

Pages 39-40: Newton Co.: L. W. & T. of CHARLES H. WILLINGHAM...
being weak in body... wife ANNY WILLINGHAM to have the plantation where
I now live... except what I have already given to my son WILKINS WILLING-
HAM... wife and children (not named)... son WILKINS WILLINGHAM, Exr.
8 July 1830... CHARLES H. WILLINGHAM (SEAL). Wit: JOHN P. LEWIS, JAMES
DOWNS, ___ DOWNS, J.P. Proven by JAMES DOWNS, 28 Dec. 1830.

Pages 41-42:   L. W. & T. of SARAH FIELDER of Newton Co... being now of good health and sound mind... to my granddaughter SARAH AN LOYALL.. daughter MARIAH MONTGOMERY... daughter SARAH ANN LOYALL... friend JOHN LOYALL, Exr... 4 May 1826... SARAH ANN FIELDER (X) (LS). Wit: REUBEN PHILLIPS, SETH P. STORRS, JOHN LOYALL. Proven 3 Jan. 1831.

Pages 43-44:   L. W. & T. of JOHN MIDDLEBROOKS of Newton County... son ZARA, $10... son ANDERSON, $10 ... daughter ABIGAIL STANTON, $10... son ISAAC S. MIDDLEBROOKS, 125 A whereon he now lives... to son JOHN, tract he sold to HENSON at $450... to wife MILLY, land where I now live and negroes (named), at her death to be divided among my sons ISAAC, DAVID & JOHN... sons ISAAC, DAVID & JOHN Exrs... 27 Feb. 1828... JOHN MIDDLEBROOKS (LS). Wit: JESSE M. CARTER, C. A. CARTER. Proven by JESSE M. CARTER & CHRISTOPHER A. CARTER, 7 Mar. 1831. Rec. 8 Mar. 1831.

Pages 45-46:   Newton County: L. W. & T. of THOMAS HANSON... lot where I now live, #96, 10th Dist., formerly Henry, now Newton Co. and part of #221, 9th Dist. on west side Yellow River divided between my daughter ELIZABETH and sons HENRY EVANS HANSON and JAMES JEFFERSON HANSON.. heirs of my son JOHN HANSON, dec'd. receive $1... son WILLIAM HANSON, $50... balance divided between my daughter ELIZABETH, son SAMUEL, son HENRY C. HANSON, JAMES HANSON and legal heirs of my daughter REBECCA ROGERS and JOHN A. HANSON, son of JOHN HANSON, dec'd... wife ELIZABETH, sons HENRY E. & JAMES J. HANSON & DAVID ROGERS, Exrs... 7 Feb. 1827... THOMAS HANSON (LS). Wit: ELIZ. MCSPARREN, STEPHEN ROWE. Proven by ELIZA STOVALL, formerly ELIZA MCSPARREN & S. ROWE. 2 May 1831.

Pages 46-49:   Newton County: L. W. & T. of JAMES ZACHRY somewhat advanced in years... wife POLLY ZACHRY, lot where my buildings now stand (sic) and 4 negroes (names) with his exception, will give when needed by my four youngest children a good bed and furniture equal to one given to TABITHA SIMMONS... to daughter TABITHA SIMMONS, negro and other property given to her when she went to house keeping... to daughter LOUISA, negro (named)... to son ALFRED F. ZACHRY, negro (named)... to daughter SARAH ANNE, negro (named)... to daughter MARY, negro (named)... remainder to be divided into five shares ... ASA SIMMONS to have one, the other four for support of my other four children... wife and ASA SIMMONS, Exrs... 15 Feb. 1831... JAMES ZACHRY. Wit: JOHN BOWEN, MICHAEL SMITH, BARNABAS PACE. Proven 5 Sept. 1831.

Pages 49-50:   Newton County: L. W. & T. of JOSEPH LAWS... being weak in body... wife TABITHA LAWS, all estate real and personal... to daughter SALLY WHITEHEAD, $500 to be placed in hands of her guardian (she being lunatic at times)... to son SPENCER LAWS, $50... to son JOHN LAWS, one equal part of estate... to son ISHAM LAWS, one equal part of estate... to daughter JANE MAUN (?) one equal part of estate... to daughter SINEY DUBERRY, one equal part of estate... to daughter MARTHA PENNINGTON, one equal part of my estate... to son STEPHEN LAWS, one equal part of estate... to son in law WILLIAM FINDLEY, $1... to son in law GILBERT WHITEHEAD, $1... TRESMAN WALTHALL & O. M. FIELDER, Exrs... 1 Nov. 1830... JOSEPH LAWS (SEAL). Wit: WILLIAM HOOD, JAS WITCHER, ELIJAH MIXON, ABNER F. DEARING. Prov. 23 Nov. 1831. Rec. 3 Jan. 1832.

Pages 51-52:   L. W. & T. of THOMAS B. WYATT of Newton County, being weak in body... to daughter JEMIMA MIZE, $5... to daughter NANCY MOORE, $5... to daughter MARY KELLY, $5... to daughter SUSANNAH BURGES, $5... to MARTHA MOORE (no relation stated), $5... to my daughter THURZA MOORE, $5... to daughter LUCY GAY, $5... to daughter SARAH WYATT at the death of her mother one bed and furniture... to granddaughter LURANCY (?) WYATT, one bed and furniture and one 2 year old heifer... to wife SUSANNAH WYATT, all privilege of land and premises to live on... at her death sons JOSEPH WYATT & THOMAS M. WYATT, all my land... to JOSEPH M. WYATT, upper part of land adj. SHACKLEFORD & WILBORN & to THOMAS, the other part adj. GAY & BRIDGES... sons THOS & JOSEPH Exrs... 23 Oct. 1830. THOS. B. WYATT (SEAL). Wit: NANCY BRADLEY (X), JOHN MCKISSACK, THOMAS WILBORN, J.P. Proven 2 Jan. 1832 by all 3 wit. Reg. 3 Jan. 1832.

Pages 53-54: Newton County: L. W. & T. of AZARIAH BAILEY, being low in health... tract I now live on, part of 3 lots, to JOSHUA BAILEY, JOSEPH BAILEY & EPHRAIM HEARN... lot in Henry ? County, #122, 6th Dist., to legal representatives of WILLIAM BAILEY, dec'd. and to legal representatives of CALEB BAILEY, dec'd. to be equally divided... to BENJAMIN H. BAILEY and his heirs, 1/2 of tract whereon WILLIAM HUBBARD now resides, to JOSHUA BAILEY, negroes (named)... to JOSEPH BAILEY, $400... I hold notes on THOMAS FIELDER & JOSEPH HOWARD... to grandson JESSE H. BAILEY, $130, to be kept in hands of BENJAMIN H. BAILEY... to my grand children JESSE, WILLIAM, AZARIAH, ELIZABETH & JOHN BAILEY, son of my son CALEB BAILEY, dec'd. $100... sons JOSHUA & BENJAMIN, Exrs. 19 Oct. 1831 A. BAILEY (SEAL). Wit: RICHARD Z. HARGROVE, J. W. MORROW, JAMES HODGE, JUNR. Proven 5 Mar. 1832 by all 3 wit. Reg. 10 Apr. 1832.

Pages 55-56: Newton County: L. W. & T. JOEL JONES, in good health, to wife NANCY, all real and personal estate during her life... land estate to son JOEL & JAMES... four daughters REBEKAH EVANS, NANCY SNOW, CYNTHIA RUSSEL & SUSANNAH T. NEWSOM, each $25... slaves Judy & Tom to be emancipated... children TIMOTHY JONES, ELIZABETH GREENE, POLLY GREENE, REBEKAH EVANS, NANCY SNOW, CYNTHIA RUSSEL, SUSANNAH NEWSOM, WILLIAM JONES, JOEL JONES & JAMES JONES... sons WILLIAM & JOEL, Exrs... 19 Oct. 1830. JOEL JONES (SEAL). Wit: GEORGE L. SMITH, SIMPSON BARFIELD, PHILIP C. PENDLETON. Proven by BARFIELD & PENDLETON 3 Sept. 1832. Reg. 4 Dec. 1832.

Pages 57-59: L. W. & T. of WILLIAM PATRICK of Newton County, being in good health... all of my estate for support of wife ELIZABETH H. PATRICK and children MARY E. PATRICK, LUCY A. PATRICK, MARTHA W. PATRICK, FRANCES JANE PATRICK & ABRAHAM W. PATRICK, for their education... wife may give them what she wishes when they arrive at 21 or marry... to son in law GEORGE CUNNINGHAM, negroes... ALEXANDER PHARR & JOHN C. MCLAUGHLIN, Exrs... 28 Sept. 1832. WILLIAM PATRICK (P). Wit: JOHN E. P. LYONS, THOS AUSLEY, REBEKAR AUSLEY. Proven by all 3 wit. 1 July 1833. Rec. 3 July 1833.

Pages 60-61: Newton County: L. W. & T. of JOHN FINCHER being weak in body... to daughter MARY LAMBETH, one feather bed and furniture.. to daughter MARGARET POPE, one bed and furniture ... to wife NANCY FINCHER, residue for herself and education my children... daughter LUCINDA FINCHER, son JAMES FINCHER... son JOHN J. FINCHER... daughter PERMELIA FINCHER... son LEONARD FINCHER... daughter ISBEAL FINCHER... daughter ELITHY ANN FINCHER... wife NANCY, JOHN CLARK, PRIOR REAVES, PLEASANT EVANS, Exrs... 13 Oct. 1832. JOHN FINCHER (X) (SEAL). Wit: TURMAN WALTHALL, EDWARD W. LANE, L. P. HARGROVE, JOHN CLARK, PRIOR REEVES, PLEASANT EVANS (X). Proven 1 July 1833 by CLARK & REEVES. Reg. 3 July 1833.

Pages 62-63: Newton County: L. W. & T. of THOMAS W. GARNER... to wife MARTHA, all my property during her life or widowhood... the estate my father left brother WILLIAM GARNER's children to remain in hands of my Extx. until the children come of age... eldest son WILLIAM GARNER to heave his part when he comes of age... son JOHN, daughter ANN S. GARNER, son MICAJAH THOMAS... wife MARTHA and friend JESSE OSLIN, Exrs... 1 March 1834.. THOS W. GARNER (SEAL). Wit: JOHN SELFRIDGE, ALLAN PARKER (X), JOHN GASTON (G). Proven by PARKER & SELFRIDGE 5 May 1834. Proven by GASTON & May 1834. Reg. 7 July 1834.

Pages 64-65: SAMUEL LAZOULY (?) died on 19 June 1834 at his residence in Newton Co... (nuncupative will)... wife NANCY TO have all property and at her death to be divided equally among all his children... Exrs., wife NANCY, SUSAN WHATLEY & CHARLES HUFF. Wit: ELISHA TRIMBILL, SUSANNAH MARKS, GEORGE HAYS. Proven July Term 1834... 7 July 1834.

Pages 65-66: Newton County: L. W. & T. of JAMES PHILLIPS being old and well stricken in years... to wife SARAH PHILLIPS, bed and furniture we now lie on and trunk she now keeps her clothes in and one set of earthen plates... at her death to go to my son TRISTAM PHILLIPS... to sons JOEL, JOHN and daughter MARY PHILLIPS and son DANIEL PHILLIPS and daughter SARAH HUGHS and sons SOLOMON, ELIJAH, JAMES and daughter ABIGAIL WINDHAM and heirs of my dec'd. daughter PRESSILA CARREL, all I have given them... JAMES PARNAL & TRISTAM PHILLIP, Exrs... 14 June 1834. Wit: WM. DREEL, THOS DREEL. Prov. 3 Nov. 1834 by all 3 wit. Reg. 5 Dec. 1834.

Pages 67-68: Newton Co.: L. W. & T. of CELIA KENNAN... my daughter ELIZABETH L. HINES had considerable of my property and died indebted to me, which I give to her three children MARY M., SARAH R., & THEREBY... remainder of my estate to be divided among my daughter MARY MARTIN, and sons WILLIAM, RICHARD, JOHN, CHARLES & THOMAS KENNAN... RICHARD CHARLES and THOMAS, Exrs... 8 Oct. 1831... CELIA KENNAN (SEAL). Wit: AARON G. BREWER, LEONARD FRETWELL, H. G. BEATES. Proven by HORACE G. BATES, LEONARD FRETWELL, 5 Dec. 1834. Proven by AARON BREWER 18 Dec. 1834. Reg. 9 Jan. 1835.

Pages 69-70: Newton Co.: L. W. & T. of SAMUEL STEWART... to wife REBECCA, tract I now live on... my two children WILLIAM SPENCER & RACHEL JANE... brother WILLIAM STEWART, Exr... 12 Nov. 1834... SAMUEL STEWART (X) (SEAL). Wit: WILLIAM TAYLOR, JOHN E. RAGAN, PATRICK STEWART. Proven by all 3 wit. 5 Jan. 1835. Reg. 9 Jan. 1835

Pages 70-74: Newton Co.; L. W. & T. JACOB HARMAN... to wife ANNY HARMON, my dwelling house & tract known as Hodge tract adj. premises & adj. EPPS TUCKER SR., EDWIN PAYNE & MRS. ELIZABETH BAGLY, 202 1/2 A... until my youngest child NANCY CAROLINE, who will be 4 years old in October next, becomes of age or marries... estate equally divided among my children except son JAMES who is to have $200 more than the other children on account of his being a cripple... to my daughter CLARISSA, wife of JOHN B. BAGBY, $207.45 or property if she prefers... to son LEWIS M. HARMAN, a young mare, not until he arrives at lawful age... the rest of my children THOMAS S., ELIZABETH, JACOB, WESLY, JOHN, FLETCHER & NANCY CAROLINE HARMAN... wf ANNY, JOHN B. BAGBY & son LEWIS, Exrs, 17 Sept. 1834... JACOB HARMAN (SEAL). Wit: C. F. SANDERS, WM. P. GRAHAM, H. BURGE. Proven 4 Nov. 1834. Reg. 9 Jan. 1835.

Pages 75-76: L. W. & T. of LETTIA or LETTEY PAYNE of Newton Co... to SARAH BOWMAN who has lived with me many years and has been kind, attentive and useful to me, all my personal estate... friends NESTHER (?) PITT of Jasper Co. and JESSE M. WILSON or Morgan Co., Exrs... 21 July 1834... LETTEY PAYNE (X) (SEAL). Wit: WILLIAM L. JUSTISS, HARRISON AUSTIN, BAT L. STAUNTON. Proven by all 3 wit., 5 Jan. 1835. Reg. 3 Mar. 1835.

Pages 77-78: L. W. & T. of DAVID STOVALL of Newton Co... to wife MARGARET STOVALL, negroes (named) and all my lands in Newton Co., on waters of big Haynes Creek and lot in Irwin Co., when drawn and one 40 acre lot in Paulding Co... at her death to JAMES R. MCCORLEY and his wife PELOVIA ANN ELIZABETH... JAMES R. MCCORLEY and wf MARGARET, Exrs... 17 Oct. 1835... DAVID STOVALL (LS). Wit: THOS BAKER, WM. HENRY, WM. S. ECHOLDS, J.P. Proven by all 3 wit. 2 Nov. 1835. Reg. 3 Nov. 1835.

Pages 79-80: Newton Co.: 21 May 1835... L. W. & T. of JOHN SEGLER, to wife MATILDA SEGLER, tract I live on except 50 A, lot #278, 16th Dist., originally Henry, now Newton Co... to my two daughters ELIZABETH and ANGELICO... sons MATHEW & JOHN NICHOLAS, 100 A, the west half of lot #289, 16th Dist., Henry, now Newton Co... to son WILLIAM RILEY, 50 A of Lot $278... wife MATILDA, ELIJAH RAGSDALE, SENR. & R. W. WOOD, JR., Exrs... JOHN SEGLER (SEAL). Wit: MATILDA SELER (sic) (X), ELIJAH RAGSDALE SENR. (X), R. W. WOODS, JUR. Proven by all 3 wit. 22 Dec. 1835. Reg. 6 Jan. 1836.

Pages 81-83: L. W. & T. of HEZEKIAH LUCKIE of Newton Co... wife JANE LUCKIE, negroes (named)... and present property... to son WILLIAM F. LUCKIE, negroes (named)... to son SAMUEL H. LUCKIE, negro (named)... to son ALEXANDER S. LUCKIE, negroes (named)... to daughter MARYANN PACE, negroes (named)... to daughter JULIA E. WILBURN, negroes (named)... sons WILLIAM, ALEXANDER & COLUMBUS C. PACE, Exrs... 16 Dec. 1835... HEZEKIAH LUCKEI (SEAL). Wit: REUBEN WOODRUFF, WYATT HOWELL, RICHARD ROSEBERRY. Proven 4 Jan. 1836 by all 3 wit. Reg. 6 Jan. 1836.

Pages 83-84: L. W. & T. of WILLIAM H. LOVE (LOWE, LANE??) of Covington, Newton Co... unto my beloved wife SUSAN K. LOVE (?) and to her issue by our present marriage, all of my estate... wife, father HENRY LOVE (?) of Town of Covington and my brother in law BENJAMIN K. POUDES (PONDER?) of Montgomery Co., Alabama, Exrs... 6 Dec. 1835... WILLIAM H. LOVE (?) (SEAL). Wit: ELIAS B. GOULD, E. WHITEHURST, MARYAN F. PONDER (?). Proven by MARY ANN F. PONDER (?) & Mar. 1836. Reg. 8 Mar. 1836.

Pages 85-87: Newton Co.: L. W. & T. of ELIZABETH HANSON... I have $500 loaned out, due 25 Dec. 1836, I bequeath it to DAVID ROGERS in trust for my niece JULIA MANDA SIMS... should she die without issue, to the heirs of my sister REBECCA ROGERS, the heirs of my brother JEFFERSON HANSON & SAMUEL HANSON... I have an interest in my deceased fathers estate, after the death of my mother ELIZABETH HANSON, I leave it to sd. DAVID ROGERS, Trustee appointed... JAMES K. HANSON, Exr... 19 Feb. 1836... ELIZABETH HANSON (SEAL). Wit: ROBERT B. UNDERWOOD, SAMUEL E. THOMPSON, WILLIAM P. ROGERS. Proven by all 3 wit. 1 June 1836. Reg. 22 Aug. 1836.

Pages 87-88: Newton Co.: L. W. & T. of CHARLES KEYS, believing my departure of this life is near at hand... land I have in Walker Co. to be sold and also lot in Pauldon (sic) Co., proceeds to go to wife CATHARINE KEYS... wife CATHARINE and daughter GINNEY D. KEYS, Exrs... 18 May 1836... CHARLES KEYS (X) (SEAL). Wit: THOS. A. DUKE, MARY WEIR, JOHN SMITH. Proven by THOS. A. DUKE & MARY WEIR 4 July 1836. Proven by JOHN SMITH 5 Sept. 1836. Reg. 8 Nov. 1836.

Page 89: Newton Co.: On __ Sept. 1835, ELIZABETH COLEMAN made her nuncupative will... granddaughter NANCY LANGFORD to receive $100, the balance to be divided between NANCY GWINN & JERUSHA BUTLER... GEORGE ELLAM to be paid $17 due him... land drawn in late Cherokee lottery, sold for benefit of my children... MINOR GWINN to execute will... Proven by NANCY GWIN, RACHAEL HENDERSON & MINOR GWINN 2 May 1836. Reg. 8 Nov. 1836.

Pages 90-91: Newton Co.: L. W & T. of THOMAS CHILDRESS SEN... to my son $1 (not named) ... to sons JOHN, KENNER, MARTIN, DAVID, THOMAS, and EINSLEY, each $1... to daughters LEANER, SABRENA, MARIA, each $1... to daughters ELIZABETH WOOD, negro (named)... to wife MARY, negro (named) sons EINSLEY & RICHARD W. WOOD, to take charge of my wife MARY... ELIJAH RAGSDALE & RANDAL BURNEY, Exrs... 16 July 1836... THOMAS CHILDRESS SENR. (X) (SEAL). Wit: JOHN C. RAGSDALE, SANDERS W. RAGSDALE, WM. S. ECHOLS, J.P. Proven by JOHN C. & SANDERS W. RAGSDALE & Nov. 1836. Reg. 4 Jan. 1837.

Pages 91-92: Newton Co.: L. W. & T. of THOMAS WALLIS... to wife (not named), all my property... WILLIAM WALLIS & MARK POLSOM, Exrs., to do what they think best for my widow and orphans... 31 Jan. 1836... THOMAS WALLIS (X) (SEAL). Wit: NICHOLAS H. BACON, WM. WALLIS, RABEN (sic). Proven by WM. WALLIS & JOSIAH WALLIS, & Nov. 1836. Reg. 4 Jan. 1837.

Pages 93-94: Newton Co.: L. W. & T. of ANN SHEPHERD, being quite old and infirm... to grandson ROBERT J. HENDERSON, $100... to two grandsons ROBERT J. & JOHN J. HENDERSON, two tracts in Telfor (sic) Co. and in Cobb Co.... to granddaughter FRANCES CORDUM HENDERSON, bed and furniture.. 27 Feb. 1836... ANN SHEPHERD (X) (SEAL). Wit: WOODSON P. ALLEN, ISAAC P. HENDERSON, WILLIAM RASBERRY. Proven by WOODSON ALLEN and ISAAC HENDERSON 6 Mar. 1837. Proven by RASBERRY 28 Mar. 1837. Reg. 10 Apr. 1837.

Pages 94-95: Newton Co.: 16 Sept. 1833... L. W. & T. of SAMUEL CHURCHWELL... to wife SARAH CHURCHWELL property I die seized of... the

217

girl that we have raised by the name of ROSANNAH HALL, one feather bed
and furniture and one cow and calf and a part of my estate with my
children... SAMUEL CHURCHWELL. Wit: WILLIAM WINGFIELD, SAML. WINGFIELD.
Proven by both wit. 15 July 1837.

Pages 95-97:   L. W. & T. of WILLIAM WALLACE of Newton Co... 22 Apr.
1837... to wife PENELOPE WALLACE lot we now live on, #150 originally
Talton (??) Co., now Newton Co., 250 A at her death to be divided
among my three sons JAMES, ANDREW & JOHN WALLACE... daughter MARTHA
WALLACE, LANEY WALLACE, REBECCA WALLACE & ELIZABETH WALLACE... to son
WILLIAM, $5... to daughter FRANCES, $5... sons WILLIAM, ALEXANDER &
THOMAS WALLACE, daughters FRANCES, MARGERY, ABIGAIL... WILLIAM WALLACE
(SEAL). Wit: JAMES WALLACE, JONATHAN GIBSON, REDDING C. SHIP. Proven
by all 3 wit. 3 July 1837. Reg. 10 July 1837.

Pages 97-100:   Newton Co.: L. W. & T. of MARTHA JOHNSON... to
daughter MARTHA ZEMBY DURHAM, 20 A upon which I resided last year, in
9th Dist., originally Henry, now Newton Co... purchased from MASERS (?)
L. GRAVES... (MARTHA's) daughter MARTHA WILLIAM DURHAM... I have a large
claim with the U. S Government for Indian Specolation (sic) ... $100
to female children of my daughter SARAH BROWN, $200 to female children of
my daughter ELIZA PULLEN, $200 to female children of my daughter HARRIET
GASTON, if she ever have any daughters, if not to my grandson DAVID
GASTON... MARTHA ZEMBE DURHAM, Extx... 21 Feb. 1838... MARTHA JOHNSON
(X) (SEAL). Wit: TOM S. MCCORD, ELIZABETH EUBANKS, H. J. BATES.
Proven by all 3 wit. 8 Mar. 1838. Reg. 16 Mar.1838.

Pages 100-101:   Newton Co.: L. W. & T. of MARTHA MAPPIN... all
property divided among my children and my two little granddaughters
MARTHA & MARY ELIZABETH DENHAM, daughters of my daughter ELIZABETH W.
DENHAM... my son THOMAS W. H. MAPPIN... my husband JAMES MAPPIN's estate.
JAMES WILLIS MAPPIN, Exr... 16 July 1838... MARTHA MAPPIN. Wit: DAVID
R. PERRYMAN, GEORGE SHIPLEY, GARUT SPINKS (?). Proven by SHIPLY &
SPINKS (?), 3 Sept. 1838. Reg. 16 Sept. 1838.

Pages 102-104:   L. W. & T. of JOSEPH LIVINGSTON of Newton Co... to
son ROBERT B. LIVINGSTON, lot on which I now reside & 2 negroes (named)..
to son JOSEPH $65... to daughter ELIZABETH H. TRIMBLE, $65... plantation
to wife ELIZABETH LIVINGSTON... at her death to heirs: WILLIAM LIVINGS-
TON, JAMES LIVINGSTON, JOSEPH LIVINGSTON, WILLIAM B. FOREMAN, heirs of my
daughter RUTHA DAVIS and daughter ELIZABETH H. TRIMBEL... sons JAMES,
JOSEPH & ROBT. Exrs... 21 July 1838... JOSEPH LIVINGSTON (SEAL). Wit:
JAS. HODGE, JUNR., JNO. L. GRAVES, HULL SIMS. Proven by GRAVES & SIMS.
3 Sept. 1838. Proven by HODGE 22 Sept. 1838. Reg. 25 Sept. 1838.

Pages 105-106:   Newton Co.: L. W. & T. of REUBEN CHRISTIAN, being
weak in body... to son JOHN L. CHRISTIAN, $1 in addition to what he
has heretofore had... to son in law AUSTIN WEBB, $1 in addition... to
son in law ELIJAH W. CHRISTIAN, $1... to son ABAX CHRISTIAN, $1... after
debts are paid, estate to go to wife MARY ANN CHRISTIAN and son REUBEN J.
J. CHRISTIAN... ELIJAH W. & ABAX CHRISTIAN, Exrs... 13 Dec. 1838...
REUBEN CHRISTIAN (SEAL). Wit: JAMES READ, J.P., ELISHA RAY, EPHRAIM
THORN. Proven by all 3 wit. 4 Mar. 1839. Reg. 7 Mar. 1839.

Pages 107-109:   County of ___ : L. W & T. of JAMES MCDONALD, having
been taken with the palsie on the 17th of March at night 1835 and being
weak on one side... to wife FLORAN, $10 three years after my death... to
daughter AGNESS DAY... to son CHARLES MCDONALD, $10... to son MELTON
MCDONALD, $10... to son JAMES MELVIN MCDONALD, $125... to son ROBERT
MCDONALD, $10... to daughter LUCINDA LEE DUKE, $10... to daughter
MARY STEVENSONS ehirs, by her husband JOHN STEVENSON, negroes (named)...
also there is $172 due to JOHN STEVENSON in notes on MCDOW... friend
SEABRON CLARK and son in law JOHN STEVENSON, Exrs... 10 Jan. 1839.
JAMES MCDONALD (SEAL). Wit: SILAS MCLAIN, WILLIAM H. STEPHENSON, WILLIAM
M. HULSEY. Proven in Newton Co., by all 3 wit. 7 March 1839.

Pages 110-112:   L. W. & T. of JOSIAH W. TAYLOR of Newton Co... wife
ELIZABETH, all estate real and personal, 170 A, part of lot $243, 10th
Dist., originally Henry Co., at her death, to sons ALFRED & ROBERT TAYLOR..
my two minor grandchildren ELIZABETH JANE and CHARLES TAYLOR PLUNKET,
son and daughter of ELIJAH & MARY PLUNKETT... to son WILLIAM TAYLOR, who
I presume is in the Republick (sic) of Texas, $1... JAMES LIMOND of De-
Kalb Co., Exr... Jan. 1839... JOSIAH W. TAYLOR. Wit: BARNES W. DIXON,
JAMES MCCOLLUM, W. R. MAN. Proven __ Sept. 1839. Reg. 4 Sept. 1839.

Pages 113-114:   Newton Co.: L. W. & T. of WILLIAM EDMUNDS being
in great weakness of body... youngest son JOHN EDMUNDS, all household
furniture and plantation tools and land... to my next youngest child
MARTHA CLARK, negroes (named)... my next youngest child ROSE EDMUNDS...
my next youngest son JAMES EDMUNDS... my two oldest sons FRANCIS and
WILLIAM EDMUNDS... JOHN WEBB, FRANCIS & WILLIAM EDMUNDS, Exrs... 22 Apr.
1846... WILLIAM EDMUNDS (LS). Wit: ROSE EDMUNDS, JOHN EDMUNDS, JOHN
WEBB. Proven 4 May 1840. Reg. June 1840.

Pages 115-117:   L. W. & T. of JAMES HODGE SENIOR of Newton Co...
support of my wife and son STEPHEN HODGE... balance to be divided among
my children JOHN E., ANDREW T., DAVID, AND SAMUEL HODGE: ANN CARROL,
JAMES HODGE, CASSEY, BRANNON, WESLEY HODGE, DUKE H. HODGE & the children
of RACHAEL SKELTON... sons ANDREW & DAVID, Exrs... 30 Sept. 1840... JAMES
HODGE (LS). Wit: JOHN BASS, ISAIAH C. WALLACE, THOMAS JONES. Proven
1 Nov. 1841. Reg. Nov. 1841.

Pages 118-119:   L. W. & T. of JEREMIAH MATTHEWS of Newton Co... to
wife SARAH MATHEWS, all property real and personal, house and home where
I now live... at her death, to be divided among my children WILLIAM
MATHEWS, BURREL MATHEWS, ELBERT MATHEWS, CARY J. MATHEWS, LEWIS M.
MATHEWS, ELIJAH W. MATHEWS, POLLY STRONG, JEREMIAH MATHEWS, CADY JOHNSON,
SALLY BACON... 3 Sept. 1839... JEREMIAH MATHEWS (SEAL). Wit: ISAM GOSS,
JESSE M. MELTON, THOMAS J. GRAY. Proven 5 Sept. 1842. Reg. 10 Sept.
1842.

Pages 120-121:   Newton Co.: L. W. & T. of JOHN JONES of Newton
Co... to wife NANCY H. JONES, negros (named) and real and personal prop-
erty... wife NANCY, Extx... 3 Sept. 1842... JOHN JONES (SEAL). Wit:
PETER GRINNELL, PURMEDUS REYNOLDS, JOHN J. FLOYD. Proven by GRINNELL
& FLOYD. Reg. 15 Nov. 1842.

There is no page numbered 122.

Pages 123-125:   Newton Co.: L. W. & T. of RICHARD FRETWELL... to
grandson RICHARD FRETWELL, negro (named)... to grandson LEONARD FRETWELL,
negro (named)... to son LEONARD FRETWELL, in trust for granddaughter
PATSEY H. BROWN, negro (named)... to son LEONARD in trust for granddaughter FRANCES KENNON, wife of M. L. KENNON, negro (named)... to
LEONARD in trust for granddaughter MARY FRETWELL, negro (named)... to
grandson WILLIAM A. J. FRETWELL, son of LEONARD FRETWELL, negro (named)...
to grandson PHILLIP Z. FRETWELL, son of LEONARD, negro (named)... to daughter in law POLLY FRETWELL, wife of LEONARD, negro (named)... to daughters LUCY CLIFTON, NANCY BURGE & PATSEY HARWELL, $5... son LEONARD &
grandson RICHARD, Exrs... 16 Aug. 1842... RICHARD FRETWELL (+) (SEAL).
Wit: JOHN HARRIS, REUBEN RANSOM. Proven 2 Jan. 1843. Reg. 12 Jan. 1843.

Pages 126-128:   Newton Co.: L. W. & T. of DANIEL SCOTT... weak
of body... to wife GEMIMA SCOTT, all lands whereon I now live, 650 A
and negroes (named)... those children who remain single to be made equal
with those that are married in portions advanced... son SAMUEL SCOTT is
appointed trustee for my daughter JANE LINDLEY, because of want of confidence in son in law ELISHA LINDLEY, as he is standing security... to son
DANIEL, my D. B. shot gun and watch... my seven children JANE, WILLIAM,
SAMUEL, ELIZABETH, JAMES, JOHN & DANIEL... sons WILLIAM and SAMUEL Exrs..
10 Oct. 1842... DANIEL SCOTT (LS). Wit: SAMPSON GIBSON, SOLOMON GIBSON,
WILLIAM GIBSON, Proven by SAMPSON and WILLIAM GIBSON 3 July 1843. Reg.
July 1843.

Page 129:   L. W. & T. of JOHN T. SNIDER of Newton Co... wife JANE
SNIDER, all that remains after payment of debts... friend SAML BRYAN,
Exr... J. T. SNIDER. Wit: JAMES O. ANDREW, R. WATKINS LOVETT. Oxford,
Ga., 28 Mar. 1842. Proven by LOVETT 4 Oct. 1843.

Pages 130-131:   L. W. & T. of ROBERT A. STEELE of Newton Co... to
my mother MARY D. BROWN, negro Ben... after her death, to be sold and
money given to Georgia Conference Missionary Society for benefit of
Collard (sic) missions in Ga. Conference... to my mother lot #36, 2nd
Sect., 11th Dist., Cherokee & lot #137, 12th, Carrol... to MARTIN M. HAYS
& ANN M. HAYS, jointly, my horse, Carriage and Harness... to ANN M.
HAYES, two notes on ELONZA D. BROWN... to ELONZA D. BROWN... to ELONZA
D. BROWN & CLOVER P. BROWN, $5 each... 10 Feb. 1844... ROBERT A. STEELE
(LS). Wit: M. KENDREE TUCKER, GEORGE HAYS, ROBERT L. HAYS. Proven by
all 3 wit. 4 Mar. 1844. Reg. 8 Mar. 1844.

Pages 132-133:   L. W. & T. of JOSEPH HOLLINGSWORTH of Newton Co...
to son GEORGE, land on W of spring branch and the spring and 1/2 acre to
the best convenience of the spring...remainder distributed among the
children... MOSES & AARON HOLLINGSWORTH, Exrs... 20 June 1839... JOSEPH
HOLLINGSWORTH (LS). Wit: ROBERT PLUNKET, JAMES FARMER. Proven by
FARMER 6 May 1844. Proven by PLUNKET 11 May 1844.

Page 134:   Newton Co.: L. W. & T. of JANE REES... 2 negroes to
daughter MARY MCLUNG, at her death to go to my granddaughter NANCY MCLUNG,
negro Cary to grandson WILLIAM REES MCLUNG... 7 Oct. 1843... JANE REES
(X) (SEAL). Wit: JAMES PLUNKET, DAVID T. WHITE, J. P. Proven May term
1844.

Pages 135-136:   L. W. & T. of ELIZABETH BASS of Newton Co... to son
JOHN BASS, negro Henry, bed and furniture, money notes, one dozen silver
teaspoons... wearing apparell to children of my deceased daughter
TABITHA WILBURN... to grandson JOHN ALPHEUS WILBURN, $1... to grandson
FRANCIS MARION BASS, six silver teaspoons... to grandaughter LAVENIA JONES,
six silver teaspoons... son JOHN BASS, Exr... 27 Sept. 1844... ELIZABETH
BASS (X). Wit: HENRY GAITHER, DAVID KOLB, JOHN C. BASS. Proven by
GAITHER 24 Sept.1844. Proven by KOLB & BASS 5 Nov. 1844.

Pages 137-138:   Newton Co.: L. W. & T. of WILLIAM WALLIS... to
wife SARAH WALLIS, plantation where I now live, 400 A and negroes (named)
to make JOHN ZAPHNAPHPAANAH (sic) and WILLIAM WRILEY, my grandson equal
to my son NICHOLAS WALLIS, as they become 21... daughters MARY, ELIZABETH,
REBECCAH A., SARAH A. S., MARGARETT M., ASENIAH VANBUREN, son ZEPH-
NATHPAANAH (sic), $50... 19 June 1840, WM. WALLIS (LS). Wit: J. L.
BAKER, JOHN MEDOWS, PATRICK H. NORRIS (X). Proven by BAKER & MEADOWS
5 May 1845. Rec. June 1845.

Pages 139-142:   Newton Co.: L. W. & T. of WILLIAM HEATH... to son
in law WILLIAM B. ALLEN, negro Elmira, valued at $450... to son CICERO
HEATH, negro Burrell, valued at $450... to son ERASMUS T. HEATH, negro
Easter, valued at $450... to son EPENETUS HEATH, negro Boston valued at
$450... to son WILLIAM HEATH, $400... to son HENRY HEATH, negro Colquett,
valued at $400... to son JOHN HEATH, negro Dick, valued at $425... to
daughter MARY CAROLINA CAMP, negro Maria, valued at $350... to daughter
HARRIET REBECCA FLOYD, negro Amy, valued at $500... to son EPENETUS in
trust for my daughter SARAH JANE TURNER, negro Narcisa, valued at $300
to be equally divided between her and her husband JOHN A. TURNER, should
she die without issue... to wife MARY HEATH in trust for my daughters
SUSAN FRANCES & ADELLA HEATH, 2 negroes, when they arrive at age... to
wife MARY, negroes (named)... to daughter EMILY ALLEN and her female heirs,
friend WILLIAM C. DAVIS and wf. MARY, Exrs... 5 Feb. 1845... WILLIAM
HEATH (SEAL). Wit: A. W. EVANS, F. M. NIX, EDWARD NIX. Proven by
AUGUSTUS W. EVANS, FRANCIS M. NIX & EDWARD NIX & July 1845. Rec. 16
July 1845.

Pages 143-144:   L. W. & T. of ALEXANDER BENNET... to wife NANCY,
land including dwelling house, on old boundary of formerly Jasper County,
on road to HOGGS old Mill, adj. SAML MARKS line, PERRY's land, NELSON's

line, 125 A... to daughter ELIZABETH, negro Carolina, bed & furniture, and $100... to my dear children MARY LUNSFORD, FRANCES STARR, SARAH LUNSFORD, ALLA HOUGINS, AMALIA HARWELL, AMANDA DOBSON & WILLIAM BENNET, negroes (named)... WILLIAM GIBSON & WILLIAM BENNET Exrs... 20 Sept. 1845. A. BENNETT (SEAL). Wit: JOHN F. JACKSON, THOMAS J. CURTIS, JOSIAH PERRY. Proven by all 3 wit., 3 Nov. 1845. Rec. 19 Nov. 1845.

Pages 145-148: Newton Co.: L. W. & T. of RICHARD LOYALL... to wife all estate real and personal... as my children become of age or marry, wife to give them what she sees fit... if wife marries, her husband is not to be guardian of my children... wife TINSEY C. LOYALL, Extx. and half brother LAURENS BAKER, Exr... 17 May 1843. RICHARD LOYALL (LS). Wit JOHN N. WILLIAMSON, LEWIS ZACHARY, G. W. ADAIR. Proven by GEORGE W. ADAIR. 24 Oct. 1845. Proven by WILLIAMSON and ZACHARY 29 Oct. 1845.

Pages 149-150 are missing on film.

Page 151: Newton Co.: Personally appeared THOMAS BABER, ISAAC S. MIDDLEBROOKS & DAVID F. MONTGOMERY, who witnessed the will of BATT SHORT STANTON... 12 Jan. 1846. Reg. 15 Jan. 1846.

Pages 152-154: Newton Co.: L. W & T. of REBECCA HAMILTON... being weak and feeble in body... estate to sons in law WILLIAM WARREN, LITTLE-TON MANNING, ISAIAH W. D. BOHANNON, AMON VINCENT, son GEORGE K. HAMILTON, heirs of my son CADER HAMILTON, dec'd. vizt. JOHN W., HEZEKIAH N., JULIA ANN, MARY R., ROBERT L., GEORGE L. & MARTHA... son GEORGE K. HAMILTON of DeKalb Co., and son in law LITTLETON MANNING of Newton no., Exrs... 26 Oct. 1845... REBECCA HAMILTON (X). Wit: SEABORN J. CLARK, JAMES RUSSEL, GEORGE SHIPLEY. Proven by all 3 wit. 24 Nov. 1845. Reg. 16 Jan. 1846.

Pages 155-156: Georgia, Morgan Co.: L. W. & T. of GEORGE BROOKS.. to my children, all my land and negroes in Newton Co., also an estate in North Carolina if obtained, also one lot in Cherokee... to wife ELIZA H. BROOKS, formerly ELIZA. H. SHEPHERD, the property that I have or may receive from the estate of TALMON W. SHEPHERD... JOSEPH M. EVANS of Morgan Co., and JOHN L. GRAVES of Newton Co., Exrs... 29 July 1837... GEORGE BROOKS (LS). Wit: JO. H. WATTS., CHARLES N. HORNE, JAMES L. HORNE. Proven in Newton Co. by JAMES L. HORNE 3 Nov. 1845, and by CHARLES N. HORNE 29 Dec. 1845. Rec. 22 Jan. 1846.

Pages 157-158: Newton Co.: L. W. & T. of MARTHA BROWN, being of advanced age and believing that I must shortly depart from this world... to my granddaughter SALINA MCDOWELL, one bed, bedstead furniture... to son ASA BROWN, one bed and furniture, and 1/7 part of my property... to son BENJN. BROWN, one horse Billy and 1/7 of my property... to son JOSIAH BROWN, 1/7 of property... to daughter PRECILLA PLESS and her husband ANDREW PLESS, 1/7 of my property... to daughter CLARKEY HARTSFIELD and her husband ISAAC J. HARTSFIELD, 1/7 part of my property... to my daughter ELIZABETH WORD and her husband, WM. B. WORD, 1/7 part of my property... to my daughter MELTHY MCDONALD, wife of MELTON MCDONALD and to her children free from possession of her husband, 1/7 part of my property... son JOSIAH Trustee for Melthy & Exr... 21 Feb. 1846... MARTHA BROWN (X) (LS). Wit: ALEX PRUET, THOMAS C. HANSON. Proven by both sit. 4 May 1846. Rec. May 1846.

Page 159: Newton Co.: L. W. & T. of GEORGE LEEKE... to wife SARAH, negro LOUISA, furniture and $47 due me from JESSE ANSLEY... remainder to be taken by friends SILAS STARR, SR. and SILAS STARR, JR. for my children JOHN K. C. STARR LEAKE, SILAS B. LEAKE, WILLIAM B. LEAKE, JAMES A. LEAKE, BENJAMIN A. LEAKE... THOS. ANSLEY, SILAS STARR SR. and SILAS STARR, JR., Exrs... 7 July 1846... GEORGE W. LEEK. Wit: JNO. L. GRAVES, THOMAS D. TERRELL, A. BELCHER. Proven by TERREL & GRAVES 8 Sept. 1846. Rec. 15 Sept. 1846.

Pages 160-163: L. W. & T. of JOSEPH PERRY of Newton Co., being afflicted in body... to wife CLARISSA, negroes (named) and as much land

as she sees fit to cultivate... to WILLIAM H. CHISLOM, negroes (named)...
to son WALTER B. PERRY, negroes (named) and 1/5 of my library, one lot
in 20th Dist., 3rd Section, Cherokee, #286... to son JESSE M. PERRY,
negroes (named), land in Newton Co., adj. CURTIS and others, known as
Hodnett place, 490 A, and 1/5 of my library... to daughter AMANDA PERRY,
negroes (named), bed and furniture... to daughter SARAH PERRY, negroes
(named), bed and furniture... to son JOSIAH, negroes (named), and 1/5
of my library... to son HENRY BRADFORD PERRY, negroes (named) 5 shares
and 12 1/2 hundredth of Georgia Railroad Stock... to CLARISA PERRY,
negroes (named), 5 share and 12 1/2 hundredth of Ga. RR Stock... wife
Exr... 5 Mar. 1846. JOSIAH PERRY (LS). Wit: FELIX HARDMAN, JNO W.
PITTS, NESTOR PITTS. Proven by all 3 wit. 7 Sept. 1846.

Pages 164-167: Newton Co.: L. W. & T. of JAMES ROSEBURY... to
wife MARTHA ROSEBURY, tract I now live on in Newton Co.. 202 1/2 on
Wild Cat Creek adj. LEVINGSTON, COWEN, THOMPSON & MILLER, and two slaves
(named), one now loaned to REUBEN WOODRUFF... to JOHN N. WILLIAMSON of
Covington in trust for my son RICHARD ROSEBURY, undivided 1/2 of tract
upon which I now reside... in trust for son WILLIAM ROSEBURY, other 1/2
of tract... negroes (named) in possession of my son in law JAMES M.
KNIGHT, son in law JOHN PERGERSON and son WILLIAM to be evaluated and
divided... my daughter MARY KNIGHT... my daughter MARTHA PERGERSON...
daughter FRANCES WOODRUFF... to wife MARTHA, 1/2 of lot in 9th Dist.,
Henry, now Newton Co., on which my son RICHARD ROSEBURY now resides,
reference to a deed from HARRY CAMP to myself and JAMES D. ROSEBURY dated
6 Jan. 1842... grandsons ROBERT ROSEBURY & WM. ROSEBURY, sons of RICHARD
friend JOHN WEBB, Exr... 25 Nov. 1842... JAMES ROSEBURY (X) (SEAL). Wit:
ROBERT COWEN, CHESLEY KINNEY, ROBERT THOMPSON. Rec. 13 Nov. 1846.

Pages 168-169: Newton Co.: L. W. & T. of ROBERT LORD, weak in
body... to wife PATIENCE LORD, 1/3 of land including buildings on west
end and the balance to remain until my children come to age... beloved
son THOMAS to have $1... son WILLIAM B. LORD to have one mare colt... to
my daughter MARY ANN LORD and my daughters TILLITHA, SARAH JANE, REBECCA
ELEANOR LORD, one bed and furniture as they marry or become of age...
sons GEORGE W., JAMES M., and ROBERT G., $20 when they become of age...
wife PATIENCE, Exr... 25 May 1846... ROBERT LORD (X) (SEAL). Wit: ABDA
CHRISTIAN, ANDERSON VEAL (X), MOSES MANN. Proven by VEAL & MANN, 2 Nov.
1846.

Pages 170-171: Newton Co.: L. W. & T. of SOLOMON WORRELL...to
wife MARTHA, the house which I now occupy in the village of Oxford and
negroes (named)... my children OLIN, IVERSON, JANE, WILEY, SANFORD &
ALLEN... to my daughter HARRIET, negroes (named)... friend DOCTOR HENRY
GAITHER, Exr. 6 June 1845... SOLOMON WORRELL (SEAL). Wit: A. B. LONG-
STREET, GEO. G. SMITH, GEORGE W. W. STONE. Proven by all 3 wit.
Nov. Term. 1846. Rec. 13 Nov. 1846.

Pages 172-175: Newton Co.: L. W. & T. of HENRY A. HARPER, being
of advanced age... to wife RHODY negro Esther, 2 feather beds, furniture
(several items named), the Swaringame lote, 202 1/2 A, #181, 11th Dist.,
Henry now Newton Co., cattle & swine.... to son EDWARD in trust for his
children free from all embarrassments of my son EDWARD, negroes (named)..
to my daughter MARGARETT ANN and her children by her present husband
DAVID M. PARKER or any future husband, free from the disposition of her
husband, negro Franklin... son NUEL M. HARPER in trust for his children,
negro Jacob... to daughter SARAH ANN and her husband (not named), negro
Burrell... lot #205, 11th Dist., Henry now Newton Co., and 100 A adj.
part of lot #180, in sd. Dist... wf RHODY, son EDWARD & DAVID M. PARKER,
Exrs... 7 Sept. 1846... HENRY A. HARPER (LS). Wit: ARCHIBALD GILMER,
DAVID PARKER, SAMUEL D. NIGHT. Proven by PARKER & NIGHT 2 Nov. 1846. Rec.
17 Nov. 1846.

Pages 176-177: Newton Co., I, JOHN A. DUNCAN, will all my settlement of lands in Newton Co., to SIMEON DUNCAN, MARGARETT DUNCAN, PATIENCE
E. LANDERS, also one lot in Randolph Co. and 2 lots in Cherokee to main-
tain LUCINDA DUNCAN during her life... $170 to my father SAMUEL DUNCAN...

19 Dec. 1846... JOHN A. DUNCAN. Wit: JOHN J. RABB, W. W. HOLDER, REUBEN WOODRUFF. Proven by RABB, 28 Dec. 1846. Proven by HOLDER & WOODRUFF 4 Jan. 1847. Rec. 19 Jan. 1847.

Pages 178-179: Newton Co.: L. W. & T. of JUDITH W. COOK... 1/8 of estate of sister SALLY's son WILLIAM M. MOSELY... 1/8 of estate of sister SALLY's daughter SARAH E. MOSELY... 1/8 of estate to sister SARAH daughter MARY S. MOSELY... 1/8 of estate to sister SARAH daughter MARTHA F. MOSELY... 1/8 of estate to sister JANE's daughter MARY J. MATTHEWS... 1/8 of estate to sister JANE's daughter MARTHA J. MATTHEWS... 1/8 of estate to sister JANE's daughter SARAH S. MATHEWS... 1/8 of estate to sister JANE's daughter ALMEADEA (sic)... JOSEPH C. MOSELY, Exr. 28 Oct. 1846... JUDITH W. COOK (X) (SEAL). Wit: B. C. W. WHATLEY, JAMES D. JOHNSON, J. W. HEWELL. Proven by J. D. JOHNSON & JESSE W. HEWELL, 11 Jan. 1847. Rec. 21, Jan. 1841.

Pages 180-181: Newton Co.: L. W. & T. of WM. P. BERRY, being in great weakness of body... to wife CYNTHA ANN BERRY, all estate real and personal... wf CYNTHA ANN, Extx... 1 Apr. 1846... WM. P. BERRY (SEAL). Wit: ETHER BREWER, F. H. HEARD, JOHN P. THOMPSON. Proven 1 Mar. 1847, by BREWER & THOMPSON. Rec. Mar. 1847.

Pages 181-183: Newton Co.: L. W. & T. of ALLEN SUMMERS... all estate real and personal to wife MARGARETTE SUMMERS... lot that my sister ELIZABETH SUMMERS now lives on adj. JACKSON, BOSTWICK & others to be sold, also 50 A on which LEWIS HINTON now lives on W side of Lawrence-ville Road adj. JOURDAN BAKER & JESSE L. BAKER, land on which WILLIAM B. HUDSON now lives, also 5 A besides what will be due me after allowing 100 feet for the Georgia Railroad part of lot formerly owned by WILLIAM K. BAGBEE... my three youngest children JAMES, THOMAS & EAMLINE ELIZA-BETH SUMMERS... son ANDREW JACKSON SUMMERS to see to the education of my 3 youngest children... to my daughter MARTHA ANN REBECCA SUMMERS, negroes (named)... 5 Jan. 1847. A. SUMMERS (LS). Wit: JOHN B. HENDRICK, HENRY LESTER, ZADOK C. BAKER. Proven by all 3 wit. 1 Mar. 1847. Rec. March 1847.

Pages 184-185: Newton Co.: L. W. & T. of ROBERT MATHERS, being weak in body... to friend ALEXANDER JOHNSON in consideration of his attention and toward cares me during my long affliction, balance of my estate after debts paid... note given by STEPHEN DAY on 27 Feb. 1847... ALEXANDER JOHNSON, Exr... 14 Apr. 1847... ROBERT MATHERS. Wit: GEORGE W. JOHNSON, DAVID T. WHITE, J.P. Proven by both sit. 3 May 1847.

Pages 186-187: L. W. & T. of ELIZABETH SHELL of Newton Co., being in the decline of life... $500 in the hands of ZERE MIDDLEBROOK's willed to my children ISHAM M. SHELL, SOPHA (sic) MIDDLEBROOK, EDMON SHELL's heirs, JOHN E. SHELL, and DREWREY J. SHELL... to grandson HENEREY W. SHELL, $60... to granddaughter MARTHEY ANN HOGH, $60... to grandson JOHN A. SHELL, $60... ZERE MIDDLEBROOK, Exr... 30 Aug. 1845. ELIZABETH SHELL (SEAL). Wit: A. B. MIDDLEBROOK, J. C. MIDDLEBROOK, WM. W. CRUMBLEY, ISAAC S. MIDDLEBROOK. Proven by JOHN C. and ISAAC S. MIDDLEBROOKS, 3 May 1841. Rec. May 1847.

Pages 188-189: Newton Co.: L. W. & T. of JOHN SHIP, 4 Feb. 1847... all estate (among items was a still) to wf IZABELLAH SHIP for the benefit of my minor children JOHN FRANCIS STEPHEN and BAILY ARNOL & ABNER LETTY JANE & ROBERT SHIP... JNO SHIP (LS). Wit: J. M. HAMILTON, GEORGE W. LESTER. Proven by LESTER L Mar. 1847. Proven by HAMILTON 23 Mar. 1847. Rec. July 1847.

Pages 190-191: L. W. & T. of MARGARET BUCKANAN of Newton Co... to MARY ANN ISABELLA BALKE, daughter of ISABELLA BLAKE, negroes (named) to WILLIAM M. BLAKE, negro Joe to make him equal to his brothers and sister JANE BELL BLAKE... 19 June 1847... MARGARET BUCKANON (X) (SEAL). Wit: ARCHIBALD E. LORD, MARTHA KILLPATRICK, ROBERT H. FARMER, J.P. Proven by all 3 wit. 5 July 1847.

Pages 192-194:   Newton Co.: L. W. & T. of MARTHA ROSEBERRY... to
JAMES KNIGHT for his wife MARY KNIGHT, negro West... to JOHN PERGUSON
in trust for his wife MARTHA, negro Vanse and my bed... to RICHARD ROSE-
BERRY, a bed stead known as his Fathers... to WILLIAM ROSEBERRY, bed-
stead and furniture and $300... land where RICHARD ROSEBERRY lives to be
sold... JOHN PERGESON to pay to RICHARD FLOYD $6 annually... friend
COLUMBUS D. PACE, Exr... 15 July 1847... MARTHA ROSEBERRY (X). Wit:
C. KINNEY, H. J. PARKER, JOHN THOMPSON. Proven by CHESLY KINNEY & H. J.
PARKER. 6 Sept. 1847.

Pages 195-197:   Newton Co.: L. W. & T. of JORDON BAKER... to wife
(not named), all property of every nature brought by her into the
coveture... property sold and divided among DANIEL NEWNAN BAKER my son;
JESSE L. BAKER, my son; THOMAS BAKER, my son; my son WILEY BAKER and his
children; my son in law CHARLES HUTSON and my daughter ELIZABETH HUTSON...
my daughter FANNY MCLENDON; my daughter ZIPPORA GOSS; daughter ALIS BAGBY,
JESSE L. & DANIEL N. BAKER, Exrs... 22 Oct. 1847... JORDON BAKER (SEAL).
Wit: JOHN N. WILLIAMSON, JOHN HARRIS, CARY WOOD. Proven by all 3 wit.
10 Jan. 1848.

Page 198:   Newton Co.: L. W. & T. of HENRY WILSON, being weak in
body... to wife SARAH WILSON, all property real and personal... to
brother WILLIAM WILSON, one rifle gun... 28 Mar. 1848... HENRY WILSON (X).
Wit: JOHN B. THOMPSON, DAVID T. WHITE, J.P., JESSE DANIEL. Proven by
THOMPSON & DANIEL May term 1848.

Pages 199-200:   Newton Co.: L. W. & T. of GEORGE W. LANE... estate
for maintenance of wife and children (not named) and education of my
children... LUCUS L. WILTICK, Exr... 29 Aug. 1846... GEO W. LANE (SEAL).
Wit: A. MEANS, J. C. SIMMONS, JOHN A. H. HARPER. Proven by SIMMONS &
HARPER 6 Nov. 1848. Rec. Nov. Term 1848.

Pages 201-202:   Newton Co.: L. W. & T. of WILLIAM WORREL, being
very old and weak in body... to wife DELILA WORREL, one negro Juda, 66
A on which I now live of the old lot... son SIMEON WORREL... 1/2 part
of my daughter MARY NELSM, daughter NANCY MELTON, son WM. G. WORREL,
daughter SARAH STALLINGS, daughter ELIZABETH HAMBY, daughter ELIZA DAVIS,
THOMAS NELMS & ISAAC N. STALLINGS, Exrs... 19 Nov. 1844... WILLIAM
WORRELL (SEAL). Wit: JOHN NAILE, EDWARD P. NIXSON, WILLIAM W. NELMS.
Proven by HAILE & NELMS, 8 Jan. 1849. Rec. Jan. Term 1849.

Pages 203-205:   Newton Co.: L. W. & T. of NATHAN JOHNSON of
feeble health... to wife ELIZABETH, all property of whatever nature she
was possessed of at our intermarriage, also 100 A on which I now live...
said land to be divided among the heirs of my son THOMAS JOHNSON... to
wife 30 barrels of corn and 1000 lbs of pork... my son ALEXANDER and my
daughter NANCY ANN NIX, I have already given... I have given to JAMES
WHITE, as trustee for my son GEORGE W. JOHNSON's family... to my son
LUKE & to my son WILLIAM S., $275... to my daughter MARY WOODS and my
daughter ELIZABETH GAY... sons ALEXANDER & LUKE, Exrs... 8 July 1848...
NATHAN JOHNSON (SEAL). Wit: NICHOLAS H. BACON, PETER B. ALMAND, DAVID
B. ALMAND. Proven by DAVID B. ALMOND 16 Mar. 1849. Proven by BACON
3 Apr. 1849. Rec. Apr. term 1849.

Pages 206-207:   Newton Co.: L. W. & T. of NANCY HAMMOCK, being
of advanced age and knowing that I must shortly depart this life... son
in law JOHN C. SLOCUMB, negroes (named)... to son BURRELL MILLER, negro
Warren... to son ROBERT C. MILLER negro girl CHANY... friends PETER
KIMBLE, WILLIAM SLOCUMB, Exrs... 18 Mar. 1849. NANCY HAMMOCK (X) (LS).
Wit: B. RICE, ELIJAH CLARK, 7 May 1849.

Pages 208-209:   Newton Co.: L. W. & T. of JOHN COWEN, June 30th.
1849... wife NANCY to have benefit of my premises... Children (not
named) shall enjoy advantage of a good english education... brother
ALEXANDER COWEN, Exr... JOHN COWEN (LS). Wit: JOHN S. PRESLEY, SAMUEL
A. BELLAH, ROBERT M. COWEN. Proven by BELLAH & COWEN, 3 Sept. 1849.
Rec. Sept Term 1849.

Pages 210-212: Newton Co.: L. W. & T. of JOHN SAWYER, being of advanced age... to wife MARY, all estate real and personal... if she marry, equal division made among children and she should receive a child's part... whatever my wife gives to my daughter SARAH A., wife of HARRY CAMP, shall be for her and her children, not subject to the debts of her husband... wife MARY and sons JOHN L., FRANCIS & THOMAS, Exrs.... 6 Aug. 1849. JOHN SAWYER (X) (LS). Wit: ROBERT G. HARPER, HORACE J. BATES, HARMAN KIRKPATRICK (X). Proven by HARPER & KIRKPATRICK 5 Nov. 1849. Rec. Nov. term. 1849.

Pages 213-215: Newton Co.: L. W. & T. of JOHN T. DUKE, having lived more than the usual time allotted to man, of feeble old age... to grandchildren CATHERINE WILLINGHAM, LOUISA SMITH, MARTHA NORTH & THOMAS MCCOY, lot in Macon County, to be sold and proceeds divided... to THOMAS M. DUKE & EDWIN SHEPHERD, for use of my daughter LUCY HODNETT, an equal distribution share... to son JOSEPH DUKE, THOMAS M. DUKE, PAYTON DUKE & daughters DEBORAH ALLEN & EMILY SHEPHARD, an equal distribution share... 2 June 1849... JNO. T. DUKE (LS). Wit: JOHN BASS, MCKENDREE TUCKER, FELIX HARDMAN. Proven by BASS 7 Jan. 1850. Proven by TUCKER & HARDMAN 4 Jan. 1850. Rec. Jan. Term 1850.

Pages 216-219: Newton Co.: L. W. & T. of JAMES HODGE of feeble health... to wife ALMEDA P. HODGE, $100 and property she brought into coverture (listed)... 2 children by my present wife (one named ELIZA-BETH BRADFORD HODGE, the other has no name), $750 each... to friend EZEKIEL STRICKLAND JUNR. of Henry Co., in trust for my daughter ELIZA A. MORROW and her children, negroes (named)... to daughter MARY BRAY HODGE, negroes (named)... to daughter LORENA WILLIAMSON HODGE, negroes (named)... to son CINCINATUS LYCIUGAS HODGE, negroes (named)... to son DUKE R. HODGE, negro Frank.... to son JAMES BAILY HODGE, negroes (named) my dec'd son ALEXANDER J. HODGE... estate bequeathed to me at the death of my mother (not named)... 20 July 1850... JAMES HODGE (SEAL). Wit: JOHN N. WILLIAMSON, MOSES MELTON, B. S. ANSLEY. Proven by all 3 wit. 25 Sept. 1850. Rec. Nov. term 1850.

Pages 220-221: Newton Co.: L. W. & T. of SUSANNAH M. WRIGHT... in feeble health... to my lovely daughter MARY LOWENS PARAM? LAMPKIN, $20... to son WILLIAM J. WRIGHT, in trust for my son LEGRAND S. WRIGHT, $200... to daughter FRANCES ANN REBECCA CALLOWAY and her children, negro Arnold... son WILLIAM J. WRIGHT, Exr... 11 July 1848... SUSANNAH M. WRIGHT (X). Wit: SILAS H. STARR, THOMAS W. RAKESTRAW, MILTON G. LEEK. Proven by all 3 wit. 14 Nov. 1850. Rec. Nov. term. 1850.

Pages 222-224: Newton Co.: L. W. & T. of WILLIAM NOLEN... feeble in body... to wife MARY NOLEN, the whole tract where I now live adj. Mrs. M. WARD, ISHAM WEAVER, N. WEST and Yellow River and negroes (named)... son JAMES NOLEN to superintend his mother's affairs... my oldest daughter MARY WEAVER... my youngest daughter SARAH CHAMBERS... to my second son ABNER NOLEN... my third son STEVEN NOLEN... my fourth son AUGUSTUS NOLEN... JAMES & STEVEN NOLEN, Exrs... WILLIAM NOLEN (C). Wit: JOHN WEBB WILSON L. DAVIS, JOHN B. LEE. Will made 12 Dec. 1850. Proven by all 3 wit 13 Jan. 1851. Rec. Jan term. 1851.

Pages 225-227: Newton Co.: L. W. & T. of HENRIETTA JOHNSON being of advanced age and knowning that I must shortly depart this life... to son JAMES D. JOHNSON, negroes (named)... to granddaughters MARIA WHATLEY, FRANCES WHATLEY, HENRIETTA WHATLEY and my grandson AUGUSTUS WHATLEY & ADOLPHUS WHATLEY, also to children of my son JAMES if he should hereafter marry and have children... 17 Mar. 1849... HENRIETTA JOHNSON (LS). Wit: DANIEL D. HENRY, N. E. ANDREW, W. R. HENRY. Proven by WM. R. HENRY & DANIEL D. HENRY 13 Jan. 1851. Rec. Jan. term 1851.

Pages 228-230: Newton Co.: L. W. & T. of JONATHAN BRANON... to son WILLIAM C. BRANAN, 63 3/4 A in NE corner of lot #40, 10th Dist., Henry now Newton Co.,... to son JAMES K. BRANON, 50 A and $40 pd. by CALVAN BRAN (sic)... to son CALVIN BRANA (sic), 36 3/8 A... lands in low country to be sold.. to wife MARY, balance of estate.. 29 Dec. 1847... JONATHAN BRANAN (SEAL). Wit: REUBEN WOODRUFF, MOSES TRIMBLE, J. W. HEWELL Proven by WOODRUFF & HEWELL 3 Mar. 1851, Rec. March Term 1851.

Pages 231-236:   Newton Co.:   L. W. & T. of CHARLES H. SANDERS,
being feeble in bodily health... wife SARAH ANN SANDERS, to have house
and lot on which we now live... land adj. JOHN J. FLOYD and negroes
(named)... all real estate (town lots and other lands) except what was
given to my wife sold and all personal property to be sold except negroes
and Railroad Stock... goods in my store in Sandtown may be brought to
Covington by my son in law JOHN N. HICKS... each of my children to be
equal... daughter OPHELIA J. HICKS... daughters to have their portion
when they become of age or marry... COLUMBUS D. PACE, friends STEPHEN
SHELL & NATHAN TURNER, Exrs... 24 July 1851... C. H. SANDERS (SEAL).   Wit:
JOHN J. FLOYD, CARY WOOD, J. H. MURRELL.   Proven by all 3 wit. 1 Sept.
1851.   Rec. Sept. term. 1851.

Page 1:   2 Jan. 1822, NATHANIEL HANDY of Oglethorpe Co., Ga. to
HENRY H. LUMPKIN of Co. and State afsd. and now of Jones Co. for $200,
202½ acres, lot #238 in the 12th district of Monroe Co., on the south
bounded by the Houston Co. line. Signed: NATHANIEL (X) HANDY. Wit.:
SAMUEL LUMPKIN, JASPER HAYNES. Ga. Oglethorpe Co., SAMUEL LUMPKIN
and JASPER HAYNES swore to the deed 3 Jan. __? before JOHN WYNNE J.P.
Recorded 30 May 1822.

Page 2:   Ga. Wilkes Co., 3 May 1822, JOHN OWENS of the State of
Alabama but formerly of Elbert Co., Ga. to DAVID BARRON of Elbert Co., Ga.,
for $200, 202½ acres, lot #93 in the 13th district of Monroe Co. drawn
by JOHN OWENS of Terrels District of Elbert Co. Signed: JOHN OWENS.
Wit. RICHARD AYCOCK, BENJAMIN COOK, WILLIAM ROBINSON, J.P. Recorded
30 May 1822.

Pages 2, 3:   Ga. Appling Co., 13 May 1822, JONATHAN MILLER of Co.
afsd. to W. W. ABBOTT & JOHN P. HAMMOCK of the same Co. & the County of
___.   (Note: bottom left corner of page broken off) for $380, 202½ acres,
lot #231 in the 12th district of Monroe. Signed: JONATHAN (X) MILLER.
Wit: ALEXANDER CAMPBELL, JOHN CAMPBELL, J.P. Recorded 30 May 1822.

Pages 3, 4:   1 May 1822, JOSEPH HEDRECK of Jackson Co., Ga. late of
Yancey's district Franklin Co. to JAMES WHATLEY of Monroe Co. for $100,
202½ acres, lto #133 in the 10th district granted sd. JOSEPH HENDRICK.
Signed: JOSEPH (X) HENDRICK. Wit: H. PERRY, WILLIAM MORGAN, WM.
LENDSEY J.P. Recorded 30 May 1822.

Page 4:   Ga. Greene Co., 13 May 1822, KEATON UPCHURCH of Greene Co.
to JOHN DUNCAN of Jones Co. for $250, 202½ acres, lot #46 in the 13th
district of Monroe Co. Signed: KEATON (X) UPCHURCH. Wit: ISHAM
WEATHERS, H.P. MALERY J.P. (Note: no recording date.)

Page 5:   Ga. Twiggs Co., 13 Feb. 1822, ENOCH BLACKSHEAR of Co. &
State afsd. to THOMAS C. PINCKARD of Monroe Co. for $300, lot #135 in
the 4th district of Monroe Co. Signed: ENOCH BLANCHSHEAR. Wit:
JEREMIAH AVERETT, JOHN BLACKSHEAR. Ga. Twiggs Co., JOHN BLACKSHEAR swore
to the deed before LAIRD MCMURREY J.P. 3 Feb. 1822. Recorded 30 May
1822.

Pages 5,6:   Ga., 20? Dec. 1821, JACOB MARTIN of Pitmans District
Gwinnett Co. to HENRY JEMISON of Monroe Co. for $350, 202½ acres, lot
#210 in the 13th district of Monroe Co. Signed: JACOB (X) MARTIN.
Wit: EZRA CATES, WILLIAM GREEN J.P. Recorded 30 May 1822.

Pages 6,7:   Ga., 15 Dec. 1821, ROBERT KENDRICK of Clark Co., Ga. to
HENRY JEMISON of Monroe Co. for $500, 202½ acres, lot #289 in the 13th
district of Monroe Co. Signed: ROBT. KENDRICK. Wit: H. B. WATTS,
R(UN?) FITZPATRICK, JOHN PARK J.P. Recorded 30 May 1822.

Page 7:   Ga. Twiggs Co., 25 Feb. 1822, Received of HENRY JEMISON
$500 for a negro girl Mima aged 21 years. Signed: JOSEPH WILLIAMS.
WitL: J. M. WILLIAMS, H. WATT J.P. Recorded 30 May 1822.

Page 8:   Ga. Baldwin Co., 13 Dec. 1821, JACOB MARTIN of Pitmans
District Gwinnett Co. to HENRY JEMISON for $350, lto #210 in the 13th
district of Monroe Co. Signed: JACOB MARTIN by his attorney TOMLINSON
FORT. Wit: JOHN BOON, APPLETON ROSSETER J.I.C. Recorded 1 June 1822.

Pages 8, 9:   16 Nov. 1821, Power of Attorney from JACOB MARTIN of
Pitmans District Gwinnett Co., Ga. to TOMLINSON FORT of Baldwin Co. to
sell 202½ acres, lot #210 in the 13th district of Monroe Co. Signed:
JACOB (X) MARTIN. Wit: JOHN LINVILLE, JANUS? DIAMOND J.P. Recorded 1
June 1822.

Pages 9, 10: Ga., 25 Feb. 1822, JOSEPH WILLIAMS of Twiggs Co. to HENRY JEMISON of Monroe Co. for $2000, 405 acres, lot #243 & lot $244 in the 13th district of Monroe Co. Signed: JOSEPH WILLIAMS. Wit. J.M. WILLIAMS, H. WATT J.P. Recorded 1 June 1822.

Pages 10, 11, 12: 25 March 1822, ABRAHAM RECKER of Chatham Co., Ga. to SAMUEL J. BRYAN of same for $125, 202½ acres, lot #15 in the 12th district of Monroe Co. Signed: ABM. RICKER. Wit: THOMAS A. ROBINS, JAMES EPPINGER J.I.C. Recorded 1 June 1822.

Pages 12, 13, 14: 13 April 1822, SAMUEL J. BRYAN (BRIANT in body of deed) of Chatham Co., Ga. to ROBERT BONNER of Warren Co. for $550, 202½ acres, lot $15 in the 12th district of Monroe Co. drawn by ABRAHAM RECKER of Chatham Co. Signed: SAML. J. BRYAN. Wit: JOSEPH W. LUCKITT, ISAAC RUSSELL J.P. Recorded 1 June 1822.

Pages 14, 15: Ga. Hancock Co., 23 March 1822, JOHN FERRELL of Hancock Co. and MICKLEBURY FERRELL of Jones Co. to WILLIAM HATHHORN of Monroe Co. for $600, lot #115 in the 12th district of Monroe. Signed: JOHN F RELL (Note: name blurred), MICKLEBURY FARRELL. Wit: S. S. RADNEY, ___? J. P. Recorded 1 June 1822.

Page 15: 23 April 1822, MOSES HUBBART (HUBBERT in body of deed) of Jackson Co., Ga. to DAVID LOCKETT and JAMES GASSAWAY of Wilkes Co. for $100, 202½ acres, lot #217 in the 1st district of Monroe Co. Signed: MOSES HUBBERT. Wit: JOHN J. HARPER, ARCHIBALD GRESHAM J.P. Recorded 1 June 1822.

Pages 15, 16, 17: Ga. Baldwin Co., 27 Dec. 1822, ARCHY (ARCHI in body of deed) T. OBRYAN attorney for LEWIS OBRYAN SENR. of Screven Co., Ga. to GEORGE W. ROGERS of Houston Co. for $1000?, lot #11 in the 12th district of Monroe Co. lying on big Tobasofca. Signed: ARCHY T. OBRYAN attr. for LEWIS OBRYAN SENR. Wit: C. R. ROGERS, A. YOUNG J.I.C. Recorded 1 June 1822.
Ga. Screven Co., LEWIS OBRYAN SENR. of same appoints ARCHEY T. OBRYAN of same his true and lawful attorney to sell lot #11 in the 12th district of Monroe Co. 15 Dec. 1821. Signed: LEWIS OBRYAN. Wit: ISSAC ROBERTS, R. D. MCKINNEY J.P.
Ga. Screven Co., 15 Dec. 1821, SEABORN GOODALL, Clerk of the Superior Court of the county afsd., certifies that ROBERT D. MCKINNEY is acting Justice of the Peace for the Co. afsd. "I have hereunto set my hand and private seal there being no seal of office in Jacksonborough."
Ga. Screven Co., 15 Dec. 1821, ROGER MCKINNEY one of the Justices of the Inferior Court for the Co. afsd. certifies that SEABORN GOODALL is acting Clerk of the Inferior Court for the Co. of Screven. Signed: ROBERT MCKINNEY J.I.C. Recorded 1 June 1822.

Page 17, 18: Ga. Baldwin Co., 22 Jan. 1822, WILLIAM PURIFOY of Putnam Co. to ZACHARIAH CHAMBLES of Baldwin Co. for $625, lot $160 in the 13th district of Monroe Co. Signed: WILLIAM (X) PURIFOY. Wit: JOHN EVANS, LEVI JUSTICE, DEMPSY JUSTICE, J.P. Recorded 3 June 1822.

Page 18: Ga. Madison Co., 19 March 1822, JOHN WILEY SR. of Co. afsd. to SIR JAMES PITMAN of Monroe Co. for $1400, 202½ acres, lot #132 in the 13th dist. of Monroe Co. Signed: JOHN (X) WILEY. Wit: BURREL J. WILEY, RICHARDSON HANCOCK, M.H. PUTMAN J.P. Recorded 3 June 1822.

Page 19: Ga. Twiggs Co., 13 March 1822, SAMUEL POWELL to WILLIAM SMITH both of Twiggs Co. for $300, 202½ acres, lot #51 in the 7th district of Monroe Co. Signed: SAMUEL POWELL. Wit: WILLIAM SOLOMON, HARDY DURHAM J.P. Recorded 3 June 1822.

Pages 19, 20: Ga. Warren Co., 1 Dec. 1821, THOMAS MADDUX agent for GEORGE SMITH of Co. & state afsd. to HARREL NEAL for $1000, 202½ acres, lot $232 in the 1st district of Monroe Co. Signed: THOS. MADDUX agent for GEORGE SMITH. Wit: RICHARD MYRICK?, JEREMIAH BEALL J.P. Recorded 5 June 1822.

Pages 20, 21: Ga. Monroe Co., 4 June 1822, JOHN CURETON Sheriff of Co. afsd. in obedience to a writ from the Superior Court of Pulaski Co. at the suit of PETER THOMAS for the use of JAMES C. ALLEN against MOSES PEPKIN & EDWARD DOBB sold lot #288 in the 13th district of Monroe Co., the property of EDWARD COBB to ELI S. SHORTER of Putnam Co., he being the highest bidder, for $660. Signed: JOHN CURETON Shff. Wit.: WILKINS HUNT, ROLLINS SMITH J.P. Recorded 5 June 1822.

Page 21: Ga. Monroe Co., 4 June 1822, ELI S. SHORTER of Putnam Co. to HENRY POPE of Jones Co. for $1050, 202½ acres, lot #288 in the 10th district of Monroe Co. Signed: ELI S. SHORTER. Wit: WILKINS HUNT, ROLLINS SMITH J.P. Recorded 5 June 1822.

Page 22: Ga. Twiggs Co., 13 Feb. 1822, NANCY PARKER of Twiggs Co. to FELIX STANLY (STANLEY in body of deed) of Jasper Co. for $350, 202½ acres, lot #134 in the 12th district of Monroe Co. Signed: NANCY PARKER. Wit: SOLOMON SAXO__, H. PERRYMAN J.P. Recorded 5 June 1822.

Pages 22, 23: Ga. Jones Co., 14 Jan. 1822, WILLIAM JOHNSTON of Morgan Co. to ABRAHAM WOMACK of Jones Co. for $800, lot #129 in the 13th district of Monroe Co. Signed: WILLIAM JOHNSTON. Wit: ROBERT ROLLINTER, TAYLOR H. MITCHELL, HENRY POPE. Ga. Jones Co., HENRY POPE swore to the deed and that he saw ROBERT ROLLENTER & TAYLOR H. MITCHELL subscribe the same before CHARLES WOMACK J.P. 28 March 1822. Recorded 5 June 1822.

Pages 23: 17 Dec. 1821, NANCY THOMPSON of Warren Co., Ga. to JOHN FINCH of Jasper Co., Ga. for $300, 202½ acres, lot #149 in the 5th district of Monroe Co. Signed: NANCY (X) THOMPSON. Wit: ROBERT FLEMING, NATHANIEL THOMPSON, JOSHUA DRAPER? J.P. Recorded 5 June 1822.

Page 24: Ga. Jones Co., 4 Jan. 1822, LEWIS WIMBERLY of Co. afsd. to HENRY WIMBERLY and JOHN CHILDERS of same for $650, lot #140 in the 13th district of Monroe Co. Signed: LEWIS WIMBERLY. Wit: M. M. DRAKE, JAMES WIMBERLY J.I.C. Recorded 5 June 1822.

Pages 24, 25: 7 Jan. 1822, ISAAC CLIETT JR. of Colliers District Columbia Co., Ga. to JAMES HERRING of Elbert Co., Ga. and GEORGE VIGAL of Lenkh Co., Ga. (Note: Lincoln Co., Ga.??) for $1000, 202½ acres, lot #284 in the 13th district of Monroe Co.. Signed: ISAAC CLIETT JR. Wit: JOSIAH THOMAS, JOHN MOSS, JR., JOHN MOSS J.P. Recorded 5 June 1822.

Pages 25, 26: Ga., 15 Jan. 1822, BRYANT DIXON of Putnam Co. to NEEDHAM MIMS of Baldwin Co. for $900, lot #231 in the 13th district of Monroe Co. Signed: BRYANT DIXON. Wit: ISAAC WELCH, MOSES DAVIS, GIDEON MIMS J.P. Recorded 6 June 1822.

Pages 26, 27: Ga., 22 March 1822, FRANCIS GIDEON of Lincoln Co. to NEEDHAM MIMS of Baldwin Co. for $1000, 202½ acres, lot #211 in the 13th district of Monroe Co. Signed: FRANCIS GIDION. Wit: B. SPIVY, THOMAS DOOLY, B. M. SANDERS, J.I.C. Recorded 6 June 1822.

Pages 27, 28: Ga. Baldwin Co., 6 Dec. 1821, AMOS YOUNG agent for WILLIAM WALL of Baldwin Co. to NEEDHAM MIMS of same for $50, 202½ acres, lot $72 in the 13th district of Monroe Co. on the waters of Tobesofkee. Signed: AMOS YOUNG Agt. for WILLIAM WALL. Wit.: HENRY WIMBERLY, D. G. WORSHAM, GIDEON MIMS J.P. Recorded 7 June 1822.
Ga. Twiggs Co., WILLIAM WALL of Twiggs Co. reposing special trust & confidence in my friend AMOS YOUNG appoint him my agent to sell lot #72 in the 13th district of Monroe Co. 3 Dec. 1821. Signed: WILLIAM WALL. Wit: HENRY WIMBERLY, JAMES PEARSON J.P. Recorded 7 June 1822.

Pages 28, 29: Ga. 24 Dec. 1821, WILLIAM M. BEALL of Warren Co. to NEEDHAM MIMS of Baldwin Co. for $2054, 202½ acres, lot #212 in the 13th district of Monroe Co. Singed: WM. M. BEALL. Wit: HENRY WIMBERLY, MARLOW PRYOR, J.P. Recorded 7 June 1822.

Pages 29, 30, 31: Ga. Montgomery Co., 14 Jan. 1822, HARRISON SEARS Attorney for BRYANT CALLAHAM both of Montgomery Co. to JOHN G. RAINES of same for $200, 202½ acres, lot $210 in the 7th district of Monroe Co. originally granted to BRYANT CALLAHAM JR. Signed: HARRISON (X) SEARS attorney for BRYANT CALLAHAM. Wit: JAMES ALSTON, EDWARD FEATHERSTON? J.I.C. Recorded 7 June 1822. Ga. Montgomery Co. 17 Dec. 1821, Power of Attorney from BRYANT CALLAHAM to HARRISON SEARS. Signed: BRYANT CALLAHAM. Wit: WILSON CONNER J.I.C. Recorded 7 June 1822.

Pages 31, 32: Ga. Baldwin Co., 8 Dec. 1821, WILLIAM BRESSIE of Baldwin Co. to JOHN LAMAR of Jones Co. for $1200, lot #317 in the 13th district of Monroe Co. Signed: WILLIAM BRESSIE. Wit: JOHN BOON, APPLETON ROSSETER J.I.C. Recorded 8 June 1822.

Pages 32, 33: Ga. Jones Co., 4 May 1822, JOHN LAMAR of Jones Co. to BENJAMIN B. LAMAR of Jasper Co. for $1200, 202½ acres, lot #317 in the 13th district of Monroe Co. Signed: JOHN LAMAR. Wit: WILLIAM VARNER, HENRY G. LAMAR. Ga. Jones Co., HENRY G. LAMAR swore to the deed before ORLLINS SMITH J.P. 3 June 1822. Recorded 8 June 1822.

Page 33: Ga. Jones Co., 29 Jan. 1822, WILLIAM WOOD of Morgan Co. to ROGER MACARTHY of Jones Co. for $300, 202½ acres, lot #202 in the 7th district of Monroe Co. Singed: WILLIAM WOOD. Wit: MICHAEL SULLIVAN, C. MACARTHY. Ga. Jones Co., CHARLES MACARTHY swore to the deed before D. T. MILLING J.P. 8 June 1822. Recorded 11 June 1822.

Page 34: Ga. Hancock Co., 21 Feb. 1822, RICHARD W. DAVIS of Washington Co. to H. & T. H. KINDALL of Hancock Co. for $1000, 202½ acres, lot #105 in the 5th district of Monroe Co. Signed: RICHARD W. DAVIS. Wit: J. W. RIGHT, W. RACHEL JR., L. L. SMITH J.P. Recorded 1 July 1822.

Pages 34, 35: Ga. Baldwin Co., 1 Feb. 1822, WILLIAM H. CRIDENTON of Elbert Co. to THOMAS WILLIAMS of Oglethorpe Co. for $150, lot #191 in the 10th district of Monroe drawn by WILLIAM H. CRIDENTON of Gilens? District Walton Co. Signed: WILLIAM HENRY CRIDENTON. Wit: EV__IT H. PIERCE, JAMES RAUSSEAU J.P. Recorded 2 July 1822.

Pages 35, 36: Ga. Camden Co., City of St. Marys, 4 March 1822, JOSIAH WINANS & ISRAEL GEER of Camden Co. to ISAAC BAILEY of same for $400, 202½ acres, lot #63 in the 6th district of Monroe Co. drawn by JOSHUA WINANS & Heretofore conveyed to ISRAIL GEER. Signed: JOSIAH WINANS, ISRAEL GEER. Wit: LEWIS LEVY, M. H. HEBBAN? J.P. Recorded 8 July 1822.

Page 37: Ga. Jones Co., 10 Feb. 1822, THOS. W. MORRIS of Jones Co. to JOHN STILWELL of Monroe Co., Ga. for $400, 202½ acres, lot #129 in the 6th district of Monroe Co. on waters of Rocky Creek & Towaliga. Singed: THOMAS W. MORRIS. Wit: ROBERT B. PAUL, JOHN (X) COTTON. Recorded 8 July 1822. Ga. Jones Co., ROBERT B. PAUL swore to the deed before STEPHEN RENFROE J.P. 27 April 1822. (Note: the following under the signature) "Dower record in Book D folio 234"

Page 38: Ga. Monroe Co., 29 June 1822, JAMES BAILEY of Monroe Co. to JEREMIAH BAKER of Pike Co., Alabama for $700, 202½ acres, lot #42 in the 13th district of Monroe Co. on the waters of Tobasofca adjoining MOSES LEPHAN & others. Signed: JAMES (X) BAILEY. Wit: HOWELL SHORT, GEORGE W. ROGERS J.P. Recorded 8 July 1822.

Page 39: Ga. Burke Co., 25 Feb. 1822, GIDEON HARRIS of Burke Co. to JOHN N. DAVIS of same for $313, 202½ acres, lot #186 in the 4th district of Monroe Co. on the waters of Towaliga Creek. Signed: GIDEON HARRIS. Wit: R. E. BRODNUX, JOHN BELL J.P. Recorded 9 July 1822.

Page 39: Ga. Burke Co., 18 March 1822, JOHN N. DAVIS of Burke Co. to WM. DAVIS of same for $313, 202½ acres, lot #186 in the 4th district of Monroe Co. on the waters of Towaliga Creek. Signed: JOHN N. DAVIS. Wit: JAMES HAYMANS, L. F. POWELL J.P. Recorded 9 July 1822.

Pages 39, 40: Ga. Monroe Co., 2 July 1822, JOHN CURETON Sheriff, according to a writ out of Justices Court of Columbia Co., Ga. at the suit of JAMES LAMPKIN for the use of Britton Sims bearer against GEORGE W. TOOLE, seized the tract of GEORGE W. TOOLE and sold at public auction to THOMAS WALKER, highest bidder, for $355, 202½ acres lot #42 in the 5th district of Monroe Co. Signed: JOHN CURETON Shff. Wit: CHARLES Y. CALDWELL, ABNER DURHAM J.P., BENJAMIN HOLLAND. Recorded 10 July 1822.

Pages 40, 41, 42: Ga. Monroe Co., 2 July 1822, JOHN CURETON Sheriff in obedience to a writ out of Superior Court of Twiggs Co., Ga. at the suit of POLLY ROUSE admtx. against GEORGE LITTLE, JOHN BUSBY, & BRYANT BASS sezied the property of sd. JOHN BASS and sold to JOHN TAYLOR highest bidder for $602, 202½ acres, lot $158 in the 12th district of Monroe Co. Signed: JOHN CURETON Shff. Wit: BENJAMIN HOLLAND, ABNER DURHAM J.P. Recorded 10 July 1822.

Page 43: Ga. Lawrence Co., 1 July 1822, JAMES RIGHT of same to SILVANUS WALKER of Monroe Co., Ga. for $50, 202½ acres, lot #27 in the 1st district of Monroe Co. Signed: JAMES RIGHT. Wit: HARMON B. HARGROVE, PLEASANT P. CLOPTON. Ga. Monroe Co., PLEASANT P. CLOPTON swore to the deed before ABNER DURHAM J.P. 11 July 1822. Recorded 11 July 1822.

Pages 44, 45: Ga. Jones Co., 11 Dec. 1822, WILLIAM WALL of Twiggs Co. to NEEDHAM MIMS of Baldwin Co. for $450, 202½ acres, lot #72 in the 13th district of Monroe Co. Signed: WILLIAM WALL. Wit: CHARLES BULLOCK, JAMES MOON, ISAAC WELCH. Recorded 20 July 1822.

Page 45: Ga. Baldwin Co., 2 Feb. 1822, EPHRAIM KING of Loyd's District Burke Co. to ARCHIBALD DARRAGH of Jones Co. foe %150, lot #32 in the 12th district of Monroe Co. Signed: EPHRAIM (X) KING. Wit: JNO. B. HINES, ___ ROUSSEAU J.P. Recorded 22 July 1822.

Pages 46, 47: Ga. Jones Co., 12 July 1822, HUMPHRY STRICKLAND of Liberty Co. to SOLOMON GRICE of Jones Co. for $223, 202½ acres, lot #14 in the 12th district of Monroe Co. Singed: HUMPHRY STRICKLAND by his attorney THOS. DURHAM. Wit: WILLIAM (X) BOWER, L. SANDERS NOBLES. Ga. Houston Co., WILLIAM BOWER swore to the deed before JOHN H. BEARD J.P. 18 July 1822. Ga. 14 Jan. 1822, Power of attorney from HUMPHRY STRICKLAND to THOMAS DURHAM to sell lot #14 in the 12th district of Monroe Co. Wit: P. PHILLIPS, ROBT. T. (X) PROCTER. Ga. Jones Co., ROBERT T. PROCTER swore to the power of attorney before JOHN JENKINS, J.P. 13 July 1822. Recorded 22 July 1822.

Pages 47, 48: Ga., 17 July 1822, SOLOMON GRICE of the Co. & state afsd. to ISAAC WELCH of Monroe Co. for ___ hundred dollars, 202½ acres, lot $14 in the 12th district of Monroe Co. on Tobasofca Creek drawn by HUMPHRY STRICKLAND of McCranie District Liberty Co. Signed: SOLOMON GRICE. Wit: ELIZA? T. JENKINS, JOHN JENKINS J.P. Recorded 22 July 1822.

Page 48: Ga. Hall Co., 18 Feb. 1822, HENRY JOHNSTON of Hall Co. to JOSEPH BARR of Jackson Co. for $500, 202½ acres, lot #136 in the 4th district of Monroe Co. Signed: HENRY JOHNSTON. Wit: ANDREW (X) THOMPSON, WILLIAM COWAN J.I.C. Recorded 26 July 1822.

Page 49: Ga. Baldwin Co., 24 Jan. 1822, DAVIS SMITH of Laurence Co. to ELIJAH PHILLIPS of Jasper Co. for $619, 202½ acres, lot #133 in the 4th district of Monroe Co. granted to ALEXANDER OUTLAW of Dunn's District of Lawrence Co. Signed: DAVIS SMITH. Wit: WOODY DOZIER, APPLETON ROSSITER J.I.C. Recorded 26 July 1822.

Page 50: Ga. Monroe Co., 4 March 1822, JOSEPH BARR of Jackson Co. to ELIJAH PHILLIPS of Monroe Co. for $619, 202½ acres in the 4th district of Monroe Co. drawn by HENRY JNOSTON. Signed: JOSEPH BARR. Wit.: WILLIAM GARY, MIDDLETON HARTSFIELD, BENJAMIN DAVIS. Recorded 26 July 1822.

Pages 50, 51: Ga. Putnam Co., 13 May 1822, CHARLES Y. CALDWELL of Putnam Co. to WILLIAM GIBSON of Wilkes Co. for $700, 202½ acres, lot #272 in the 11th district of Monroe Co. Signed: CHARLES Y. CALDWELL. Wit: THO.? HARDEMAN, WILLIAM WILKINS J.I.C. Recorded 29 July 1822.

Page 51: Ga. Putnam Co., 2 March 1822, JOHNSON ASHFIELD to CHARLES Y. CALDWELL both of Co. afsd. for $500, 202½ acres, lot $272 in the 11th district of Monroe Co. Signed: JOHNSON ASHFIELD. Wit: W. WILSON, JNO. I.? SMITH J.I.C. Recorded 29 July 1822.

Pages 51, 52: Ga. Jasper Co., 20 May 1822, GREENE D. BRANTLEY of Co. afsd. to SPRINGER GIBSON of Wilkes Co. for $500, 202½ acres, lot #271 in the 11th District of Monroe. Signed: GREENE D. BRANTLEY. Wit: M. PHILLIPS, JESSE LOYAL J.P. Recorded 29 July 1822.

Pages 52, 53: Ga. Wilkes Co., 29 June 1822, SPRINGER GIBSON to WILLIAM GIBSON both of Wilkes Co. for $400, 202½ acres, 1to #271 in the 11th district. Signed: SPRINGER GIBSON. Wit: ROBERT SIMPSON, JOHN SHACKELFORD J.P. Recorded 29 July 1822.

Page 53: Ga. Monroe Co., 11 Feb. 1822, JOSHUA WARD of blank County to ABNER DURHAM J.P. Recorded 29 July 1822.

Page 54: Ga., 20 Dec. 1822, BERY FORT of Walton Co. to HENRY BURT in LINSEY SHEATS both of Clark Co. for $10.50, 202½ acres, lot #91 in the 2nd District of Monroe. Signed: BERRY (X) FORT. Wit: WILLIAM HARDIN, J. BURNETT, ALLEN W. BROWN, J.P. Ga. Clarke Co., JEREMIAH BURNETT swore to the deed before ALLEN W. BROWN 17 Jan. 1822. Recorded 3 Aug. 1822.

Pages 54, 55: Ga., 11 July 1822, JOHN and AXIOM CALHOON of Lawrence Co. to THOMAS WALKER of Putnam Co. for $769, lot #41 in the 5th district of Monroe. Signed: JOHN (X) CALHOON, AXIOM CALHOUN. Wit: R. H. L. BUCHANNON, APPLETON ROSSETER J.I.C. Recorded 5 Aug. 1822.

Pages 55, 56: Ga. Putnam Co., 13 Feb. 1822, JOSHUA SMITH of Telfair Co. to JOHN W. TOMME and PRESLEY HIGHTOWER of Putnam Co. for $80, lot #17 in the 2nd district of Monroe. Signed: JOSHUA SMITH. Wit: DANIEL LOW, JNO. C. LOW J.P. Recorded 5 Aug. 1822.

Page 56: 24 April 1822, VINES HARWELL of Jasper Co., Ga. to WILLIAM JONES SENR. of same for $200, 202½ acres, lot #223 in the 2nd district of Monroe. Signed: VINIS HARWELL. Wit: M. TRUPE, M. PHILLIPS, JESSE LOYALL J.P. Recorded 5 Aug. 1822.

Pages 56, 57: 12 April 1822, WINNEY TAYLOR of Elbert Co., Ga. to JOSEPH CHIPMAN of Co. & state afsd. for $400, 202½ acres, lot #5 in the 13th district of Monroe. Signed: WINNEY (her mark) TAYLOR. Wit: JOHN S. TAYLOR, NATHAN (X) TAYLOR. Ga. Elbert Co., NATHAN TAYLOR swore to the deed before JOHN COOK J.P. 12 April 1822. Recorded 6 Aug. 1822.

Pages 57, 58: Ga., 13 July 1822, JOSEPH CHIPMAN of Elbert Co. to JOHN SIMS of Oglethorpe Co. for $600, 202½ acres, lot #5 in the 13th district of Monroe, granted to WIDOW TAYLOR of Elbert Co. Signed: JOSEPH CHIPMAN. Wit: BEVERLY ALLEN, JAMES BANKS J.P. Recorded 6 Aug. 1822.

Page 59: Ga. Richmond Co., 20 Dec. 1821, MARY DALTON widow of Co. & State afsd. to EDWARD KENT of Jackson Co. for $500, 202½ acres, lot #280 in the 9th district of Monroe "drawn in my name." Signed: MARY DALTON widow. Wit: JAMES GRAY, WILLIAM JONES, Ga. Richmond Co., JAMES GRAY swore to the deed before R. BUSH J.P. 20 Dec. 1821. Recorded 6 Aug. 1822.

Page 59: Ga. Jackson Co., 26 Dec. 1821, JOHN SAILERS (SALERS in body of deed) and WILLIAM MEGINES of Co. & State afsd. to DAVID CRAWFORD of Morgan Co. for $1000, 202½ acres, 1to #35 in the 6th district of Monroe. Signed: JOHN SAILERS, WILLIAM MCGINNES. Wit: WILLIAM SAILERS, THOMAS C. B___? J.P. Recorded 8 Aug. 1822.

Page 60: Ga. Monroe Co., 6 Aug. 1822, In obedience to a writ of feire facias issued out of a Justice Ct. of Jasper Co. at the suit of DAVID THOMPSON against BENJAMIN GARRET, JOHN CURETON Sheriff seized the property of BENJAMIN GARRET and sold to FELIX STANLEY, highest bidder, for $301, 202½ acres, lot #32 in the 11th district of Monroe. Signed: JOHN CURETON Shff. Wit: JOHN F. BEAVERS, ELBERT PHILLIPS, J.P. Recorded 8 Aug. 1822.

Pages 61, 62: Ga., Monroe Co., 6 June 1822, JOEL CATLIN, late of Wards Dist. now of Brantley's Dist. Richmond Co., Ga. to JAMES WHATLEY of Monroe Co. for $150, 202½ acres, lot $227 in the 8th district of Monroe. Signed: JOEL CATLIN. Wit: ISAAC RHODES, PRUDENCE RHODES. Ga. Monroe Co., ISAAC RHODES swore to the deed before WILLIS WHATLEY J.P. 27 June 1822. Recorded 9 Aug. 1822. Augusta, 15 June 1822. This is to certify that we have known Mr. JOEL CATLIN since the year 1817, that he has resided in this place since that time that he has a family in this place since the year 1820 and that his titles to any land that he may have drawn in the last land Lottery will be good and sufficient. Signed: BENJAMIN HALL, WM. J. HOBBY. Ga. Richmond Co., Clerk's office Superior Court & Inferior Court Office. This is to certify that JOEL CATLIN a resident of Richmond County has no Judgments or Executions against him in any Offices & I take pleasure in Stating that I believe he is entirely clear of commercial difficulties. Signed: JAMES MCLAWS Clerk Sup. & In. Court, Georgia City of Augusta Clerks office of Mayors Court. This is to certify that JOEL CATLIN of the City of Augusta is not now nor ever has been sued in the Mayors Court of this City nor is there any Judgement against him in said Court and I further certify that as a man of Sterling worth and genuine integrity no man Stands Better. Signed: WM. JACKSON Clk. Mayors Court Augusta, Georgia 15 June 1822. Recorded 9 Aug. 1822.

Pages 62, 63: Ga. Baldwin Co., 2 May 1822, WILLIAM BRUMBLOW (BROM-BLOW in body of deed) of Jackson Co. by his agent HUGH CRAFT by power of attorney dated 22 April 1822 to THOMAS STANFORD of Hancock Co. for $1200, 202½ acres, lot #56 in the 11th district of Monroe drawn by Mr. WILLIAM BROMBELOW of Pitman's district Gwinnet Co. Signed: HUGH CRAFT attorney for WILLIAM BROMBLOW. Wit: CHARLES INGRAM, APPLETON ROSSETER J.I.C. Ga. Jackson Co., 22 April 1822, Power of Attorney from WILLIAM BROMBELOW JR. to HUGH CRAFT of Baldwin Co. to sell lot #56 in the 11th district of Monroe. Signed: WILLIAM BROMBELOW. Wit: WILLIAM MATTHEWS JR., H. B. GREENWOOD J.I.C. Recorded 9 Aug. 1822.

Page 64: Ga. Monroe Co., 6 Aug. 1822, JOHN CURETON Sheriff in obedience to a writ of the Superior Court of Green Co. at the suit of BUCKNER WILLIAMS for the use of THOMAS WILLIAMSON against WILLIAM C. JOHNSON seized the property of WILLIAM C. JOHNSON and sold to BUCKNER P. WILLIAMS highest bidder for $185, 202½ acres, lot #171 in the 4th district of Monroe. Signed: JOHN CURETON Shfff. Wit: JOSEPH DUGHAN, ELBERT PHILLIPS, J.P. Recorded 14 Aug. 1822.

Pages 65, 66: Ga. Baldwin Co., 6 April 1822, SPENCER MOON* of Baldwin Co. as attorney for GEORGE RAWLINSON of Appling Co. to SAMUEL MOON for $50, 202½ acres lot #184 in the 11th district of Monroe. Signed: SPENCER MOON as attorney for GEORGE RAULISON. Wit: BRAXTON FOARD, C. MCCARTY J.P. Recorded 14 Aug. 1822. Ga. Appling Co., 5 Feb. 1822, Power of Attorney from GEORGE ROULERSON to SPENCER MOON to sell lot #184 in the 11th district of Monroe. Signed: GEORGE ROULERSON. Wit: JOSEPH LOCKALIER. JOSEPH LOCKALAR swore to the deed before JOSEPH DYALL J.P. 25 Feb. 1822. Recorded 14 Aug. 1822. (*Note: The name MOON is difficult to read. It may be MOORE.)

Pages 66, 67: Ga. Telfair Co., 4 March 1822, Power of Attorney from SAMUEL STONE of Irwin Co. to SPENCER MOON of Baldwin Co. to take out lot #148 in the 11th district of Monroe and to sell same to SAMUEL MOON $200 4 March 1822. Ga. Baldwin Co., 6 April 1822, SPENCER MOON of Baldwin Co. attorney for SAMUEL STONE of Irwin Co. to SAMUEL MOON for $200, 202½ acres, lot #148 in the 11th district of Monroe. Signed: SPENCER MOORE as attorney in fact for SAMUEL STONE. Wit: BRAXTON FOARD, C. MCCARTY J.P. Recorded 21 Aug. 1822.

233

Pages 67, 68: Ga. Baldwin Co., 1 April 1822, BENNETT FERRILL of
Wilkinson Co., Ga. to SPENCER MOORE of Baldwin Co. for $375, 202½ acres,
lot #128 in the 12th district of Monroe. Signed: BENNETT FERRELL.
Wit.: ROBT. HILL, ZACHUS WRIGHT, JOHN BARNARD. Ga. Baldwin Co., JOHN
BARNARD swore to the deed before JAMES A. PERDUE J.P. 6 April 1822.
Recorded 21 Aug. 1822.

Pages 68, 69: Ga., Baldwin Co., 3 Jan. 1822, BURWELL KENDRICK of
Putnam Co. to SPENCER MOORE for $200, 202½ acres, lot #116 in the 13th
district of Monroe on waters of Deer Creek. Signed: BURWELL KENDRICK.
Wit.: MENDA? KENDRICK, E. LOWE. Ga. Baldwin Co., EDMOND LOW swore
to the deed and that MERIDA KENDRICK was a subscribing witness. Sworn
before JAMES A. PERDUE J.P. 6 April 1822. Recorded 21 Aug. 1822.

Pages 69, 70: Ga. Monroe Co., 6 Aug. 1822, In obedience to a writ
of feire facias issued out of a justice court of the county at the suit
of RAKESTRAW & RUPERT against ZACHARIAH COLLY, I JOHN CURETON Sheriff
of the Co. afsd. lately seized the property of ZACHARIAH COLLY and sold
at public auction to SPENCER MOORE of Baldwin Co. for $430, 202½ acres,
lot #143 in the 12th district of Monroe. Signed: JOHN CURETON Shff.
Wit: JAS. NEAL, ELBERT PHILLIPS J.P. Recorded 21 Aug. 1822.

Pages 70, 71: Ga., 4 May 1822, REUBEN SUMNER of Richmond Co., Ga.
to THOS. (THOMAS in body of deed) TALMADGE of same for $200, 202½ acres,
lot #36 in the 7th district of Monroe drawn by REUBEN SUMNER of Lamars?
Dist. Richmond Co. Signed: REUBEN SUMNER. Wit: CALEB (X) MAULDEN,
R. BUSH J.P. Recorded 24 Aug. 1822.

Pages 71, 72: Ga., 4 May 1822, CALEB MAULDIN of Richmond Co., Ga.
to THOMAS TALMADGE of same for $200, 202½ acres, lot #73 in the 6th
district of Monroe drawn by sd. MAULDEN of Luthers Dist. Richmond Co.
Signed: CALEB (X) MAULDEN. Wit: REUBEN SUMNER, R. BUSH J.P. Ga.
Richmond Co., JUDITH MAULDEN wife of the within named CALEB MAULDEN
relinquished her claim of dower before R. BUSH J.P. 6 May 1822.
Recorded 24 Aug. 1822.

Pages 73, 74: Ga., 25 Jan. 1822, NATHANIEL ROBERTS attorney for
SAMUEL BRYANT of Screven Co. to AMBROSE CHAPMAN of Baldwin Co. for $400,
lot #6 in the 12th district of Monroe. Signed: NATHANIEL ROBERTS
attorney for SAMUEL BRYANT. Wit: NEAL MOSES, WM. W. CARNES, A. YOUNG
J.I.C. Recorded 2 Spet. 1822. Ga. Screven Co., 12 Jan. 1822, Power of
Attorney from SAMUEL BRYAN of Screven Co. to NATHANIEL ROBERTS of same
to sell 2 tracts of land drawn by sd. BRYAN: lot #208 in the 1st dis-
trict of Henry Co. and lot #6 in the 12th district of Monroe Co.
Signed: SAMUEL BRYAN. Wit: SEABORN GOODALL, WM. W. OLIVER J.I.C.
Recorded 2 Spet. 1822.

Pages 74, 75: Ga., 6 June 1822 JOHN A SCRODER of Chatham Co. to
AMBROSE CHAPMAN of Baldwin Co. for $350, 202½ acres, lot #29 in the 12th
district of sd. Co. Signed: JOHN A. SCHRODER. Wit: ROBERT MILES,
JOHN GADDIS, JOHN MILES J.P. Recorded 2 Sept. 1822.

Pages 75, 76: Ga. Monroe Co., 31 May 1822, HENRY HEARD & STEPHEN
HEARD of Walton Co. to WILLIAM NUNN of Co. & State afsd. for $500,
202½ acres, lot #217 in the 13th district of Monroe. Signed: HENRY
HEARD, STEPHEN (X) HEARD. Wit: WM. D. RIGHT, WILLIAM BLOUNT J.P.
Recorded 2 Sept. 1822.

Page 76: Ga. Jones Co., 1 Jan. 1822, WM. SMITH of Co. & State afsd.
appoints JOSEPH DAVIE my brother in law of the same State & Co. my
true & lawful attorney to sell lot #182 in the 13th district of Monroe.
Signed: WILLIAM SMITH. Wit: J. RUSHIN, ISAAC DUNCAN J.P. Recorded
2 Sept. 1822.

Pages 76, 77: Ga., 5 Jan. 1822, JOSEPH DAVIE attorney in fact of
Jones Co. to WILLIAM NUNN of Baldwin Co. for $600, 202½ acres, lot #182
in the 13th district of Monroe drawn by WILLIAM SMITH of Flowers Dist.

Jones Co. & conveyed by a power of attorney hereunto annexed. Signed:
JOSEPH DAVIE attorney for WILLIAM SMITH. Wit.: R. H. L. BUCHANNON,
MARLOW PRYOR J.P. Recorded 2 Sept. 1822.

Page 77, 78: Ga. Monroe Co., 8 June 1822, HENRY SMITH of Jones Co.
to ISAAC PHILLIPS of Monroe Co. for $200, 50½ acres, ¼ of lot #285 in
the 13th district of Monroe being the SE corner of above named lot one
side the lines of BRADY & HOWARD on the west side of the Oakmulgee River
and on the waters of said River. Signed: HENRY (X) SMITH. Wit.:
GEORGE VIGAL, JOHN TOMPKINS, ISAAC BAKER J.P. Recorded 3 Sept. 1822.

Pages 78,79: Ga. Jones Co., 26 Dec. 1821, RICHARD SHURLEY of Jones
Co. to ISAAC PHILLIPS of Monroe Co. for $1500, 202½ acres, lot $295
in the 13th district of Monroe On waters of Oakmulgee river. Signed:
RICHARD SHURLY. Wit: THOMAS M. PAXTON, ISAAC BAKER, CHAS. PHILLIPS
J.P. Ga. Jones Co., Sarah SHURLY relinquished her right as wife of
RICHARD SHURLEY to the above this first day named 1822. Signed: SARAH
(X) SHURLEY. Wit: BENJAMIN H. BROWN, CHAS. PHILLIPS J.P. Recorded
3 Sept. 1822.

Page 79: Ga. Hall Co., 29 April 1822, James Wilson Jr. of sd. Co.
to JAMES W. ALSTON & CADWELL W. RAINES of Monroe Co. for $362.50, 202½
acres, lot #267 in the 13th district of Monroe. Signed: JAMES WILSON
JR. Wit.: JAMES WILSON SENR., JAS. BLACKSTOCK J.P. Recorded 3 Sept.
1822.

Pages 80, 81: Ga. Monroe Co., 7 July 1822, PIERCE A. LEWIS of
Jones Co. to ISAAC BAKER of Monroe Co. for $186 sells to ISAAC PHILIPS
(Note: ISAAC is surnamed BAKER once in the deed and surnamed PHILIPS
twice in the deed) 10 acres 1 pole and ½ of land, part of lot #294 on
the w. side of Oakmulgee River in Monroe Co. Signed: P. A. LEWIS.
Wit: HARBERT LANEIR?, ISAAC BAKER J.P. Recorded 3 Sept. 1822.

Pages 81, 82: Ga., 22 March 1822, ROBERT NORTHCUT by SAML. BRIGHT
his attorney in fact of the Co. of Habersham to JOHN EVANS of Walton
Co. for $600, 202½ acres, lot #101 in the 3rd district of Monroe.
Signed: ROBERT NORTHCUT by his attorney in fact SAMUEL (X) BRIGHT.
Wit: FREDERICK BALDWIN, LUDWELL COLLINS. Ga. Monroe Co., LUDWELL COLLINS
swore to the deed before LITTLEBURY GRISHAM 2 Sept. 1822. Recorded 3
Sept. 1822.

Page 82: Ga. Monroe Co., 21 Aug. 1822, CATHERINE RAGAN appoints
LUDWELL E. COLLINS her attorney to recover from RICHARD TARVER all
debts due from sd. TARVER. Signed: CATEY RAGAN. Wit: JOHN SESSIONS.
Ga. Monroe Co., JOHN SESSIONS swore to the power of attorney before W. J.
STARLING J.P. 2 Sept. 1822. Recorded 3 Sept. 1822.

Pages 82, 83: Ga. Hancock Co., 4 May 1822, JOHN HASWELL of Hancock
Co. to MARK GONDER of same for $60, 202½ acres, lot #22 in the 1st
district of Monroe. Signed: JOHN HASWELL. Wit: WILLIAM C. SHELDON,
JAMES E. GONDER. Ga. Hancock Co., JAMES E. GONDER swore to the deed
before JOHN BINION J.P. 28 Aug. 1822. Recorded 3 Sept. 1822.

Pages 83, 84: 3 Sept. 1822, Whereas I ZACHARIAH CHAMBLIS having
purchased of WM. PURIFY lot #180 in the 13th district of Monroe Co. &
the sd. PURIFY having made title to me & whereas the sd. lot has been
since sold at Sheriffs sale to satisfy judgements other than sd. titles
& I became the purchaser but the sd. PURIFY paid the purchase money for
me & the sheriff having made the deed to me, now I do hereby relinquish
all claim, demand and right of action against the said PURIFY. Signed:
ZACHARIAH CHAMBLES. Wit: JOHN CURETON, AMOS LOVE J.I.C. of Laurens Co.
(Note: No recording date.)

Page 84, 85: Ga. Monroe Co., 3 Sept. 1822 in obedience to a writ
of feri facias issued out of the Supr. Court of Elbert Co. at the suit
of RICHARD J. EASLER & Co. for the use of ISAAC MIMS against GAINES
THOMPSON & JOHN BECK, JOHN CURETON Sheriff of Monroe Co. seized the

property of GAINES THOMPSON & sold to WILEY THOMPSON of Elbert Co., highest bidder, for $1005, 202½ acres, lot #104 in the 12th district of Monroe. Signed: JOHN CURETON Shff. Witness: ISAAC WELCH, G. W. RAINES J.I.C. (Note: No recording date.)

Pages 85, 86: Ga. Monroe Co., 3 Sept. 1822, In obedience to a writ of feri facias issued out of a Justice Court of Wilkes Co. at the suit of JOHN M. CHENNEY against EPHRAIM FRASIER JR., BARNET FRASIER & EPHRAIM FRASIER SENR., JOHN CURETON Sheriff of Monroe Co. seized the property of EPHRAIM FRASIER & sold to DANIEL OWEN for $330, 202½ acres, lot #174 in the 6th district of Monroe. Signed: JOHN CURETON Shff. Wit: WILKINS HUNT, C. W. RAINES J.I.C. Recorded 4 Sept. 1822.

Pages 86, 87: Ga. Monroe Co., 3 Sept. 1822, In obedience to a writ of feire facias issued out the Superior Court of Lawrens Co. at the suit of FUQUA & COLEMAN against JAMES BAITY, JOHN CURETON Sheriff of Monroe Co. seized the property of JAMES BAITY & sold to DANIEL OWEN, highest bidder, for $431, 202½ acres, lot #165 in the 12th district of Monroe. Signed: JOHN CURETON Shff. Wit: WILKINS HUNT, ELBERT PHILLIPS J.P. Recorded 4 Sept. 1822.

Page 87, 88: Ga. Monroe Co., 3 Sept. 1822, In obedience to a writ of fire facias issued out of a Justices Court of Burke Co. at the suit of ARTHUR BELL administrator of ANN ATKINSON dec'd. against WILLIAM KEY, JOHN CURETON Sheriff of Monroe Co. seized the land of said WILLIAM KEY & sold to BLASSINGAME G. PAULETT, highest bidder for $166, 202½ acres, lot #48 in the 7th district of Monroe Co. Signed: JOHN CURETON shff. Wit: ISAAC WELCH, C. W. RAINES J.I.C. Recorded 4 Sept. 1822.

Pages 88, 89: Ga. Monroe Co., 3 Sept. 1822, In obedience to a writ of feri facias issued out of a Justices Court of Laurens Co. at the suit of JOEL CONEY against JOHN DEAN, WM. & HENRY ALBRITTON, JOHN CURETON Sheriff of Monroe Co. did seize the property of the said JOHN DEAN & sold to ZACHARIAH CHAMBLES, highest bidder, for $1051, 202½ acres, lot #160 in the 13th district of Monroe. Signed: JOHN CURETON Shff. Wit: ISAAC WELCH, C. W. RAINES J.I.C. Recorded 5 Sept. 1822.

Pages 90, 91: Ga. Monroe Co., 7 Sept. 1822, THOMAS REES (REESE in body of deed) of Monroe Co. to JONATHAN MILNER of Oglethorpe Co. for $402, lto #244 in the 10th district of Monroe. Signed: THOMAS REES. Wit: ABNER DURHAM J.P., HENRY H. LUMPKIN, MORDECAI C. HOWARD. Recorded 7 Sept. 1822. Monroe Co., 3 Sept. 1822, Power of attorney from THOMAS REES to JONATHAN MILNER of Oglethorpe Co. to rent or to sell a parcel of land, lot #244 in the 10th district of Monroe. Signed: THOMAS REES. Wit: ROBERT R. MINTER?, C. W. ALEXANDER, ABNER DURHAM J.P. Recorded 7 Sept. 1822.

Pages 91, 92 Ga. Monroe Co., 3 Sept. 1822, In obedience to a writ of feri facias issued out of a Justice Court of Morgan Co. at the suit of JOHN EMBERSON for the use of JAS. BELL against JESSE PONDERS, JOHN CURETON seized the property of said JESSE PONDERS & sold to JONATHAN MILNER of Oglethorpe Co., highest bidder, for $300, 202½ acres, lot #229 in the 9th district of Monroe. Signed: JOHN CURETON Shff. Wit: WILLIAM HUNT, ABNER DURHAM J.P. Recorded 7 Sept. 1822.

Pages 92, 93: Ga. Warren Co., 2 Dec. 1821, GEORGE SMITH of Warren Co. to JOHN MCCORMICK of same for $100, 202½ acres, lot #232 in the 1st district of Monroe. Signed: GEORGE (X) SMITH. Wit: JOHN GILES, SAMPSON (X) WORSELY. Ga. Warren Co., JOHN GILES swore to the deed before ROBT. LAZENBY J.P. 27 April 1822. Recorded 7 Sept. 1822.

Pages 93, 94: Ga. Monroe Co., 3 Sept. 1822, In obedience to a writ of feiri facias issued out of a Justice Court of Jefferson Co. at the uist of WILLIAM HAYLES against HENRY BROWN, JOHN CURETON Sheriff of Monroe Co. seized the land of HENRY BROWN and sold to JOBE TAYLOR, highest bidder, for $198, 202½ acres, lot #23 in the 1st district of Monroe. Signed: JOHN CURETON Shff. Wit: WILKINS HUNT, ABNER DURHAM J.P. Recorded 7 Sept. 1822.

Pages 94, 95: Ga. Burke Co., 18 May 1822, ALEXANDER YOUNG of Burke Co. to JOHN CHANDLER of the State of New York for $100, 202½ acres, lot #270 in the 12th district of Monroe. Signed: ALEXANDER YOUNG. Wit: JACOB EVANS, ___? ___ J.P. Ga. Burke Co., MARGARET YOUNG wife of ALEXANDER YOUNG relinquished her interest in land in sd. deed before JOHN L. (or S.) ROYAL J.P. Signed: MARGARET (X) YOUNG. Wit: JACOB EVANS. Recorded 9 Sept. 1822.

Pages 95, 96: Ga. Monroe Co., 3 Sept. 1822, In obedience to writ of feri facias issued out of the Superior Court of Twiggs Co. at the suit of PETERSON SANDERS against JOSEPH PATTERN, JOHN CURETON Sheriff of Monroe Co. seized the property of JOSEPH PATTERN and sold to JOSEPH CHIPMAN, highest bidder, for $331, 202½ acres, lot #9 in the 6th district of Monroe. Signed: JOHN CURETON Shff. Wit: WILKINS HUNT, ABNER DURHAM J.P. Recorded 9 Sept. 1822.

Pages 96, 97: Ga. Monroe Co., 3 Sept. 1822, In obedience to a writ of feri facias issued out of a Justice Court of Jasper Co. at the suit of WILLIAM R. RUSSEL against SAMUEL HEARD, JOHN CURETON Sheriff of Monroe Co. seized the property of SAMUEL HEARD and sold to WILLIAM R. RUSSEL, highest bidder, for $177, 202½ acres, lot #27 in the 10th district of Monroe. Signed: JOHN CURETON Shff. Wit: JAMES WHATLEY, ABNER DURHAM J.P. Recorded 9 Sept. 1822.

Pages 97, 98, 99; 25 April 1822, SHADRACH HARPER of Bryan Co., Ga. to MICHAEL O. CONNOR of Chatham Co., Ga. for $50, 202½ acres, lot #64 in the 10th district of Monroe. Signed: SHARACH HARPER. Wit: WM. MOREL Not. Publ., EDMOND MAHER. Savannah 25 April 1822, Received of Mr. MICHAEL O'CONNOR the sum of $50. Signed: SHADRACH HARPER. Recorded 10 Sept. 1822.

Pages 99, 100: Ga. Monroe Co., 3 Sept. 1822, In obedience to a writ of feri facias issued out of the Superior Court of Richmond Co., Ga. at the suit of JAMES MOORE against JOHN WILLY, JOHN CURETON Sheriff of Monroe Co. seized the property of JOHN WILLY & sold to MATTHEW MCCRARY, highest bidder, for $142, 202½ acres, lot #230 in the 5th district of Monroe. Signed: JOHN CURETON Shff. Wit: ALEXANDER CHAMBLESS, WILKINS HUNT, C. W. RAINES, J.I.C. Recorded 10 Sept. 1822.

Page 100: Ga. Lawrence Co., 5 Jan. 1822, Power of attorney from BENJAMIN B. THOMPSON of Laurens Co. to CHARLES EVANS of Jones Co. to dispose of lot #153 in the 6th district of Monroe. Signed: BENJAMIN B. THOMPSON. Wit: NATHL. HOLLEY. Recorded 11 Sept. 1822.

Page 101: Ga. Monroe Co., 11 Sept. 1822, THOMAS REESE of Monroe Co. to BENJAMIN MILNER of same for $760, 202½ acres, lot #221 in the 7th district of Monroe. Sgd. THOMAS REESE. Wit: WILKINS HUNT, BENJAMIN HOLLAND, HENRY H. LUMPKIN. Recorded 19 Sept. 1822.

Page 102: Ga. Monroe Co., 3 Sept. 1822, In obedience to a writ of feri facias issued out of the Superior Court of Lawrence Co. at the suit of THOMAS MOORE against JAMES BAITY, JOHN CURETON Sheriff of Monroe Co. seized the property of JAMES BAITY & sold to JAMES WHATLEY, highest bidder, for $253, 202½ acres, lot #107 in the 10th district of Monroe. Signed: JOHN CURETON Shff. Wit: WILKINS HUNT, C. W. RAINES J.I.C. Recorded 12 Sept. 1822.

Page 103: Ga. Monroe Co., 3 Sept. 1822, In obedience to a writ of feri facias issued out of the Superior Court of Wilkinson Co. at the suit of the administrators of DAVID CLAY dec'd. against THOMAS SHERRER, JOHN CURETON Sheriff of Monroe Co. seized the property of THOMAS SHERRER & sold to JAMES WHATLEY, highest bidder, for $105, 202½ acres, lot #24 in the 8th district of Monroe. Signed: JOHN CURETON Shff. Wit: WM. R. RUSSELL, ABNER DURHAM J.P. Recorded 13 Sept. 1822.

Page 104: Ga. Jasper Co., 14 Jan. 1822, EDMOND DAVIS to JOURDAN COMPTON both of State afsd. for $300, 202½ acres, lot #250 in the 3rd district of Monroe. Signed: EDMUND DAVIS. Wit: WM. D. JARRATT, P. COMPTON J.P. Recorded 14 Sept. 1822.

Pages 104, 105: Ga. Jasper Co., 29 July 1822, Know all men by these presents I HEZEKIAH BROWN (BROUN in body of power of attorney) of Laurence Co. appoint NOAH SMITH of the Co. afsd. my attorney to recover 202½ acres, lot #73 in the 4th district of Monroe. Signed: HEZEKIAH BROWN. Wit: P. COMPTON J.P. Ga. Jasper Co., 2 Aug. 1822, NOAH SMITH attorney in fact for HEZEKIAH BROWN to WILLIAM M. COCHRAN both of Co. & State afsd. for $200, 202½ acres, lot #73 in the 4th district of Monroe. Signed: NOAH SMITH. Wit: A. PONDER J.P., C. COMPTON J.P. Recorded 14 Sept. 1822.

Pages 105, 106: Ga. Monroe Co., 3 Sept. 1822, In obedience to a writ of feri facias issued out of a Justice Court of Jefferson Co. at the suit of FONTAINE & NEAL against WM. BARROW, JOHN CURETON Sheriff of Monroe Co. seized the property of WILLIAM BARROW & sold to SOLOMON STEPHENS of Monroe Co., highest bidder, for $315, 202½ acres, lot #9 in the 10th district of Monroe. Signed: JOHN CURETON Shff. Wit: WILLIAM HUNT, JOHN GRESHAM J.P. Recorded 17 Sept. 1822.

Pages 106, 107: Ga. Madison Co., 25 May 1822, BERRY HENDRICK of Madison Co. to JAMES HAMMETT of Monroe Co. for $20, 10t #259 in the 13th district of Monroe. Signed: BERRY HENDRICK. Wit: JAMES LONG, ROBERT GROVES J.P. Recorded 18 Sept. 1822.

Pages 107, 108: Ga. Hancock Co., 21 Feb. 1822, H. & T. H. KINDALE of Sate & Co. afsd. to THOMAS PINCKARD of Greene Co., Ga. for $1,150, 202½ acres, lot #105 in the 5th district of Monroe. Signed: H. & T. H. KENDALL. Wit: J. A. WRIGHT, W. RACHEL JR., L. L. SMITH J.P. Recorded 19 Sept. 1822.

Pages 108, 109: Ga. Walton Co., 29 April 1822, JONATHAN REEVES of Walton Co., Ga. to ISAAC BARNES of Jasper Co., Ga. for $100, 2021/2 acres, lot #155 in the 13th district of Monroe. Signed: JONATHAN REEVES. Wit: JOHN P. WINN, MALICHI REEVES. MALACHI REEVES swore to the deed before ANDREW BOYD J.P. 29 April 1822. Recorded 20 Sept. 1822.

Pages 109, 110: Ga. Walton Co., 29 April 1822, MALACHI REEVES of Walton Co., Ga. to ISAAC BARNES of Jasper Co. for $165, 202½ acres, lot #181 in the 11th district of Monroe. Signed: MALACHI REEVES. Wit: JOHN REEVES, ANDREW BOYD. Recorded 21 Sept. 1822.

Page 110: Ga. Monroe Co., 27 Dec. 1821, ELIAS GOFF of Hall Co., Ga. to JOHN H. PONDER of Co. afsd. for $200, 202½ acres, lot #129 in the 13th district of Monroe on Rockey Creek. Signed: ELIAS (X) GOFF. Wit: BENJN. JOURDAN, F. W. ARNOLD, JOSEPH MORTON J.P. Recorded 23 Sept. 1822.

Pages 110, 111: Ga., 26 Dec. 1821, JOHN E. GARDNER of Washington Co., Ga. to THOMAS PINCKARD of Greene Co., Ga. for $750, lot #104. Signed: JOHN E. GARDNER. Wit: JNO. R. SMITH, MARLOW L. PRYOR J.P. Recorded 24 Sept. 1822.

Pages 111, 112: Ga. 3 Sept. 1822 in obedience to a writ of feire facias issued out of the Justice Court of Wilkerson Co. at the suit of JOHN BROOKS against ROBERT WELBORN (WILBORN), JOHN S. PLATT & MATTHEW SHARP, JOHN CURETON Sheriff of Monroe Co. seized the tract of ROBERT WELBORN and sold to SAMUEL REID of Jasper Co. for $96, 202½ acres, lot #155 in the 3rd district of Monroe. Signed: JOHN CURETON Shff. Wit: IRVIN LAWSON, ABNER DURHAM J.P. Recorded 1 Oct. 1822.

Pages 112, 113: 14 Aug. 1822, HENRY MATTHEWS of Chatham Co. to THOMAS ELKINS for $200, 202½ acres, lot #299 in the 13th district of Monroe. Signed: HENRY MATHEWS. Wit: BARNARD KOCHLER, JOHN DELLON J.P. Recorded 1 Oct. 1822.

Pages 113, 114, 155: 12 March 1822, WILLIAM SMITH, House Carpenter of Chatham Co., Ga. to RICHARD R. CUYLER? Attorney at Law, for $40,

202½ acres, lot #34 in the 2nd district of Monroe. Signed: WILLIAM
SMITH. Wit: WILLIAM WILLIAMS, JESSE BANDY. Ga. Chatham Co., WILLIAM
WILLIAMS of Chatham Co., Ga. swore to the deed before ISAAC RUSSELL
J.P. 29 July 1822. Recorded 1 Oct. 1822.

Page 116: Ga. Wilkerson Co., 29 Dec. 1821, JOSEPH STEPHENS SENR.
of Co. afsd. to GEORGE STEPHENS of Twiggs Co., Ga. for $101.25, 101¼
acres, part of lot #169 in the 6th district of Monroe. Signed: JOSEPH
STEVENS SENR. Wit: ETHELRED PITTMAN, PHILIP PITMAN J.P. Recorded 2
Oct. 1822.

Pages 116, 117: Ga. Monroe Co., 1 Oct. 1822, In obedience to a
writ of fieri facias issued out of a Justice Court of Washington Co. at
the suit of WILLIAM WALLER against JOHN BRANNAH, JOHN CURETON Sheriff
seized the tract of said JOHN BRANNAN and sold to JOHN C. WALTERS for
$137, 202½ acres, lot #19 in the 14th district of Monroe. Signed: JOHN
CURETON Shff. Wit: WILKINS HUNT, ELBERT PHILLIPS J.P. Recorded 2 Oct.
1822.

Page 118: Ga. Monroe Co., 3 Sept. 1822, In obedience to a writ of
fieri facias issued out of the Justice Court of Elbert Co. at the suit
of NEIL & LEWIS MCMULLAN against JOHN DAVIS, JOHN CURETON Sheriff seized
the tract of JOHN DAVIS and sold to JOHN C. WALTERS of Monroe Co. for
$23, 202½ acres, lot #80 in the 15th district of Monroe. Signed: JOHN
CURETON Shff. Wit: WILKINS HUNT, THOMAS BUSTION J.P. Recorded 2 Oct.
1822.

Page 119: Ga. Monroe, 1 Oct. 1822, In obedience to a writ of fieri
facias issued out of the Superior Court of Chatham Co. at the Suit of
the Planters Bank of the State of Ga. for the use of Bryan & Brother
against B. & G. Lathrop, JOHN CURETON Sheriff of Monroe Co. seized the
tract of land of B. & G. LATHROP and sold to JOHN C. WALTERS for $60.06¼
202½ acres, lot #36 in the 8th district of Monroe. Signed: JOHN CURETON
Shff. Wit: MORDECAI C. HOWARD, WILKINS HUNT, ELBERT PHILLIPS J.P.
Recorded 3 Oct. 1822.

Page 120: 28 June 1822, ROBERT BUCKERSTAFF of Jasper Co., Ga. to
LITTLEBURY GRESHAM of Monroe Co. for $500, 202½ acres, lot #81 in the
14th district on the District line on the Towaliga River. Signed:
ROBERT BECKERSTAFF. Wit: BENJAMIN JORDAN, WILLIAM SCOTT. WILLIAM
SCOTT swore to the deed before ABNER DURHAM J.P. L Sept. 1822. Recorded
4 Oct. 1822.

Pages 120, 121: Ga. Jones Co., 23 Aug. 1822, NANCY Z. GAMMAGE of
Wilkes Co. to SEABORN J. WHATLEY of Jones Co. for $450, 202½ acres, lot
#186 in the 5th district of Monroe. Signed: ANCY (X) Z. GAMMAGE.
Wit: WILLSON WHATLEY, WILLIAM WHATLEY. Recorded 8 Oct. 1822.

Pages 121, 122: Ga., 19 Dec. 1821, BARNETT R. POWEL of Twiggs Co.
to HARDY LASSETER of Jasper Co. for $750, 202½ acres, lot #100 in the
14th district of Monroe, drawn by me the said BARNETT R. POWIL of Blackshear's district Twiggs County. Signed: BARNETT R. POWELL. Wit:
THOMAS REASSEAU, JAMES REAUSSEAU. Recorded 8 Oct. 1822.

Pages 122, 123: 18 Sept. 1822, DAVID BUSBIN of Oglethorpe Co., Ga.
to WILLIAM L. FAMBROUGH of Clark Co. for $600, 202½ acres, lot #61 in
the 6th district of Monroe on waters of rocky Creek. Signed: DAVID (X)
BUSBIN. Wit: WILLIAM FAMBROUGH SENR., WILLIAM FAMBROUGH J.P. Recorded
8 Oct. 1822.

Page 123: Ga., 30 March 1822, SEABORN CHRISTOPHER of Greene Co.
to JOEL FORISTER of Green Co. for $250, 202½ acres, lot #211 in the 2nd
district of Monroe. Signed: SEABORN (X) CHRISTOPHER. Wit: DOUGLASS
WATSON, THOMAS M. WILLIAMS, SARAH WATSON. Ga. Greene Co., DOUGLASS
WATSON swore to the deed before ROBERT NEWSOM a Magistrate of Green Co.
8 June 1822. Recorded 8 Oct. 1822.

Pages 123, 124: Ga. Baldwin Co. 28 Aug. 1822, AMBROSE CHAPMAN of Baldwin Co. to THOMAS H. WYNN of Monroe Co. for $676, 20½ acres, lot #142 in the 13th district of Monroe. Signed: AMBROSE CHAPMAN. Wit: THOMAS YOUNGBLOOD, TURNER HUNT, J.I.C.

Pages 124, 125: Ga. Putnam Co., 20 Dec. 1821, WILLIAM ROGERS of Putnam Co. to THOMAS P. SWANN of same for $250, the SW half of 202½ acres, lot #150 in the 5th district of Monroe. Signed: WILLIAM (X) ROGERS. Wit: BENJAMIN F. WARD, HARMON (X) CHANNEL, FRANCIS WARD. Ga. Monroe Co., HARMON CHANNEL swore to the deed before MOSES DUMAS J.P. 3 Aug. 1822. Recorded 9 Oct. 1822.

Pages 125, 126: Ga. Monroe Co., 5 Sept. 1822, JOHN SMITH of Appling Co. to JOHN FINCH of Monroe Co. for $250, 202½ acres, lot #77 in the 5th district of Monroe. Signed: JOHN SMITH by his Attorney. JAMES (X) TAYLOR. Wit: C. W. COODY, ROLLINS SMITH J.P. Ga. Jones Co., 12 June 1822, Power of Attorney from JOHN SMITH of Appling Co. to JAMES TAYLOR SENR. of Jones Co. to sell lot #77 in the 5th district of Monroe. Signed: JOHN SMITH. Wit: WILLIAM R. SAYERS J.P. Recorded 9 Oct. 1822.

Pages 126, 127: Ga. Jasper Co., 21 May 1822, JOHN BIRD SENR. by his attorney in fact WILLIAM D. BIRD of Hall Co. to THOMAS HOLLIS of Jasper Co. for ___? Hundred sixty nine dollars, lot #191 in the 12th district of Monroe. Signed: JOHN BYRD SENR. By his attorney in fact WILLIAM D. BYRD. Wit: JAMES WILLSON JR., E. DODSON J.P. Ga. Hall Co., Power of Attorney from JOHN BYRD SENR. of Hall Co. to WILLIAM D. BYRD of same to sell lot #191 in the 12th district of Monroe and to convert the same to his won proper use & benefit & behoof. Signed: JOHN BYRD. Wit: JOHN G. BRYAN, D. G. MCCLESKEY J.P. Recorded 9 Oct. 1822.

Page 128: Ga., 4 Dec. 1821, NATHANIEL JACKSON of Morgan Co. to WILLIAM SANDERS of Hancock Co. for $900, lot #197 in the 13th district of Monroe. Signed: NATHANIEL JACKSON. Wit: RICHARD GRAY, MARLOW PRYOR J.P. Recorded 9 Oct. 1822.

Pages 128, 129: Ga. Richmond Co., 7 Feb. 1822, BENJAMIN KENAH of Richmond Co. to BOLEN SMITH of Jasper Co. for $650, 202½ acres, lot #199 in the 13th district of Monroe. Signed: BENJAMIN (X) KENAH. Wit: DANIEL DILL, WILLIAM M. PICKRON, AN. J. DILL, Ga. Richmond Co., ANDREW J. DILL swore to the deed before PHILIP H. MANTZ J.P. 9 Feb. 1822. Recorded 9 Oct. 1822.

Page 130: Ga. Monroe Co., 1 Aug. 1822, BOLIN SMITH of Jasper Co. to WILLIAM SANDERS of Monroe Co. for $1000, 202½ acres, lot #199 in the 13th district of Monroe. Signed: BOLIN SMITH. Wit: JOHN MARTIN, ___?, ___? J.I.C. Recorded 9 Oct. 1822.

Page 131: Ga. Putnam Co., 13 Sept. 1822, RICHARD W. FOX of Putnam Co. to ELI HARRIS of same for $600, 202½ acres, lot #46 in the 5th district of Monroe. Signed: RICHARD W. FOX. Wit: LAIRD W. HARRIS, WILLIAM GAY J.P. Recorded 24 Oct. 1822.

Pages 131, 132: Ga., 23 Aug. 1822, HENRY BURT of Clark Co. to HEZEKIAH BLANKENSHIP of same for $250, half of lot #91 in the 2nd district originally granted BERRY FORT and since conveyed to HENRY BURT. The lot to be divided into equal parts & the afsd H. BLANKENSHIP is to have that part which himself & LINDSEY SHEETS the owner of the other half shall agree on. Signed: HENRY BURT. Wit: JAMES HINTON, WILLIAM PRITCHARD. HENRY BURT swore to the deed before W. WHITE J.P. 21 Oct. 1822. Recorded 24 Oct. 1822.

Pages 132, 133: Ga. Gwinnett Co., 18 Oct. 1822, WILLIAM BAILEY of Gwinnett Co. to WILLIAM HINNARD of Clark Co. for $1000, lot #137 in the 5th district of Monroe. Signed: WILLIAM BAILEY. Wit: JOHN HINNARD, M. H. COGBURN J.P. Recorded 24 Oct. 1822.

Pages 133, 134: Ga. Clark Co., 2 Sept. 1822, WILLIS WHATLEY of Clark Co. to JOSEPH HUDDLESTON of Baldwin Co. for $500, lot #153 in the

5th district of Monroe. Signed: WILLIS (X) WHATLEY. Wit: DANIEL
SUMMERS. WILLIAM STROUD J.P. Ga. Clark Co., CATHARINE (X) WHATLEY
relinquished her dower before WILLIAM STROUD. Recorded 25 Oct. 1822.

Pages 134, 135: Ga. Monroe Co., 3 Sept. 1822, In obedience to a
writ of fieri facias issued out of a Justice Court of the Co. of Jones
at the suit of JOEL RUSHIN against LUKE PETTY, JOHN CURETON Sheriff of
Monroe Co. seized the property of LUKE PETTY and sold to JOHN G. LUMSDALE
for $165, 202½ acres, lot #226 in the 3rd district of Monroe. Signed:
JOHN CURETON Shff. Wit: IRVINE LAWSON, ABNER DURHAM J.P. Recorded 25
Oct. 1822.

Page 135: Ga. Monroe Co., 3 Sept. 1822, In obedience to a writ of
fieri facias issued out of a Justice Court of Morgan Co. at the suit of
WILLIAM BARTOW against MOSES W. YOUNG, JOHN CURETON Sheriff of Monroe
Co. seized the land of MOSES W. YOUNG and sold to JOHN G. LUMSDEN for
$202, 202½ acres, lot #11 in the 3rd district of Monroe. Signed: JOHN
CURETON Shff. Wit: ANDERSON HOLT, C. W. RAINES J.I.C.

Pages 136: Ga. Jasper Co., 22 Oct. 1822, DAVID HELDREBRAND
(HELDEBRAND in body of deed) of Jasper Co. to ABNER CHAPMAN SENR. of same
for $350, 202½ acres, lot #93 in the 14th district of Monroe. Signed:
DAVID HELDEBRAND. Wit: MARHACH TEEL, WOODY DOZIER J.I.C. Recorded 31
Oct. 1822.

Page 136, 137: Ga., 30 July 1822, WILLIAM HARDMAN of Oglethorpe
Co. to WILEY BARRON (BARROW?) of Jones Co. for $1000, 202½ acres, lot
#6 in the 13th district of Monroe on the waters of Little Tobasofca.
Signed: WILLIAM HARDMAN. Wit: RICE DURRETT, SAMUEL BARRON. Ga. Jones
Co., SAMUEL BARRON swore to the deed before CHARLES NAMECK J.P. 15
Sept. 1822. Recorded 31 Oct. 1822.

Page 138: Ga. Liberty Co., 7 Feb. 1822, To all whom it may concern
I, A. FANNEY SMITH widow of State & Co. afsd. hath this day appointed
JACOB HARNEDGE of same my legal attorney to sell, rent or lease lot
#192 in the 13th district of Monroe Co. drawn by me in the late land
lottery. Signed: A. FANNEY (X) SMITH. Wit: MOSES WESTBERY J.P.,
JOSEPH SMITH. Recorded 31 Oct. 1822.

Pages 138, 139: Ga. Appling Co., 31 July 1822, JACOB HARNEDGE of
Liberty Co. as attorney for A. FANNEY SMITH wid. of McCraneys district
Liberty Co. to ISAAC MOODY of Appling Co. for $400, 202½ acres, lot
#192 in the 13th district of Monroe. Signed: JACOB (X) HARNEDGE. Wit:
SAMUEL E. SEVELLY J.P., POLLY SEVELLY. Recorded 31 Oct. 1822.

Page 139: Ga. Clark Co., 23 Oct. 1822 HUMPHREY HURST of Clark Co.
to RICHARD HAMLIN of Jones Co. for $500, 202½ acres, lot #61 in the
13th district of Monroe, on the Waters of Tobasofca Creek. Signed:
HUMPHREY HURST. Wit: WILLIAM EUBANK, ADAM CARSON J.P. Recorded 31 Oct.
1822.

Page 140: Ga. Jones Co., 27 Feb. 1822, WILLIS ROBINSON of McIntosh
Co. to PEARCE A. LEWIS of Jones Co. for $500, all of lot #249 in the 13th
district of Monroe. Signed: WILLIS ROBINSON. Wit: FOUCHE CLEVELAND,
FELIX LEWIS. Recorded 27 Nov. 1822.

Pages 140, 141: Ga. Baldwin Co., 21 Jan. 1822, NATHAN BROWN OF
Emanuel Co. to PEARCE A. LEWIS of Jones Co. for $500, 202½ acres, lot
$110 in the 5th district of Monroe. Signed: NATHAN BROWN. Wit:
THOMAS BASS, APPLETON ROSSETER J.I.C. Recorded 1 Nov. 1822.

Pages 141, 142: Ga. Greene Co., 13 Jan. 1822, MARTHA CATCHING of
Co. & State afsd. to JOSEPH CATCHING of same for $200, 202½ acres, lot
#115 in the 5th district of Monroe on Clantons Creek granted to MARTHA
CATCHING. Signed: MARTHA (X) CATCHING. Wit: PHILLIP CAUSEY, JAMES
GREER, WILLIAM WINFIELD J.P. Recorded 3 Nov. 1822.

Pages 142, 143: Ga., 2 Feb. 1822, JAMES G. DAVIS of Twiggs Co. to ZACHA. BOOTH SENR. of Jones Co. for $150, 202½ acres, lot #149 in the 7th district of Monroe. Signed: JAMES G. DAVIS. Wit: JOHN W. H. HOBSON, JOHN T. BOOTH, Ga. Monroe Co., JOHN T. BOOTH swore that he saw JAMES G. DAVIS assign the within deed to ZACHARIAH BOOTH. Recorded 5 Nov. 1822.

Pages 143: Ga. Warren Co., 28 May 1822, ELEMUEL B. SKEGGS of Putnam Co. to JOHN LYNN of the Co. & State of the other part. Witnesseth that the said JOHN LYNN hath this day bargained & swapt lot #216 in the 9th district of Monroe for 10t #49 in the 8th district of Monroe with ELEMUEL B. SKEGGS, lot #49 containing 202½ acres. Signed: LEMUEL B. SKEGGS. Wit: BENJA. IVY. BENJA. SANDFORD J.P.

Page 144: Ga. Clark Co., 6 July 18 (omitted), TIMOTHY WILLIAMS of Co. afsd. to JOHN MALUOM (MALOOM in body of deed) of Morgan Co. for $300, 202½ acres, Lot #264 in the 12th district of Monroe. Signed: TIMOTHY (X) WILLIAMS. Wit: LEWIS WILLIAM, JAMES CATES J.P.

Pages 144, 145: Ga. Jackson Co., 7 Dec. 1821, JOSEPH PRICE of Co. & State afsd. to TATUM MANIFEE & ALLEN LAWHORN of same for $50, 250 acres, lot #263 in the 13th district of Monroe. Signed: JOSEPH PRICE. Wit: SELMUS LYLE, JAMES SELLERS J.P. Recorded 18 Nov. 1822.

Page 145: Ga. Jackson Co., 26 Oct. 1822, TATUM MANIFEE of Co. afsd. to ALLEN LAWHORN for $500, 202½ acres, all of lot #263 in the 13th district of Monroe. Signed: TATUM MANIFEE. Wit: ANDREW J. SCOTT, M. D. MARTIN J.P. Recorded 18 Nov. 1822.

Pages 145, 146, 147: 13 Jan. 1822, ISAAC SCUDER of Chatham Co., Ga. to WILLIAM HEAD of Jasper Co. for $500, 202½ acres, lot #98 in the 14th district of Monroe surveyed by ISADORE STEASSON? Signed: ISAAC SCUDDER. Wit: B. DOBBINS J.P., JAMES PONDER. Recorded 9 Nov. 1822.

Pages 147, 148: Ga., 19 Feb. 1822, LABON C. POOL, attorney for JOHN MCVEAN Rev. of Baldwin Co. to AMBROSE CHAPMAN of Baldwin Co. for $350, 202½ acres, lot #142 in the 13th district of Monroe. Signed: LABON C. POOL attorney for JOHN MCVEAN Rev.. Wit: WM. DANIEL, JAMES A. HILL, JOHN MILES J.P. Recorded 20 Nov. 1822.

Pages 148, 149: Ga. Monroe Co., 5 Nov. 1822. In obedience to a writ of fiare facias issued out of a Justice Court of blank County at the suit of NICHOLASON VARNEY against ISAIAH PARKER, JOHN CURETON Sheriff of Monroe Co. seized the land of sd. PARKER & sold to FELIX STANLEY of Jasper Co. for $55, 202½ acres, lot #185 in the 6th district of Monroe. Signec: JOHN CURETON Shff. Wit: WILKINS HUNT, ABNER DURHAM J.P. Recorded 20 Nov. 1822.

Pages 149, 150: Ga. Monroe Co., 5 Nov. 1822, In obedience to a writ of fire facias issued out of a Justice Court of Washington Co. at the suit of WILLIAM MURPHREY Against SOLOMON TARVER, JOHN CURETON Sheriff of Monroe Co. seized the tract of land of sd. TARVER and sold to WILLIAM MURPHREY of Washington Co. for $37, 202½ acres, lot #246 in the 8th district of Monroe. Signed: JOHN CURETON Shff. Wit: WILKINS HUNT, ALLEN COCHRAN, ABNER DURHAM J.P. Recorded 20 Nov. 1822.

Pages 150, 151: Ga. Monroe Co., 8 Feb. 1822, ISIAH B. AVENT of Washington Co. appoints his trusty friend DAVID WRIGHT his true and lawful attorney to sell lot #83 in the 14th district of Monroe to ZACHARIAH PHILLIPS. Signed: I. B. AVENT. Wit: SARAH (X) ("his mark") MCSWAIN, JAMES WOODRUFF.

Pages 151, 152: Ga. Jasper Co., 21 Feb. 1822, DAVID WRIGHT attorney for ISAIAH B. AVENT of Washington Co. to ZACHARIAH PHILLIPS of Monroe Co. for $350, 202½ acres, lot #83 in the 14th district of Monroe. Signed: David Wright. Wit: JAMES WOODRUFF, T. D. KING. Recorded 21 Nov. 1822.

Pages 152, 153: 19 June 1822, LEVI BOWEN of Tatnall Co., Ga.
Capt. Johnstons district appoints DANIEL MARTIN of Franklin Co. his
lawful attorney to sell 202½ acres, lot #94 in the 5th district of
Monroe. Signed: LEVI (X) BOWIN. Wit: REBECCA (X) THOMPSON, WILLIAM
THOMPSON. Recorded 20 Nov. 1822.

Page 153: 5 July 1822, LEVI BOWIN of Johnsons District of Tatnall
Co. by his attorney DANIEL MARTIN to WILLIAM FERRELL of Habersham Co.
for $155, 202½ acres, lot #94 in the 5th district of Monroe. Signed:
LEVI BOWIN by his attorney in fact DANIEL MARTIN. Wit: JOHN H. GEORGE,
D. T. MILLING J.P. Recorded 20 Nov. 1822. (Note: Grantee written
TERRELL as well as FERRELL).

Page 154: Ga., 3 Jan. 1822, JAMES GRAHAM of Lawrens Co. to NEILL
MONROE of same for $125, 202½ acres, lot #121 in the 8th district of
Monroe Granted to sd. GRAHAM. Signed: JAMES (X) GRAYHAM. Wit: J.
BLACKSHEAR, JOHN BUYTON J.I.C. Recorded 20 Nov. 1822.

Pages 154, 155: 1 March 1822, WYLEY HIX of Habersham Co., Ga. to
LEONARD HARTWICK of same for $150 lot #56 in the 7th district of Monroe.
Signed: WYLY HIX. Wit: SAMUEL (X) WARD, AMILY WATTS. Ga. Habersham
Co., MILLY WATTS (she) swore to the deed before ABSALOM HOLCOMB J.P.
19 Aug. 1822. Recorded 20 Nov. 1822.

Pages 155, 156: 5 June 1822, ANDERSON WORTHY of Capt. Tatis
District Franklin Co., Ga. to WILLIAM TERRELL of Habersham Co. for $150,
202½ acres, lot #132 in the 15th district of Monroe. Signed: ANDERSON
(X) WORTHY. Wit: TH. HOLLINGSWORTH, JOSEPH DUNLAP J.P. Recorded 21
Nov. 1822.

Pages 156, 157: 23 Aug. 1822, DANIEL MARTIN of Franklin Co., Ga.
to WILLIAM TERRELL of Habersham Co. for $260, 202½ acres, lot #121 in
the 8th district of Monroe drawn by JAMES GRAHAM of McClendon's District
Lawrens Co. Signed: DANIEL MARTIN. Wit: SAMUEL JACKSON, ABSALOM
HOLCOMB J.P. Recorded 21 Nov. 1822.

Page 157: 25 March 1822, LENORD HARTWICK of Habersham Co., Ga. to
WILLIAM TERRELL of Co. afsd. for $300, all of lot #56 in the 7th district
of Monroe Co. drawn by WILEY HIX of Captain Riches District in sd. Co.
Signed: LEONARD (X) HARTWICK. Wit: SAMUEL HOLCOMB, ABSALOM HOLCOMB J.P.
Recorded 21 Nov. 1822.

Pages 158: Ga. Laurens Co., 6 Aug. 1822, NEILL MUNROE of Lawrens
Co. to DANIEL MARTIN of Franklin Co. for $200, 202½ acres, lot #121 in
the 8th district of Monroe granted to JAMES GRAHAM of Laurens Co.
Signed: NEILL MUNROE. Wit: JOHN THOMAS, AMOS LOVE J.I.Ct. Recorded
21 Nov. 1822.

Page 159: Ga. Twiggs Co., 13 Sept. 1822, JOSIAH HOMES (HOLMES
in body of deed) of Twiggs Co. to DAVID ADAMS of Jasper Co. for $600,
202½ acres, lot #26 in the 11th district of Monroe. Signed: JOSIAH
HOMES. Wit: D. D. COPP, DAVID GRAHAM J.P. Recorded 22 Nov. 1822.

Page 159, 160: Ga. Twiggs Co., 29 Aug. 1822, HENRY TARVER of
Twiggs Co. to JOSIAH HOMES of same for $600, 202½ acres, lot #26 in the
11th district of Monroe. Signed: HENRY TARVER. Wit: JAMES VISAGE,
HARDY DURHAM J.P. Recorded 22 Nov. 1822.

Page 1:   3 Aug. 1822, JOHN C. ADAMS of Elbert Co., to ROBERT BROWN
of Co. & State aforesaid for $270...202½ A. in Monroe Co., 13th District,
#56, JOHN C. ADAMS (SEAL). Test: J. M. CLEAVELAND, WM. DOOLEY, JP.
Rec. 11 Sept. 1823.

Pages 2, 3: State of Ga., Monroe Co. In obedience to a writ of
fiere facias issued out of the Superior Court of Elbert County at the
suit of WILLIAM WOODS against JOHNSON S. PLEDGER, I, JOHN CURETON, Shff.
of the Co. aforesaid, did seize the property of sd. JOHNSON S. PLEDGER,
and sold on the 1st Tues. in Aug. 1823 to one JAMES OLIVER, for $152,
lot #74, 4th Dist. 202½ A. JOHN CURETON, Shff (SEAL. Wit: WILEY JONES,
JOHN STILWELL. Rec. 11 Sept. 1823.

Pages 3,4: State of Ga., Monroe Co.: In obedience to a writ of
fiere facias issued out of the justice court of Chatham County, at the
suit of MOSES HERBERT against SAMUEL HINE, JOHN CURETON, Shff. did
seize the tract of sd. HINE and did place it at public sale 7 Jan. 1823,
sold to the highest bidder, one JAMES MAY, for $308 and this indenture
made 11 Sept. 1823, 202½ A, 6th Dist., lot #224 of Monroe County. JOHN
CURETON Shff (SEAL). Wit: ANGUS M. D. KING, HENRY MIMS, J.I.C. Rec.
11 Sept. 1823.

Pages 4-6: Georgia, Appling Co.: 1 Oct. 1822, WILLIAM TOMLINSON
of Appling Co., to JOHN W. PHILLIPS of Monroe Co., for $900, 1to #106,
4th Dist., Monroe Co., WILLIAM TOMLINSON (SEAL). Wit: WILLIAM RIDDLE,
DEMSEY PHILLIPS (X).
Proven before MURDOCK SHAW, one of the Justices of the peace, by
DEMSEY PHILLIPS, 9 Dec. 1822. Rec. 11 Sept. 1823.

Page 6: Georgia, Wilkes County, 19 Oct. 1822, POLLY STAMPER,
widow of Wilkes Co., to JOHN CHANDLER of Augusta, Ga., Richmond Co., for
$144, being paid in one horse and waggon at $125 and taking the plat &
grant out of the office which was $19, 202 A in Monroe Co., on waters of
Ichocans Creek #36, 11th Dist., POLLEY STAMPER (X) (SEAL). Wit: MARY
B. WINGFIELD, JOHN B. LENNARD, J.I.C. Rec. 11 Sept. 1823.

Page 7: Ga., Monroe Co., 30 Dec. 1822, JOHN BASS of Gwinnett County,
to JOSEPH SENTELL of Monroe Co., for $500, #96, 14th District, JOHN BASS
(X) (SEAL). Wit: HALCUT ALFORD, JAMES CARGILL, ALSEY DURHAM.
Proven by JAMES CARGILL before LITTLEBERRY GRESHAM, J.I.C. 22 Sept.
1823. Rec. 11 Sept. 1823.

Page 8: Georgia, Clark County, 23 Oct, 1872. JOHN FLOYD of Co.
aofresd. to THOMAS EVANS of Baldwin Co., for $520, 202½ A. lot #49, 12th
Dist. Monroe Co. JOHN FLOYD (SEAL). Wit: JULIUS C. ALFORD, J. M.
DOBBINS, J.P. Rec. 11 Sept. 1823.

Pages 8-10: Ga., Monroe Co.: In obedience to a writ of fira
facious [sic]out of the justices court of Jasper County at the suit of
JEFFRY BURKSDALE against ISAAC SIMMONS, JOHN CURETON, Shff did seize
tract of sd. SIMMONS & on 5 Nov. 1822 expose to public sale, sold to
sd. JEFFRY BARKSDALE of Hancock Co., for $170, 202½ A lot #34, 11th
Dist. JOHN CURETON Shff (SEAL). Wit: FELIX STANLEY, ABNER DURHAM, JP.
Rec. 11 Sept. 1823.

Pages 10-11: Ga., Twigs Co. 5 Nov. 1822, WILLIAM F. CHERRY of Co.
aforesd. to JESSE NEWBY, JR. of Jones County for $100, Lot #222, 6th
Dist. Monroe Co., WILLIAM F. CHERRY (SEAL. Wit: PETER BAILEY, GEORGE
H. CHERRY.
Proven before JOHN STILWELL, a JP, by WILLIAM T. CHERRY 3 June 1823,
WILLIAM T. CHERRY (X). Rec. 11 Sept. 1823.

Pages 11-12: Ga., Jasper County, 12 Nov. 1822, ALSEA HOLIFIED to
JOHN L. S. FOSTER, both of sd. county, for one Negro Cithishal, lot #31,

5th Dist. of Monroe Co., 202½ A. A. HOLIFIELD. Wit: STEPHEN G. HEARY, JESSE LOYALL J.P. Rec. 11 Sept. 1823.

Pages 12-13: Baldwin Co., 11 Feb. 1822, SAM MCNEAL of Jefferson Co., to DAVID THRASH of Putnam Co., for $250, lot #75, 5th Dist. Monroe Co. SAMUEL MCNEAL (LS). Wit: JOSIAH V.(?) BLACKWELL, APPLETON ROSSETER, J.I.C. Rec. 22 Nov. 1823.

Pages 13-14: 11 Feb. 1822, DAVID THRASH of Putnam Co. from WILLIAM LONG of Jefferson Co., for $300(?), lot #329, 5th Dist., Monroe Co., WILLIAM LONG by SAMUEL MCNELL his attorney. Wit: JOSIAH V. BLACKWELL, APPLETON ROSSETER, J.I.C. Rec. 22 Nov. 1823.

Pages 14-15: Georgia, 28 Mar. 1822, WILLIAM FLEMING of Madison Co. to DAVID THRASH of Putnam Co., for $119, lot #58, 5th Dist. 202½ A. granted to sd. FLEMING 11 Feb. 1822, WM. FLEMING (SEAL). Wit: JEREMIAH CLARK, JAS M. DUNN, J.P. Rec. 22 Nov. 1823.

Pages 16-17: Monroe Co., 6 Oct. 1823, SILAS TATUM of Lincoln Co., to JOSEPH COTTON of the state first mentioned, for $500, 101¼ A. north half of Lot #93, 13 Dist., Monroe Co., SILAS TATUM (LS). Wit: W. C. MAYS, GEORGE W. ROGERS, J.P.
Monroe Co.; MARTHA W. TATUM, wife of sd. SILAS TATUM relinquish dower, 6 Oct. 1823. Wit: GEORGE W. ROGERS JP. Rec. 22 Nov. 1823.

Pages 17-18: Georgia, 5 Jan. 1822, JAMES TINDELL & CASSINDRA TINDELL of Montgry Co. to THOMAS CLOWER of Baldwin Co., for $500, lot #253, 13th Dist., Monroe Co., JAMES TINDEL (SEAL), CASSINDRA TINDEL (SEAL). Wit: WILLIS BEN, DAVID CHAMBERS, J.P. Rec. 22 Nov. 1823.

Pages 18-19: Georgia, 28 Dec. 1821, STOUTON HAYMAN of Bryan(?) Co. to JAMES HEARD of Jasper Co., for $163, 202½ A granted 28 Dec. 1821, lot #149, STOUTON HAYMAN (X) (LS). Wit: Z. LAMAR, MARLOW L. PRYOR, J.P. Rec. 23 Nov. 1823.

Pages 19-20: Lincoln Co., Ga.: 7 Dec. 1822, EVANS F. FRANCE to JOHN ZELLNER both of Co. aforesd. for $200, 202½ A. granted to sd. EVANS FOLERANCE, 12th Dist., lot #260, EVANS FLORENCE (X) (SEAL). Wit: J. HOLMES, R. BOOKER J.P. Rec. 23 Nov. 1823.

Pages 20-21: Monroe Co. JOHN MILLER of Monroe Col to JAMES WASHING-TON for his son JAMES WASHINGTON, both of Chatham Co., for $500, one negro SAUNEY about 45 years old, JNO MILLER (LS). Wit: WILLIAM WOODARD, ANDERSON BALDWIN, JP. Dated 21 Nov. 1823, Rec. 23 Nov. 1823.

Pages 21-22: Georgia, Jasper Co., 1 Sept. 1823 ARTHUR SMITH, JUNR. to ISAAC HILL for $500, lot #2, 5th Dist. Monroe Co. 202½ A. ARTHUR SMITH JUNR. (SEAL). Wit: GREEN F. CILL, JAMES BEALE, WILLIAM B. HILL.
Monroe Co. proven by JAMES BEALL before NADERSON BALDSIN JP. 2 Dec. 1823. Rec. 2 Dec. 1823.

Pages 22-23: 28 Oct. 1823, JAMES STOC of Franklin Co., to FLEMING F. ADRIAN of Hall Co., for $500, lot #28, 6th Dist. Monroe Co., 202½ A on Rocky Creek, granted to sd. STOC, JAMES STOC (X) (LS). Wit: JOHN JOHNSON, J.P., SAMUEL JOHNSON. Rec. 22 Dec. 1823.

Pages 23-24: Wilkes Co., Ga. 1 Apr. 1823 SAMUEL HEARTS of Co. aforesd. to SAMUEL LOVEJOY & ELEAZAR LOVEJOY of Jasper Co., for $225, lot #133, 6th Dist. Monroe Co., 202½ A. SAMUEL HURST (SEAL). Wit: WALTER L. CAMPBELL, SAML RICE, J.P. Rec. 23 Nov. 1823.

Pages 24-25: State of Georgia 3 Jan. 1823 ANDERSON HUNT of Greene Co. to MAXCY BROOKS of Wilkerson Co., for $900, 202½ A, lot #177, 6th Dist., Monroe Co., on Matthews Creek, by waters of big Toby(?) Saka(?), granted by JOHN CLARK, Gov. 12 Oct. 1823. ANDERSON HUNT (X) (SEAL). Wit: WM. TUCKER (X), WM. WINFIELD J.P. Rec. 24 Nov. 1823.

Pages 25-26: Warren Co., Ga. WILLIAM CASTLEBERRY, Tax Collector of sd. county to ABNER H. MCORMICK purchaser of collector's sale, for $30.75 on 8 Nov. 1823, lot #55, 11th Dist., Monroe Co., property of DANIEL W. NEWSOM to satisfy an execution for taxes, WILLIAM CASTLEBERRY (SEAL). Wit: WILLIAM JONES, JOHN NEAL, J.P. Rec. 8 Dec. 1823.

Pages 27-28: Monroe County, In obedience to a writ of fiere facias issued out of the Superior Court of Gwinnett County at the suit of MEREWETHER BEAL & Co. against JAMES W. SIBLES(?), JOHN CURETON Shff did seize tract of sd. SIKES(?) nad on 1st Tues. in Dec. one ISAAC HILL was the highest bidder, for $1, 202½ A, lot #242, 6th Dist., Monroe Co. JOHN CURETON Shff (LS). Wit: WILKINS HUNT, ANDERSON BALDWIN, J.P. Rec. 8 Dec. 1823.

Pages 28-29: Monroe Co., In obedience to a writ of fiere facias issued out the Superior Court of Morgan Co., at the suit of Philip ALSTON against LUDISELL(?) WATTS, JOHN CURETON Shff did seel on 5 Aug. 1823, to JOHN FINCH highest bidder, for $70, 202½A, lot #78, 11th Dist. Monroe Co. JOHN CURETON (LS). Wit: THOMAS C. RUSSELL, TURNER HUNT, J.I.C. Rec. 8 Dec. 1823.

Page 30: Georgia, Gwinnett Co., I, ELIAS HOLLIS of Co. aforesd. do sell unto WILLIAM PERRY of state aforesd., lot #69, 11th Dist. Monroe County for $100, 28 Jan. 1823. ELIAS HOLLIS (SEAL). Wit: DAVID WATSON, JAMES HUDSON(?).
Pike Co., Ga. Proven before WM. MITCHELL, J.I.C. by JAMES HUDSON(?), 8 Dec. 1823, Rec. 8 Dec. 1823.

Pages 30-32: Ga., Baldwin Co., 8 Aug. 1823 GEORGE STEPHENS of Monroe Co. to JAMES NASWORTHY of Hancock Co., for $1000, 101¼ A in 6th Dist., Monroe Co., part of lot #169 adj. lots #168, 152, 184. GEORGE STEPHENS (SEAL). Wit: C. R. PIRTCHARD, APPLETON ROSSETER, J.I.C.
Monroe Co., EASTER STEPHENS, widow of sd. GEORGE STEPHENS relinquished dower 18 Dec. 1823. EASTER STEPHENS (X) (SEAL). Wit: JOHN STILWELL, J.P. Rec. 18 Dec. 1823.

Pages 32-33: 30 Dec. 1822 ABRAHAM NORTH of Oglethorp Co., Ga. to JAMES GARLINGTON of Jasper Co., for $200, 202½ A in Monroe Co., lot #47, 13th Dist., grant made out to sd. NORTH 2 Dec. 1822. ABRAHAM NORTH (SEAL). Wit: JOHN WISE, CUTHBERT COLIER, JOSIAH JORDAN J.P. Rec. 18 Dec. 1823.

Page 33: Monroe Co. JANE NASWORTH wife of within named JAMES NASWORTH relinquished dower 12 Dec. 1823. JANE NASWORTH (X) (SEAL). Wit: JOHN STILWELL, J.P. Rec. 18 Dec. 1823.

Pages 33-35: 21 Jan. 1823 JONATHAN PEARREA of Columbia Co., Ga. to JOHN SIMS of Oglethorp Co., for $500, lot #5, 12th Dist., Monroe Co., 202½ A drawn by JONATHAN PEARREA of Gaitrales Dist., Columbia Co. JONATHAN PEARREA (SEAL). Wit: WM. M. STOKES, JAMES WHITSELL, ABRAM CROWLEY (X).
Oglethorpe Co. p oven by WM. STOKES before ROBERT GILLESPIE, Esqr. 25 Jan. 1823. (No rec. date.)

Pages 35-36: Ga., 2 Dec. 1823, WILLIAM WILLIAMS, Admr. of THOMAS WILLIAMSON late of Putnam Co., decd., to JOHN VAUGHAN of Monroe Co. for $703, lot #94, 6th Dist. 202½ A, land sold at public outcry in town of Eastonton, Putnam Co., WM. WILLIAM, Admr. of THOS WILLIAMSON decd. Wit: SAMUEL PEARSON, JNO. J. SMITH, J.I.C. Preceding deed rec. 18 Dec. 1823.

Pages 36-37: Ga., Hall Co., I, JOHN MCKEN, do appoint SAMUEL B. TURNER my lawful attorney to have grant, sell & convey a lot in 11th Dist., Monroe Co. (not dated). JOHN MCKEN (SEAL. Wit: JAMES GAILEY, PLEASANT HULSEY.
Proven before JESS DOBBS, J.P. by JAMES GAILEY, 6 Apr. 1822. Rec. 18 Dec. 1823.

Pages 37-38: Morgan Co., 21 Dec. 1822, SAMUEL B. TURNER for JOHN MACKIN to LITTLETON TALLERS for $200, lot #23, 202½ A, 11th Dist., Monroe Co., SAMUEL B. TURNER for JOHN MCKIN (SEAL). Wit: CHARLES JETER, LARKIN TURNER.
Proven by LARKIN TURNER before JOHN P. MACH(?), J.P. Rec. 18 Dec. 1823.

Pages 38-39: Jones Co., 5 Dec. 1822 ALEXANDER WATSON of Early Co. to THOMAS FREEMAN of Jones Co. for $400, lot #68, 13th Dist. Monroe Co., 202½ A. A. M. WATSON (SEAL). Wit: THOMAS WYNN (X), ARCHD. MCDONALD, WILLIAM GAY, J.P. Rec. 18 Dec. 1823.

Pages 39-41: Monroe Co., In obedience to a writ of fiere facias issued out of the Superior Court of Franklin Co., at the suit of MCDON & POSER(?) for the use of MCKINNE LAMPKIN against JOHN MADDIN & GREEN W. SMITH, Security, JOHN CURETON Shff did seize tract, property of sd. JOHN MADDIN, sold 7 Oct. 1823 in Monroe Co. this indenture 9 Nov. 1823 for $10001, pd. by ISAAC WELCH, 202½ A, lot #22, 13th Dist., Monroe Co. JOHN CURETON Shff (LS). Wit: W. HUNT, GEORGE W. ROGERS. Rec. 18 Dec. 1823.

Pages 41-42: Ga., 29 Nov. 1823, ISAAC WELCH of Monroe Co., to JOHN CURETON of same, for $1000, lot #22, 13th Dist., 202½ A. ISAAC WELCH (SEAL). Wit: A. LAWHUION, GEORGE W. ROGERS J.P. Rec. 18 Dec. 1823.

Pages 42-43: Clark Co., 19 Dec. 1822, THOMAS BELL to JOSEPH SUMMERLIN & HENRY BURT for $250, land in 10th Dist., granted to sd. BELL, THOMAS BELL (X) (SEAL). Wit: JAS OATES, J.P. RD. WYATT OATES. Rec. 18 Dec. 1823.

Pages 43-44: 15 July 1822, SALLEY BECKER to WILLIAM BECKER of Green Co. for $100, lot #116, 6th Dist. SALLEY BECKER (X) (SEAL). Wit.: G. W. FOSTER, JOHN BETHUNE, JOHNSTON WALKER.
Proven by G. W. FOSTER & JOHN BETHUNE 31 May 1823. A. H. LIRK(?), JP. Rec. 18 Dec. 1823.

Pages 44-45: 1 June 1822, MASTIN HATCHER to CHURCHILL GIBSON, HATCHER of Gasper [sic] Co. and GIBSON of Warren Co. for $225 lot #148 7th Dist. Monroe Co. MASTIN HATCHER (X) (SEAL). Wit: JOSEPH BRANTLY, JOHN BRANSFORD, DAVID FREADWELL, J.P. Rec. 18 Dec. 1823.

Pages 45-46: Warren Co., ROBERT ELLIS for $380 to JAMES SANDERS, 202½ A. ROBERT ELLIS (LS). Wit: RANDOLPH IVY, JOSHUA DRAPER J.P. Rec. 18 Dec. 1823.

Page 46: 12 Feb. 1823, JAMES JAMESON of Twiggs Co. to CHURCHHIL GIBSON of Warren Co. for $500, lot #142, 7th Dist., Monroe Co. JAMES JAMESON (SEAL). Wit: B. P. STUBBS, JAS. FLEMING. Rec. 18 Dec. 1823.

Pages 47-48: Scriven Co., 19 Jan. 1822 HENRY B. NELSON to WILLIS YOUNG both of Scriven Co. for $150, 202½ A in Monroe Co. lot #39, 13th Dist. HENRY B. NELSON (LS). Wit: BARNELD NEWTON, ALEX HENDERSON(?) J.P. Rec. 18 Dec. 1823.

Pages 48-49: Ga., 1 Feb. 1822 WILLIS YOUNG of Scriven Co. to DAVID YOUNG of same for $250, lot #39, 13th Dist. 202½ A drawn by HENRY B. NELSON, WILLIS YOUNG (SEAL). Wit: JAMES COCKRAN, HUGH COCHRAN (X), HANNAH COCHRAN (X). Preceding deed proven by WILLIS YOUNG before ALEX. HENDERY, J.P. 4 Nov. 1823. Rec. 18 Dec. 1823.

Pages 49-50: 30 Dec. 1822 ABNER T. TURMAN of Elbert Co. to WILLIAM HARRIS of Monroe Co. for $500, lot #79, 5th Dist. Monroe Co., ABNER T. TURMAN (SEAL). Wit: ROBERT TURMAN, JAMES BELL, JOHN COOK J.P. Rec. 18 Dec. 1823.

Pages 50-51: Monroe Co., 23 Dec. 1822 ROBERT SURLS of Lincoln Co. to BENJAMIN BRANTLEY of Warren Co. for $450, lot #22, 12th Dist. Monroe

Co. drawn by sd. ROBERT SURLES in the lottery of 1821, ROBT SEARLS (SEAL).
Wit: LEE GIBSON, D. DENNIS J.P. Rec. 18 Dec. 1823.

Pages 51-52: 6 Apr. 1822, MARY BIRD, widow of Morgan Co. Manows
Dist. to GEORGE L. BIRD of same for $1000, lot #152, 13th Dist. Monroe
Co. adj. lots 153, 151, 121, 202 A. MARY BIRD (X) (SEAL). Wit: DAVID
M. CROCKET, ROBERT BROWN, ABRAHAM LEE (X). Ackn. before D. LANIER,
J.P. Rec. 22 Dec. 1823.

Pages 52-54: Monroe Co., In obedience to a writ of fiere facias
issued out of a Justices Court of Warren Co. at the suit of BAKER &
HEATH against DANIEL W. NEWSOM, JOHN CURETON, Shff. on 7 Jan. 1823 at
public sale in Monroe Co. did sell to one SAMUEL REED the highest bidder
lot #55, 11th Dist. JOHN CURETON Shff (LS). Wit: JAMES HIGHTOWER,
WILLIAM TUGGH.
Proved by JAMES HIGHTOWER 15 Dec. 1823 before JOHN WHITE, J.P.
Rec. 22 Dec. 1823.

Pages 54-55: Ga., 28 Nov. 1822 WILLIAM BROWN of Camden Co. to JOSEPH
BELL of Montgomery Co. for $500, lot #191, 4th Dist. Monroe Co., granted
10 Sept. 1822. WILLIAM BROWN (LS). Wit: THOMAS HUGHS, ROBERT PAXTON,
J.P. Rec. 25 Dec. 1823.

Pages 55-56: Ga., Muro Co., 13 Dec. 1823, JESSE PATTERSON &
HENRY PATTERSON of Jackson Co., to JESSE JOHNSON for $300, 202½ A, lot
#49, 6th Dist. Monroe Co. HENRY PATTERSON(LS), JESSE PATTERSON (P)
(LS). Wit: W. H. HOUSE, JOHN LASSETTER, ABNER DURHAM, J.P. Rec. 25
Dec. 1823.

Pages 56-57: 29 Oct. 1823, JAMES WASHINGTON to JESSE JOHNSON,
WASHINGTON of Chatham Co., for $300, ½ of tract, lot #57, 101¾ A drawn
by SUSAN HUTHINSON of Mills' Dist., Chatham Co., 6th Dist., Monroe Co.
on path from ANDERSON GRIFFINGS across a new road leading to FORSYTH,
JAMES WASHINGTON (LS). Wit: THOMAS M. HARRIS, JOHN HARRIS.
Proven by JOHN HARRIS before WM. PAYNE J.P. 25 Dec. 1823. Rec.
25 Dec. 1823.

Pages 58-59: Monroe Co., 13 Jan. 1823, HOWELL CHERRY of Monroe Co.,
to JOHN DILLARD of same for $331, lot #234, 6th Dist. adj. lots 235,
233, drawn in the late land lottery by CALEB SMITH of Wilkerson Co.,
202½ A. HOWELL CHERRY (LS). Wit: HENRY MIMS, J.I.C., STEPHEN BLOUNT.
Rec. 25 Dec. 1823.

Pages 59-60: Newton Co., 26 Dec. 1822 EDWARD BASS of Jones Co. to
BENJAMIN MAGUIRK of Co. aforesd. for $500, lot #114, 4th Dist. Monroe
Co. 202½ A. EDWARD BASS (LS). Wit: WELDON JONES, BURREL MATTHEWS J.P.

Pages 60-61: Greene Co. 10 July 1822 WILLIAM P. CATO of Green Co.
to ALSEA HOLIFIELD of Jasper Co. for $419, lot #31, 5th Dist. 202½ A.
WILLIAM P. CATO (LS). Wit: JOHN L. SWINNEY, JOHN L. S. FOSTER.
Proven by JOHN L. S. FOSTER before JESSE LOYALL, J.P. in Jasper
Co. 12 Nov. 1822. Rec. 25 Dec. 1823.

Pages 61-63: Monroe Co., 3 July 1823 PERMELIA POOLE to JOHN
BARNET both of Monroe Co for certain articles of agreement, lot #42,
14th Dist., 202½ A. PARMELIA POOLE (X) (SEAL). Wit: LYDIA WATKINS,
JNO PEABODDY.
Washington Co., Proven by JOHN PEABODY who said he saw Mrs. LYDIA
WATKINS sign. 12 July 1823 before C. WILLIAMSON, J.I.C.W.C. Rec. 26
Dec. 1823.

Pages 63-64: Ga., 28 Feb. 1822 WILLIAM FLANIGAN SENIOR of Hall Co.
to CARTER W. SPARKS of Morgan Co. for $400, lot #89, 12th Dist. Monroe
Co. WILLIAM FLANIGAN (X) (SEAL). Wit: HIRAM HALSEY, JOHN HEAD, J.P.
Rec. 26 Dec. 1823.

Pages 64-65: 20 Nov. 1823 CARTER W. SPARKS of Morgan Co. to SIMON

BROOKES of Baldwin Co. for $750, lot #89, 12th Dist. CARTER W. SPARKS
(LS). Wit: A. MEANS, J. CULBERSON, J.P. Rec. 27 Dec. 1823.

Pages 65-66: Jackson Co., Ga. 25 Sept. 1823 MELTON MATTHEWS of
Co. aforesd. to JAMES HEARING of Monroe Co. for $1300 landin Monroe Co.
at time of survey now in Bibb Co., lot #283, 13th Dist. Monroe Co., 202½
A. MELTON MATTHEWS (SEAL). Wit: STEPHEN C. DURRAM,JOHN BRISTOW(?)
(X). Rec. 27 Dec. 1823.

Pages 66-67: Jones Co., 25 Jan. 1823 ARCHIBALD DARRAGH of Jones Co.
to JOHN COURSON of Houston Co. for $300, lot #32, 12th Dist. Monroe Co.
drawn by EPHRAIM KINE of Loyd's Dist. Burke Co. A. DARRAGH. Wit:
THOMAS BATES, NICHOLAS W. WELLS. Rec. 27 Dec. 1823.

Pages 67-68: Monroe Co., 13 Dec. 1822 JAMES FLEMING of Co. aforesd.
to JAMES TURNER of Jasper Co. for $275, 101¼ A. part of lot #275, 7th
Dist. JAMES FLEMING (SEAL). Test: BARTLET SIMS, JOHN MAYS J.P.
Rec. 27 Dec. 1823.

Pages 68-69: Jones Co., EDWARD H. GRESHAM to JEPTHA HILL both of
same county for $1300, lot #142, 5th Dist. Monroe Co. 1 May 1822
EDWARD H. GRESHAM (LS). Wit: HENRY AVENT (X), JOHN T. POPE J.P. Rec.
27 Dec. 1823.

Pages 69-70: Greene Co. 3 Jan. 1823 MICAJAH MCMILLIN of Green
Co. to THOMAS CLOWEN of Monroe Co. for $500, lot #224, 13th Dist., 202½
A. MICAJAH MCMILLIN (SEAL). Wit: JOHN W. AMUS(?), WILLIAM WINGFIELD J.P.
Greene Co., MARY MCMILLEN wife of sd. MICAJAH relinquish dower,
3 Jan. 1823. MARY MCMILLEN (X) (SEAL). Wit: WILLIAM WINGFIELD J.P.
Rec. 1 Jan. 1824.

Pages 71-72: 2 Dec. 1823 EMANUEL SHEROUSE of Effingham Co & wf.
LYDIA to JONATHAN MILLER of same for $150, 202½ A in 11th Dist., lot #85
EMANUEL SHEROUSE (LS). Wit: MATTHEW HEIDT (X), FURNEY WELLS, J.I.C.
LYDIA SHEROUSE relinquish of dower 2 Dec. 1823 before FURNEY
WILLIS, J.I.C. E.C. Rec. 1 Jan. 1824.

Pages 72-73: 24 Jan. 1823 ELDREAD SWAIN of Emanuel Co. to WILLIAM
Y. COURY for $300, 202½ A., 14th Dist., lot #28. ELDREAD SWAIN (LS).
Wit: JAMES BARFIELD, MARLOW PRYOR J.P. Rec. 9 Jan. 1824.

Pages 73-74: 29 Jan. 1823 JOHN HUCKABY of Walton Co. to GREEN
INGLISH of Jones Co. for $250. E. half of lot #167, 5th Dist. Monroe
Co. JOHN HUCKABY (X) (LS). Wit: GUSTAVES HENDRICK, D. T. MILLING,
J.P. Rec. 9 Jan. 1824.

Pages 74-75: Early Co. 3 Feb. 1823 JOHN E. PARRAMORE to WYATT
SINGLETON of Jones Co. for $100, lot #124, 6th Dist. Monroe Co., 202½ A.
JOHN E. PARRAMORE (LS). Wit: ABNER W. SINGLETON, WILLIAM TILLEY.
Proven by ABNER SINGLETON before MORDICAI JACOBS, J.P. 12 Feb. ___.
Rec. 9 Jan. 1824.

Pages 76-77: 14 Feb. 1822 CHARLES EVANS attorney for BENJAMIN R.
THOMPSON of Jones Co to JESSE EVANS for $40, lot #153, 6th Dist. Monroe
Co. CHARLES EVANS (SEAL). Wit: NATHL. HOLLEY, JOHN VANCE, J.P.
Rec. 9 Jan. 1824.

Pages 77-78: Jones Co., 15 Oct. 1822 SILAS GAMMON of Monroe Co. to
JOHN POE of Jones Co. for $400, 202½ A. lot $218, 5th Dist., Monroe Co.
SILAS GAMMON (SEAL). Wit: JOHN PERKINS, WILLIS MOYE, THOMAS MCGEHEE,
J.P. Rec. 9 Jan. 1824.

Pages 78-79: Camden Co., 9 Jan. 1823, MARGET HOPPS of Wyne Co.
to JOSEPH CONE of Co. aforesd. for $500, lot in 4th Dist. Monroe Co.
#238. MARGAT HOPPS (SEAL) (X). Wit: JOHN GIBSON, HANNAH STAFFORD,
THOMAS HAGEN.
Proven before ROBERT PAXTON a JP by THOMAS HAGEN, 18 Oct. 1823.
THOMAS HAGIN. Rec. 9 Jan. 1824.

Page 80: Jasper Co. 29 July 1822 BENJAMIN MAGOUIRK of Newton Co. to JOSIAH KING of Jasper Co. for $460, lot $185, 5th Dist. Monroe Co. 202½ A. BENJAMIN MAGOUIRK. Wit: BURWELL GREENE, JUNR., JAMES RAMSEY, J.P. Rec. 9 Jan. 1824.

Page 81: 20 Jan. 1822, ROLIN THOMASON of Hancock Co. to EDMUND M. BUTLER of Co. aforesd. for $550, lot #80, 5th Dist., Monroe Co., granted to sd. TOMASON in the late lottery 14 Jan. 1822. ROLIN TOMASON (X) (LS). Wit: S. DUGGAR, WILLIAM D. LUCAS, J.P. Rec. 9 Jan. 1824.

Pages 82-83: Monroe Co. In obedience to a write of fiere facias issued of the Justice Court of Jasper Co. at the suit of BALEY & MABRY against MABRY HARRIGAN, JOHN CURETON, Shff, did seize tract of sd. HARRIGAN & sold to JOHN K. SIMMONS at public outcry for $21 this indenture made 7 Jan. 1823, 202½ A, lot #147, 12th Dist. Monroe Co. JOHN CURETON Shff (SEAL). Wit: ANDERSON HOLT, WILLIAM HATHORN.
Jasper Co. Proven by ANDERSON HOLT, 2 June 1823 before JESSE LOYAL, J.P. Rec. 9 Jan. 1824.

Page 84: Monroe Co. 26 Mar. 1823 DAVID WOOD of Chatham Co. to JAMES THWEATT of Monroe Co. for $1350, lot in 13th Dist., #64, 202½ A. DAVID WOOD (LS). Wit: DAVID C. ATWOOD, TURPIN G. ATWOOD, JAMES GRAY, J.I.C. Rec. 9 Jan. 1824.

Page 85: Monroe Co., 14 Jan. 1822, JOHN TUCKER to HARDY HOBSON for $100, 25 A, lot #223 the NE corner of sd. lot, 6th Dist., Monroe Co. JOHN TUCKER (X) (LS). Wit: WILKINS HUNT, ANDERSON BALDWIN, J.P. Rec. 14 Jan. 1824.

Page 86: Elbert Co., I, LARKIN CLARK of Elbert Co. for love & affection to my grnad daughter MILLEY ELIZABETH CLARK daughter of my son WILLIAM B. CLARK of Monroe Co. do give her a certain Negro Benn, about 4 or 5 years old. 8 Nov. 1823. LARKIN CLARK (LS). Wit: ROBERT ROEBUCK, THOMAS AKIN, JOSEPH RUCKER(?) J.P. Rec. 14 Jan. 1824.

Pages 86-87: Ga., 29 Jan. 1823 JOHN HUCKABY of Walton Co., to ISAIAH HORNIDE of Jones Co. for $250, lot #167, 5th Dist. Monroe Co. 101¼ A. JOHN HUCKABY (LS). Wit: GUSTAVES HENDRICK, D. T. MILLING, J.P. Rec. 3 Jan. 1824.

Pages 87-89: 12 Apr. 1823 JOHN T. BOOTH of Jones Co. to the Hon. Justices of the Inferior Ct. of Monroe Co. for $700, lot $171, 6th Dist., drawn by sd. BOOTH in the last lottery. JOHN T. BOOTH (SEAL). Wit: JOHN T. PATTERSON, MARK PATTERSON, J.P.
Jones Co. HENRITTA M. BOOTH wife of sd. JOHN T. BOOTH relinquish dower 12 Apr. 1823. HENRIETTA M. BOOTH (SEAL). Wit: MARK PATTERSON, J.P. Rec. 2 Jan. 1824.

Pages 89-90: Columbia Co. 15 Mar. 1823 LEMUEL SHIPP to JOHN PITMAN both of Co. aforesd. for $220, lot #85, 5th Dist. LEMUEL SHIPP (LS). Wit: WILLIAM S. DUNN, GEORGE S. ROBERT, BASEL NEAL J.P. Rec. 3 Jan. 1824.

Pages 90-92: Monroe Co. 15 Aug. 1823 JOHN FINCH to JOHN PITMAN both of Co. aforesd. for $500, lot #77, 5th Dist., 202½ A. JOHN FINCH (SEAL). Wit: ROBERT WATSON, JAMES JOHNSON.
Proven by JAMES JOHNSON 10 Jan. 1824 before MOSES DUMAS J.P. HENRIETTA FINCH wife of sd. JOHN FINCH relinquish dower 10 Jan. 1824. HENRIETTA FINCH (X) before MOSES DUMAS. (No Rec. date).

Page 92: Monroe Co. Rec'd. of GEO. OWEN, $145 for a certain tract 4th Dist., #18, 17 Mar. 1823. WILLIS KELLUM (SEAL). Wit: WM. HOLIFIED, JOHN FOSTER J.P.

Page 93: 15 Oct. 1823 HENRY R. STEMBRIDGE of Hancock Co. to HOPE H. TIGNER of Monroe Co. lot #88, 13th Dist., HENRY R. STEMBRIDGE (SEAL). Wit: GEORGE CARR, WM. TRIPPE, WM. GREEN MACON J.I.C. Rec. 3 Jan. 1824.

Page 94: Baldwin Co. 19 Nov. 1822 JOHN REED of Colubmia Co. to
HINCHER THOMAS of Lincoln Co. for $500, 202½ A. lot #21 on waters of
Beaverdam Cr. JOHN REED (SEAL). Wit: THOMAS W. MURRAY, REM. REMSON
J.I.C. Rec. 3 Jan. 1824.

Page 95: Monro Co. 9 Jan. 1824 MATTHEW WALKER to JORDAN LESUIER both
of Co. aforesd. for $1000 land on Beaverdam Creek 13th Dist. lot #229.
MATTHEW WALKER (SEAL), RUTH WALKER (SEAL). Wit: DRURY M. LESUEUR,
JAMES HERRING, JOHN PRATT, J.I.C. Rec. 3 Jan. 1824.

Pages 96-97: Ga., 27 Feb. 1823 HINCHER THOMAS of Lincoln Co. to
MEADE LESUEUR of Baldwin Co. for $600, lot #193, 13th Dist. HINCHER
THOMAS (LS). Wit: L. ATKISON, MARLOW PRYOR, J.P. Rec. 3 Jan. 1824.

Pages 98-99: Walton Co. 4 Mar. 1822, WILLIAM JOLLY of Walton Co. to
JACOB GIDER of Waton Co. for $100 land in 11th Dist. lot #21, 202¼ A.
WILLIAM JOLLY (X) (SEAL). Wit: ISAAC AUSTIN, JAMES LINDLEY J.P. Rec.
6 Jan. 1824.

Page 100: Baldwin Co. 26 Aug. 1823 NATHANIEL COOK of Elbert Co. to
THOMAS WALKER of Monroe Co. for $500, lot #39, 5th Dist. Monroe Co. 202½
A. NATHANIEL COOK (X) (SEAL). Wit: B. P. STUBBS, ___ FLEMING J.P.
Rec. 6 Jan. 1824.

Pages 101-102: Ga. 10 Oct. 1823 WILLIAM HARRIS of Augusta to
THOMAS WALKER of Monroe Co. for $700, lot #122, 5th Dist. Monroe Co.
202½ A. WILLIAM HARRIS (SEAL). Wit: ALONZO B. BIGELOW, RALPH KETCHUM(?),
J.I.C. Rec. 6 Jan. 1824.

Pages 102-103: 6 Oct. 1823 SILAS TATOM of Lincoln Co. to WILLIAM
RHYMES of Monroe Co. for $300 lot #93, 13th Dist. Monroe Co. SILAS
TATOM (LS). Wit: W. O. MAYS, GEORGE W. ROGERS J.P. Rec. 6 Jan. 1824.
    Monroe Co. MARTHA W. TATOM wife of sd. SILAS relinquished dower
6 Oct. 1823. MARTHA TATOM (SEAL). Wit: GEORGE W. ROGERS J.I.C. Rec.
6 Jan. 1824.

Pages 103-104: Jones Co. 15 May 1823 WILLIAM GRADY of Hall Co. to
MACAJAH HASPIT of Jones Co. for $400, 202½ A., 6th Dist., lot #230.
WILLIAM GRADY (SEAL). Wit: JAMES ALLEN, GEORGE HARPER.
    Jones Co., Proven by JAMES ALLEN 10 Jan. 1824 before WM. MCMATH J.P.
Rec. 6 Jan. 1824.

Page 105: Liberty Co., Ga. I, WILLIAM NETTLES appoint ELI MCFAIL
my lawful attorney to convey unto MESHACK TURNER 202½ A in 6th Dist.
Monroe Co. lot #5. 3 Nov. 1823. WM. NETTLES (LS). Wit: JOSHIAS
HASSEL(?), ROBT HENDRY JR., J.P. Rec. 6 Jan. 1824.

Pages 105-106: 31 Dec. 1823 WILLIAM NETTLES of Liberty Co. to
MESHACK TURNER of Jasper Co. for $575, lot #5, 6th Dist. Monroe Co.
ELI MCFAIL (LS). Wit: HIRAM PHINESEE, EATON BANKS J.P. Rec. 6 Jan.
1824.

Pages 106-105: Pulaski Co. 9 Oct. 1823 PATRICK YOUNG of Pulaski
Co. to SAMUEL POOL of Monroe Co. for $350 lot #88, 11th Dist. Monroe Co.
PATRICK YOUNG (X) (SEAL). Wit: ELIAS O. HAWTHRON, WM. BRYAN (X).
    Pulaski Co., Proven by WM BRYAN. 10 Oct. 1823. BAKER ADAMS J.P.
Rec. 6 Jan. 1824.

Page 105-106: Jackson Co. I, MICHAEL AUSTIN appoint WILLIAM SPRUCE
of Co. aforesd. my lawful attorney to sell lot #131 drawn by MICHAEL
OSTON, title to be made to WILLIAM SHIP of Jackson Co. when he does
produce the grant. 26 Feb. 1822. MICHAEL AUSTIN (LS). Wit: WILLIAM
BALKE, JOHN HILL.
    Gwinnett Co., Proven by WILLIAM BLAKE 5 Mar. 1822 before JOSEPH
THOMPSON JP. Rec. 6 Jan. 1824.
    (N.B. There are two pages numbered 105 and 106 each.)

251

Pages 106-107: Jefferson Co., I. WILLIAM LONG of Co. aofresd. appoint SAMUEL MCNEIL of same, my attorney to sell lot #229 drawn in my own name gave in Capt. Halls Dist, Co. aforesd. to sell to DAVID THRASH. 12 Feb. 1822. WILLIAM LONG. Wit: W. CASON J.P. Rec. 6 Jan. 1824.

Pages 107-108: Monroe Co. In obedience to a writ of fiere facias issued out of the court of Oglethrop Co. at the suit of FLEMING & REUBIN JORDAN against WADE GOOLSBY. JOHN CURETON Shff, did seize property sold on 6 Jan. 1824 for $65, lot #237, 7th Dist. Monroe Co. sold to sd. FLEMING & REUBIN. JOHN CURETON Shff (LS). Test: AMOS P. PERRY, ANDERSON BALDWIN J.P. Rec. 6 Jan. 1824.

Page 109: Warren Co. 21 Jan. 1823 ELISHA HATTAWAY to ROBERT DICKINS both of Co. aforesd. for $619, lot #181, 6th Dist. Monroe Co., 202½ A. ELISHA HATTAWAY (LS). Wit: ISAAC DOWNS, REUBEN MAY J.P. Rec. 7 Jan. 1824.

Pages 110-111: Monroe Co. 6 Jan. 1824 ROBERT DICKINS of Monroe Co. to THOMAS WILSON for $800, 202½ A., lot #181, 6th Dist. Monroe Co. ROBERT DICKINS (LS). SALLY DICKINS (X) (SEAL). Wit: A. WILLINGHAM, ANDERESON BALDWIN J.P.
SALLY DICKINS, wife of ROBERT relinquish dower 6 Jan. 1824. SALLY DICKINS (X) Re.c 7 Jan. 1824.

Pages 111-113: 2 Sept. 1823 GEROGE DRISKILL of Monroe Co. to DAVID B. DRISKILL of sd. Co. for $500, lot #65, 14th Dist. GEORGE DRISKILL (LS). Wit: FELIX GRESHAM, ATHONY COZART. Rec. 7 Jan. 1824.
Proven by ANTHONY COZART before LITLEBERRY GRISHAM J.I.C. Rec. 7 Jan. 1824.

Pages 113-114: Lincoln Co. 18 Jan. 1823 HAMBELTON REMSON to JAMES HINES for $1200, 202½ A in Monroe Co., lot #105, 12th Dist. HAMBLETON REMSON (LS). Wit: R. REMSON, S. BROWN, J.P., SILAS TATOM J.P. Rec. 9 Jan. 1824.

Pages 114-115: Twiggs Co., 16 Feb. 1822 THEOPHILUS PENNEY of Co. aforesd. to WILLIAM S. CONNALLY for $1000, lot #___, 6th Dist., adj. lots 77, 79, 83, 51. THEOPHILUS PENNY (LS). Wit: DRURY CHRISTIAN, ALFRED PENNY.
Madison Co., proven by DRURY CHRISTIAN before JOHN CLEHORN a magistrate. 3 Feb. 1823. Rec. 10 Jan. 1824.

Pages 115-116: Monroe Co., 24 May 1823 WOOD MORELAND to ISAAC MORELAND of Putnam Co. for $200, ½ of lot #28, 5th Dist. Monroe Co. WOOD MORELAND (LS). Wit: JAMES HIGHTOWER, ELISHA HIGHTOWER, JOHN BROWN J.P. Rec. 10 Jan. 1824.

Pages 116-118: Monroe Co. In obedience to a writ of fiere facias issued out of a Justices Court of Madison Co. at the suit of JAMES MONEY against JOHN RAY on 7 Oct. sold to highest bidder for $12. RICHARD LAWRENCE, JOHN CURETON Shff (LS). Wit: ALLEN COCHRAN, ELISHA N. WALDROP.
Proven by ALLEN COCHRAN before ANDERSON BALDWIN JP. 10 Jan. 1824. Rec. 10 Jan. 1824.

Pages 118-119: Ga., 9 Aug. 1823 MICAJAH PALK JUNR of Lawrence Co. to BENJ. YATES for $219 lot #20, 5th Dist. Henry Co. BENJAMIN YATES of Monroe Co. MACGER PAULK (SEAL). Wit: HENRY TOWNSEND, S. B. HESTER J.P. Rec. 10 Jan. 1824.

Page 120: Jasper Co. 14 Jan. 1823 NATHANIEL BABER of Monroe Co. to DANIEL W. PEARSON of Jasper Co. for $750 lot #23, 6th Dist. NATHANIEL BARBER (LS). Wit: JOHN M. PEARSON, M. KOPENAN(?), MAT WHITFIELD J.P. Rec. 12 Jan. 1824.

Pages 121-122: Burke Co., 25 Jan. 1823 HARVEY ANDREWS to ZACHARIAH S. FRYER for $800, 202½ A lot #131, 13th Dist. Monroe Co. HARVEY ANDREWS (LS). Wit: WILLIAM F. FRYER, JOSIAH MATTHEWS, ELIJAH BOYD.

Burke Co., CLERISSA ANDERS wife of sd. HARVEY relinquish dower, 25 Jan. 1823. CLERISSA ANDREWS (+) (LS). Wit: JOSIAH MATTHEWS, WM. F. FRYER, ELIJAH BOYD.
Proven by WM. FRYER 8 Jan. 1824 before Z. P. POWELL, J.P. Rec. 14 Jan. 1824.

Pages 123-125: Ga., In obedience to a writ of fiere facias in Jasper County Justices Court, suit of JAMES HILL against WILEY A. WHATLEY, JOHN CURETON Shff, did seize tract of sd. WHATLEY, sold on 1st Tues. in April bought by THOMAS WALKER in Monroe Co. for $400, 202½ A lot #133, 5th Dist. JOHN CURETON Shff (SEAL). Wit: BENJAMIN HOLLAND, CHARLES Y. CALDWELL.
Proven by both wit. 6 Oct. 1823 before JOHN BROWN J.P. Rec. 15 Jan. 1824.

Pages 125-126: Monroe Co., 27 Sept. 1823 GILLAM MILES of Co. aofresd. to THOMAS WALKER for $280, 101¼ A, lot #56, 5th Dist. Monroe Co. GILLMAN MILES (X) (SEAL). Wit: DANIEL MCKAY, MOSES DUMAS J.P.
Monroe, SENTHY MILES wife of sd. GILLAM MILES relinquish dower 27 Sept. 1823. SENTHY MILES (X) (SEAL. Wit: DANIEL MCKAY, MOSES DUMAS, J.P. Rec. 16 Jan. 1824.

Pages 127-128: Richmond Co., 11 Oct. 1823 ALFRED HUNTINGTON & wf CAROLINA of Augusta to THOMAS WALKER of Monroe Co. for $450, lot #53, 202½ A. A. J. HUNTINGTON (LS), CAROLINE E. HUNTINGTON (LS). Wit: GEO. W. HUNTINGTON, RALPH KETCHUM, J.P.
CAROLINE HUNTINGTON relinquish dower 11 Oct. 1823 before RALPH KETCHUM, J.P., J.I.C.R.C. Rec. 14 Jan. 1824.

Pages 128-130: Ga., 13 Feb. 1823 JAMES B. HALL & JANE LILLY of Richmond Co. to PAYTON HAIRES(?) for $200, lot #124, JAMES B. HALL. Wit: JOHN HOLLINGSHEAD, F. GREEN J.P. (LS).
Richmond Co., Mrs. JANE LILLY HALL relinquish dower, 13 Feb. 1823 before F. GREEN J.P. JANE L. HALL (LS). Rec. 6 Jan. 1824.

Pages 130-132: Ga., 20 Jan. 1823 JOSEPH BOND of Hall Co. to THOMAS P. SWAIN of Monroe Co. for $245, lot #151, 5th Dist. Monroe Co., 202½ A. JOSEPH B. BOND (SEAL), SALLY BOND (+). Wit: JAMES BOND, JOHN FINCH, LARKIN HOLCOMB (her mark +), JAMES EDMONDSON J.P.
Gwinett Co., SALLY BOND relinquished dower 7 Jan. 1823 before JAMES EDMONDSON, J.P.
Monroe Co., Proven by JOHN FINCH 16 Jan. 1824 before MOSES DUMAS J.P. Rec. 17 Jan. 1824.

Pages 133-134: DeKalb Co., 8 Oct. 1823 REUBEN CONE of DeKalb Co. to CHARLES J. SHELTON of Telfair Co. for $350, lot #202, 12th Dist., Monroe Co. REUBEN CONE (LS). Wit: GEORGE HEA__, JOSEPH HUBBARD, J.P. Rec. 17 Jan. 1824.

Pages 134-135: Monroe Co., 27 Feb. 1823 JONATHAN BONNER of Pike Co. to JOHN WOODALL of Monroe Co. for $400, lot #250, 6th Dist. Monroe Co. JONATHAN BONNER (LS). Wit: N. DAVIS, SILUS PONDER (+). Rec. 17 Jan. 1824.

Pages 135-136: Jasper Co., 5 Aug. 1823 GREEN D. BRANTLEY of Monroe Co. to ALSEA HOLIFIELD of Co. first mentioned for $400, lot #67, 5th Dist., Monroe Co., 202½ A. GREEN D. BRANTLY. Wit: LAWRENCE SMITH, JOHN HILL, J.P. Rec. 17 Jan. 1824.

Pages 136-138: Jasper Co., 5 Dec. 1823 JAMES THOMPSON of Jasper Co. to GREEN C. BRANTLY of Monroe Co. for $400, lot #68, 5th Dist. Monroe Co., 202½ A. JAMES THOMPSON (SEAL). Wit: ANDERSON THOMPSON, WILLIAM L. THOMPSON.
Jasper Co., proven by WILLIAM L. THOMPSON 8 Dec. 1824, before JOHN HILL, J.P. Rec. 17 Jan. 1824.

Pages 138-140: Oglethorpe Co., 24 July 1823 EDWARD COX of Co. aforesd. attorney for DUDLEY DUNN of Lawrence Co., Ala. to GREEN D.

BRANTLY of Monroe Co. for $400, lot #67, 5th Dist. Monroe Co. EDWARD COXE (SEAL). Attorney for DUDLEY DUNN. Wit: ELIAS BEALL, WILLIAM LATIMAR.
Monroe Co., proven by ELIAS BEALL before JOHN HILL, J.P. 26 July 1823. Rec. 18 Jan. 1824.

Pages 141-142: Jones Co., 7 Sept. 1823 MARK PATTERSON of Jones Co. to JOEL MIZELL of sd. Co. for $280, 202½ A Lot #188, 13th Dist., Monroe MARK PATTERSON (SEAL). Wit: MICHAEL DUSKIN, ASA MIZELL.
SALLY PATTERSON wife of MARK relinquish dower 20 Dec. 1823. SALLY PATTERSON (+) before STEPHEN RENFROE J.P.

Jones Co. proven by ASA MIZELL 10 Sept. 1822 before R. HUTCHING J.P. Rec. 18 Jan. 1824.

Pages 142-144: Jones Co., 14 Nov. 1823 BENJAMIN MILNER of Jones Co. to IVAN H. MILNER of same for $300, lot in 7th Dist., waters of Touchaga River, 607½ A. lot #221. BENJAMIN MILNER (LS). Wit: PITT MILLNER, REASON GAY. Rec. 23 Jan. 1824.
PENELOPE MILNER wife of sd. BENJAMIN relinquished dower ___ 1823.

Pages 144-145: Monroe Co., ELIZABETH SALTER (SATTER?) wife of ROBERT relinquished dower on lot #134 which her husband conveyed unto sd. WARNER 23 Dec. 1822. 8 Jan. 1824. JESSE PITTMAN J.P. ELIZABETH SATTER (X). Rec. 22 Jan. 1824.

Pages 145-146: Monroe Co., In obedience to a writ of Fira Facias issued out of the Superior Court of Washington Co. at the suit of MORGAN BROWN against THOMAS ARNOLD, JOHN CURETON Shff did seize tract of sd. ARNOLD & sold on 2 Sept. 1823. MORGAN BROWN being the highest bidder for $50, 202½ A lot #218, 7th Dist. JOHN CURETON Shff (LS). Wit: J. WHITE, LITTLEBERRY GRESHAM J.P. Rec. 22 Jan. 1824.

Pages 147-148: Monroe Co., In obedience to a writ of Fira ficas issued out of the Justice Court of Jasper Co. at the suit of ELISHA KINDALL against BUD COMBS, JOHN CURETON Shff did seize lot of sd. COMBS & sold 6 July 1822. ELISHA KINDALL being the highest bidder, this indenture made 20 Jan. 1824 for $197 lot #18, 10th Dist. JOHN CURETON Shff (LS). Wit: M. F. MILLER, WM. W. MOORE J.P. Rec. 23 Jan. 1834.

Pages 148-149: 1 July 1823 JOSEPH BARR of Jackson Co., Ga. to FELIX GRESHAM and ANTHONY COZART of Monroe Co. for $200, lot #49, 14th Dist., 202½ A. JOSEPH BARR (LS). Wit: DAVID B. DRISKILL, LITTLEBERRY GRESHAM J.I.C. Rec. 23 Jan. 1824.

Page 150: Monroe Co. An article of agreement made between ANTHONY COZART and FELIX GRISHAM both of same place, division of above lot. ANTHONY COZART (LS), FLEIX GRISHAM (LS). Wit: PASCHAL GRISHAM, LITTLEBERRY GRISHAM J.I.C. Rec. 23 Jan. 1824.

Pages 150-151: Monroe Co., 19 Jan. 1824, JAMES DEES to JOHN C. JOHNSON for $100, lot #140, 3rd Dist. JAMES DEES (LS). Wit: EDMOND STEVENS, ANDERSON BALDWIN J.P. Rec. 23 Jan. 1824.

Pages 152-153: Ga., JAMES MADDOX, BENJAMIN HOLLAND, CHARLES Y. CALDWELL, ASA COX, WILLIAM SIMMONS & WILLIAM C. ROBISON are bound to Gov. GEORGE M. TROUP for $20,000, 23 Jan. 1824. JAMES MADDOX on 5 Jan. 1824 was elected sheriff. JAMES MADDOX (SEAL. BENJAMIN HOLLAND (LS), CHARLES Y. CALDWELL (LS), ASA COX (LS), WILLIAM SIMMONS (LS), WILLIAM ROBINSON (LS). Wit: LITTLEBERRY GRESHAM J.I.C., TURNER HUNT J.I.C., JOHN PRATT J.IC. Rec. 27 Jan. 1824.
Monroe Co., I do solemnly swear that I will faithfully execute all writs, warrants, etc. Sheriff of County of Monroe. 23 Jan. 1824. JAMES MADDOX. Rec. 27 Jan. 1824.

Pages 153-155: Oglethorpe Co., 29 Nov. 1823 MATTHEW GALLAWAY of Co. aofresd. to THOMAS LIGHTFOOT of Jones Co. for $500, 202½ A. lot #163,

13th Dist. Monroe Co. MATTHEW GALLAWAY (SEAL). Wit: WILLY GALLOWAY, WM. M. STOKES J.P.
Oglethrope Co., POLLY GALLAWAY wife of sd. MATTHEW relinquish dower 29 Nov. 1823 before W. M. STOKES J.P. POLLY GALLAWAY (+) (SEAL). Rec. 27 Jan. 1824.

Pages 155-156: Monroe Co., 27 Oct. 1823 THOMAS LIGHTFOOT of Jones Co. to JOHN H. PICKARD of Co. aforesd for $1000, lot #163, 13th Dist. Monroe Co. THOMAS LIGHTFOOT (LS). Wit: WILLIAM L. MCREE, JACKSON PICKARD.
Jones Co., RENNY LIGHTFOOT wife of sd. THOMAS relinquish dower 7 Nov. 1823. RENNEY LIGHTFOOT. Wit: MATH: SHIRLY, S. W. SMITH, J.P.

Page 157: Monroe Co., 9 Jan. 1824 JOHN H. PICKARD of Co. aforesd. to JACKSON PICKARD of same for $300 lot #163, 13th Dist. JOHN H. PICKARD (+) (LS). Wit: WILL: L. MCREE, WILLIAM A. BELL, PENELOPE B. DISANBLEAUX. Rec. 27 Jan. 1824.

Pages 158-159: Baldwin Co., JOSEPH HUDDLESTONE of Co. aofresd. & wf. ELIZABETH for $500 to JOHN L. MARTIN of same, lot #153, 5th Dist. on Rum Creek, 25 Feb. 1822. JOSEPH HUDDLESTON (LS), ELIZABETH HUDDLES-TON (SEAL). Wit: JOHN F. DODDS, JANE HUDDLESTON (+), JOHN MILES J.P.
ELIZABETH HUDDLESTON relinquish dower 12 May 1823. Wit: JOHN MILES, J.P. Rec. 27 Jan. 1824.

Pages 159-160: Putnam Co., 20 Aug. 1822 JOEL WISE of Jasper Co. to HARDY GLAWN of same for $500, lot #345, 6th Dist. Monroe Co. JOEL WISE (+) (SEAL). Wit: JAMES CANNON(?), JAMES E. REY(?), J.P. Rec. 27 Jan. 1824.

Pages 160-161: Telfair Co., 5 Jan. 1824 HENRY HULETT JUNR. to REDDING PANAMOOR(?) of Monroe Co. for $100, lot #7, 5th Dist. Monroe Co. HENRY HULETT JR. (LS). Wit: DUNCAN CURRY J.P. WILLIAM HATTEN J.P. Rec. 28 Jan. 1824.

Pages 162-163: Telfair Co., 3 Sept. 1822 JOHN RAINEY to JOHN PARRIMORE for $500 lot #118, 12th Dist. Monroe Co. 202½A. JOHN RAINEY (SEAL). Wit: BENJAMIN HUETT (+), REDDING PARRAMORE.
Proven by P. W. PARRAMORE, 10 Jan. 1824 before J. L. LAMKIN, J.I.C. Rec. 28 Jan. 1823.

Pages 163-164: Monroe Co., 5 Jan. 1824 JOHN SPRATLAN to WILLIAM BROWN both of Monroe Co for $220, lot #33, 11th Dist. JOHN SPRATLIN (LS). Wit: W. B. HEETH, WM. S. CLAR. Rec. 28 Jan. 1824.

Pages 164-166: 8 Nov. 1822 JAMES NORRIS of Monroe Co. to ELIJAH BRITTINGHAM of same for 250, lot #107, 12th Dist. JAMES NORRIS (SEAL). Wit: JOHN LOFLIN, JOHN QUIN.
Proven by JOHN LOFLIN before AMBROSE CHAPPMAN J.P. 24 Nov. 1823. Rec. 29 Jan. 1824.

Pages 166-167: Telfair Co., 21 Aug. 1823 ISAAC ALLEN to JOHN PARRAMORE for $100, lot #50, 4th Dist., 202½ A. ISAAC ALLEN. Wit: REBECCA WILLIAMS (+), R. W. PARRAMORE.
Proven by REDDIN W. PARRAMORE 10 Jan. 1824. Rec. 29 Jan. 1824.

Pages 168-169: Walton Co., 14 Aug. 1823. JAMES J. BENTLY & WM. BENTLY of Walton Co. to CHARLES K. KENNON of Jasper Co. for $650, lot #173, 6th Dist. Monroe Co., 202½ A. JAMES J. BENTLY (LS), WM. BENTLY (LS). Wit: WM. C. THOMAS, JOHN H. BRANTLY.
Proven by JOHN H. BRANTLY in Jasper Co. before ROBERT E. RICHARDSON J.P. on 17 Jan. 1824. Rec. 29 Jan. 1824.

Pages 169-170: Ga., 2 June 1823 RICHARD LOVING of Newton Co. to JAMES J. BRANTLY & WM. BRANTLEY of Walton Co. for $300, lot #173, 6th Dist., Monroe Co. RICHARD LOVING (SEAL). Wit: JESSE KING(+), JOSIAH BENTLY.

Walton Co., proven by JOSIAH BENTLY 7 June 1823 before C. STROWD J.P. Rec. 29 Jan. 1824.

Page 171: Jasper Co., 9 Dec. 1823 JAMES B. MARTIN & MINERVA his wife to EDWARD A. ELDER for $600, lot #85, 14th Dist., 202½ A. JAMES B. MARTIN (LS), MINERVA MARTIN (LS). Wit: FLEMING JORDAN, THOMAS GASTON J.P. Rec. 2 Feb. 1824.

Page 172: 19 Sept. 1822 ROBERT WOODWARD of WOODARD [sic] of Morgan Co. to DANIEL TOMLINSON of Jasper Co. for $320, lot #20, 4th Dist., 202½ A. Monroe Co. ROBERT WOODARD (SEAL). Wit: ELIZABETH G. GILBERT, JOHN R. WOOD, JOS. RICHARDS, JNO(?) GILBURT(?) J.P. Rec. 2 Feb. 1824.

Page 173: Twiggs Co., 1 Oct. 1823 JOHN CAMPBELL to HENRY CARLETON (CAMPBELL of Twiggs Co.) (CARLETON of Monroe Co.) for $800, lot #17, 5th Dist., Monroe JOHN CAMPBELL (LS). Wit: SAMUEL M. GRANBERY, JAMES PEARSON J.P. Rec. 2 Feb. 1824.

Pages 174-175: Ga., 4 Jan. 1823 DANIEL ROBERTS of Laurens Co., Ga. to DANIEL TOMLINSON of Monroe Co. for $300 lot #34, 14th Dist., 202½ A DANIEL ROBERTS (SEAL). Wit: NIELL MONROE, THOMAS MOOR J.P. Rec. 2 Feb __

Pages 175-176: 10 June 1823, JAMES HOLLAWAY of Monroe Co. to BENJAMIN JORDAN of Putnam Co. for $50, ½ of lot $51, 13th Dist. Monroe Co. given to me for my services in obtaining the sd. lot for the State from ALLEN HUDSON who drew the lot fraudulently, 50½ A. JAMES HOLLOWAY (SEAL). Wit: THOMAS J. VASS, HORATIO SHIELD, JESSE M. WHITE.
Putnam Co., proven by THOMAS J. VASS, 6 Sept. 1823, before WMSON ROBY J.P. Rec. 2 Feb. 1824.

Pages 177-178: Monroe Co., 27 Dec. 1823 GREEN D. BRANTLY to JOB TAYLOR of Jones Co. for $550 lot #68, 5th Dist. Monroe Co., 202½ A GREEN D. BRANTLY (SEAL), Wit: WILKINS HUNT, WILLIAM BAYM J.P. Rec. 4 Feb. 1824.

Pages 178-179: Baldwin Co., 7 June 1822 JOHN MURKSON of Washington Co. to JOB TAILOR of Jones Co. for $180, lot #102, 6th Dist., Monroe Co. 202½ A. JOHN MURKISON (LS). Wit: CHARLES INGRAM, APPLETON ROSSETER J.P. Rec. 4 Feb. 1824.

Pages 18-181: 29 July 1822 ELIJAH ETHREDGE of Jones Co. to JOB TAILOR of same for $200, lot #115, 6th Dist., Monroe Co. 202½ A. surveyed 10 Aug. 1821 ELIJAH ETHERIDGE (SEAL). Wit: DANIEL MALONE J.P., JOHN SORRELL. Rec. 4 Feb. 1824.

Pages 181-182: 5 Nov. 1822 JAMES W. POE of Monroe Co. to JOB TAILOR of Jones Co. for $800, 202½ A lot #69, 5th Dist. JAMES W. POE (SEAL). Wit: DANIEL MALONE J.P., MARTHA MALONE. Rec. 4 Feb. 1824.

Pages 182-183: 28 Oct. 1823 WILLIAM WRIGHT of Monroe Co. to JOB TAILOR of Jones Co. for $469, 202½ A, lot #84, 6th Dist. WILLIAM WRIGHT (SEAL). Wit: THOMAS B. STUBBS, JAMES FLEMING J.P. Rec. 4 Feb. 1824.

Page 184: Monroe Co., 30 July 1822 THOMAS STAPLETON of Jefferson Co. to GEORGE PARKER of Monroe Co. for $200, 202½ A, lot #107, 6th Dist. on Popes Creek, THOMAS STAPLETON (SEAL). Wit: ISOOM BRAZEAL (X), GEORGE W. ROGERS J.P. Rec. 4 Feb. 1824.

Pages 185-186: Ga., 17 Jan. 1822 ANDREW FULWOOD of Warren Co. to GEORGE PARKER of Baldwin Co. for $300, 202½ A, lot #86 drawn by sd. FULWOOD of Edwards Dist. Telfair Co., but now is a resident of Warren Co. ANDREW FULLWOOD (LS). Wit: THOMAS H. KENAN, JAMES C. HUMPHRIS J.I.C. Rec. 4 Feb. 1824.

Pages 186-187: Monroe Co., 5 Mar. 1824 WILEY BUCKNER of Co. aforesd. to ISAAC HENDRICK of same, for $500, lot #116, 12th Dist., WILLEY BUCKNER

(LS). Wit: ROBERT MCGENTY, WM. BAYNE J.P. Rec. 6 Feb. 1824.

Pages 187-188: Jackson Co., 21 May 1823 JOHN PARK to WILLIAM
HOLLIS of Morgan Co. for $350, lot #152, 5th Dist., Monroe Co., 202½ A.
JOHN PARK (SEAL). Wit: BERRY W. GIDEON, T. MITCHELL, J.I.C. of Clark
County. Rec. 6 Feb. 1824.

Pages 188-189: Ga., 17 June 1823 WILLIAM HOLLIS of Morgan Co. to
THOMAS HOLLIS of Jasper Co. for $300 lot #152, 5th Dist. Monroe Co.
WILLIAM HOLLIS (SEAL). Wit: J. W. DODSON, E. DODSON J.P. Rec. 6 Feb.
1824.

Pages 189-190: Ga., 24 Nov. 1823 NORBORN B. POWELL of Jasper Co.
BENJAMIN HASTING of Monroe Co. for $500, lot #229, 12th Dist., Monroe
202½ A. to JOHN MAYS of Lincoln Co. NORBORN B. POWELL (SEAL). BENJAMIN
HASTING (SEAL). Wit: RICHARD HOLMES, JOHN HILL J.P.
Jasper Co. ELIZA A. POWELL wife of NORBORN relinquish dower 24
Nov. 1823. ELIZA A. POWELL (LS). before JOHN HILL, J.P.

Pages 191-192: Ga., 10 Feb. 1824 HENRY R. PHILLIPS of Jasper Co. to
ELEAZAR ADAMS of Monroe Co. for $1500 lot #10, 11th Dist. Monroe Co.
HENRY R. PHILLIPS (LS). Wit: MATTHEW PHILLIPS, E. DODSON J.P. Rec. 11
Feb. 1824.

Pages 192-193: 23 July 1823 GEORGE W. HARMON of Elbert Co. to
BENJAMIN COOK of same for $250, lot #72, 12th Dist. 202½ A. GEORGE W.
HARMON (SEAL). Wit: NATHANIEL NELLUMS (X), WM. DOOLY J.P. Rec. 11
Feb. 1824.

Pages 193-199: City of Savannah, 18 May 1822, GEORGE MILLER & wf.
of Savannah to JOHN ADAMS of same for $5130 one tract in 8th Dist., Henry
#241 drawn by JOHN A. STEPHENS JUNR. one tract in 15th Dist. of Houston(?)
Co. #77 drawn by sd. JOHN A. STEPHENS JR. one tract in 17th Dist. Henry
Co., #117 drawn by RENICE CLOVIS PETIT also one tract in 17th Dist.
Henry Co. #199, drawn by one JOSEPH BRANTLEY also one tract in 14th Dist.,
Henry Co. #66, drawn by one DEMPSEY GRIFFIN..also one tract in 13th Dist.,
Monroe Co., #153 drawn by on JOHN DERRICK, also one tract in the 8th
Dist. of Monroe, #187 drawn by one WILLIAM MARSH(?), one tract in 7th
Dist. of Monroe Co., #188, also one tract in 12th Dist. of Houston Co.,
#207 drawn by one THOMAS EPOLETT(?), one tract in 6th Dist. Henry Co.
#161, drawn by one JOHN BATESTE (BAPTIST?), also one tract in 15th Dist.
Houston Co., #154 drawn by one JOHN COSTEN, also one tract in 11th Dist.,
of Dooly Co., #253 drawn by JOHN MITCHELL, also one tract in 16th Dist.,
Henry Co., #78 drawn by PETER WHITE, one tract in 2nd Dist., Monroe Co.,
#57, drawn by sd. PETER WHITE, tract in 4th Dist., Dooly Co., #128,
drawn by HENRY MATHEWS, one tract in 13th Dist., Henry Co., #201 drawn by
JAMES CRANE, one tract in 4th Dist., Houston Co., #158 drawn by one
SOLOMON DASHER, also one tract in 10th Dist., Houston #238 drawn by
SOLOMON DASHER, also one tract in 19th Dist. of Early Co., #132 drawn by
one EZRA KENT, also one tract in 7th Dist., Henry Co. #227 drawn by one
KYNCAID STRICKLAND, one also one tract in 12th Dist., Houston Co., drawn by
sd. KYNCAID STRICKLAND, #162, also one tract in 8th Dist., Monroe Co.,
#100, drawn by one RODERICK W. MCKINNON, tract in 5th Dist., Henry Co.,
#47 drawn by ___ HASELTON, lot in 7th Dist., Monroe Co., #60 drawn by
GIDEON HAMILTON, tract in 15th Dist., Houston Co., #8, drawn by GEDION
HAMILTON, tract in 9th Dist., Houston drawn by one HAMET JOHNSTON #164
tract in 4th Dist., Houston Co., #164 drawn by JOSEPH BOCACAN(?), tract
in 4th Dist., Dooly Co. lot #56 drawn by one WILLIAM BUTLER, tract in
4th Dist. Henry Co., #76 drawn by one LEWIS MILLS, tract in 8th Dist.,
Early Co. #76 drawn by WILLIAM O. MILLS, tract in 14th Dist., Monroe Co.,
#99 drawn by one JOSEPH FERAND, tract in 1st Dist., Appling Co., #372,
drawn by JOHN BEASOM, tract in 11th Dist., Dooly Co., #248 drawn by one
BRYSON DOBBINS, lot in 14th Dist., Fayette Co., #7 drawn by JOHN W.
ALSTON, tract in 4th Dist. Henry Co., #104 drawn by JOHN KEENE, one
tract in 8th Dist., Dooly Co., #115 drawn by ELIZABETH KEEN, tract in
18th Dist., Henry Co., #10 drawn by ELEANOR MILLAR(?), GEO. MILLER (LS),
ELIZA JANE W. MILLER (LS), JOHN ADAMS (LS). Wit: IVORY STACKPOE, WM.
C. BARTON, J.P.

Chatham Co., ELISA JANE W. MILLER wife of GEORGE relinquish dower 17 May 1822, WM. GARLON J.P. Rec. 17 Feb. 1824.

Pages 200-201: 11 Mar. 1823, CORBITT STEVENS of Putnam Co. to SAMUEL BARBER of Jasper Co. for $300 lot #195, 6th Dist. Monroe Co. CORBITT STEVENS (SEAL). Wit: JOHN RIVERS, JAMES PATTON.
Jasper Co., proven by JAMES PATTON 23 Feb. 1824. Before OBADIAH EDGE, J.P.

Pages 201-202: 24 Mar.1823 JOHN CHANDLER of Richmond Co. to THOS. CRAYTON of same for $100, lot #36, 11th Dist. 202½ A drawn by POLLY STAMPER widow of Wilks Co. JOHN CHANDLER (SEAL). Wit: WM. MCMILLAN, R. BUSH J.P. Rec. 18 Feb. 1824.

Pages 202-204: Monroe Co., 21 May 1823 THOMAS JOHNSON of Green Co. to ARCHIBALD SWAN of Monroe Co., for $300, lot #48, 6th Dist., Monroe Co., 101¼ A. ½ of sd. lot. THOS. JOHNSON (SEAL). Wit: ISAAC LIVINGSTON, AARON LIVINGSTON.
Monroe Co., proven by AARON LIVINGSTON, 25 Dec. 1823 before WM. B. CLARK J.P.

Pages 204-205: Burke Co., 7 Jan. 1824 JOHN BRIGHAM of Co. aforesd. to JOHN ADAMS of Savannah Chatham Co., for $500, 202½ A lot #128, 5th Dist., Monroe Co. JOHN BRIGHAM (LS). Wit: SETH ROYAL, JACOB ELLISON J.P. Rec. 18 Feb. 1824.

Pages 205-206: 26 March 1822 ANN MOORE to EDWARD CROSS both of Washington Co. for $500 lot #146, 4th Dist., Monroe Co. ANN MOORE (SEAL) (X). Wit: WILLIAM STONE, OWEN JENKINS (X).

Georgia, 89th Dist., Washington Co. Proven by WILLIAM STONE before FRDK GRADDY J.P. Rec. 19 Feb. 1824.

Pages 206-207: Monroe Co., 21 May 1823 THOMAS JOHNSON of Green Co. to SAMUEL LEVINGSTON for $400, ½ of lot #48, 6th Dist. Monroe Co. THOMAS JOHNSON (SEAL). Wit: ISAAC LEVINGSTON, AARON LEVINGSTON.
Proven by AARON LEVIGSTON before WM. B. CLARK J.P. 25 Dec. 1823. Rec. 20 Feb. 1824.

Page 208: Jones Co., 31 Dec. 1822 WILLIAM EVANS of Putnam Co. to THOMAS MORRIS of Co. aforesd. for $800, lot on waters of Rocky Creek 13th Dist., #91 adj. JOSEPH COTTON & others. WILLIAM EVANS (LS). Wit: LEROY HARVEY, D. R. MILLING. Rec. 20 Feb. 1824.

Page 209: Ga., 25 Nov. 1823 ISAAC BAILEY of Jasper Co. to WILLIAM RUSSEL of Jasper Co. for $700, lot #63, 6th Dist., Monroe Co. ISAAC BAILEY (SEAL). Wit: SAMUEL HUSTON, JOHN HILL J.P. Rec. 24 Feb. 1824.

Page 210: Clark Co. 17 Sept. 1823 JAMES WILLIAMSON of Co. aforesd. to SILVANOUS WALKER of Monroe Co. for $600, lot #190, 4th Dist., Monroe Co. JAMES WILLIAMSON (SEAL). Wit: MIDDLETON HARTSFIELD, STEWART FLOYD, ELIJAH PHILLIPS, J.I.C. Rec. 20 Feb. 1824.

Pages 210-211: Ga., 2 Oct. 1823 ROBERT ELLIS attorney for ELISHA WINN of Gwinett Co., to WILLIAM HUCKABY of Jones Co. for $400, 202½ A granted 14 Feb. 1822 to JOSEPH HIGGINS of Ellisons Dist., Gwinett Co., conveyed to ELISHA WINN lot #126, 12th Dist. ROBERT ELLISON (X) attorney for ELISHA WINN (SEAL). Wit: THOS C. MCDOWELL, STEPHEN EILAND J.P. Rec. 21 Feb. 1824.

Page 212: Ga., 24 Sept. 1823 JEFFREY BARKSDALE of Hancock(?) Co. to JAMES TURNERof Monroe Co. for $2000, lot #34, 11th Dist., 202½ A. JEFFREY BARKSDALE (+) (SEAL). Wit: M. PHILLIPS, CLAUDE BELLAH, BENJAMIN WILLIAMS(?), (B). Rec. 21 Feb. 1824.

Page 213: Morgan Co., 29 Jan. 1820(?), JOHN VASON of Co. aforesd. to PHILLIMON OGLETREE of Jasper Co., for $700, lot #76, 13th Dist., Monroe Co., JOHN VASON (LS). Wit: WM. MERRITT, JAMES H? SPURE, JESSE THOMAS J.P. Rec. 21 Feb. 1824.

Page 213-214: Jones Co., 14 May 1823 JOHN JONES of sd. Co. to JAMES
BRANTLY of same, for $1500, lot #262, 12th Dist., 202½ A. JOHN JONES
(SEAL). Wit: ROBERT BEASLEY, WM. HEADS J.P. Rec. 21 Feb. 1824.

Pages 214-215: State of S. C.: I, WILLIAM MILLER of York Dist.,
for $340, pd. by NOAH NELSON of Morgan Co., Ga. have sold 202½ A.,
lot #144, 6th Dist., Monroe Co., granted to LEWIS KENAN, 24 Mar. 1823.
WILLIAM MILLER (LS). Wit: JOSEPH LEWIS, JOSEPH GUTHREE.
 Chester Dist., S. C. Proven by JOSEPH LEWIS before P. WYLIE, J.P.
Rec. 21 Feb. 1824.

Pages 215-216: Morgan Co., 4 Feb. 1822 JOHN WORTHY of Morgan Co.
to EQUILLA CHANCEY of same for $208, lot $127, 12th Dist., 202½ A on
waters of ___. JOHN WORTHY (X) (LS). Wit: ANDREW BROWN, JOSEPH
MORROW J.P. Rec. 24 Feb. 1824.

Pages 216-217: Monroe Co., 3 Mar. 1824, REUBEN CONE ot JOHN
PERMENTER for $800, lot #179, 6th Dist., Monroe Co., REUBEN CONE (LS).
Wit: JAMES M. WRIGHT, A. BALDWIN J.P. Rec. 3 Mar. 1824.

Pages 217-219: Chatham Co., 20 Feb. 1824 JAMES TETSON of Beauford
Dist., St. Peter's Parish, S. C. to ABNER DURHAM of Monroe Co., Ga. for
$150, 10t #226, 7th Dist., Monroe Co., drawn in the late lottery by
CHRISTOPHER TETSON(?) of Hingham(?) Co., now deceased, sd. JAMES M.
TETSON is the legal representative. JAMES M. TETSON (LS). Wit: JOHN
GWINNETT, JAS. EPPINGER J.P. Rec. 3 Mar. 1824.

Page 220: Wilkison Co., 17 Jan. 1822 JAMES DAVIDSON for $500 make
over all title to tract drawn by NANCY WINN(?) of Twiggs Co. to JOSEPH
DAVIDSON JUNR. of Lawrence Co., lot #125, 12th Dist., Monroe Co., JAMES
DAVIDSON (LS). Wit: A. JORDAN, WILLIAM DAVIDSON (X). Rec. 3 Mar. 1824.
 Proven by A. W. GORDIAN, 1 Mar. 1824. Before ALFRED PEACOCK J.P.
Rec. 5 Mar. 1824.

Page 221: 19 Sept. 1823 RICHARD LETTERELL of Hall Co. to JACOB
M. SCUDDER of the Cherokee Nation & Limits of the same state for $250
sd. LETTERELL & wf LUCRETIA, lot #230, 6th Dist. RICHARD LETTERELL (SEAL)
(X), LUCRETIA LETTELL (X) (SEAL). Wit: WILLIAM CAIN, JOSEPH CAIN J.P.
Rec. 6 Mar. 1824.

Pages 222-223: 2 Feb. 1824 BENJAMIN COOK of Elbert Co. to JAMES
WILDER of Monroe Co for $500, lot in 12th Dist., #72, BENJA. COOK (LS).
Wit: DAVID BARRON, JORDAN JONES J.P.
 Elbert Co., Before JORDAN JONES, J.P., ELIZABETH D. COOK relinquish
of dower as wife of BENJAMIN COOK, 2 Feb. 1824. ELIZABETH D. COOK (LS).
Rec. 6 Mar. 1824.

Pages 223-224: Monroe Co., 30 Mar. 1823 ALEXANDER BRYAN of Chatham
to JAMES WILDER of Monroe Co., for $100, lot #132, 7th Dist., Monroe Co.,
202½ A, drawn by JOHN CORRAN, ALEXANDER BRYAN (LS). Wit: S. PERRY,
DAVID BRYAN (X), WILLIAM B. FILES, J.P. Rec. 6 Mar. 1824.

Pages 224-225: Monroe Co., 5 Jan. 1824 WILLIAM & JANE BARNES of
Monroe Co. to THOMAS WALKER of same for $600, lot #134, 5th Dist. WILLIAM
BARNES (LS), JANE BARNES (X) (LS). Wit: GARRETT HUDMAN, WM. BAYNE J.P.
 JANE BARNES relinquished dower 23 Jan. 1824 before MOSES DUMAS
J.P.

Pages 226-227: 26 Feb. 1823, HENRY GOLDEN of Warren Co., to BENJA-
MIN REESE of Monroe Co., for $500, lot #259, 12th Dist., Monroe Co.
HENRY GOLDEN (X) (SEAL). Wit: JOHN M. ALLEN, H. ALLEN, J.I.C.
Rec. 6 Mar. 1824.

Pages 227-228: Jasper Co., 3 Jan. 1822 WILLIAM LAWLESS of Jasper
Co. to JONATHAN F. BRIDGES of same for $500, lot #132, 6th Dist. Monroe
Co. WILLIAM LAWLESS (X) (SEAL). Wit: WILLIAM ARMSTRONG, J. MCCLENDON
J.P. Rec. 6 Mar. 1824.

Pages 228-229: Jones Co., 23 Feb. 1824 WILLIAM CABANESS of Jones Co. to JONATHAN F. BRIDGES of Monroe Co. for $500 lot #67, 6th Dist., 202½ A. WM CABANISS (SEAL). Wit: JOHN H. FANNIN, JOHN T. POP J.P. Rec. 6 Mar. 1824.

Pages 229-230: Monroe Co., 16 Dec. 1823 SAMUEL JOHNSON of Early Co. to MOSES HARRIS of sd. Co. for $350, lot #188, 6th Dist., 202½ A. SAMUEL JOHNSON (SEAL), Wit: T. B. ULFORD, WILL L. MCREE J.P. Rec. 6 Mar. 1824.

Pages 230-231: Alabama, Autauga Co., 20 Feb. 1824 BENJAMIN TEMPLE of Co. aforesd. to HOPE H. TIGNOR of Monroe Co., Ga. for $150, 106 #88, 10th Dist., Monroe Co., drawn by WILLIAM STEMBRIDGE of Putnam Co. BEN. TEMPLE (SEAL). Wit: WM. WOMACK, WILIE WOMACK, COLLIN ROGERS.
    Proven by COLLEN RODGERS 27 Feb. 1824 in Monroe Co. before WILLIAM BLOUNT, J.P. Rec. 6 Mar. 1824

Pages 231-232: Monroe Co. 5 Jan. 1824 JEREMIAH PIERSON of Co. aforesd. to WILLIAM BAYNE of same, for $50, part of lot in 12th Dist., #81, 5 A. JER. PIERSON (LS). Wit: JOHN REDDING, WM. W. MOORE, J.P. Rec. 6 Mar. 1824.

Pages 232-233: Monroe Co., 6 Dec. 1823 NICHOLAS THOMPKINS of Putnam Co. to WILLIAM SHARP of Monroe Co. for $500, lot #222, 13th Dist., NICHOLAS THOMPKINS (LS). Wit: JOHN J. PATTERSON, MARK PATTERSON J.P. Rec. 6 Mar. 1824.

Page 233: Newton Co., I, GILLES J. ADAMS appoint THOMAS CAMP my attorney to make titles to ½ of lot in 12th Dist., #81, 6 Nov. 1822, GILLES J. ADAMS (SEAL). Wit: ARCHD. RITTEL(?), M. BRASWELL J.P. Rec. 6 Mar. 1824.

Pages 234: Monroe Co., 16 Nov. 1822 THOMAS CAMP of Monroe Co., to WILLIAM BAYNE of Jones Co. for $300, 10t #81, 12th Dist., ½ of sd. lot, 101¼ A. THOMAS CAMP for GILLES J. ADAMS (SEAL). Wit: WM. PEIRSON, SILAS MONK, GEORGE W. ROGERS, J.P. Rec. 6 Mar. 1824.

Pages 234-235: Putnam Co., 25 Nov. 1823 NICHOLAS THOMPKINS of Putnam Co. from PLEASANT WRIGHT of same for $5000, lot #222, 13th Dist., PLEASANT WRIGHT (X) (SEAL). Wit: JOHN TOMPKINS, JAMES JOHNSON, JOHN E. MORROW J.P. Rec. 6 Mar. 1824.

Pages 235-236: Ga., 25 Dec. 1823 JOHN BOLTON of Wilkes Co. to HENRY H. LUMPKIN of Monroe Co., for $210, lot #203, 6th Dist. JOHN BOLTON (SEAL). Wit: WM C. BOREN, J. C. HOLMES.
    Wilkes Co., Proven by JOSIAH B. HOLMES, 29 Dec. 1823 before REUBIN ECHOLS J.P. Rec. 6 Mar. 1824.

Pages 236-237: Ga., 6 Mar. 1823 JEREAMIAH MOORE of Greene Co., to LEONARD GREER of Monroe Co. for $300, lot #101, 5th Dist. JEREMIAH MOORE (SEAL). Wit: THOMAS F. GIBBS, JOHN PARK J.P. Rec. 6 Mar. 1824.

Pages 237-238: Ga., 28 Oct. 1822 JAMES A. WOOTEN of Green Co. to MOSES MATHIS of Monroe Co. for #800, lot #261, 13th Dist. JAMES A. WOOTEN (SEAL). Wit: ALEXANDER PERKINS, THOMAS JOHNSON J.P. Rec. 6 Mar. 1824.

Pages 238-239: 26 Feb. 1824, WILLIAM BRIANT to PHILIP H. BURFORD for $500, lot #24, 12th Dist., drawn by sd. BRIANT, WILLIAM BRIANT (X) (SEAL). Wit: JAMES SPRATLING, WILLIAM COLBURN (X), STEPHEN BUNNERLS, WILEY CARTER J.P. Rec. 13 Mar. 1824.

Pages 239-240: 15 Jan. 1825 CHARLES CRAWFORD of Jones (?) Co. to ROBERT M. BROWNING of Morgan Co. for $350, lot #102, 6th Dist., Monroe Co. CHARLES CRAWFORD (SEAL). Wit: (illegible). Rec. 18 Mar. 1824.

Page 240:   27 Nov. 1823, WILLIAM ULLINS of Hall Co. to JAMES HAMMETT of Pike Co. for $400, lot #54, 6th Dist., 202½ A.   WILLIAM MULLINS (SEAL).   Wit: WM. HEAD, JAMES PONDER, JAMES D. HEAD.

Jasper Co., Proven by JAMES D. HEAD before WM HANCOCK J.P.   30 Dec. 1823.   Rec. 18 Mar. 1824.

Page in Marriage Book - (PMB)   Marriage Date - (MD)
Marriage Performed By - (MPB)   Title - (Title)

GROOM	BRIDE	PMB	MD	MPB	TITLE
Austin, Thomas C.	Deborilla Mulican	25	11-27-27	Charles Collins	JIC
Adcock, Anderson W.	Nancy Sharp	46	11-3-26	Jas. H. Williams	JP
Averca, William	Elizabeth Peacock	58	12-4-25	Wm. Ward	JP
Alford, James	Dorcas W. Pegg	59	3-5-26	Finley G. Stewart	JIC
Adcock, Anderson W.	Mahala Harrington	64	11-4-28	Com. Ward	JP
Austin, John	Mary Gunling	77	1-13-29	Middleton M. Antony	JP
Allums, Hopson	Ann McMullen	86	1-13-29	Chas. Holsey	JP
Austin, Jesse	Mary Powell	107	1-13-29	Com. Pegg	JIC
Allen, Elijah P.	Eliza T. Harris	104	10-25-27	Elijah Waynes	JP
Averca, William	Cara Walker	109	2-10-28	Com. Ward	JP
Alldridge, Thomas P.	Cincy Williamson	112	6-29-28	J. D. Wann	JIC
Allen, Coleman A.	Matilda W. Harris	141	3-6-31	Elijah Hanes	JP
Anthony, James	Lucinda Lassiter	147	9-29-31	Elijah Hanes	JP
Barrow, Henry	Lucretia Watson	159	2-23-32	Zadock Davis	JP
Burnsides, William	Jane Drigars	157	12-8-31	Wm. Reaves	JP
Bowen, Matther	Anna Parker	142	3-25-31	Wm. Reaves	JP
Berryhill, Pleasant	Martha Right	5	12-23-23	Wm. Harknes	JP
Betterton, Joshua	Peggy Finley	10	9-2-24	Ephriam Pennington	JP
Betterton, Nathan	Deborah Finley	11	11-11-24	Ephraim Pennington	JP
Bland, James E.	Winney Pate	20	6-14-27	Robert Tucker	JP
Bowers, Stephen	Temperance Kelley	26	9-18-28	George Wane	JP
Beavers, Awlsey	Nancy West	27	9-18-26	Elijah Hanes	JP
Beck, James	Lurany Gilbert	45	12-13-26	Elijah Hanes	JP
Bohannon, Henderson	Agnes Watkins	45	2-8-26	J. Head	MG
Boatright, William	Lucinda Gilbert	46	7-19-25	Elijah Hanes	JP
Brown, Jesse C.	Sarah Kindall	55	12-12-26	C. McCarty	MG
Burnsides, William	Lavina Grier	78	3-19-29	Wm. Reaves	JP
Brown, Fannen	Matilda Davis	95	12-30-29	Wm. Wakefield	JP
Blackstock, Kendall	Elizabeth Cook	96	12-30-29	Wm. Wakefield	JP
Betterton, William	Mary Ann Glenny	101	2-4-30	Wm. Wakefield	JP
Beck, Jeffery	Katherin Shadux	103	10-7-27	Elijah Hanes	JP
Bentley, John	Jane Betsill	108	12-26-27	Robert Tucker	JP
Bates, Matthew	Passify T. Nelson	110	5-12-25	A. Roberts	JP
Burrus, John C.	Louiza Madden	128	10-28-30	Isaiah Derham	JP
Burrow, John J.	Sarah Bonton	130	12-5-30	Jesse Ward	JP
Baker, Matthew	Martha Drennan	133	1-4-31	Finley G. Stewart	JIC
Barnett, John C.	Christina Eastin	136	2-3-31	Isaiah Derham	JP
Barton, Thomas	Mary Berry	137	2-24-31	Edward J.G. Johnson	JP
Betterton, Henry	Mary Finley	139	2-24-31	"	JP
Cunningham, J. H.	Emily L. P. Alford	3	10-3-23	James S. Brown	JIC
Clements, James	Rebeccah Linvisa	5	1-5-24	Wm. Harkins	JP
Craig, Andrew	Peggy Pike	6	2-6-24	Wm. Harkins	JP
Cooper, James	Lurana Reeves	8	3-14-24	Wm. Harkins	JP
Cockville, William	Nancy Cox	18	3-24-25	James Strown	JIC
Casey, Daniel	Sarah Morris	36	1-13-26	James Strown	JIC
Copeland, Archibald H.	Lucretia Muligan	48	12-23-27	James McBride	JP
Cook, Rolin	Katherine Mosely	83	10-9-27	E. P. Allen	JP
Carter, Benjamin P.	Martha Barber	83	2-21-28	James Head	MG
Cox, John	Elizabeth Harkins	84	12-18-28	George Ware	JP
Chambers, Samuel	Mary Berry	86	7-5-27	James Head	MG
Cleckler, Jacob	Edney Head	93	10-28-29	John Ganeson	JP

GROOM	BRIDE	PMB	MD	MPB	TITLE
Cox, Thomas	Martha Cockville	96	12-1-29	Eli Edmondson	JP
Cummings, Benjamin	Nancy Weathers	100	1-13-30	G. B. Davis	JP
Coleman, Jesse H.	Elizabeth Laurence	105	11-29-27	Charles Collins	JIC
Coleman, James	Katharine Drennan	127	9-28-30	Eli Edmondson	JP
Clements, Lovic P.	Martha Mannen	128	10-21-30	George Ware	JP
Coal, James	Martha Smith	131	11-30-30	Wm. Reeves	JP
Cox, Samuel	Malinda Burnett	132	11-2-30	Eli Edmondson	JP
Carter, Stephen	Temack Adams	133	12-23-30	George Ware	JP
Copeland, Samuel	Elizabeth Christian	140	3-17-21	Geo. McEackern	JP
Cole, John	Eliza G. Cummings	142	4-7-31	J. H. Williams	JIC
Davis, John C.	Jerush Lamberth	2	9-8-23	Wm. Morgan	JIC
Dunn, John	Rachel Edwards	14	12-4-24	Robert Tucker	JP
Dunn, John Jr.	Patsey Lambert	14	10-8-24	Robert Tucker	JP
Davis, James G.	Roany Mathis (?)	19	5-29-28	Wm. McBride	CC
Dent, John	Elizabeth Sparks	35	7-15-25	Edwin	JP
Davis, Thomas	Polly Shellnut	38	10-4-27	Caleb Garrison	JP
Dorman, Alfred	Gracy Ann Padgett	47	2-15-27	Jas. T. Wakes	JIC
Dukes, William	Mary Norman	49	4-17-27	Ben. McLandow	JP
Davis, William	Sarah Dunn	54	11-23-28	John Lambert	JP
Daniel, Burges	Katharine Nelson	62	2-7-26	Elijah Hanes	JP
Davis, John	Mary Yates	63	7-19-26	Silas King	MG
Daniel, Jesse	Milly Pate	72	2-18-29	Elijah Hanes	JP
Dedwilder, Lindsey	Mary Walker	73	1-22-29	Wm. Ward	JP
Duty, Thomas	Mary Hearn	75	2-6-29	David D. Smith	JP
Davis, Henry	Rebeccah Shellnut	79	3-29-29	Wm. Wakefield	JP
Dorman, Hiram	Miriah Cox	81	2-26-29	J. D. Mann	JP
Dodson, Constantine	Elizabeth T. Moore	98	12-9-29	Elijah D. Dodson	JP
Davis, William C.	Martha Reeves	108	12-17-27	G. B. Davis	JP
Dodson, William	Elizabeth Brown	115	11-2-28	Elijah J. Dodson	JP
Dodson, Elijah	Mahaley C. Moore	119	11-24-30	John M. Forbes	JP
Denham, Ansler	Manerva Spradlin	124	8-26-30	Geo. Coare	JP
Davis, Harmon	Elizabeth Twzerviss	137	2-9-31	Edward Johnson	JP
Davis, Charles	Matilda Whatley	150	11-22-31	Geo. Ware	JP
Davis, John	Susannah Dunn	154	1-17-32	Eli Edmondson	JP
Edmondson, Eli	Jane McBride	16	2-1-25	Wm. H. Dickson	JIC
Eason, Edmond	Mary Gay	72	1-22-29	E. P. Allen	JIC
Fowler, Elbert	Nancy Tredwell	13	2-6-25	Andrew Craig	JP
Ford, Richard	Sally C. Dewsberry	22	10-16-28	E. D. Vaughn	JP
Falkner, Jefferson	Sarah Ann Byrd	70	12-6-28	Jas. McBride	JP
Faulkner, William	Nancy Parker	109	2-26-28	Jas. McBride	JP
Fowler, Dennis	Louisa Nichols	113	8-31-28	Geo. Ware	JP
Formsby, Thompson	Deborah Cox	127	9-9-30	Eli Edmondson	JP
Finley, James	Martha Yates	141	3-10-31	Wm. Henderson	MG
Gilliland, William	Sarah Allen	7	3-25-24	Elijah Hanes	JP
Garrett, Benjamin	Polly Piles	12	1-27-25	Eph. Pennington	JP
Garrett, James	Vicey Hammock	37	8-2-25	Edwin Lambert	JP
Gunn, Thomas H.	Mary Ingram	50	2-11-27	William Peig	JIC
Garrett, Moses	Hannah Morris	54	12-29-25	James Strown	JIC
Garrison, Henry B.	Rachel Bosworth	68	8-10-26	John Hunter	MG
Garrison, James F.	Abigail Bonner	68	8-24-26	James T. Waber	JIC
Glass, Lovinski	Lydia May	69	2-19-29	Geo. Ware	JP
Ginnings, William	Nancy Franklin	75	1-6-29	David D. Smith	JP
Gurley, Ezekiel	Elizabeth Gray	76	2-9-29	Middleton W. Antony	JP
Getters, John D.	Margaret Pegg	85	5-4-26	Jas. Strown	JIC
Gentry, Mason	Milly Seals	91	11-22-29	Sylvanus Walker	JP
Gray, Absolom	Sarah Matthews	95	12-23-29	G. B. Davis	JP
Griggs, Bryan	Rosalina Herrin	121	4-21-30	Zadcock Davis	JP
Gibson, Stafford	Elizabeth Adcock	122	4-1-30	Jas. H. Williams	JP
Gilland, John	Lucretia Burgs	126	9-22-30	Ed. Johnson	JP
Goodwin, Lewis D.	Elizabeth Ann McNeil	131	12-9-30	A. McEachem	JP

GROOM	BRIDE	PMB	MD	MPB	TITLE
Graves, Charles	Elizabeth Cleckler	132	11-25-30	Eli Edmondson	JP
Graves, John	Susan Cleckler	135	1-11-31	Eli Edmondson	JP
Gilliland, Lucas	Elizabeth Hunt	152	12-25-31	Elijah P. Allen	JIC
Harris, William	Mariah Smallwood	145	7-24-31	Zadcock Davis	JP
Harkins, John L.	Martha T. McCarty	1	Within 10 days	W. Harkins	JP
Hendrix Reuben	Sarah Davis	4	10-16-23	Jas. Strown	JIC
Ham, David	Elizabeth Lassiter	5	11-13-23	Eph.Pennington	JP
Harkins, Joseph T.	Sarah Clements	10	12-12-24	Wm. Parks	JP
Hinnard, William	Lucinda Davis	24	11-11-28	Jeremiah D. Mann	
Harris, Jesse	Mary Bell	26	3-18-27	Jas. Reeves	MG
Heardon, Benjamin	Rebeccah Hudgins	32	5-31-25	Jas. West	JP
Hobb, William	Fanny Parker	33	4-16-27	Wm. Pegg	JIC
Hammock, Thomas	Elizabeth Nelson	3	1-3-26	Finley G. Stewart	JIC
Haisten, Daniel E.	Judy Terry	34	11-4-26	G. B. Davis	JP
Howard, James	Sarah Powell	37	4-16-27	Jas. McBride	JP
Howell, William	Carolyn Craigs	40	1-1-26	Finley Stewart	JIC
Hawkins, Nathaniel	Charlotte Cox	56	9-23-27	Caleb Johnson	JP
Hanson, George	Jerusha Lambreth	60	5-8-25	Larkin Landrim	
Hutchinson, Tumey	Nancy Antony	65	10-17-27	E. P. Allen	JP
Harris, James	Malinda Lapiton	69	12-3-28	E. P. Allen	JP
Hadley, Thomas	Delaney Mullins	71	1-4-29	Jas. Williams	JP
Harris, Robert W.	Rhoda Gilliland	73	2-5-29	Elijah Hanes	JP
Hearndon, Elijah	Minny Cannady	74	2-7-29	David D. Smith	MG
Hearndon, Enoch	Manerva Yarborough	84	10-6-28	James Head	JP
Hancock, James	Margaret Evans	85	12-28-28	Elijah Hanes	JP
Houston, Johnson	Rachel Davis	90		Finley Stewart	JIC
Head, Benjamin	Nancy Derham	98	12-11-29	John Ganion	
Hightower, John	Elizabeth Hunter	99	12-24-29	Aaron Turner	MG
Hammock, Aaron	Mary Carrol	99	1-7-30	George Ware	JP
Hanson, William	Martha Dunn	107	12-11-27	Edward Lowrith	JP
Houston, John	Nicey Fowler	110	3-6-28	Finley Stewart	JIC
Huie, Alexander	Margaret Hancock	126	6-3-30	Elijah Hanes	JP
Head, Elijah	Martha Head	129	11-26-30	Archibald Eachem	JP
Hinton, James	Charlotte Powell	138	2-10-31	Eli Edmondson	JP
Ivy, Travis	Serena Donavin	152	12-20-31	Aaron Turner	MG
Jones, Thomas	Permillia Reeves	57	6-5-27	Com. Nance (?)	JP
Jones, William	Charlotte Adkinson	69	1-2-25	Finley G.Stewart	JIC
Jentry, Harvey	Nancy Dodson	102	4-24-25	Com, Gilliland	JP
Killcrease, Nathan	Kitty Killcrease	22	8-7-23	James Strown	JIC
Killcrease, Lewis	Matilda Williams	33	8-24-23	James Strown	JIC
Kelly, Lemuel	Pamella Harrell	89	7-23-29	George Ware	JP
Kelly, Denny	Eliza Smallwood	92	12-28-28	George Ware	JP
Key, Alford	Sarah Gunn	130	8-12-30	W. W. Baggin	JP
Knox, Rier	Sarah Padgett	153	12-27-31	Eli Edmondson	JP
Knowles, Edmond Jr.	Mary Denson	157	1-2-32	Jesse Ward	JP
				(Rev. Turner added that he married 18 person on this date)	
Lasseter, Elisha	Sarah Powell	21	12-4-27	Wm. Mosely	MG
Lumpkin, John C.	Nancy Hill	30	7-26-27	Caleb Field	JIC
Lile, John	Mary Simmons	34	5-12-25	Edwin Lambreth	JP
Lochlear, Jesse	Mary Gunn	35	8-27-27	Wm. Maddox	MG
Lambreth, John	Permillia W. Garrison	43	8-24-26	Jas. Wafer	JIC
Lancaster, Henry	Elizabeth B. Pegg	44	10-31-27	Finley Stewart	JIC
Leopard, John	Sarah Skinner	49	3-15-27	Beniah McLeadorp	JP
Leopard, Luke	Abigail Fowler	51	4-17-27	Beniah McLeadorp	JP
Lee, Bud	Elizabeth Finch	89	12-3-29	Benj. Garrett	JP
Lyle, Stephen D.	Elizabeth Graves	97	11-8-29	William McBride	CCO
Lancaster, Henry	Sarah Terry	97	12-20-29	Eli Edmondson	JP

GROOM	BRIDE	PMB	MC	MPB	TITLE
Leopard, John	Mary Blake	107	12-17-27	G. B. Davis	JP
Lochlear, William	Ann Morris	112	5-12-28	Jas. McBride	JP
Lee, William	Monica Stubs	114	9-20-28	Jesse Ward	JP
Lett, Wyatt	Rebeccah Ann Wells	148	6-30-31	Finley Stewart	JP
Moman, William	Hannah Miles	6	12-5-23	Henry Lansford	JIC
Miller, Joel	Mary Denson	6	1-1-24	John W. Smith	JP
Maddox, William	Nancy West	11	12-22-24	Wm. Morgan	JIC
McQuire, Riley	Lucinda Banister	18	3-10-25	John Hicks	JP
Mitchell, Jonathan	Sarah Hightower	41	3-29-27	William Pegg	JIC
Morgan, William	Henrietta Bridges	42	11-22-27	G. B. Davis	JP
Mulligan, Tandy	Nancy Parrish	48	1-4-28	Jas. McBride	JP
Moore, Thomas C.	Cinthia Smith	56	5-13-27	Caleb Garrison	JP
McEachern, Archibald	Abey Ann Post	58	8-16-26	Jas. T. Wafer	JIC
Morgan, Hiram	Elizabeth Hasting	60	1-22-26	Willis B. Noll	MG
Miller, Samuel	Elizabeth Bowen	62	3-15-27	Samuel Ward	JP
McIntosh, Jesse D.	Margaret A. L. Head	65	1-1-29	William Ward	JIC
McCormick, William	Martha A. Dickson	66	2-23-26	William Dickson	JP
Mitchell, Daniel B.	Elizabeth Mann	80	12-10-28	J. D. Mann	JIC
McPhirson, Ezra	Nancy Jannon	82	12-27-27	James Head	MG
Moore, Sandford	Mary Ann F. Fuller	94	10-15-29	Elijah Dodson	JP
Mitchell, Hardy	Rebeccah Post	104	10-25-27	Caleb Garrison	JP
Miller, Sidney	Jane Houston	111	5-3-28	Jas. McBride	JP
McHargus, Seaborn	Margaret Ann Bannon	115	9-2-29	James Head	MG
Maddox, Samuel	Elizabeth Chambers	116	2-2-30	James Head	MG
McCantry, Benjamin	Elizabeth Bonner	118	3-4-30	Edwin Lamberth	JP
McClain, John	Rebeccah Cavendah	120	5-13-30	John Gillcoat	MG
Moulder, William	Martha Chambers	120	5-26-30	John Gillcoat	MG
McElhannon, Cooper	Anna Mannin	123	8-12-30	George Ware	JP
Mullkey, George W.	Elizabeth Padgett	129	12-1-30	N. H. Rhodes	MG
Mitchell, Asa B.	Mary Willford	131	1-6-31	George Ware	JP
Morris, William	Charity Gunn	134	1-11-31	Eli Edmondson	JP
Mulican, Cary	Mary Norton	144	1-1-30	William Ward	JIC
Mosely, George	Thunsy M. Man	149	11-7-38?	Elijah P. Allen	JIC
Mann, Peter D.	Elizabeth S. King	153	12-28-31	Finley G. Stewart	JIC
Manning, Lewis	Jane Spencer	158	2-21-32	George Ware	JP
Nelson, Peter	Temperance Bridges	121	4-27-30	Robert M. Steele	MG
Owen, William A.	Harriet Nichols	100	1-14-30	J. D. Mann	JP
Orsborn, William	Susan Green	140	3-1-31	R. M. Steel	MG
Powell, William	Sarah Mays	157			
Pate, Hollis M.	Jincey Hughes	154	1-19-32	Ed Johnson	JP
Phillips, Harrington	Sophia Gay	151	12-15-31	Wm. Reeves	JP
Pearson, Joshua	Rachel Dukes	149	9-22-31	Wm. Reeves	JP
Peters, Jesse	Charlotte Holden	143	6-7-31	Benj. Garrett	JP
Post, Allen	Kathern Davis	3	6-31-23	Wm. Morgan	JIC
Poe, Gilbert	Delila Betterton	4	12-2-23	Eph. Pennington	JP
Presnols, Jacob	Elizabeth Right	7	2-25-24	Wm. Harkins	JP
Parsons, Samuel P.	Lucy Eason	15	2-18-24	A. Thorpe	JP
Post, Martin	Sarah Ann McNeil	19	8-17-26	Jas. T. Wafer	JIC
Pruit, Samuel	Mary Braswell	21	3-2-25	Wm. H. Dickson	JIC
Piles, Peter	Mariah Davis	24	6-25-26	Elijah Hanes	JP
Pilkington, William	Jinny Heandron	27	4-19-25	James Hicks	JP
Pace, John	Jincey McDonald	28	6-7-27	Jas. H. Williams	JP
Piles, James	Mary Betsill	39	4-9-28	Robert Tucker	JP
Pate, George W.	Mary Simmons	42	12-25-27	Charles Collins	JIC
Pate, Seaborn	Mary Weather	43	10-25-27	Jas. H. Williams	JP
Pate, Charles	Charlotte Pritchett	50	5-11-26	William Head	JP
Pitman, Jeremiah	Julian Gaggett	51	9-9-27	Elijah Hanes	JP
Pollard, Irvin	Malinda Walker	57	3-4-27	Samuel Ward	JP
Pearson, Joseph	Mary Cox	61	2-25-27	James McBride	JP
Pate, William	Rachel Pearce	79	3-12-29	William Reeves	JP
Patterson, Francis	Mariah Reeves	87	11-21-26	Woodson, Hubbard	JP

GROOM	BRIDE	PMB	MD	MPB	TITLE
Pitman, Telghman	Elizabeth Holland	92	9-17-29	William McBride	JP
Pitman, Irvin	Elisa Johnson	106	11-8-27	Caleb Garrison	JP
Pope, Hardy	Kitty Renfrow	117	2-24-30	Moses Padgett	JIC
Padgett, James W.	Susan Simmons	118	3-19-30	Jeremiah Moses	JP
Padgett, Henry	Phebe Boring	119	4-14-30	Nathan Rhodes	MG
Pyle, Nicholas	Mary Westbrook	135	1-2-31	Elijah Hanes	JP
Prestridge, Joel	Joanah Gay	136	1-3-31	A. McEachern	JP
Quick, Eli	Drucilla Turner	70	6-14-28	James McBride	JP
Rountree, Wiley	Cumfort Hanes	8	3-18-24	Ephriam Pennington	JP
Roundtree, Cador	Jean Strawden	25	8-16-27	Ep. Allen	JP
Reed, James	Elizabeth Townsend	28	8-10-26	Robert Tucker	JP
Richard, William	Margaret Webster	47	8-26-25	James West	JP
Rentfrow, Council	Nancy Shadux	90	12-23-25	Jas. T. Wafer	JIC
Roberts, Avery	Clementine Andrew	93	9-6-29	Elijah Hanes	JP
Rentfrow, Henry	Tracey Rountree	94	7-19-29	Elijah P. Allen	JP
Robinson, Mordica	Unice Robinson	122	6-30-30	Zadock David	JP
Spradlin, Seaborn	Nancy Bearden	146	8-4-31	George Ware	JP
Sanders, James	Flora Skaggs	156	2-14-32	Eli Edmondson	JP
Smith, Alexander	Patricia Cobb	158	2-14-32	Aaron Turner	JP
Stearn, James	Lucinda Knowles	159	2-25-32	Edward N. Johnson	JP
Smith, Jeptha	Nancy C. Dickson	6	4-29-24	James Strown	JIC
Shellnut, William	Nancy Lambreth	20	11-21-25	Edwin Lambreth	JP
Smith, Isaac	Elizabeth Turner	23	7-17-28	Wm. Wakefield	JP
Stewart, William	Mary Beck	29	3-15-27	Jas. Blackstocks	JP
Shepherd, John W.	Sarah Robinson	32	7-5-27	Aaron Turner	MG
Shellnut, Thomas	Jane Wakefield	41	10-3-27	Caleb Garrison	JP
Smith, Henderson	Mary McIntosh	52	10-23-25	Jas. Strown	JIC
Smith, Henry	Susan Ledlow	53	10-9-25	William Pegg	JIC
Sharp, John F.	Martha Adcock	53	12-29-25	James Head	MG
Spradlin, Joshua	Manerva Williford	55	11-27-28	George Ware	JP
Smith, Laurence	Mary McLendon	59	7-26-27	Jas. T. Wafer	JIC
Stett, Robert M.	Elendor Sharp	61	1-18-27	James H. Williams	JP
Stewart, James G.	Elizabeth Huston	64	1-27-29	Eli Emundson	JP
Sims, James	Nancy Nobles	70	8-6-28	James McBride	JP
Strawn, Absalom	Susan Steen	74	1-1-29	E. P. Allen	JIC
Swinford, Jonathon C.	Martha David	76	12-10-28	David D. Smith	JP
Sparks, Ettiene	Elizabeth Lyle	78	12-24-26	Edwin Lambreth	JP
Smallwood, Mark	Elizabeth Walden	80	10-14-28	William Ward	JP
Spradlin, Oliver	Matilda Harris	91	12-11-28	George Ware	JP
Swan, Bishop	Sarah Lyle	102	5-1-25	Finley G. Stewart	JIC
Strickland, Gales	Ailsey Kerbo	113	8-4-28	Middleton W. Antony	JP
Smith, Asberry	Makaby Hulsy	123	8-25-30	Eli Edmondson	JP
Strother, Berry	Julian Derham	125	6-27-30	Elijah Dodson	JP
Stewart, Gideon	Ruth Inby	137	2-11-31	E. D. Vaughn	JP
Smith, Benjamin	Mary Hannah	143	5-5-31	Sheldrake McCombs	JP
Tilghman, Aaron	Nancy Cleckley	1	4-10-23	Wm. Harkins	
Tucker, Bartlett	Jane Finch	12	12-24-24	Robert Tucker	JP
Tucker, Coleman	Rachel Finch	13	12-27-24	Robert Tucker	JP
Tredwell, John	Delila Strickland	15	11-7-24	Andrew Craig	JP
Tredwell, Henry	Nancy Parish	38	7-6-28	William Mosely	MG
Thornton, Middleton	Adalin Watkins	39	6-1-28	J. D. Mann	JIC
Turner, Silas	Elizabeth Bannister	111	5-11-28	James McBride	JP
Turner, Thomas	Lucinda Willkinson	125	8-25-30	E. D. Mann	JP
Thomas, James E.	Jan Kindall	144	11-2-30	William Ward	JIC
Thompson, William	Minerva Hinman	148	8-18-31	Jesse Ward	JP
Vickery, William	Susannah Yarbo	23	8-30-25	James T. Wafer	JIC
Vowel, Malichia	Nancy Leopard	67	1-30-27	Beniah McLendon	JP
Wilkins, David L.	Sarah Sparks	1	5-18-23	William Harkens	JP
Wood, Winston	Dicey Gay	7	2-12-24	James Strown	JIC

GROOM	BRIDE	PMB	MD	MPB	TITLE
Watson, Harmon	Sarah Lawrence	9	6-24-24	Eph. Pennington	JP
Wallis, Elijah	Susan Chavions	22	2-21-28	Jas. H. Williams	JP
Williams, Avington	Penelope Harvy	29	12-27-28	Willis B. Noel	MG
Willson, Samuel	Mary Fleming	30	1-11-27	William Pegg	JIC
Watson, William	Virginia Head	31	2-14-27	Jas. T. Wafer	JIC
Williams, James	Malinda Daley	31	12-8-27	Jas. Blcokstock	JP
Williams, John	Carrey Millsap	40	3-30-26	Aquilla Hardy	JP
Walden, William H.	Martha Hamilton	52	1-11-27	William Ward	JP
Williams, Isaac	Mary Harrison	63	11-7-26	Jas. Williams	JP
Wilkins, James	Ailsey Austin	66	5-21-25	William Richards	JP
Ward, Miles	Livia McLeod	81	3-19-29	Eli Edmondson	JP
Wharton, Leibus	Elizabeth Daughtry	82	5-27-26	James McBride	JP
Watson, William C.	Martha Callico	87	1-22-29	Robert Tucker	JP
Williford, King H.	Lucy Mannen	88	5-23-29	George Ware	JP
Wilson, William	Nancy Houston	88	7-9-29	Eli Emondson	JP
Weathers, William	Rachel Lee	103	8-14-27	Jas. H. Williams	JP
Wood, Miles	Elizabeth Cochran	106	10-28-27	Caleb Garrison	JP
Wells, William A.	Louise Barron	114	10-8-28	James Head	MG
Whaley, Madison	Martha Renfrow	116	1-20-30	Elijah Hanes	JP
Willson, Thomas B.	Martha Williams	117	1-25-30	James Head	MG
Walldrop, Martin G.	Elizabeth Davis	124	8-31-30	Wm. Henderson	MG
Westbrook, Bartholomew	Elizabeth Hill	138	2-24-31	Thomas H. Cliett	MG
Wood, Benjamin	Lucinda Walldrop	145	4-7-31	Jesse Ward	JP
Watts, Robert B.	Elizabeth Thomas	146	8-7-31	Zadock Davis	JP
West, James	Nancy F. Ward	147	10-6-31	Benjamin Garrett	JP
Wilf, Tense	Sarah Knowes	150	11-17-31	Jesse Ward	JP
Williford, William P.	Ruth Williford	155	1-22-32	Geroge Ware	JP
Westbrook, Joseph	Eliza Hill	156	1-27-32	A. McEachern	JP
Weathers, Jesse	Elizabeth Reeves	157	1-24-32	William Reeves	JP
Young, Willson	Nancy Wood	4	10-23-23	John Williams	JIC
Yarbrough, William	Cinthia Pace	16	8-31-24	John Richards	JP
*Yarbrough, Reuben	Cinthia Short				
*Yates, Irvin	Elizabeth Bunion				
*Yarbrough, ___	Malinda Hearn				

* These cannot be found in Fayette Co., Ga. or Pike County, Ga.

DOCKET OF THE COURT OF ORDINARY, FAYETTE COUNTY, GEORGIA

NOTE: There is no page 36; however, there are 2 pages numbered 38 as in the Original Docket Book.

1829-1854 Adm., Admx., Exor., Orphans, Deceased	Securities	Court Term	Cash Involved	1829-1854 Returns Made For
Page 1				
Joshua Hanes & Elizabeth Rountree, Adm. & Admx. of the estate of Roba Rountree	James Hanes & Elijah Hanes	July, 1829		1843
Gainey Joseph & James Westbrook, Adm. of the estate of Moses Westbrook, Junior	John D. Stell & J. Lamberth	Nov. 1834		1839
Zachariah Petty, Adm. of Archable Booth, deceased	A. McBride & William Herring	March, 1840	Amt. on hand $146.45/4	1842
Benjamin Neal, Adm. of John Nickols, deceased	A. Nichols & William Morgan	July, 1840	Amt. $696.15	1845 (Left 1846)
Andrew McBride & Seaborn J. Weaver, Executors of the estate of Thomas Carroll, deceased		Jan. 1841		1849
Page 2				
Josiah R. Bosworth, guardian for Thomas C. Bosworth, orphan of James Bosworth, deceased	Jeptha Landrum & George Ward	Jan. 1841	Amt. due $529.87	1849
Nancy Glass & James D. Glass, executor & exrx. of Richard Glass, deceased		Letters issued Jan. 1841	Amt. due $2795.0½	1842
Daniel D. Denham, guardian of the orphans of Phillip Easten, deceased	E. P. Nickson & J. H. Elder	Jan. 1841	Amt. due $750.00	1841
John D. Stell, guardian of the orphans of Samuel W. Cox, deceased	E. P. Allen & A. McBride	Jan. 1841		1851
Lucinda Wooton, guardian of the orphans of William B. Wooton, deceased	Jesse Ward & A. McBride	July, 1841		1851-1854
Page 3				
Janet Handley, exrx. of the estate of Abraham Coker		Sept. 1841	Amt. due $308.38	1842

Adn., Admx., Exor., Orphans, Deceased	Securities	Court Term	Cash Involved	Returns Made For
William C. Champion, guardian of the orphans of Abner Champion, deceased	Willis Champion & Francis Champion	Jan. 1832		1851-1854
Jeptha Landrum, gurardian of the orphans of David Lay	Larkin Landrum & Josiah R. Bosworth	Jan. 1842		
Hope Ogletree, guardian of the orphans of Sherod B. Johnson, deceased	Absalum Ogletree, Jr. Thomas Ogletree Solomon Bearden Elijah Glass	Jan. 1842	Amt. Due $97.00	1842
George H. Page, guardian of William Vaugh, orphan of Patrick DeVaughn, deceased	Wm. R. Head	June 1842	Amt. due $165.28	1842
Page 4 Gay Upchurch, Adm. of the estate of Joseph Y. Barnes, deceased	J. H. Johnson & I. Whaley	March 1842	Amt. due $516.92	1846
Jane Landrum & Josiah R. Bosworth, executor & Exrx. of the estate of Larkin Landrum, decd.		July 1842	Amt. due $1021.51	1843
John Huie, Administrator of the estate of Isaac Hughes, deceased	T. M. Jones G. C. King Eli Edmondson	July, 1842		
Burket Rentfrow, Administrator of the estate of James Wilfs, deceased	R. Rentfrow	July 1844		
John Williams & Perthena Millsap, Adm. of Reuben Millsap, deceased				1852-1853 Dismissed 1856
Page 5 Harvey Pate, guardian of Willis A., minor child of Herod Pate			Amt. due $224.75	1845
Martha McLeroy, Administratix of John McLeroy, deceased	Eli Edmondson		Amt. due $690.05	
Jeptha Landrum, Adm. of Warren H. Cooper, deceased	John Huie			

271

Adm., Admx., Exor., Orphans, Deceased	Securities	Court Term	Cash Involved	Returns Made For
Rowland Stubbs, Adm. of the estate of Micheal I. Kener				1851-1852
P. H. Allen, Adm. of the estate of John Whaley	Jesse Ward		Over paid $2.30	1847
Page 6 Thomas Mathewes & Mary Mathewes, Adm. of the estate of Robert C. Mathewes, deceased		Appointed July, 1832		
Gainey, Joseph & James Westbrook, Adm. of Moses Westbrook, deceased		Appointed Nov. 1834		
Charles Clements, guardian of Howell, Sterling, Mary E. & Martha A., orphans of Sterling Elder		Appointed May 1835		Return for Martha 1846
Mary May, guardian of the orphans of Levy May		July 1836		
Josiah F. Reeves, guardian of the orphans of William P. Willson, deceased		July 1836	Amt. due $114.08½	1842
Page 7 Gay Upchurch & John M. Osburn, Executors of the estate of William Osburn, deceased	Jethro H. Barns John L. Dodd	Appointed May, 1838	Amt. due $366.31	1848
John Q. Alford & P. O. Beall, Administrators of A. R. Beall, deceased	Almen Stratten James F. Johnson	Nov. 1838	Amt. due $96.00	1847
Phillip Fitzgerald, guardian of the orphans of James Fitzgerald, deceased		March 1849		1852, 1853 1854
Elisha Hill, guardian of E. Hill's orphans and minors	Wm. L. Chambers			1847
Larkin Landrum & Samuel H. Elvin, Adm. of the estate of David Lay, deceased	Jeptha Landrum		Amt. due $715.63	1841

Adm., Admx., Exor., Orphans, Deceased	Securities	Court Term	Cash Involved	Returns Made For
Page 8 Charles Cheek & Phillip Fitzgerald, Adm. of the estate of Elisha Cheek, deceased		Jan. 1840	Amt. due $171.61	1842
Peterson Hubbard & Phillip Fitzgerald, Adm. of the estate of Henry Hubbard, Sr., deceased		Jan. 1840	Amt. due $166.91	1843
Alexander L. Huie, Adm. of the estate of Albert G. Hancock, deceased		March, 1847		1850-1851
William Watson, Adm. of the estate of Thomas Watson, deceased		March 1847	Amt. due 2 cents	1850
Ishmael Dunn & Martha W. Sellers, Adm. of John Sellers, deceased		Jan. 1847		1851-1853
Page 9 James H. Williams, Adm. of the estate of A. B. Williams, deceased		May 1852		1851-1854
Jesse Ward, guardian of Nancy, orphan of M. T. Bishop, deceased	Eli Edmundson Wm. Sparkman	Sept. 1847		1851, 1852 1854
James Graves, guardian of Amanda, orphan of M. T. Bishop, deceased		March 1838	Amt. due $56.04	1845
Rebecca Brogden, guardian of the orphans of John Brogden, deceased	Alfred Brown Blackmon Thorington	Jan. 1847		
James F. Johnson, Adm. Debonis of the estate of James Ryal, deceased	Jeptha Landrum	Jan. 1847		
Page 10 William N. Hill, guardian of Elizabeth, orphan of Pitt. W. Milner, deceased	Eli Edmondson J. V. May	May 1847		
William N. Hill, guardian of Susan, orphan of Pitt Milner, deceased	Eli Edmondson J. V. May	May 1847		1851-1853

273

Adm., Admx., Exor., Orphans, Deceased	Securities	Court Term	Cash Involved	Returns Made For
Thomas Mathewes, guardian for the orphans of A. B. Williams	John Westmoreland C. E. Westmoreland	Nov. 1847		1854
Jesse Jones, guardian for Harrison and Robert Jones	John McLean Wm. B. Jones	Nov. 1847		
James F. Johnson, Adm. Debonis, of the estate of Pitt W. Milner, deceased				1851-1853
Page 11 Charles Clements, Adm. of the estate of E. P. Nickson	Josiah R. Bosworth	Jan. 1849		
Wyatt L. Reeves, Adm. of D. A. Reeves	Thomas Henderson	Jan. 1848		1850
A. J. Mundy, Adm. of the estate of Kinchen Strickland, deceased	Jesse Ward Reuben Wallis	March 1848		1852
John L. Holliday, Adm. & Mildred Ward, Admx. on the estate of George Ward, decd.	Robert Holliday Eli Edmondson	July 1849		1851-1853
James Haines, Jr., Executor of the last will and testament of Jesse Lassiter, dec'd.		Nov. 1848		1852-1854
Page 12 Jeptha Landrum, Sr., Adm. of Edward Bearden, deceased	Thomas J. Head W. W. Bearden Walter J. Campbell Thomas E. Campbell	Nov. 1848		1851-1854
Calvin L. Westmoreland & Thomas C. Mathewes, Adm. of the estate of John Westmoreland, dec'd.	John A. Smith Jas. H. Westmoreland	Nov. 1848		1851
William H. Blalock, Adm. of Wyatt McGuirt, deceased.	Jesse L. Blalock	May 1849		
Lemuel M. Murphy, guardian of Martha A. E. Hayes, orphan of John A. Hayes, deceased	David Hanes	March 1849		1851-1854

Adm., Admx., Exor., Orphans, Deceased	Securities	Court Term	Cash Involved	Returns Made For
P. H. Brasell, guardian of Joseph H. Cavinder, orphan of Wade H. Cavinder, deceased	John C. Brasell	March 1849		1851-1854
Page 13 B. O. Jones, guardian of the orphans of Bryant Griggs	T. M. Jones	May 1849		Jane 1851 1852
Ishmael Dunn, guardian of Louisa Sellers, orphan of John Sellers, deceased	Chris. C. Bowen	May 1849		1850
James F. Johnson, Adm. of Rocella Vernon, decd.	John L. Holliday	July 1849		1851, 1852
James F. Johnson, Adm. Debonis, of the estate of Bryant Griggs, deceased	T. D. King Patrick Allen	July 1849		1851-1853
William P. Smith & Elizabeth Smith, Adm. of the estate of Isaiah Smith, deceased		July 1849		
Page 14 Sterling J. Elder, Adm. of the estate of Thomas R. Pearsons, deceased	Jesse L. Blalock Jas. F. Johnson Wm. H. Blalock	Sept.		1851-1854
William Jinnings, Adm. of Allen Jinnings, deceased with will annexed	Wm. Whatley Wm. Jinnings, Sr. A. M. Parker	Nov. 1849		1851-1852
Mark W. Westmoreland, guardian of S. J. Westmoreland, orphan of John Westmoreland, decd.	Thomas C. Mathewes	Nov. 1849		1851, 1852 Letters dismissory 1853
John W. Reeves, guardian of Mary Ann Reeves, orphan of Dempsey A. Reeves, deceased	Wm. Reeves	Nov. 1849		1851, 1852
John H. Williams, guardian of Thomas J. Williams (idiot) son of John H. Williams	James H. Williams	Nov. 1849		1853
Page 15 Kissiah Watterman, Adm. of Daniel L. Watterman, deceased	Reuben Wallis A. J. Mundy	March 1850		1853, 1854

Adm., Admx., Exor., Orphans, Deceased	Securities	Court Term	Cash Involved	Returns Made For
William W. Bearden, guardian of Vicey Bearden, orphan of Edward Bearden	Wm. Watson Jeptha Landrum, Sr.	March 1850		1851-1854
Wm. J. Russell, Adm. Debonis on the estate of Thomas Herring, deceased	Charles Clements	Jan. 1850		1851, 1852
Andrew McBride, guardian of Mary McLeroy, orphan of John McLeroy, deceased	Eli Edmondson	Nov., 1849		
Gideon F. Mann, guardian of the orphans of James Christian, deceased	Isaac M. Christian Harriett Christian	March 1850		1851-1854
Page 16 William J. Russell, Adm. Debonis on the estate of James Loyd, deceased	Wm. H. Blalock T. C. Mathewes Wm. N. Hill Charles Clements John Loyd Mitten Loyd	March 1850		1851-1852
William Sparkman, Adm. of Joseph Anthoney, deceased with will annexed	Rowland Hutcherson Funcey Hutcherson	March 1850		1850, 1854
John Murphey, Adm. of James Murphey, dec'd.	Andrew Murphey Elisha Hill Wm. N. Hill Thos. B. Gay	March 1850		1851
John C. Brasell, guardian of Martha M. Cavender, orphan of Wade H. Cavender, dec'd.	Jabez M. Brasell L. D. Padgett	Jan. 1850		1851, 1853
Jabez M. Brasell, guardian of John H. Cavender, orphan of Wade H. Cavender, dec'd.	John C. Brasell	Jan. 1850		1851-1853
Page 17 P. B. Cox, Adm. Debonis of Catharine Molder, deceased	Almen Stratten	May 1850		
Robert C. Porter, guardian of Andrew M. Henderson, orphan of Mitchal Henderson, dec'd.	Hugh Porter	May 1850		1851-1853

Adm., Admx., Exor.,.. Orphans, Deceased	Securities	Court Term	Cash Involved	Returns Made For
John Buse, Adm. of Wm. Buse, deceased	William Wiggins	May 1850		
Andrew J. Sweat, Adm. of James Hunter, dec'd.	Ephraim Sweat	May 1850		
Ishmael Dunn, guardian of Sarah Baily, a person deaf & dumb of age	C. C. Bowen	May 1850		
Page 18 Hiram Travis, guardian of Richard & Thomas Umphrey, orphans of William Umphrey, dec'd.	James Jones	May 1850		
John Loyd, guardian of Thomas E. & Sarah F. Loyd, orphans of James Loyd, deceased.	Sarah Loyd Mary Fernander James Loyd J. L. Jones	July 1850		1851-1854
R. Manson Stell, Adm. on the estate of James J. Stell, deceased	John D. Stell T. D. King	July 1850		1851, 1852
Rebecca Murphey & Joseph H. Murphey, Adm. with the will annexed on the estate of Simon P. Murphey, deceased	Thomas E. Murphey Jeptha M. Murphey Nathan Eason E. M. Murphey	July 1850		1851-1855
Jarell I. Whitaker, guardian of Jasper & Newton Loyd, orphans of James Loyd, deceased	John I. Whitaker Simon T. Whitaker	July 1850		1851-1854
Page 19 O. J. Head & David P. Elder, Administrators on the estate of William R. Head, deceased	Joshua Elder S. T. Whitaker	July 1850		1851-1854
John Shelnut, Adm. on the estate of Andrew Shelnut, deceased	John Ward	July 1850	Amt. due $445.63	1850
Alfred Dorman, Adm. on the estate of John Dorman, deceased	T. D. King	July 1850		1851-1854
A. W. Stone, Adm. Debonis, on the estate of Burrell Ware, late of Texas deceased	John L. Holliday	Nov. 1850		1851, 1852

Adm., Admx., Exor., Orphans, Deceased	Securities	Court Term	Cash Involved	Returns Made For
C. C. Bowen, Adm. of the estate of Pascheal E. Collins, deceased	John Bowen	Nov. 1850		1851-1853
Page 20				
Warren N. Glass, Adm. of Uriah Glass, dec'd.	Geo. M. Perry, Wiley W. Glass	Nov. 1850		
James Loyd, guardian of Samuel Loyd, orphan of James Loyd, deceased	John Loyd, William Whatley, Walter J.Campbell	Nov. 1850		1851-1854
William Jinnings, guardian of Elizabeth Jinnings, orphan of Allen Jinnings, dec'd.	Nathaniel Stinchcomb, Burrel A. Ware	Nov. 1850		1851-1853
Mildred Ware, guardian of Richard Ware & Ann Eliza Ware, orphans of George Ware, dec'd.	John L. Holliday, Burrel A. Ware	Nov. 1850		1851-1854
John L. Holliday, guardian of Emily H. Ware, orphan of George Ware, deceased	Robert K. Holliday	Nov. 1850		1851, 1852
Page 21				
Burrel A. Ware, guardian of James Ware & Catharine Ware, orphans of George Ware, dec'd.	John L. Holliday	Nov. 1850		1851-1854
Zadock Blalock, guardian of Barbary E. Avria & Mary Jane Avria	Isaac B. Avria	Nov. 1850		
Talten Holland, guardian of the heirs of Talten & Susan Holland	L. C. Smith	Nov. 1850		1852
James L. Hobgood, Adm. Debonis of Wright Martin, deceased	Nathan Camp, Lewis Hobgood	Jan. 1851		1851, 1853
Elijah Glass, Adm. of James Turner, dec'd.	John Murphey, Wm. N. Hill	Jan. 1851		1851-1854
Page 22				
Edmond Knoles, guardian of Benjamin F. Knoles, orphan of Benjamin E. Knoles	Eli Edmondson, A. McBride	Jan. 1851		

Adm., Admx., Exor., Orphans, Deceased	Securities	Court Term	Cash Involved	Returns Made For
Charles W. Wilerford, guardian of Wilson A. Wilerford, orphan of Wilson P. Wilerford, deceased	Daniel D. Denham	Jan. 1851		1851
Floyd Gamage, guardian of Thomas M. Gamage, orphan of Wm. Gamage, deceased	F. M. Nix	March 1851		
Allen Reeves, adm. of William Reeves, dec'd.	James H. Williams O. J. Head	May 1851		
Washington Wilson, guardian of Nancy & John Wilson, minors of said Washington Wilson	John L. Holliday	July 1851		1852
Page 23 James L. Hobgood, Adm. of Wright Martin, dec'd.		Sept. 1851		1853
Samuel H. Elenen, Adm. of Mack Smallwood, dec'd.	D. D. Denham Littleton Stokes Janot Handley	Sept. 1851		1852, 1853
Council Rentfrow, Adm. of John W. Pledger, dec'd.	Elijah Glass	May 1852		1852, 1853
Zadock Blalock, Adm. of Barbary McDanold, dec'd.	Wm. H. Blalock	May 1852		
Rowland Stubbs, Debonis on the estate of Wm. Stubbs, deceased	R. K. Holliday	May 1852		
Page 24 Parker Eason, guardian of William L. Milner, orphan of Pitt W. Milner, deceased.	William Brown	Jan. 1848		1851-1855
Martha C. Small, Admx. of the estate of Robert C. Small, deceased	John D. Stell Robert McCatchen	Jan. 1848		1849, 1852 1853
William N. Hill, Adm. of the estate of James A. Newton, deceased	Wm. J. Russell Wm. H. Blalock	June 1852		1853
William Malone, Adm. on the estate of William W. Bishop, late of Montgomery, State of Alabama, deceased.	C. L. Westmoreland	July 1852		

Adm., Admx., Exor., Orphans, Deceased	Securities	Court Term	Cash Involved	Returns Made For
Edmond Knoles, guardian of James M. Knoles, orphan of Benjamin E. Knoles, deceased	Wm. N. Hill	July 1852		
Page 25 William H. Blalock, guardian of Jefferson Bearden, orphan of Edward Bearden, dec'd.	Wm. J. Russell Z. Blalock	Aug. 1852		1853, 1854
William H. Blalock, guardian of Quiller Bearden, orphan of Edward Bearden, dec'd.	Wm. J. Russell Z. Blalock	Aug. 1852		1853, 1854
William H. Blalock, guardian of Larkin Bearden orphan of Edward Bearden, dec'd.	Wm. J. Russell Z. Blalock	Aug. 1852		1853, 1854
William H. Blalock, guardian of Pertheney Bearden, orphan of Edward Bearden, dec'd.	Wm. J. Russell Z. Blalock	Aug. 1852		1853, 1854
William H. Blalock, guardian of Sarah Ann Bearden, orphan of Edward Bearden, dec'd.	Wm. J. Russell Z. Blalock	Aug. 1852		1853, 1854
Page 26 William H. Blalock, guardian of Asa J. Bearden, orphan of Edward Bearden, dec'd.	Wm. J. Russell Z. Blalock	Aug. 1852		1853-1854
Drury B. May, Adm. of the estate of Hiram Moses, deceased.	Jeptha V. May	Oct. 1852		1852-1854
John B. Kenedy, Adm. of the estate of William W. Kenedy, deceased	George R. Kenedy William Z. Corine	Oct., 1852		1853
Jesse Hubbard, Adm. on the estate of Elbert Bishop, deceased	John O. Dickson	Nov. 1852		1852-1854
Perry Chandler & Wyatt Chandler, Executors of the last will & testament of Asa Chandler, deceased		Nov. 1852 Letters of Adm.		
Page 27 Willis Brasell, Executor of the last will and testament of James Brasell, dec'd.		Dec. 1852		1853, 1854

Adm., Admx., Exor., Orphans, Deceased	Securities	Court Term	Cash Involved	Returns Made For
Simon L. Whitaker & Dennis Stubbs, Adm. on the estate of Sarah Stubbs, deceased	Oliver J. Head John O. Dickson John D. Stell	Nov. 1851		1852-1854
Lorenzo D. Padgett, guardian of James T. Brassell, orphan of James Brassell, dec'd.	Alford Brown	Jan. 1853		1854
William Jinnings, guardian of Emily Turner, orphan of James Turner, dec'd.	James Jones	Jan. 1853		1853, 1854
Malinda Graves, Administratrix of David Graves, deceased	Minten Graves John Graves Hilby Cleckler Jesse Ward	Jan. 1853		1853, 1854
Page 28 Jasper Kinebrew & Benjamin H. Fortson, Executors of the last will & testament of Henry Kinebrew, deceased.		Feb. 1853		1854 Letters of dismissory 1854
Martha E. McLean, Executrix & Joseph M. McLean, Exor. of the last will & testament of John McLean, deceased		Appointed M. E. McLean Nov. 1850 J. M. McLean Feb. 1853		1853, 1854
Nicholas F. Powers, guardian of Thomas F. G. Powers	George Powers	March 1853		
Jesse Barintine, guardian of James Thompson, son of Allen Thompson	James F. Johnson	May 1853		
Marcelus k. McIntosh, guardian of Andrew J. McBride, & Lochland S. McBride, minors of William McBride	A. C. McIntosh	June 1853		
Page 29 Andrew J. Mundy & Reuben T. Mundy, Adm. on the estate of Jesse Lasseter, deceased	John O. Dickson Wm. J. Russell.	July 1853		1853, 1854

281

Adm., Admx., Exor., Orphans, Deceased	Securities	Court Term	Cash Involved	Returns Made For
Elijah Glass, guardian of Nathan Turner, orphan of James Turner, deceased		July 1852		1853
Elijah Glass, guardian of Sampsen Turner, orphan of James Turner, deceased		July 1852		1853
Elijah Glass, guardian of Zachariah Turner, orphan of James Turner, deceased		July, 1852		1853
Page 30 Elizabeth Graves, Executrix of the last will and testament of Charles Graves, dec'd.		Aug. 1853		1854
Robert C. Porter, Executor of the last will and testament of Mitchel Henderson, dec'd.				1851-1854
William N. Hill, guardian of Pitt W. Milner, orphan of Pitt W. Milner, dec'd.				1851-1853
William N. Hill, guardian of John H. Milner, orphan of Pitt W. Milner, dec'd.				1851
William N. Hill, guardian of James M. Milner, orphan of Pitt W. Milner, dec'd.				1851-1853
Page 31 Jeptha Landrum, Sr., Executor of the last will and testament of Holland Leopard, dec'd.				1851-1854
P. H. Allen, guardian of A. J. Hayes, orphan of Lewis Hayes, deceased				1851-1854
Wm. J. Russell, guardian of Marcus Herring, orphan of Thomas Herring, deceased				1851-1854
Wm. J. Russell, guardian of Francis Herring, orphan of Thomas Herring, deceased				1851-1854
Wm. J. Russell, guardian of Jonathan Herring, orphan of Thomas Herring, deceased				1851-1854

Adm., Admx., Exor., Orphans, Deceased	Securities	Court Term	Cash Involved	Returns Made For
Page 32 Elijah Cleckler, Executor of the last will and testament of Silas G. Eastin, dec'd.				1851-1853
Rowland Hutcherson, guardian of John D. Anthony				1852-1854
William J. Kimberly, Adm. of Isaac Kimberly, deceased	Charles E. Kimberly James M. Kimberly	Jan. 1849		1852
Abner Camp, Executor of the last will and testament of Morris Harris, deceased.				1852-1854
Wm. W. Mathewes, Executor of the last will and testament of Alexander Smith, dec'd.				1852
Page 33 Rowland Stubbs, Adm. of the estate of William Stubbs				1852
Mathew Jones, guardian of William Thompson	Wm. J. Russell			1854
Wm. B. Fuller, guardian of Mary Thompson and Martha Thompson	M. M. Tidwell John O. Dickson John L. Holliday			1854
Thomas B. Gay & Isaac T. Gay, Executors of Gilbert Gay				1853, 1854
Samuel Kisler, guardian of John H. Mathews	Allen Reeves			
Martha A. Reeves, guardian of Wm. F. Reeves				1854
Page 34 Martha A. Reeves, guardian of Henry C. Reeves				1854
Martha A. Reeves, guardian of Amos W. Reeves				1854
Martha A. Reeves, guardian of Robert H. Reeves				1854
Martha A. Reeves, guardian of Sarahan Reeves				1854

283

Adm., Admx., Exor., Orphans, Deceased	Securities	Court Term	Cash Involved	Returns Made For
Martha A. Reeves, guardian of Martha W. Reeves				1854
Page 35				
Wyatt L. Reeves, guardian of Letha Ann Reeves	Allen Reeves			
Wm. H. Flowers, Adm. of <u>Milas Scott</u>	E. M. Pool			
Sarah F. Jennings, Admx. of will of <u>John A. Jennings</u>		Dec. 1853		
Abner Camp, testamentary guardian of Matilda Allen Appraisers appointed Dec., 1853		Dec. 1853		
Andrew J. Mundy, Adm. of Francis M. Jones Temporary letters Dec. 1853, Permanent Letters Feb. 1854		Feb. 1854		1854
Page 37				
Hugh Porter, Adm. of <u>Samsen Roberts</u>	Eli Edmondson H. F. Underwood	Temp. letters Dec. 1853 Perm. letters Feb. 1854		1854
Martha Owens, guardian of Martha A. Owens	William Owens	Jan. 1854		1854
Martha Owens, guardian of Sarah E. Owens	William Owens	Jan. 1854		1854
Martha Owens, guardian of Matilda C. Owens	William Owens	Jan. 1854		1854
Martha Owens, guardian of Lucinda C. Owens	William Owens	Jan. 1854		1854
Martha Owens, guardian of Robert M. Owens	William Owens	Jan. 1854		1854
Page 38				
James W. Tally, guardian of Kindrick D. Little	Jordan Williams James L. Lovejoy	May 1854		
Sidney D. Mann, Adm. Debonis of Peter Mann	Reuben Wallis	May 1854		1854
Hugh Porter, guardian of Sarah T. Roberts	H. F. Underwood	May 1854		

Adm., Admx., Exor., Orphans, Deceased	Securities	Court Term	Cash Involved	Returns Made For
Hugh Porter, guardian of James L. Roberts	H. F. Underwood	May 1854		
Hugh Porter, guardian of Lewis E. H. G. Roberts	H. F. Underwood	May 1854		
Hugh Porter, guardian of Griffin A. Roberts	H. F. Underwood	May 1854		
Page 38				
Gideon F. Mann, Executor of Sarah Mann		Jan. 1854		1854
James Hanes, Jr., guardian of Elizabeth Lasseter	S. T. W. Miner	Feb. 1854		1854, 1855
James Hanes, Jr., guardian of Elisha Lasseter	S. T. W. Miner	Feb. 1854		1854, 1855
Hugh Porter, guardian of Mary A. P. Roberts	H. F. Underwood	Feb. 1854		
Hugh Porter, guardian of Wm. H. Roberts	H. F. Underwood	Feb. 1854		
Page 39				
Andrew McBride, Administrator of Samuel Martin	Edward Conner	March 1854		
Haywood Ozburn, Adm. of William K. Ozburn	Henry Rentfrow	March 1854		
Elizabeth Cook & Wm. N. Cook, Exec. of Harbord Cook		June 1854		1854
Mel M. Mathews, Adm. of Racheal Mathews	Samuel Kislin	June 1854		1854
John A. F. Hankins, guardian of Michael A. E. Collins	John T. Whitaker S. T. Whitaker	June 1854		
John A. F. Hankins, guardian of Romalus D. Collins	John T. Whitaker S. T. Whitaker	June 1854		
Page 40				
John A. F. Hankins, guardian of Emily C. Collins	John J. Whitaker S. T. Whitaker	June 1854		
John A. F. Hankins, guardian of James A. Collins	J. J. Whitaker S. T. Whitaker	June 1854		

Adm., Admx., Exor., Orphans, Deceased	Securities	Court Term	Cash Involved	Returns Made For
John A. F. Hankins, guardian of Pascheal Collins	J. J. Whitaker S. T. Whitaker	June 1854		
John A. F. Hankins, guardian of Martin Collins	J. J. Whitaker S. T. Whitaker	June 1854		
John A. F. Hankins, guardian of Elizabeth Collins	J. J. Whitaker S. T. Whitaker	June 1854		
Simon T. Whitaker, guardian of Francis A. E. Neal	John J. Whitaker O. J. Head	June 1854		
Page 41 Simon T. Whitaker, guardian of Amelia H. Neal	John J. Whitaker O. J. Head	June 1854		
Simon T. Whitaker, guardian of Benjamin F. Neal	John J. Whitaker O. J. Head	June 1854		
Simon T. Whitaker, guardian of Sarah Jane Neal	John J. Whitaker O. J. Head	June 1854		
Simon T. Whitaker, guardian of John Neal	J. J. Whitaker O. J. Head	June 1854		
Simon T. Whitaker, guardian of George Neal	J. J. Whitaker O. J. Head	June 1854		
Simon T. Whitaker, guardian of Pocahontas Neal	J. J. Whitaker O. J. Head	June 1854		
Simon T. Whitaker, guardian of James Neal	J. J. Whitaker O. J. Head	June 1854		
Page 42 Andrew McBride, guardian for M. L. Carrol				1853
M. P. Devaughan, Executor of Henry McLeroy	W. P. Allen P. H. Allen Wm. E. Tucker	Feb. 1855		1853, 1854

286

Adm., Admx., Exor., Orphans, Deceased	Securities	Court Term	Cash Involved	Return Made For
John J. Whitaker, Adm. of Elbert Harris	S. T. Whitaker	Sept. 1854		1854
William E. Tucker, Adm. of Joshua S. Calloway	W. P. Allen	Dec. 1854		1854
Mary Waldrup, Executrix of Thomas D. Waldrup	Winslow G. Norton Miles Norton	March 1855		
James McConnell, Adm. of Emily McLeroy	M. B. Devaughan Elijah Glass	March 1855		
Page 43 Wm. N. Hill, Adm. of Saphrona Hill	J. P. Allen	April 1855		
James Hanes, guardian of Sopha Lasseter	Jas. F. Johnson	April 1855		
Jesse Barantine, Adm. of Sarah E. Barantine	Wm. H. Blalock	March 1855		
Newton M. Fitts, Adm. of Walker Fitts				1854
George J. Miles, Adm. of Theora F. Miles	Wm. Miles			1854
Page 44 Phillip H. Brasell, guardian of John H. Cavender				
James Hanes, guardian of Lofton Lasseter				

287

Askew, Wm. H.
Alford, J. Q. A.
Allen, Robert
+Alexander, M. A.
  (John G. Hill, Trustee)
Askew, Joseph B.
Allen, J. Y.
Alexander, James L.
+Alexander (Mrs.) (James L.
  Alex., Agent for)
Alexander, L. P.
Aycock, William
Alexander, Adam
Alford, A.
Alexander, George

Bennett, J. A. K.
Block, Elias
Beck, Lewis
+Beck, Dobbins & Co.
+Beck, Dobbins & Claude
Baird, Wm. D.
Bullard, R. W.
Baker, Richmond
Bullard, John K.
Beall, P. O.
Burtody, Thomas
Bowdin, M. A.
Bellamy, A.
Bloodworth, Wiley
Booth, Robert
Beall, Wm.
Buntyn, Joseph
Bloodworth, S. W.
Beeks, James A.
Beeks, John C.
+Mrs. Beeks (John C. Beeks,
  Agent for)
+Beeks, John C. (Trustee for
  above)
Bunlyn, James
Hunter & Beeks
Brever, L. R.
Bloodworth, D. M.
Brown, David
Buster, James
Blankenship, ?
Baker, Henry

+City Hall (Stephen
  Williams, Trustee for)
Carter, Willis M.
Cummins, Francis
Cherry, L. S.
Beck, Dobbins & Claude
Cline, Wm. M.
+Chapman, W. W. (John G.
  Hill, Agent for)
Cline, William
Cohson, Felix G.
Chambers, Wm. H.
Chambers, Wm. B.
Coker, Garlington

Cox, P. B.
+Cox, R. R. (P. B. Cox,
  Agent for)
+Cox, P. B. (Agent for Wm. Herring)
Carpenter, Henry
Cox, G. H.
Corbin, James W.
Crenshaw, John S.
Colbert, A. G.
Carpenter, Alfred
Consdon, C.
Consdon, Daniel
Clark, Geo. W.
Clark, Jefferson (Geo. W.
  Clark, Agent for)
Clark, Geo. W. (Agent for
  Jefferson Clark)
Claude, Aaron
Chambers, Thomas
Coker, Henry
Caldwell, O. H. P.
Crowley, Gineshan
Crow, John W.
Coppedge, John W.
Cherry, Samuel
Coker, Harvey
Conner, T. (Estate of)
Crenshaw, David
Callaway, J. M.
Crenshaw, Cornelius (This
  name struck)
Beck, Dobbins & Claude
C. Day & Co.

Doe, Benjamin W.
+Dyer, Thos. H.
Dyer, Easter (James Hilsman,
Beck, Dobbin & Co.   Gdn. for)
Beck, Dobbin & Claude
Deone, Henry L.
+C. Day & Company (C. Lewis
  Jointly Interested)
Dugan, George
Dulin, A. B.
Dickens, Fred
Dobbins, M. G.
Durham, Ruffin
Dobbins, Com.

*Limerick & Eady (colored)
  (C. W. Wright, Gdn. for)
Espy, James W.
Eason, Parker

Faulkner, Thos.
Fox, Samuel D.
Foster, Edward G.
Fleming, William

Gray, A.
+Gray, A. - (Gdn. for Barbory
  & Lewis)
Gray, Schulman & Schulman

288

Goulding, A. A.
Green, Berry
Griffin, John W.
Gilbert, Thos.

Hilsman, James
+Hilsman, James (Gdn. for
  Easter & Thos. Dyer)
Howland, Merrit & Co.
Woodruff & Hughey
Hughey, W. W.
Holland, Moses
Hatton, Lewis
Hatton, E.
Holliday, Henry B.
*Hill, John G.
  1st. Emily Lake
  2nd. Eliz (Manson) Beck
    (Widow of Lewis Beck)
Hill, John. G. & Co.
  "   "   " (Guardian)
+"   "   " (Trustee for M. A.
  Alexander)
  "   "   " (Agent for W. W.
  Chapman)
  "   "   " (Agent for M. R.
  Reese)
+ "   "   " (Agent for
  Martin & Reese)
Huson, Amelia
Hicks, Thomas E.
Hicks, Thomas E. (Trustee)
Huff, Whitfield
Huff, Francis M.
Herronton, Wm. S.
Huson, Francis A.
Herring, William (P. B.
  Cox, Agent for)
Hollingsworth, Joe
Hollingsworth, Levi
Haywood, Wiley M.
Haywood, George
Holland, E. L.
Hunter & Beeks
Harbum, (?) Macon, Ga.
Hatton, A. H.
Harris, Thos.

Ison, Francis M.
Ison, John

Jones, John W.
Johnson, David
Johnson, Thomas J.
+Johnson, Jones & Peck
Jones, James S.
Johnson, Joseph W.
Johnson, Tandy
Johnson, George
Jones, Stephen
James, Spruill

Kennedy, A.
Kennedy, A. (Agent)

Lanier, Robert
Lanier, Sampson

Lewis, C. (Jointly interested
  in C. Day & Co.)
Lewis, C. (Trustee for
  Jane Lewis)
  "   " , Jane (C. Lewis
    Trustee for)
Lovinggood, John
Leak, William (often times
  pronounced Lake)
Leake, William
Leak, Wesley
Leak, Rufus
Lowe, John
Legg, Thomas
Legg, John
Long, James S.
Lindsey, William
Lewis, J. T.

Howland, Merrit & Co.
Merritt, Augustus
+Martin, Reese, John G. Hill
  (Agent for)
Martin, J. R.
Martin & Company
McDonald, John
McAllister
Mason, John
Mason, Richard
Mann, R. F. W.
Moore, Wm. F. (son of Matthew
  Moore, b. 1790 in Va. died
  1852 Jones Co., Ga.)

Nall, A. M.
Neely, A. J.

Oglesby, Joseph L.
Orr, Simeon
Oglesby, G.
Oglesby, Wm.
Osburn, C. H.
Oglesby, Thos. H.
Orr, Matthew
Oglesby, S. H.

Porter, A. A.
Porter, Hugh
Johnson, Jones & Peck
Pegg, Wm. H.
Presley, E.
Peck, Jonathon M.
Polhill, L. T.
Powell, John
Powell, Mrs.
Pace, Solomon (Wiley Rogers
  Agent for)
Perry, Wm.
Perry, Amos

Rosier, Mrs.
Reese, M. R.
Roberts, B. F.
Rope, Henry
Rogers, Wiley
+Rogers, Wiley (Agent for John S.
  Travis)

+Reese, M. R. (John G. Hill,
   Agent)

Shulman
   or   Barbary & Lewis
Schulman (A. Gray Gdn. for)
Springer, James M.
Scott, John
Scott, John (Trustee for
   R. A. Scott)
Scott, R. A. (John Scott,
   Trustee for)
Surry, Jordan S.
Sargent, J. B.
Sargent, J. B. & Co.
Sargent, H. J.
Stough, Robt. W.
Spruill, John
Shivers, J. H.
Shackelford, John
Spear, Henry
Stewart, John
Stewart, David
Settle, John M.
Salmond, L. S. (often times
   written Salmon, Salmons and
   Sammons)
*Starr, Benjamin (Married
   Charlotte Pinkston 1807
   Wilkes Co., Ga.)
Shackleford, J. B.
Smith, C. H.

Thweatt, John L.
Terry, Samuel
Tedd, Henry
Trice, Ezekiel
Turner, Chas.
Threlkeld, J.
Terry, John C.
Terry, Robt. W.
+Travis, John S. (Wiley
   Rogers Agent for)
Trommell, John

Williams, Stephen (Trustee for
   City Hall)
Williams, Stephen
Woodruff, W. W.
Wright, C. W. C.
Wright, C. W. C. (Trustee)
+Wright, C. W. C. (Guardian for
   Lemerick & Eady) Colored
Wright, Franklin
Worde, James M.
Westmoreland, M.
Westmoreland, W.
Wood, James S.
Waters, Thos. M.
Williams, Joseph B.
Williams, John
Wooten, Seaborn L.
Wooten, A. A.
Wooten, A. A. & Co.

Worthy, Colonel
Woodruff, John
Weems, S. A.
Whittle, L. N.
Wilson, John W.
Whitehead, Elijah

Youngblood, John L.

290

TAX RETURNS FOR 1846

CITY OF GRIFFIN, PIKE COUNTY, GEORGIA

Alexander, George
Aycock, Wm.
Alexander, L. P.
Alexander, Jas. L. (Agent
  for Mrs. M. Alexander)
Allen, Robt.
Alexander, Adam
Askew, Wm. H.
Askew, Joseph B.
Allen, J. Y.

Bledsoe, Lemuel
Butler, James
+Beck, Dobbins & Co.
Beasley, John
*Burr, Jason (Trustee for
  Nancy J. Burr b. in
  Morgan Co., Ga.
Burr, Jason (Agent for
  H. L. Jewitt)
Banks, Henry
Bloodworth, S. W.
Bloodworth, W. B.
Baird, Wm. B. (Name
  drawn thru)
Bunting, James E. (Natural
  Gdn.)
Brewer, Osbon
Booth, Tobert
Bellamy, A.
+Hunter, Beeks
+Beeks, John C. (Trustee)
+Beeks, John C. (Agent for
  Mrs. S. Beeks)
+Beeks, John C. (Agent for
  L. N. Whittle)
Bertody, Thomas
Beall, Dr. Wm. E.
Beeks, James A.
Bloodworth, D. M.
Buntyn, Joseph (Name
  struck thru)
Brown, David
Block, Elias
Brewer, L. R.
Bass, Wm.
Bass, James O.
Bass, John C.
Bowdin, M. A.
Benton, B. E.
Black, Jas.
Bullard, R. B.

Cummins, F. D.
Cox, John M.
Calloway, J. M.
Cherry, Samuel
Cherry, L. S.
Curtis, S. W.
Curtis, A.
Cline, Wm.
Crozier, John

Corbin, J. W.
+Clark, Geo. W. (Agent for
  Jefferson Clark)
Clark, Jefferson (Geo. W. Clark
  Agent for)
Crenshaw, John S.
Coker, Henry
Coker, Harvey
Carpenter, Alford
Carpenter, Henry
Crawley, Ginethan
Gordon, Daniel (Name struck)
+City Hall (Stephen Williams
  Trustee)
Conner, T. (Estate of)
Cox, P. B. (Agent for R. R. Cox)
Cox, R. R. (P. B. Cox, Agent for)
+Cox, P. B. (Agent for Wm. Herring)
Colbert, A. T.
Condon, Caleb
Cline, Wm. M.
Coker, Garlington
Coppedge, J. W.
+Caldwell, Dr. J. J. (Dr. James S.
  Long Agent.)
+Collier, C. C. (C. Lewis
  Agent for)
Cohson, Felix G.
Crenshaw, David
Cox, G. H. (Agent P. B. Cox)
Cox, P. B. (Agent for H. Cox)

Dobbins, M. G.
Beck, Dobbins & Co.
Doe, Benj. W.
Dyer, Thos. H.
Dulin, A. B.
+C. Day & Co. (C. Lewis Jointly int.)
Dobbins, Wm.
Deane, Henry L.
Dugan, George
Daniel E. P. (Stephen Williams,
  Agent)
Douglas, H.
Durham, Ruffin

Ellis, Jas. T.
+Easter, (Jas. Hiesman, Gdn.)
Eason, P.
Espy, Jas. W.

Futral, Richard
+Neely, Fleming & Co.
Fleming, Wm.
Foster, E. G.
Freeman, Wm.
Ferrill, B. W.

Goulding, A. A.
+Shannon & Goulding
Gray, A. (Agent)

291

Hilsman, Jas. (Gdn. for
   Easter)
Hatton, Lewis
Hatton, E.
Hatton, A. H.
Herronten, Wm. S.
*Hill, John G.
John G. Hill & Co. (Agent
   for Martin & Reese)
Holland, M.
Hollingsworth, Levi
Howard, Daniel
Huff, Whitfield
Huff, Francis M.
Humphrey, C. A. (Struck
   thru)
Harbum, Mr. (Macon)
Hollingsworth, Joseph
Holliday, H. B.
+Herring, Wm. (P. B. Cox,
   Agent for)

Ison, F. M.
Ingram, Benj.
Ison, John

Johnson, N. B.
Johnson, D. H.
Jones, John W.
+Johnson, Jones & Peck
Johnson, Joseph W.
Johnson, Thomas W.
Jones, Jas. S.
Johnson, Thos. J.

Kennedy, A.
Knight, Lloyd

Latimer, Robt.
Leak, Wesley
Lawson, P. A.
Low, A. J.
+Lewis, C. (Jointly Int.
   with C. Day & Co.)
Lewis, C. (Trustee for
   Jane Lewis)
Lewis, Jane (C. Lewis
   Trustee for)
Lewis, J. T.
Leak, Wm. M.
Ligon, Woodson M.
Lake, John
Lovingood, John
Lanier, Robt. S.
+Long, Dr. James S. (Agent
   for Dr. J. J. Caldwell)

Miller, John M.
Murray, A. G.
Martin, J. R.
Merritt, A.
McLendon, J. P.
McDonald, John
Moore, Major Henry
Milburn, D.
Moore, Wm. F.
McAllister, H. S.

+Martin & Reese (John G.
   Hill & Co.)

*Nall, A. M.
+Neely, Fleming & Co.
Neely, H. I.

Orr, Matthew
Ogilby, G. L.
Orr, Simeon
Ogilby, Mrs. Martha
Ogilby, Wm. E.
Oglesby, T. J.

Piper, A. M.
Piper, Jas. A.
Peck, J. M.
+Pace, Solomon (Wiley Rogers
   agent for)
Pearce, Wm. R.
Perry, Amos
Perry, Wm. J.
Pritchard, S. C.
Parsons, J. M.
Polhill, F. T.
Presley, E.
Porter, Hugh
Porter, A. A.
Pope, Wm. M.
+Johnson, Jones & Peck

Rope, Henry
Richardson, Jas.
Ready, Jackson
+Sargent, Richardson & Co.
+Martin & Reese (John G. Hill
   & Co. Agent for)
+Rogers, Wiley (Agent for
   Solomon Pace)

Sargent, H. J.
Sharp, H. T.
+Shannon & Goulding
Shin, B.
Sargent, J. B.
Spruill, James
Settle, John M.
+Sims & Threlkeld
Sims, Richard H.
*Starr, Benj.
Schackleford, Jas. B.
Stern, D. G. & Brothers
Shulman, Lewis
Scott, R. A. J. (John Scott,
   Trustee for)
Smith, C. H.
*Salmond, L. S.
+Spear, Mrs. J. (John T.
   Thweatt, Agent for)
Stough, Robt. W.
Shannon, Evann
Stewart, David
Spruill, John
+Sargent, Richardson & Co.
Shannon, P.

Thweatt, John T. (Agent for
   Mrs. J. Spear)

Terry, Samuel
Travis, John S.
Tidd, H. J.
Terry, Robt. W.
Threlkeld, T. J.
+Sims & Threlkeld
Trice, E. (Agent for
  T. Trice)
Thompson, John

Underwood, M. (Dr. Jas.
  S. Long, Agent for)

Varner, Henly

Weems, S. R.
Whittle, L. N.
Williams, John
White, Wm. H.
White, G. W.
Wilson, John W.
Westmoreland, C. S.
Westmoreland, M.
Woodruff, W. W.
Word, Jas. M.
Williams, Jas. B.
Wright, C. W. C. (Trustee
  for J. Franklin Wright)
Westmoreland, W.
Wood, Jas. S.
+Whittle, L. N. (John C.
  Beeks, Agent for)
Wagner, George
White, Henry M.
Whitehead, Elijah
Worthy, Col. L.
+Williams, Stephen (Trustee
  for City Hall)
+Williams, Stephen (Agent for
  E. P. David)

Yoleson, M. B. (Struck thru)
  added explanation Going out
  of (Corporation?)
Youngblood, John L.

INDEX

Prepared by
Flora C. Hendricks Curd
ElPaso, Texas
1978

Brinson,Jason 187
Brirson,John 249
Britain,
  George 30,103
  Henry 207
  Susan 112
Britt,
  Baldy 192
  David J. 149
  Edward 149
  Thomas 131
Britten,
  John 50
  Mahoney H. 122
  Marion F. 122
  Sarah J. 136
Brittenham,Narcissa 21
Brittingham,Elisha 180,255
Britton,
  Emanuel 108
  George 31,77,81
  Henry 114,119
  James 112,141
  John 76
  Lucy Ann 114
  Martha Jane 129
  Mary 76,119,123
  Sandford 76
Brocher,Wilser 74
Brock,
  Christopher 149
  Jonas(?) 171
  William 151
Brockman,George M.T. 60,69
Broddas,Thomas 74
Broddus, E.A. 199
Brodnux,R.E. 230
Brogdon,
  David 58
  John 273
  Peterson G. 107
  P.G. 90
  Rebecca 273
Brokton,Gideon H. 186
Bronson,T. 37
Brookes,Simon 249
Brooking,Isaac 73
Brookins,Benjamin 154
Brookling,S.L. 128
Brookman,M.T. 55
Brooks,
  A. 30,196
  Aaron 99,197,198,199
  C. 158
  Charity 110
  Charles 56
  Elisha 100,190
  Eliza H. 221
  George 221
  Hannah R. 123
  Hellery 208
  Hillary 129
  Holbry 208
  John 182,203,238
  Joseph 83
  Martha E. 132
  Maxey 245
  Micajah 193
  Moses 175,198
  Nancy P. 123
  Samuel 95
  Sarah L.J. 120
  Thomas 198
  William 35,40,41
Broughan,James 118
Broughton,Mary Ann 111
Brown,
  A. 99
  Abel 173
  Alfred 273
  Alford 281
  Allen W. 232
  Anderson 90,92

Brown(con't)
  Andred M. 188
  Andrew 169,170,191,195,
    196,259
  Asa 221
  A.W. 75
  Ben A. 75
  Benjamin 88,221,235
  Bill 144
  Bolin 68
  Cherry 76
  Clover P. 220
  Christopher 179
  David 190
  Daniel 157
  E.G. 195
  Eliphalet E. 11
  Elizabeth 108,265
  Elonza D. 220
  Fanny Moss 212
  George 198
  Glenn 133
  Henry 19,76,138,236
  Hezekiah 238
  Hugh 192
  Isaac 74,76,85,99,100,
    196,197,264
  Jemmie 143
  John 47,83,90,91,108,
    184,253,254
  Josiah 221
  Lucinda 107
  Malinda 133
  Margaret 109
  Mariah 143
  Martha 32,76,221
  Martin H. 2
  Mary 20,22,220
  Milton 145
  Morgan 169,178,254
  Nancy 19,23,107,124
  Nancy Welsher 211
  Nathan 241
  Noah 143
  Patsey H. 219
  R. 36,42,43
  Richanry 109
  Richmond 32
  R.L. 131
  Robert 30,36,42,47,48,
    50,59,72,77,81,104,
    244,248
  Rowland 197
  S. 149
  Sarah 218
  Sarah Ann 20
  Samuel 78,203
  Simon 142
  Susan 122
  Thomas 159,200
  Tilman 209
  Uriah 162
  William 105,109,119,
    182,248,255,279
  W.T. 125
  W.W. 179
  Wyatt 203
Brownholn,W. 151,174
Browning,Robert M. 260
Brownlee,
  Amanda R. 143
  App 143
  Catherine 126
  Elizabeth 131,141
  George 127
  James 55,128
  Jane 121
  Lou 145
Bruce,Martha 22
Brumbelow,
  Lavinia 28
  Tabitha 22
Brumblow,Wm. 233

Brunah,Eli 164
Brunnet,Mary M. 28
Bryan,
  Alexander 196,198,200,
    204,206,259
  Alsa B. 119
  David 259
  Elizabeth 82
  George H. 101
  G.H. 101
  Jacob 172
  James 124,196
  Jesse 176
  John 176,240
  Royal 182
  Samuel J. 82,120,168,
    172,182,205,206,220,
    228
  Solomon 206
  William 251
Bryans,Samuel L. 80
Bryant,
  Archibald 78,98,104
  Bohling 104
  Bolin 98,104
  Isaac 175
  James 80
  Jaret 34
  Jesse 182
  John 175
  Malinda 119
  Martha 134
  Mary 80,166
  R.R. 39,40,41
  Samuel 81,234
  Willis 201
  William 186
Buchannon,R.H.L. 232,235
Buck,
  Hannah 172
  Joseph 74
  Nancy 172
Buckanan,
  Charles G.J. 122
  John 66.67
  Joseph 74
  Margaret 223
  Silas B. 77
  Thomas E. 109
Buckehanon,John 211
Buckhannon,W.B. 181
Buckhanon,Elizabeth 211
Buckhalter,
  Isham R. 164
  Jer. 164
Buckerstaff,Robert 239
Buckner,
  Freeland 170
  Eli 49
  Emily 139
  Martha M. 119
  Wiley 256
Buffington,John J. 141
Buford,
  Frank 144
  G.P. 59,61
  Judith 123
  Samuel P. 39,60
  T.B. 51
  Thomas B. 47
Bugg,E. 45
Bull,John 76
Bullar,
  Bullard,James 66
  James 66
  John 47,102,127
Bullock,
  Charles 231
  Eleanor 24
  Eliza 14
  Elizabeth 209
  James 59,209
  Mary A. 23

Davis(con't)
  Jonathan W. 154
  Joseph 234,235
  Kathern 267
  Lucinda 266
  Maj. 5
  Maria 23
  Mariah 267
  Martha 111
  Mary 107
  Matilda 264
  Miles 73
  Moses 229
  N. 253
  Nancy 114
  Nehemiah 176
  Purmelia B. 116
  Rachel 266
  Rebecca 12
  Richard 165,169
  Richard W. 230
  Rutha 218
  Sarah 266
  Telitha G. 116
  Thomas 179
  Thomas N. 138
  William 115,159,191,209,
    230
  William C. 220
  William E. 165
  William H. 55
  William J. 165
  Willis 92
  Wilson L. 225
  Zachariah 192
  Zadock 264,265,266,269
Dawkins,
  George 71
  Thomas J. 126
Dawson,
  Henry T. 38
  H.T. 38
  John 62,109
  Joseph 69
  Simon 139
  W.C. 42,43
  William C. 190
Dawns,Shelby 83
Day,
  Agnes 218
  Joseph 55
  Stephen 223
Dearing,
  Abner F. 214
  H.G. 139
  Lucy Ann 119
  Sara 130
Deas,John 60
Dean,John 236
Deason,
  Ambrose 97
  Benjamin 97,110
  Coker 39
  John 108
  Margaret 143
  Martha J. 129
  Mary A. 128
  Mathilda 121
  Nancy Jane 125
  Zachariah 89,97
Debingport,John 184,185
Deck,Obediah 172
Dees,
  James 254
  John 53
  Martha 23
DeDeen,Frederick 182
Deen,Frederick 182
Deets,John J. 182
Delamar,Joanne 113
Delemar,Amanda 115
Delemer,James C. 117
Dellon,John 138

Delmar,
  Elizabeth 110
  Sally 123
Dempsey,Harry W. 118
Deneaux,Lydia 114
Denham,
  Daniel D. 270,278
  Elizabeth W. 218
  Martha 218
  Mary Elizabeth 218
Denmark,James 161
Denning,
  Nathaniel 56
  William 56
Dennis,
  Abbey 24
  D. 204,248
  E.C. 56,60,64
  Elizabeth C. 58,63
  Elizabeth Charlott 55,56
  J.F. 134
  John 55,56,58,60,63,95,
    122
  Johnson 95
  Peter 55,63,64
  Richard G. 123
  William 55,60,63,134
Denson,Mary 266,267
Dent,
  M.S. 78,98
  Nancy 102
  Thomas 149
Derden,B.H. 46
Derdin,Frances 120
Derham,
  Isaiah 264
  Julian 268
  Nancy 266
Derrick,John 257
Deshazo,William 40
Desmatta,J.Jr. 197
Detwyler,Martin 93
DeVaughn,Patrick 271
Devaughn,M.B. 287
Devaughan,M.P. 286
Dewsberry,Sally C. 265
Dewitt,Ann M.C. 23
Diamond,Janus 227
Dick,
  James 186
  William L. 121
  William M. 140
Die,James 110
Dicken,
  Hampton T. 114
  James 162
  John 110
  Marion M. 118
  N.D. 161
  Patsy 144
Dickerson,
  Abe 146
  C.M. 141
  Frances 142
  Martha 122
  R.L. 180
  Sarah 134
  Wiley R. 127
  William B. 68
  William T. 127
Dickins,
  Robert 253
  Sally 253
Dickinson,Eliza 123
Dickson,
  Anna 3
  Benjamin 3
  Claricia 28
  Elizabeth 3
  Emma W. 131
  John O. 280,281,283
  Josiah 3
  Martha A. 267

Dickson(con't)
  Mary 23
  Michael 153
  Moses 160
  Nancy C. 268
  Robert 3
  Sarah 25
  Thomas 3
  William 6
  William H. 265,267
Dill,
  An.J. 240
  Andrew J. 240
  Daniel 240
Dillard,
  Elizabeth 23
  Fielding 48
  John 248
  Joseph B. 36
  Martha 36
  Nancy 26
  Phoeba 23
  Rhoda 21,23
  Theophilus 168
Dillon,
  Catherine R. 126
  J. 163
  John 149,152,163
  Mary A. 122
  Sarah M. 120
Dimick,John 186
Dinick,Andrew 206
Dinger,John 70
Disanbleaux,Penelope B.
    255
Dismukes,James 170
Dixon,
  Abe 145
  Barnes W. 219
  Bryant 229
  Jeremiah 154
Dobb,Edward 229
Dobbs,Jess 246
Dobbins,
  B. 157,187,242
  Bryson 257
Dobson,Amanda 221
Doby,Silas 131
Dodd,
  Isabella 120
  John L. 272
  Julia 114
  Julia (Mrs.) 141
  Marcella 121
Dodds,John F. 255
Dodson,
  Charles 122,126,130
  E. 162,181,240,257
  Elijah D. 265,267,268
  James 124
  J.W. 257
  Martha 131
  Nancy 266
  Mary J. 131
Dogget,
  Levicia 126
  Mary 126
Doles,Sarah 23
Dolley,Thomas 164
Dolson,Margaret C. 213
Donalson,John W. 176
Donaldson,
  Lavinia 118
  Mary N. 112
Donavin, Serena 266
Donelson,William H. 118
Doolittle,Abram 206
Dooly,Thomas 229
Dooley,William 165,244,
    257
Doomis,Jennie 146
Dopson,Caty Ann 6
Dorman,

Harkness(con't)
  Partianah 135
  Queen 145
  R.N. 103
  Robert V. 59
  R.W. 37,39,40,44,89,105
  Robert 39,46
  Robert W. 41,47,72,96,
    100
  Rosannah 126,193
  Sallie J. 135
  Sarah E. 132
  Simon 144
  Thomas M. 115,126
  William 53,264
  W.William S.B. 112
  Zachariah T. 129
Harleson,Benjamin 89
Harman,
  Elizabeth 216
  Fletcher 216
  Jacob 212,216
  James 216
  John 216
  Lewis M. 216
  Nancy Caroline 216
  Thomas S. 216
  Wesley 216
Harmon,
  Anny 216
  George W. 257
  Joseph 50,71,110
  Sherwood B. 112
  William 37,138
Hermedge,Jacob 241
Harold,Thomas 163
Harp,
  Cullin 195
  Samuel 109
Harpe,Cullen 197
Harper,
  Benjamin L. 116
  Edward 222
  Elizabeth 21
  Elizabeth D. 109
  Elizabeth F. 122
  George 251
  H.G. 200
  Henry A. 165,222
  John 83,102
  John A.H. 224
  John J. 228
  M.C. 181
  Margarett Ann 222
  Nuel.M. 222
  Reuben J. 116
  Rhoderick 174,191
  Rhody 222
  Richard 55,91
  Richard M. 134
  Robert G. 225
  Roderick 158
  Sarah 107
  Sarah Ann 222
  Shadrack 152,237
  Thomas 174,191
  Wilkins 99
  William 31,34,40,42,46,
    47,48,49,50,51,57,64,
    65,68,69,99,100,107,
    112,114
  William H. 65
Harralld,Henry 181
Harrel,
  Green Berry 6
  Hardy 6
  James H. 6
  James Jardy 6
Harrell,
  Dotson 169
  Jethro 166,187
  John 6
  Joseph 187
  Pamella 266

Harrell(con't)
  William E. 6
Harrigan,Mabry 250
Harris,
  B.F. 140
  David 212,213
  Eleanor 20
  Eli 240
  Eliza T. 264
  Elizabeth 24,25,140
  Elizabeth Gober 212
  Ellen H. 4
  Elvay 131
  Gabriel 158
  Gideon 230
  Hannah 213
  Henry 58
  Hiram E.C. 150
  J.N. 131
  John 47,219,224,248
  Joshua 203
  Laird W. 158,240
  Lanford 213
  Lard H. 190
  M.J. 130
  Mary H. 119
  Matilda W. 264,268
  Morris 283
  Moses 260
  Sally 109
  Seaborn J. 122
  Silas 150
  Thomas 105,115
  Thomas M. 248
  Thomas W. 203
  Tyre 213
  Wiley 138
  William 41,247,251
  Young.R. 58,59,70
Harrington,
  Caroline 122
  Charles 155
  Drewry 151
  Eliza 7
  Mahala 264
Harrison,
  Ann 60
  Benjamin 34,92,102
  E.W. 173
  Eli W. 166,210
  Elizabeth 121
  James 60,65,109
  James W. 5
  Jane 112
  Mary 113,269
  Mary Ann 133
  Margaret 117
  Nathaniel 80
  Rachel Ann 65,114
  Reuben 161
  W. 45
  William 45,65,87,97

Harrold,Hardy 174
Harry,
  John 162
  William 187
Hart,
  Elizie 144
  Mary Berry 211
  Thomas 160
  Thomas W. 190
  Warren 55
Harvey,
  Eliza 3
  H.H. 136
  Isaac 3
  Leroy 258
  Martha 3
  Penelope 269
  Sarah Napier 7
  Tabitha N. 20
Harvie,Isabel 82
Hartiman,John G. 14

Hartsfield,
  Andrew 163
  Clarkey 221
  Elizabeth 118
  Frances E. 125
  G.M. 70
  Isaac J. 221
  Lizzie 141
  Mary 109
  Middleton 231,258
  Mrs. 38,41
  Susan 129
  William 31
  William T. 107
Harwick,Hulda A. 145
Harwell,
  Amelia 221
  Dottson 182
  Jackson 211
  Patsey 219
  Richard 211
  Vines 232
Hasbury,William 209
Haspit,Macajah 251
Hassel,Josiah 251
Hasting,Benjamin 257
Hastings,Elizabeth 267
Hasty,
  Obediah 40
  Obediah A. 108
  Thomas P. 109
Haswell,John 235
Hatcher,
  Bethany 85
  Daniel 197,198
  Hetty 24
  James 185
  John 185,197,198
  Kitty 24
  Mastin 247
  Wilmouth 24
Hately,
  F. 46,47
  H. 36,40,46,51,59,66,
  Frances 43
  Henry 36,37,38,39,41,44,
    46,47,59,62,69
  Sarah 116
Hathorn,William 250
Hattaway,Elisha 253
Hatten,William 255
Hatton,Jno. 40
Haughton,William M.S. 204
Hawthron,Elias O. 251
Hay,
  John 197
  Mary Ann 128
  Sarah A. 130
  Washington 65
Hayes,
  A.J. 282
  John A. 274
  John R. 8
  Lewis 282
  Martha A.E. 274
  William 63
Haygood,
  Green W. 16
  Martha 16
  Lewis 175
Hayles,William 236
Hayman,Stouton 245
Haymans,James 230
Haynes,
  A.G. 47,61
  Henry 175,197
  James W. 203
  Jasper 227
  John 80
  Robert H. 114
  Thomas 203
  William D. 203
Haynood,Thomas 208
Hays,

Kicker,W.G. 123
Kicks,Margaret 27
Kidd,James H. 94
Kight,Stephen 77,83,90
Kights,Samuel 76,88,105
Kilcrease,
 Jackson 116
 Rilzy Ann 111
 Robert 58
Kilgore,
 Henrietta 125
 John 88
Killcrease,Kitty 266
Killeress,Elizabeth 109
Killgore,
 Allen 207
 Charles A.70
Killingsworth,
 Elizabeth 23
 Mary 28
 Sarah 25
 Sophia 21
Killpatrick,Martha 223
Killum,Willis 250
Kilpatrick,
 Hugh 159
 William 159
Kimbell,
 Benjamin 105
 Benjamin F. 123
 D. 105
 F.T. 133
 Finney M. 121
 James G. 117
 Margaret,Mrs. 140
 Margaret T. 133
 Mary W. 123,137
 Robert 105
Kimberley,
 Amson 182
 Anson 167,182
 Charles E. 283
 Isaac 283
 James M. 283
 William J. 283
Kimble,
 James G. 126
 Peter 224
Kimbole,Margaret 110
Kimbree,David 69
Kimbro,John 31
Kimbrough,
 Adaline 115
 C.M. 127
 Elvira 111
 James 83,152,170,171,172
  173,174,188,192,194,
  195,196,197,201
 John 41,59,104,115,163
 Leroy J. 15
 Louisa 112
 Mary Ann 115
 W.C. 125
 William 102,154,156,162
  198,201
Kinard,
 Barned 203
 Christinia 118
 John 203
 Martha 117
 Miley A. 118
 Owen H. 157
 Serena 114
 Terisa 114
Kindale,
 H. 238
 T.H. 238
Kindall,
 Elisha 254
 H. 230
 Henry 72,73
 Jan 268
 Sarah 264

Kindall(con't)
 T.H. 159,230
 Thomas H. 72,73,159
Kinchen,Uriah 72
Kindrick,
 Adeline J. 127
 Burwell 89
 John 102
 Mary 126
 R. 59
 Sarah C. 137
 Sylvanus 101,102
Kine,
 Ephriam 249
 W. 14
Kinebrew,
 Henry 281
 Jasper 281
King,
 Abner H. 182
 Alex. 161
 Alfred H. 114
 Angus M.D. 244
 Barrington 102
 Benjamin 85
 Bennington 105
 Caroline 3,26
 Elizabeth F. 128
 Elizabeth S. 267
 Ephriam 231
 F.R. 132
 Frances 123
 G.C. 271
 Henry 170,182,210
 Henry H. 128
 J. 55
 Jacob W. 185
 Jackson Esly 3
 James 49,78,81,99,134,
  152
 James A. 136
 James H. 3
 James M.D. 80
 James N. 19
 Jesse 255
 Josiah 250
 John 3,103,144,168
 John G. 109
 Mary 173
 Mary A. 185
 Mary F. 122
 Maryetta 133
 Nancy A. 139
 Olivia 144
 Parnale 3
 Priscilla 103
 Rebecca C. 129
 Rebecca H. 12
 Silas 265
 Sobrina 110
 Susanna 19
 T.D. 242,275,277
 Thomas 19
 William 199
 William J. 212
 Winefer 3
 Wineford 28
 Y.P. 161
Kink,Ezra 186
Kinmon,Charles 82
Kinney,Chesley 222,224
Kinnon,H.I.M. 108
Kinsey,Lucy 25
Kinzy,Henry M. 58
Kirby,John L. 154
Kirkpatrick,
 Harman 225
 J.H. 199
 James 197
 John 197
Kirksey;
 E.S. 47,53,57,64,90
 Franklin 93

Kirksey(con't)
 Gideon 62,65,109
 Margaret 112
 Nancy 109
 West A. 93
Kirksey & Hendrick 68
Kisler,Samuel 283
Kislin,Samuel 285
Kitchen,
 Joseph 171
 William 79
Kitchens,
 A.S. 139
 Adline M. 130
 Elizabeth 132
 Frances 130
 Henry 117
 James 197
 John 134
 Loucinda 135
 Nelson 120
 Thomas 130
Kittle,James Smith 82
Knight,
 Aletha 111
 Annath 206
 C.F. 33,42,43,54,65,98
 Calvaron 39
 Calvery 98
 Calvery F. 46,63,102
 Eli 65
 H.D. 46,60,63,76,93
 J.C.˙59,66
 James 224
 James A. 15
 James M. 222
 Jarrushed 189
 Joel 49,61
 Mary 224
 Mary H. 176
 Mary Rosebury 222
 Richard 42,43,46,49,54,
  61
 Stephen 95,189,206
 Water T. 35,36,37,38
 Wiley 145
 William 43,55,78
 Wood 60
 Woody 41
 Woody K. 107
 Woody R. 176
 Zachariah T. 46
Knoles,
 Benjamin 278,280
 Edmond 278,280
 James M. 280
Knols,H.W. 37
Knowes,Sarah 269
Knowland,Anna E. 141
Knowles,
 J. 55
 James B. 129
 Lucinda 268
 Parker 191
Knox, A.P. 181
Kochler,Barnard 238
Kolb,David 220
Kopeman,M. 253
Kuchhill,J.A. 162
Laddon,Jepe 109
Lacy,
 Henry 136
 Martha 24
 Nathan 137
 Patience 22
Lain,
 Edward 53
 James 103
Lam,Patsy Burge 211
Lamar,
 Basil 11
 Benjamin B. 2,8,10,230
 Eliza 8,10

O'Nail(con't)
Zachariah 45
Orr,
C. 175
Matthew 68
Orea,Robert 55
Orme,
John 167
M. 202
Osborn,
Daniel 59,66,68
Ella 136
George 168
John 179
Osborne,Reps. 191
Osburn,
Alexander 124
Daniel 64
John M. 272
William 272
Oslin,Jesse 215
Outlaw,Alexander 231
Owen,
Aaron 35,36
Daniel 236
Elizabeth 110
George 250
Hardaman 181,182
Jesse L. 10,11
L.L. 5
Molly 139
Moorefield 160
Peter 56
Rebecca 109
Thomas 92,94
Owens,
Alfred 110
Benjamin Franklin 4
David 80
Elmyria A. 4
George 39,86,92,94
J.L. 12
Jno.G. 38,41
John 227
Lucinda C. 284
Martha 284
Matilda C. 284
Obbey J. 133
Robert M. 284
Sarah E. 284
William 284
Wm.Henry 4
Oxford,Edward B. 64,65,114
Ozburn,
Haywood 285
William K. 285
Pace,
Adeline F. 120
Baziel 208
Barnabas 212,214
C.D. 102
Cinthia 269
Columbus C. 217
Columbus D. 224,226
George W. 157
Hardy 48,58,65
Julia A. 128
Lucinda 157
Malinda 109
Mary Ann Luckie 216
Mary R. 123
Matilda 157
Paris 35,43
Perneten J. 26
Rebecca J. 26
Samuel 6
Thomas 2
Thomas J. 157
Welborn 179
William 179
William A. 126
Zachariah 157
Padgett,

Padgett,
Elizabeth 267
Gracy Ann 265
L.D. 276
Lorenzo D. 281
Moses 268
Sarah 266
Page,
George H. 271
Nancy 20
Pain,
Henry D. 82
Reuben 69
William H. 132
Palack,David 82
Palk,Micajah 253
Palmer,
Amasa 45
Amasa E. 51
Ann 45,51
Asbury W. 51
Christopher 160
Jesse A. 45,51
John 51
Martin 160,162
Matthew G. 51
Robert T. 51
Sally 45,46,47,51
T. 172
William W. 51
Pam,Bridgett 103
Paramore,N. 167
Parham,
Dickson 89
John 68
Par(harm?),John 209
Parich---,
William 213
Parish,
Jonathan 55
Sanford 166
Park,
John 179,227,257,260
Susan 6
William T. 79
Parker,
A.M. 275
Aaron 170,180,208
Allan 215
Anna 264
Boswell 17
David M. 222
Dicey 160
Eldetio 28
Emily 20,133
Eveline 110
Fanny 266
G. 17
George 89,256
H.J. 224
Isaiah 242
J.F. 137
John 47,54,110
John C. 129
Lemuel 90
Lucinda 24
Mary S. 123
Mile 111
Nancy 81,229,265
Pheraby 25
Richard 88,105
Sanford 90
Sarah 21
Susannah 133
W.C. 73
William 93.160
William B. 8
William C. 74,77,81,88,
105,106
William H. 30
Willwm L. 105
W.R. 131
William T. 79

Parkers,Israel 193
Parks,
Eli 59,68
Isaac 59,67,68
Harriett 135
John 4
Milly 26
William 193,266
Parmenter,Capt. 165
Parmer,George 152,184
Parnal,James 216
Parnell,
G. 41
James 139
Parramore,
John E. 188,249
N. 150
P.W. 255
Reddin W. 150
Redding 255
Parrimore,John 255
Parris,Nathan 162
Parrish,
J. 58
Jonathan 56,60
Nancy 267,268
S. 58
Parrodice,William 164
Parrot,Benjamin 59
Partain,Kindred 155
Partridge,Jesse 169
Paskel,John H. 63
Pate,
Edward 187
Harvey 271
Herod 271
Milly 265
William 83,170,177
Willis A. 271
Winney 264
Patrick,
Abram P. 13
Abraham W. 215
Alexander 68
Andrew 211
Chloe Ann 119
Elizabeth H. 215
Frances Jane 215
Jane Elizabeth 13
John 36
John C. 32,33
John J,Kirk 125
Lucy A. 215
Luke 58,58,59,159
Martha 32,33,107
Martha W. 215
Mary E. 215
Sarah F. 132
Solomon 208
Susan 32,33,107,130
Thomas J.D. 13
William 13,215
Pattern,Joseph 237
Patterson,
D.S. 70
Elizabeth 28,114
Henry 248
Jesse 248
Job 63
Job C. 55,64
John J. 260
John T. 250
Mark 250,254,260
Sally 254
Wiley 60
Patton,
Alexr.E. 7
Elizabeth 20
James 258
Jane 27
Sally S. 24
Sarah 25
Pattrick,

Young(con't),
  Andrew 183
  D. 193
  Daniel 172
  David 161,247
  Edward B. 5
  F. 66
  Frederick 59
  Hannah
  Jak T. 36
  John 59,171,193
  Johh T. 48,50,51
  Margaret 237
  Martha 24
  Moses W. 241
  Patrick 251
  Robert 154,158
  William S. 122
  Willis 247
  Willy 176
Youngblood,
  Martha 24
  Thomas 240
Zachary,Lewis 221
Zachery,
  A.C. 57
  William 57
Zachry,
  Alfred F. 214
  James 214
  Louisa 214
  Mary 214
  Polly 214
  Sarah Ann 214
Zaphnaphpaanh,
  John 220
Zellner,John 245

Slave Index

Aberdeen 6
Abram 18,211
Adaline 1,11
Adam 5
Adams 16
Addy 5
Adolphus 12
Aggy 5,10,212
Alexander 5,11
Alford 10
Alfred 11,35,43
Alice 12
Allen 7,10,14
Ally 9
Alonzo 19
Amanda 5,7
America 12
Amos 7
Amy 1,220
Anabella 7
Anaka 7
Anchy 4
Andrew 4,10
Angelina 7
Anica 18
Ann 2,6,10,19,100,102
Anna 16
Anthony 14,35,43,45
Arnold 11,225
Asa 103
Austin 1,14
Baldy 9
Barnett 11
Becca 4
Becky 6
Bedy 10
Betta 103
Benjamin 11
Benn 250
Ben 1,3,7,10,11,45,220
Bet 10
Betsy 7,12
Betsy Ann 11
Betty 6,10,52
Bill 3,11,18
Boney 15
Burrell 222
Bob 6
Boston 220
Brister 15
Brown 4
Byrd 9
Caleb 19
Caliner 12
Canada 9
Candis 11
Caroline 7,9,10,11,12,19,
  221
Carver 9
Cary 220
Catherine 212
Caty 3
Chance 2,13
Chaney 2,13,224
Charity 19
Charles 11,15
Charlotte 4,30,32,78
Cithishal 244
Claborn 78
Clark 30
Clarisa 35
Collins 17
Colquett 220
Coulis 10
Cuty 9
Cynthia 13,105
Cyrus 13
Daniel 5,7,10,11
David 8,49
Davy 8,49

Debary 9
Dianna 4
Dicey 211
Dick 7,10,11,220
Diley 10
Dinah 55
Dolly 1,78
Eady 3
Easter 2,10,194,220
Edmond 3,11
Edneah 196
Edward 10
Elijah 35
Ellick 10
Eliza 7,11
Elizabeth 10,212
Eliza Jane 4
Elmira 220
Elvira 11
Emanuel 13,14
Emeline 11,16
Emily 9,10,15
Emory 1
Ephriam 4,11,149
Esswx 211
Ester 11
Esther 222
Eva 10
Fanny 6,7,10,13,18
Fed 9
Felix 18
Fenby 104
Fillis 10
Flora 6
Floyd 7
Frances 7
Frank 7,10,18,225
Franklin 222
Genny 35
George 1,11,13,14,49,211
Gilbert 212
Giles 10
Grace 7
Granville 10
Greene 30
Griffin 11
Hagar 103
Hampton 9
Hannah 1,5,14,211
Hardy 16
Harriet 4,7,11,16,18,30,
  55,104
Harriet Ann 11
Harrison 16
Harry 1,3,11,35
Harvey 15
Henrietta 10,15
Henry 10,11,104,220
Hester 5
Hetty 11
Hiram 103
Holland 10
Isaac 1,55
Isam 10
Isabel 43
Isham 10,13,14
Israel 10
Jack 7,12,45,55
Jackson 241
Jacob 4,10,15,222
Jaicy 10
James 9,15
Janah 1
Jane 11,12,13,18
Janet 11
Jarrett 13
Jefferson 7
Jeney 13
Jenny 244
Jerry 11,35